Gendered Lives, Sexual Beings

We dedicate this book to our friends and families, who have supported us through this arduous process and loved us every step of the way. Thank you especially to David, Amina, and Rabi, Casey, Emerson, and Tucker, and, of course, Hattie.

Sara Miller McCune founded SAGE Publishing in 1965 to support the dissemination of usable knowledge and educate a global community. SAGE publishes more than 1000 journals and over 800 new books each year, spanning a wide range of subject areas. Our growing selection of library products includes archives, data, case studies and video. SAGE remains majority owned by our founder and after her lifetime will become owned by a charitable trust that secures the company's continued independence.

Los Angeles | London | New Delhi | Singapore | Washington DC | Melbourne

Gendered Lives, Sexual Beings

A Feminist Anthology

Edited by

Joya Misra
University of Massachusetts, Amherst

Mahala Dyer Stewart
University of Massachusetts, Amherst

Marni Alyson Brown
Georgia Gwinnett College

Los Angeles | London | New Delhi
Singapore | Washington DC | Melbourne

FOR INFORMATION:

SAGE Publications, Inc.
2455 Teller Road
Thousand Oaks, California 91320
E-mail: order@sagepub.com

SAGE Publications Ltd.
1 Oliver's Yard
55 City Road
London EC1Y 1SP
United Kingdom

SAGE Publications India Pvt. Ltd.
B 1/I 1 Mohan Cooperative Industrial Area
Mathura Road, New Delhi 110 044
India

SAGE Publications Asia-Pacific Pte. Ltd.
3 Church Street
#10-04 Samsung Hub
Singapore 049483

Acquisitions Editor: Jeff Lasser
Content Development Editor: Gabrielle Piccininni
Editorial Assistant: Adeline Wilson
Production Editor: Jane Haenel
Typesetter: C&M Digitals (P) Ltd.
Proofreader: Chris Dahlin
Cover Designer: Scott Van Atta
Marketing Manager: Kara Kindstrom

Printed in the United States of America

Library of Congress Cataloging-in-Publication Data

Names: Misra, Joya, editor. | Stewart, Mahala Dyer, editor. | Brown, Marni Alyson, editor.

Title: Gendered lives, sexual beings : a feminist anthology / edited by Joya Misra, University of Massachusetts, Amherst, Mahala Dyer Stewart, University of Massachusetts, Amherst, Marni Alyson Brown, Georgia Gwinnett College.

Description: Thousand Oaks, CA : SAGE, [2018]

Identifiers: LCCN 2017005240 | ISBN 9781506329345 (pbk. : alk. paper)

Subjects: LCSH: Sex role. | Sex. | Feminist theory. | Feminism. | Women's studies.

Classification: LCC HQ1075 .G467165 2018 | DDC 305.3—dc23
LC record available at https://lccn.loc.gov/2017005240

This book is printed on acid-free paper.

SUSTAINABLE FORESTRY INITIATIVE

Certified Chain of Custody
Promoting Sustainable Forestry
www.sfiprogram.org
SFI-01268

SFI label applies to text stock

17 18 19 20 21 10 9 8 7 6 5 4 3 2 1

Contents

Preface

S tudying gender and sexuality is exciting and challenging as they present complicated problems and inequalities while manifesting important possibilities of change and resistance. We have designed an anthology that pays tribute to theories and presents knowledge significant to the field, as well as addressing new insights. We do this through employing an "Intersectional, Masculinities, Transgender, and Global (IMTG) Framework" throughout the text. Readings situated in this framework highlight systematic and institutional experiences of gender and sexuality, with the hope of encouraging better understanding of the complexities of gender, gender identity, and sexuality.

Gendered Lives, Sexual Beings draws from many collective years of teaching and research experience in the fields of gender and sexuality. We have experienced how and why texts do or do not work in the classroom. We have watched students succeed with certain readings and assignments while struggling with others. We have seen the field change from being primarily text based, with a few notable films that might be screened in class, to one where a range of materials, podcasts, video clips, and data are regularly assigned both inside and outside the classroom. We have observed students' frustrations as well as been inspired by them in teaching gender and sexuality courses. Our pedagogy and experience with students have guided this text just as much as our cumulative familiarity with the field.

This anthology and framework is responsive to shifts and advancements in scholarship. Students who sign up for classes in gender and/or sexuality often arrive knowing bits and pieces of gender scholarship, potentially from an introductory-level course or from coverage in the media. Our book is intentionally designed to connect gender and sexuality to all areas of social life.

Course prep is one of the most time-consuming aspects of teaching. We have drawn on our experiences in the classroom, both behind the scenes and on the stage, to put together a website that supplements the reader for ease in course preparation. We offer teaching resources organized to be useful for lectures, discussions, and direct assignments to students. These materials provide a wide range of information to assist in classroom preparation for each section of the reader. We provide film suggestions, media clips, podcasts, and further readings, all intended to expand the conversation and knowledge building around gender and sexuality in the 21st century.

Introduction

Gender, gender identity, and sexuality affect every element of social life. In this anthology, we present works that analyze the gendered and sexualized processes that shape individual experiences and the organization of society in the 21st century. Indeed, it is critical to recognize that ideas about gender and sexuality suffuse interactions, institutions, and the societies in which we live. Major recent changes in the field of gender and sexuality include intersectional frameworks that recognize that gender intersects in meaningful ways with race, class, sexuality, nationality, ability, and other factors. Scholarship also includes greater focus on masculinities, transgender and gender minorities, and gendered processes from a global and transnational lens.

In this anthology, we have collected cutting-edge scholarship on gender and sexuality in the 21st century. In each section of the book, we engage with four frameworks: *intersectionality, masculinity, transgender*, and *global/transnational* (IMTG) *research*. Rather than segmenting these issues, we ensure consistent attention to all of these cross-cutting emphases in gender and sexuality research throughout the book. Intersectional research allows us to understand that women, for example, do not experience being a woman the same way; gender is experienced differently based on one's other identities. Research on masculinity emphasizes that gender analyses do not only apply to women. Gender is reflected in societal expectations around both masculinity and femininity and applied to all people. *Transgender* studies, and understandings of the experiences of gender minorities more broadly, is also critical to 21st-century gender research. Transgender- and gender-nonconforming research highlights the socially constructed nature of sex and gender and the challenges faced by those whose sex assigned at birth does not match their gender performance and gender identity. A *global/transnational* perspective illustrates that gendered and sexualized processes are not standardized, but vary based on location. We emphasize that gender and sexuality cannot be analyzed globally as "traditional" or "modern," but must instead be situated to show that these processes are affected by all aspects of their context.

Intersectionality conceptualizes the interlocking nature of race, gender, class, sexuality, and other structures that shape the lives of all people. Intersectional perspectives show that gender and sexuality are not experienced in the same way by all the members of a particular group. An intersectional lens shows that a White working-class lesbian woman experiences *both* her gender *and* sexuality very differently from a Black working-class lesbian woman. Although both women are lesbians from the same class location, their race impacts their experience of their class, gender, and sexuality. Making these connections highlights how these categories shape our lives in ways that are similar and distinct. Intersectionality draws attention to variations in how gender and sexuality are experienced, while emphasizing the power and privilege that shape these inequalities. Interconnected oppressions and privileges shape social identities, communities, regions, nations, and global society.

Masculinity studies emerged over the last several decades, as scholars realized that women are not the only people who possess a gender or are encouraged to enact gendered lives. Masculinity studies considers what it means to be masculine and how masculinity is achieved across bodies. The field also draws from intersectional studies to consider the variations among men, the ways that certain men are privileged and others are disadvantaged in our stratified gender system. Masculinity may differ from time to time, as well as from context to context, so that masculinity may be enacted differently among software engineers and among musicians. Masculinity studies have thus become critical to gender and feminist research.

Transgender studies emerged over the last few decades, as scholars recognized that gender and gender identity are more complex and nuanced than previously theorized. While initially folded into studies of sexuality, transgender research now emphasizes the important distinctions between gender, sex, and sexuality, while highlighting the experiences of gender minorities. These people are those who are moving across gender identities, challenging gender norms, and often transforming the meaning of gender in social institutions such as families, schools, workplaces, sports, laws, and politics. Transgender issues are increasingly visible in local, national, and global political debates and allow for deeper understanding of *what* gender actually is, how it is accomplished and recognized, as well as how gender, sex, and sexuality are linked and yet distinct.

The media often presents a fairly homogenous view of other countries as "civilized" or "backwards," which may lead to thinking that there are specific, correct ways gender and sexuality should be accomplished. Yet, expectations around gender and sexuality affect lives everywhere in multiple shapes and forms. *Global* scholarship provides a broader perspective, showing how global contexts link to the experience of gender and sexuality and map variations in gender and sexuality. Global research highlights how nations and countries around the world structure and order gender and sexuality on interactional and institutional levels, making clear how these processes are socially constructed.

Organization of the Book

The book considers how we theorize gender and sexuality and how researchers go about producing knowledge about these topics. We address how gender and sexuality are reflected in bodies and identities. Yet, the book is also organized to address many of the major institutions in social life, such as popular culture, religions, families and intimate relations, schools, workplaces, sports, systems of violence, crime, and law, as well as politics and social movements. By showing that gender and sexuality matter in all of these arenas, we hope to help identify the centrality of scholarship on gender, sexuality, and gender identity for making sense of the world in which we live.

Each section has an introductory section describing the articles and demonstrating how they fit together within our IMTG frame. We use this framework consistently to highlight how gender and sexuality are produced and reproduced in the United States and around the world. The book reflects both classic statements on gendered and sexualized processes and the most up-to-date research on gender and sexuality, demonstrating recent groundbreaking changes in how gender and sexuality order societies and influence daily interactions.

In Part I, the book provides a number of key statements on theorizing gender and sexuality and further developing our IMTG framework. Our aim is to give students conceptual tools that will be useful in reading the rest of this anthology. This section introduces how gender is enacted and achieved through interactions, as well as how gender is central to how we are seen in all dimensions of our lives, including visibility in social institutions. We also include readings emphasizing the importance of theorizing race, class, and gender oppressions as intersecting and analyzing masculinity as dynamic. We include a reading on the work done to emphasize and support transgender gender identity, showing again how gender is dependent on social interaction. And we end this section with a reading that emphasizes the complexity and variation in gender inequalities by country and region.

In Part II, the book considers research and knowledge production around gender and sexuality. Feminist researchers emphasize subjectivity rather than objectivity in research and recognize biases in who produces knowledges. We provide pieces that point out how taking an intersectional approach can enrich understanding and empathy as well as create networking and coalition building. These chapters consider how to carry out research on gender and sexuality thoughtfully, being open to how the researcher's identity shapes the research process. We also include a piece that emphasizes the importance of recognizing the knowledge being produced about gender and sexuality from different global locations.

Parts III and IV discuss bodies and identities, as well as culture and media, although these sections are deeply intertwined. In Part III, we consider the socially constructed nature of gendered and sexualized bodies and the expectations that people face, conform to, and sometimes resist. We also include pieces that theorize body labor and how body labor may differ based on context—in terms of how people both use and fashion their bodies. In Part IV, we consider how culture and media shape our lives, often reinforcing gendered and sexualized expectations, through films, magazine articles, and news media. We also consider how subcultures emphasize particular performances of gender and sexuality, depending on the messages they are trying to convey.

In Parts V and VI, we consider the social institutions of religion and family and their role in reflecting and influencing performances of gender and sexuality. In Part V, we analyze religion as a central institution organizing social life, including gender and sexuality. Religion is often thought of as enforcing traditional notions of gender and sexuality and may seem somewhat inflexible. Yet other readings emphasize how religion may have a more complex and differentiated function and can be used strategically by certain groups. In Part VI, we consider families and intimate relationships, analyzing how gender and sexuality are practiced in these contexts. Intimate relationships often carry gendered notions of what people should be doing, although expectations vary by race, class, sexuality, and location. Understanding how relationships operate for lesbian, gay, bisexual, transgender, and queer families helps provide more evidence for the complex ways gender and sexuality intertwine, yet are distinct.

In Parts VII, VIII, and IX, we consider the institutions of education, sports, and work, aimed at understanding how gender and sexuality remain salient in these settings. In Part VII, the readings analyze how students experience schools and universities in differing ways, based on their race and gender, and how gender influences decisions around educational debt. These readings also consider how schooling arrangements and practices may intentionally or unintentionally reinforce or resist particular assumptions around gender, gender identity, and sexuality. Part VIII considers how gender, sexuality, and gender identity play out among athletes, with spectators, among family members, and at sporting events. In these settings, athletes perform gender and sexuality in complex and contradictory ways. Part IX examines these processes in work settings, identifying the variety of ways in which assumptions about gender, sexuality, and race shape workplace hierarchies. Rather than creating workers whose gender, gender identity, and sexuality are unimportant, workplaces reinforce very particular expectations for workers.

In Parts X and XI, we consider how gender, gender identity, and sexuality are reflected in both the criminal justice system and in politics and activism. In Part X, the chapters touch on a range of issues in the field of crime, violence, and social control from the sexual violence girls come to expect as normal to the differences in how correction officers understand criminals as gendered beings. Readings also address the gendered racialized criminalization of Black and Latino boys by the criminal justice system, as well as the xenophobic construction of "honor killings" by the media. We also consider gendered violence experienced by transgender communities, as well as the experiences of transgender prisoners. Part XI examines how politics reflects inequalities by gender and sexuality, as well as inequalities by race and class. This part also considers how activists and social movements mobilize in ways that call on, and sometimes undermine, gendered assumptions. These assumptions may be used to garner support for particular groups, as when an immigrants' rights group emphasizes men as loving fathers. Even where politics is exclusionary, groups can mobilize in ways that allow them greater political power.

Additional Resources

This reader is also aimed at recognizing the way that students learn in the 21st century, going beyond the text. Students no longer only read outside of class and listen to lectures inside of class. Classes increasingly use hybrid approaches, such as the "flipped classroom" or "team-based learning" where students engage in concrete activities to clarify concepts. Students are also looking for classes to offer connections to everyday, real-world experiences. Students not only read materials, they also engage with podcasts, videos, films, new stories, and blogs inside and outside of class, with the aim of having these materials reinforce the concepts they are learning.

The open access website for the book provides suggestions for films, short videos, podcasts, and blogs that pair well with the readings and is consistent with our IMTG framework. At the same time, we provide suggestions for additional readings, data sources, updated statistics, and images. We also offer resources for finding other blogs, films, videos, and podcasts, so that students and instructors can seek out other materials. Instructors can use these materials in preparing class sessions, assigning students to view or listen to materials, or design research projects using the sources we provide.

We see the course website as a way to effectively bridge the divide between course readings and the "real world," as well as regularly provide updated materials as new issues or policy changes arise. This allows instructors to update their courses quickly and easily and offers students access to the most recent and relevant research and media discussions of gender and sexuality. The website allows us to receive feedback from users about the materials that work best in the classroom, as well as suggestions for additional materials to ensure consistently updated content. In this way, we hope the website serves as a resource for all those interested in learning and teaching about gender, gender identity, and sexuality.

Possibilities

We hope that this anthology provides theoretically grounded and empirically rich research for the study of gender and sexuality in the 21st century. The frameworks of intersectionality, masculinity, transgender, and global experiences allow students to learn about the central developments in gender and sexuality scholarship over the past several decades. Our open access website, filled with multimedia resources that complement the reader, meets the realities of our changing classrooms and student populations. We have selected research that considers a multitude of ways that gender and sexuality matter in everyday life, from bodies and identities to social institutions and social movements. We have designed these materials to emphasize how gender and sexuality are central to shaping the world we inhabit, as well as offering possibilities for positive social change.

Acknowledgments

Writing and coordinating an anthology is no easy task. This effort would not have been possible without the help of partners in our homes and families, colleagues in the Sociology Department at the University of Massachusetts, Amherst, and Georgia Gwinnett College, and beyond. We thank all who have helped see this project to fruition.

We are so thankful for our publishing team at SAGE. First, we would like to thank Jeff Lasser and the entire SAGE Publishing crew, including Gabrielle Piccininni, Adeline Wilson, Jane Haenel, Scott Van Atta, and Kara Kindstrom.

This work would not be possible without our students. Our students bring inspiration to the scholarship we do, read, and teach, while grounding our teaching in the contemporary social world. They also offer insight on scholarship that is accessible and teachable and help us better understand the lived experiences of the world we study, reminding us, as bell hooks says, that "teaching can transgress." We have teaching experience from varied schools and different student populations; we all agreed on the importance of making central, highly regarded scholarship readable for our undergraduates. We want to honor what our students have shared with us in the classroom by offering this collection of high-quality gender and sexuality scholarship.

We are delighted to present the work of so many wonderful scholars who do important social science research on gender, gender identity, and sexuality. Thank you for sharing your knowledge and research.

SAGE Publishing thanks the following reviewers:

Valerie Chepp, *Hamline University*

Jason Lee Crockett, *Kutztown University of Pennsylvania*

Michelle Deming, *University of South Carolina*

Matthew B. Ezzell, *James Madison University*

Michelle Hughes Miller, *University of South Florida*

Laura Hunter, *University of Arizona*

Robert B. Jenkot, *Coastal Carolina University*

Katherine Lineberger, *Florida International University*

Krista McQueeney, *Merrimack College*

Harmony D. Newman, *University of Northern Colorado*

Naomi J. Pinion, *Northern Arizona University*

Maura Ryan, *Georgia State University*

PART I

Theorizing Gender and Sexuality in the 21st Century

Feminist theory provides a framework for thinking about gendered lives and sexual beings. Theory provides us with a map, a way of analyzing and understanding the terrain around us. Maps might highlight roads, or political borders, or physical terrain, like mountains, rivers, and lakes. In this opening section, we provide several different maps that examine gender from the perspectives of intersectionality, masculinity, transgender, and global (IMTG) processes. We focus on these areas specifically because of their importance to understanding the experience of gender and sexuality at the levels of interactions, organizations, and broader institutional structures.

Candace West and Don Zimmerman's groundbreaking work, "Doing Gender," introduced gender as a verb, an action and accomplishment, as opposed to a "natural" or biological characteristic. Rather than being born as gendered, we learn how to enact gender through every interaction, day in and day out. "Doing Gender" is thus an activity that is taught, rehearsed, and achieved according to social expectations and interactions. We are held accountable by other people and institutions to meet the expectations for our assumed gender, and these norms are created and embedded in social structures. Thus, seeing gender as something that is "done," rather than something that exists, helps convey new understandings of gender relations.

In "Framed Before We Know It," Cecilia Ridgeway builds a social psychological argument for how gender is a primary frame in an individual's interactional and institutional life, influencing both their opportunities and disadvantages. Culturally hegemonic beliefs (e.g., men are smart, women are caring) about gender are not only held by individual people but also institutionalized through media depictions and planted in organizations. Key to Ridgeway's argument, though, is that contexts shape how gender affects our experiences. In a setting culturally typed as masculine (e.g., the military), gender beliefs will bias judgments in favor of men, but where they are culturally typed as feminine (e.g., a preschool classroom), they may bias judgments in favor of women. Ridgeway argues that understanding gender as a frame leads to a multidimensional understanding of how gender matters at individual, institutional, and societal levels.

In "Defining Black Feminist Thought," Patricia Hill Collins elucidates intersectional theory as a framework that begins by centering Black women's experiences. The theory demonstrates the importance of Black women defining their own realities for both empowerment and resistance of race, gender, and class oppression, while recognizing the varied ways differently positioned Black women can participate in this project. Yet while emphasizing the importance of Black women's intellectual leadership, Collins also recognizes the importance of partnerships with other groups, such as Black men, White women, and other groups with particular standpoints. Collins seeks to deconstruct all forms of domination through dialogue and coalition-building with other groups, working toward a humanist community of belonging.

Claire Duncanson's "Hegemonic Masculinity and the Possibility of Change in Gender Relations" builds upon the important concept of hegemonic masculinity developed by Raewyn Connell. Many studies show that, even with more inclusive notions of hegemonic masculinity, these forms continue to marginalize and stratify other groups, such as painting certain men as hypermasculine and violent, or women as dependent and passive, while valorizing other men as peaceful and enlightened. Yet Duncanson critiques the notion that hegemonic masculinity is so powerful that it necessarily always maintains patriarchal gender inequality, arguing that there are possibilities for social change in which a more feminized version of masculinity becomes hegemonic, leading to gender equality. Yet, it is important to be vigilant that new versions of masculinity do not also create new forms of oppression.

In "Gender Labor," Jane Ward examines gender as a form of labor within relationships, including sexual relationships. Through examining narratives of the labor involved in femme lesbians' relationships with transgender men, she finds that women perform emotional carework through validating their partner's masculinity and play support roles in trans subculture. Ward argues that emotional carework is feminized in ways that require such work from straight women, femme lesbians, feminine gay men, and other groups. The research demonstrates the gendered dynamics within romantic relationships through which carework continues to be expected and naturalized as feminized work, even within queer communities.

Christine Bose's "Globalizing Gender Issues" introduces multifaceted and intersecting gender issues that exist around the world. Bose explains that gender issues, including a wide array of inequalities, vary by country and region and cannot be simply reduced to dualistic scenarios of societies that are "empowered" or "disempowered." Bose shows how transnational processes—such as the global political economy and migration—and regional processes—such as the development of the African Union or gender mainstreaming—reflect, transform, and reinforce gender inequalities. There are also national processes specific to particular location, as well as cross-cutting themes such as HIV/AIDS, religion, or war, that could lead to coalition-building across regions. As she argues, it is critical to take a more nuanced and inquisitive approach to understanding variations in gender inequality worldwide.

Through these pieces, we aim to introduce readers to a variety of conceptual frameworks that can be used to analyze gender and gender inequalities in the rest of this volume. When trying to understand the role of gender in the different institutions of social life, we hope that these pieces provide a foundational and contemporary feminist toolkit that emphasize intersectionality, masculinity, transgender, and global and transnational (IMTG) processes.

Doing Gender

Candace West and Don H. Zimmerman

[...]

Our purpose in this article is to propose an ethnomethodologically informed, and therefore distinctively sociological, understanding of gender as a routine, methodical, and recurring accomplishment. We contend that the "doing" of gender is undertaken by women and men whose competence as members of society is hostage to its production. Doing gender involves a complex of socially guided perceptual, interactional, and micropolitical activities that cast particular pursuits as expressions of masculine and feminine "natures."

When we view gender as an accomplishment, an achieved property of situated conduct, our attention shifts from matters internal to the individual and focuses on interactional and, ultimately, institutional arenas. In one sense, of course, it is individuals who "do" gender. But it is a situated doing, carried out in the virtual or real presence of others who are presumed to be oriented to its production. Rather than as a property of individuals, we conceive of gender as an emergent feature of social situations: both as an outcome of and a rationale for various social arrangements and as a means of legitimating one of the most fundamental divisions of society.

[...]

To elaborate our proposal, we suggest at the outset that important but often overlooked distinctions be observed among *sex, sex category*, and *gender. Sex* is a determination made through the application of socially agreed upon biological criteria for classifying persons as females or males. The criteria for classification can be genitalia at birth or chromosomal typing before birth, and they do not necessarily agree with one another. Placement in a *sex category* is achieved through application of the sex criteria, but in everyday life, categorization is established and sustained by the socially required identificatory displays that proclaim one's membership in one or the other category. In this sense, one's sex category presumes one's sex and stands as proxy for it in many situations, but sex and sex category can vary independently; that is, it is possible to claim membership in a sex category even when the sex criteria are lacking. *Gender*, in contrast, is the activity of managing situated conduct in light of normative conceptions of attitudes and activities appropriate for one's sex category. Gender activities emerge from and bolster claims to membership in a sex category.

Candace West and Don H. Zimmerman. 1987. "Doing Gender." *Gender & Society* 1(2):125–51.

We contend that recognition of the analytical independence of sex, sex category, and gender is essential for understanding the relationships among these elements and the interactional work involved in "being" a gendered person in society.

[. . .]

Sex, Sex Category, and Gender

Garfinkel's (1967, pp. 118–40) case study of Agnes, a transsexual raised as a boy who adopted a female identity at age 17 and underwent a sex reassignment operation several years later, demonstrates how gender is created through interaction and at the same time structures interaction. Agnes, whom Garfinkel characterized as a "practical methodologist," developed a number of procedures for passing as a "normal, natural female" both prior to and after her surgery. She had the practical task of managing the fact that she possessed male genitalia and that she lacked the social resources a girl's biography would presumably provide in everyday interaction. In short, she needed to display herself as a woman, simultaneously learning what it was to be a woman. Of necessity, this full-time pursuit took place at a time when most people's gender would be well-accredited and routinized. Agnes had to consciously contrive what the vast majority of women do without thinking. She was not "faking" what "real" women do naturally. She was obliged to analyze and figure out how to act within socially structured circumstances and conceptions of femininity that women born with appropriate biological credentials come to take for granted early on. . . . Agnes's case makes visible what culture has made invisible—the accomplishment of gender.

Garfinkel's (1967) discussion of Agnes does not explicitly separate three analytically distinct, although empirically overlapping, concepts—sex, sex category, and gender.

Sex

Agnes did not possess the socially agreed upon biological criteria for classification as a member of the female *sex*. Still, Agnes regarded herself as a female, albeit a female with a penis, which a woman ought not to possess. The penis, she insisted, was a "mistake" in need of remedy (Garfinkel 1967, pp. 126–27, 131–32). Like other competent members of our culture, Agnes honored the notion that there *are* "essential" biological criteria that unequivocally distinguish females from males. However, if we move away from the commonsense viewpoint, we discover that the reliability of these criteria is not beyond question (Money and Brennan 1968; Money and Erhardt 1972; Money and Ogunro 1974; Money and Tucker 1975). Moreover, other cultures have acknowledged the existence of "cross-genders" (Blackwood 1984; Williams 1986) and the possibility of more than two sexes (Hill 1935; Martin and Voorhies 1975, pp. 84–107; but see also Cucchiari 1981, pp. 32–35).

More central to our argument is Kessler and McKenna's (1978, pp. 1–6) point that genitalia are conventionally hidden from public inspection in everyday life; yet we continue through our social rounds to "observe" a world of two naturally, normally sexed persons. It is the *presumption* that essential criteria exist and would or should be there if looked for that provides the basis for sex categorization. Drawing on Garfinkel, Kessler and McKenna argue that "female" and "male" are cultural events—products of what they term the "gender attribution process"—rather than some collection of traits, behaviors, or even physical attributes. Illustratively they cite the child who, viewing a picture of someone clad in a suit and a tie, contends, "It's a man, because he has a pee-pee" (Kessler and McKenna 1978, p. 154).

Translation: "He must have a pee-pee [an essential characteristic] because I see the *insignia* of a suit and tie." Neither initial sex assignment (pronouncement at birth as a female or male) nor the actual existence of essential criteria for that assignment (possession of a clitoris and vagina or penis and testicles) has much—if anything—to do with the identification of sex category in everyday life. There, Kessler and McKenna note, we operate with a moral certainty of a world of two sexes. We do not think, "Most persons with penises are men, but some may not be" or "Most persons who dress as men have penises." Rather, we take it for granted that sex and sex category are congruent—that knowing the latter, we can deduce the rest.

Sex Categorization

Agnes's claim to the categorical status of female, which she sustained by appropriate identificatory displays and other characteristics, could be *discredited* before her transsexual operation if her possession of a penis became known and after by her surgically constructed genitalia (see Raymond 1979, pp. 37, 138). In this regard, Agnes had to be continually alert to actual or potential threats to the security of her sex category. Her problem was not so much living up to some prototype of essential femininity but preserving her categorization as female. This task was made easy for her by a very powerful resource, namely, the process of commonsense categorization in everyday life.

The categorization of members of society into indigenous categories such as "girl" or "boy," or "woman" or "man," operates in a distinctively social way. The act of categorization does not involve a positive test, in the sense of a well-defined set of criteria that must be explicitly satisfied prior to making an identification. Rather, the application of membership categories relies on an "if-can" test in everyday interaction (Sacks 1972, pp. 332–35). This test stipulates that if people *can be seen* as members of relevant categories, *then categorize them that way*. That is, use the category that seems appropriate, except in the presence of discrepant information or obvious features that would rule out its use. This procedure is quite in keeping with the attitude of everyday life, which has us take appearances at face value unless we have special reason to doubt (Schutz 1943; Garfinkel 1967, pp. 272–77; Bernstein 1986). It should be added that it is precisely when we have special reason to doubt that the issue of applying rigorous criteria arises, but it is rare, outside legal or bureaucratic contexts, to encounter insistence on positive tests (Garfinkel 1967, pp. 262–83; Wilson 1970).

Agnes's initial resource was the predisposition of those she encountered to take her appearance (her figure, clothing, hair style, and so on), as the undoubted appearance of a normal female. Her further resource was our cultural perspective on the properties of "natural, normally sexed persons." Garfinkel (1967, pp. 122–28) notes that in everyday life, we live in a world of two—and only two—sexes. This arrangement has a moral status, in that we include ourselves and others in it as "essentially, originally, in the first place, always have been, always will be, once and for all, in the final analysis, either 'male' or 'female'" (Garfinkel 1967, p. 122).

[...]

Gender

Agnes attempted to be "120 percent female" (Garfinkel 1967, p. 129), that is, unquestionably in all ways and at all times feminine. She thought she could protect herself from disclosure before and after surgical intervention by comporting herself in a feminine manner, but she also could have given herself away by overdoing her performance. Sex categorization and the accomplishment of gender are not the same. Agnes's categorization could be secure or suspect, but did not depend on whether or not she lived up to some ideal conception of femininity. Women can be seen as unfeminine, but that does not make them "unfemale." Agnes faced an ongoing task of *being* a woman—something beyond style of dress (an identificatory display) or allowing men to light her cigarette (a gender display). Her problem was to produce configurations of behavior that would be seen by others as normative gender behavior.

Agnes's strategy of "secret apprenticeship," through which she learned expected feminine decorum by carefully attending to her fiancé's criticisms of other women, was one means of masking incompetencies and simultaneously acquiring the needed skills (Garfinkel 1967, pp. 146–47). It was through her fiancé that Agnes learned that sunbathing on the lawn in front of her apartment was "offensive" (because it put her on display to other men). She also learned from his critiques of other women that she should not insist on having things her way and that she should not offer her opinions or claim equality with men (Garfinkel 1967, pp. 147–48). (Like other women in our society, Agnes learned something about power in the course of her "education.")

Popular culture abounds with books and magazines that compile idealized depictions of relations between women and men. Those focused on the etiquette of dating or prevailing standards of feminine comportment are meant to be of practical help in these matters. However, the use of any such source *as a manual of procedure* requires the assumption that doing gender merely involves making use of discrete, well-defined bundles of behavior that can simply be plugged into interactional situations to produce recognizable enactments of masculinity and femininity. The man "does" being masculine by, for example, taking the woman's arm to guide her across a street, and she "does" being feminine by consenting to be guided and not initiating such behavior with a man.

Agnes could perhaps have used such sources as manuals, but, we contend, doing gender is not so easily regimented (Mithers 1982; Morris 1974). Such sources may list and describe the sorts of behaviors that mark or display gender, but they are necessarily incomplete (Garfinkel 1967, pp. 66–75; Wieder 1974, pp. 183–214; Zimmerman and Wieder 1970, pp. 285–98). And to be successful, marking or displaying gender must be finely fitted to situations and modified or transformed as the occasion demands. Doing gender consists of managing such occasions so that, whatever the particulars, the outcome is seen and seeable in context as gender-appropriate or, as the case may be, gender-*in*appropriate, that is, *accountable*.

[. . .]

Resources for Doing Gender

Doing gender means creating differences between girls and boys and women and men, differences that are not natural, essential, or biological. Once the differences have been constructed, they are used to reinforce the "essentialness" of gender. In a delightful account of the "arrangement between the sexes," Goffman (1977) observes the creation of a variety of institutionalized frameworks through which our "natural, normal sexedness" can be enacted. The physical features of social setting provide one obvious resource for the expression of our "essential" differences. For example, the sex segregation of North American public bathrooms distinguishes "ladies" from "gentlemen" in matters held to be fundamentally biological, even though both "are somewhat similar in the question of waste products and their elimination" (Goffman 1977, p. 315). These settings are furnished with dimorphic equipment (such as urinals for men or elaborate grooming facilities for women), even though both sexes may achieve the same ends through the same means (and apparently do so in the privacy of their own homes). To be stressed here is the fact that:

> The *functioning* of sex-differentiated organs is involved, but there is nothing in this functioning that biologically recommends segregation; *that* arrangement is a totally cultural matter . . . toilet segregation is presented as a natural consequence of the difference between the sex-classes when in fact it is a means of honoring, if not producing, this difference. (Goffman 1977, p. 316)

[. . .]

Gender may be routinely fashioned in a variety of situations that seem conventionally expressive to begin with, such as those that present "helpless" women next to heavy objects or flat tires. But, as Goffman notes, heavy, messy, and precarious concerns can be constructed from *any* social situation, "even though by standards set in other settings, this may involve something that is light, clean, and safe" (Goffman 1977, p. 324). Given these resources, it is clear that any interactional situation sets the stage for depictions of "essential" sexual natures. In sum, these situations "do not so much allow for the expression of natural differences as for the production of that difference itself" (Goffman 1977, p. 324).

[. . .]

Individuals have many social identities that may be donned or shed, muted or made more salient, depending on the situation. One may be a friend, spouse, professional, citizen, and many other things to many different people—or, to the same person at different times. But we are always women or men—unless we shift into another sex category. What this means is that our identificatory displays will provide an ever-available resource for doing gender under an infinitely diverse set of circumstances.

[. . .]

We have sought to show that sex category and gender are managed properties of conduct that are contrived with respect to the fact that others will judge and respond to us in particular ways. We have claimed that a person's gender is not simply an aspect of what one is, but, more fundamentally, it is something that one *does*, and does recurrently, in interaction with others.

[. . .]

Sex and Sexuality

What is the relationship between doing gender and a culture's prescription of "obligatory heterosexuality" (Rubin 1975; Rich 1980)? As Frye (1983, p. 22) observes, the monitoring of sexual feelings in relation to other appropriately sexed persons requires the ready recognition of such persons "before one can allow one's heart to beat or one's blood to flow in erotic enjoyment of that person." The appearance of heterosexuality is produced through emphatic and unambiguous indicators of one's sex, layered on in ever more conclusive fashion (Frye 1983, p. 24). Thus, lesbians and gay men concerned with passing as heterosexuals can rely on these indicators for camouflage; in contrast, those who would avoid the assumption of heterosexuality may foster ambiguous indicators of their categorical status through their dress, behaviors, and style. But "ambiguous" sex indicators are sex indicators nonetheless. If one wishes to be recognized as a lesbian (or heterosexual woman), one must first establish a categorical status as female. Even as popular images portray lesbians as "females who are not feminine" (Frye 1983, p. 129), the accountability of persons for their "normal, natural sexedness" is preserved.

Gender, Power, and Social Change

Let us return to the question: Can we avoid doing gender? Earlier, we proposed that insofar as sex category is used as a fundamental criterion for differentiation, doing gender is unavoidable. It is unavoidable because of the social consequences of sex-category membership: the allocation of power and resources not only in the domestic, economic, and political domains but also in the broad arena of interpersonal relations. In virtually any situation, one's sex category can be relevant, and one's performance as an incumbent of that category (i.e., gender) can be subjected to evaluation. Maintaining such pervasive and faithful assignment of lifetime status requires legitimation.

But doing gender also renders the social arrangements based on sex category accountable as normal and natural, that is, legitimate ways of organizing social life. Differences between women and men that are created by this process can then be portrayed as fundamental and enduring dispositions. In this light, the institutional arrangements of a society can be seen as responsive to the differences—the social order being merely an accommodation to the natural order. Thus if, in doing gender, men are also doing dominance and women are doing deference (cf. Goffman 1967, pp. 47–95), the resultant social order, which supposedly reflects "natural differences," is a powerful reinforcer and legitimator of hierarchical arrangements. Frye observes:

> For efficient subordination, what's wanted is that the structure not appear to be a cultural artifact kept in place by human decision or custom, but that it appear *natural*—that it appear to be quite a direct consequence of facts about the beast which are beyond the scope of human manipulation. . . . That we are trained to behave so differently as women and men, and to behave so differently toward women and men, itself contributes mightily to the appearance of extreme dimorphism, but also, the *ways* we act as women and men, and the *ways* we act toward women and men, mold our bodies and our minds to the shape of sub-ordination and dominance. We do become what we practice being. (Frye 1983, p. 34)

If we do gender appropriately, we simultaneously sustain, reproduce, and render legitimate the institutional arrangements that are based on sex category. If we fail to do gender appropriately, we as individuals—not the institutional arrangements—may be called to account (for our character, motives, and predispositions).

[. . .]

The sex category/gender relationship links the institutional and interactional levels, a coupling that legitimates social arrangements based on sex category and reproduces their asymmetry in face-to-face interaction. Doing gender furnishes the interactional scaffolding of social structure, along with a built-in mechanism of social control. In appreciating the institutional forces that maintain distinctions between women and men, we must not lose sight of the interactional validation of those distinctions that confers upon them their sense of "naturalness" and "rightness."

Social change, then, must be pursued both at the institutional and cultural level of sex category and at the interactional level of gender. Such a conclusion is hardly novel. Nevertheless, we suggest that it is important to recognize that the analytical distinction between institutional and interactional spheres does not pose an either/or choice when it comes to the question of effecting social change. Reconceptualizing gender not as a simple property of individuals but as an integral dynamic of social orders implies a new perspective on the entire network of gender relations.

[. . .]

Gender is a powerful ideological device, which produces, reproduces, and legitimates the choices and limits that are predicated on sex category. An understanding of how gender is produced in social situations will afford clarification of the interactional scaffolding of social structure and the social control processes that sustain it.

References

Bernstein, Richard. 1986. "France Jails 2 in Odd Case of Espionage." *New York Times*, May 11.

Blackwood, Evelyn. 1984. "Sexuality and Gender in Certain Native American Tribes: The Case of Cross-Gender Females." *Signs: Journal of Women in Culture and Society* 10:27–42.

Cucchiari, Salvatore. 1981. "The Gender Revolution and the Transition from Bisexual Horde to Patrilocal Band: The Origins of Gender Hierarchy." Pp. 31–79 in *Sexual Meanings: The Cultural Construction of Gender and Sexuality*, edited by S. B. Ortner and H. Whitehead. New York: Cambridge.

Frye, Marilyn. 1983. *The Politics of Reality: Essays in Feminist Theory*. Trumansburg, NY: The Crossing Press.

Garfinkel, Harold. 1967. *Studies in Ethnomethodology*. Englewood Cliffs, NJ: Prentice-Hall.

Goffman, Erving. 1967 [1956]. "The Nature of Deference and Demeanor." Pp. 47–95 in *Interaction Ritual*. New York: Anchor/Doubleday.

Goffman, Erving. 1977. "The Arrangement Between the Sexes." *Theory and Society* 4:301–31.

Hill, W. W. 1935. "The Status of the Hermaphrodite and Transvestite in Navaho Culture." *American Anthropologist* 37:273–79.

Kessler, Suzanne J. and Wendy McKenna. 1978. *Gender: An Ethnomethodological Approach*. New York: Wiley.

Martin, Kay M. and Barbara Voorhies. 1975. *Female of the Species*. New York: Columbia University Press.

Mithers, Carol L. 1982. "My Life as a Man." *The Village Voice* 27(October 5):1ff.

Money, John and Anke A. Erhardt. 1972. *Man and Woman/Boy and Girl*. Baltimore, MD: Johns Hopkins.

Money, John and Charles Ogunro. 1974. "Behavioral Sexology: Ten Cases of Genetic Male Intersexuality with Impaired Prenatal and Pubertal Androgenization." *Archives of Sexual Behavior* 3:181–206.

Money, John and John G. Brennan. 1968. "Sexual Dimorphism in the Psychology of Female Transsexuals." *Journal of Nervous and Mental Disease* 147:487–99.

Money, John and Patricia Tucker. 1975. *Sexual Signatures*. Boston, MA: Little, Brown.

Morris, Jan. 1974. *Conundrum*. New York: Harcourt Brace Jovanovich.

Raymond, Janice G. 1979. *The Transsexual Empire*. Boston, MA: Beacon.

Rich, Adrienne. 1980. "Compulsory Heterosexuality and Lesbian Existence." *Signs: Journal of Women in Culture and Society* 5:631–60.

Rubin, Gayle. 1975. "The Traffic in Women: Notes on the 'Political Economy' of Sex." Pp. 157–210 in *Toward an Anthropology of Women*, edited by R. Reiter. New York: Monthly Review Press.

Sacks, Harvey. 1972. "On the Analyzability of Stories by Children." Pp. 325–45 in *Directions in Sociolinguistics*, edited by J. J. Gumpen and D. Hymes. New York: Holt, Rinehart & Winston.

Schutz, Alfred. 1943. "The Problem of Rationality in the Social World." *Economics* 10:130–49.

Wieder, D. Lawrence. 1974. *Language and Social Reality: The Case of Telling the Convict Code*. The Hague: Mouton.

Williams, Walter L. 1986. *The Spirit and the Flesh: Sexual Diversity in American Indian Culture*. Boston, MA: Beacon.

Wilson, Thomas P. 1970. "Conceptions of Interaction and Forms of Sociological Explanation." *American Sociological Review* 35:697–710.

Zimmerman, Don H. and D. Lawrence Wieder. 1970. "Ethnomethodology and the Problem of Order: Comment on Denzin." Pp. 287–95 in *Understanding Everyday Life*, edited by J. Denzin. Chicago, IL: Aldine.

Framed Before We Know It

How Gender Shapes Social Relations

Cecilia L. Ridgeway

[. . .]

Gender as a Primary Frame

What does it mean to say that gender is a primary cultural frame for organizing social relations (Ridgeway 1997, 2006, 2007)? As we know, people depend on social relations with others to attain most of what they want and need in life. Social relations pose a well-known problem, however. To relate to another to accomplish a valued goal, we have to find some way to coordinate our behavior with that other. Classic sociologists such as Goffman (1967) and contemporary game theorists (Chwe 2001) have arrived at the same conclusion about what it takes to solve this coordination problem. For you and me to coordinate effectively, we need shared, "common" knowledge to use as a basis for our joint actions. Common knowledge is cultural knowledge that we all assume we all know. I have argued that actually, we need a particular type of common, cultural knowledge (Ridgeway 2007). We need a shared way of categorizing and defining "who" self and other are in the situation so that we can anticipate how each of us is likely to act and coordinate our actions accordingly.

Coordination and Difference

Systems for categorizing and defining things are based on contrast, and therefore, difference. Something is this because it is different from that. Defining *self* and *other* to relate focuses us on finding shared principles of social difference that we can use to categorize and make sense of one another. The coordination problem inherent to organizing social relations drives populations of people who must regularly relate to one another to develop shared social-category systems based on culturally defined standards of difference.

Cecilia L. Ridgeway. 2009. "Framed Before We Know It: How Gender Shapes Social Relations." *Gender & Society* 23(2):145–60.

To manage social relations in real time, some of these cultural-category systems must be so simplified that they can be quickly applied as framing devices to virtually anyone to start the process of defining *self* and *other* in the situation. In fact, studies of social cognition suggest that a very small number of such cultural-difference systems, about three or so, serve as the primary categories of person perception in a society (Brewer and Lui 1989; Fiske 1998). These primary categories define the things a person in that society must know about someone to render that someone sufficiently meaningful to relate to him or her.

Sex/gender, of course, is a form of human variation that is highly susceptible to cultural generalization as a primary category for framing social relations (Ridgeway 2006, 2007). It yields a cultural-difference system that is relevant to sexuality and reproduction and that delineates a line of difference among people who must regularly cooperate with one another. Thus, the male–female distinction is virtually always one of a society's primary cultural-category systems (Glick and Fiske 1999). In the United States, race and age are also primary categories (see Schneider 2004, 96).

Social-cognition studies show that in fact, we automatically and nearly instantly sex categorize any specific person to whom we attempt to relate (Ito and Urland 2003; Stangor et al. 1992). We do this not just in person but also over the Internet and even imaginatively, as we examine a person's résumé or think about the kind of person we would like to hire. Studies show that Americans categorize others they encounter on Black or white race almost instantly as well (Ito and Urland 2003). When we categorize another, we by comparison implicitly make salient our own sex and race categorization as well.

We so instantly sex-categorize others that our subsequent categorizations of them as, say, bosses or coworkers are nested in our prior understandings of them as male or female and take on slightly different meanings as result (Brewer and Lui 1989; Fiske 1998). This initial framing by sex never quite disappears from our understanding of them or ourselves in relation to them. Thus, we frame and are framed by gender literally before we know it. Importantly, however, the extent to which this preframing by gender shapes what happens in a specific situation depends greatly on what else is going on in that situation. As we will see, this is a point at which the gender frame interacts with institutional context. But first, I need to say more about how the gender frame coordinates behavior.

Cultural Beliefs About Gender

Primary categories of person perception, including sex category, work as cultural frames for coordinating behavior by associating category membership with widely shared cultural beliefs about how people in one category are likely to behave compared to those in a contrasting category. These cultural beliefs are shared stereotypes, as in "men are from Mars and women are from Venus." Gender stereotypes are our beliefs about how "most people" view the typical man or woman (Eagly and Karau 2002; Fiske 1998; Fiske et al. 2002). We all know these stereotypes as cultural knowledge, whether or not we personally endorse them. But the point is, because we think "most people" hold these beliefs, we expect others to judge us according to them. As a result, we must take these beliefs into account in our own behavior even if we do not endorse them. In this way, these shared cultural beliefs act as the "rules" for coordinating public behavior on the basis of gender (Ridgeway and Correll 2004).

The use of sex or gender as a primary cultural frame for defining *self* and *other* drives the content of gender stereotypes to focus on presumed gender differences. *Difference* need not logically imply inequality. Yet, among groups of people who must regularly deal with one another, difference is easily transformed into inequality through any of a variety of social processes (Ridgeway 2006). Once inequality is established between groups of people, however, it will reshape the nature of the differences that are culturally perceived as characteristic of the higher and lower status groups (Fiske et al. 2002; Jackman 1994). The content of our gender stereotypes shows the characteristic pattern of status inequality in which the higher status group is perceived as more proactive and agentically competent ("from Mars") and the lower status group is seen as more reactive and emotionally expressive ("from Venus"; Conway, Pizzamiglio, and Mount 1996; Glick and Fiske 1999; Wagner and Berger 1997). Thus, difference and inequality codetermine each other in our shared gender beliefs, and coordination on the basis of them produces social relations of inequality as well as difference (Wagner and Berger 1997).

[...]

The familiar, widely known gender stereotypes that I have called the rules of gender are not just individual beliefs. They are culturally *hegemonic* beliefs for two reasons. First, these beliefs are institutionalized in media representations, in the images of men and women implied by laws and government policies, and in a wide variety of taken-for-granted organizational practices. Second, the content of these gender beliefs, while they purport to be universal depictions of the sexes, in fact represent most closely the experiences and understandings of gender by dominant groups in society—those who most powerfully shape our institutions. The men and women we see in gender stereotypes look most like white, middle-class heterosexuals. Yet, as Shelley Correll and I have argued, in public places and with strangers, these hegemonic cultural beliefs about gender act as the default rules of gender (Ridgeway and Correll 2004). This makes the public enactment of gender that much more complicated for those who are not white, middle-class heterosexuals.

Although we all know hegemonic gender beliefs, many of us also hold alternative beliefs about gender that we share with a subgroup of similarly minded others—fellow feminists, a racial or ethnic group, or an immigrant group. Some evidence suggests that these alternative cultural beliefs about gender, rather than the hegemonic ones, shape our behavior and judgments most clearly when we are relating to others we believe share those beliefs (Filardo 1996; Milkie 1999). This makes sense if we are using these beliefs to coordinate our behavior with those others. It remains for future research to investigate the contexts in which we systematically rely on alternative gender beliefs, rather than hegemonic beliefs, to guide our behavior.

[...]

Effects of the Gender Frame

Research shows that sex categorization unconsciously primes gender stereotypes in our minds and makes them cognitively available to shape behavior and judgments (Blair and Banaji 1996; Kunda and Spencer 2003). The extent to which they actually do shape our behavior, however, can vary from negligible to substantial depending on the nature of the particular situation and our own motives or interests. What matters is the extent to which the information in gender beliefs is diagnostic for us in that it helps us figure out how to act in the situation. Research shows that some basic principles guide how this works.

When people in the situation differ in sex category, cultural beliefs about gender become effectively salient and measurably affect behaviors and judgments unless something else overrides them (see Ridgeway and Smith-Lovin 1999). Also, in either mixed or same-sex contexts, gender stereotypes implicitly shape behavior and judgments to the extent that gender is culturally defined as relevant to the situation, as, for instance, with a gender-typed task such as math (Ridgeway and Correll 2004; Ridgeway and Smith-Lovin 1999). The effects of gender beliefs on an actor's behavior will also be greater to the extent the actor consciously or unconsciously perceives the game of gender to be relevant to his or her own motives or interests in the situation (Fiske 1998).

Pulling these arguments together, we can see that the way the gender frame brings cultural beliefs about gender to bear on our expectations for self and other, on our behavior, and on our judgments produces a distinctive pattern of effects. In mixed-sex settings in which the task or context is relatively gender neutral, cultural beliefs that men are more agentically competent and more worthy of status will advantage them over otherwise similar women, but only modestly so. In settings that are culturally typed as masculine, gender beliefs will bias judgments and behaviors more strongly in favor of men. In contexts culturally linked with women, biases will weakly favor women except for positions of authority. A wide variety of research supports this general pattern of effects (see Ridgeway and Correll 2004; Ridgeway and Smith-Lovin 1999).

These effects largely describe the way the gender frame introduces implicit biases into expectations and behaviors that affect gender inequality in the setting. The enactment of inequality, however, is accomplished through the enactment of gender difference (e.g., agentic competence vs. reactive warmth) that implies and creates the inequality. The enactment of gender difference or inequality is fed by the interests the gender frame gives people in understanding themselves as appropriately gendered as well as by the way the gender frame causes them to react to and judge the behaviors of others. As institutionalized cultural "rules," gender beliefs about difference and inequality have a prescriptive edge that people enforce by sanctioning explicit violations. Women are typically sanctioned for acting too domineering and men for being too yielding or emotionally weak (Eagly and Karau 2002; Rudman and Fairchild 2004).

[...]

The Interaction of the Gender Frame and Institutional Structure

The extent to which the gender frame flavors or biases the performance of institutional role identities depends on two general factors. The first is the salience and relevance of the gender frame in the situation. As we can infer from above, this depends on the gender composition of the institutional context and the extent to which the activities and roles in the context are themselves culturally gendered. When organizational activities are gendered, the background gender frame becomes more powerfully relevant for actors, and the biases it introduces shape how people carry out those activities and how they fill in the details not clearly specified by institutional rules. The gendering of institutional tasks or roles, then, empowers the background gender frame in the situation to become a significant part of the process by which people enact their institutional roles. Scholars such as Patricia Martin have given us powerful illustrations of this process (Martin 2003).

A second factor that affects the impact of the gender frame is the extent to which organizational rules and procedures constrain individual discretion in judgments and behavior. The more constrained individuals' actions are, the less scope the gender frame has to implicitly shape their behavior on its own. For this reason, many scholars have recommended formal rules and procedures as devices to suppress stereotype bias and discrimination in employment (Bielby 2000; Reskin and McBrier 2000). On the other hand, feminist scholars have also long pointed out that apparently neutral formal rules and procedures can embody bias in their application or effect (e.g., Acker 1990; Nelson and Bridges 1999; Steinberg 1995).

The gender-framing perspective suggests that whether formal personnel procedures do more good than bad depends not only on the extent to which bias is built into the procedures but also on how powerfully disadvantaging the gender frame would be for women if actors were not constrained by formal procedures. Thus, there is no simple answer to the "are formal rules best" question. But a consideration of the joint effects of the gender frame and the organizational frame allows us to specify how the answer to this question varies systematically with the nature of the context. . . .

To the extent that cultural beliefs about gender do shape behavior and social relations in an institutional context, either directly through the gender frame acting on individuals or indirectly through biased procedures, these gender beliefs will be reinscribed into new organizational procedures and rules that actors develop through their social relations in that setting (Ridgeway 1997; Ridgeway and England 2007). In this way, the gendered structure of society can be projected into the future through new organizational procedures and forms that reinvent it for a new era.

My argument suggests that the background gender frame is the primary mechanism by which material, organizational structures become organized by gender. By the same token, these organizational structures sustain widely shared cultural beliefs about gender. To the extent that economic, technological, and political factors change these structures and the material arrangements that they create between men and women, these material changes create gradual, iterative pressure for change in cultural beliefs about gender as well.

[. . .]

Conclusion

. . . Although the gender frame acts through the sense-making of individuals as they try to coordinate their behaviors, it does more than add texture and detail to a structural account of gender and society. When considered jointly with an institutional or structural analysis, the effects of the gender frame help us see how gender becomes embedded in new organizational forms and material arrangements. This analysis also suggests that change in the gendered system of a society will be iterative and may not always proceed smoothly. The forces for change come from political, economic, and technological factors that alter the everyday material arrangements between men and women in ways that undercut traditional views of status differences between men and women. The initial impact of such material changes is often blunted because people reinterpret the meaning of these changes through the lens of their existing, more conservative gender beliefs. Yet, even as people do this, the material changes make those more conservative gender beliefs harder and harder to sustain as meaningful representations of men and women in everyday life. If, over time, changes in the material arrangements between men and women continue to accumulate, the traditional content of cultural beliefs about gender will gradually change as well. A single wave does not move a sandbar, but wave after wave does.

References

Acker, Joan. 1990. "Hierarchies, Jobs, and Bodies: A Theory of Gendered Organizations." *Gender & Society* 4:139–58.

Bielby, William T. 2000. "Minimizing Workplace Gender and Racial Bias." *Contemporary Sociology* 29:120–28.

Blair, Irene V. and Mahzarin R. Banaji. 1996. "Automatic and Controlled Processes in Stereotype Priming." *Journal of Personality and Social Psychology* 70:1142–63.

Brewer, Marilynn and Layton Lui. 1989. "The Primacy of Age and Sex in the Structure of Person Categories." *Social Cognition* 7:262–74.

Chwe, Michael Suk-Young. 2001. *Rational Ritual: Culture, Coordination, and Common Knowledge.* Princeton, NJ: Princeton University Press.

Conway, Michael M., Teresa Pizzamiglio, and Lauren Mount. 1996. "Status, Communality, and Agency: Implications for Stereotypes of Gender and Other Groups." *Journal of Personality and Social Psychology* 71:25–38.

Eagly, Alice H. and Stephen J. Karau. 2002. "Role Congruity Theory of Prejudice Towards Female Leaders." *Psychological Review* 109:573–79.

Filardo, Emily K. 1996. "Gender Patterns in African American and White Adolescents' Social Interactions in Same-Race, Mixed-Sex Groups." *Journal of Personality and Social Psychology* 71:71–82.

Fiske, Susan T. 1998. "Stereotyping, Prejudice, and Discrimination." In *The Handbook of Social Psychology.* Vol. 2. 4th ed. edited by D. T. Gilbert, S. T. Fiske, and G. Lindzey. Boston, MA: McGraw-Hill.

Fiske, Susan T., Amy J. Cuddy, Peter Glick, and Jun Xu. 2002. "A Model of (Often Mixed) Stereotype Content: Competence and Warmth Respectively Follow from Perceived Status and Competence." *Journal of Personality and Social Psychology* 82:878–902.

Glick, Peter and Susan T. Fiske. 1999. "Gender, Power Dynamics, and Social Interaction." In *Revisioning Gender*, edited by M. M. Ferree, J. Lorber, and B. B. Hess. Thousand Oaks, CA: Sage.

Goffman, Erving. 1967. *Interaction Ritual.* Garden City, NY: Doubleday.

Ito, Tiffany A. and Geoffrey R. Urland. 2003. "Race and Gender on the Brain: Electrocortical Measures of Attention to the Race and Gender of Multiply Categorizable Individuals." *Journal of Personality and Social Psychology* 85:616–26.

Jackman, Mary R. 1994. *The Velvet Glove: Paternalism and Conflict in Gender, Class, and Race Relations.* Berkeley, CA: University of California Press.

Kunda, Ziva and Steven J. Spencer. 2003. "When Do Stereotypes Come to Mind and When Do They Color Judgment? A Goal-Based Theoretical Framework for Stereotype Activation and Application." *Psychological Bulletin* 129:522–44.

Martin, Patricia Y. 2003. "'Said and Done' Versus 'Saying and Doing': Gendering Practices, Practicing Gender at Work." *Gender & Society* 17:342–66.

Milkie, Melissa A. 1999. "Social Comparison, Reflected Appraisals, and Mass Media: The Impact of Pervasive Beauty Images on Black and White Girls' Self-Concepts." *Social Psychology Quarterly* 62:190–210.

Nelson, Robert and William Bridges. 1999. *Legalizing Gender Inequality: Courts, Markets, and Unequal Pay for Women in America.* New York: Cambridge University Press.

Reskin, Barbara and Debra Branch McBrier. 2000. "Why Not Ascription? Organizations' Employment of Male and Female Managers." *American Sociological Review* 65:210–33.

Ridgeway, Cecilia L. 1997. "Interaction and the Conservation of Gender Inequality: Considering Employment." *American Sociological Review* 62:218–35.

Ridgeway, Cecilia L. 2006. "Gender as an Organizing Force in Social Relations: Implications for the Future of Inequality." In *The Declining Significance of Gender?* edited by F. D. Blau, M. C. Brinton, and D. B. Grusky. New York: Russell Sage Foundation.

Ridgeway, Cecilia L. 2007. "Gender as a Group Process: Implications for the Persistence of Inequality." In *The Social Psychology of Gender*, edited by S. J. Correll. New York: Elsevier.

Ridgeway, Cecilia L. and Lynn Smith-Lovin. 1999. "The Gender System and Interaction." *Annual Review of Sociology* 25:1991–216.

Ridgeway, Cecilia L. and Paula England. 2007. "Sociological Approaches to Sex Discrimination in Employment." In *Sex Discrimination in the Workplace: Multidisciplinary Perspectives*, edited by F. J. Crosby, M. S. Stockdale, and A. S. Ropp. Oxford, UK: Blackwell.

Ridgeway, Cecilia L. and Shelley J. Correll. 2004. "Unpacking the Gender System: A Theoretical Perspective on Gender Beliefs and Social Relations." *Gender & Society* 18(4):510–31.

Rudman, Laurie A. and Kimberly Fairchild. 2004. "Reactions to Counterstereotypic Behavior: The Role of Backlash in Cultural Stereotype Maintenance." *Journal of Personality and Social Psychology* 87:157–76.

Schneider, David J. 2004. *The Psychology of Stereotyping*. New York: Guilford.

Stangor, Charles, Laure Lynch, Changming Duan, and Beth Glass. 1992. "Categorization of Individuals on the Basis of Multiple Social Features." *Journal of Personality and Social Psychology* 62:207–18.

Steinberg, Ronnie J. 1995. "Gendered Instructions: Cultural Lag and Gender Bias in the Hay System of Job Evaluation." In *Gender Inequality at Work*, edited by J. A. Jacobs. Thousand Oaks, CA: Sage.

Wagner, David G. and Joseph Berger. 1997. "Gender and Interpersonal Task Behaviors: Status Expectation Accounts." *Sociological Perspectives* 40:1–32.

Defining Black Feminist Thought

Patricia Hill Collins

[...]

Who Can Be a Black Feminist?
The Centrality of Black Women Intellectuals
to the Production of Black Feminist Thought

I aim to develop a definition of Black feminist thought that relies exclusively neither on a materialist analysis—one whereby all African-American women by virtue of biology become automatically registered as "authentic Black feminists"—nor on an idealist analysis whereby the background, worldview, and interests of the thinker are deemed irrelevant in assessing his or her ideas. Resolving the tension between these two extremes involves reassessing the centrality Black women intellectuals assume in producing Black feminist thought. It also requires examining the importance of coalitions with Black men, white women, people of color, and other groups with distinctive standpoints. Such coalitions are essential in order to foster other groups' contributions as critics, teachers, advocates, and disseminators of a self-defined Afrocentric feminist standpoint.

Black women's concrete experiences as members of specific race, class, and gender groups as well as our concrete historical situations necessarily play significant roles in our perspectives on the world. No standpoint is neutral because no individual or group exists unembedded in the world. Knowledge is gained not by solitary individuals but by Black women as socially constituted members of a group (Narayan 1989). These factors all frame the definitional tensions in Black feminist thought.

Black women intellectuals are central to Black feminist thought for several reasons. First, our experiences as African-American women provide us with a unique standpoint on Black womanhood unavailable to other groups. It is more likely for Black women as members of an oppressed group to have critical insights into the condition of our own oppression than it is for

Patricia Hill Collins. 1990. Chapter 2 from *Black Feminist Thought: Knowledge, Consciousness, and the Politics of Empowerment*. New York: Routledge.

those who live outside those structures. One of the characters in Frances Ellen Watkins Harper's 1892 novel, *Iola Leroy*, expresses this belief in the special vision of those who have experienced oppression:

> Miss Leroy, out of the race must come its own thinkers and writers. Authors belonging to the white race have written good books, for which I am deeply grateful, but it seems to be almost impossible for a white man to put himself completely in our place. No man can feel the iron which enters another man's soul. (Carby 1987, 62)

Only African-American women occupy this center and can "feel the iron" that enters Black women's souls, because we are the only group that has experienced race, gender, and class oppression as Black women experience them. The importance of Black women's leadership in producing Black feminist thought does not mean that others cannot participate. It does mean that the primary responsibility for defining one's own reality lies with the people who live that reality, who actually have those experiences.

Second, Black women intellectuals provide unique leadership for Black women's empowerment and resistance. In discussing Black women's involvement in the feminist movement, Sheila Radford-Hill points out the connections among self-definition, empowerment, and taking actions in one's own behalf:

> Black women now realize that part of the problem within the movement was our insistence that white women do for/with us what we must do for/with ourselves: namely, frame our own social action around our own agenda for change. . . . Critical to this discussion is the right to organize on one's own behalf. . . . Criticism by black feminists must reaffirm this principle. (1986, 162)

Black feminist thought cannot challenge race, gender, and class oppression without empowering African-American women. "Oppressed people resist by identifying themselves as subjects, by defining their reality, shaping their new identity, naming their history, telling their story," notes bell hooks (1989, 43). Because self-definition is key to individual and group empowerment, using an epistemology that cedes the power of self-definition to other groups, no matter how well-meaning, in essence perpetuates Black women's subordination. As Black feminist sociologist Deborah K. King succinctly states, "Black feminism asserts self-determination as essential" (1988, 72).

Stressing the importance of Black women's centrality to Black feminist thought does not mean that all African-American women exert this leadership. While being an African-American woman generally provides the experiential base for an Afrocentric feminist consciousness, these same conditions suppress its articulation. It is not acquired as a finished product but must continually develop in relation to changing conditions.

Bonnie Johnson emphasizes the importance of self-definition. In her critique of Patricia Bell Scott's bibliography on Black feminism she challenges both Scott's categorization of all works by Black women as being Black feminist and Scott's identification of a wide range of African-American women as Black feminists: "Whether I think they're feminists is irrelevant. *They* would not call themselves feminist" (Clarke et al. 1983, 94). As Patrice L. Dickerson contends, "a person comes into being and knows herself by her achievements, and through her efforts to become and know herself, she achieves" (personal correspondence, 1988). Here is the heart of the matter. An Afrocentric feminist consciousness constantly emerges and is part of a self-conscious struggle to merge thought and action.

Third, Black women intellectuals are central in the production of Black feminist thought because we alone can create the group autonomy that must precede effective coalitions with other groups. This autonomy is quite distinct from separatist positions whereby Black women withdraw from other groups and engage in exclusionary politics. In her introduction to *Home Girls: A Black Feminist Anthology*, Barbara Smith describes this difference: "Autonomy and separatism are fundamentally different. Whereas autonomy comes from a position of strength, separatism comes from a position of fear. When we're truly autonomous we can deal with other kinds of people, a multiplicity of issues, and with difference, because we have formed a solid base of strength" (1983, xl). Black women intellectuals who articulate an autonomous, self-defined standpoint are in a position to examine the usefulness of coalitions with other groups, both scholarly and activist, in order to develop new models for social change. However, autonomy to develop a self-defined, independent analysis does not mean that Black feminist thought has relevance only for African-American women or that we must confine ourselves to analyzing our own experiences. As Sonia Sanchez points out, "I've always known that if you write from a black experience, you're writing from a universal experience as well. . . . I know you don't have to whitewash yourself to be universal" (in Tate 1983, 142).

While Black feminist thought may originate with Black feminist intellectuals, it cannot flourish isolated from the experiences and ideas of other groups. The dilemma is that Black women intellectuals must place our own experiences and consciousness at the center of any serious efforts to develop Black feminist thought yet not have that thought become separatist and exclusionary. bell hooks offers a solution to this problem by suggesting that we shift from statements such as "I am a feminist" to those such as "I advocate feminism." Such an approach could "serve as a way women who are concerned about feminism as well as other political movements could express their support while avoiding linguistic structures that give primacy to one particular group" (1984, 30).

By advocating, refining, and disseminating Black feminist thought, other groups—such as Black men, white women, white men, and other people of color—further its development. Black women can produce an attenuated version of Black feminist thought separated from other groups. Other groups cannot produce Black feminist thought without African-American women. Such groups can, however, develop self-defined knowledge reflecting their own standpoints. But the full actualization of Black feminist thought requires a collaborative enterprise with Black women at the center of a community based on coalitions among autonomous groups.

Coalitions such as these require dialogues among Black women intellectuals and within the larger African-American women's community. Exploring the common themes of a Black woman's standpoint is an important first step. Moreover, finding ways of handling internal dissent is especially important for the Black women's intellectual community. Evelyn Hammond describes how maintaining a united front for whites stifles her thinking: "What I need to do is challenge my thinking, to grow. On white publications sometimes I feel like I'm holding up the banner of black womanhood. And that doesn't allow me to be as critical as I would like to be" (in Clarke et al. 1983, 104). Cheryl Clarke observes that she has two dialogues: one with the public and the private ones in which she feels free to criticize the work of other Black women. Clarke states that the private dialogues are the ones that "have changed my life, have shaped the way I feel . . . have mattered to me" (p. 103).

Coalitions also require dialogues with other groups. Rather than rejecting our marginality, Black women intellectuals can use our outsider-within stance as a position of strength in building effective coalitions and stimulating dialogue. Barbara Smith suggests that Black women develop dialogues based on a "commitment to principled coalitions, based not upon expediency, but upon our actual need for each other" (1983, xxxiii). Dialogues among and coalitions with a range of groups, each with its own distinctive set of experiences and specialized thought embedded in those experiences, form the larger, more general terrain of intellectual and political discourse necessary for furthering Black feminism. Through dialogues exploring how relations of domination and subordination are maintained and changed, parallels between Black women's experiences and those of other groups become the focus of investigation.

Dialogue and principled coalition create possibilities for new versions of truth. Alice Walker's answer to the question of what she felt were the major differences between the literature of African-Americans and whites offers a provocative glimpse of the types of truths that might emerge through an epistemology based on dialogue and coalition. Walker did not spend much time considering this question, since it was not the difference between them that interested her, but, rather, the way Black writers and white writers seemed to be writing one immense story, with different parts of the story coming from a multitude of different perspectives. In a conversation with her mother, Walker refines this epistemological vision: "I believe that the truth about any subject only comes when all sides of the story are put together, and all their different meanings make one new one. Each writer writes the missing parts to the other writer's story. And the whole story is what I'm after" (1983, 49). Her mother's response to Walker's vision of the possibilities of dialogues and coalitions hints at the difficulty of sustaining such dialogues under oppressive conditions: "'Well, I doubt if you can ever get the *true* missing parts of anything away from the white folks,' my mother says softly, so as not to offend the waitress who is mopping up a nearby table; 'they've sat on the truth so long by now they've mashed the life out of it'" (1983, 49).

What Constitutes Black Feminism? The Recurring Humanist Vision

A wide range of African-American women intellectuals have advanced the view that Black women's struggles are part of a wider struggle for human dignity and empowerment. In an 1893 speech to women, Anna Julia Cooper cogently expressed this alternative worldview:

> We take our stand on the solidarity of humanity, the oneness of life, and the unnaturalness and injustice of all special favoritisms, whether of sex, race, country, or condition. . . . The colored woman feels that woman's cause is one and universal; and that . . . not till race, color, sex, and condition are seen as accidents, and not the substance of life; not till the universal title of humanity to life, liberty, and the pursuit of happiness is conceded to be inalienable to all; not till then is woman's lesson taught and woman's cause won—not the white woman's nor the black woman's, not the red woman's but the cause of every man and of every woman who has writhed silently under a mighty wrong. (Lowenberg and Bogin 1976, 330–31)

Like Cooper, many African-American women intellectuals embrace this perspective regardless of particular political solutions we propose, our fields of study, or our historical periods. Whether we advocate working through separate Black women's organizations, becoming part of women's organizations, working within existing political structures, or supporting Black community institutions, African-American women intellectuals repeatedly identify political actions such as these as a *means* for human empowerment rather than ends in and of themselves. Thus the primary guiding principle of Black feminism is a recurring humanist vision (Steady 1981).

Alice Walker's preference for the term *womanist*, a term she describes as "womanist is to feminist as purple is to lavender," addresses this notion of the solidarity of humanity. To Walker, one is "womanist" when one is "committed to the survival and wholeness of entire people, male and female." A womanist is "not a separatist, except periodically for health" and is "traditionally universalist, as is 'Mama, why are we brown, pink, and yellow, and our cousins are white, beige, and black?' Ans.: 'Well, you know the colored race is just like a flower garden, with every color flower represented'" (1983, xi). By redefining all people as "people of color," Walker universalizes what are typically seen as individual struggles while simultaneously allowing space for autonomous movements of self-determination.

In assessing the sexism of the Black nationalist movement of the 1960s, Black feminist lawyer Pauli Murray identifies the dangers inherent in separatism as opposed to autonomy, and also echoes Cooper's concern with the solidarity of humanity:

> The lesson of history that all human rights are indivisible and that the failure to adhere to this principle jeopardizes the rights of all is particularly applicable here. A built-in hazard of an aggressive ethnocentric movement which disregards the interests of other disadvantaged groups is that it will become parochial and ultimately self-defeating in the face of hostile reactions, dwindling allies, and mounting frustrations.... Only a broad movement for human rights can prevent the Black Revolution from becoming isolated and can insure ultimate success. (Murray 1970, 102)

Without a commitment to human solidarity, suggests Murray, any political movement—whether nationalist, feminist or antielitist—may be doomed to ultimate failure.

bell hooks's analysis of feminism adds another critical dimension that must be considered: namely, the necessity of self-conscious struggle against a more generalized ideology of domination:

> To me feminism is not simply a struggle to end male chauvinism or a movement to ensure that women will have equal rights with men; it is a commitment to eradicating the ideology of domination that permeates Western culture on various levels—sex, race, and class, to name a few—and a commitment to reorganizing U.S. society so that the self-development of people can take precedence over imperialism, economic expansion, and material desires. (hooks 1981, 194)

Former assemblywoman Shirley Chisholm also points to the need for self-conscious struggle against the stereotypes buttressing ideologies of domination. In "working toward our own freedom, we can help others work free from the traps of their stereotypes," she notes. "In the end, antiblack, antifemale, and all forms of discrimination are equivalent to the same thing—antihumanism.... We must reject not only the stereotypes that others have of us but also those we have of ourselves and others" (1970, 181).

This humanist vision is also reflected in the growing prominence of international issues and global concerns in the works of contemporary African-American women intellectuals (Lindsay 1980; Steady 1981, 1987). Economists Margaret Simms and Julianne Malveaux's 1986 edited volume, *Slipping Through the Cracks: The Status of Black Women*, contains articles on Black women in Tanzania, Jamaica, and South Africa. Angela Davis devotes an entire section of her 1989 book, *Women, Culture, and Politics*, to international affairs and includes essays on Winnie Mandela and on women in Egypt. June Jordan's 1985 volume, *On Call*, includes essays on South Africa, Nicaragua, and the Bahamas. Alice Walker writes compellingly of the types of links these and other Black women intellectuals see between African-American women's issues and those of other groups: "To me, Central America is one large plantation; and I see the people's struggle to be free as a slave revolt" (1988, 177).

The words and actions of Black women intellectuals from different historical times and addressing markedly different audiences resonate with a strikingly similar theme of the oneness of all human life. Perhaps the most succinct version of the humanist vision in Black feminist thought is offered by Fannie Lou Hamer, the daughter of sharecroppers, and a Mississippi civil rights activist. While sitting on her porch, Ms. Hamer observed, "Ain' no such thing as I can hate anybody and hope to see God's face" (Jordan 1981, xi).

Taken together, the ideas of Anna Julia Cooper, Pauli Murray, bell hooks, Alice Walker, Fannie Lou Hamer, and other Black women intellectuals too numerous to mention suggest a powerful answer to the question "What is Black feminism?" Inherent in their words and deeds is a definition of Black feminism as a process of self-conscious struggle that empowers women and men to actualize a humanist vision of community.

References

Carby, Hazel. 1987. *Reconstructing Womanhood: The Emergence of the African American Woman Novelist.* New York: Oxford University Press.

Chisholm, Shirley. 1970. *Unbought and Unbossed.* New York: Avon.

Clarke, Cheryl, Jewell L. Gomez, Evelyn Hammonds, Bonnie Johnson, and Linda Powell. 1983. "Conversations and Questions: Black Women on Black Women Writers." *Conditions: Nine* 3(3):88–137.

hooks, bell. 1981. *Ain't I a Woman? Black Women and Feminism.* New York: Routledge.

hooks, bell. 1989. *Talking Back: Thinking Feminist, Thinking Black.* Boston, MA: South End Press.

hooks, bell. 1984. *Feminist Theory: From Margin to Center.* Boston, MA: South End Press.

Jordan June. 1981. *Civil Wars.* Boston, MA: Beacon.

King, Deborah K. 1988. "Multiple Jeopardy, Multiple Consciousness: The Context of a Black Feminist Ideology." *Signs* 14(1):42–72.

Lindsay, Beverly, ed. 1980. *Comparative Perspectives of Third World Women: The Impact of Race, Sex, and Class.* New York: Praeger.

Lowenberg, Bert J. and Ruth Bogin, eds. 1976. *Black Women in Nineteenth Century American Life.* University Park, PA: Pennsylvania State University Press.

Murray, Pauli. 1970. "The Liberation of Black Women." Pp. 87–102 in *Voices of the New Feminism*, edited by M. L. Thompson. Boston, MA: Beacon.

Narayan, Uma. 1989. "The Project of Feminist Epistemology: Perspectives from a Non-Western Feminist." Pp. 256–69 in *Gender/Body/Knowledge: Feminist Reconstructions of Being and Knowing*, edited by A. M. Jaggar and S. Bordo. New Brunswick, NJ: Rutgers University Press.

Radford-Hill, Sheila. 1986. "Annie Mae in Academe." *Women's Studies Quarterly.*

Smith, Barbara. 1983. "Introduction." Pp. xix–lvi in *Home Girls: A Black Feminist Anthology*, edited by B. Smith. New York: Kitchen Table Press.

Steady, Filomina Chioma. 1981. "The Black Woman Cross-Culturally: An Overview." Pp. 7–42 in *The Black Woman Cross-Culturally,* edited by F. C. Steady. Cambridge, MA: Schenman.

Tate, Claudia, ed. 1983. *Black Women Writers at Work.* New York: Continuum Publishing.

Walker, Alice. 1983. *In Search of Our Mothers' Gardens We Find Our Own.* New York: Harcourt Brace Jovanovich.

Walker, Alice. 1988. *Living by the Word.* New York: Harcourt Brace Jovanovich.

Hegemonic Masculinity and the Possibility of Change in Gender Relations

Claire Duncanson

© iStockphoto.com/Mari

Hegemonic masculinity was introduced as a concept which, due to its understanding of gender as dynamic and relational and of power as consent, could explain both the persistence of male power *and* the potential for social change. Raewyn Connell, one of the originators and key proponents of the concept, maintains that in its formulation it allows for more equitable relations between dominant and subordinate groups (Connell 2005, 1818; Connell and Messerschmidt 2005, 853). Yet, when hegemonic masculinity is applied in empirical cases, it is most often used to demonstrate the way in which hegemonic masculinity shifts and adopts new practices in order to enable some men to retain power over others (Ehrenreich 1984; Demetriou 2001; Hooper 2001; Messner 2007; Messerschmidt 2010). . . . My particular

Claire Duncanson. 2015. "Hegemonic Masculinity and the Possibility of Change in Gender Relations." *Men and Masculinities* 18(2):231–48.

contribution is to build on an emergent and underdeveloped strand of Connell's work on hegemonic masculinity: how change might be theorized.

The term hegemonic masculinity is well established in gender and sexuality studies. Since its introduction in the 1980s (Carrigan, Connell, and Lee 1985; Connell 1987), many theorists have built on the insight that masculinities exist in relations of hierarchy, dominated by a loosely coherent and evolving hegemonic form which dominates not through force, but through consent (Donaldson 1993; Connell 1995; Connell 2002; Hearn 2004; Connell and Messerschmidt 2005). It "occupies a uniquely privileged positioning within the field" (Beasley 2012, 753) and is used in a wide variety of contexts (Messerschmidt 2012) to explain the persistence of male dominance in a context of multiple and dynamic masculinities.

I argue that hegemonic masculinity remains a useful concept, but that the process through which "hegemony may fail" (Connell and Messerschmidt 2005, 853) requires rethinking. I make this argument by exploring and working through empirical material on military masculinities, drawing on both my own research and critical analysis of the literature. Militaries are important sites for the investigation of hegemonic masculinities. Constructions of masculinity and femininity in the military context arguably shape the entire gender order. The idea that men take life while women give it underpins the ideology of gender difference, especially in cultures where military myth and the military as an institution play a significant role in national pride (Muir 1993; Morgan 1994; Segal 1997). "No other arena," as Connell (1995, 213) puts it, "has been more important for the definition of hegemonic masculinity in European and American culture." If the concept of hegemonic masculinity is to be of use in theorizing the potential of social change as well as understanding the persistence of the gender order, it needs to work here.

. . . For the unraveling of hegemonic masculinity, men must be encouraged not so much to *change their ways* as to *change the way in which they negotiate their identities in relation to others*. Rather than forge their identities through relations of opposition or domination, men and subjects in general need to construct their identities through recognition of similarity, respect, interdependence, empathy, and equality with others. The importance of ideas of interdependence and empathy in undoing hierarchical gender relations is not a new insight, but detailed theorization of how this process of change could occur is missing from Connell and others' accounts. There has been since the 1980s a focus on gender as practice, but as Deutsch perceptively notes, the language inherent in the phrase "doing gender" has "undermined the goal of dismantling gender inequity by, perhaps inadvertently, perpetuating the idea that the gender system of oppression is hopelessly impervious to real change and by ignoring the links between social interaction and structural change" (Deutsch 2007, 107). It is the aim of this article to develop these links and to develop Connell's theorizing of the dynamics of gender relations and the possibility of social change.

[. . .]

Hegemonic Masculinity in Militaries Scholarship

The concept of hegemonic masculinity has . . . been used extensively in order to capture the way in which certain ideas about being a soldier and a man dominate in army cultures, with important implications for the gender order as a whole. These ideas differ slightly in different times and places but are generally ideas connected to combat: strength, physical fitness, aggression, action, competitiveness, and the ability to dehumanize the enemy and defeat them in combat, along with some not so directly connected to combat: heterosexual (and actively so) and hard drinking, for example. The argument is not that all soldiers fit this model or even that the majority do—rather, that this model acts as a cultural ideal, in more or less overt ways, and all negotiate their masculinity in relation to it (Enloe 1983, 1993; Morgan 1994; Hockey 2003; Higate 2003; Woodward and Winter 2007).

The workings of hegemonic masculinity are complex. At times it acts as a glue: A shared respect and admiration for the idealized model provides the common ground to mask the differences of class, rank, and age; at the same time, however, hegemonic masculinity is the result of the power struggles and rivalries between different groups of men and their efforts to prove their masculinity (Enloe 1993, 98). Moreover, these power struggles are expressed in gendered—often misogynist and homophobic—terms: the threat of being feminized is used to downgrade and police groups of men—which we see in army training with the archetypal use of "woman," "girl," "queer," and "faggot" to put down those who are failing to complete the various physical challenges associated with manliness (Segal 1997; McManners 1993; Woodward 1998; Higate 2003; Hockey 2003). Importantly, these strategies of feminization—although directed at men—have an impact on women by reinforcing "feminized" qualities with inferiority.

It is clear from the terms used to feminize others that sexuality has also been at issue in the power struggles. Heterosexuality has been central to Connell's concept of hegemonic masculinity as a practice which has enabled men's dominance over women and subordinate men to continue. The policing of the boundaries between heterosexual and homosexual has been a central dynamic in the construction of hegemonic masculinity: "gayness, in patriarchal ideology, is the repository of whatever is symbolically expelled from hegemonic masculinity . . ." (Connell 1995, 78). This has perhaps particularly been so in many western military contexts, where some allege the insecurities brought about by a homosocial culture have at times engendered an acute homophobia (Judd 2014).

The dominance of this combat-oriented masculinity, which is associated with toughness, force, and heterosexual prowess, has had material effects. When this way of being a man is valorized, so too are the practices of militarization and war—military solutions to problems which are arguably better solved in other ways. The association of masculinity with toughness, aggression, and war, and femininity with weakness, passivity, and peace privileges "tough" responses to conflict and feminizes nonviolent alternatives, reinforcing the systems of war and militarism (Tickner 1992; Hooper 2001; Enloe 2007; Cockburn 2010). The dominance of this particular model of military masculinity has also been linked to violence against women by soldiers including the use of rape as a weapon of war (Eriksson Baaz and Stern 2009; Meger 2010), domestic violence (Lutz 2004), and the sexual exploitation of women on peacekeeping operations (Whitworth 2004; Higate 2007). Finally, it maintains the very idea that gender is a dichotomous structure, with that which is masculine valorized over that which is feminine, not just in military contexts but beyond.

Western militaries have of course changed much over recent decades. They have shifted focus from traditional warfare to more complex operations, often with a peacebuilding or stabilization agenda (Moskos, Williams, and Segal 2000; Elliot and Cheeseman 2004). They have downsized, modernized, and increased in their professionalism, with implications for masculinities (King 2013). Furthermore, militaries do not exist in isolation from wider society, and military masculinities have thus been influenced by changes in masculinities in civilian culture (Woodward and Winter 2007). In feminist studies of these shifts in military masculinities, however, what is emphasized is the superficiality of any change in hegemonic masculinity. Hegemonic masculinity—both cultural ideal and patterns of practice of real men—is acknowledged to have changed, but new hierarchies have been formed. In other words, there is a softening of hegemonic masculinity, through the adoption of new practices and styles of soldiering, but with little in the way of shifts of power from privileged men and masculinist foreign policies. . . .

Hegemonic Masculinity and the "Flexibility of the Machinery of Rule"

Steve Niva (1998, 118) identifies a new hegemonic masculinity in the US military at the time of the 1991 US invasion of Iraq in which an "openly articulated sense of manly vulnerability and human compassion" appeared to have replaced "bravado or stern invincibility." The First Gulf War enabled the US army and nation to reclaim their masculinity in response to its emasculation in the wake of Vietnam, he argues, but this masculinity was significantly different. Military spokespersons' constant references to worrying about the safety of "our troops" and media coverage which avoided jingoist militarism are interpreted by Niva as evidence of a feminization of military masculinity, through the construction of a "tough and aggressive, yet tender-hearted masculinity" (Niva 1998, 118). The way in which, for example, General Colin Powell "openly wept at his high school reunion," and General Norman Schwarzkopf "spoke of his love for the opera and his family and even donned traditional Saudi robes on occasion in a display of multicultural sensitivity" suggests that American soldiers could be "tough but tender" (Niva 1998, 118). The construction was based on race as well as gender, with the liberal and compassionate white masculinity of the US soldiers contrasted with Saddam Hussein, who became an "Oriental Hitler," and a positioning of Arab men in general as backward in their macho and hypermasculine ways (Niva 1998, 119). Rather than fundamental change, then, this shift was nothing more than "a redefinition of masculinity in man's favour through an expansion of the concept of legitimate masculinity and thus an extension of masculinity's power over women and deviant men who do not measure up to this new paradigm" (Niva 1998, 121). The result is another "hybrid masculinity," combining aggressiveness *and* sensitivity, in order to ensure the position of elite men is harder to challenge. Niva's conclusion details the negative consequences:

> This new masculinity can counter critics who claim it seeks to denigrate women or sharply define itself against the feminine. It can hold itself out as superior to and more easily justify its actions, however ill intentioned, against those men and masculinities in different social and cultural contexts that are still associated with traditional patriarchal social orders. And it can do all this without having to radically question the persistent fact that men, particularly elite western men, still dominate the major institutions, decision making bodies of international authority and power that, however enlightened their agendas and concerns, still shape the agenda of world politics. (Niva 1998, 122)

Feminists have identified similar tough but tender masculinities in the discourse surrounding 1990s peacekeeping, peacebuilding, and humanitarian operations (Orford 1999; Razack 2004; Whitworth 2004). Both Sherene Razack and Sandra Whitworth argue compellingly that Canadian peacekeepers in Somalia in 1993 constructed their masculinity in relation to the Somalis they were supposed to be protecting. The positioning of Somalis as barbaric and primitive, ungrateful and immoral, enabled a Canadian peacekeeper masculinity that was civilized, advanced, and heroic, reinforcing ideas of Canada as an ethical middle power, an expert at peacekeeping (Razack 2004, 24–27; Whitworth 2004, 85–118). Even after the murder of a sixteen-year-old Somali boy at the hands of two Canadian peacekeepers, it was noticeable how quickly the narrative returned to one in which a "gentle, peacekeeping nation was betrayed by a few unscrupulous men" (Razack 2004, 4). Razack (2004, 14) argues that what the Somalia Affair teaches us is that "the dehumanization of others is more easily accomplished and condoned when we understand those others to be different and when we understand ourselves to be standing outside of the world's crises as impartial and compassionate observers." It thus reinforces racism and provides a "smokescreen for a new politics of containment in peripheralized regions" (Pieterse 1998, 236). Here, "peripheralized" conveys "the legacy of authoritarianism, the supremacy of security in politics, surplus armaments, and a tradition of politics of polarization—in many cases overlaid upon the authoritarian legacy of colonialism" (Pieterse 1998, 236) which are obscured by the "powerful and seductive story of the West bringing human rights and democracy to non-Western countries" (Razack 2004, 47). Similarly, in the narratives justifying intervention in Bosnia, Ann Orford argues that the intervening forces are imagined as "white knights," heroic agents of progress, democratic values, peace, and security, while the locals are "oppressors, criminals or primitive barbarians" (leaders or elites), "engaged in child-like squabbles, motivated by unsatisfied ambitions, and cannot govern themselves" (ethnic groups) or "starving, powerless, suffering, abused, helpless victims" (women and children; Orford 1999, 698–99). She concludes, "The constant linking of violence to local passions and chaotic nationalism masks the more far-reaching forms of violence that are now conducted through massive restructuring and social upheaval in the name of free trade or economic liberalism" (Orford 1999, 710).

[. . .]

It is clear that there has also been a considerable degree of change in terms of gender relations *within* western militaries in the last decades. This is not just with respect to the inclusion of women, where all North Atlantic Treaty Organization militaries, with the current exception of the United Kingdom, have opened up combat positions to female personnel. It is also evident in terms of attitudes to sexuality. The US policy of Don't Ask Don't Tell was repealed in 2011. Recent findings that the repeal had no overall negative impact on cohesion, recruitment, retention, assaults, harassment, or morale (Belkin et al. 2013) indicate that the US military is now a more tolerant place for LGBT personnel. The United Kingdom's Code of Social Conduct conceptualizes sexual orientation as a private matter for the individual, ending the compulsory discharge of known homosexuals, and indicating the UK military too is becoming more accepting of diversity (Judd 2014; Bindel 2012).

One could conclude that heterosexuality is no longer so obviously the quintessential practice of hegemonic masculinity, and homosexuality the subordinated, as was once the case. Here too, however, commentators suggest that progress is not straightforward. LGBT personnel are clearly still more tolerated than celebrated. Sarah Bulmer's conclusion of the UK case posits the idea that LGBT inclusion in the military could be understood as "homonormative," whereby only certain "acceptable queers," ones who are discreet and keep their sexuality private, are accepted (Bulmer 2013). . . . We arguably have another case of old hierarchies being replaced by new ones: respectable, discreet queers and problematic, offensive, "out" queers.

The key point to note here is that all these cases reinforce the claims of many feminist and postcolonial scholars that race, class, nation, and sexuality need to be considered in any analysis of gender relations. "Softer" or hybrid masculinities appear to always entail new race or class or sexuality oppressions. Discussing masculinity in isolation from other practices can thus "obscure rather than illuminate both structural inequalities and progressive changes" (Hooper 2001, 73). Attentiveness to intersectionality, not just masculinities and femininities, is vital to ensure that change in gender relations is progressive and that any challenge to hegemonic masculinity is meaningful. As Michael Messner concludes, although drawing from a different context (the hybrid masculinity of California Governor Arnold Schwarzenegger):

The success of this new man leadership style is at once a visible sign of the ways that liberal feminist critiques of hypermasculinity have been incorporated and embodied into many professional-class men's interactional styles and displays. What results is a rounding of the hard edges off of hypermasculinity and a visible softening of powerful men's public styles and displays. But this should not be seen necessarily as a major victory for feminism. Rather, if I am correct that this more sensitive, new man style tends to facilitate and legitimize privileged men's wielding of power over others, this is probably better seen as an example of feminism's being co-opted into new forms of domination—in this case, class and race domination. (Messner 2007, 477)

Conceptualizing Change: Positive Hegemonic Masculinity, a Contradiction in Terms?

The view that unravelling masculinities is a utopian aspiration because new hegemonic masculinities are always being refigured—often across multiple axes of identity—is dominant in empirical studies. . . . As Hooper (2001, 61) puts it, "Hegemonic masculinity gets transformed, through constant challenges and struggles, to resemble whatever traits happen to be most strategically useful for the getting and keeping of power." The risk is that we come to our analysis of gender relations with a framework within which progressive change cannot be conceptualized.

. . . It is as if any shift in gender relations is inevitably hegemony at work; and there is little point in asking whether such shifts might be signs of progressive change, and, more importantly, how they could be furthered. Connell's work never has this pessimism. From initial theorizing about hegemonic masculinity to her more recent work, she argues that hegemonic masculinity is capable of radical reform—of being *dismantled,* so that there are no remaining hierarchical relations between masculinity and femininity. Two questions immediately arise. Is Connell attentive enough to intersectionality, that is, does she address the way in which challenges to hegemonic masculinity often in practice involve new hierarchical relations across other and multiple axes of identity? Second, how is this dismantling to come about? The most explicit articulation of this commitment to the possibility of dismantling hegemonic masculinity appears in Connell and Messerschmidt's (2005) revisiting of the concept, where they argue that gender relations are always areas of tension, of contestation, and that, crucially, "hegemony may fail":

> Put another way, the conceptualization of hegemonic masculinity should explicitly acknowledge the possibility of democratizing gender relations, of abolishing power differentials, not just of reproducing hierarchy. A transitional move in this direction requires an attempt to establish as hegemonic among men [. . .] a version of hegemony open to equality of women. In this sense, it is possible to define a hegemonic masculinity that is thoroughly "positive" [. . .]. Recent history has shown the difficulty of doing this in practice. A positive hegemony remains, nevertheless, a key strategy for contemporary efforts at reform. (Connell and Messerschmidt 2005, 853)

They are quite clear, then, that the concept of hegemonic masculinity should not imply that masculinity's dominance over femininity or men's dominance over women is inevitable. Gender relations can be democratized, made more equal. As for the how, the suggestion is that it is possible to have a "positive hegemonic masculinity"—positive in the sense that it is "open to equality with women" and hegemonic in the sense that it remains "hegemonic among men."

What is being proposed is a two-step process: a "transitional stage" in which a version of masculinity is established which is open to equality with women as hegemonic among men, then, second, eradicating relations of hierarchy, presumably through allowing the hegemonic masculinity to construct those relations of equality.

[. . .]

I argue that, if there are to be two stages, the transitory stage would be more likely to be one where the hegemonic masculinity shifts to adopt traits, practices, and values which are conventionally associated with femininity. Rather than the disposition toward equality and democracy coming first—which is the difficult challenge—the more achievable and therefore more likely first step is the incorporation of the "feminine." This, of course, is the phenomenon identified in much of the literature, as outlined earlier, where it was found to be problematic—constituting a new hybrid hegemonic masculinity which relied on the subordination of others while pretending to progressive change. Yet, I argue that it is a mistake to confuse these particular examples with a problem with the concept itself. Although in many cases hegemonic masculinity shifts to retain power, it can be more fundamentally challenged—dismantled, in Connell's terms. The softening of hegemonic masculinities, identified across many contexts, is not always inevitably a superficial change, masking the retention of power and the creation of new hierarchies. The difference can be illustrated with reference to changing military masculinities in the British Army.

British Military Masculinities Constructed Through Relations of Equality

. . . As a result of an increased focus on peace support or stabilization operations, we can identify an alternative British military masculinity to the combat model; a masculinity that is associated as much with conflict resolution as conflict, with the skills and practices of communication, negotiation, humanitarianism, sensitivity, compassion, and empathy (Duncanson 2009, 2013). The attempts to construct an alternative masculinity—a peacebuilder masculinity—have potentially important lessons for theorizing how the more radical transformatory challenge to hegemonic masculinity can be achieved. Here we see practices traditionally associated with femininity, such as communication, sensitivity, and compassion, included in the model of masculinity. As a step, it is necessary but far from sufficient, given the analysis of the softening of masculinities detailed previously. To be part of a process of radical change, peacebuilder masculinity must be constructed in a way that does not create new hierarchical identities across any axes of identity.

[. . .]

There are examples of British soldiers in Bosnia taking women's groups seriously as political actors, subverting the positioning of women as passive victims in warzones, and of British soldiers in Iraq and Afghanistan building relations of empathy and mutual respect with local people and the soldiers of the local security forces (see Duncanson 2009, 2013). In such cases, hierarchical gender dichotomies are not merely replaced with others, but the structure of hierarchical gender relations begins to be dismantled. It has to be restated that these instances are rare, and far overshadowed by evidence of soldiers constructing masculinities through "radical Othering." Nonetheless, it is important to consider the disruptions to the rule because of the insight they give us into the possibility and mechanics of change which would actually dismantle hegemonic masculinity.

There is evidence from other contexts of gender relations increasingly being forged through relations of equality and respect, such as rock music subcultures (Schippers 2007); some American University fraternities that are shifting away from the laddish "frat boy culture" (Anderson 2008, 616–17); and families who are making concerted efforts to divide housework and childcare equally, redefining family roles in the process (Risman 1999). In these cases, it is not just that hegemonic masculinities shift to incorporate practices associated with femininity, it is that crucially the masculinities are being constructed through relations of equality and respect, thus dismantling hegemony.

In sum, I agree with Connell that positive change is possible, that "hegemony might fail," but disagree over the way in which it can happen. As I have argued, the idea of a masculinity hegemonic among men retaining its hegemony but being open to relations of equality with women is contradictory. The idea that a softer, more feminized form of hybrid masculinity (in the sense that it has incorporated traits and practices associated with women and femininity) can become hegemonic, however, is theoretically possible and empirically observable in many situations. This phenomenon has the potential to be dangerous—masking new oppressions by seeming to be progressive—or more positive. It is positive if, and only if, it is constructed through relations of empathy and respect.

Conclusion: Pushing at Contradictions and Encouraging Relational Thinking

[. . .]

To conclude, to dismantle hegemonic masculinity, hierarchical relations must be replaced with relations of equality, mutual respect, or empathy. Dismantling can happen in stages, as Connell argues, but the transitory stage cannot be the one she suggests, where a version of masculinity open to equality with women becomes hegemonic among men. Given the means by which hegemonic masculinity is formed, through the subordination—often feminization—of others, that suggestion is incoherent. Instead, the transitory stage has to be one where traditionally disparaged, feminized traits are newly valued and incorporated into "softer" or hybrid masculinities. The forging of more equal relations is the ultimate, more challenging stage. The hybrid stage may make it more likely that relations of equality, mutual respect, empathy, and so on, are formed, however, so rather than dismiss the New Man syndrome in all its contexts, assuming it always camouflages the continuation of patriarchy, militarism, and neoliberalism, we can look to expose its contradictions and to push for those relations of equality.

References

Anderson, Eric. 2008. "Inclusive Masculinity in a Fraternal Setting." *Men and Masculinities* 10:604–20.

Beasley, Chris. 2012. "Problematizing Contemporary Men/Masculinities Theorizing: The Contribution of Raewyn Connell and Conceptual-terminological Tensions Today." *The British Journal of Sociology* 63:747–65.

Belkin, Aaron, Morten G. Ender, Nathaniel Frank, Stacie R. Furia, George Lucas, Gary Packard, Steven M. Samuels, Tammy Schultz, and David R. Segal. 2013. "Readiness and DADT Repeal: Has the New Policy of Open Service Undermined the Military?" *Armed Forces & Society* 39:587–601.

Bindel, Julie. 2012. "For Lesbian and Gay Recruits, The UK Military Has Been Transformed." *The Guardian,* July 5. World news. Retrieved June 15, 2014 (www.theguardian.com/ world/2012/jul/05/ uk-military-generals-attend-lgbt-conference).

Bulmer, Sarah. 2013. "Patriarchal Confusion? Making Sense of Gay and Lesbian Military Identity." *International Feminist Journal of Politics* 15:137–56.

Carrigan, T., R. W. Connell, and J. Lee. 1985. "Toward a New Sociology of Masculinity." *Theory and Society* 14:551–604.

Cockburn, Cynthia. 2010. "Gender Relations as Causal in Militarization and War." *International Feminist Journal of Politics* 12:139–57.

Connell, R. W. 1987. *Gender and Power: Society, the Person and Sexual Politics.* Cambridge, MA: Polity Press.

Connell, R. W. 1995. *Masculinities.* Cambridge, UK: Polity Press.

Connell, R. W. 2002. *Gender.* Cambridge, UK: Polity Press.

Connell, R. W. 2005. "Change Amongst the Gatekeepers: Men, Masculinities, and Gender Equality in the Global Arena." *Signs: Journal of Women in Culture and Society* 30:1802–25.

Connell, R. W. and James W. Messerschmidt. 2005. "Hegemonic Masculinity: Rethinking the Concept." *Gender and Society* 19:829–59.

Demetriou, Demetrakis Z. 2001. "Connell's Concept of Hegemonic Masculinity: A Critique." *Theory and Society* 30:337–61.

Deutsch, Francine M. 2007. "Undoing Gender." *Gender and Society* 21:106–27.

Donaldson, Mike. 1993. "What Is Hegemonic Masculinity?" *Theory and Society* 22:643–57.

Duncanson, Claire. 2009. "Forces for Good? Narratives of Military Masculinity in Peacekeeping Operations." *International Feminist Journal of Politics* 11:63–80.

Duncanson, Claire. 2013. *Forces for Good? Military Masculinities and Peacebuilding in Afghanistan and Iraq.* Basingstoke, UK: Palgrave Macmillan.

Ehrenreich, Barbara. 1984. *The Hearts of Men: American Dreams and the Flight from Commitment.* Reprinted. Garden City, NY: Anchor Books.

Elliot, Lorraine and Graeme Cheeseman. 2004. *Forces for Good: Cosmopolitan Militaries in the Twenty-first Century.* Manchester, UK: Manchester University Press.

Enloe, Cynthia. 1983. *Does Khaki Become You?* Boston, MA: South End Press.

Enloe, Cynthia. 1993. *The Morning After: Sexual Politics at the End of the Cold War.* Berkeley, CA: University of California Press.

Enloe, Cynthia. 2007. *Globalization and Militarism: Feminists Make the Link.* Lanham, MD: Rowman and Littlefield.

Eriksson Baaz, Maria and Maria Stern. 2009. "Why Do Soldiers Rape? Masculinity, Violence and Sexuality in the Armed Forces in the Congo." *International Studies Quarterly* 53:495–518.

Hearn, Jeff. 2004. "From Hegemonic Masculinity to the Hegemony of Men." *Feminist Theory* 5:49–72.

Higate, Paul. 2003. *Military Masculinities: Identity and the State.* Westport, CT: Praeger.

Hockey, John. 2003. "No More Heroes: Masculinity in the Military." Pp. 27–42 in *Military Masculinities,* edited by P. Higate. Westport, CT: Greenwood Publishing Group.

Hooper, Charlotte. 2001. *Manly States: Masculinities, International Relations, and Gender Politics.* New York: Columbia University Press.

Judd, Terri. 2014. "How the Forces Finally Learnt to Take Pride." *The Independent.* Retrieved June 15, 2014 (www.independent.co.uk/news/uk/home-news/how-the-forces-finally-learnt-to-take-pride-1762057.html).

King, Anthony. 2013. *The Combat Soldier: Infantry Tactics and Cohesion in the Twentieth and Twenty-first Centuries.* Oxford, UK: Oxford University Press.

Lutz, Catherine. 2004. "Living Room Terrorists." *Women's Review of Books* 21:17–18.

McManners, Hugh. 1993. *The Scars of War.* London, UK: HarperCollins.

Meger, Sara. 2010. "Rape of the Congo: Understanding Sexual Violence in the Conflict in the Democratic Republic of Congo." *Journal of Contemporary African Studies* 28:119–35.

Messerschmidt, James W. 2010. *Hegemonic Masculinities and Camouflaged Politics: Unmasking the Bush Dynasty and Its War Against Iraq.* Boulder, CO: Paradigm Publishers.

Messerschmidt, James W. 2012. "Engendering Gendered Knowledge: Assessing the Academic Appropriation of Hegemonic Masculinity." *Men and Masculinities* 15:56–76.

Messner, Michael. 2007. "The Masculinity of the Governator: Muscle and Compassion in American Politics." *Gender and Society* 21:461–80.

Morgan, David. 1994. "Theatre of War: Combat, the Military, and Masculinities." Pp. 165–82 in *Theorising Masculinities,* edited by H. Brod and M. Kaufman. London, UK: Sage.

Moskos, Charles, John Allen Williams, and David R. Segal. 2000. *The Post Modern Military: Armed Forces After the Cold War*. Oxford, UK: Oxford University Press.

Muir, Kate. 1993. *Arms and the Woman*. London, UK: Coronet Books.

Niva, Steve. 1998. "Tough and Tender: New World Order, Masculinity and the Gulf War." Pp. 109–28 in *The "Man Question" in International Relations*, edited by M. Zalewski and J. Parpart. Boulder, CO: Westview.

Orford, Anne. 1999. "Muscular Humanitarianism: Reading the Narratives of the New Interventionism." *European Journal of International Law* 10:679–711.

Pieterse, J. N. 1998. *World Orders in the Making: Humanitarian Intervention and Beyond*. Basingstoke, UK: Macmillan.

Razack, Sherene. 2004. *Dark Threats and White Knights: The Somalia Affair, Peacekeeping and the New Imperialism*. Toronto, Canada: University of Toronto Press.

Risman, Barbara J. 1999. *Gender Vertigo: American Families in Transition*. New Haven, CT: Yale University Press.

Schippers, Mimi. 2007. "Recovering the Feminine Other: Masculinity, Femininity, and Gender Hegemony." *Theory and Society* 36:85–102.

Segal, Lynne. 1997. *Slow Motion: Changing Masculinities, Changing Men*, vol. 2. 2nd ed. London, UK: Virago.

Tickner, J. Ann. 1992. *Gender in International Relations: Feminist Perspectives on Achieving Global Security*. New York: Columbia University Press.

Whitworth, Sandra. 2004. *Men, Militarism and UN Peacekeeping: A Gendered Analysis*. Boulder, CO: Lynne Rienner.

Woodward, Rachel. 1998. "'It's a Man's Life!' Soldiers, Masculinity and the Countryside." *Gender, Place and Culture* 5:277–300.

Woodward, Rachel and Patricia Winter. 2007. *Sexing the Soldier: The Politics of Gender and the Contemporary British Army*. New York: Routledge.

Gender Labor

*Transmen, Femmes, and
Collective Work of Transgression*

Jane Ward

I n 2004, I took a newly out bisexual woman friend of mine to a queer bar in Los Angeles. She had little experience with queer subculture, but that night at the bar she met a trans-identified guy, an FTM, and went home with him to have sex. As for myself, like many queer femmes who witnessed and supported the explosion of transgender identification among dykes in the early 2000s, I had become fairly conversant in the politics and erotics of transgender alliance. In fact, in the eyes of my neophyte friend, my two brief relationships with FTMs made me an expert, and her mentor in all things genderqueer. The next day, as planned, she called to tell me about the previous night's events. But to my surprise, she sounded ashamed and disappointed as she reported that everything had gone well until the moment when she had naively referred to her lover's cock using the word "plastic." His instantly cold response made her feel rejected and under-skilled. After recounting all of the details, she said, "Why didn't you tell me about this? Why didn't you tell me that I was supposed to treat the dildo like a *real* body part? Why didn't you teach me about transgender cock?" Regrettably, having forgotten my own queer training, I responded, "Wasn't it *obvious?*"

Yet by the end of our conversation we had clarified what we both already knew. Of course it is not obvious how to interact with queer bodies and genders, just as we do not naturally or automatically know how to engage normative genders and their accoutrement. Successfully recognizing and affirming the gender of the other—whether the normative or transgressive other—involves a significant amount of training, study, and practice—which, like all forms of work, can be very pleasurable, theatrical, and dynamic, or it can be tedious, failure-ridden, and compulsory.

This project takes femme/FTM sexual relationships as a point of departure to consider gender itself as a form of labor, or to illustrate how gender subjectivities are constituted by various labors required of, and provided by, intimate others. My analysis focuses on examples of work that women do in relationships with transgendered men, specifically the work that they do to

Jane Ward. 2010. "Gender Labor: Transmen, Femmes, and Collective Work of Transgression." *Sexualities* 13(2):236–54.

validate and celebrate their partners' masculinity and to suppress the complexity of their own gender and sexual subjectivity in the service of this goal. Though numerous theorists have accounted for the ways in which gender is constructed, performed, and disciplined, such approaches have yet to theorize fully the relational and feminized labors that reproduce gender and nurture new genders (or new gender formations) into public and private being. These collective labors are distinct from the repetitive and involuntary acts that constitute the subject, or that take form as unwilled labors of the *self* (Butler, 1990, 1997). In contrast, I use the term gender labor to describe the affective and bodily efforts invested in *giving gender* to others, or actively suspending self-focus in the service of helping others achieve the varied forms of gender recognition they long for. Gender labor is the work of bolstering someone's gender authenticity, but it is also the work of co-producing someone's gender irony, transgression, or exceptionality.

The Collective Work of Queer Transgression

The wave of transgender identification among dykes that occurred in the late 1990s and early 2000s exemplifies a new gender formation made possible in part by collective efforts to nurture, witness, and celebrate those occupying an emergent and threatened gender category. In 2003, the lesbian magazine *Curve* described this mass emergence of FTM genders and its relational effects for femme-identified lesbians and their "sense of self":

> Dykes are coming out in droves as transgendered, whether as "TG butches," "bigendered," "FTMs," or everything in between. There is a lot of support for female born boys, but as the community is learning, partners of people in transition—particularly femme-identified lesbians—often get left in the dust when it comes to dealing with their own gender and sense of self. (Szymanski, 2003)

Drawing on tensions between an exceptionalized gender and one "left in the dust," this article explores gender as a relation between people, one characterized not only by countless gestures that are interactively accomplished (West and Zimmerman, 1987) and performatively reiterated (Butler, 1990), but also by tedious acts of emotional, physical, and sexual "support" that are undertaken to co-produce the gender coherence and/or transgression of others.

[. . .]

Gender as Labor

My first aim here is to consider the relational, intimate, and sexual labor that has produced transgender subjectivity and to show how this labor is undertaken by people who fall both within and outside of the boundaries of transgenderism. . . . Notably, Susan Stryker and Stephen Whittle's (2006) 720-page anthology, *The Transgender Studies Reader*, gives virtually no attention to the intimate relations of transgender world/home-making or the "wifely" and/or maternal care that often keeps genders, and masculinity in particular, in motion. Here I place labor at the center of my analysis of femme/FTM relationships in order to focus attention not only on the affective labors that constitute these relations (e.g., compassion, nurturing, witnessing), but also the physical and feminized labors that contribute to the production of queer (and normative) genders (e.g., cooking, sexual services, nursing care, administering gender technology/hormones, chest-binding).

My second aim is to reveal the applications of linking gender and labor not only for queer analyses, but also for understanding the collective work that produces masculinities and femininities in all of their various iterations. Indeed, examples of gender labor abound. Women friends, across the lines of race and class, rehearse for one another the self-effacing scripts associated with female validation ("I wish I had your body," or "no, you don't look fat, but I do"). Women of color come home from work and care for men of color, helping to ease their partners' presumably greater racial burden. Femme dykes labor to treat butches and FTMs like men; and butches and FTMs labor to treat femmes (and sometimes all women) like queens. That these efforts are often "labors of love" enacted for and by people who are denied gender validation within mainstream culture (women, men of color, queers) must not elide the ways in which gender is reproduced through routinized forms of care work. As I will show, these routine efforts . . . often result in the recurring misrecognition or diminishment of the laborer. As I will demonstrate, all genders demand work, and therefore all people both give and require gender labor. However, some genders, principally those that are masculine and especially those that intersect with other forms of power (such as wealth and whiteness), make their demands less visible and more legitimate, or deliver them with more coercive force. Gender labor, like other forms of caring, weighs down most heavily on feminine subjects, the people for whom labors of love are naturalized, expected, or forced (Glenn, 2004).

Giving Gender

A growing body of feminist research has examined the relationship between labor, intimacy, and gender—particularly in the context of sex work, domestic work, and care work. Intimate labors, whether paid or unpaid, are those that increase the use-value of the person who performs them, but they are also marked by elements of trust, privacy, secret knowledge, special access, or shared memories (Zelizer, 2007). As Viviana Zelizer has explained, intimate labor frequently involves the work of providing support in the face of denials of dignity or compensating for someone's shortcomings—shortcomings that may be emotional, interpersonal, physiological, or otherwise material in nature. Intimate labor, most commonly done by women, also includes offering temporary connection and authenticity (Bernstein, 2007), which can involve "faking" or giving someone what they want, even when the lack of "realness" is implicitly recognized by both participants (Augustin, 2007). Though these feminized labors are integral components of social life and subject to increasing demand, they are also regularly denied the status of work due to "social expectations about what women should undertake out of love, kinship, or obligation" (Boris and Parreñas, 2007).

To the extent that gender is always a shortcoming or never-achieved ideal, I want to suggest that gender is always already bound up with the search for people and things that will offer relief, compensate for failure, enhance dignity, and create moments of realness. In this sense, gender labor is the act of giving gender to others in an attempt to fulfill these needs. Though these acts of giving, like care work in general, are performed by people across the spectrum of feminine and masculine genders, feminine subjects (straight women, femme lesbians, transwomen, feminine gay men, faggy boys/bois, and so on) are held particularly responsible for the work of gendering. This is because the duties that comprise gender labor—witnessing, nurturing, validating, fulfilling, authenticating, special knowing, and secret-keeping—have long been relegated to the sphere of female work (Hochschild, 2003 [1983]).

Several feminists have explored the intersections of gender, sex acts, and labor by investigating the range of contexts (marriage, dating, the workplace) in which sex is exchanged for financial resources and other forms of capital (e.g., Levy, 2005). In this vein, it is useful to consider the ways in which sexualized forms of gender labor can be conceptualized as sex work, or as the output of sexual energy in the service of production. Like other forms of intimate labor, the output of sex as a means of recreating subjects, culture, and nations has a feminized history and meaning (Faier, 2009). Laboring subjects, most often women, accept and perform sex acts that offer new value or meaning to others; assist in remaking sexual pasts; and recreate their own sexual desires, sexual vocabulary, and erotic identity in relation to external demands. Such examples demonstrate the complex interaction between sex work and gender work.

[. . .]

The Labor of Being "The Girl"

In FTM identity narratives, trans masculinity has frequently been described as the experience of not being, or not wanting to be, a girl. As has been explored in other research on FTMs (Devor and Devor, 1997; Dozier, 2005), "not wanting to be a girl" speaks to an awareness, often beginning in childhood, of a gendered self and body that does not fit social, cultural, and familial expectations associated with girlhood: "I didn't want to wear dresses," "I always felt more like a boy," "I hated my breasts," and so on. Yet beyond not wanting to be *a* girl, many FTM (and butch) identity narratives also describe the experience of not wanting to be *the* girl in a particular relational context, often during sex. In Dozier's (2005: 312) study, for example, "Dick," a white FTM, explains why his transition led to a new sexual interest in men by stating, "what I figured out a lot later was that it wasn't about not wanting to be with a guy; it was about not wanting to be the girl."

[. . .]

The coherence of butch and FTM identity narratives depends upon the existence of a feminine subject who experiences female embodiment, sexual submission, and sexism as more natural or trouble-free than the butch/trans subject. My interest here is the way this reliance on the satisfied feminine other—whether as an abstraction ("somewhere out there, other women like being girls") or specified within a relationship ("my girlfriend loves being a girl")—has produced a demand for the labor of becoming this satisfied girl. Needless to say, many butches and FTMs do not have relationships with femmes (or feminine people, for that matter); however the figure of the girl nonetheless remains an important element of the narrative of trans and butch difference. In cases in which FTMs do have femme partners, the interviews I conducted suggest that the latter are often compelled to embody this girl subjectivity, or to work to enhance their own femininity and its apparent seamlessness in order to reinforce the masculinity of their partners. Keaton, a 32-year-old white FTM, told me:

> [I think some transguys] want their girlfriend or their partner, if they're dating a woman, to re-emphasize their masculinity. These two FTMs [I know] who are both dating women . . . apparently had both asked their girlfriends to grow their hair out long since their transitions. . . . And [my girlfriend] has long hair, so they asked her if I did the same thing, and she's like, "no, and if he did, I'd cut it all off."

Jimmy, a 40-year-old Asian American FTM, told me about a conflict that he and his femme-identified partner had with one of their FTM friends. He said:

We had a friend who was . . . very warm and loving and wonderful in a lot of ways, but has this very clear sense of what he feels he needs to be as a man, as an FTM person, and has really imposed his sense of the world on us as a couple. . . . And I think he saw my wife as, "OK, you're the female, you need to be the one who's doing clearly feminine tasks in support of your man." . . . He really wanted to disregard her and put her in her place, and like snap at her or whatever, and disrespect her.

Femmes also told similar stories about being compelled to occupy the position of the girl so as to bolster trans masculinity. For example, Melinda, a 37-year-old white femme talked about her experience meeting transmen online (through dating websites). She said:

I heard from three transguys in a row who all made comments about liking my photographs, and specifically aspects of my appearance that were super feminine. And they all said "I want to learn more about you" and followed up . . . with some variation of "tell me why trans-people do it for you" and in one case "tell me why trans-people are better for you, hotter for you than anybody else on the planet." That was a very explicit solicitation for my femininity to prop up their masculinity or validate it in some way, and it was really revolting and at that point I decided, "no trans-people, no trans-men."

Similarly, another femme named Jennifer told me:

In my relationships with people who are trans-identified, there's been less room for the politics around *my* gender. . . . They really wanted my identity to be femme, and they really wanted the person they were with to help bolster their own gender.

[. . .]

Undoubtedly there are cases in which being the girl is a reflection of femmes' own sense of comfortable alignment with the conventions of femininity (with being in the kitchen, having long hair, and so on). Yet the foregoing narratives also indicate that being the girl is a form of intimate labor that is undertaken to produce the masculinity of the other and to keep the social, emotional, and erotic structure of femme/FTM relationships intact. Femme labor not only involves embodying feminine contrast (if I'm the girl, then you are the boy), but also discovering, acknowledging, encouraging, fulfilling, validating, nurturing, and initiating masculine complexity. Like other forms of intimate and sexualized labor, femmes *give gender* to FTMs through efforts that augment masculine authenticity, offer moments of realness, and compensate for gendered shortcomings.

The Labor of Forgetting

Several of the FTMs interviewed for this project explained that new sexual relationships with femmes go through a kind of testing phase in which FTMs assess whether or not they can trust their new partner to interact with them, and their bodies, as male. In some cases, this involves developing trust that the femme partner has forgotten, or does not see, signs of femaleness.
[. . .]
Some participants explained that they teach femme partners to learn a new trans vocabulary of the body, including ways of talking about sex, talking about the past, gender code-switching

when FTMs are not out to family or co-workers, and a new gendered division of labor (such as asking femmes to always buy the tampons, place them in the bathroom, but never speak about them). Forgetting, in this case, is not the opposite of having knowledge, but is a new kind of gendered knowing that includes a new vocabulary and a new set of gendered practices (Halberstam, 2006). These relations of forgetting and knowing are marked by many of the elements Zelizer (2007) attributes to intimate labor: trust, privacy, secret knowledge, and special access.

[. . .]

The corollary of the labor of forgetting femaleness is the labor of establishing trust that femmes see, know, and understand trans masculinity and can deploy and communicate this understanding through particular sex acts. Countless sex columns in queer magazines and websites now instruct readers on how to have sex with the trans or genderqueer body ("how to fuck a boi," "how to suck cock," "mommy/boy role-play," and so on). These advice columns often stress the importance of relating to trans masculinity as authentic, as well as the importance of ensuring that one's sex cannot be mistaken for lesbian feminist sex (circa 1970), which is typically represented as boring, unsexy, power-neutral, or passé. For example, the magazine *On Our Backs: The Best of Lesbian Sex* instructs readers about "how to suck cock" by stating: "Get Real: treat the dildo like a real penis—focus on the things that feel good to bio men; stroke the vein along the bottom, tongue the slit, gently tickle the balls" (Venning, 2002). Femmes can learn how to affirm the gender identity of FTM partners not simply by forgetting or de-emphasizing their partners' past femaleness, but also by demonstrating knowledge of male physiology and desire. In some cases, interview participants shared stories of successful male recognition, such as R.J., a 42-year-old African American FTM:

> My girlfriend tells me, "You're not a lesbian. . . . When I talk to you there's no woman there. . . . You're just male, you know. I don't relate to you like I've related to butch lesbians." She says, "I don't relate to you the same way. Nothing's the same." So I feel very lucky in that sense.

Yet, in other cases, femmes described the trans/femme erotic script as a site of negotiation, confusion, and hard work, one that is subject to an unspoken and often changing set of rules, particularly with respect to sex. Bridgette, one 26-year-old white femme dating an FTM in Los Angeles told me:

> The question of breasts and what I'm allowed to do to them has always felt very confusing to me. . . . I can remember moments where every so often [one of my partners] would sort of be like, "hey, I have boobs too" and I would be like "oh, right, right, right" but I think there was this way that I had been given other messages. . . .

[. . .]

The Labor of Alliance

One of the effects of the aforementioned labors is that they solidify a trans-gender/fixed-gender binary in which femmes are firmly located outside of a gender dysphoric experience, and often outside the realm of the queer or transgressive. . . . Within trans subculture, femmes have been positioned in the outsider categories of "ally" or "SOFFA." In order to be understood as legitimate stakeholders in trans politics, some accounts suggest that femmes are compelled to participate as "gender supporters," quietly celebrating female masculinity while remaining silent as femininity is de-queered or pathologized.

[. . .]

In emphasizing the work of alliance, my aim is to show the ways in which femmes labor at being gender supporters not only within intimate, sexual relations, but also within the more collective realm of FTM political and cultural public space. The laborious quality of alliance stems primarily from the silences and misrecognitions that femmes manage in order to help preserve the momentum of FTM exceptionalism. The femme-as-ally or SOFFA construction typically erases feminine forms of gender fluidity or dysphoria, an erasure that causes many femmes to assert and reassert their experiential alignment with trans narratives. For instance, Jennifer, a femme in Los Angeles who also identifies as a "tough broad," told me that being an ally does not capture her own identification with the trans experience. She said:

> When I was partnered with folks who were FTM identified, sometimes it was complicated for me to understand "ok, what is this ally thing?" . . . Because [in the trans community,] I found for the first time a real comfort in my own queerness. I had similar feelings [as trans folks] about walking into dyke space and [being] both an insider and an outsider. I came into the trans community not as a partner to anybody, but as an individual. But it felt like I was being pigeonholed as, "well, the only way a bio female can be in this community then is as an ally or as a SOFFA." But my only place wasn't as an ally, because the trans relationship to gender and sexuality and queerness was really familiar to me. . . . Just because it's femininity and not masculinity, I [still] had similar things going on.

As Jennifer points out, feminine forms of gender trouble pose a challenge to the very construction of FTM community by drawing attention to the permeability of trans identification. Given the fixity of trans boundaries, femmes' efforts to locate themselves within trans politics frequently involves adopting, and adapting to, the ill-fitting role of gender supporter. Like other forms of affective labor, performing the role of SOFFA not only entails elements of scripted "faking," it also requires suspending truer accounts of oneself in the service of the other.

Femmes who are critical of being assigned the position of gender supporter have drawn heavily upon feminist frameworks to intervene in the sexism they experience in their relationships with transmen or within trans political spaces. In contrast, many FTM discourses place the FTM subject outside or beyond feminist analysis, emphasizing instead the ways in which FTMs' refusals of femininity and/or the forces of sexism stem from a natural calling to masculine gender rebellion. The resultant polarization of feminist and trans frameworks has dissonant effects within femme/FTM relationships, particularly given the ways in which FTMs' disidentificatory narratives about female embodiment and objectification often ring true for femmes (and for women in general). Though it has become something of a taboo to draw comparisons between the gender dysphoric feelings of FTMs (i.e., I hated my female body and the sexism it elicited) and those of non-trans women (i.e., I hate my female body and the sexism it elicits), both femmes and FTMs reported in interviews that such comparisons nonetheless emerge, especially when two female-coded bodies share intimate sexual space. For instance, R.J., an African American FTM, explained:

> [My girlfriend] says, "You make [being female] sound so disgusting. I hope you don't think that of me." And I was like, no, . . . it's not that I think that about you. It's just that, you know, I love these things about you, but I don't want them on me. Like my chest, I call them cow sacks, you know. Something like that. I use those kind of really negative terms.

[. . .]

As in most forms of service work, the story about the needs of the recipient also tells a story about the satisfied laborer. The laborer not only fulfills others' needs, but also arrives on the scene satisfied and ready to work, presumably without possessing similar needs of her own. As Hochschild explains (2003 [1983]), this is the justifying logic that naturalizes the "second shift": women manage their own emotional needs throughout the course of a day's work, and arrive home from paid labor ready to provide intimate care for others. Similarly, the SOFFA construction implies a resolved and natural gender, one that arrives on the scene ready to nurture masculinity into being.

Discussion

Focusing on gender labor draws attention to the collective work that produces and sustains gender. Though we already know that genders exist inside an interdependent gender system, little attention has been given to the laborious quality of reproducing other people's genders in daily life, and we remain without a clear mapping of the training, skills, duties, and specific efforts that various genders require. Here I have shown that in many cases, FTM identities remain reliant upon the labors of femininity that nurture and witness them, both within, and outside of, intimate sexual relations. It is not simply that femmes provide support to transmen (and butches); they also reproduce a trans/not-trans binary by training to be the girl in new and particular ways, many of which they are compelled to experience as easy and natural. In some cases, femmes learn to actively forget their partner's differently gendered past, to study up on male desire and male physiology, and to master a new set of sexual practices and erotic scripts. Transsupportive and feminist-identified femmes also learn how to occupy the role of ally or SOFFA, often through silence regarding their own gender dysphoria. In sum, femme labor describes not only the emotional, physical, and sexual work of reproducing FTM subjectivity; it also refers to the work of adjusting one's own gendered self in relation to this process—such as the work of transitioning from femme to transsensual femme.

. . . I have attempted to show the ways in which many elements of gender labor—offering sexual validation, coconstructing realness, forgetting other possibilities, maternal nurturing, keeping one's complex personhood to oneself—mirror the practices of intimate labor generally assigned to women. This confluence reveals the ways in which gender itself takes form through feminized acts of service done for others, often at the expense of the laborer's own recognition, dignity, or assistance with gendered shortcomings. To the extent that these labors are performed within intimate spheres and through gestures of bodily, emotional, and sexual care, they are embedded in the historical and political-economic structures of women's work. . . . I have attempted to underscore the ways in which all genders may be bound up in intimate dependencies and feminized relations of nurture, giving, and collectivity.

References

Augustin, Laura Maria. 2007. "A Multiplicity of Acts, Acting and Caring: The International Sex Industry." Paper presented at Intimate Labors: An Interdisciplinary Conference on Domestic, Care, & Sex Work. UC Santa Barbara, 4–6 October 2007.

Bernstein, Elizabeth. 2007. *Temporarily Yours: Intimacy, Authenticity, and the Commerce of Sex.* Chicago, IL: University of Chicago Press.

Boris, Eileen and Rhacel Parreñas. 2007 "Conference Program." *Intimate Labors: An Interdisciplinary Conference on Domestic, Care, & Sex Work*. UC Santa Barbara, 4–6 October 2007. Retrieved December 20, 2009 (www.ihc.ucsb.edu/intimatelabors/)

Butler, Judith. 1990. *Gender Trouble: Feminism and the Subversion of Identity*. New York: Routledge.

Butler, Judith. 1997. *The Psychic Life of Power: Theories in Subjection*. Stanford, CA: Stanford University Press.

Devor, Aaran and Holly Devor. 1997. *FTM: Female-to-Male Transsexuals in Society*. Bloomington, IN: Indiana University Press.

Dozier, Raine. 2005. "Beards, Breasts, and Bodies: Doing Sex in a Gendered World." *Gender & Society* 19(3):297–316.

Faier, Lieba. 2009. *Intimate Encounters: Filipina Women and the Remaking of Rural Japan*. Berkeley, CA: University of California Press.

Halberstam, Judith. 2006. "Notes of Failure," Keynote Address at the *Failure: Ethics and Aesthetics Conference*, 3 March, University of California, Irvine.

Hochschild, Arlie Russell. 2003 [1983]. *The Managed Heart: Commercialization of Human Feeling*. Berkeley, CA: University of California Press.

Levy, Ariel. 2005. *Female Chauvinist Pigs: Women and the Rise of Raunch Culture*. New York: Free Press.

Nakano Glenn, Evelyn. 2004. *Unequal Freedom: How Race and Gender Shaped American Citizenship and Labor*. Cambridge, MA: Harvard University Press.

Stryker, S. and S. Whittle. 2006. *The Transgender Studies Reader*. New York: Routledge.

Szymanski, Zak. 2003. "Out on the Web: Affirm Your Identity." *Curve Magazine*, February: 14.

Venning, Rachel. 2002. "How to Suck Dyke Cock." *On Our Backs,* December/January: 11.

West, Candace and Don Zimmerman. 1987. "Doing Gender." *Gender & Society* 1(2):125–51.

Zelizer, Viviana. 2007. Keynote presented at *Intimate Labors: An Interdisciplinary Conference on Domestic, Care, & Sex Work*. UC Santa Barbara, 4–6 October 2007.

Globalizing Gender Issues

Many Voices, Different Choices

Christine E. Bose

[. . .]

My starting point is the question: Why are the important gender inequality issues, as revealed in research and movement activism, different in various countries around the world? In asking this question, I am not by any means suggesting that major issues of gender inequality are or should be the same in every nation. By now, we recognize that just as there is a wide diversity among individual women's and men's concerns, based on their intersecting axes of age, race, ethnicity, class, marital status, sexuality, religion, or other sources of difference, there is also global diversity in the conditions that are the focus of feminist or gender research. On the flip side, I also am not suggesting that significant gender inequalities are entirely unique in every country or locality, either. Certainly there are commonalities that arise from shared experiences.

Rather, I outline a framework through which to understand some of the patterned differences across nations in their significant gender inequalities. To illustrate and support this perspective, I rely on examples drawn from a broad array of extant research about women's and men's issues and gender inequalities in various world regions (including Africa, Asia and the Middle East, Latin America and the Caribbean, and Europe) or specific nations. . . .

One of my basic arguments is that there are a series of intersecting dynamics, or as Patricia Hill Collins (1990) might say, intersecting axes of oppression, which shape the types of gender inequality visible in any given nation. While most analyses of gender inequality are focused on the particularities of a single nation's economic, political, social, or cultural conditions and history, I want to suggest that these features can be separated more fruitfully into the four major intersecting axes of transnational, regional, cross-cutting thematic, and unique national conditions that shape the variety of important feminist concerns within any given country. Using this approach, the inequalities located

Christine E. Bose. 2011. "Globalizing Gender Issues: Many Voices, Different Choices." Eastern Sociological Society Presidential Address. *Sociological Forum* 26(4):739–53. Blackwell Publishing Ltd.

in any given nation, including the United States, can be interpreted or framed in multiple simultaneous contexts. Although these four axes may sound merely geographic, they are much more complex and reflect underlying sociopolitical patterns. Indeed, my goal is to move us beyond the concepts of the Global North and Global South, both because empirical studies show that many gender inequalities do not differentiate themselves globally in this manner, and because theoretical developments over the last several decades have shown us that, although quite useful, these geographic dichotomies often tend to homogenize real conditions. For example, as we well know, significant inequalities still persist, even among the most powerful nations around the globe.

[...]

Transnational Sources of Inequality

Transnational sources of inequality persist across most nations, and feminist researchers or activists describe them, in one form or another, almost everywhere. The bulk of national and international gender scholarship makes it possible for me to argue that the two primary sources of global gendered inequalities are economic conditions and violence. In the current global era, I also include issues of gendered migration, which are tightly intertwined with economic conditions. . . .

Perhaps the most pervasive factor shaping worldwide similarities in gender research agendas is the globalized political economy, formed by the movements of corporate capital and labor around the globe. . . . The contemporary "free market" ideological push that dominates the global economy and keeps promoting privatization policies is leading many nations, including the United States, to relinquish many of their responsibilities for the welfare of their citizens. . . .

To take one example of the outcomes of economic globalization, one can look at Africa, where from the mid-1980s through the 1990s structural adjustment policies were enacted in more than 40 nations. Gender research in this region reveals that as the civil service and other formal-sector occupations began to shrink during this period, more and more women, even those with university degrees, turned to the informal sector to support themselves and their families (Darkwah, 2002). Scholars also note that SAPs have contributed to exacerbating an already crippling brain drain from Africa, including women who left positions in universities, hospitals, and other government bureaucracies to obtain more stable employment abroad (Osirim et al., 2009). . . .

A second global dynamic that affects women's lives and feminist research agendas is the steadily rising rate of migration, a global labor flow that has become increasingly feminized over the last few decades. . . . By 2010, women were 49% of those who migrate internationally. . . . About 75% of all international migrants are located in 30 countries of the world. This new "equality" in migration rates is based largely on the increased number of women who migrate on their own as contract workers—people who go to another country for a specified time period, often to work in fields like domestic or child-care work, food and lodging services, factory assembly lines, or entertainment. Their migration is a key feature of the global economy because they create new, low-cost labor supplies (Sassen, 2002) and, since the 1980s, through the remittances they send back home, women transnational migrants have become an important source of income for their families. They are a frequent subject of global gender research that examines low-wage carework, especially across the Asian region, or on women in global export processing zones. Among the common themes that appear in these studies are transnational families and transnational motherhood (Hondagneu-Sotelo and Avila,

1997), the international division of reproductive labor (Parreñas, 2000), issues of citizenship and surveillance (Cheng, 2003), and environmental or occupational health concerns.

[. . .]

Although the global economy forms a background for all gender inequalities, a third and almost universal critical worldwide feminist issue is violence against women. Research on this topic is found in almost every country, although the form of violence that becomes a primary feminist research concern may focus on particular national problems, including wife beating; date rape, stranger rape, or rape during war; military prostitution; genital cutting; bride burning (when dowries are perceived as being too small) or acid violence; and many others. For example, domestic violence against women is a worldwide problem, with between 15–70% of women in each nation indicating that they were physically abused by a male partner or intimate.

[. . .]

Regional Sources of Inequality

Regional sources of gender inequality can reflect similar geographically based political or economic conditions, but they also are shaped by transnational forces. On the one hand, the largely deregulated nature of global capitalism has sustained uneven power relations between the highly industrialized and the developing nations—differences that often parallel earlier colonial ones. On the other hand, the interaction between regions and transnational capital also has caused other changes, such as the opening up of national markets in China or Vietnam, the heightened global importance of production in China and India, the rising flows of contract labor and marriage migration within Asia, and the increasing contact between resident citizens of Asia, Latin America, and Africa with their diasporic populations.

. . . The formation of the African Union, as a nascent transnational body, has opened a unique opportunity for African women to shape their rights, and to do this based on their own experiences, but with full knowledge of what has or has not worked elsewhere. Regional governance mechanisms, like the African Union or the European Union, help combat problems not well handled by individual states, even though some of the current problems in those two regions may be significantly different. . . .

A related regional political trend, also common both to European Union and African Union countries, is the concept of gender mainstreaming, which was first introduced at the 1985 Women's World Conference in Nairobi and was propelled forward as a new intergovernmental strategy after the 1995 Beijing Conference. The goal of this approach is to adopt a gender perspective in all government policies and programs that assesses the impact on women and men of any planned action, and also promotes gender equality as its ultimate goal (United Nations, 2002:5). These programs have the potential to influence arenas that are not usually associated with women, such as trade policies or the military. Considerable feminist research, especially in Europe, concerns the opportunities and limitations in implementing gender mainstreaming. The political dilemma for them is deciding how to strategically incorporate gender mainstreaming into policy making, while simultaneously maintaining feminist agendas outside the government that challenge patriarchal domination, especially by suggesting entirely new policies.

There are other important regionally related dimensions of inequality, especially women's access to education, property ownership, and good jobs—these are fundamental equity issues for women in the developing regions of Africa, the Middle East, Southeast and South Asia, and large portions of Latin America and the Caribbean.

[. . .]

Unique National Sources of Inequality

Despite the importance of the first two transnational and regional axes, gender inequality in any particular country is not shaped only from the outside by large-scale forces. In many nations there are unique localized political, economic, or cultural dynamics that intersect with those broader patterns.

[. . .]

There are also national-level difficulties in the creation and distribution of feminist research on gender inequality—related to reaching national and/or international audiences. One barrier pertains to language or terminology. For example, the word "gender" is novel in some countries such as China, whose language is not rooted in a Latin or romance language system (Chow et al., 2009). In those countries, feminists deal with the issue of terminology either by inventing new terms or adapting existing ones, while also trying to avoid linguistic postcolonialism and the political charge that their gender or feminist research is merely a "Western import." More generally, though, there is a reverse problem, where language barriers and monolingualism hinder feminist thoughts that are developed in non-English-speaking Global South countries from even reaching feminists in the Global North (Knapp, 2009).

[. . .]

Cross-Cutting Themes of Gender Inequality

Transnational scholars have considered global factors, area studies scholars have researched regional factors, and country specialists have focused on national factors that shape the worldwide variation in gender inequalities. I suggest a new fourth factor or axis that is based on what I term the "cross-cutting themes" that influence just a few countries, which are scattered across several regions. I argue that this type of gendered inequality could give impetus to cross-regional alliances among women's groups. . . .

Health concerns are probably the most highly visible inequities because of global concerns over the transmission of HIV/AIDS to women and children. Although every region has AIDS cases, infection rates vary considerably across the nations within any region. For instance, HIV and AIDS are critical problems in Africa, where infection rates are among the world's highest and there is a unique overrepresentation of women suffering from them. Nonetheless, looking across Sub-Saharan Africa, over 20% of adults are infected in Botswana, but less than 5% in many nations of Western Africa, such as Nigeria, Niger, Mali, and Chad, or the Democratic Republic of the Congo and Angola. HIV and AIDS also are key feminist concerns in selected nations within other regions, such as the Southeast Asian countries of Thailand and Vietnam, or the Latin American nation of Brazil, where prostitution is legal and there is a well-established sex tourism industry. This suggests to me that cross-regional alliances between African and Asian women from the most AIDS-plagued nations could prove useful.

[. . .]

A second issue that cross-cuts regions is the engendered relationship between religion and the state, found in a variety of countries ranging from Catholic-dominated ones, through those with strong fundamentalist Protestant movements, to fundamentalist Islamic countries. To take a European example, because of the activist role of the Catholic Church during the transformation of Poland from a socialist to a capitalist nation, it was possible for aspects of Catholic morality to be inserted into the new postcommunist national constitution. One of many outcomes was that the existence of lesbians, gays, bisexuals, or transgender individuals was legally denied—these groups have few rights and some argue that they are rendered largely invisible (Mizielińska, 2001).

Other examples can be found in the application of Islam to family law, especially in North Africa, the Horn of Africa, and some regions of Francophone and Anglophone West Africa. In Senegal, the practice of Islam is central in the secular state, and it affects laws related to marriage, divorce, death, and inheritance, as well as women's right to work. . . . Not surprisingly, African gender studies scholars and transnational feminist networks have been very concerned with the relationship between women's rights and the state under Islam (see, e.g., Osirim et al., 2009; Salime, 2010). International activist groups such as Women Living Under Muslim Laws (WLUML) already have been uniting women in Africa and the Middle East to modify some of the inequalities created when conservative interpretations of Islam infuse national laws.

A final example of issues that cross-cut regions is war and/or the militarization of a society. The devastating effects of this kind of military violence have caused many women to become single mothers, experience forced migration, live in internment or refugee camps, or suffer various forms of "noncombatant" violence, such as genocidal war-related rape and its consequences. In addition, many young boys have been forced to become soldiers in various conflict zones throughout Africa. At any one time, some regions may experience more conflict than others. In recent years, African and Middle Eastern nations have had more conflict than Europe, but within Europe, the Balkan conflict and the break-up of the former Yugoslavia was significant in the late twentieth century, especially for the global impact of the subsequent international trials concerning war rape and ethnic cleansing.

Nonetheless, ever since the year 2000, some countries in every region have experienced periods of major armed conflict or ethnic tensions. There have been ethnic tensions, violence, and human rights struggles by indigenous populations within Latin America, especially in Mexico and Guatemala; and in Indonesia, Tibet, and Burma within Asia. There also have been civil conflicts, famine, hunger, kidnappings, and, sometimes, genocide in Rwanda, Sudan, Ethiopia, Somalia, and Eritrea within Africa. More recently, we have seen democratization protests and concomitant government violent responses in several Middle Eastern countries, among them Egypt, Lebanon, Syria, Iran, and Libya; as well as international interventions such as the U.S. "war against terror" in Afghanistan and Iraq.

[. . .]

Conclusion: Bringing the Intersections Together

[. . .]

In conclusion, let me discuss how my four intersecting axes integrate themselves into global patterns of gender inequalities. When discussing an individual's position in a single society, I might say that his or her gender, race, class, sexuality, age, religion, citizenship, and other sources of difference intersect simultaneously and are so intertwined that they are hard to separate, even though certain life settings might bring to the fore one or two of these dimensions more than others. The parallel construction would be to explain the gender inequalities of any single nation as a function of their global, regional, and national situations, combined with any cross-cutting themes, including those that were mentioned above.

But I am interested in a different angle on this latter question, which is: What factors allow us to group some nations together based on their similar gender inequality issues, the bulk of their research, or their movement activism? . . . Complex global, regional, national, and thematic issues not only interact, but also are layered. Global and regional dynamics are the interrelated foundations on which broad gender inequalities are built.

[. . .]

It is all too easy to use a broad brush in painting global gender inequalities as either all the same or as all unique—and my goal is to challenge that type of Global North–Global South dichotomy. U.S. gender researchers need to become more attuned to the different voices of women, domestically and globally, recognizing their agency and the particular choices they make in their own daily lives because, as many now agree (Tripp, 2006), the cutting edge of the women's movement is no longer in the United States. Rather, the new key issues are being defined in the regions that have historically been considered the "developing" ones of Africa, Asia, Latin America, and the Caribbean.

References

Cheng, Shu-Ju Ada. 2003. "Rethinking the Globalization of Domestic Service: Foreign Domestics, State Control, and the Politics of Identity in Taiwan." *Gender & Society* 17(2):166–86.

Chow, Esther Ngan-Ling, Naihua Zhang, and Wang Jinling. 2009. "Promising and Contested Fields: Advancing Women's Studies and Sociology of Women/Gender in Contemporary China." Pp. 73–91 in *Global Gender Research: Transnational Perspectives*, edited by C. E. Bose and M. Kim. New York/London: Routledge.

Collins, Patricia Hill. 1990. *Black Feminist Thought: Knowledge, Consciousness, and the Politics of Empowerment*. Boston, MA: Unwin Hyman.

Darkwah, Akosua K. 2002. "Trading Goes Global: Ghanaian Market Women in an Era of Globalization." *Asian Women* 15:31–49.

Hondagneu-Sotelo, Pierrette and Ernestine Avila. 1997. "I'm Here, but I'm There: The Meanings of Latina Transnational Motherhood." *Gender & Society* 11(5):548–71.

Knapp, Gundrun-Axeli. 2009. "Traveling Theories—Situated Questions: Feminist Theory in the German Context." Pp. 261–77 in *Global Gender Research: Transnational Perspectives*, edited by C. E. Bose and M. Kim. New York/London: Routledge.

Mizielińska, Joanna. 2001. "'The Rest Is Silence . . .': Polish Nationalism and the Question of Lesbian Existence." *European Journal of Women's Studies* 8(3):281–97.

Osirim, Mary, Christine E. Bose, and Minjeong Kim. 2009. "Introduction to Gender Research in Africa." Pp. 11–15 in *Global Gender Research: Transnational Perspectives*, edited by C. E. Bose and M. Kim. New York/London: Routledge.

Parreñas, Rhacel Salazar. 2000. "Migrant Filipina Domestic Workers and the International Division of Reproductive Labor." *Gender & Society* 14(4):560–80.

Salime, Zakia. 2010. "Securing the Market, Pacifying Civil Society, Empowering Women: The Middle East Partnership Initiative." *Sociological Forum* 25(4):725–45.

Sassen, Saskia. 2002. "Global Cities and Survival Circuits." Pp. 254–274 in *Global Woman: Nannies, Maids, and Sex Workers in the New Economy*, edited by B. Ehrenreich and A. R. Hochschild. New York: Henry Holt.

Tripp, Aili Mari. 2006. "The Evolution of Transnational Feminisms: Consensus, Conflict, and New Dynamics." Pp. 51–75 in *Global Feminism: Transnational Women's Activism, Organizing, and Human Rights*, edited by M. M. Ferree and A. M. Tripp. New York/London: New York University Press.

United Nations. 2002. *Gender Mainstreaming: An Overview*. New York: United Nations, Office of the Special Adviser on Gender Issues and Advancement of Women.

PART II

Knowledge Production and the Methods of Feminist Research

How do we know what we know? What is feminist knowledge? In this section, we address how feminist researchers approach doing research about gender, gender identity, and sexuality. Feminist researchers think deeply about how to carry out their research in ways that allow them to portray the complexities of gendered and sexualized experiences, while sensitively representing the perspectives of those they study. While much traditional scholarship treats the researcher as being objective and almost omniscient, feminist scholarship recognizes the researcher as being subjective and achieving only partial understanding. Knowledge is ongoing, not perfect or complete, yet how do we carry out research in ways that thoughtfully depict how gender and sexuality are experienced? We highlight the rigor and multiplicity of feminist methodologies that examine the multiple ways gender and sexuality matter.

In "Practicing Intersectionality in Sociological Research," Hae Yeon Choo and Myra Marx Ferree address what it means to practice intersectionality through sociological research. Drawing on two important studies that address multiple inequalities, the authors assess how an intersectional lens would deepen these works. When scholarship contains assumptions, such as that White, middle-class family formation is "normal," whereas other types of family formation are not, much potential insight is lost. Similarly, if "race" is only analyzed when discussing Black families, even though White families also possess a race, the effects of race are not fully interrogated. Analyzing marked as well as unmarked categories (such as Whiteness), while recognizing the nuanced differences in the ways that intersecting categories operate, leads to stronger, more discerning research.

Penner and Saperstein's "Engendering Racial Perceptions" uses longitudinal data to examine how survey researchers attribute race differently, based on the experiences and gender of those they survey. Interestingly, the survey researchers mark down a respondent's race, rather than asking for self-identification. They make the determination at the end of the survey, and—over time—appear to change how they classify respondents' race. Both men and women are more likely to be classified as White if they live in the suburbs or are married, and as Black if they have been unemployed, are poor, live in inner cities, or are single parents. Such findings demonstrate how race has institutionalized practices, institutions, and locations by skin color. In addition, by using an intersectional framework, Penner and Saperstein show how incarceration is associated with men being identified as Black or not White, while welfare receipt is associated with women being identified as Black or not White. These gendered stereotypes, then, influence survey researchers' perception of men's and women's race differently over time. Such work demonstrates the complicated, intertwined, and unequal ways in which social relations and status operate.

"Becoming a 'Trusted Outsider,'" by Sandra Meike Bucerius, examines the feminist methodological tension around a researcher's insider/outsider status. Using the example of her ethnographic study of a group of second-generation immigrant men in Germany, the author argues that her outsider status as a native-born woman was not the liability it would commonly be assumed to be. The young men did not view Bucerius the same way they might a woman of their community, but this made her someone whom they could talk to and ask questions about women, giving them insights into women's thoughts and expectations. At the same time, Bucerius could use her difference to build rapport with the young men. Being an outsider actually afforded her different and important data that would not have been available to a researcher afforded insider status.

In "Studying Each Other," Tey Meadow reflects on her ethnographic research with transgender children and their families to elucidate central tensions experienced in conducting feminist ethnographic research. Meadow points out the complexity of positions that those she interviews represent; a parent may be read as challenging gender binaries or maintaining gender binaries, depending on how you interpret their actions. As an ethnographer, Meadow argues, the aim should be to observe how they understand the world and their own community rather than placing them as "this" or "that." At the same time, she focuses on how her own gender presentation affected those she was researching and how they studied her just as she studied them. For Meadow, feminist researchers need to remain attentive and reflexive in how they negotiate the research process and their own identities while doing research. Meadow's work reminds us that ethnographic research is interactional and relational.

Finally, "The Sociology of Gender in Southern Perspective," by Raewyn Connell, examines the sociological field of gender research, with particular focus on gender theory and research from the Global South. Examining the historical trajectory of gender relations, Connell points out how colonial and postcolonial processes have meant that feminist researchers in the Global North have mined the Global South for data, while ignoring the powerful and grounded theorizing emerging from those locations. This also reflects a global power system that prioritizes theory from Europe and North America. This piece offers an analysis of feminist knowledge production that demonstrates the significance of engaging in dialogue across national divides to develop feminist theory at the global level, while also requiring decolonizing practices that recognize the important contributions to gender theory from the Global South.

Overall, the articles in this section emphasize the challenges of doing intersectional feminist research, the importance of recognizing our positionality as researchers, the complexity of our relationships with those we study, and the way that the politics of knowledge shape feminist scholarship. Doing gender research, then, requires taking great care that we do not simply reproduce existing ways of understanding gender, gender identity, and sexuality. Our aim should be to create new angles of vision, while also identifying the inequalities inherent in the production—and recognition—of knowledge.

Practicing Intersectionality in Sociological Research

A Critical Analysis of Inclusions, Interactions, and Institutions in the Study of Inequalities

Hae Yeon Choo and Myra Marx Ferree

R ecent feminist scholarship increasingly presents race, class, and gender as closely intertwined and argues that these forms of stratification need to be studied in relation to each other, conceptualizing them, for example, as a "matrix of domination" (Collins 1990) or "complex inequality" (McCall 2001). Scholars have referred to this nonadditive way of understanding social inequality with various terms, including "intersectional" (Crenshaw 1991), "integrative" (Glenn 1999), or as a "race-class-gender" approach (Pascale 2007). Feminist scholarship has embraced the call for an intersectional analysis but largely left the specifics of what it means indistinct, leading Kathy Davis (2008) to call intersectionality a theoretical "buzzword" with as yet unrealized analytic bite. Moreover, whether such feminist appeals have practical consequences for sociology is hard to estimate without more precisely defining what this agenda implies for the conduct of research.

This article addresses the question of what it means to practice intersectionality sociologically as a theoretical and methodological approach to inequality. . . . We select . . . outstanding works of qualitative research that are engaging with multiple inequalities at a conceptual level and use them as our data for considering the methodological implications of bringing in particular styles of intersectional analysis. . . . We point out how each of these studies could become richer in their empirical findings than they already are: if they had emphasized the inclusion of perspectives, not only persons, from the margins of society; if they had problematized relationships of power for unmarked categories, such as whiteness and masculinity; or if they had treated inequalities as multiply-determined and intertwined rather than assuming one central institutional framework.

[. . .]

Hae Yeon Choo and Myra Marx Ferree. 2010. "Practicing Intersectionality in Sociological Research: A Critical Analysis of Inclusions, Interactions, and Institutions in the Study of Inequalities." *Sociological Theory* 28(2):129–49.

Intersectionality as a Method of Analysis

In order to demonstrate how theories of intersectionality can illuminate the methodological choices that analysts make, we turn now to consider highly regarded sociological monographs on social inequalities—*Promises I Can Keep* (Edin and Kefalas 2005)... and *Unequal Childhoods* (Lareau 2003). We use their data and analysis to highlight how more attention to system-level complexity can enrich microlevel analysis, tightening the connections among power relations, institutional contexts, and lived experience.

... [These] prize-winning monographs rely on qualitative methods, are deeply concerned with social justice, and offer insightful analyses of multidimensional inequality. Yet while each is strongly inclusive, and some attend to the processes of inequality as having intersectional effects, none adopts a complex view of mutually constitutive intersectional processes in the setting they study. Rather than revealing a process by which each relationship of inequality works on and through the others, each of these books offers a look at particular social locations marked as outside the mainstream, obscures the relationship of the unmarked categories to the highlighted group, and sets the power relations that create these processes outside the picture. By making use of the rich data presented in these exemplary studies, we point to where an intersectional analysis could move to reveal more of the complex, contextual, and comparative relations in the data that the authors themselves present.

[...]

Inclusion and the Rhetoric of Voice:
[. . .] *Promises I Can Keep*

[...]

Edin and Kefalas's way of telling the stories of poor single mothers also privileges the view of middle-class readers concerned with morality and unfamiliar with poverty. Examining the cultural logic of poor women who put motherhood before marriage, Edin and Kefalas find that these single mothers put a high symbolic value on marriage as a luxury to be enjoyed after they achieve a successful livelihood but they see children as necessary to bring meaning and value to their lives right now. They present this cultural logic of motherhood with rich ethnographic detail, but make comparisons only to a thin and stereotypical version of a middle-class moral standard. If, when, and why middle-class women of a similar age group value children and why they (oddly?) put marriage before childbearing appear only as unquestionable norms against which these women are implicitly measured. For example, Edin and Kefalas conclude: "It is the perceived low costs of early childbearing and the high value that poor women place on children—and motherhood—that motivate their seemingly inexplicable inability to avoid pregnancy" (p. 171). Since the authors do not raise the question of what makes the decision "inexplicable," the women's choices are converted invisibly into an "inability."

The point is not that these authors need to do a comparative ethnography, but rather that an intersectional perspective on the women's decision making as a process would place their structural location into relation with others, eliciting counterfactual questions that disturb the naturalness of existing arrangements—such as what is absent in middle-class, college-aged women's lives that would lower the cost of early childbearing for them? What motivates their "inexplicable" decision to wait to marry first and risk later infertility?

If not to meet a middle-class norm of respectability, why should poor women try to "avoid pregnancy"? This is actually the unanswered question. When directly asked, "what would your life be like without children?" their interviewees say: "I'd be dead or in jail," "I'd be in the streets," "I wouldn't care about anything," "My child saved me," and "It's only because of my children that I'm where I am today" (p. 184). Edin and Kefalas argue that even if mothers are better off by having children, their choice is harmful: "although having children early may not affect a young mother's life chances much, it may diminish the life chances of her children" (p. 216). But this framing of the problem places "the children" on one side of a moral divide, where the readers' desire to care for them is assumed, and frames poor mothers (and fathers, p. 217) as potentially dangerous parents, whose own interests are less significant. Despite Edin and Kefalas's intention to "give voice" to these poor mothers, their own needs are discursively marginalized.

Interactions and the Logic of Comparison: Power and Process in *Unequal Childhoods*

Unequal Childhoods by Annette Lareau offers an insightful analysis of the cultural logic in American childrearing in middle-class and working-class families through a systematic comparison across class, race, and gender. Yet, despite its merits, the methodological approach that guides Lareau's data analyses is intersectional only in the static sense of street-corner-like locations where the different forces of inequality cross.

Unequal Childhoods claims that there are highly significant social class differences in childrearing with distinctive cultural logics that influence children's sense of self in relation to society, and successfully shows that the categorical approach to social class, rather than a continuous variable such as mother's education, better explains differences in the childrearing logics of these families. Lareau then points to gender and racial differences as an "addition" to these core differences by class:

> To be sure, other things also mattered in addition to social class. Gender differences were particularly striking. Girls and boys enjoyed different types of activities. Girls had more sedentary lives compared to boys. They also played closer to home. . . . Race also played a role, particularly as racial segregation of residential neighborhoods divided children into racially segregated informal play groups (although race did not influence the number of activities children had). (p. 36)

There are two interrelated analytic problems that arise from treating gender, race, and class as separate variables and trying to find which has the "biggest" effect. First, because the "main effects" of gender, race, and class are studied as essentially unaffected by each other, the interaction among them is not apparent as a *process,* even when the families that populate each intersectional *location* are examined in a type of "multiple jeopardy" analysis. Second, the effects of class, race, and gender are primarily seen in the experiences of those in the subordinated or "marked" category in each dimension. We take up each of these in turn.

In the subsection titled "the intersection of race and class," Lareau goes into detail about the particularity of the middle-class black families as compared to their white counterparts. Yet despite these rich descriptions, the analysis suggests a choice must be made between race and class as "the" primary dimension. She frames this as an analytic decision between two variables, rather than unpacking any interaction between them:

> Still, the biggest differences in the cultural logic of child rearing in the day-to-day behavior of children in this study were between middle-class children on the one hand . . . and working-class and poor children on the other. As a middle-class black boy, Alexander Williams had much more in common with white middle-class Garrett Tallinger than he did with less-privileged Black boys, such as Tyrec Talyer or Harold McAllister. (p. 241)

Making a comparison between the amounts of inequality by class or race to see which has more effect means defining them as independent and separate "main effects" while limiting the visibility of dynamic intersections of these processes. More attention to how each process, as a process, is inflected and transformed by its intersection with the other might draw out some richer consideration from the same data.

Consider how gender and race dynamics actually interact in the stories of mothers' carework in the middle-class black families. Although Lareau presents white and black middle-class parents' active intervention in school as similar, her data suggest their motives for and nature of intervention vary in important ways. Both mothers of the two middle-class black children, Alexander Williams and Stacey Marshall, provide the intensive attention for which the class logic of "cultivation" calls, but what they do and how they do it is deeply intertwined with race. Alexander's mother monitors every activity in which her son enrolls to make sure he is not "the only black kid." Stacey's mother is concerned about whether teachers might have lower expectations because of her race and worries about how to deal with the school bus driver who makes all black children sit in the back of the bus (p. 179).

Lareau recognizes this burden of black mothers' carework: "This vigilance meant that Black middle-class parents, mothers especially, undertook more labor than did their white middle-class counterparts, as they worried about the racial balance and the insensitivity of other children, and framed appropriate responses to their own children's reactions" (p. 181). However, this is framed as an added burden ("more labor"), not a qualitatively distinctive logic of race-aware childrearing in a racist society. Lareau makes this explicit: "Nevertheless, race did not appear to shape the dominant cultural logic of child rearing in Alexander's family or in other families in the study" (p. 133). In this succinct statement, the complexities in the black middle-class mothers' antiracist work are subsumed under the "big picture" of "class-based advantage" of middle-class parents (p. 180), and a chance also to look for if and how race-aware parenting transforms class logics and vice versa is lost.

Unequal Childhoods also allows its emphasis on inclusion and difference to divert attention from the *unmarked categories*. Even though there is systematic comparison with middle-class experiences, which are themselves theorized, each comparison in *Unequal Childhoods* is formulated to explain only the difference of the nondominant groups from the dominant. For example, the effect of race is elaborated in the case of blacks, but there is no theoretical account given for the workings of race for whites. Similarly, for gender, only the girls' differences from boys are pointed out. The opportunity for a gender analysis of masculinity and femininity for both boys and girls that might expose a process producing and reproducing gender advantage in class and race specific ways is squandered.

Instead, consider the structure of *Unequal Childhoods*, where detailed stories of one specific family are told in each chapter. Only in the accounts of black families is there a race-related subsection (entitled "role of race" for Harold's and Alexander's families and "race: constant worries, intermittent interventions" for Stacey's). This analytic design implicitly theorizes race as a particularity added only to black lives, as if whiteness is not racial and its relationships meaningful in the lives of parents and children. Yet the data themselves point in another direction, as in the following example of a mention of varying degrees of racial seg-regation as a "fact of life" for white families:

> Billy Yanelli's home is in an all white neighborhood, but the street demarcating the begin-ning of an all-Black neighborhood is only a few blocks away. . . . His third-grade teacher, Ms. Green was African American, as was the school counsellor. . . . At home, he mostly plays with white children. . . . (p. 224)

The implications of race for the cultural logic of childrearing for white families is under-mined by failing to consider how it could be that Billy's home is "only a few blocks away" from those of black children but nonetheless he "mostly plays with white children." Is there parental work, and if so, of what sort, involved in creating and maintaining such segregated experience for white children?

If race were explicitly theorized as a more fully intersectional process of the exercise of power, it would be easier to ask about the ways that racialized relationships are being formed through cultural logics of childrearing as well. How is racialization and racial segregation understood by white parents and how do they succeed or fail in transmitting these expectations of differences in status and social distance to their children? Leaving the unmarked category of whiteness uninterrogated in racial terms makes the conclusion that race "has less effect" than class almost a foregone conclusion, since class is the only relationship viewed as effective for all families. Similarly, gender also emerges in the data more than it does in the analysis. Consider the story Lareau tells of Wendy, a working-class white girl. Possibly having a learning disorder, Wendy is seriously behind in her reading, and her teacher laments the insufficient attention paid to Wendy's needs, using racialized and gendered language to do so:

> Wendy, I think, slipped through the cracks. . . . I firmly believe that if Wendy was a little Black girl that she should already have been in a special education type of situation. A kid in fourth grade who can't read a first-grade reader, something is dreadfully wrong here. . . . And Wendy is so cute and so sweet. She has a smile for everybody, and I think somehow or other, I think they did her a terrible disservice by just letting her go forward. (p. 213)

What does the teacher mean by "if Wendy was a little Black girl" she would have been helped? Is he implying that the assumption of academic competence that comes with white-ness hindered recognition of Wendy's special needs? Is it the pervasive racial tracking in the schools that makes him call this help "special education type of services" rather than simply "special education"? What does the perception of Wendy as "so cute and so sweet" and having "a smile for everybody," invoking the people-pleaser image of good white girls, have to do with this? Although Wendy's case is analyzed in the book by focusing on her class, an inter-sectional analysis would also question how her experience is also racialized and gendered in the structure of the school, creating issues for her parents to respond to (or not).

Since we can see in the data that issues of segregation and academic expectations arise for both white and black families, both sets of parents must have some ways of dealing with race, but these do not emerge as a "logic" that shapes their process of parenting intersectionally with the logics of class and gender. Identifying and comparing dynamic processes as such, rather than families that simply sit at the crossroads of intersecting inequalities, would tend to make the unmarked categories more useful for explaining power structures and relational experiences, which is Lareau's goal.

[. . .]

Conclusion

Although being critical of the . . . studies we selected, we do so not to diminish their contributions but to concretize the potential that more attention to complex intersectionality could offer analytically. We have tried to take the authors' own theoretical goals seriously in each case, while also suggesting ways in which their undertheorization of what intersectionality means in their case limits the power of their analysis. . . . While we are sympathetic to the need to include the voices of the marginalized in mainstream sociological thought, we take these studies as evidence that it is still easier to include multiply-marginalized groups than to analyze the relationships that affect them intersectionally. We suggest that seeing the hardly touched opportunities for intersectional analysis in even strong studies—particularly in seeing stratification processes nonhierarchically and understanding the multilevel co-determination of racialization and gendering processes with those of class—will help sociologists think about how their work might better address these challenges.

We have highlighted the specific losses in these studies that can be attributed to adopting a rhetoric of voice, a locational rather than process understanding of intersectionality, a strategy of comparing main effects with "additional" interactions, an implicitly hierarchical understanding of social processes, and a single-level analytic focus. Our own theoretical preferences lead us to believe that if intersectionality is approached methodologically as relational rather than locational, as transforming the processes affecting the "mainstream" as well as identifying select interactions for the "special" cases, and as implying a flow of knowledge and power across levels of social organization rather than a nested hierarchy of stratification processes, sociology as a whole would profit. . . .

Overall, we believe that attention to intersectional inequalities in future studies could become more methodologically appropriate and theoretically productive if the specific assumptions that the researcher makes about intersectionality were made more explicit. We do not suggest that doing studies aimed at "giving voice" to often-excluded groups are misguided, but we do think that theoretically considering the challenges of intersectionality would direct attention to methodological choices that might avoid placing an unmarked standard in the position of exercising normative power, for example, by questioning the values that readers might bring to the account of these "different" groups. A good example of this can be found in Hays's (2003) discussion of the ways in which college students are prone to the drug use and sexual activity that are so strongly condemned among poor teens. A research project that compares main effects and interactions as processes in a particular setting might examine how interactions appear for the dominant as well as for the subordinate groups and what assumptions about the hierarchical relationships among these processes are being made. A good example of this can be found in Roth's study (2004) of the "separate roads" to feminism taken by women in the social movements of the 1960s, in which white women and white-central groups are analyzed as no less race specific than Latina and African-American organizations and gender dynamics.

However, we also suggest that many studies would benefit from adopting a still more complex view of intersectionality, in which the focus is on the feedback loops among processes at multiple levels that create interactions among them as inherent parts of how they are constituted. We argue that the complexity of multiple institutions that feed back into each other—both positively and negatively—can become obscured when the macrostructures of inequality are separated from the micro-structures of social construction of meaning. . . . In the end, the better sociology we seek will be constructed by those scholars who take the theoretical challenge of intersectionality as a spur to improve how their own research is designed.

References

Collins, Patricia H. 1990. *Black Feminist Thought: Knowledge, Consciousness, and the Politics of Empowerment*. Boston, MA: Unwin Hyman.

Crenshaw, Kimberlé. 1991. "Mapping the Margins: Intersectionality, Identity Politics, and Violence Against Women of Color." *Stanford Law Review* 43:1241–99.

Davis, Kathy. 2008. "Intersectionality as Buzzword: A Sociology of Science Perspective on What Makes a Feminist Theory Successful." *Feminist Theory* 9:67–85.

Edin, Kathryn and Maria Kefalas. 2005. *Promises I Can Keep: Why Poor Women Put Motherhood Before Marriage*. Berkeley, CA: University of California Press.

Glenn, Evelyn N. 1999. "The Social Construction and Institutionalization of Gender and Race: An Integrative Framework." Pp. 3–43 in *Revisioning Gender*, edited by M. M. Ferree, J. Lorber, and B. B. Hess. New York: Sage.

Hays, Sharon. 2003. *Flat Broke With Children: Women in the Age of Welfare Reform*. New York: Oxford University Press.

Lareau, Annette. 2003. *Unequal Childhoods: Class, Race, and Family Life*. Berkeley, CA: University of California Press.

McCall, Leslie. 2001. *Complex Inequality: Gender, Class and Race in the New Economy*. New York: Routledge.

Pascale, Celine-Marie. 2007. *Making Sense of Race, Class and Gender: Commonsense, Power and Privilege in the United States*. New York: Routledge.

Roth, Benita. 2004. *Separate Roads to Feminism: Black, Chicana, and White Feminist Movements in America's Second Wave*. New York: Cambridge University Press.

Engendering Racial Perceptions

An Intersectional Analysis of How Social Status Shapes Race

Andrew M. Penner and Aliya Saperstein

For many gender scholars there is an inherent tension between survey-based, quantitative methods and the study of intersectionality. As McCall (2005) notes, there is considerable scorn for the mathematical language ("additive" vs. "multiplicative") often used to describe the insights of intersectionality and frustration at the implication that the entire paradigm can be reduced to a series of "interaction effects" in a multivariate model. At the same time, research from a traditional stratification perspective is often dismissive of insights gleaned from case studies and personal narratives, arguing that claims about how systems of inequality operate cannot be validated without more generalizable data. As a result, conversations across these methodological, epistemological, and disciplinary divides remain limited, despite shared interest in understanding the mechanisms that perpetuate social difference and division (McCall 2005).

We aim to further the study of intersectionality by demonstrating that statistical modeling is not necessarily antithetical to examining the intersections of race, class, and gender. In doing so, we take seriously recent critiques that stress the importance of asking dynamic, process-oriented, and relational questions about how race, gender, and social class divisions overlap in people's lives (Choo and Ferree 2010). Drawing on nearly 20 years of longitudinal data from the National Longitudinal Survey of Youth (NLSY, 1979 cohort), we examine whether changes in how people are perceived racially by others are influenced by social class position in ways that differ by gender. Specifically, we ask: If Americans are more likely to be seen as Black and less likely to be seen as white after experiencing decreases in status, such as becoming incarcerated or impoverished (Saperstein and Penner 2012), are these effects stronger for women or men? Or do different sets of class-relevant factors matter depending on the gender of the person being racially classified?

Andrew M. Penner and Aliya Saperstein. 2013. "Engendering Racial Perceptions: An Intersectional Analysis of How Social Status Shapes Race." *Gender & Society* 27(3):319–44.

Our results highlight that an individual's position in the "matrix of domination" (Collins 1990) is not necessarily fixed. Consistent with the idea that race is a changeable marker of status encoded onto the body (Omi and Winant 1994), we find that class mobility can trigger racial mobility, both upward and downward, and the specific trajectories often vary for women and men. For example, while some status cues, such as living in the suburbs, make both women and men more likely to be seen as white, others have differential effects either in magnitude, significance, or both, as when receiving welfare makes women (but not men) more likely to subsequently be seen as Black and incarceration makes men (but not women) less likely to subsequently be seen as white. These findings not only illustrate how intersectional processes affect individuals in their everyday lives, they also provide further evidence, nationally representative and longitudinal, of one of the central claims of the field: that race and class are gendered, and gender and class are racialized.

Implementing an Intersectional Analysis

Over time, both the "what" and the "how" of studying intersectionality have been in dispute. . . .

A growing quantitative literature directly engages intersectionality and evaluates its empirical claims (e.g., Harnois 2010; Steinbugler, Press, and Dias 2006). Yet, it is often implied, if not explicitly stated, that qualitative research methods are the most appropriate means of studying the intersectional complexity of social difference, in part because they tend to be better suited to identifying mechanisms and process rather than broad patterns (Choo and Ferree 2010).

A common critique of quantitative studies of inequality is that, even when they consider the effects of race, class, and gender (and/or other categories of difference), they often assess each effect independently and ask which axis of stratification is most prominent in a given situation. This approach goes against the claim that the various dimensions are inextricably intertwined and always operating in conjunction. We adopt an intermediate position, in line with others (e.g., Browne and Misra 2003; Timberlake and Estes 2007), that asserts the extent of the co-constitution of race, class, and gender inequality is an empirical question and may vary across contexts. Following Glenn (2002), we use standard racial and class categories as "anchors," without assuming that they are static, and explore how they change relative to one another over an individual's life course. That is, we are both questioning the categories' essentialism and using their purported existence for analytical leverage to demonstrate how boundaries are drawn between them.

Data and Methods

Our data come from the 1979 cohort of the NLSY, a representative sample of 12,686 U.S. men and women who were 14 to 22 years of age when first surveyed in 1979. . . . We utilize data from 1979 to 1998, the most recent year in which the interviewers recorded their racial classification of the respondents. To define our study populations, we use the respondent's self-reported sex from 1979.

Our dependent variable is the interviewer's classification of the respondent's race, which was collected in all but one survey year from 1979 to 1998. Interviewers were instructed to classify the respondent's race at the end of the interview. Thus, we do not have their first impression of the respondent's race; we have a classification colored by the respondent's answers during the survey interview. This is ideal for assessing the effects of social status on racial classification, because the interviewer heard a range of information about the respondent, from their income and education to their employment and marital history, prior to recording the respondent's race.

Interviewers were not given any special instructions as to how to classify the respondents by race (NLS 2006); the categories available to them were "Black," "White," and "Other." . . .

Of the observations where respondents have racial classifications in consecutive survey years, 6 percent are described by a different race than in the previous person-year, and 20 percent of the individuals in the sample experienced at least one change in how they were racially classified between 1979 and 1998.

It is possible that these changes in respondents' racial classification from one survey year to the next were the result of mistakes made by the interviewers if, for example, they were in a hurry to complete their remarks and meant to check "White" but mistakenly checked "Black." To the degree that the mistakes were randomly distributed, this explanation would decrease the signal-to-noise ratio in our analyses, making it difficult to find evidence of a relationship between gender, social position, and racial classification. . . .

However, we do not assume that the interviewer's classification is "true" or correct in any objective sense. We also do not assume that the interviewer's racial classification necessarily aligns with how the respondent would self-identify; rather we view self-identification and classification by others as capturing different information about an individual's race and racial experiences (Saperstein 2008). We regard the interviewer's racial classification as a measure of how the respondent is likely to be perceived, and presumably treated, by others. Indeed, some scholars have argued that racial classification is actually a more appropriate measure than self-identification for understanding phenomena such as discrimination (Telles and Lim 1998). For this reason, understanding who gets racially classified as what, and under what circumstances, is an important question for sociological analysis.

Changes in Race Over Time

Previous research has documented the existence of fluidity in racial classification in the United States for the same individuals at different points in their life course (Brown, Hitlin, and Elder Jr. 2007; Saperstein and Penner 2012). However, whether the level or patterns of change differ by gender has yet to be empirically explored. . . . [On] average 1.3 percent of women who were classified as Black in the previous year are classified as white in the current year. Similarly, on average 3.7 percent of women classified as white in the previous year are currently classified as other. Comparing the results for women . . . and men . . . reveals that the overall level of change in racial classification is almost identical. It is not the case that only women, or only men, experience changes in racial classification. Rather, racial fluidity characterizes the lived experience of race equally for women and men. . . .

Among respondents who have ever been classified as Black, 14 percent of individuals experience a change in classification from Black to white in consecutive interviews, and 4 percent experience a change from Black to other. Among respondents ever classified as white, 5 percent experience a change from white to Black in consecutive interviews, while 19 percent experience a change from white to other. Finally, among respondents ever classified as other, 88 percent experience at least one classification shift from other to white, and 8 percent experience a shift from other to Black in consecutive interviews. Like the fluidity observed in the year-to-year changes, the likelihood of ever experiencing a particular racial transition does not vary by gender.

The Effects of Social Status on Race

Having established that both women and men experience racial fluidity, we now turn to modeling which social factors influence racial classification. Though changes in race are equally likely for women and men overall, it does not necessarily follow that the changes for men and women are driven by the same factors, as we demonstrate below.

Table 8.1 presents odds ratios from two sets of logistic regression models estimating how interviewers racially classified women and men, alongside p values from fully interacted models testing whether the coefficients for women and men differ. The first two models examine the odds of being classified as white (vs. all else) separately for women and men. The third column in the table presents the p value from a model in which all independent variables were interacted with gender to test whether the differences in odds ratios for women and men are statistically significant (full model results available upon request). The other three columns in the table present analogous models examining the odds of being classified as Black (vs. all else).

Table 8.1 Odds Ratios From Logistic Regression Models Predicting Racial Classification by Interviewer

	Classified as White			Classified as Black		
	Women	Men	p Value of Women-Men	Women	Men	p Value of Women-Men
Ever long-term unemployed	0.71*** (−9.59)	0.77*** (−7.33)	.062	1.52*** (6.38)	1.33*** (3.66)	.129
Ever below poverty line	0.74*** (−7.03)	0.65*** (−10.07)	.011	1.34*** (4.09)	1.527*** (5.33)	.207
Ever incarcerated	1.00 (−0.01)	0.64*** (−5.93)	.090	0.88 (−0.26)	1.57** (2.95)	.278
Ever received welfare	0.75*** (−5.97)	0.93 (−1.45)	.000	1.47*** (4.61)	1.09 (0.87)	.019
Married with children	1.261** (4.68)	1.37*** (7.27)	.213	0.77** (−3.10)	0.70*** (−4.19)	.466
Married without children	1.42*** (5.90)	1.53*** (7.61)	.356	0.81 (−1.82)	0.58*** (−3.92)	.078
Unmarried with children	0.65*** (−7.78)	0.85 (−1.95)	.009	1.72*** (4.97)	1.58* (2.30)	.739
Four or more children	0.67*** (−3.95)	0.80 (−1.45)	.306	1.41 (1.93)	1.07 (0.24)	.371
Lives in an inner city	0.62*** (−5.10)	0.65*** (−5.14)	.311	1.88*** (5.44)	1.49*** (3.39)	.053
Lives in a suburb	1.17** (2.59)	1.22** (3.20)	.182	0.88 (−143)	0.87 (−147)	.662

(Continued)

Table 8.1   (Continued)

	Classified as White			Classified as Black		
	Women	Men	p Value of Women-Men	Women	Men	p Value of Women-Men
Education (years)	0.97** (−2.84)	1.02* (2.48)	.000	1.06** (2.71)	0.98 (−0.95)	.008
Same race previously	160.50*** (58.00)	173.19*** (52.99)	.324	4189.2*** (74.55)	5913.6*** (79.88)	.011
Hispanic in 1979	1.10 (0.54)	1.11 (0.55)	.961	0.19*** (−5.69)	0.21*** (−4.14)	.760
Multiple races in 1979	1.72*** (7.87)	1.70*** (6.82)	.870	0.69** (−2.81)	0.68** (−2.96)	.947
Born outside the US	0.88 (−0.98)	1.05 (0.30)	.290	1.17 (0.65)	0.60 (−155)	.093
Lives in the South	0.63*** (−5.54)	0.63*** (−5.77)	.787	1.87*** (7.49)	1.79*** (6.47)	.523
Age (years)	1.11** (2.61)	1.01 (0.22)	.052	0.86* (−2.00)	1.04 (0.57)	.050
Age-squared	1.00* (−2.28)	1.00 (−0.52)	.145	1.00 (182)	1.00 (−0.43)	.085
Female interviewer	1.30 (105)	1.33 (166)	.968	0.57 (−178)	0.67 (−1.44)	.394
Interviewer age (years)	1.01 (183)	1.01 (172)	.379	1.01 (1.94)	1.01 (171)	.540
Interviewer some college	0.94 (−0.45)	0.95 (−0.40)	.946	1.00 (−0.04)	1.07 (0.49)	.581
Interviewer college grad	1.09 (0.68)	0.98 (−0.15)	.233	0.81 (−1.89)	1.13 (0.83)	.022
Black interviewer	0.34*** (−7.44)	0.31*** (−9.58)	.489	3.14*** (6.18)	3.31*** (5.47)	.801
Other interviewer (non-black, non-white)	0.56 (−1.44)	0.64 (−113)	.595	0.97 (−0.09)	0.59 (−1.68)	.292
Observations (person-years)	81,237	79,297		81,233	79,297	

Source: 1979 National Longitudinal Survey of Youth.

Note: All models include survey year fixed effects and indicators for missing data. z statistics account for clustering on interviewers. "Same race previously" indicates whether respondents were classified as white in the previous interview in the models predicting classification as white, and whether respondents were classified as Black in the previous interview in the models predicting classification as Black. The columns labeled "Women" and "Men" report odds ratios from separate models for women and men, and the column labeled "p value of Women-Men" reports the p value from a fully interacted model testing whether the effect of each variable was the same for men and women.

*$p < .05$, **$p < .01$, ***$p < .001$.

For both women and men, racial classification is influenced by a wide variety of status characteristics. Looking first at column 1, the odds ratio for having ever experienced long-term unemployment (.705) indicates that, net of all other measured factors, including whether she was classified as white in the previous year, having been unemployed reduces the odds of a woman being classified as white in the current year by roughly 30 percent. In fact, for women, all but one of our status variables is a significant predictor of being classified by the interviewer as white. The second model presents the analogous results for men, and 8 of the 11 status variables are statistically significant predictors of being classified as white among men. Results from the other pair of models can be interpreted similarly, with odds ratios greater than one indicating that a given factor increases the odds of being classified as Black, and odds ratios less than one indicating that factor decreases the odds of being classified as Black. Overall, 30 of the 44 possible associations between social position and racial classification are statistically significant and in the expected direction, demonstrating the inextricable link between race and class in the United States.

Focusing specifically on gender differences in the relationship between social position and racial classification, we examine p values comparing the odds ratios for women and men (see columns 3 and 6). A statistically significant p value ($p < .05$) for the gender interaction of a given characteristic indicates that there is a measurable difference in the effect of that characteristic on the racial classifications of women and men. We find six instances where the odds ratios are significantly different at the .05 level and four additional factors with gender differences that are approaching significance ($p < .10$). Poverty, for example, decreases both women's and men's odds of being classified as white, but the p value indicates that having ever been in poverty has a stronger effect (indicated by the odds ratio furthest from 1) on the racial classification of men compared to women. Finding that poverty has a stronger effect for men is consistent with traditional gender roles that emphasize men's responsibility as breadwinners (Reskin and Padavic 1994). Likewise, consistent with gendered stereotypes around welfare (Timberlake and Estes 2007), we see that women who ever received welfare benefits have lower odds of being seen as white and higher odds of being seen as Black, whereas men's racial classifications are not affected by reporting a history of welfare receipt (e.g., food stamps, SSI, and other public assistance).

However, there are also characteristics that significantly predict racial classification for both women and men where the estimated effects do not differ significantly by gender. Nonsignificant p values in columns 3 and 6 suggest that some status cues affect racial classification equally for everyone. For example, both women and men are significantly more likely to be seen as white if they are married (with or without children), or live in the suburbs, and significantly less likely to be seen as white if they live in the inner city.

It is also worth noting that the factors that affect whether people are seen as white are not necessarily the same factors that affect whether they are seen as Black. For example, living in a suburb increases both women's and men's odds of being classified as white, but does not affect their odds of being classified as Black. We also find that the odds ratio for having been classified as Black in the previous year is significantly larger for men. This suggests that "Blackness" in general is stickier for men: net of the status variables examined here, a man classified as Black this year has higher odds of being classified as Black again next year than a woman who is classified as Black this year.

The results from our analysis of gender differences in the relationship between social position and racial classification can be summarized by three broad patterns, illustrated in Figure 8.1. First, as depicted in the pair of bars on the left, there are some status distinctions, such as living in the inner city, that are gender neutral; they affect racial classification similarly for women and men, both in terms of their magnitude and statistical significance. Second, some factors have

Figure 8.1   Gendered Patterns in How Social Status Shapes Race

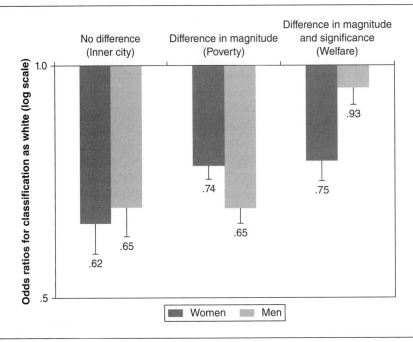

Note: Odds ratios are from models predicting classification as white separately for women and men (see Table 8.1). Error bars represent 1 standard error.

statistically significant effects for both women and men, but the magnitude of the effect differs. For example, as depicted in the middle pair of bars, having ever lived in poverty reduces the odds of being classified as white for both women and men, but the effect is significantly stronger for men. Third, some factors differ in both magnitude and statistical significance, as seen in the pair of bars on the right, where a history of welfare receipt affects the odds of women being classified as white, but has no significant net effect for men.

Overall, the results are consistent with a priori expectations of how common racial stereotypes are gendered. For status distinctions that tend to affect men and women equally, such as being married, we find no gender differences in their effects on racial classification. However, where status distinctions and their associated stereotypes are strongly gendered, as with welfare or incarceration, we find significant status effects on racial classification only for the expected group. Between these extremes are factors like poverty and parenthood, with stereotypes that can be applied to both men and women but are often deployed unequally (or asymmetrically), as when out-of-wedlock births are seen as a problem only for women of color (Furstenberg 2003).

We can also read the content of our racial stereotypes and their gendered dimensions backward, inferring them from the significant effects in Table 8.1. From this perspective, our results suggest that Blackness is associated with unemployment, poverty, unmarried parenthood, and inner city residence, for both men and women. Whiteness, on the other hand, is associated with living in the suburbs and being married (regardless of parental status). By focusing on the *p* value testing for significant differences in the effects of a given factor, one can also infer the degree to which racial stereotypes are gendered. The primary example here is welfare, which has significant gender differences in its effects on being classified as white and Black, with significant effects for women but not men.

Our results imply that the stereotypes shaping racial classifications vary by gender, and thus suggest that factors triggering racial discrimination are also likely to vary. This echoes social psychological research on racial prototypicality showing that the more characteristics someone has that are associated with Blackness the more likely they are to be discriminated against (Eberhardt et al. 2006). However, our work also supports previous research finding that the prototypical Black woman and Black man (or white woman and white man) are not identical (cf. Timberlake and Estes 2007). Taken together, our study calls attention to the fact that before racial discrimination can occur, potential discriminators must first racially classify their targets, and the factors that inform these classifications vary by gender. Revealing a history of welfare receipt may put a woman at greater risk for racial discrimination, because it increases the likelihood that she will be perceived as Black, but the same is not true for men. From a policy perspective, it is important to understand how the antecedents of discrimination might vary, especially if other axes of difference (e.g., gender, sexuality, class, disability) are subject to similar classification processes.

Destabilizing Categories or Reinforcing Hierarchy?

The micro-level processes discussed above do not simply reflect macro-level structures of inequality, they actively "(re)constitute broader relations of inequality" (Pyke 1996, 546). As such, finding that changes in race are tied to social mobility in gendered ways has important implications for how we think about macrostructural aspects of intersectionality. In particular, our results highlight that changes in race, gender, or class status do not necessarily imply a significant weakening of boundaries or an undermining of categories, as has often been predicted in previous research (e.g., see Alba 2005; Wilkins 2004). Instead, our findings reveal a deeply intertwined system of inequality in which individual fluidity can perversely reinforce existing structural inequalities.

To illustrate, we take Collins's (1990) metaphor of the "matrix of domination" literally, invoking a multidimensional array of cells that encode a hierarchy of social status. . . .

Typically, the boundaries separating categories, or cells, along the dimension of race (or gender) are seen as static and rigid, restricting mobility and causing individuals' experiences to be shaped or constrained by their social location. So, when people experience class mobility, moving into the cells above or below their current structural position, it is assumed their trajectory is restricted to the same racialized column of cells. Our results reveal the potential for diagonal movement between cells, as social mobility can involve multiple dimensions of stratification simultaneously. For example, when a man's income falls below the poverty line, our results show that this not only affects his class position but also lowers his odds of being classified as white and raises his odds of being classified as Black.

However, highlighting the permeability of racial boundaries is not necessarily the same as saying they become blurred or unstable. We argue instead that these unexpected patterns of mobility are serving, intentionally or not, to maintain perceived differences between groups. When confronted with counter-stereotypical status shifts, the larger system of inequality can be stabilized by redefining individuals—moving them between cells of the existing matrix—instead of redefining the categories or their associated stereotypes and lived experiences. Rather than revise tropes about Black women and welfare, the matrix is reinforced as the racial categorizations of women who are (and are not) on welfare get reinterpreted.

Indeed, we suggest the strength of these social boundaries is in their selectivity, not their impermeability per se. If the movement of individuals across cell (or category) boundaries is selective and based on status characteristics, the social meaning of the categories will remain in equilibrium, and their associated stereotypes will continue to be reinforced over time. . . .

Conclusion

This study demonstrates how longitudinal survey data, with repeated measures of key axes of stratification, can help further efforts to understand the dynamics of intersectional inequalities in the United States. Choo and Ferree argue that, by examining changes over time, "macrostructures of inequality" can be linked to "microstructures of social construction of meaning," revealing feedback loops among the various axes of stratification (Choo and Ferree 2010, 146). Our results illuminate one such loop by identifying gendered patterns in how class relevant factors shape racial classification in the United States. In some cases, the gendered effects match a priori expectations based on widespread stereotypes about criminal propensities and "welfare queens." In others, they point to unexplored variation in how women and men experience both social and racial mobility. . . .

To fully understand how race, class, and gender interact, in "a process by which each relationship of inequality works on and through the others" (Choo and Ferree 2010, 36), it is crucial for future research on these issues to be developed iteratively and from a range of methodological perspectives.

References

Alba, Richard. 2005. "Bright vs. Blurred Boundaries: Second-Generation Assimilation and Exclusion in France, Germany, and the United States." *Ethnic and Racial Studies* 28:20–49.

Brown, Scott J., Steven Hitlin, and Glen H. Elder, Jr. 2007. "The Importance of Being Other: A Natural Experiment About Lived Race Over Time." *Social Science Research* 36:159–74.

Browne, Irene and Joya Misra. 2003. "The Intersection of Gender and Race in Labor Markets." *Annual Review of Sociology* 29:487–513.

Choo, Hae Yeon and Myra Marx Ferree. 2010. "Practicing Intersectionality in Sociological Research." *Sociological Theory* 28:129–49.

Collins, Patricia Hill. 1990. *Black Feminist Thought.* London, UK: HarperCollins. *etin*

Eberhardt, Jennifer L., Paul G. Davies, Valerie J. Purdie-Vaughns, and Sheri Lynn Johnson. 2006. "Looking Deathworthy: Perceived Stereotypicality of Black Defendants Predicts Capital-Sentencing Outcomes." *Psychological Science* 17:383–86.

Furstenberg Jr., Frank E. 2003. "Teenage Childbearing as a Public Issue and Private Concern." *Annual Review of Sociology* 29:23–39.

Glenn, Evelyn Nakano. 2002. *Unequal Freedom.* Cambridge, MA: Harvard University Press.

Harnois, Catherine E. 2010. "Race, Gender, and the Black Women's Standpoint." *Sociological Forum* 25(1):68–85.

McCall, Leslie. 2005. "The Complexity of Intersectionality." *Signs* 30:1771–1800.

Omi, Michael and Howard Winant. 1994. *Racial Formation in the United States.* New York: Routledge.

Pyke, Karen D. 1996. "Class-Based Masculinities: The Interdependence of Gender, Class, and Interpersonal Power." *Gender & Society* 10:527–49.

Reskin, Barbara F. and Irene Padavic. 1994. *Women and Men at Work.* Thousand Oaks, CA: Pine Forge Press.

Saperstein, Aliya. 2008. "(Re)modeling Race: Moving From Intrinsic Characteristic to Multidimensional Marker of Status." In *Racism in Post-race America: New Theories, New Directions*, edited by C. Gallagher. Chapel Hill, NC: Social Forces.

Saperstein, Aliya and Andrew M. Penner. 2012. "Racial Fluidity and Inequality in the United States." *American Journal of Sociology* 118:676–727.

Steinbugler, Amy C., Julie E. Press, and Janice Johnson Dias. 2006. "Gender, Race, and Affirmative Action: Operationalizing Intersectionality in Survey Research." *Gender & Society* 20(6):805–25.

Telles, Edward and Nelson Lim. 1998. "Does It Matter Who Answers the Race Question? Racial Classification and Income Inequality in Brazil." *Demography* 35:465–74.

Timberlake, Jeffrey M. and Sarah Estes. 2007. "Do Racial and Ethnic Stereotypes Depend on the Sex of Target Group Members?" *Sociological Quarterly* 48:399–433.

Wilkins, Amy C. 2004. "Puerto Rican Wannabes: Sexual Spectacle and the Marking of Race, Class, and Gender Boundaries." *Gender & Society* 18:103–21.

Becoming a "Trusted Outsider"

Gender, Ethnicity, and Inequality in Ethnographic Research

Sandra Meike Bucerius

© iStockphoto.com/UberImages

Ethnographers have written extensively about the various roles they assume when conducting research and the implications these roles have for their fieldwork experiences and findings (Gans 1968; Gold 1958). . . . Underlying these roles is the degree of belonging a researcher achieves, which is influenced by his or her participation in group activities, commitment to group values and norms, and level of group affiliation. While achieving "insider" status, or becoming completely integrated into a field setting, can enhance a researcher's access to key informants and information, it can also provoke issues of role conflict (Brannick and Coghlan 2007, 70) and role confusion (Asselin 2003). Given these potential

Sandra Meike Bucerius. 2013. "Becoming a 'Trusted Outsider': Gender, Ethnicity, and Inequality in Ethnographic Research." *Journal of Contemporary Ethnography* 42(6):690–721.

issues, I suggest that ethnographers do not necessarily need to strive for insider status or to avoid an outsider role. Instead, I suggest that being an outsider is not a liability one must over-come, because achieving status as an outsider trusted with "inside knowledge" may provide the ethnographer with a different perspective and different data than that potentially afforded by insider status.

[...]

The development of trust in the research process . . . does not *necessarily* depend on insider status. . . . However, it is still commonly assumed that an ethnographer's ability to gain the trust of group members depends on his or her degree of similarity to them. . . . Criminological researchers widely believe that male researchers have an easier time conducting research in the often violent and male-dominated world of drug dealers and street criminals. Thus, being different from one's research participants is often viewed as a research liability, and being a *woman* who does ethnographic research on drug dealers is regarded as an even more daunting burden to overcome. Feminist ethnographers who study male-oriented social worlds have often commented on the extreme power struggles and sexual tensions present in the research process, suggesting that these dynamics are not only common in their research on men engaged in illicit activities but also in women's investigations of male populations (Arendell 1997; Grenz 2005; Pascoe 2007).

[...]

I address the question of how ethnographers, particularly if they are women, can best establish a rapport with groups operating in informal economies. Building on five years of ethnographic research with an all-male group of 55 second-generation Muslim immigrants involved in the informal economy in Frankfurt, Germany, I demonstrate that (1) being a trusted outsider can facilitate in-depth understanding of a group while being an insider can be a liability and (2) being a woman is not necessarily the greatest impediment in research with male-dominated groups involved in illicit activities; instead, it can facilitate insights about the research participants potentially unavailable to male researchers. While my gender, ethnicity, and class played an important role in the research process, particularly in gaining access, my transition from mere outsider to an outsider trusted with inside knowledge did not depend on my adoption of a masculine style.

[...]

Background and Methods

[...]

To gain a nuanced understanding of the lived experiences of young, male, Muslim immi-grants, I pursued an ethnographic approach, believing this to be the most effective and nonthreatening way of connecting with them. Because of their negative experiences in Germany, they were unaccustomed to forming long-term positive relationships with mem-bers of so-called mainstream society. Thus, I engaged the young men in their own social environment to maximize the possibility of collecting useful and meaningful data.

Initially, I met the group at a local community youth center. Over approximately two-and-a-half years, I spent roughly six hours each day, three afternoons per week, with the young men, usually at the youth center. After having established an initial rapport, I also participated in their activities two or three nights a week. I depended on group members to take me along to various evening activities: hanging out in the streets, bars, and cafés; cruising around in cars without a specific destination; or going to clubs. After the first two-and-a-half years, the young men stopped using the community youth center as their main meeting point, and I had to become flexible. I started to meet the group on certain street corners in the evenings.

My field notes were a daily record of my observations of, and countless conversations and interactions with, the young men. I had the opportunity to witness many types of drug transactions (purchase, drug delivery, storage, negotiations, etc.), fights within the group and with outsiders, as well as family interactions. Moreover, I conducted 105 in-depth interviews; some men I spoke with several times, others only once. In these interviews, the young men disclosed their thoughts and feelings about their social environment, sense of belonging, and participation in the informal drug economy. I audio recorded some of these interviews, but mostly only took notes during and after the interviews since many of the young men felt less comfortable in the presence of a recording device—they often attempted to alter their vocabulary and tone (e.g., they tried to sound more formal), and some of them became quite nervous.

In the first months of my research, I conducted approximately twenty interviews using an interview guide I developed before the start of the project. As the project continued, however, I often used prompts instead of a guide to gain a deeper and more nuanced understanding of certain aspects of the young men's lives that I needed clarification on. Of these more in-depth but less-structured interviews, approximately twenty-five focused on the specifics of the drug trade; thirty on relationships to women, marriage, family, and the future; and thirty on the men's experiences living as second-generation immigrants in Germany. Using prompts in all interviews allowed the young men to decide for themselves what they wanted to emphasize in their replies and allayed the tension created by a more formal interview process. Furthermore, by the time I started conducting these interviews after two years in the field, the young men and I had already built a strong rapport, making the use of a more formal interview style awkward. I also collected letters from three of the five young men who were incarcerated during the research period; they wrote to me from jail. In addition to relying on my field notes, interviews, and the letters from incarcerated men, I received feedback from three of the young men who agreed to peruse some of my notes and supply additional information where needed.

[. . .]

Participants and Researcher

I recruited fifty-five young men between the ages of 16 and 31 (the mean age was 23) for this study. These men were primarily the sons of parents who were recruited by the government as guest workers between the late 1950s and early 1970s to rebuild the economy after World War II. Because of the restrictive citizenship laws, both parents and sons typically did not have German citizenship.

The young men were from heterogeneous cultural backgrounds. The largest subgroup in the sample ($n = 27$) was of Turkish descent, followed by those of Kosovo-Albanian ($n = 8$) and Moroccan descent ($n = 6$). The remainder of the group was composed of young men who came from Croatia, Bosnia, Serbia, and Germany, some of whom had multinational backgrounds.

Despite these national differences, they had many commonalities. Their primary language for communication was German; in fact, most of the young men claimed their German language skills exceeded their mother tongue fluency. They also had the following characteristics in common: their neighborhood, their immigrant status, a Muslim heritage (although they did not necessarily engage in Muslim religious practices), disadvantaged educational and socioeconomic backgrounds, and involvement in drug dealing activities (e.g., they typically sold marijuana and cocaine to a fairly steady customer base).

Although my gender was the most obvious feature that set me apart from the all-male group, I was also distinguished by my German-Christian heritage, level of education, and middle-class background. . . . I found that my identity was fluid over time and that I was perceived differently depending on whom I was with and in what context we found ourselves. Ultimately, however, all of the young men treated me like a "buddy-researcher" (Snow, Benford, and Anderson 1986). This meant that I could behave as their friend while also retaining a certain degree of professional distance. . . .

For the young men, my German background buoyed their assumptions that I had enjoyed more opportunities in life than they had. (They blamed Germans for much of their social, political, and economic exclusion.) Indeed, I initially represented for them what they called "bad people." The fact that I was a PhD student meant that class also influenced their initial perceptions of me—more so even than if I had been a social worker. Given that the young men's main—and often only—source of income was drug dealing (none of them had a steady job within the formal economy), graduate work represented something elite and outside of their realm. . . . When I explained that my intention was to write a book about their lives, they were actually quite responsive to the idea, much to my relief. Many ethnographers have documented this effect: marginalized peoples are often quite open to having their stories and histories told. In Scheper-Hughes's words, I became the "minor historian" for people who otherwise would have no history (1992, 29). The fact that I was German *and* earnestly interested in them and their lives seemed to work in my favor since hitherto most of them had had only negative experiences with Germans.

I believe the fact that I was Christian and not Muslim also worked to my advantage. The young men's Islamic backgrounds were important to their identity. They had very clear ideas of what behaviors and activities complied with their religion, and although most of what they believed to be "Islamic" would never hold true in a traditional Islamic context, they took their self-created rules very seriously. For example, they believed that women—and Muslim women specifically—should be protected from becoming "impure" through exposure to other men, drugs, and violence, and therefore made efforts to shield Muslim women from their activities. Thus, my outsider status as a Christian woman helped to exempt me from their rules: because I did not directly contravene their views on gender, I was permitted access to their world.

Nevertheless, as a woman researching an all-male group, gender dynamics definitely affected my ability to build rapport with the group. My gender was most salient during drug deals when, in most cases, I was the only woman present. Truth be told, my gender was salient to some degree in all my exchanges with the young men. In spite of the fact that I was conducting research in a city where I myself was living, I faced barriers to access and trust reminiscent of dynamics in classical ethnographic studies conducted by anthropologists. The gender dynamics were also complicated and compounded by my age: when I started my fieldwork I was 23, the same age as the group average. This meant that the men perceived me as a potential sexual partner, which undoubtedly influenced the process of establishing relationships with them. Some attempted to flirt during the first few months of the research; however, because I had not garnered their full respect yet, these attempts were always in one-on-one situations rather than in front of the group.

At the same time, I did not cohere with their image of the "perfect woman"—an ideal the young men discussed at great length. They arrived at a general consensus about the traits she ought to possess: she must obey and please her partner, not intrude into his private life by asking too many questions, be good-looking, and excel as a housewife. In light of my religious and social background, my liberal ideas about gender relations, and my physical dissimilarity to the pictures of women in pornographic magazines strewn across the center, I did not fall into their "perfect woman" category. Consequently, they did not flirt with me overtly; the ubiquitous presence of pornography, however, added a sexual charge to the environment, and although the young men did not see me as an appropriate romantic partner, they nevertheless projected their sexual needs onto me (see Grenz 2005). This is not uncommon; many feminist scholars have discussed the sexualized dimensions of gender dynamics when female researchers study male research participants. For example, Arendell (1997) describes how she encountered sexism and inappropriate gestures when interviewing divorced men.

By the later stages of the research process, I had become an integral part of the group; the sexual overtones had disappeared. Yet despite the underlying sexual charge that generally characterizes mixed-gender research contexts, my status as a woman also enabled me to act as sort of relationship counselor without having to act as a "wise adult."

[. . .]

Initial Interactions With the Group: Gender, Ethnicity, and Inequality at Play

. . . My first day at the youth center was relatively uneventful. The director introduced me as an intern, and over the first few hours the young men and I mostly surveyed one another from a distance. When I made attempts at small talk, they were largely ignored.

My gender played a significant role in how I was received and likely rendered both parties—myself and the young men—additionally insecure at the outset. The group was used to new male social workers cycling through the center—they knew how to respond to and test the trustworthiness of a male "intruder" in their space. Finding a woman in their midst, however, presented them with an utterly unfamiliar situation. According to 23-year-old Rahim, who had a Turkish background:

> Let's face it X: You're just showing up but nobody knows you—not a single fucking person around here! And, of course, you're saying that you're a student and want to write a book about us and all that bullshit. I mean, that's all nice but honestly, who is supposed to believe that shit? And how are we supposed to know whether you're cool or not? Let's face it: this could have been the biggest nonsense! . . . You are a woman . . . we can't check you out the same way we'd do it with a guy. Nobody around here is going to beat up females or threaten them big time or something like that. That's why everyone was just staring at you for the first couple of days and everyone was waiting for you to leave again by yourself. When that didn't happen, something just had to be done about it.

Furthermore, pursuing amicable relationships with females, as Jetmir would later explain to me, was an alien concept to most of the young men: "Nobody here has girlfriends to just hang out with. I've always thought that a friendship between men and women is just not possible" (Jetmir, 24 years, Albanian descent).

Although the subject of women was one of the most discussed topics within the group, women were rarely present amongst the group members. Not only did they meet at the community youth center as an all-male group, but they also had limited contact with women more generally—even with their girlfriends—outside of the facility. When I asked why that was, Ibor (25 years, Bosnian descent) offered two explanations:

Ibor: You never want to fight about a bitch with your friends. That's just not on. If girls are around, politics will start. That's no good for anyone.

Me: What do you mean by that?

Ibor: Well, some idiots may get horny because your girl is around. And then, what do you do? Beat up your friends? Or they behave totally primitively. Or whatever.

As Ibor mentions, the young men did not want to fight over women, which made their presence undesirable. At the same time, some of the young men admitted that the girls they dated did not live up to their idea of "the perfect woman," which led them to think they should not introduce them to the group. While the young men seemed to agree about what comprised this idealized image, they also recognized that being in a relationship requires compromises. Yet, this admission was only ever discussed with me during one-on-one conversations, never publicly within the group. In this context, my outsider status enabled me to access information that was not openly shared among so-called insiders (Fonow and Cook 1991). Consider Georgio, for instance, who revealed to me why he would never introduce his girlfriend to the other men or discuss any relationship details with them: "Well, then you have the guys laughing at you because they think her ass is too big or because they think she's not listening to you or whatever. I don't want that happening" (Georgio, 22 years, multinational background).

Given that the young men talked so much about women and our gender difference was one of our "major status traits" (Hughes 1945), it is not surprising that they tested me against their idealized image in every possible way. Almost every conversation we had returned at some point to women, gender roles, and why I did not fulfill their criteria of a "real" woman. I was aware that many of these conversations were attempts to incite reactions and even impress me (for similar experiences, see Kauffman 1994, 180), but I couldn't help feeling awkward when they made remarks about my physical appearance, my clothing, or my lack of "female" personality. As much as I wished that comments like "X, did you gain weight? Your legs look a little fat today" would have had no effect on me whatsoever, I caught myself thinking about those comments more than once.

During the first stages of my research, I tried to minimize any signs of my sexuality by purposely wearing extremely baggy sweatshirts, worn-out jeans, and no make-up whatsoever (see Maher 1997). This ended up backfiring; I was constantly subjected to negative comments about my appearance and femininity. Although I endured their taunts, I often wished I could appear as my usual self. The first time I wore a long skirt, which only happened several months into my research, the young men commented on my appearance incessantly and kept referring to the "unfeminine" clothing I typically sported. I wondered if I had made too strong a statement with my clothing, ironically triggering the very conversations I wanted to avoid. Ironically enough, instead of using my clothes as a means of sexualizing me, the young men talked about how unsexy I was. As many feminist researchers have pointed out, gender is always salient (e.g., Arendell 1997; Presser 2005); however, in those early days I mistakenly believed I could somehow "ease the tension" by trying to efface signs of my femininity.

Although the young men talked about women constantly, they did not talk *with* women about intimate matters, and their relationships rarely lasted more than a few weeks. In fact, over the course of my five-year study, only five group members were in relationships that lasted longer than three months. Nevertheless, they were all sexually active on a regular basis—if not with their current girlfriends then with prostitutes, or they had one-night stands.

In many ways, I assumed the role of a sexual educator: they expected me to offer a female perspective on romantic relationships and gender relations. In contrast to the men Horowitz

(1986) studied, who initially identified her as "the lady" and refused to discuss sexual matters in front of her, the young men in my study constantly discussed sex and women (so long as they were sexual partners and not steady girlfriends) in front of me and sought my opinions. Their intense interest in my sex life and sex in general was not only amplified by their naivety about female sexuality but also by the fact that, for the first time in their lives, they were on familiar terms with a woman and could ask her (me) intimate questions. Significantly, this presented me with an opportunity to impress the young men and earn their trust: I had information to offer that they could not easily access from anyone else.

Thus, my status as a German woman who was relatively educated about sexuality worked in my favor and became the unexpected basis for establishing trusting rapports. The young men were fond of repeating how they could have never asked "their own" women the same kinds of questions they asked me. For example:

Rahim: "X, come here, we're having an argument."

Me: "What's it about?"

Ibor: "We're talking about how often a woman has her period and this moron thinks it's 4 times a year! I've been telling him it's just twice."

Rahim: "Whatever you idiot! X, tell him I'm right!"

Because of the young men's avid interest in sexual matters, I was in a position to answer their questions and share my knowledge, which allowed me to bring my own personality into the research relationship—a strategy that many feminist ethnographers have encouraged others to incorporate into the investigative process (Oakley 1981).

Given the young men's ideas about how women ought to behave, our views often clashed. Especially in the early stages of the project, the group members took personal offense to what they regarded as my constant disavowal of my "female duties," like when I refused to acquiesce to their demands to "clean this fucking place." My nonconformity to their gender norms often led to discussions wherein the young men reaffirmed pernicious stereotypes about how women *should* behave.

[. . .]

Because we each held views about one another's opinions that were informed by our different cultural attitudes about gender, many of the discussions served to test our respective positions while providing a basis for growing familiarity. In essence, we used these situations to learn about each other's worlds. My outsider status facilitated my ability to gain inside knowledge while our differing perspectives allowed us to maintain a helpful degree of social and intellectual distance, forging the "space" in which "the actual work of the ethnographer gets done" (Adler and Adler 1987, 17). . . .

Gender and Ethnicity in the Field

Although our diverging opinions on gender roles provided a basis for establishing trust, it was not the only strategy that permitted me to gain everyone's confidence. In spite of sharing many common cultural reference points, the young men did not comprise a uniform group; they were a heterogeneous bunch. Although the social workers had emphasized the importance of targeting the leaders in order to succeed in gaining the group's trust, I had to work to secure the trust of each individual and subgroup, which required me to respect different paces and employ a variety of tactics. My identity markers—gender, ethnicity, class, non-Muslim status— always played a role in every interaction, but the degree to which they were salient varied depending on the individual or subgroup.

Within the group there was one small subgroup of four older youths—Aissa (24 years, Moroccan descent), Rafet (23 years, Turkish descent), Mustaffer (24 years, Turkish descent), and Nermin (21 years, Moroccan descent)—who were highly respected because of their education and lifestyle choices. Unlike the others, they had not only earned high school diplomas but had also completed vocational programs and been legally employed at least once. They didn't take drugs or drink alcohol, and worked out at the gym almost every day. Younger group members viewed them as role models and admired them for their athletic bodies, their disciplined diet and exercise routines, and their education; older group members respected them for how they successfully avoided the "bum" lifestyle. All four were also considered to be tough to the extent that other members of the group avoided physical confrontations with them.

From the outset, these particular young men took an interest in me. Two of them were considering quitting their jobs and going back to school, and the fact that I was a student piqued their interest and opened up the communication channels. The first time we talked, they were very engaged and directed the conversation; they inquired about me, my personal life, and my role at the center. They also conveyed their unequivocal doubt that I would have any success conducting research at the center:

> Let's face it: you just can't handle this! You're just clueless about us, why do you even try? They will scare you off within two weeks and I swear, you will be running away crying like hell and wishing you had never started all this. Don't ever say that we did not warn you about that! Why don't you just look for a kindergarten to work at? . . . Play with little kids who listen to you! This is just a little bit too big for you! (Nermin, 22 years, Moroccan descent)

These early interactions were predictors of our future relationship. When we spoke, they constantly alternated between positioning themselves as insiders— affiliating themselves with the rest of the group—and as outsiders who could teach me and share inside knowledge about the group, something usually only reserved for insiders. As might be expected, they pivoted depending on which role suited them best in a given situation. This kind of vacillation demonstrates clearly that insider and outsider identities are not fixed categories but are instead quite fluid (Mullings 1999, 340). Although the group's ethos was quite patriarchal and sexualized, for instance, the young men regularly distanced themselves from these attitudes in one-on-one conversations with me.

Two weeks into my fieldwork, I was fortunate to have had an opportunity, quite by chance, to build a rapport with these four young men and gain the respect of many of the younger men in the process. The center had organized an outing to a nearby lake and I was tasked with putting air in the air mattresses. Nermin and Mustaffer stood beside me from start to finish and monitored my efforts with a defective air pump. After I finished filling the last two mattresses, they seized them and were about to run off. I had already decided not to swim on the trip, especially after listening to their highly sexual and chauvinistic comments about the bodies of other women at the lake; I did not want to give them the gratification of seeing me in a bathing suit. But when they took for granted that the remaining two mattresses belonged to them, I changed my mind. I stopped them from leaving and asked whether their behavior did not seem strange to them—taking the last two mattresses and leaving me without one even though I had done all the work to pump them up. In hindsight, this comment probably had a positive effect on my relationship with these young men; however, it was nonetheless primarily a sign of my own insecurity in that moment. I wanted to show the group that I would not submit to their chauvinistic perception of women (see Bucerius 2008, 254). I thought I would only be able to build a strong relationship with them if they viewed me as an equal, but my demand for equality at the lake outing was premature. . . .

In hindsight, Nermin and Mustaffer would have probably claimed the two mattresses even had I been male. From their perspective, they had not taken the mattress from a female researcher but from an outsider. After I protested, they looked at me in surprise and explained that filling the air mattresses was one of my tasks as an intern, and that I should not be entitled to use a mattress if the supplies did not permit. . . .

We had a very impassioned discussion about whether I was actually in a position to make any kind of request. Looking back, I definitely was not. Finally, they agreed to a compromise by suggesting a swimming race. In the unlikely event of my victory, I could claim a mattress. They were very surprised when I accepted their challenge. Prior to the race, they made sure that everyone was aware of my "outrageous" request for a mattress and my honor-offending assumption that I had any chance at all of winning the race.

As we prepared for the race, the discussion became increasingly sexist. They were adamant that they would "rather die than lose against a woman" and accused me of having completely underestimated their "Turkish and Moroccan blood," which was "invincible—especially when it came to women." Walking to the lake, they double-checked several times that I could actually swim (being solicitous while still performing their bravado): "Don't think that we care if you drown over there" (Mustaffer). Moreover, they assured me that while I may be "smart enough to do useless book things," they were the ones who knew how to compete on a physical level. Once we arrived at the lake, they generously let me choose the race course, but reiterated that I was going to make a fool of myself and that it would be my own fault.

They lost the race. They did not know that I had been a competitive swimmer for many years, a fact that I only revealed to them after the race. Contrary to my expectations, this revelation did not change their perception of the loss. I had been confident that I would win all along, and expected them to feel betrayed by my secret and claim that the race was unfair. Instead, they clung vehemently to their views about women and "useless book people" and did not even question the fairness. Naturally, other group members watched the race, so defeat was especially embarrassing for Mustaffer and Nermin. When I reached the half-way point in the race, I switched to backstroke so that I could wave to the other young men on the shore as Mustaffer and Nermin tried to keep up. After we reached the finish line, they appealed to me to never mention the race again.

Before I began my research, I had planned to avoid any strategies that would explicitly or inadvertently reinforce patriarchal power plays. . . . The swimming race illustrates how I earned some initial respect, especially among the younger group members who seemed to admire my victory, in ways I never would have imagined. It appeared that I had accomplished something that they themselves secretly yearned to achieve: "I can't believe you ripped them apart! Man, if only I could swim that well" (Ayan, 21 years, Moroccan background). Others found the defeat amusing. My win had no lasting influence, however, on my status with anyone except the younger group members and the subgroup composed of Aissa, Rafet, Nermin, and Mustaffer. Unlike the others, competition and sport was very important to these four, so my win impressed them and had a lasting impact. This marked the beginning of their trust.

They began taking me into their confidence about some aspects of their lives, but I only gained fuller access to their information about the drug market many months later once I had established a more solid field presence.

After this event, however, these four young men started to distinguish themselves from the others: they participated less when the group started indulging in patriarchal or sexualized taunts, and toned down their jousting during our one-on-one conversations. Our most intimate conversations always occurred when they assumed relative "outsider" positions to analyze my position within the group and told me that I will never be successful at gaining trust. Yet, when particular group members engaged me, these four young men sometimes still joined in, criticizing or insulting me. After such events they would often evaluate how adept or clumsy my reactions had been to other members' verbal provocations. For example, after a long conversation about women's social roles and how a "real woman" should serve "her man" in which I offered a counter-perspective, Rafet said: "I swear this will never work out if you're always giving them such an aggressive reaction. Take it easy sometimes. . . . Relax! . . . Just let them talk shit. If you try to respond, you're only giving them what they want." My dynamic with this particular subgroup was complicated and sometimes difficult to navigate. At times it seemed as if they wanted to help me gain access, while at others they participated in discussions of my ability—or rather, inability—to live up to perceived gender expectations.

[. . .]

Conclusion

[. . .]

It is not surprising that being a woman at once facilitated access (it permitted me to serve as relationship counselor, for example) and also impeded it in other circumstances (I could not follow the young men into brothels and observe their interactions with sex workers, who were among their biggest cocaine clients). Overall, however, being a woman allowed me to participate in conversations about women and sex, and serve as a sexual educator whenever required, all of which helped me secure their confidence and respect. As a German woman, an identity upon which many project very particular and denigrating stereotypes, I could obtain certain information that a male or a non-German would likely not have been able to access. Importantly, the men I studied did not equate me with "the typical German robot woman" who "only cares about her career, career, career and nothing else" and "never laughs, hates her children, and can't cook at all" (Talat). In fact, they had trouble identifying me with all the negative and xenophobic connotations they associated with what it meant to be "German," particularly since my interest in the group signaled to the young men that I was not xenophobic. Unlike the assimilationist efforts they experienced at school, my interactions with them never signaled a desire to promote their assimilation into German culture (Heitmeyer, Müller, and Schröder 1997, 21). They recognized over time that I was honestly interested in them, and they were continuously asking about "the book." . . . In many ways, this study demonstrates that ethnographic research in criminological fields of inquiry across gender, ethnic, and class lines in fact opens up opportunities for gaining access and trust, and ultimately a deeper and more nuanced understanding of the research group. Researchers often make a mistake by assuming that the identity markers which render us as outsiders will compromise our efficacy—that they are liabilities we must overcome. In fact, I discovered quite the opposite—they were key to garnering "insider" information and to facilitating effective research.

[. . .]

References

Adler, Patricia and Peter Adler. 1987. *Membership Roles in Field Research.* Newbury Park: Sage.

Arendell, Terry. 1997. "Reflections on the Researcher-Researched Relationship: A Woman Interviewing Men." *Qualitative Sociology* 20:341–68.

Asselin, Marlene. 2003. "Insider Research: Issues to Consider When Doing Qualitative Research in Your Own Setting." *Journal for Nurses in Staff Development* 19:99–103.

Brannick, Teresa and David Coghlan. 2007. "In Defense of Being 'Native': The Case of Insider Academic Research." *Organizational Research Methods* 10:59–74.

Bucerius, S. 2008. "Drogendealer im Spannungsfeld Zwischen islamischen Werten, Alltag in Deutschland und Kriminalität" (Drug Dealers in Between Islamic Values, Everyday Life and Crime). *Zeitschrift für Soziologie* 03/08:246–65.

Fonow, Mary and Judith Cook. 1991. *Beyond Methodology.* Bloomington, IN: Indiana University Press.

Gans, Herbert. 1968. "The Participant Observer as a Human Being." Pp. 300–317 in *Institutions and the Person*, edited by H. Becker. Chicago, IL: Aldine.

Gold, Raymond. 1958. "Roles in Sociological Observations." *Social Forces* 36:217–33.

Grenz, Sabine. 2005. "Intersections of Sex and Power in Research on Prostitution." *Signs: Journal of Women in Culture and Society* 30(4):2091–113.

Heitmeyer, Wilhelm, Joachim Müller, and Helmut Schröder. 1997. *Verlockender Fundamentalismus.* Frankfurt am Main: Suhrkamp.

Horowitz, Ruth. 1986. "Remaining an Outsider: Membership as a Threat to Research Rapport." *Journal of Contemporary Ethnography* 14:409–30.

Hughes, Everett. 1945. "Dilemmas and Contradictions of Status." *American Journal of Sociology* 50:353–59.

Kauffman, Karen. 1994. "The Insider/Outsider Dilemma." *Nursing Research* 43:3.

Maher, Lisa. 1997. *Sexed Work.* Oxford, UK: Clarendon Press.

Mullings, Beverly. 1999. "Insider or Outsider, Both or Neither." *Geoforum* 30:337–50.

Oakley, Ann. 1981. "Interviewing Women: A Contradiction in Terms." Pp. 30–61 in *Doing Feminist Research*, edited by H. Roberts. London, UK: Routledge.

Pascoe, Cheri. 2007. *Dude You're a Fag.* Berkeley, CA: University of California Press.

Presser, Lois. 2005. "Negotiating Power and Narrative in Research: Implications for Feminist Methodology." *Signs: Journal of Women in Culture and Society* 30(4):2067–90.

Scheper-Hughes, Nancy. 1992. *Death Without Weeping.* Berkeley, CA: University of California Press.

Snow, David, Robert Benford, and Leon Anderson. 1986. "Fieldwork Roles and Informational Yield." *Journal of Contemporary Ethnography* 14:377–408.

Studying Each Other

On Agency, Constraint, and Positionality in the Field

Tey Meadow

© iStockphoto.com/CREATISTA

Can we ever fully prepare ourselves for the fieldwork moments in which our pre-conceived interests, ideas, and questions meet the complex realities of our subjects' lives? . . . [I]n what follows I use examples from my own (one might say "progressive") ethnographic study of families with transgender and significantly gender nonconforming children to elaborate two features of the fieldwork dynamics endemic to most complex analyses of human life: the constant tension between agency and constraint, and how an individual's identity and appearance structure every significant interpersonal relationship, including those in the field. The stories I include here come from a multi-sited "ethnography of a category" (Valentine 2007), the transgender child, which I shadowed through its life as both a personal identity and a diagnostic classification within biomedicine and psychiatry. Over the course of twenty-four months, from

Tey Meadow. 2013. "Studying Each Other: On Agency, Constraint, and Positionality in the Field." *Journal of Contemporary Ethnography* 42(4):466–81.

2008 to 2010, I observed the work of activist organizations that do advocacy work on behalf of children, participated in conferences and workshops for families and physicians across the country, and visited parent support groups, schools where individual children were transitioning from one gender category to another, and a clinic where families received psychological services. I interviewed physicians and mental health workers, activists, and parents or guardians of gender nonconforming and transgender children.

These families, with the support of their doctors, are engaging in novel forms of parenting. They call female children male names (and vice versa), allow them to wear whatever clothing they choose, and even approach the state to alter the gender designation on their passports and birth certificates. More than progressive, some even call these children radical destabilizers of our entire gender order (Ablow 2011; Brown 2011). Yet, had I remained fixated on their potential to disrupt conventional gender expectations, I would have missed some crucial parts of what I found them actually doing. Their stories engaged discourses I myself consider normative and others I would frame as revolutionary. And the multiplicity of those discourses was my greatest source of data on social change at work. I also found I understood their parenting practices in a deeper way by examining their interactions with and interpretation of me.

In what follows, I . . . offer two conclusions about the business of feminist (and, really, any) ethnography: first, constraint and agency are always at play, no matter whether the social context is conservative or progressive, and the interplay between those forces outlines the contours of communities of practice. Second, as we labor to place ourselves at some distance from those we wish to analyze, they are also laboring, watching us, making meaning of us. These interpersonal processes should be treated as an important form of data, one that allows us to redress a weakness common to some strains of feminist thought—accounting for the individual women who choose life conditions we ourselves might consider oppressive. In this way, it is the individual feminist who must practice reflexivity, and not the institution of feminism, if one exists.

Entering the Field

The moment I met Madeleine Frank, I lost control of the conversation. My hours of careful planning, my premeditated introduction, my initial questions composed to sound thoughtful and informed all fell away, as she strode towards me, hand extended, with a look of quiet suspicion. . . . I began asking her about the program for the evening and the history of the school, and before I got halfway through my first sentence, she interrupted to fire a string of questions at me about who I am, how I envision the frame of the project, and what sort of things it is I'll want to know. Madeleine's distrust was immediately palpable, on the surface. I found myself utilizing queer vernacular and my nontraditional gender presentation more than I ever had before with other research informants. I thought positioning myself as an insider might make me a safer interlocutor. Yet, Madeleine seemed to dismiss me quickly, content to have me observe, but not particularly interested in engaging with me in any substantive way, even after the presentation as I drove away from the school in her car.

I spent the better part of a two-week trip trying to nail down a time to sit down with her for a one-on-one conversation. She evaded my attempts, finally sending me a one-line text message on the last day of my trip to offer up a single hour-long window. I quickly jumped at the chance, and boarded a train and headed 40 minutes outside the city to meet her near her home. Had I simply decided, rather than questioning openly, her reasons for trepidation, I might have missed an important part of Madeleine's story, and her read of me. When I asked her about our initial interaction, she told me that her early attempts at advocacy were roundly criticized by transgender adults, who feared a political backlash would result from talking openly about gender diversity in children. She had equal skepticism about journalists and media in general, and often felt misrepresented in their accounts of her work. I realized my own nontraditional gender presentation didn't necessarily make me appear safe, that her read of me as gender nonconforming in my own way didn't automatically position me as an ally.

Indeed, I learned in that conversation that there is reason to wonder what anyone, no matter how transparent their politics, will come to make of this emergent identity group and the group of adults affirming them. So-called conservative and liberal academics, clinicians, and pundits have internal disagreements about what transgender children represent. Are they the ultimate challenge to patriarchy and heteronormativity, or are they yet stronger evidence that the sex/ gender system retains its vise-like grip on our social order? Indeed, which possibility would even be socially desirable? Depending on one's political perspective and personal philosophy, it's possible to view transgender children as change agents responsible for blurring our social boundaries between men and women, or as cultural dupes further reinforcing the current patriarchal gender order. Even among those who call themselves feminists and agree that disestablishing hegemonic gender norms is a socially desirable goal, some posit that transgender identities represent the usurpation of uniquely female power by men (Eichler 1987; Irvine 1990; Raymond 1977, 1979). Others, including many who identify with transgender or queer communities, argue that transgender identities have the power to disrupt and destabilize binary gender fundamentally (Bornstein 1995; Butler 2004; Connell 2012; Gagne and Tewksbury 1998; Garber 1997; Halberstam 1998; Stone 1991; Stryker 1995).

So, is this community of parents raising transgender children progressive or conservative? It depends entirely on whom you ask. . . . [W]e cannot enter the field believing our subjects to be allies or foes, or assuming they will believe any particular thing about us. . . . I found . . . that the extent of an individual's culpability in constructing, reproducing, or resisting the patriarchal social order is itself an empirical question.

For example, I interviewed Patti on the night before her fourteen-year-old child Avery was scheduled to receive his first injection of Lupron, a synthetic GNRH (or gonadotropin-releasing hormone) antagonist, one of a class of drugs used to suppress the body's production of sex hormones to pause puberty. Patti told me the recent few weeks had been the most difficult time for her around Avery's gender. She compared Avery to transgender children she knows frequently during our conversation. She described other children who said, often with confidence, that they absolutely *are* girls, that there was some sort of mistake when they were born with the bodies they have. Avery used different language. She felt he was less confident in general, and that came across in his more reserved, less forceful responses about gender. But it also left Patti feeling uncertain about whether to proceed with blockers for him, or instead, to let him go through puberty just to "see what happens." She told me she spent a lot of time wondering if perhaps Avery was just gay—wishing in fact, that he would be gay.

> I worry a little bit about the pain for him and the shot but that's not, the bigger thing is . . . here he is 15 years-old still not even knowing what gender he identifies with. And having that be such an enormous part of his life. I mean, the gender. You know, the gender issue, his whole life is about this gender thing. You have to go into the city. We have to get shots. We talk about this all the time because he has to talk about it. He's got a year before a decision's gonna be made on cross-sex hormones if he wants to be able to present himself as female as an adult without any questions. Right? So I guess the

worry is that we'll run out of time to make the right decision. And [our doctor] will say to me, you can transition at any time in your life. And my answer is yes, but then you look like a transsexual, you know? You have this body and everyone can just tell.

Patty and many other parents describe a feeling of working against the clock, in conditions of great uncertainty, while trying to decide whether to help their children forestall or allow them to experience their natal puberty. On one hand, they fear the unknown long-term consequences of hormone therapies; on the other, they have copious amounts of evidence suggesting that previous generations of transgender adults suffer mightily when their bodies and identities don't match in the eyes of others. One might read the above passage and think that Patty was at the very vanguard of postmodern parenting. Or, one might argue that her investment in Avery passing is a re-articulation of hegemonic gender norms.

The field my subjects inhabit is no monolith—it is a hodgepodge of structure, constraint, agency, capitulation, and resistance. The job of the ethnographer is precisely to analyze the spatial and symbolic boundaries of communities, their ways of understanding the world and their internal cultures (Blumer 1969; Geertz 1973). . . .

Studying Each Other

Early on in my fieldwork, I spent several hours in the empty lobby of a conference hotel interviewing one of the most controversial psychologists involved in research and treatment with gender-variant youth. During our talk, he puzzled over the connections between gender identity and sexual orientation. He presented a digital camera, on which he displayed an image of a young adult formerly in his care for severe gender identity disorder (GID). A soft and solemn face gazed into the camera, and as this psychologist continued describing his "adult outcome," I struggled to discern the work this image was supposed to do. Was I supposed to look for evidence of continued femininity? Was he an example of a "successful" male-identified adult?

As we concluded the formal part of our conversation and I switched off my recording device, he presented the camera again and showed me several more photographs. He then asked me if he could take my picture. I asked him why he wished to do that, and he responded, "I just like taking pictures," and proceeded to pull up several others, one of his own child smiling into the screen. I felt immediately uncomfortable, exposed, at issue. I took a mental inventory of my own gender transgressions that day—

+1: I had just gotten a haircut

−1: I was wearing a women's shirt

And I wondered if the young person in the initial photo felt similarly exposed when faced with his camera. Though I acquiesced, I wondered what I would become an example of for the next curious investigator. I became newly aware that he was the first of my subjects to ask if he could also record our discussion, and his tape recorder sat on the table beside mine. It was in this moment I realized that we were studying each other.

This was not the only time I felt my own gender presentation enter the dialogic space between others and myself. Gender could render me suspect, ally, or even data, depending on who was on the other side of my table. Sometimes this reality was made explicit; often it took the form of veiled questions about the origins of the project, my interest, or aspects of my appearance. Indeed it became clear to me that, much like the child subjects of my research, I too lacked control over the meanings made by others of my body and my identity. But it was clear to me that it mattered to my research subjects just who and what I am. They engaged in intentional labor to decipher my identity, relationship to communities with which they identified, and political perspective on their choices to facilitate gender nonconformity in their children. In short, they returned my gaze, and the ways they did so were themselves valuable data on how individuals make sense of gender in others, and how that sense-making affects interactions and relationships.

In the frame of this doctor's camera lens, I felt as if I had moved from the space of colleague, interlocutor, or even just researcher and into the realm of study object, of case example: a gender variant in my own right. In some ways, this taste of objectification offered me the closest approximation of what I imagine the children parented by my research subjects experience—objectification in the service of affirmation. My decision to relent to the lens offered me continued access to this clinician, and it was an important methodological choice. But it wasn't one without emotional consequence for me.

It is a central tenet of feminist ethnography that "knowing is itself determined by the relationship of knower to known" (Visweswaran 1994, 48). The products of the ethnographic endeavor are always "situated knowledges" (Haraway 1988, 1990) or "partial truths" (Clifford 1986); every body (and everybody) has gender, and so gender always frames both the perceptions of the researcher and research endeavor by those who are studied and the knowledge produced by person-to-person encounters. An ethnographer is "a positioned subject, who occupies a position of structural location and observes with a particular angle of vision" (Rosaldo 1989, 19). Feminist standpoint theory long ago elaborated not merely the effect of the researcher's gender (Casper 1997; Harding 1991), but also her life experiences and even her embodiment (Hartsock 1983; Reich 2003; Smith 1990, 1997) on the products of ethnographic inquiry. What this means is that our informants are always looking to us and at us and gauging how to interact. This is not a methodological obstacle; this is a social and empirical fact.

My own gender presentation structured my experience of my research subjects in important and occasionally conflicting ways. From the noted psychologist who framed me as his own research subject, to the parents of transgender youth who endeavored strategically to either expose or remove their children from my presence, to the children who often asked questions or made comments about my body, my gender became a topic of frequent commentary and speculation. Such scrutiny was an unavoidable characteristic of the ethnographic process. The subjects of my research—parents, doctors, and psychologists—were actively seeking to understand the very same phenomenon I was, yet with vastly different epistemological orientations and for different sets of reasons. We were participants in what Judith Stacey (1988) calls a "collaborative, reciprocal quest for understanding." Indeed, we were co-creating the very questions we sought to resolve. In this context, who we each were in relation to the material became deeply important.

I witnessed complex processes of identification and disidentification with what group members perceive to be the meanings of transgender created by previous generations. Gender nonconforming adults, myself included, were deeply symbolic in a variety of conflicting ways for many of the parents. We functioned as floating signifiers for the hopes and fears parents attach to their children's uncertain futures. For some parents, the deep pain and pervasive discrimination faced by transgender adults was too much to bear emotionally. For others, it was the notion that their child might cultivate an oppositional identity, one that radically departs from social norms, that was of primary concern. These parents attempt to disassociate their child from dominant cultural images of transgender adults. For still others, constructing taxonomies of different forms of adult gender variance allowed them to exert more careful control over precisely what *sort* of influence connections to the adult transgender community might have on their children's evolving self-understandings. It was around these issues of identification and disidentification that I felt my own gender presentation become most salient for my interview respondents, and navigating those moments proved treacherous, both methodologically and emotionally.

Jerri, the grandmother and primary parent of a nine-year-old transgirl, expressed concern that the dominant cultural images of transgender people, and in fact, the dominant self-representations she saw them present in community spaces, emphasized transgression over assimilation. Jerri worries this would be the sole representation her granddaughter, Phoebe, has access to, and that she might grow up thinking she has to form an oppositional identity herself.

> You know, I'll be really blunt with you. I don't want to offend you or anyone else, but the truth is a lot of trans people, a lot of trans adults are fringe, right? They're not fully accepted in society. A lot of them present themselves as being different and wanting to be different. Some of them present themselves as being freaks. And if that's their path and they're happy, good for them. And if that's Phoebe's path and she's happy, good for her. But I want her to know that she has many possible paths. And so I don't want her to go into the trans community and just see the fringe people and so that's my only path. I want her to know that she can be an Olsen twin if she wants to! Or she can be a freak if she wants to. You know, she can have any of those paths.

For a number of parents like Jerri, strategic exposure to certain forms of gender nonconformity functions as a way to manage anxiety about the ambiguity of their child's identity.

Colten's mom, Deirdre, tells me her biggest fear is that Colten will spend a lifetime hiding the truth of his body from potential intimate partners. Deidre hopes that exposing Colten to gender-queer adults who live openly and without making full medical and social transitions might provide him with a sufficient model for how to articulate his own gender, thus alleviating his desire to make a full transition himself. As we conclude our interview, she asks me if I would join them for lunch that afternoon. She says she doesn't want to assume anything about my identity, but she'd really like me to spend some time with Colten. I ask why she thinks that would be important.

> My feeling is, the more varied kinds of people that Colten talks to, the better. I want him to see more and more of those people in the gray area. I want him to meet more people that are like him. I want him to meet more people that are female but not at that end of female. In that way, it's kind of like when I discover somebody who speaks Italian, because my husband is Italian, it's like, *Oh, speak Italian to him, please. Speak French to him. He can do it.*

She paused, made direct eye contact and said, slowly and meaningfully, "So *please*. . . . Speak gender stuff to him in a way that I can't."

Other parents of masculine girls (generally of middle school age, and generally those who have yet to fully make a social transition) approached me during my fieldwork at conferences and asked me to spend time with their child. Twelve-year-old Eve's mother and I talked for a long time about her newly emerging gender identity and her own sense of isolation as she struggled to cope with her feelings about it. She asked if I would talk with her husband and with Eve during the lunch break at the conference. I agreed that I would, and she replied, "Oh, that's great. Because here you are, smart and successful and writing a book . . . and you're not a man." She seemed then to pause as if looking to me to confirm my identity. I smiled at her, but didn't reply.

When I met Eve later that day, she was wearing a striped boys rugby shirt, crisp white shorts, and impeccably clean running shoes. The burnt embers of her red hair were cropped short around her ears, longer and disarrayed around her forehead. She had disarming blue-green eyes, and seemed at once shy, quiet, and utterly self-possessed. We discussed some of the older youth at the conference who left behind unsupportive family to attend. At one point, she leaned in conspiratorially to whisper to me, "I feel so bad for them. They couldn't get blockers and had to go through puberty, and now, they have breasts so they don't look so good." I saw her parents glance at one another out of the corner of my eye. They were watching us carefully, as if prepared to witness something important, revelatory. And then, in unison, they both looked down at my chest.

While there are examples of moments when I felt called upon to minimize aspects of my own gender difference and politicized identity, there were others where it was valuable capital as well. My gender, my gender-queerness, was a resource I could mobilize in the field—sometimes through its amplification and other times through minimizing it. I've no doubt it both garnered me access to certain people and conversations and precluded my access to others. I would argue that this is true for everyone. I worried upon entering the field that research subjects might impute political or psychological motives that would affect my field-work interactions. And I cannot say for certain that those encounters were not transformed. Perhaps most tellingly, at many moments, I found myself thinking about Loïc Wacquant's ethnography of the "pugilistic craft" of boxing in *Body and Soul*, particularly the use of his body as an ethnographic instrument (2004). Wacquant's notion of "carnal ethnography," of learning the other through the acquisition of bodily habitus felt apt as my own body became a *tabula rasa* for the gendered fantasies of others. But for me, it wasn't the taking on of a gender different than my own that constituted the learning; it was the management of others' reactions to it and to me, their assumptions, discomforts, and interest. It was in those self-conscious moments that I believe I came closest to knowing the gender nonconforming child, by which I mean living the experience of having one's body and identity be the object of a particular type of searching gaze, one tinged with worry, fear, and expectation. This is precisely the kind of scrutiny politically inflected ethnographic research fixes on the lives of those we seek to understand, and it is a mistake to think that our subjects don't feel that gaze.

The recent emergence of transgender children provides sociologists with a unique opportunity to watch an emergent social category in formation. Yet contemporary struggles to understand and define the category itself inflect ethnographic encounters with a sense of urgency for the research subjects themselves. The desire for epistemological clarity leads parents, physicians, and children to investigate the gender of those around them with incredible nuance. I found this gaze impossible to escape, even as I tried to turn it back on those who directed it toward me. . . .

Because the gender categories and identities I studied are in a process of active iteration, I discovered that they were surprisingly porous and susceptible to contamination by the ethnographic encounter itself. This presented me with certain methodological challenges in the field that warrant examination. Would I participate in organizing activities for the children, knowing that it was in the context of their shared community that many of them labored to form coherent identities? Would my presence and participation ultimately overdetermine what it is I would find? These moments and questions from my fieldwork with families and clinicians reveal both how individuals engage in the process of making new social categories and the many ways gender structures relationships in the ethnographic field.

Conclusions

. . . What I've come to believe fundamentally is that the goal of feminist ethnography, and perhaps for ethnography more generally, is to be "for, not merely about" (Risman 1993) the particular individuals we study. By this, I mean that we must take seriously the self-understandings of our participants and the extent to which they share our political and social goals and ideals.

I found my subjects fully enmeshed in competing social forces; they navigated the realities of a "patriarchal" sex/gender system at individual, interpersonal, and institutional levels, and yet they worked diligently and often successfully to transform the contours of that very system. Sometimes they were complicit in enacting forms of gender regulation; at other times they were downright deconstructionist. Part of the work of my analysis involved sorting out the social conditions under which struggles for recognition over-determined a particular response. . . .

Like some other scholars, I do not view transgender phenomena as prima facie reproductions or contraventions of social order, but rather, in more nuanced fashion, as individual actions within a given cultural field, ones that involve struggles over intelligibility, safety, status, and desire (see, e.g., Eyre et al. 2004). Indeed, the denaturalization of male/female difference can, in some cases, disrupt hegemonic norms, and in others, serve to reconsolidate them (Butler 1993, 125). Paying careful attention to the content of my interactions with my research subjects brings to the fore the processual nature of relationship building in the field (Emerson 2009). Communities are structured by practices (Shapira 2010) as much as they are by politics. Talking with our informants openly not only about what they are doing, but how they understand what they are doing, garners far more interesting data than relying on a priori assumptions . . . This insight does not relieve the difficulties of negotiating our different selves with our informants, but it does clarify why recording the ways we negotiate these selves garners even more useful data. Neither does any form of reflexive ethnography grant us escape from a problem that still vexes many feminists—namely, how to interpret those moments when we (women, queers, researchers, humans) come into contact with others who envision a fundamentally different life as desirable, good, or even liveable than we do.

[. . .]

References

Ablow, Keith. 2011. "J. Crew Plants the Seeds for Gender Identity." *Fox News*, April 11. Retrieved January 25, 2013 (www.foxnews.com/health/2011/04/11/j-crew-plants-seeds-gender-identity).

Blumer, Herbert. 1969. *Symbolic Interactionism: Perspective and Method.* Englewood Cliffs, NJ: Prentice Hall, Inc.

Bornstein, Kate. 1995. *Gender Outlaw: On Men, Women, and the Rest of Us.* New York: Routledge.

Brown, Erin R. 2011. "J. Crew Pushes Transgendered Child Propaganda: Women's Clothing Company Highlights Pink Nail-Polish Wearing Boy in Promotional Email." *Culture and Media Institute*, April 8. Retrieved January 25, 2013 (www.mrc.org/cmi/articles/2011/JCREW_Pushes_Transgendered_Child_Propaganda_.html).

Butler, Judith. 1993. *Bodies That Matter: On the Discursive Limits of "Sex."* New York: Routledge.

Butler, Judith. 2004. *Undoing Gender*. New York: Routledge.

Casper, Monica 1997. "Feminist Politics and Fetal Surgery: Adventures of a Research Cowgirl on the Reproductive Frontier." *Feminist Studies* 23:232–63.

Clifford, James. 1986. "Introduction: Partial Truths." Pp. 1–26 in *Writing Culture: The Poetics and Politics of Ethnography*, edited by J. Clifford and G. E. Marcus. Berkeley, CA: University of California Press.

Connell, R. W. 2012. "Transsexual Women and Feminist Thought: Toward New Understanding and New Politics." *Signs: Journal of Women in Culture and Society* 37(4):857–81.

Eichler, Margit. 1987. "Sex Change Operations: The Last Bulwark of the Double-Standard." Pp. 67–78 in *Gender Roles: Doing What Comes Naturally?* edited by E. Salamon and B. William Robinson. Toronto, Canada: Methuen.

Emerson, Robert M. 2009. "Ethnography, Interaction and Ordinary Trouble." *Ethnography* 10(4):535–48.

Eyre, Stephen L., Rebecca de Guzman, Amy A. Donovan, and Calvin Boissiere. 2004. "'Hormones Is Not Magic Wands': Ethnography of a Transgender Scene in Oakland, California." *Ethnography* 5(2):147–72.

Gagne, Patricia and Richard Tewksbury. 1998. "Conformity Pressures and Gender Resistance Among Transgendered Individuals." *Social Problems* 45:81–101.

Garber, Marjorie. 1997. *Vested Interests: Cross-Dressing and Cultural Anxiety*. New York: Routledge.

Geertz, Clifford. 1973. *The Interpretation of Cultures*. New York: Basic Books.

Halberstam, Judith. 1998. *Female Masculinity*. Durham, NC: Duke University Press.

Haraway, Donna. 1988. "Situated Knowledges: The Science Question in Feminism and the Privilege of Partial Perspective." *Feminist Studies* 14:575–99.

Haraway, Donna. 1990. *Simians, Cyborgs and Women: The Reinvention of Nature*. New York: Routledge.

Harding, Sandra. 1991. *Whose Science? Whose Knowledge? Thinking from Women's Lives*. Ithaca, NY: Cornell University Press.

Hartsock, Nancy C. M. 1983. "The Feminist Standpoint: Developing the Ground for a Specifically Feminist Historical Materialism." In *Discovering Reality: Feminist Perspectives on Epistemology, Metaphysics, Methodology and Philosophy of Science*, edited by S. Harding and M. B. Hintikka. Dordrecht, The Netherlands: Reidel Publishing.

Irvine, Janice. 1990. *Disorder and Desire: Sex and Gender in Modern American Sexology*. Philadelphia, PA: Temple University Press.

Raymond, Janice. 1977. "Transsexualism: The Ultimate Homage to Sex-Role Power." *Chrysalis* 3:11–23.

Raymond, Janice. 1979. *The Transsexual Empire: The Making of the She-male*. New York: Teachers College Press.

Reich, Jennifer. 2003. "Pregnant with Possibility: Reflections on Embodiment, Access and Inclusion in Field Research." *Qualitative Sociology* 26(3):351–67.

Risman, Barbara. 1993. "Methodological Implications of Feminist Scholarship." *The American Sociologist* 24(3/4):15–25.

Rosaldo, Renate. 1989. *Culture and Truth: The Making of Social Analysis*. Boston, MA: Beacon Press.

Shapira, Harel. 2010. "Waiting for Jose: The Minutemen and the United States/Mexico Border." Unpublished dissertation, Columbia University, NY. On file with author.

Smith, Dorothy. 1990. *The Conceptual Practices of Power: A Feminist Sociology of Knowledge*. Boston, MA: Northeastern University Press.

Smith, Dorothy. 1997. "Comment on Hekman's 'Truth and Method: Feminist Standpoint Theory Revisited.'" *Signs* 22:392–99.

Stacey, Judith. 1988. "Can There Be a Feminist Ethnography?" *Women's Studies International Forum* 11:21–27.

Stone, Sandy. 1991. "The Empire Strikes Back: A Posttransexual Manifesto." In *Body Guards: The Cultural Politics of Gender Ambiguity*, edited by K. Straub and J. Epstein, 280–311. New York: Routledge.

Stryker, Susan. 1995. "Transsexuality: The Postmodern Body and/as Technology." *Exposure: Journal of the Society for Photographic Education* 30:38–50.

Valentine, David. 2007. *Imagining Transgender: An Ethnography of a Category*. Durham, NC: Duke University Press.

Visweswaran, Kamala. 1994. *Fictions of Feminist Ethnography*. Minneapolis, MN: University of Minnesota Press.

Wacquant, Loïc. 2004. *Body and Soul: Notebooks of an Apprentice Boxer*. New York: Oxford University Press.

The Sociology of Gender in Southern Perspective

Raewyn Connell

G ender research is, today, one of the major fields of sociology, both academic and applied. The sociology of gender has had significant impact in the education and health sectors, in violence prevention, antidiscrimination and equal opportunity policy. As an organized field, however, it is not yet strongly influenced by the postcolonial revolution in knowledge.

In this article I explore how the sociology of gender can be developed in the light of Southern theory and Southern research. This is not a small task, not a matter of creating a postcolonial corner inside the sociology of gender. The issue concerns foundational concepts and methods, global relations of power and centrality in knowledge production. The analysis must be grounded in an understanding of the history of sociology, but also needs to engage contemporary global developments in feminist thought.

[. . .]

Northern Gender Analysis and the Global Dimension

[. . .]

If we look back into the history of gender research, it is clear that data acquired by European colonial conquest and postcolonial dependency have been very important to metropolitan theorists. Mohanty's famous essay "Under Western Eyes" (1991) revealed the colonial gaze that constructed a false image of the "third world woman." But even this understated the importance of knowledge from the periphery.

The colonized world provided raw material for metropolitan feminist debates about the origin of the family, matriarchy, the gender division of labour, the Oedipus complex, third genders, male violence and war, marriage and kinship, gender symbolism—and now, of course, globalization. Such pivotal feminist texts as Mitchell's *Psychoanalysis and Feminism* (1974), Rubin's "The Traffic in Women" (1975) and Chodorow's *The Reproduction of Mothering* (1978)

Raewyn Connell. 2014. "The Sociology of Gender in Southern Perspective." *Current Sociology Monography* 62(4):550–67.

would be inconceivable without the colonial knowledge on which Freud, Lévi-Strauss and other mighty men of the metropole built their theories.

Gender analysis, then, is involved in a global political economy of knowledge. Global imperialism left no culture separate or intact, not even the culture of the imperialists. The colonial encounter, continuing as the encounter of contemporary communities with globalized power, is itself a massive source of social dynamics—including intellectual innovation.

This is the territory now being explored in a vigorous literature on the global dynamics of knowledge. The strands of this literature include research on Southern theory (Connell, 2007; Meekosha, 2011), alternative traditions in social science (Alatas, 2006; Patel, 2010), postcolonial sociology (Bhambra, 2007; Reuter and Villa, 2010), indigenous knowledge (Odora Hoppers, 2002), the psychology of liberation (Montero, 2007), decolonial thought (Mignolo, 2007; Quijano, 2000), the decolonization of methodology (Smith, 1999) and more. In the context of this article it would be superfluous to discuss this whole terrain, but my analysis of the sociology of gender has a specific starting-point within it. This is the global sociology of knowledge developed by the Beninese philosopher Paulin Hountondji in *Endogenous Knowledge* (1997; see Connell, 2011).

Hountondji observes that imperialism created a global division of labour in the sciences, in which data were collected in the colonies and concentrated in the metropole, where theory was developed and the data were processed. This division of labour persisted after decolonization. The global periphery still exports data and imports applied science, the global metropole is still the centre of theory and methodology. An international circulation of knowledge workers accompanies the international flows of data, concepts and techniques. Workers from the periphery travel to the metropole for doctoral training, sabbaticals, conferences or better jobs; workers from the metropole frequently travel to the periphery to collect data, rarely to get advanced training or to learn theory.

One of the most striking parts of Hountondji's analysis concerns the attitude of knowledge workers in the global periphery resulting from this global structure. This attitude he calls "extraversion"—being oriented to external sources of intellectual authority. Extraversion is seen in practices such as citing only metropolitan theorists, publishing preferentially in metropolitan journals, joining "invisible colleges" centred in the metropole, and acting as native informants for metropolitan scientists who are interested in the periphery.

We can add to Hountondji's analysis the powerful influence of neoliberal politics and management. Neoliberal agendas are currently deepening extraversion by locking the universities of the periphery into market competition and global ranking systems—in which the elite universities of the United States and Europe always appear on top, defining the "excellence" others must strive for. Scholars in the periphery are now under heavier pressure than ever to publish in metropolitan journals, gain recognition in the metropole and form partnerships with prestigious centres.

Extraversion in this sense is as widespread in gender studies as in other fields of knowledge. Metropolitan texts about gender are translated and read in the periphery, and treated as authorities. Gender researchers from the periphery travel to the metropole for qualifications and recognition. Whole frameworks, terrains of debate and problematics are liable to be imported.

[. . .]

But there is always some friction between the intellectual perspectives created in the imperial centres, and the realities of society and culture in the colonized and postcolonial world. Nelly Richard (2004 [1993]), importing French postmodernist thought to feminism in Chile, notes that these ideas have to be "re-worked" in the periphery.

We could put this more strongly. The re-working requires a critique and transformation of the metropolitan frameworks themselves. The debates about decolonial thought, Southern theory, indigenous knowledge and postcolonial thought, though they have mostly not been gender-informed, are now vital resources for developing the sociology of gender.

Southern Thematics for Gender Analysis

The necessary starting-point is imperialism itself. Gender dynamics take specific forms in colonial and postcolonial contexts because, as María Lugones (2007) states, they are interwoven with the dynamics of colonization and globalization. As Valentine Mudimbe (1994) has argued, the colonizing power, in order to establish itself, had to create a new society. It is important to register that the large majority of the world's people live in such societies with colonial, neocolonial and postcolonial histories. The global metropole is the exception, not the norm. Analysis informed by what Lugones has usefully called "the coloniality of gender" should be the mainstream of the sociology of gender.

Recognition of the fact of colonization has already polarized postcolonial gender analysis. In reaction against Northern feminism, more exactly a simplified version of it, one school of thought asserts that "gender" is itself a product of colonialism, imposed on societies which previously did not organize themselves in gendered ways. Perhaps the best-known example is Oyeronke Oyewumi's *The Invention of Women* (1997), which contrasts Western sex dichotomy with "a Yoruba stance" that does not classify people on the basis of bodies. Accordingly, gender is not a structure of precolonial Yoruba society and "women" does not exist as a social category. This argument has been criticized in Africa as both an inaccurate account of precolonial society, and as replacing an essentialism of bodies with an essentialism of culture that helps to legitimize postcolonial patriarchy (Bakare-Yusuf, 2003; Lewis, 2002). Powerful men in postcolonial regimes can, and do, fend off demands for gender equality by branding feminism as a neocolonial intrusion.

Uma Narayan (1998: 103), whose critique of cultural essentialism is exemplary, defends legitimate generalizations about gender: "virtually every community is structured by relationships of gender that comprise specific forms of social, sexual, and economic subjection of women." This view is complicated by research that shows precolonial conceptions of gender to be complex and structured differently from European conceptions. Thus Sylvia Marcos (1998), examining the metaphorical religious thought of Mesoamerican communities in surviving colonial-era documents, finds powerfully embodied conceptions that emphasize duality, integration and the absence of barriers. On the other hand, oral-history evidence from Aboriginal people and anthropologists about precolonial society in Australia points to ritual separation of women and men, as well as a marked gender division of labour, in that very different civilization (Berndt, 1974).

Whatever the precolonial situation, it was transformed by colonialism, and not gently. Gendered violence played a formative role in the shaping of colonial and postcolonial societies. Colonization itself was a gendered act, carried out by imperial workforces, overwhelmingly men, drawn from masculinized occupations such as soldiering and long-distance trade. The rape of women of colonized societies was a normal part of conquest. The colonial state was built as a power structure operated by men, based on continuing force. Brutality was built into colonial societies, whether they were settler colonies or colonies of exploitation. The level of gendered violence in postcolonial societies is now a central issue in global feminism, from international policy forums (Harcourt, 2009) to local research and action agendas—illustrated by the emphasis on gender violence in the women's studies programmes in Costa Rica (Cordero, 2008). Saffioti's (2004) later work paid close attention to the issue; she quotes survey data showing about half of Brazilian women have experienced gender-based violence.

In a powerful paper, Amina Mama (1997) recalls the violence of imperial patriarchy, the creation of colonial economies that marginalized women, and the gender dimension of the struggles for independence in Africa. Women widely supported the nationalist movements, but once in power, few of the nationalist regimes defended women's interests. With the economic crisis of the post-independence states that began in the 1970s, very harsh conditions were created for women, and high levels of violence against women became apparent.

Mama argues convincingly that the feminist strategies against gender violence developed in the metropole do not apply in this context, because these strategies presuppose a well-functioning state and a coherent gender order; neither of which is experienced by Black and working-class women in postcolonial Africa. Nina Laurie (2005) makes a similar point when discussing masculinity politics in the contemporary Andes, that research in the global South cannot presuppose a consolidated gender order. Jane Bennett (2008: 7) in South Africa describes the specificity of gender research in conditions where "relative chaos, gross economic disparities, displacement, uncertainty and surprise" are the norm not the exception.

Gender analysis from the global South thus, in a sense, must invert the problematic of recent gender theory in the global North, where a deconstructionist agenda is hegemonic. In the colonial and postcolonial world the *making* of gender orders, or the attempts to make them, are central issues. Establishing colonial gender arrangements required, as well as formative violence, a sustained cultural and organizational effort on the part of the colonizers. This is rightly emphasized by Lugones (2007), though I think she is mistaken to describe gender arrangements as "imposed" on the colonized. Active responses by the colonized were also involved; and the active responses by women of colonized societies are now well recognized in feminist historiography and indigenous critique (Moreton-Robinson, 2000).

Less recognized in most of the gender literature are the active responses also made by men. This issue is explored by Ashis Nandy, whose book *The Intimate Enemy: Loss and Recovery of Self Under Colonialism* (1983) is a classic study of the social construction of masculinity. Nandy traces how the pressure of British conquest and the colonial regime re-shaped Indian culture, including its gender order. The response to this pressure called out specific elements of Indian tradition, over-valuing the *Kshatriya* or warrior category, to justify essentially new patterns of masculinity in a modernizing process. Equally important, Nandy shows how the colonial encounter re-shaped models of masculinity among the colonizers. As the regime settled into a permanent governing structure during the nineteenth century, a distinctive culture emerged that exaggerated gender and age hierarchies. This produced a simplified, dominance-oriented, and often violent masculinity as the hegemonic pattern among the British, despising weakness, suspicious of emotion, concerned to draw and police rigid social boundaries.

More recently, the making of masculinities and negotiation of gender relations in colonial and postcolonial transitions has been the subject of intense research in southern Africa (Epstein et al., 2004; Morrell, 2001). This research goes far to establishing two important conclusions. The first is the sheer diversity of masculinities that are under construction at the same time in the one national territory. Postcolonial gender reality cannot be captured by generalized models of "traditional" vs "modern" manhood. The second is how intimately the making of masculinities is bound up with the vast and continuing transformations of postcolonial society as a whole. Gender is not off to the side in a cupboard of its own. It is enmeshed with the changing structure of power and shifts in the economy, the movement of populations and the creation of cities, the struggle against Apartheid and the 1990s lurch to neoliberalism, the institutional effects of mines, prisons, armies and education systems.

This illustrates a tendency in postcolonial gender analysis towards a sociological view of gender. . . .

This can be seen, for instance, in Chilean discussions of voice and identity. Julieta Kirkwood's feminist classic *Ser política en Chile* (1986) concerns the establishment of women's political voice in twentieth-century Chile. This could be treated in terms of cultural identity, but it is not. A key step in Kirkwood's research was an interview study with women's movement activists under the dictatorship, and she constructs the history of Chilean feminism as a collective story of social struggle. The emergence of women as a political subject, in her narrative, was closely bound up with the features of a postcolonial political order, and the changing ways in which Chile's socioeconomic formation was articulated with the world economy and international politics. Sonia Montecino (2001) similarly emphasizes that gender identities are collective constructions, in their diversity; indeed, she suggests that an understanding of identity as emerging from social struggle is characteristic of Latin American thought.

As I have argued in *Southern Theory* (Connell, 2007), the issue of land is crucial in understanding colonial society, and this applies to gender relations. Marcia Langton (1997), a leading Aboriginal intellectual in Australia, shows one dimension of this. Australian Aboriginal culture has been portrayed as patrilineal and patriarchal, but this account mainly comes from male anthropologists convinced of women's inferiority. Women have increasingly demonstrated that women's rights were embedded in precolonial land tenure systems. In the conditions of violent conquest, and the extreme pressure on most Aboriginal cultures that followed, this land-and-gender order was badly disrupted. Langton argues that it was women's traditions and ties to place—"Grandmothers' law"—that were the more resilient, and proved crucial in holding Aboriginal society together. Older women thus became the key to social survival.

Land is also central to the analysis of gender relations in agricultural society in the Indian subcontinent by Bina Agarwal, whose *A Field of One's Own* (1994) is one of the great classics of modern gender analysis. Agarwal is professionally an economist, but *A Field of One's Own* is actually a rich interdisciplinary exploration of peasant society, involving regional and legal history, sociology of the family, studies of political movements, and more. Land is shown to be a crucial element in gender practices ranging from kinship alliance and inheritance to the constitution of patriarchal power structures. Agarwal documents a vigorous gender politics including collective mobilizations by women for land ownership and land use, and widespread, sometimes violent, resistance by men.

To argue there are common themes that emerge from Southern gender studies is not to imply there is a single Southern gender order. Very certainly, there is not—neither before nor after colonization. Indeed, recognition of the diversity of gender orders is an important consequence of the arguments of Southern feminists in forums such as the UN world conferences on women, from Mexico City in 1975 to Beijing in 1995. Critique of unexamined universalism in Northern gender theory has been a persistent theme in African feminist studies (Arnfred et al., 2004), and the arguments apply also within the global South.

Gender analysis from the global South therefore poses the question of diversity, the multiplicity of gender forms, not at the level of the individual, but at the level of the gender order and the dynamic of gender relations on a societal scale.

Conditions and Configurations of Knowledge

Thematics are one thing, practicalities another. One of the big differences between gender research in the global North and the global South is the scale of resources available for scholarship. There are some well-resourced universities in the periphery, such as the federal university system in Brazil, the elite universities in India, the "sandstones" or "Group of Eight" in Australia, the "historically white" universities in South Africa and the National University of Singapore. Public investment in higher education, currently static or contracting in the North, has grown in China and Brazil especially. Smaller resources, multiplied, might still amount to a significant asset: across Africa, about 30 universities were teaching gender studies in the early 2000s (Mama, 2005).

None of this, however, is comparable to the scale and wealth of the higher education systems in Europe and the United States, the publishing industries of the metropole, the corporate and state-funded research centres (including census bureaux), and therefore the workforce potentially engaged in gender research in the global North. With the crisis of the postcolonial developmental state and the advent of global neoliberalism, gender research in the South depends to a large degree on NGOs and development aid programmes. As Mama notes, the African university programmes have been struggling with contradictory demands, staff in need of qualifications and erratic institutional support. Continent-wide networks and capacity-building programmes have been created, but the situation is precarious.

[. . .]

Taking these initiatives and examples together, we can imagine a global configuration of gender research very different from the Northern-centred patterns of the past generation. It has gradually been accepted that there are irreducible differences between feminist perspectives. But it is also argued that dialogue across such divides is possible (Bulbeck, 1998). Not only dialogue, but active political cooperation across national borders, and conceptions of feminism on a global scale, are increasingly visible elements of gender politics (Naples and Desai, 2002). Chandra Talpade Mohanty (2003) nicely summarizes this in the idea of "feminism without borders."

Ashwini Tambe (2010) has recently offered an intriguing model of "transnational feminist studies" that contests the metropole-centred narrative of development, the homogenizing vision of essentialist global feminism, and even the kind of metropole/periphery model used in this article. Local feminisms differ from national, she rightly observes, and may have distant links. Mara Viveros (2007) also notes the importance of South–South alliances in getting beyond the mosaics of liberal conceptions of difference and the hierarchies that are the legacy of colonialism. To change social structures still requires a decolonizing practice; and in this practice, the connection between the personal and the political can be re-established.

[. . .]

References

Agarwal, B. 1994. *A Field of One's Own: Gender and Land Rights in South Asia*. Cambridge, MA: Cambridge University Press.

Alatas, S. F. 2006. *Alternative Discourses in Asian Social Science: Responses to Eurocentrism*. New Delhi, India: Sage.

Arnfred, S., B. Bakare-Yusuf, E. Waswa Kisiang'ani, et al. 2004. *African Gender Scholarship: Concepts, Methodologies and Paradigms*. Dakar: CODESRIA.

Bakare-Yusuf, B. 2003. "'Yorubas Don't Do Gender': A Critical Review of Oyeronke Oyewumi's *The Invention of Women: Making an African Sense of Western Gender Discourses.*" *African Identities* 1:119–40.

Bennett, J. 2008. "Editorial: Researching for Life: Paradigms and Power." *Feminist Africa* 11:1–12.

Berndt, C. H. 1974. "Digging Sticks and Spears, or, the Two-sex Model." Pp. 64–84 in *Woman's Role in Aboriginal Society.* 2nd ed., edited by F. Gayle. Canberra: Australian Institute of Aboriginal Studies.

Bhambra, G. K. 2007. "Sociology and Postcolonialism: Another 'Missing' Revolution?" *Sociology* 41(5):871–84.

Bulbeck, C. 1998. *Re-orienting Western Feminisms: Women's Diversity in a Postcolonial World.* Cambridge, MA: Cambridge University Press.

Chodorow, N. 1978. *The Reproduction of Mothering: Psychoanalysis and the Sociology of Gender.* Berkeley, CA: University of California Press.

Connell, R. 2007. *Southern Theory: The Global Dynamics of Knowledge in Social Science.* Cambridge, MA: Polity.

Connell, R. 2011. *Confronting Equality: Gender, Knowledge and Global Change.* Sydney, Australia: Allen and Unwin Australia.

Cordero, T. 2008. "Aportes investigativos del programa de posgrado maestría regional en estudios de la mujer." *Revista casa de la mujer,* 2nd series, 14:14–29.

Epstein, D., R. Morrell, R. Moletsane, and E. Unterhalter. 2004. "Gender and HIV/AIDS in Africa South of the Sahara: Interventions, Activism, Identities." *Transformation* 54:1–16.

Harcourt, W. 2009. *Body Politics in Development: Critical Debates in Gender and Development.* London, UK: Zed Books.

Hountondji, P. J. 1997. "Introduction: Recentring Africa." Pp. 1–39 in *Endogenous Knowledge: Research Trails,* edited by P. J. Hountondji. Dakar: CODESRIA.

Kirkwood, J. 1986. *Ser política en Chile: Las feministas y los partidos.* Santiago, Chile: FLACSO.

Langton, M. 1997. "Grandmothers' Law, Company Business and Succession in Changing Aboriginal Land Tenure Systems." Pp. 84–116 in *Our Land Is Our Life,* edited by G. Yunupingu. St. Lucia: University of Queensland Press.

Laurie, N. 2005. "Establishing Development Orthodoxy: Negotiating Masculinities in the Water Sector." *Development and Change* 36(3):527–49.

Lewis, D. 2002. "African Gender Research and Postcoloniality: Legacies and Challenges." Paper presented to CODESRIA Gender Institute.

Lugones, M. 2007. "Heterosexism and the Colonial/Modern Gender System." *Hypatia* 22(1):186–219.

Mama, A. 1997. "Sheroes and Villains: Conceptualizing Colonial and Contemporary Violence Against Women in Africa." Pp. 46–62 in *Feminist Genealogies, Colonial Legacies, Democratic Futures,* edited by M. J. Alexander and C. T. Mohanty. New York: Routledge.

Mama, A. 2005. "Gender Studies for Africa's Transformation." Pp. 94–116 in *African Intellectuals: Rethinking Politics, Language, Gender and Development,* edited by T. Mkandawire. Dakar: CODESRIA Books.

Marcos, S. 1998. "Embodied Religious Thought: Gender Categories in Mesoamerica." *Religion* 28(4):93–114.

Meekosha, H. 2011. "Decolonizing Disability: Thinking and Acting Globally." *Disability and Society* 26(6):667–81.

Mignolo, W. D. 2007. "Delinking." *Cultural Studies* 21(2/3):449–514.

Mitchell, J. 1974. *Psychoanalysis and Feminism.* New York: Pantheon Books.

Mohanty, C. T. 1991. "Under Western Eyes: Feminist Scholarship and Colonial Discourses." Pp. 51–80 in *Third World Women and the Politics of Feminism,* edited by C. T. Mohanty, A. Russo, and L. Torres. Bloomington, IN: Indiana University Press.

Mohanty, C. T. 2003. *Feminism Without Borders: Decolonizing Theory, Practicing Solidarity.* Durham, NC: Duke University Press.

Montecino, S. 2001. "Identidades y diversidades en Chile." Pp. 65–98 in *Cultura y desa-rollo en Chile,* edited by M. A. Garretón. Santiago, Chile: Andres Bello.

Montero, M. 2007. "The Political Psychology of Liberation: From Politics to Ethics and Back." *Political Psychology* 28(5):517–33.

Moreton-Robinson, A. 2000. *Talkin' Up to the White Woman: Indigenous Women and Feminism.* St. Lucia: University of Queensland Press.

Morrell, R. 2001. *From Boys to Gentlemen: Settler Masculinity in Colonial Natal 1880–1920.* Pretoria, SA: University of South Africa.

Mudimbe, V. 1994. *The Idea of Africa.* Bloomington, IN: Indiana University Press.

Nandy, A. 1983. *The Intimate Enemy: Loss and Recovery of Self Under Colonialism.* New Delhi, India: Oxford University Press.

Naples, N. and M. Desai, eds. 2002. *Women's Activism and Globalization: Linking Local Struggles and Transnational Politics.* New York: Routledge.

Narayan, U. 1998. "Essence of Culture and a Sense of History: A Feminist Critique of Cultural Essentialism." *Hypatia* 13(2):86–106.

Odora Hoppers, C. A., ed. 2002. *Indigenous Knowledge and the Integration of Knowledge Systems.* Claremont, SA: New Africa Books.

Oyewumi, O. 1997. *The Invention of Women: Making an African Sense of Western Gender Discourses.* Minneapolis, MN: University of Minnesota Press.

Patel, S., ed. 2010. *ISA Handbook of Diverse Sociological Traditions.* London, UK: Sage.

Quijano, A. 2000. "Coloniality of Power and Eurocentrism in Latin America." *International Sociology* 15(2):215–32.

Reuter, J. and Villa, P.-I., eds. 2010. *Postkoloniale Soziologie: Empirische Befunde, theoretische Anschlüsse, politische Intervention.* Bielefeld: Transcript.

Richard, N. 2004 [1993]. *Masculine/Feminine: Practices of Difference(s).* Translated by S. R. Tandeciarz and A. A. Nelson. Durham, NC: Duke University Press.

Rubin, G. 1975. "The Traffic in Women: Notes on the 'Political Economy' of Sex." Pp. 157–210 in *Toward an Anthropology of Woman,* edited by R. R. Reiter. New York: Monthly Review Press.

Saffioti, H. I. B. 2004. *Gênero, patriarcado, violência.* São Paulo: Fundação Perseu Abramo.

Smith, L. T. 1999. *Decolonizing Methodologies: Research and Indigenous Peoples.* London, UK: Zed Books.

Tambe, A. 2010. "Transnational Feminist Studies: A Brief Sketch." *New Global Studies* 4(1):Article 7.

Viveros, M. 2007. "De diferencia y diferencias. Algunos debates desde las teorías feministas y de género." Pp. 175–190 in *Género, mujeres y saberes en América Latina,* edited by L. G. Arango and Y. Puyana. Bogotá: Universidad Nacional de Colombia.

PART III
Bodies and Identity

In this section, we acknowledge the interconnected relationship among bodies and identity, including how these are socially constructed. We emphasize the role culture and society play in manufacturing the ways bodies are recognized and identity changes over time. We dedicate readings to the control, regulation, and constant (re)interpretation of the body and identity. The IMTG framework focuses on how body- and identity-centered research has shifted in the 21st century, addressing sexuality, social control, labor, and gender management.

Karin Martin's "Becoming a Gendered Body" shows how the preschool classroom becomes space that constructs and controls bodily behavior, leading to specific gendered practices and expectations. Martin empirically shows how "doing gender" occurs in preschool classrooms, providing rich examples of how boys and girls learn to meet teachers' expectations for how they use their bodies. Girls and boys learn how to "dress up" differently, while teachers also spend more time adjusting girls' clothing and hair. Teachers also police how boys and girls use their bodies, for example, allowing boys to sprawl across the floor, or encouraging girls to sit up straight, in ways that reinforce gender differentiation and the use of space. Teachers discipline how boys and girls use their voices, with girls expected to be quieter and use nicer tones of voice. Martin shows exactly how gendered bodies are made and regulated, through these processes that teach boys and girls how to use their bodies "appropriately."

Breanne Fahs's "Perilous Patches and Pitstaches" examines experiences with and responses to women's body hair growth. Fahs conducts two studies: one where she asks women to imagine letting their body hair grow out, and another where women volunteer to stop shaving their body hair. Women that imagine growing their body hair see body hair as a trivial personal choice, even as they display negative responses to women's body hair growth and justify their removal of body hair. Women who grow their body hair recognize the larger social expectations, the objections of family and friends, and how they relate to homophobia and internalized feelings of disgust. The studies, and their differences, show how gender deviance in body performance leads to serious negative social repercussions for women.

In "The Managed Hand," Miliann Kang uses an intersectional lens to study the emotional and body labor performed by immigrant Asian women in nail salons. By studying interactions between Korean nail salon workers and customers in three different locations—a luxury nail salon located in a mostly White upper and middle-class neighborhood, an artistic nail salon located in a predominantly Black working and lower middle-class neighborhood, and a cheap, standard nail salon located in a racially mixed middle-class neighborhood—Kang examines how both emotional and body labor differ depending on the clientele, and the niche the salons aim to serve. Kang deftly demonstrates that nail salon workers do not follow one script; they provide different types of service and engage in relationships that reflect the classed and racialized context in which they carry out their work. It is clear that nail salon workers' experiences vary by context and location. In a global market, Asian immigrant women learn to enact particular forms of gender and race that shape the kind of body labor they perform.

Tristan Bridges in "Gender Capital and Male Bodybuilders" considers the multiple possibilities of hegemonic masculinity, most often based on body type, among men who are bodybuilders. These men take pride in their strength and musculature, which can be a source of status, as when they work as bouncers, or can expose them to ridicule in other settings, where they are viewed as "freaks." Black bodybuilders note that police appear to view them as particularly threatening. Even within the gym, some powerlifters, who value strength, refer to bodybuilders who value definition and size as "fags" focused on their bodies, while some bodybuilders see powerlifters as "jocks" who use powerlifting to relive their high school triumphs. Bridges thoughtfully shows that men bodybuilders recognize that their muscular and physical development can be viewed as deviant, yet they are still deeply invested in building their bodies. Bridges explores how masculinity is defined, negotiated, and utilized in this subculture.

In "Body Modification and Trans Men," Katelynn Bishop focuses on interviews and YouTube videos to examine partners' experiences of intimacy with trans men undergoing transition. This piece focuses on the changes that occur in trans men's bodies, including the changes produced by testosterone (T) and by surgery. Partners worry how T might change their partners and how to adjust to changes in their partners' voices and bodies. Bishop argues that desire and intimacy must also be navigated as their partners' bodies change, particularly when they are used to desiring women's bodies. Bishop's study demonstrates how partners of transmen focus on their intimate relationships with their partners and their personhood to navigate the bodily changes that occur with transition.

Kimberly Hoang's "Competing Technologies of Embodiment" explores how Vietnamese women are directly involved in constructing bodies that will appeal to Western tourists as well as local and Asian elites. These workers employ different technologies of embodiment, such as plastic surgery, skin lightening, or tanning solutions to appeal to different groups of tourists. Rather than mimicking Western beauty standards, Vietnamese entertainment workers who target Western tourists tan their skin and portray themselves as poor, Third-World victims to appeal to these men's ideals of Vietnamese women as subjugated and traditional. On the other hand, they emphasize light skin and high fashion when working with Asian clientele to appeal to these men's ideals of modern Asian culture in ascendancy over the global economy. While both groups of women engage in cosmetic surgery to meet the needs of their clientele, these surgeries differ based on the market they serve.

All in all, these pieces aim to focus attention on how deeply implicated bodies are in constructions of gender and sexuality from lived experience, interactions, and institutional arrangements. We learn to use our bodies in gendered ways, even in preschools, and we are policed in how we perform gender with our bodies, as when women allow their body hair to grow. Korean women working in nail salons perform body and emotion work differently, depending on their clientele. As people actively transform and change their bodies—as with bodybuilders, transmen transitioning, or among sex workers attempting to attract particular clientele—both gender and sexuality are negotiated.

Becoming a Gendered Body

Practices of Preschools

Karin A. Martin

© iStockphoto.com/FatCamera

S ocial science research about bodies often focuses on women's bodies, particularly the parts of women's bodies that are most explicitly different from men's—their reproductive capacities and sexuality (E. Martin 1987; K. Martin 1996; but see Connell 1987, 1995). Men and women in the United States also hold and move their bodies differently (Birdwhistell 1970; Henley 1977; Young 1990); these differences are sometimes related to sexuality (Haug 1987) and sometimes not. On the whole, men and women sit, stand, gesture,

Karin A. Martin. 1998. "Becoming a Gendered Body: Practices of Preschools." *American Sociological Review* 60(4):494–511.

walk, and throw differently. Generally, women's bodies are confined, their movements restricted. For example, women take smaller steps than men, sit in closed positions (arms and legs crossed across the body), take up less physical space than men, do not step, twist, or throw from the shoulder when throwing a ball, and are generally tentative when using their bodies (Birdwhistell 1970; Henley 1977; Young 1990). Some of these differences, particularly differences in motor skills (e.g., jumping, running, throwing) are seen in early childhood (Thomas and French 1985). Of course, within gender, we may find individual differences, differences based on race, class, and sexuality, and differences based on size and shape of body. Yet, on average, men and women move differently.

[. . .]

Our bodies are also one *site* of gender. Much postmodern feminist work (Butler 1990, 1993) suggests that gender is a performance. Microsociological work (West and Zimmerman 1987) suggests that gender is something that is "done." These two concepts, "gender performance" and "doing gender," are similar—both suggest that managed, adorned, fashioned, properly comported and moving bodies establish gender and gender relations.

Other feminist theorists (Connell 1987, 1995; Young 1990) argue that gender rests not only on the surface of the body, in performance and doing, but becomes *embodied*—becomes deeply part of who we are physically and psychologically. According to Connell, gender becomes embedded in body postures, musculature, and tensions in our bodies.

> The social definition of men as holders of power is translated not only into mental body-images and fantasies, but into muscle tensions, posture, the feel and texture of the body. This is one of the main ways in which the power of men becomes naturalized. . . . (Connell 1987:85)

Connell (1995) suggests that masculine gender is partly a feel to one's body and that bodies are often a source of power for men. Young (1990), however, argues that bodies serve the opposite purpose for women—women's bodies are often sources of anxiety and tentativeness. She suggests that women's lack of confidence and agency are embodied and stem from an inability to move confidently in space, to take up space, to use one's body to its fullest extent. Young (1990) suggests "that the general lack of confidence that we [women] frequently have about our cognitive or leadership abilities is traceable in part to an original doubt of our body's capacity" (p. 156). Thus, these theorists suggest that gender differences in minute bodily behaviors like gesture, stance, posture, step, and throwing are significant to our understanding of gendered selves and gender inequality. This feminist theory, however, focuses on adult bodies.

Theories of the body need gendering, and feminist theories of gendered bodies need "childrening" or accounts of development. How do adult gendered bodies become gendered, if they are not naturally so? Scholars run the risk of continuing to view gendered bodies as natural if they ignore the processes that produce gendered adult bodies. Gendering of the body in childhood is the foundation on which further gendering of the body occurs throughout the life course. The gendering of children's bodies makes gender differences feel and appear natural, which allows for such bodily differences to emerge throughout the life course.

I suggest that the hidden school curriculum of disciplining the body is gendered and contributes to the embodiment of gender in childhood, making gendered bodies appear and feel natural. Sociologists of education have demonstrated that schools have hidden curriculums (Giroux and Purpel 1983; Jackson 1968). Hidden curriculums are covert lessons that schools teach, and they are often a means of social control. . . . This curriculum demands the practice of bodily control in congruence with the goals of the school as an institution. It reworks the students from the outside in on the presumption that to shape the body is to shape the mind (Carere 1987). In such a curriculum teachers constantly monitor kids' bodily movements, comportment, and practices. Kids begin their day running wildly about the school grounds. Then this hidden curriculum funnels the kids into line, through the hallways, quietly into a classroom, sitting upright at their desks, focused at the front of the room, "ready to learn" (Carere 1987; McLaren 1986). According to Carere (1987), this curriculum of disciplining the body serves the curriculums that seek to shape the mind and renders children physically ready for cognitive learning.

I suggest that this hidden curriculum that controls children's bodily practices serves also to turn kids who are similar in bodily comportment, movement, and practice into girls and boys, children whose bodily practices are different. Schools are not the only producers of these differences. While the process ordinarily begins in the family, the schools' hidden curriculum further facilitates and encourages the construction of bodily differences between the genders and makes these physical differences appear and feel natural. Finally, this curriculum may be more or less hidden depending on the particular preschool and particular teachers. Some schools and teachers may see teaching children to behave like "young ladies" and "young gentlemen" as an explicit part of their curriculums.

Data and Method

The data for this study come from extensive and detailed semistructured field observations of five preschool classrooms of three-to five-year-olds in a midwestern city.

[. . .]

A total 112 children and 14 different teachers (five head teachers and nine aides) were observed in these classrooms. All teachers were female. Forty-two percent of the kids were girls and 58 percent were boys, and they made up similar proportions in each classroom. There were 12 Asian or Asian American children, 3 Latino/a children, and 4 African American children. The remaining children were white. The children primarily came from middle-class families.

A research assistant and I observed in these classrooms about three times a week for eight months. . . .We observed girls and boys for equal amounts of time, and we heeded Thorne's (1993) caution about the "big man bias" in field research and were careful not to observe only the most active, outgoing, "popular" kids.

We focused on the children's physicality—body movement, use of space, and the physical contact among kids or between kids and teachers. . . . Excerpts from field notes are presented throughout and are examples of representative patterns in the data. Tables presenting estimates of the numbers of times particular phenomena were observed provide a context for the field note excerpts. . . .

Results

Children's bodies are disciplined by schools. Children are physically active, and institutions like schools impose disciplinary controls that regulate children's bodies and prepare children for the larger social world. While this disciplinary control produces docile bodies (Foucault 1979), it also produces gendered bodies. As these disciplinary practices operate in different contexts, some bodies become more docile than others. I examine how the following practices contribute to a gendering of children's bodies in preschool: the effects of dressing-up or bodily adornment, the gendered nature of formal and relaxed behaviors, how the different restrictions on girls' and boys' voices limit their physicality, how teachers instruct girls' and boys' bodies, and the gendering of physical interactions between children and teachers and among the children themselves.

Bodily Adornment: Dressing Up

Perhaps the most explicit way that children's bodies become gendered is through their clothes and other bodily adornments. Here I discuss how parents gender their children through their clothes, how children's dress-up play experiments with making bodies feminine and masculine, and how this play, when it is gender normative, shapes girls' and boys' bodies differently, constraining girls' physicality.

Dressing up (1). The clothes that parents send kids to preschool in shape children's experiences of their bodies in gendered ways. Clothes, particularly their color, signify a child's gender; gender in preschool is in fact color-coded. On average, about 61 percent of the girls wore pink clothing each day (Table 12.1). Boys were more likely to wear primary colors, black, fluorescent green, and orange. Boys never wore pink.

> The teacher is asking each kid during circle (the part of the day that includes formal instruction by the teacher while the children sit in a circle) what their favorite color is. Adam says black. Bill says "every color that's not pink." (Five-year-olds)

Fourteen percent of three-year-old girls wore dresses each day compared to 32 percent of five-year-old girls (Table 12.1). Wearing a dress limited girls' physicality in preschool. However, it is not only the dress itself, but knowledge about how to behave in a dress that is restrictive. Many girls already knew that some behaviors were not allowed in a dress. This knowledge probably comes from the families who dress their girls in dresses.

> Vicki, wearing leggings and a dress-like shirt, is leaning over the desk to look into a "tunnel" that some other kids have built. As she leans, her dress/shirt rides up exposing her back. Jennifer (another child) walks by Vicki and as she does she pulls Vicki's shirt back over her bare skin and gives it a pat to keep it in place. It looks very much like something one's mother might do. (Five-year-olds)

> Four girls are sitting at a table—Cathy, Kim, Danielle, and Jesse. They are cutting play money out of paper. Cathy and Danielle have on overalls and Kim and Jesse have on dresses. Cathy puts her feet up on the table and crosses her legs at the ankle; she leans back in her chair and continues cutting her money. Danielle imitates her. They look at each other and laugh. They put their shoulders back, posturing, having fun with this new way of sitting. Kim and Jesse continue to cut and laugh with them, but do not put their feet up. (Five-year-olds)

Dresses are restrictive in other ways as well. They often are worn with tights that are experienced as uncomfortable and constraining. I observed girls constantly pulling at and rearranging their tights, trying to untwist them or pull them up. Because of their discomfort, girls spent much time attuned to and arranging their clothing and/or their bodies.

Table 12.1 Observations of Girls Wearing Dresses and the Color Pink:
Five Preschool Classrooms

Observation	N	Percent
Girls wearing something pink	54	61
Girls wearing dresses	21	24
3-year-old girls	6	14
5-year-old girls	15	32
Number of observations	89	100
3-year-old girls	42	47
5-year-old girls	47	53

Note: In 12 observation sessions, what the children were wearing, including color of their clothing, was noted. The data in Table 12.1 come from coded field notes. There were no instances of boys wearing pink or dresses, and no age differences among girls in wearing the color pink.

. . . Teachers were much more likely to manage girls and their clothing this way—rearranging their clothes, tucking in their shirts, fixing a ponytail gone astray. Such management often puts girls' bodies under the control of another and calls girls' attentions to their appearances and bodily adornments.

Dressing up (2). Kids like to *play* dress-up in preschool, and all the classrooms had a dress-up corner with a variety of clothes, shoes, pocketbooks, scarves, and hats for dressing up. Classrooms tended to have more women's clothes than men's, but there were some of both, as well as some gender-neutral clothes—capes, hats, and vests that were not clearly for men or women—and some items that were clearly costumes, such as masks of cats and dogs and clip-on tails. Girls tended to play dress-up more than boys—over one-half of dressing up was done by girls. Gender differences in the amount of time spent playing dress-up seemed to increase from age three to age five. We only observed the five-year-old boys dressing up or using clothes or costumes in their play three times, whereas three-year-old boys dressed up almost weekly. Five-year-old boys also did not dress up elaborately, but used one piece of clothing to animate their play. Once Phil wore large, men's winter ski gloves when he played monster. Holding up his now large, chiseled looking hands, he stomped around the classroom making monster sounds. On another occasion Brian, a child new to the classroom who attended only two days a week, walked around by himself for a long time carrying a silver pocketbook and hovering first at the edges of girls' play and then at the edges of boys' play. On the third occasion, Sam used ballet slippers to animate his play in circle.

When kids dressed up, they played at being a variety of things from kitty cats and puppies to monsters and superheroes to "fancy ladies." Some of this play was not explicitly gendered. . . . Children often seemed to experiment with both genders when they played dress-up. The three-year-olds tended to be more experimental in their gender dress-up than the five-year-olds, perhaps because teachers encouraged it more at this age.

Everett and Juan are playing dress-up. Both have on "dresses" made out of material that is wrapped around them like a toga or sarong. Everett has a pocketbook and a camera over his shoulder and Juan has a pair of play binoculars on a strap over his. Everett has a scarf around his head and cape on. Juan has on big, green sunglasses. Pam (teacher) tells them, "You guys look great! Go look in the mirror." They shuffle over to the full-length mirror and look at themselves and grin, and make adjustments to their costumes. (Three-year-olds)

The five-year-old children tended to dress-up more gender normatively. Girls in particular played at being adult women.

> Frances is playing dress-up. She is walking in red shoes and carrying a pocketbook. She and two other girls, Jen and Rachel, spend between five and ten minutes looking at and talking about the guinea pigs. Then they go back to dress-up. Frances and Rachel practice walking in adult women's shoes. Their body movements are not a perfect imitation of an adult woman's walk in high heels, yet it does look like an attempt to imitate such a walk. Jen and Rachel go back to the guinea pigs, and Frances, now by herself, is turning a sheer, frilly lavender shirt around and around and around trying to figure out how to put it on. She gets it on and looks at herself in the mirror. She adds a sheer pink and lavender scarf and pink shoes. Looks in the mirror again. She walks, twisting her body—shoulders, hips, shoulders, hips— not quite a (stereotypic) feminine walk, but close. Walking in big shoes makes her take little bitty steps, like walking in heels. She shuffles in the too big shoes out into the middle of the classroom and stops by a teacher. Laura (a teacher) says, "don't you look fancy, all pink and purple." Frances smiles up at her and walks off, not twisting so much this time. She goes back to the mirror and adds a red scarf. She looks in the mirror and is holding her arms across her chest to hold the scarf on (she can't tie it) and she is holding it with her chin too. She shuffles to block area where Jen is and then takes the clothes off and puts them back in dress-up area. (Five-year-olds)

[. . .]

Other types of responses to girls dressing up also seemed to gender their bodies and to constrain them. For example, on two occasions I saw a teacher tie the arms of girls' dress-up shirts together so that the girls could not move their arms. They did this in fun, of course, and untied them as soon as the girls wanted them to, but I never witnessed this constraining of boys' bodies in play.

Thus, how parents gender children's bodies through dressing them and the ways children experiment with bodily adornments by dressing up make girls' and boys' bodies different and seem different to those around them. Adorning a body often genders it explicitly—signifies that it is a feminine or masculine body. Adornments also make girls movements smaller, leading girls to take up less space with their bodies and disallowing some types of movements.[2]

Formal and Relaxed Behaviors

[. . .]

I identified several behaviors that were expected by the teachers, required by the institution, or that would be required in many institutional settings, as formal behavior. Raising one's hand, sitting "on your bottom" (not on your knees, not squatting, not lying down, not standing) during circle, covering one's nose and mouth when coughing or sneezing, or sitting upright in a chair are all formal behaviors of preschools, schools, and to some extent the larger social world. Crawling on the floor, yelling, lying down during teachers' presentations,

Table 12.2 Observations of Formal and Relaxed Behaviors, by Gender of Child: Five Preschool Classrooms

Type of Behavior	Boys		Girls		Total	
	N	Percent	N	Percent	N	Percent
Formal	16	18	71	82	87	100
Relaxed	86	80	21	20	107	100

Note: Structured/formal behaviors were coded from references in the field notes to formal postures, polite gestures, etc. Relaxed/informal behaviors were coded from references to informal postures, backstage demeanors, etc.

and running through the classroom are examples of relaxed behaviors that are not allowed in preschool, schools, work settings, and many institutions of the larger social world (Henley 1977). Not all behaviors fell into one of these classifications. When kids were actively engaged in playing at the water table, for example, much of their behavior was not clearly formal or relaxed. I coded as formal and relaxed behaviors those behaviors that would be seen as such if done by adults (or children in many cases) in other social institutions for which children are being prepared.

In the classrooms in this study, boys were allowed and encouraged to pursue relaxed behaviors in a variety of ways that girls were not. Girls were more likely to be encouraged to pursue more formal behaviors. Eighty-two percent of all formal behaviors observed in these classrooms were done by girls, and only 18 percent by boys. However, 80 percent of the behaviors coded as relaxed were boys' behaviors (Table 12.2).

These observations do not tell us *why* boys do more relaxed behaviors and girls do more formal behaviors. Certainly many parents and others would argue that boys are more predisposed to sloppy postures, crawling on the floor, and so on. However, my observations suggest that teachers help construct this gender difference in bodily behaviors. Teachers were more likely to reprimand girls for relaxed bodily movements and comportment. Sadker and Sadker (1994) found a similar result with respect to hand-raising for answering teachers' questions—if hand raising is considered a formal behavior and calling out a relaxed behavior, they find that boys are more likely to call out without raising their hands and demand attention:

Sometimes what they [boys] say has little or nothing to do with the teacher's questions. Whether male comments are insightful or irrelevant, teachers respond to them. However, when girls call out, there is a fascinating occurrence: Suddenly the teacher remembers the rule about raising your hand before you talk. (Sadker and Sadker 1994:43)

This gendered dynamic of hand-raising exists even in preschool, although our field notes do not provide enough systematic recording of hand-raising to fully assess it. However, such a dynamic applies to many bodily movements and comportment:

The kids are sitting with their legs folded in a circle listening to Jane (the teacher) talk about dinosaurs. ("Circle" is the most formal part of their preschool education each day and is like sitting in class.) Sam has the ballet slippers on his hands and is clapping them together really loudly. He stops and does a half-somersault backward out of the circle and stays that way with his legs in the air. Jane says nothing and continues talking about dinosaurs. Sue, who is sitting next to Sam, pushes his leg out of her way. Sam sits up and is now busy trying to put the ballet shoes on over his sneakers, and he is looking at the other kids and laughing, trying to get a reaction. He is clearly not paying attention to Jane's dinosaur story and is distracting the other kids. Sam takes the shoes and claps them together again. Jane leans over and tells him to give her the shoes. Sam does, and then lies down all stretched out on the floor, arms over his head, legs apart. Adam is also lying down now, and Keith is on Sara's (the teacher's aide) lap. Rachel takes her sweater off and folds it up. The other children are focused on the teacher. After about five minutes, Jane tells Sam "I'm going to ask you to sit up." (She doesn't say anything to Adam.) But he doesn't move. Jane ignores Sam and Adam and continues with the lesson. Rachel now lies down on her back. After about ten seconds Jane says, "Sit up, Rachel." Rachel sits up and listens to what kind of painting the class will do today. (Five-year-olds)

Sam's behavior had to be more disruptive, extensive, and informal than Rachel's for the teacher to instruct him and his bodily movements to be quieter and for him to comport his body properly for circle. Note that the boys who were relaxed but not disruptive were not instructed to sit properly. It was also common for a teacher to tell a boy to stop some bodily behavior and for the boy to ignore the request and the teacher not to enforce her instructions, although she frequently repeated them.

The gendering of body movements, comportment, and acquisitions of space also happens in more subtle ways. For example, often when there was "free" time, boys spent much more time in child-structured activities than did girls. In one classroom of five-year-olds, boys' "free" time was usually spent building with blocks, climbing on blocks, or crawling on the blocks or on the floor as they worked to build with the blocks whereas girls spent much of their free time sitting at tables cutting things out of paper, drawing, sorting small pieces of blocks into categories, reading stories, and so on. Compared to boys, girls rarely crawled on the floor (except when they played kitty cats). Girls and boys did share some activities. For example, painting and reading were frequently shared, and the three-year-olds often played at fishing from a play bridge together. Following is a list from my field notes of the most common activities boys and girls did during the child-structured activity periods of the day during two randomly picked weeks of observing:

Boys: played blocks (floor), played at the water table (standing and splashing), played superhero (running around and in play house), played with the car garage (floor), painted at the easel (standing).

Girls: played dolls (sitting in chairs and walking around), played dress-up (standing), coloring (sitting at tables), read stories (sitting on the couch), cut out pictures (sitting at tables).

Children sorted themselves into these activities and also were sorted (or not unsorted) by teachers. For example, teachers rarely told the three boys that always played with the blocks that they had to choose a different activity that day. Teachers also encouraged girls to sit at tables by suggesting table activities for them—in a sense giving them less "free" time or structuring their time more.

It's the end of circle, and Susan (teacher) tells the kids that today they can paint their dinosaur eggs if they want to. There is a table set up with paints and brushes for those who want to do that. The kids listen and then scatter to their usual activities. Several boys are playing blocks, two boys are at the water table. Several girls are looking at the hamsters in their cage and talking about them, two girls are sitting and stringing plastic beads. Susan says across the classroom, "I need some painters, Joy, Amy, Kendall?" The girls leave the hamster cage and go to the painting table. Susan pulls out a chair so Joy can sit down. She tells them about the painting project. (Five-year-olds)

These girls spent much of the afternoon enjoying themselves painting their eggs. Simon and Jack joined them temporarily, but then went back to activities that were not teacher-structured.

Events like these that happen on a regular basis over an extended period of early childhood serve to gender children's bodies—boys come to take up more room with their bodies, to sit in more open positions, and to feel freer to do what they wish with their bodies, even in relatively formal settings. Henley (1977) finds that among adults men generally are more relaxed than women in their demeanor and women tend to have tenser postures. The looseness of body-focused functions (e.g., belching) is also more open to men than to women. In other words, men are more likely to engage in relaxed demeanors, postures, and behaviors. These data suggest that this gendering of bodies into more formal and more relaxed movements, postures, and comportment is (at least partially) constructed in early childhood by institutions like preschools.

Controlling Voice

Speaking (or yelling as is often the case with kids) is a bodily experience that involves mouth, throat, chest, diaphragm, and facial expression. Thorne (1993) writes that an elementary school teacher once told her that kids "reminded her of bumblebees, an apt image of swarms, speed, and constant motion" (p. 15). Missing from this metaphor is the buzz of the bumblebees, as a constant hum of voices comes from children's play and activities. Kids' play that is giggly, loud, or whispery makes it clear that voice is part of their bodily experiences.

Voice is an aspect of bodily experience that teachers and schools are interested in disciplining. Quiet appears to be required for learning in classrooms. Teaching appropriate levels of voice, noise, and sound disciplines children's bodies and prepares them "from the inside" to learn the school's curriculums and to participate in other social institutions.

The disciplining of children's voices is gendered. I found that girls were told to be quiet or to repeat a request in a quieter, "nicer" voice about three times more often than were boys (see Table 12.3). This finding is particularly interesting because boys' play was frequently much noisier. However, when boys were noisy, they were also often doing other behaviors the teacher did not allow, and perhaps the teachers focused less on voice because they were more concerned with stopping behaviors like throwing or running.

Table 12.3 Observations of Teachers Telling Children to Be Quiet, by Gender of Child: Five Preschool Classrooms

Gender	N	Percent
Girls	45	73
Boys	16	26
Total	61	100

Note: Coded from references in the field notes to instances of teachers quieting children's voices.

Additionally, when boys were told to "quiet down" they were told in large groups, rarely as individuals. When they were being loud and were told to be quiet, boys were often in the process of enacting what Jordan and Cowan (1995) call warrior narratives:

> A group of three boys is playing with wooden doll figures. The dolls are jumping off block towers, crashing into each other. Kevin declares loudly, "I'm the grown up." Keith replies, "I'm the police." They knock the figures into each other and push each other away. Phil grabs a figure from Keith. Keith picks up two more and bats one with the other toward Phil. Now all three boys are crashing the figures into each other, making them dive off towers. They're having high fun. Two more boys join the group. There are now five boys playing with the wooden dolls and the blocks. They're breaking block buildings; things are crashing; they're grabbing each other's figures and yelling loudly. Some are yelling "fire, fire" as their figures jump off the block tower. The room is very noisy. (Five-year-olds)

Girls as individuals and in groups were frequently told to lower their voices. Later that same afternoon:

> During snack time the teacher asks the kids to tell her what they like best in the snack mix. Hillary says, "Marshmallows!" loudly, vigorously, and with a swing of her arm. The teacher turns to her and says, "I'm going to ask you to say that quietly," and Hillary repeats it in a softer voice. (Five-year-olds)

These two observations represent a prominent pattern in the data. The boys playing with the wooden figures were allowed to express their fun and enthusiasm loudly whereas Hillary could not loudly express her love of marshmallows. Girls' voices are disciplined to be softer and in many ways less physical—toning down their voices tones down their physicality. Hillary emphasized "marshmallows" with a large swinging gesture of her arm the first time she answered the teacher's question, but after the teacher asked her to say it quietly she made no gestures when answering. Incidents like these that are repeated often in different contexts restrict girls' physicality.

It could be argued that context rather than gender explains the difference in how much noise is allowed in these situations. Teachers may expect more formal behavior from children sitting at the snack table than they do during semistructured activities. However, even during free play girls were frequently told to quiet down:

> Nancy, Susan, and Amy are jumping in little jumps, from the balls of their feet, almost like skipping rope without the rope. Their mouths are open and they're making a humming sound, looking at each other and giggling. Two of them keep sticking their tongues out. They seem to be having great fun. The teacher's aide sitting on the floor in front of them turns around and says "Shhh, find something else to play. Why don't you play Simon Says?" All three girls stop initially. Then Amy jumps a few more times, but without making the noise. (Five-year-olds)

By limiting the girls' voices, the teacher also limits the girls' jumping and their fun. The girls learn that their bodies are supposed to be quiet, small, and physically constrained. Although the girls did not take the teacher's suggestion to play Simon Says (a game where bodies can be moved only quietly at the order of another), they turn to play that explores quietness yet tries to maintain some of the fun they were having:

> Nancy, Susan, and Amy begin sorting a pile of little-bitty pieces of puzzles, soft blocks, Legos, and so on into categories to "help" the teacher who told them to be quiet and to clean up. The three of them and the teacher are standing around a single small desk sorting these pieces. (Meanwhile several boys are playing blocks and their play is spread all over the middle of the room.) The teacher turns her attention to some other children. The girls continue sorting and then begin giggling to each other. As they do, they cover their mouths. This becomes a game as one imitates the other. Susan says something nonsensical that is supposed to be funny, and then she "hee-hees" while covering her mouth and looks at Nancy, to whom she has said it, who covers her mouth and "hee-hees" back. They begin putting their hands/fingers cupped over their mouths and whispering in each others' ears and then giggling quietly. They are intermittently sorting the pieces and playing the whispering game. (Five-year-olds)

Thus, the girls took the instruction to be quiet and turned it into a game. This new game made their behaviors smaller, using hands and mouths rather than legs, feet, and whole bodies. Whispering became their fun, instead of jumping and humming. Besides requiring quiet, this whispering game also was gendered in another way: The girls' behavior seemed to mimic stereotypical female gossiping. They whispered in twos and looked at the third girl as they did it and then changed roles. Perhaps the instruction to be quiet, combined with the female role of "helping," led the girls to one of their understandings of female quietness—gossip—a type of feminine quietness that is perhaps most fun.

Finally, by limiting voice teachers limit one of girls' mechanisms for resisting others' mistreatment of them. Frequently, when a girl had a dispute with another child, teachers would ask the girl to quiet down and solve the problem nicely. Teachers also asked boys to solve problems by talking, but they usually did so only with intense disputes and the instruction to talk things out never carried the instruction to talk *quietly*.

> Keith is persistently threatening to knock over the building that Amy built. He is running around her with a "flying" toy horse that comes dangerously close to her building each time. She finally says, "Stop it!" in a loud voice. The teacher comes over and asks, "How do we say that, Amy?" Amy looks at Keith and says more softly, "Stop trying to knock it over." The teacher tells Keith to find some place else to play. (Five-year-olds)
> [. . .]

We know that women are reluctant to use their voices to protect themselves from a variety of dangers. The above observations suggest that the denial of women's voices begins at least as early as preschool, and that restricting voice usually restricts movement as well.
[. . .]

Conclusion

Children also sometimes resist their bodies being gendered. For example, three-year-old boys dressed up in women's clothes sometimes. Five-year-old girls played with a relaxed comportment that is normatively (hegemonically) masculine when they sat with their feet up on the desk and their chairs tipped backward. In one classroom when boys were at the height of their loud activity—running and throwing toys and blocks—girls took the opportunity to be loud too as the teachers were paying less attention to them and trying to get the boys to settle down. In individual interactions as well, girls were likely to be loud and physically assertive if a boy was being unusually so:

> José is making a plastic toy horse fly around the room, and the boys playing with the blocks are quite loud and rambunctious. José flies the toy horse right in front of Jessica's face and then zooms around her and straight toward her again. Jessica holds up her hand and waves it at him yelling, "Aaaarrrh." José flies the horse in another direction. (Five-year-olds)

These instances of resistance suggest that gendered physicalities are not natural, nor are they easily and straightforwardly acquired. This research demonstrates the many ways that practices in institutions like preschools facilitate children's acquisition of gendered physicalities.

Men and women and girls and boys fill social space with their bodies in different ways. Our everyday movements, postures, and gestures are gendered. These bodily differences enhance the seeming naturalness of sexual and reproductive differences, that then construct inequality between men and women (Butler 1990). As MacKinnon (1987) notes, "Differences are inequality's post hoc excuse..." (p. 8). In other words, these differences create a context for social relations in which differences confirm inequalities of power.

This research suggests one way that bodies are gendered and physical differences are constructed through social institutions and their practices. Because this gendering occurs at an early age, the seeming naturalness of such differences is further underscored. In preschool, bodies become gendered in ways that are so subtle and taken-for-granted that they come to feel and appear natural. Preschool, however, is presumably just the tip of the iceberg in the gendering of children's bodies. Families, formal schooling, and other institutions (like churches, hospitals, and workplaces) gender children's physicality as well.

Many feminist sociologists (West and Zimmerman 1987) and other feminist scholars (Butler 1990, 1993) have examined how the seeming naturalness of gender differences underlies gender inequality. They have also theorized that there are no meaningful natural differences (Butler 1990, 1993). However, how gender differences come to feel and appear natural in the first place has been a missing piece of the puzzle.

Sociological theories of the body that describe the regulation, disciplining, and managing that social institutions do to bodies have neglected the gendered nature of these processes (Foucault 1979; Shilling 1993; Turner 1984). These data suggest that a significant part of disciplining the body consists of gendering it, even in subtle, micro, everyday ways that make gender appear natural. It is in this sense that the preschool as an institution genders children's bodies. Feminist theories about the body (Bordo 1993; Connell 1995; Young 1990), on the other hand, tend to focus on the adult gendered body and fail to consider how the body becomes gendered. This neglect may accentuate gender differences and make them seem natural. This research provides but one account of how bodies become gendered. Other accounts of how the bodies of children and adults are gendered (and raced, classed, and sexualized) are needed in various social contexts across the life course.

[...]

References

Birdwhistell, Ray. 1970. *Kinesics and Contexts*. Philadelphia, PA: University of Pennsylvania Press.

Bordo, Susan. 1993. *Unbearable Weight*. Berkeley, CA: University of California Press.

Butler, Judith. 1990. *Gender Trouble*. New York: Routledge.

Butler, Judith. 1993. *Bodies That Matter*. New York: Routledge.

Carere, Sharon. 1987. "Lifeworld of Restricted Behavior." *Sociological Studies of Child Development* 2:105–38.

Connell, R. W. 1987. *Gender and Power*. Stanford, CA: Stanford University Press.

Connell, R. W. 1995. *Masculinities*. Berkeley, CA: University of California Press.

Foucault, Michel. 1979. *Discipline and Punish: The Birth of the Prison*. New York: Vintage Books.

Giroux, Henry and David Purpel. 1983. *The Hidden Curriculum and Moral Education*. Berkeley, CA: McCutchan.

Haug, Frigga. 1987. *Female Sexualization: A Collective Work of Memory*. London, UK: Verso.

Henley, Nancy. 1977. *Body Politics*. New York: Simon and Schuster.

Jackson, Philip W. 1968. *Life in Classrooms*. New York: Holt, Rinehart, and Winston.

Jordan, Ellen and Angela Cowan. 1995. "Warrior Narratives in the Kindergarten Classroom: Renegotiating the Social Contract." *Gender and Society* 9:727–43.

MacKinnon, Catharine. 1987. *Feminism Unmodified*. Cambridge, MA: Harvard University Press.

Martin, Emily. 1987. *The Woman in the Body*. Boston, MA: Beacon Press.

Martin, Karin. 1996. *Puberty, Sexuality, and the Self: Boys and Girls at Adolescence*. New York: Routledge.

McLaren, Peter. 1986. *Schooling as a Ritual Performance: Towards a Political Economy of Educational Symbols and Gestures*. London, UK: Routledge and Kegan Paul.

Sadker, Myra and David Sadker. 1994. *Failing at Fairness: How America's Schools Cheat Girls*. New York: Charles Scribner and Sons.

Shilling, Chris. 1993. *The Body and Social Theory*. London, UK: Sage.

Thomas, Jerry and Karen French. 1985. "Gender Differences Across Age in Motor Performance: A Meta-Analysis." *Psychological Bulletin* 98:260–82.

Thorne, Barrie. 1993. *Gender Play: Girls and Boys in School*. New Brunswick, NJ: Rutgers University Press.

Turner, Bryan S. 1984. *The Body and Society: Explorations in Social Theory*. New York: Basil Blackwell.

West, Candace and Don Zimmerman. 1987. "Doing Gender." *Gender and Society* 1:127–51.

Young, Iris. 1990. *Throwing Like a Girl*. Bloomington, IN: Indiana University Press.

Perilous Patches and Pitstaches

Imagined Versus Lived Experiences of Women's Body Hair Growth

Breanne Fahs

© iStockphoto.com/MrKornFlakes

W omen's bodies have often served as contested terrain in battles over agency, control, power, and identity. . . . Does removing body hair represent a decision made by individuals who *choose* to do so, or does it reflect larger cultural mandates that require the compliance and obedience of women and their bodies? Can women who have never grown body hair accurately imagine the personal and social consequences of having a hairy body, or must they experience the growth of body hair to understand the kinds of social penalties they might encounter with such "transgressions"? Do different groups of women face different outcomes for body hair, or is the norm of depilation so pervasive that few women remain exempt from the demands for hairlessness?

Breanne Fahs. 2014. "Perilous Patches and Pitstaches: Imagined Versus Lived Experiences of Women's Body Hair Growth." *Psychology of Women Quarterly* 38(2):167–80.

[. . .]

The pervasiveness and normalization of body hair removal in the Western world—particularly the United States—suggest that body hair removal has transitioned from an optional form of body modification to a relatively universal expectation placed upon women. Recent studies suggest that between 91% (Kenyon & Tiggemann, 1998) and 97% (Lewis & Tiggemann, 2004) of Australian women shaved their legs, 93% of Australian women shaved their underarms (Kenyon & Tiggemann, 1998), and over 99% of women in the United Kingdom have removed body hair at some point in their lives (Toerien, Wilkinson, & Choi, 2005). . . . Pubic hair removal—a practice that largely stopped in the late 19th century but restarted in the 1980s (Ramsey, Sweeney, Fraser, & Oades, 2009)—has also shown a dramatic increase in recent years, with younger and partnered women in the United States removing pubic hair at a growing rate (Herbenick, Schick, Reece, Sanders, & Fortenberry, 2010) and pornography and popular culture idealizing hairless and prepubescent female genitals (Schick, Rima, & Calabrese, 2011). . . .

Whenever a body norm becomes this pervasive, questions arise about the reasons for its compulsory status. . . . Across all social identity groups, hairless female bodies have entered the cultural imagination as a compulsory ideal, in part generated by mass media and marketing campaigns that feature Brazilian waxes, eyebrow waxes, permanent hair removal, and body hair removal creams as positive choices for body modification, particularly within industrialized countries (Hodgson & Tiggemann, 2008; Whelehan, 2000). . . . The notion that women's hairiness equals dirtiness or even abomination has a firm grip on the contemporary cultural imagination about women's body hair.

[. . .]

My two studies ask three central research questions. (a) Because women's hairlessness represents an invisible yet compulsory social norm, how do women think about, talk about, and experience violations of that norm? (b) What narrative differences appear when women *imagine* growing their body hair compared with those who actually *grow* their body hair? (c) Finally, how do women conceptualize freedom, agency, and choice when imagining and experiencing body hair norm violations?

Study 1: Imagined Experiences

[. . .]

In Study 1, I utilized qualitative data from a sample of 20 adult women . . . recruited in 2011 from a large metropolitan Southwestern U.S. city. Participants were recruited through local entertainment and arts listings distributed free to the community as well as from the "volunteers" section of the local online section of Craigslist.

[. . .]

A purposive sample was selected to provide greater demographic diversity; sexual minority women and racial/ethnic minority women were intentionally oversampled, and a diverse range of ages was represented (11 women aged 18–31; 5 women aged 32–45; and 4 women aged 46–59). The sample included 11 White women and 9 women of color, including 3 African American women, 4 Mexican American women, and 2 Asian American women. For self-reported sexual identity, the sample included 12 heterosexual women, 7 bisexual women, and 2 lesbian women (though women's reported sexual behavior often indicated far more same-sex eroticism than these self-categorized labels suggest).

[...]

Participants were interviewed using a semistructured interview protocol that lasted for approximately 1.5 to 2 hours and during which they responded to 36 questions about their sexual histories, sexual practices, and feelings and attitudes about sexuality.

[...]

Women were asked four questions about women's body hair: (a) "Women describe different feelings about having body hair, particularly leg, armpit, and pubic hair. How have you negotiated your body hair and how do you feel about shaving or not shaving?" (b) "Have you ever not shaved during your life? If so, did you face any social punishments? If not, what would it be like to not shave? Is not shaving empowering or disempowering?" (c) "Do you feel that shaving is a choice or a requirement?" (d) "What do you think of women who do not shave their bodies?"

[...]

The community sample of women who imagined body hair growth and discussed their feelings about other women who did not shave described responses that clustered around three themes: (a) belief that body hair removal represented a trivial personal choice rather than a strong social requirement, (b) language of disgust toward other women's choices to grow body hair, and (c) refusal to voluntarily grow their body hair and justification for always removing body hair. . . .

Theme 1: Personal Choice

When I asked women directly whether they felt that shaving represented a choice or a requirement, 15 of 20 said frankly that body hair removal was a choice, 2 others said it was a requirement, and the remaining 3 said that it was both a choice and a requirement. Women overwhelmingly constructed body hair removal as something they, and others, chose to do, even though a few acknowledged the complexity of blending choices and requirements together. Most women unequivocally stated that body hair removal represented a choice for themselves, such as April (a 27-year-old Latina lesbian) who said, "It's a choice. I don't feel like it's a requirement. I just prefer to shave." Dessa (a 19-year-old Latina heterosexual woman) said, similarly, "It's a choice, yeah, a choice. I do it only out of my own preference." Tania (a 25-year-old White heterosexual woman) reflected on the way body hair removal felt compulsory by saying, "I think it's a choice that I make a requirement," whereas Keisha (a 34-year-old African-American woman) said, only half-jokingly, "It's a choice, but if it gets out of hand it *should* be a requirement to shave, especially if you have body odor. It should be required!"

Some women indicated that they wanted others to accept them without judgment, although they still found body hair disgusting and repulsive. Inga (a 24-year-old White bisexual woman) admitted that she felt body hair removal was a choice but still struggled with letting her hair grow: "I'd probably feel gross if I grew it out. It's just one more thing I have to try to keep tidy and clean because I'm kind of OCD, and because society doesn't feel it's attractive and my girlfriend doesn't feel it's attractive." Similarly, Kelly (a 23-year-old White heterosexual woman) firmly believed that body hair removal represented her personal choice, and even though she said she would not judge others, she acknowledged the disgust she felt toward body hair: "If I didn't shave, I don't think my boyfriend would like that but I don't think I would either. People would be grossed out and he wouldn't be comfortable with it." When I asked her what she thought of other women who did not shave, she said, "I think it's fine and great. Everyone deserves to live the way they want to live, but if I was their partner, I don't know if I'd be comfortable."

[...]

Theme 2: Disgust

Although women mostly discussed depilation as a choice, they overwhelmingly considered not removing body hair an undesirable choice. Disgust toward other women appeared frequently, particularly as women constructed body hair as "dirty" and "unclean." Some women described distaste for hair that they projected onto other women, such as Cris (a 22-year-old White lesbian) who said, "I think women who don't shave are a little gross. Because sometimes, like if people don't shave their entire lives, that's just a little too much to handle for me. I always shave. I don't like hair. I shave everything." Similarly, Abby (a 26-year-old White heterosexual woman) wanted to accept other women's choices but ultimately found unshaved women disgusting:

> I know there are people who choose not to shave. I wouldn't want to subject other people to that. There's kind of a stigma, maybe being unclean or something, and I think people would have those thoughts. I wonder what their partners think about it, whether they are "hippies." I guess their partners don't care.

Mei (a 22-year-old Asian American heterosexual woman) showed the vast contradictions in women's narratives about depilation as she simultaneously described some disgust toward women who did not shave, combined with acceptance for not removing body hair, while also admitting that depilation caused her problems:

> I had laser hair removal because I had really bad ingrown hairs from shaving and they would get pimply and pus-filled. . . . I feel shaving is a requirement in this society and women should shave everything except for their heads. You don't want to see women with hairs on their fingers or arms. It depends on which culture they're in. I'm very open to whether you do or don't shave, but some people I know really care.

Even when women claimed that they did not judge other women for not removing body hair, their statements often indicated otherwise.
[. . .]
Leticia (a 41-year-old Latina bisexual woman) said that women could choose not to shave but then added:

> Hairy legs and hairy armpits look gross. I just think it's gross. It signifies a woman being lazy and not taking care of herself. Maybe they're not involved with someone, that's just their culture, but it bothers me. Why doesn't she just *shave*? You know what I mean?

Theme 3: Refusal and Justification

Discussions of managing the unruly, "smelly," and "dirty" body appeared frequently in women's narratives about body hair removal. Shantele admitted that she always needed to keep her body in control to manage her anxieties:

> I never let it get out of control. When I don't shave I'm not aroused, I'm not turned on. I always do my armpits because of the smell. If I go a few days without shaving my armpits have a different smell so you have to use deodorant more often and that's not good. And then my legs, if it gets too long it starts to actually hurt, doesn't feel good, so then I'll shave that off too. It doesn't actually get long ever.

Tania worried that she would harm others by having body hair: "It's got a lot to do with cleanliness, and you know, there's nothing stuck down there. You can actually hurt the other person, or they get caught in your hair, and it just kind of makes a mess otherwise."

Justifying body hair removal based on attractiveness to men also appeared frequently in women's narratives. Sometimes this appeared more directly as women said they faced direct social penalties for not removing body hair. For example, Zhang (a 36-year-old Asian American bisexual woman) noted that her boyfriend "gets upset when I don't shave because it turns him off and he will get cranky all day." More often, women described this tension more subtly, such as April who conflated the notion of personal choice and (heterosexual) social norms when "confining" her body hair to please her male partner: "I think women are expected to shave but it's still my choice. I could stop shaving if I wanted but my boyfriend wouldn't like it. It makes me feel more comfortable anyway."

As another fusion of personal choice rhetoric with pleasing men, Rhoda (a 57-year-old White heterosexual woman) who said earlier in the interview that she "cleaned up" her pubic area but generally thought shaving a bore, described contradictions of both shaving for men and shaving for herself: "When I don't have a man around, I don't shave. I think it's a personal choice. I feel better if I am shaved. I just think it looks better, feels better. Smooth feels better than stubbly." . . .

Although women often removed body hair, they sometimes reported internal conflicts about the social and technical meanings assigned to hair. Jean (a 57-year-old White heterosexual woman) recalled that body hair norms had changed significantly in her lifetime:

> When I was younger and first got out into the world it was free love and all that stuff. I didn't shave much and I didn't have to. Then I got into the corporate world and I started shaving. I didn't realize that hair was even bad until then, that it was unattractive, until the times changed. Now I have everything shaved.

Patricia (a 28-year-old African American woman) also described always removing her pubic hair despite having some conflicts about the function of pubic hair and others' treatment of her as a prepubescent girl:

> I like the way I look shaved and I hate when it grows back. Even though they'll say keeping your hair keeps stuff from going down in there, at the same time it can cause moisture and I don't like that. You don't want to start smelling. It keeps you cool down there in the summer to not have hair. When I started having sex, I was 18 but I looked like I was 14 at the time because I didn't have any hair down there. So guys would be like, "Man, you know you really look like a little girl, like I'm robbing the cradle!" That was frustrating.

Finally, Jane (a 59-year-old White heterosexual woman) admitted that, though she admired women who resisted depilation, she could never do it herself:

> If I wanted to make a statement, it's not going to be about body hair. I'm going to save my soapbox for something a little more important than about whether I shave or not. I think that women who don't shave are so comfortable in their own skin. They're not trying to be someone else. That's great if they can carry that off and they feel comfortable doing that. I just can't.

[...]

Notably, women in Study 1 framed body hair primarily within the realm of personal choice, citing it as something that women can or cannot choose to grow. Their narratives often ignored larger social critiques and stories about removing body hair as a social requirement or a mandatory social norm to avoid punishment. The fascinating contradiction between framing body hair as a relatively benign personal choice and then talking about hairy women with strong disgust and rejection reveals the way social norms may embed themselves silently and invisibly in women's lives. In other words, women may find themselves in a familiar quandary: "I feel like I can choose whatever I want but I still choose to conform." This opens up many new questions, particularly the notion of what would happen if women actually grew out their body hair and faced the social punishments for actually violating the norm rather than merely imagining such a violation. Study 2, then, reveals the experiential facets of growing body hair, giving a stark contrast to the relatively casual assessments portrayed in Study 1.

Study 2: Lived Experiences

[...]

The findings from Study 2 emerged from a thematic analysis of a written class assignment undertaken by women enrolled in an elective upper division women's studies course at a large public southwestern university.... The sample for Study 2—the 62 participating women—included 23 (37%) women of color (primarily Latina and African American) and 39 White women.... Roughly 40 (65%) described having exclusively male partners or suggested a heterosexual identity, whereas roughly 13 (21%) described having exclusively female partners or mentioned a lesbian identity, and 9 (14%) described both male and female partners and/or a bisexual identity.

Materials and Procedure

During the fall 2010, spring 2011, and fall 2011 semesters, students were asked to participate in an extra credit assignment that asked them to grow out their body hair (underarm and leg hair) for a period of 10 weeks. Students kept weekly logs of their personal reactions to their body hair, others' reactions to their hair, changes in their own or others' behavior, and thoughts about how changes in body hair affected them....

Although I did not solicit information from students about their current body hair removal habits, five students disclosed that they already did not depilate (they were excluded from the study and not included among the 62 participants); all other women engaged in at least semifrequent body hair removal prior to beginning this assignment. There were no requirements about making the hair visible or discussing the assignment with others; students could choose if/when to disclose to others about this assignment (although most eagerly discussed it).

[...]

Women in Study 2, who actually grew their body hair, discussed these experiences by relating their body hair experiences to the social and cultural expectations placed upon women. Many women reflected on how, although they initially framed body hair as a (sometimes insignificant or casual) personal choice prior to doing the assignment, they changed their views once they grew their body hair. Four themes (sometimes overlapping) appeared in women's discussions: (a) new perspectives on the social meanings of body hair, (b) encounters with homophobia and heterosexism, (c) anger from family members and partners about growing body hair, and (d) internalized feelings of being "disgusting" and "dirty."

Theme 1: Social Meanings

. . . Any students initially felt that the assignment would be "no big deal" and that they had a vast array of personal choices about body hair. At the end of the semester, several women described new perspectives, changes of heart, or more solidified consciousness about the relationship between body hair and social norms.

[. . .]

Kelci (a White heterosexual woman) reflected on her conflicted feelings about the social meanings of her body hair:

> I really did gain a lot from the project. I learned about people and what society has deemed as outcast behavior. I did kind of feel like an outcast when people freaked out about it, but at the same time I felt like a bad ass because I stuck it out and just kind of accepted my hair as a badge of honor. . . . I love making other people step back and have a good look at real issues, issues that affect the way society has trained us all to believe that shaving is expected of women. I've been asking myself if I feel the need to conform too much to the expectations of society.

Nichole (a Latina bisexual woman) admitted that a dialectic between personal choice and social norms appeared often for her during the assignment:

> When this assignment was first given to the class, I thought it was useless. I felt that shaving was entirely my own decision and that regardless of how society plays into my life, I was the one who willingly took razors to my legs and armpits. . . . After completing this assignment, I have realized that having body hair has allowed me to see things through a deeper lens. If the males are content on putting the pressure on us, we should all rise above them and stick it to them—with our hairy legs and armpits.

Theme 2: Heterosexism and Homophobia

Women's encounters with homophobia and heterosexism—something that appeared only subtly in Study 1—typically involved one of the two scenarios: either women encountered people who explicitly said that they would not "get a man" or "find a man" if they grew body hair (heterosexism), or they encountered negative comments that body hair had directly signaled a lesbian or nonheterosexual identity (homophobia). As an example of the former, Leila (a bisexual White woman) wrote about a Facebook interaction with a male acquaintance after she posted about growing body hair:

Him: Good thing you're single right now. GULP.

Me: That is so fucking insensitive and offensive.

Him: Why offensive? Mainly my thoughts were that any girl wanting to take part in that project would be tough. Most guys don't like their girls all hairy.

Me: Body hair is not gross, first of all. It's HAIR. I'm not covering myself with leeches or refusing to use toilet paper.

Him: It's part of a daily personal care routine, like saying don't take a shower for X days.

Me: Body hair doesn't smell. I'm still showering!

Him: I and the rest of the world have this viewpoint. It's an inconvenience for you and your boyfriend or any other couple.

As an example of direct homophobia, Noelle (a White bisexual woman) described her boss's negative reaction to her body hair: "My supervisor made some lesbian jokes. He knows I am pretty vocal about feminism and gay rights, so he makes lots of jokes about my body hair, saying, 'Are you trying to tell me something?'"
[. . .]

Theme 3: Anger From Others

Several women recounted "horror stories" of their partners and families reacting with anger, disgust, and outrage about the body hair assignment. In particular, women sometimes felt pressured to seek permission from partners (especially male partners), which elicited a variety of responses. For example, Marina (a White bisexual woman) recounted her boyfriend's adamant resistance to the assignment:

When I brought up the idea of doing the project, he was automatically opposed. First I got, "Ew, no. I won't let you do that." Then I got a joking but upsetting "I will not engage in any sexual acts with you until you shave." Obviously upset and hurt that my partner would put my shaved body on such a pedestal, I decided right away that I *would* be taking part in this project. After this verbal assault on my womanhood, he went on to say how "it was pointless" and "women can do whatever they want now because it is 2011." . . . I explained that there was obviously an issue with women's body hair and that he had just qualified it in his mini panic attack over my wanting to stop shaving.

As another example of negative partner reactions, Liz (a White heterosexual woman) recalled that her boyfriend became angry and hostile when she first mentioned the assignment:

My boyfriend started yelling when I first told him, not at me but he was upset that my teacher was trying to interfere with my life in this way. He is really attracted to legs and that is a big part of our sex life. His anger made me cry.

Still, both women proceeded with the assignment and noted that it served a pivotal role in deciding whether to stay in a relationship with a man who would not accept their hairy bodies. By the end of the semester, Marina stayed with her boyfriend, whereas Liz had left the relationship.

Family reactions also revealed the powerful ways that parents and siblings monitored and controlled women's choices about their bodies. As found in previous research (Fahs & Delgado, 2011), women of color received particularly harsh judgments from their families when growing body hair. Lola, a Latina heterosexual woman, recalled how her mother found it "amusing" when the project was temporary, but when Lola threatened to do it forever, her mother became enraged: "Her voice changed from content and happy to shocked and appalled. She told how underarm hair is 'for men only' and how it makes girls look 'sloppy' and how she 'did not raise a sloppy daughter.'"

[. . .]

As an unexpected twist on family rejection, Michelle (also Latina and heterosexual) noted that her daughters (both "tweens") also conveyed these same messages of respectability: "My eldest daughter said it was gross of me not to shave for that long. She rubs my hairy legs. I heard her calling her sister names and referred to her as being disgusting like my legs."

Theme 4: Internalized Feelings

Many women struggled with feeling disgusting, dirty, and sexually unattractive, even when others did not provide that direct feedback. Anika (a White heterosexual woman) who admitted that she would readily take a pill to stop all hair growth on her body, recalled feeling preoccupied with how "gross" she felt:

My legs looked ugly and fat with their hair on. I constantly thought about my gross hair, especially at the gym. Every time I was taking a shower, every time I changed my clothes, it was always on my mind. I couldn't believe how much time I spent thinking about my hair. It was insane!

Rosa, too, felt disgusted by her armpit hair such that the mere disclosure of having it upset her: "I will never ever show anyone my pit hair. I really don't want anyone else to ever know that I ever had pit hair. Ever."

Some women also reflected on how they wanted to feel more confident about growing body hair but nevertheless caught themselves with feelings of doubt, anxiety, and self-directed disgust. Rux (a biracial bisexual woman) admitted that she wanted to feel freer than she did:

I feel like women are trained to oppress themselves, that we're brainwashed to a point that even when we question, there is still something inside us which recoils from that questioning. That's the way I felt. Even though I knew what I was doing was supposed to be freeing, and it *was* to a point, mostly I felt embarrassed and ill-defined.

[. . .]

Cat (a White bisexual woman) also expressed similar conflicts, noting that she fluctuated between feeling attractive and unattractive with body hair, even while ultimately seeing it as rebellious:

Since I am not heterosexual and somewhat actively looking for a girlfriend, will my hair growth appeal or repulse another? Today I saw some women walk by and every single one of them had their legs shaved. My initial reaction was, "Eww." That kinda took me by surprised and I laughed a bit. Kinda cool that I had that reaction.

As a final example, Leila did some soul searching after some particularly difficult encounters with coworkers:

It's hard. My coworker told me I was "brave" and she said she'd never have the courage to do that. People act like I'm standing up to Hitler! Another guy said that I should tell the teacher to go fuck herself. I'm still deciding what I want my form of resistance to be. To what extent am I going to "play by the rules"? Will I pretend to be a good member of society while actually revolting against it? My body hair remains a work in progress.

[. . .]

Women in Study 2, who faced the challenges of actually growing their body hair, had new perspectives about the meaning of body hair, particularly the compulsory aspects of needing to remove it. Women faced heterosexism and homophobia as well as anger from family members and partners about growing body hair, and they internalized feelings of "disgust" and "dirtiness" about themselves. In contrast to Study 1, the women in Study 2 discussed their violation of body hair norms as having severe consequences for them. In addition to the affective responses it provoked in others, it clearly challenged their own comfort with, and agency around, their bodily choices. In particular, it made visible the intersections between social identities like sexual identity, race, and class while also provoking them to assess their own comfort with pushing back against social norms about women's bodies.

General Discussion

[. . .]

My studies were designed to interrogate the notable differences in women's narratives about body hair when they thought intellectually and imaginatively about choice from a more abstract perspective ("How do you feel about body hair when you have not actually grown out body hair?") compared with the perspectives that emerge from the lived experiences of women growing body hair ("How do you feel about body hair after having temporarily grown out your own body hair?"). Such a contrast makes a case for the kinds of differences found when examining the rhetoric of choice from an abstract versus lived experience and from outside and within academic settings dedicated to critical thinking and feminist interrogation.

The ultimate strengths of my studies lie in their unique comparative consideration of imagined versus lived experiences of the body because most existing research on body hair has focused on attitudes about hairy (or shaved) bodies rather than on women's lived experiences of body hair (Basow & Willis, 2001; Basow & Braman, 1998; Kenyon & Tiggemann, 1998; Lewis & Tiggemann, 2004; Toerien & Wilkinson, 2004). By using qualitative research to assess the "messiness" of how women imagine the range of bodily choices available to them—both with and without actually testing the social penalties they face for deviating from social norms—we can better understand the challenges present in merely imagining issues of embodiment from afar (particularly in the classroom). A hypothetical consideration of a "deviant" body works quite differently than a tangible and literal enactment of "deviance."

[. . .]

Body hair represents an avenue into tougher and more painful discussions about gender, bodies, power, social control, invisibility of patriarchy, the fusions between heterosexism and sexism (seen vividly in men's and family members' reactions to women's body hair), and overlaps among classism, racism, ageism, homophobia, and sexism. . . . Conversations about body hair hold up a mirror to otherwise unseen aspects of gender and sexuality, making the seemingly benign ("fluffy tufts," "fuzzy patches") suddenly endowed with the power to unsettle and transform.

[. . .]

References

Basow, S. A. and A. Braman. 1998. "Women and Body Hair: Social Perceptions and Attitudes." *Psychology of Women Quarterly* 22:637–45.

Basow, S. A. and J. Willis. 2001. "Perceptions of Body Hair on White Women: Effects of Labeling." *Psychological Reports* 89:571–76.

Fahs, B. and D. A. Delgado. 2011. "The Specter of Excess: Race, Class, and Gender in Women's Body Hair Narratives." Pp. 13–25 in *Embodied Resistance: Breaking the Rules, Challenging the Norms*, edited by C. Bobel and S. Kwan. Nashville, TN: Vanderbilt University Press.

Herbenick, D., V. Schick, M. Reece, S. Sanders, and D. Fortenberry. 2010. "Pubic Hair Removal Among Women in the United States: Prevalence, Methods, and Characteristics." *The Journal of Sexual Medicine* 7:3322–30.

Hodgson, S. and M. Tiggemann. 2008. "The Hairlessness Norm Extended: Reasons for and Predictors of Women's Body Hair Removal at Different Body Sites." *Sex Roles* 59:889–97.

Kenyon, S. and M. Tiggemann. 1998. "The Hairlessness Norm: The Removal of Body Hair in Women." *Sex Roles* 39:873–85.

Lewis, C. and M. Tiggemann. 2004. "Attitudes Toward Women's Body Hair: Relationship and Disgust Sensitivity." *Psychology of Women Quarterly* 28:381–87.

Ramsey, S., C. Sweeney, M. Fraser, and G. Oades. 2009. "Pubic Hair and Sexuality: A Review." *The Journal of Sexual Medicine* 6:2102–10.

Schick, V. R., B. N. Rima, and S. K. Calabrese. 2011. "Evulvalution: The Portrayal of Women's External Genitalia and Physique Across Time and the Current Barbie Doll Ideals." *Journal of Sex Research* 48:74–81.

Toerien, M. and S. Wilkinson. 2004. "Exploring the Depilation Norm: A Qualitative Questionnaire Study of Women's Body Hair Removal." *Qualitative Research in Psychology* 1:69–92.

Toerien, M., S. Wilkinson, and P. Y. L. Choi. 2005. "Body Hair Removal: The 'Mundane' Production of Normative Femininity." *Sex Roles* 52:399–406.

Whelehan, I. 2000. *Overloaded: Popular Culture and the Future of Feminism*. London, UK: Women's Press.

The Managed Hand

The Commercialization of Bodies and Emotions in Korean Immigrant-Owned Nail Salons

Miliann Kang

© iStockphoto.com/RichLegg

The title of Hochschild's (1983) groundbreaking study of emotional labor, *The Managed Heart,* provides a rich metaphor for the control and commercialization of human feeling in service interactions. The title of this article, "The Managed Hand," plays on Hochschild's to capture the commercialization of both human feelings and bodies and to introduce the concept of body labor, the provision of body-related services and the

Miliann Kang. 2003. "The Managed Hand: The Commercialization of Bodies and Emotions in Korean Immigrant-Owned Nail Salons." *Gender & Society* 17(6):820–39.

management of feelings that accompanies it. By focusing on the case study of Korean immigrant manicurists and their relations with racially and socioeconomically diverse female customers in New York City nail salons, I broaden the study of emotional labor to illuminate its neglected embodied dimensions and to examine the intersections of gender, race, and class in its performance. . . . What are the dimensions of body labor, and what factors explain the variation in the quality and quantity of its performance? An embodied perspective on gendered work highlights the feminization of the body-related service sector and the proliferation of intricate practices of enhancing the appearance of the female body. A race, gender, and class perspective highlights the increasing role of working-class immigrant women in filling body-related service jobs and the racialized meanings that shape the processes of emotional management among service workers.

[. . .]

Emotional Labor in Body Service Work: Race, Gender, and Class Intersections

Work on the body requires not only physical labor but extensive emotional management, or what Hochschild's (1983) seminal work describes as emotional labor.

The concept of body labor makes two important contributions to the study of emotional labor: (1) It explores the embodied dimensions of emotional labor and (2) it investigates the intersections of race, gender, and class in shaping its performance. By bringing together an embodied analysis of emotional labor with an integrative race, gender, and class perspective, I show how this case study of nail salon work retheorizes emotional labor to have greater applicability to gendered occupations dominated by racialized immigrant women. . . .

While the study of beauty and the beauty industry presents a rich opportunity to explore the emotional work involved in servicing female bodies, this literature has focused attention almost exclusively on the experiences of middle-class white women consumers and their physical and psychological exploitation by the male-dominated beauty industry (Banner 1983; Bordo 1993; Chapkis 1986; Wolf 1991), neglecting the substandard working conditions, unequal power relations, and complex emotional lives of the women who provide these services. . . .

In addition to neglecting emotional work in body service jobs, the literature on emotional labor has framed the processes of interactive service work primarily through a gender lens and paid less attention to the crosscutting influences of gender, race, and class. . . .

My research expands this work not only in its empirical focus on immigrant women of color doing gendered, emotional labor but through the theoretical framework of race, gender, and class as "interactive systems" and "interlocking categories of experience" (Anderson and Hill Collins 2001, xii). This framework critiques additive models that append race and class to the experiences of white middle-class women and instead highlights the simultaneity and reciprocity of race, gender, and class in patterns of social relations and in the lives of individuals (Baca Zinn 1989; Collins 1991; hooks 1981; Hurtado 1989; Glenn 1992; Chow 1994). Thus, I demonstrate that different expectations or "feeling rules" (Hochschild 1983, x) shape the performance of emotional labor by women according to the racial and class context. . . .

By investigating the understudied area of body-related service occupations through an intersectional race, gender, and class analysis, this study of body labor reformulates the concept of emotional labor to dramatize how the feeling rules governing its exchange are shaped by interlocking oppressions that operate at the macro level (Collins 1991) and then emerge as different styles of emotional service at the micro level.

Research Design and Method

The data collection for this project involved 14 months of fieldwork in New York City nail salons. The research design included in-depth interviews ($N = 62$) and participant observation at three sites: (1) "Uptown Nails," located in a predominantly white, middle- and upper-class commercial area; (2) "Downtown Nails," located in a predominantly Black (African American and Caribbean) working- and lower-middle-class commercial neighborhood; and (3) "Crosstown Nails," located in a racially mixed lower-middle and middle-class residential and commercial area. I spent at least 50 hours at each salon over the course of several months. In the case of Crosstown Nails, which was located near my home, visits were shorter (2 to 3 hours) and more frequent (several times a week). The other two salons required long commutes, so I usually visited once a week for 6 to 7 hours.

In addition to hundreds of unstructured conversational interviews conducted as a participant-observer, the research included in-depth structured interviews with 10 Korean nail salon owners, 10 Korean nail salon workers, 15 Black customers, and 15 white customers. . . .

In-depth interviews averaged 45 minutes for customers and two hours for owners and workers. Customers were interviewed in English at the salon while they were having their manicures, and when necessary, a follow-up meeting or telephone interview was arranged. Owners and workers were interviewed in both Korean and English, depending on their preference and level of fluency.

The Contours of Body Labor

Body labor involves the exchange of body-related services for a wage and the performance of physical and emotional labor in this exchange. My study's findings illustrate three dimensions of body labor: (1) the physical labor of attending to the bodily appearance and pleasure of customers, (2) the emotional labor of managing feelings to display certain feeling states and to create and respond to customers' feelings regarding the servicing of their bodies, and (3) variation in the performance of body labor as explained through the intersection of gender with race and class. These dimensions vary across the different research sites and emerge as three distinct patterns of body labor provision: (1) high-service body labor involving physical pampering and emotional attentiveness serving mostly middle- and upper-class white female customers, (2) expressive body labor involving artistry in technical skills and communication of respect and fairness when serving mostly working- and lower-middle-class African American and Caribbean female customers, and (3) routinized body labor involving efficient, competent physical labor and courteous but minimal emotional labor when serving mostly lower-middle and middle-class racially mixed female customers. The data presentation admittedly flattens some of the variation within each site to clarify distinctions between them, but this typology highlights the dominant physical and emotional style of service at each salon.

Uptown Nails: High-Service Body Labor

A seasoned Korean manicurist who has worked at Uptown Nails for nearly 10 years, Esther Lee is in high demand for her relaxing and invigorating hand massages. She energetically kneads, strokes, and pushes pressure points, finishing off the massage by holding each of the customer's hands between her own and alternately rubbing, slapping, and gently pounding them with the flare that has wooed many a customer into a regular nail salon habit. Margie, a white single woman in her mid-30s who works for an accounting firm, smiles appreciatively and squeezes Esther's hand: "I swear, I couldn't stay in my job without this!" Esther reciprocates a warm, somewhat shy smile.

Uptown Nails boasts leafy green plants, glossy framed pictures of white fashion models showing off well-manicured hands, recent fashion magazine subscriptions stacked neatly on a coffee table, and classical CDs on the stereo system. The salon has been in operation for 13 years, and three of the six employees have worked there for more than 10 years. The customers sit quietly sipping their cappuccinos, updating their appointment books, or at times politely conversing with each other about the weather or the color of the nail polish they are wearing. Located in a prosperous business district of Manhattan, an Uptown Nails manicuring experience involves not only the filing and polishing of nails but attention to the customer's physical and emotional comfort. From the gentle removal of undernail dirt, to the careful trimming of cuticles and buffing of calluses, to the massaging of hands and feet, Korean manicurists literally rub up against their customers, who are mostly white middle- and upper-class women. The owner, one of the earliest pioneers in the nail salon industry, currently operates six very profitable salons in prime Manhattan locations and visits this salon only once a week to take care of paperwork. The owner, manager, and employees are all middle-aged Korean women with fluent English-language ability, reflecting the greater expectations for communications with customers. The physical dimensions of body labor in Uptown Nails, including hot cotton towels, bowls of warm soaking solution, sanitized utensils, and calming background music, all indicate considerable attention to creating a pleasurable sensory experience for the customer. Particular attention is given to avoiding nicks and cuts and sterilizing and apologizing profusely when they occur.

In addition to this extensive physical pampering, Uptown Nails prioritizes the emotional needs of customers regarding the servicing of their bodies. The mostly white middle-class customers at this salon place great importance on emotional attentiveness as a crucial component of the service interaction. Kathy, a personal trainer, elaborated,

> Having them done is a pleasure, a luxury. Doing them myself is tedious, having them done is a treat. It's the whole idea of going and having something nice done for myself. If I do them myself, it's just routine upkeep of my body—like washing your hair or keeping your clothes clean. . . . Of course it makes it more enjoyable if they are friendly and can talk to you. If they can't remember my name that's okay, but I think they should recognize me.

The proper performance of body labor thus transforms a hygienic process, otherwise equated with washing hair or clothes, into a richly rewarding physical and emotional experience. The satisfaction Kathy experiences from the manicure derives not only from the appearance of the nails but the feeling of being special that accompanies attentive body servicing. To generate this feeling, customers expect the manicurist to display a caring demeanor and engage in pleasant one-on-one conversation with them.

Service providers recognize customers' high expectations with regard to both the physical and emotional dimensions of body labor, and they respond accordingly. Judy Cha, a 34-year-old who immigrated in 1993, describes the emotional and physical stressors that accompany high-service body labor, particularly giving massages to earn tips and engaging in conversation.

> Three years ago we didn't give a lot of massages but now customers ask more and more. It makes me weak and really tired. . . . I guess because I don't have the right training to do it in a way that doesn't tire my body. Some manicurists give massage all the time to

get tips, but sometimes I don't even ask them if I'm tired. Owners keep asking you to ask them, but on days I'm not feeling well, I don't ask. . . . One of my biggest fears working in the salon is, what if I don't understand what the customer is saying? They don't really talk in detail, just say, "how is the weather." But in order to have a deeper relationship, I need to get past that and to improve my English. It makes it very stressful.

Thus, manicurists work hard to conform to the high-service expectations of middle-class white women, but while the performance of caring, attentive emotional labor is noticeably higher than that afforded in the other research sites, it often does not meet customers' expectations. In particular, many Uptown Nails customers disapprove of the use of Korean language by the manicurists as a violation of proper attentiveness in beauty service transactions and suspect that they are being talked about (Kang 1997).

Cathy Hong, a 32-year-old manicurist who immigrated in 1999, sums up the assumptions many of the Uptown Nails customers have regarding access to a regular manicure delivered with high-service body labor: "These women get their nails done regularly because it has become a habit to them, they take if for granted. Just as we wash our face daily, American women get their nails done."

Downtown Nails: Expressive Body Labor

Entering another borough, the scene inside Downtown Nails differs as radically as the neighborhoods in which these two salons are located. Squeezed between a Caribbean bakery and a discount clothing store, a worn-out signboard displays the single word "NAILS" and a painting of a graceful, well-manicured hand holding a long-stemmed rose and pointing to a staircase leading to the second-story entrance. Upon being buzzed in through the locked door, the customer is greeted with a display of hundreds of brightly colored airbrushed nail tips lining an entire wall. The noise level in the salon is high, as various electronic nail-sculpting tools create a constant buzz to match the flow of the lively conversations among the mostly Black customers. On a weekend afternoon, Downtown Nails is filled to capacity, and the wait for a preferred "nail artist" can be more than an hour. Mostly Caribbean and African American women, the customers engage in animated conversations while sharing coco buns and currant rolls from the downstairs bakery. The banter ranges from vivid accounts of a recent mugging near the salon to news about the pay freeze in the nearby hospital where many of the women work as nurses or technicians.

A far cry from the spa-like pampering experience of Uptown Nails, a nail job at Downtown Nails is closer to a stint on a factory assembly line: highly mechanized and potentially toxic. Absent are the elaborate sanitizing machines and solutions, let alone the soft pampering touches. Despite these appearances, body labor at Downtown Nails involves a complex mix of physical and emotional labor that accommodates customers' desires to express a unique sense of self through their nail designs and their expectations that service providers demonstrate both individual respect and appreciation to the community. . . .

The importance of the physical appearance of the nails themselves as opposed to the pampering experience of receiving these services is dramatized by customers' concern with the design of the nails versus the massage and other services that customers at Uptown Nails regard as integral and Downtown Nails customers view as extraneous. Jamilla, a 26-year-old African American part-time student and waitress, proudly displays her inch-and-a-half-long nails, each one adorned with the skyline of New York City in bold black, framed by an orange and yellow sunset. A regular patron of Downtown Nails for six years, she explains why she is willing to spend "$50–$60 every two weeks" for elaborate hand-painted designs:

> Because I don't like looking like anyone else. My nails say "me." They're the first thing people notice about me. I have big hands for a female. I never had those long, thin lady-like fingers. My father used to say my hands were bigger than his. I want long nails because they make my hands look more feminine.

Indicating a preference for nails that reflect very different norms of femininity than the demure, pastel tones prevalent at Uptown Nails, Jamilla elaborates further on her nail aesthetics. "It all depends on my mood. Like this design makes me feel like I'm on top of the city, like it can't bring me down [laughing]. . . . No one's gonna mess with you when you got nails like these." Jamilla's pride in having originally designed nails that no one else can reproduce suggests the importance of her nails as an expression of her individuality that also communicate a sense of self-efficacy and protection, as indicated in her comments that no one would "mess" with a woman with nails like hers. To meet the expectations of customers such as Jamilla, body labor at Downtown Nails calls for development of expertise in sculpting and painting original nail designs rather than in the soothing, pampering services offered at Uptown Nails. Thus, the physical demands of body labor are not less but simply of a different type.

Similarly, the emotional dimensions of body labor at Downtown Nails are not different in degree so much as kind. The customer's race and class location intersect to produce much lower expectations among working-class Black customers for emotional attentiveness than the white middle-class women at Uptown Nails. While it is clearly less attentive, Serena, an African American grocery store cashier, assesses the emotional labor at Downtown Nails positively.

> It's very good, I'm satisfied with it. They really just do the nails, no massages. That's fine with me. I just go in with my Walkman and listen to some good music and maybe just have a little basic conversation.

Customers at Downtown Nails rarely are on a first-name basis with the service providers, and their preference for a particular manicurist is based much more on her technical skills than her emotional attentiveness. . . .

Emotional labor at Downtown Nails calls less for sensitivity to pampering of individual customers and more for demonstration of values of respect and fairness that recognize the complex dynamics of Korean businesses operating in Black neighborhoods. This includes efforts such as sponsoring a Christmas party to thank customers for their patronage, participating in community events, displaying Afrocentric designs, and playing R&B and rap music. Mrs. Lee, the co-owner of the salon, allows regulars to run an informal tab when they are short of money and keeps a change jar that customers dip into for bus fare, telephone calls, or other incidentals. It is not uncommon for customers to drop by even when they are not getting their nails done to use the bathroom or leave shopping bags behind the front desk while they complete errands. These efforts at "giving back to the community" entail a distinct form of emotional labor that conforms not to white middle-class women's feeling rules of privilege and pampering but to Black working-class women's concerns about being treated with respect and fairness. . . .

Expressive body labor thus prioritizes both the meanings of the nails as a form of self-expression to working-class Black customers and the expression of symbolic but tangible efforts to respond to the feeling rules of respect and fairness governing Korean immigrant service providers in predominantly Black working-class neighborhoods.

Crosstown Nails: Routinized Body Labor

Located on the second floor above a fashionable boutique, Crosstown Nails is clean but sparse and utilitarian. In many ways, this salon is representative of the most prevalent style of service offered in Korean-owned nail salons: fast, cheap, basic manicures and pedicures with no frills. The McDonald's of the nail salon industry, Crosstown Nails offers a manicure that is standardized and predictable in both its physical and emotional aspects.

This salon often has customers waiting, but even when it is busy, the line moves quickly as each customer is whisked in and out of the manicuring seat with crisp efficiency. The customer chooses her nail color, presents it to the manicurist who asks her to specify the desired shape of the nail, and then soaks her nails briefly in a softening solution. Depending on her preference, her nails are either trimmed or pushed back. The manicurist offers to give a massage, but it is perfunctory and lasts usually not more than a minute. After carefully layering on two coats of polish and a quick-drying topcoat, the customer moves to a heated hand dryer where she converses with other customers or more often "zones out."

Many customers come from the neighboring hospital during lunch hour or after work. Situated on the edge of a fashionable, high-rent, racially diverse residential district and a lower-income but also racially mixed neighborhood, Crosstown Nails captures the broad range of customer interactions that many Korean service providers negotiate in a given day. In large, high-immigrant-receiving cities such as New York, service interactions often involve multiracial rather than binary interactions between Koreans and Blacks or Koreans and whites. . . .

The secret of Crosstown Nails's success is its ability to appeal to customers who lack excess disposable income and normally would not indulge in a professional manicure but are attracted by the convenience and price. Julia, a white bartender, commented,

I'm kind of a ragamuffin, so it kind of surprises me that I get them done as often as I do, which is still much less than most people in the city. It's just so easy to do here, and cheap.

Julia's description of herself as a "ragamuffin" suggests that she does not adhere to strict codes of femininity in her dress or other beauty routines, as indicated by her casual peasant skirt and no makeup. Nonetheless, easy and cheap access draws her into purchasing regular manicures.

Many customers at Crosstown Nails seek manicures not as a pampering experience or as creative expression but as a utilitarian measure to enhance their self-presentation at work. Merna, an Afro-Caribbean clinical researcher, explained,

I only get them done about every two months. I don't want to get attached to it. For some women it's such a ritual, it becomes a job—maintaining the tips and stuff. I'm presenting my hands all day long so it's worth it to me to spend some time and money to make sure they look good.

Merna regards manicured nails as a professional asset more than a core aspect of a gendered self. Thus, the style of her nails and the meaning she gives to them are more similar to the white middle-class customers at Crosstown Nails than to the Black working-class customers at Downtown Nails.

In general, middle-class Black customers like Merna mostly exhibited similar nail aesthetics to those of middle-class white women, suggesting the greater importance of class over race in influencing nail styles and expectations of body labor, particularly in routinized settings such as Crosstown Nails.

Discussion

In what ways is nail salon work gendered? In what ways are these gendered work processes remolded by race and class? Understanding the influence of race and class on the gendered performance of body labor in Korean-owned nail salons illuminates how gendered work processes reflect and reproduce racial and class inequalities at the level of social structures. Nail salon work is gendered in four major dimensions: (1) It involves mostly female actors, as both service providers and customers; (2) it focuses on the construction of beauty according to feminine norms; (3) it is situated in feminized, semiprivate spaces; and (4) it involves the gendered performance of emotional labor.

In describing each of these dimensions, I do not emphasize how socialized gender roles are acted out in these establishments, but rather how gender operates as a social institution that lays the groundwork for the very existence of these businesses and frames the interactions that occur within them. . . .

I argue that as gendered institutions, they cannot be separated from forces of racial and class inequality.

If, as Paul Gilroy (1993, 85) asserted, "gender is the modality in which race is lived," then race, and I argue class as well, are lived in these nail salons and other body-service sites as differences in gendered styles of body labor. Interactions in Korean female immigrant-owned nail salons illustrate how the gendered practices of body labor become the locus of expressing and negotiating race and class hierarchies between white, Black, and Asian women. High-service body labor, as performed at Uptown Nails, is similar to the style of caring, attentive emotional labor practiced by Hochschild's flight attendants and conforms to the feeling rules of white middle-class women. Expressive body labor focuses on the physical appearance and artistry of the nails and the communication of respect and fairness in serving mostly working- and lower-middle-class African American and Caribbean women customers at Downtown Nails. Routinized body labor stresses efficiency, predictability, affordability, and competency in physical labor and a courteous but no-frills style of emotional labor geared toward mostly lower-middle- and middle-class racially mixed female customers at Crosstown Nails.

These patterns of body labor conform to the racial and class positions of the customers and the associated feeling rules that define their service expectations. At Uptown Nails, race, gender, and class intersect to produce an emotionally and physically pampering form of body labor that conforms to the expectations of white, professional women for caring and attentive service. These women have high expectations regarding massages, cleanliness, sensitive touch, and friendly conversation while Black, working-class women at Downtown Nails expect minimal pampering and focus on the appearance, originality, and durability of the nails themselves. At Crosstown Nails, class prevails over race as both Black and white women of middling socioeconomic status view the nails instrumentally as a no-nonsense professional asset rather than conforming to traditional notions of pampered femininity. Thus, they trade off the physical pleasure and emotional attentiveness of high-service treatment for the convenience and price of routinized body labor.

Black middle-class women at Crosstown Nails share this instrumental view of nails and a preference for a routinized, hassle-free manicure. The style of nails and the meaning given to them by Black middle-class women radically differ from the working-class Black women at Downtown Nails, who value nail art as a form of self-expression and demand emotional labor that communicates respect and fairness. This contrast between the Black middle-class and working-class women customers at Crosstown and Downtown Nails again suggests the greater salience of class over race in determining the type of body labor.

What structural factors explain the differences in the provision of body labor in these three sites? These body labor types, while enacted at the micro level, reflect the social conditions of the neighborhoods in which the salons are located and the clientele they serve. Because of the reliance on tips in white middle-class neighborhoods, service providers have greater incentive to cater to the emotional needs of customers such as those at Uptown Nails to increase their earnings. In the Black working-class neighborhoods where tipping is not a widespread practice, nail salon workers guarantee their economic livelihood by establishing a base of regular customers who seek them out for their technical and artistic abilities more than their emotional or physical attentiveness. In routinized body labor settings serving lower-middle-class women of mixed races, service providers maximize their earnings by generating a high turnover of customers who receive satisfactory but not special emotional and physical treatment.

These patterns of body labor service reflect and reproduce racial and class inequalities between women. Korean service providers learn to respond to white middle- and upper-class customers' emotional pampering and physical pleasure, thereby reinforcing the invisible sense of privilege claimed by these customers. The expressive practices of creating artful nails and troubleshooting potential problem with Black working-class customers, while helping to smooth relations, can also serve to emphasize racial meanings in these interactions and enforce a sense of difference. The routinized style of body labor reflects the generic social position of women whose bodies are neither privileged nor pathologized but simply treated with routine efficiency.

Conclusions

[I]n mapping out the racial, gendered, and classed complexity of body labor, this article highlights a kernel of social change that lies in negotiating service interactions between women of different classes, racial and ethnic backgrounds, and immigrant statuses. While these interactions often mimic structures of power and privilege, they also create opportunities to contest these structures. The Korean salon owner of Downtown Nails learns to respect and show appreciation for Black working-class patrons. Korean manicurists at Uptown Nails assert their knowledge and expertise over their white middle-class customers. Routinized service at Crosstown Nails equalizes treatment of women across race and class.

From the customer's side, a weekly trip to the local nail salon can become a lesson in relating to a woman of a radically different social position, whom she would rarely encounter in her own milieu. As these emotional and embodied interactions reflect larger systems of status and power, by rewriting the unspoken feeling rules of these interactions, women can take small but important steps in the creation of more equal relations with other women. Glenn (2002, 16–17) wrote that "contesting race and gender hierarchies may involve challenging everyday assumptions and practices, take forms that do not involve direct confrontation, and occur in locations not considered political." Exchanges involving body labor in Korean-owned nail salons are one such location where these everyday assumptions and practices can be recognized and possibly renegotiated.

References

Anderson, Margaret and Patricia Hill Collins. 2001. *Race, Class, and Gender: An Anthology.* Belmont, CA: Wadsworth.

Baca Zinn, Maxine. 1989. "Family, Race, and Poverty in the Eighties." *Signs: Journal of Women in Culture and Society* 14:856–74.

Banner, Lois. 1983. *American Beauty.* New York: Alfred A. Knopf.

Bordo, Susan. 1993. *Unbearable Weight: Feminism, Western Culture and the Body.* Berkeley, CA: University of California Press.

Chapkis, Wendy. 1986. *Beauty Secrets.* Boston, MA: South End.

Chow, Esther Ngan-Ling. 1994. "Asian American Women at Work." In *Women of Color in U.S. Society*, edited by M. B. Zinn and B. D. Thornton. Philadelphia, PA: Temple University Press.

Collins, Patricia Hill. 1991. *Black Feminist Thought: Knowledge, Consciousness, and the Politics of Empowerment.* New York: Routledge.

Gilroy, Paul. 1993. *The Black Atlantic: Modernity and Double Consciousness.* Cambridge, MA: Harvard University Press.

Glenn, Evelyn Nakano. 1992. "From Servitude to Service Work: Historical Continuities in the Racial Division of Paid Reproductive Labor." *Signs: Journal of Women in Culture and Society* 18:1–43.

Glenn, Evelyn Nakano. 2002. *Unequal Freedom: How Race and Gender Shaped American Citizenship and Labor.* Cambridge, MA: Harvard University Press.

Hochschild, Arlie. 1983. *The Managed Heart: The Commercialization of Human Feeling.* Berkeley, CA: University of California Press.

hooks, bell. 1981. *Ain't I a Woman: Black Women and Feminism.* Boston, MA: South End.

Hurtado, Aida. 1989. "Relating to Privilege: Seduction and Rejection in the Subordination of White Women and Women of Color." *Signs: Journal of Women in Culture and Society* 14:833–55.

Kang, Miliann. 1997. "Manicuring Race, Gender, and Class: Service Interactions in New York City Korean Nail Salons." *Race, Gender, and Class* 4:143–64.

Wolf, Naomi. 1991. *The Beauty Myth: How Images of Beauty Are Used Against Women.* New York: William Morrow.

Gender Capital and Male Bodybuilders

Tristan S. Bridges

© iStockphoto.com/Kappri

I have to keep on being a bodybuilder. I can't use my street credit anywhere else. This is the only place it works. . . . No one else gets us. We're the freaks to lots of people, but here, we're like gods.

Chris, 255 lb, professional bodybuilder,
36, physical trainer, 18 years on the bench

Bodybuilders are in the business of developing a "physical" (Shilling, 1993) or "bodily" capital (Wacquant, 1995). This is a capital that has greater relative value within specific fields of practice but would be identified as "masculine" in almost any setting. However, what that masculinity is worth varies by context. As the quote above illustrates, some bodybuilders understand their bodily capital as contextually significant in the distribution of cultural

Tristan S. Bridges. 2009. "Gender Capital and Male Bodybuilders." *Body & Society* 15(1):83–107.

status. Utilizing Bourdieu's notion of cultural capital, this work builds on the conceptualization of hegemonic masculinity by developing a new hybrid concept: gender capital.

Cultural capital is part of a larger theory of the social character of "taste" that gained widespread popularity following its original conceptualization (Bourdieu and Passeron, 1977). Most broadly, cultural capital refers to the resources (e.g., knowledge, body image, tastes) that individuals employ to gain status in certain contexts. Hegemonic masculinity is another theoretical concept that has received celebratory attention since it was proposed (Carrigan et al., 1985; Connell, 1987). The concept was established to recognize status asymmetries in inter- and intragender relations (Connell, 1998). Thus, it was first conceptualized to discuss the ways that men can be more or less "manly." Both concepts have since been reexamined and re-articulated. The purpose of this article is to build on the theoretical strength of both concepts by developing "gender capital."

Bodybuilders have also received scholarly attention, particularly among those interested in gender, sport and studies of the body (e.g., Gillett and White, 1992; Klein, 1993; Monaghan, 1999, 2001; Wiegers, 1998). They provide an example of the utility of gender capital. Cultural capital and hegemonic masculinity are strategies for making sense of systems of valuation that vary between and among groups, and by context (Bourdieu, 1984; Connell, 1987, 1995). The development of both concepts enabled studies of not only inter-group variation (e.g., men relative to women), but intra-group relations (e.g., men relative to other men).

In this article, I address two main issues: (1) What is gender capital and how does it build on cultural capital and hegemonic masculinity? (2) How do relations among bodybuilders and between bodybuilders and other men (and women) illustrate the utility of gender capital? Gender capital refers to the value afforded contextually relevant presentations of gendered selves. It is interactionally defined and negotiated. Thus, gender capital—similar to both cultural capital and hegemonic masculinity—is in a state of continuous (though often subtle) transformation. This article illustrates that bodybuilders are often aware of the different contextually contingent and gender-political messages their massive figures send.

A Methodological Note

Daren pointed at me and, talking with the three men he was working out with, said, "This man over here think he can study us. . . . I hope he likes hanging out at the gym." (from author's field notes)

This article emerged from a one-year ethnography of four "hard-core" bodybuilding gyms in two US East coast cities carried out in 2004–5. One city was a smaller, less urban environment, while the other was a major metropolitan city.

I use pseudonyms when referring to the sites I studied, which I am conceptually combining into one gym—"Mount Olympus"—for heuristic purposes. . . . Despite disparate physical locations, these bodybuilders occupy one "field" with a set of transferable capital, an aesthetic disposition, and tastes all their own. . . .

My purposive sample is composed of 43 aspiring, amateur and professional male bodybuilders. A large component of this study was participant observation, but I interviewed a number of participants as well. More than half of the interviews came from the larger city (23), as there were more bodybuilders in these gyms. Eleven interviews were performed in the smaller city. The remaining participants (9) were observed but not interviewed. Some men figure more prominently in the research than others: 12 men form the bulk of my observations.

Interviews ranged from 20 minutes to approximately two hours in length, averaging 35 minutes.

[...]

Why Study Bodybuilders?

[...]

The task for sociologists is not only to discuss the ways that bodybuilders have a relationship with a hegemonic masculine form, but also to discuss the ways that they physically and discursively manage capital field-specifically. Here, I am not interested in cultural, bodily or gender capital per se, but in the ways that the status and meanings of these capitals vary not only between and within groups, but by context as well. For instance, bodybuilders often have high status in the gym. However, their gender capital purchases a different sort of masculinity outside the gym. While it is not new to argue that bodybuilders are peculiar on more than one level (Gillett and White, 1992; Klein, 1986; Wiegers, 1998), this article will explore the ways that their peculiarities are delicately tied to the transformative quality of gender capital.

[...]

Before defining cultural capital we must first clarify what it is that Bourdieu means when he defines "capital" as:

[A]n energy which only exists and only produces its effects in the field in which it is produced and reproduced, each of the properties attached to class is given its value and efficacy by the specific laws of each field. (1984: 113)

By defining capital as energy, Bourdieu allows its impact to vary. Capital has much more to do with the perceptual status of—and relations between—resources than it does with the objective resources themselves. *Cultural capital* refers to specific repertoires of knowledge, tastes, dispositions and objects of desire that individuals within particular social spaces perceive and employ for status accumulation. The content of cultural capital only matters as it is evaluated in social practice. It will differ by the individual making use of it, and actors will employ it differently—or employ different situationally relevant cultural resources—in different contexts.

[...]

Connell's theory is concerned with the distinction between gender categories and gender relations: "The key is to move from a focus on difference to a focus on *relations*. Gender is, above all, a matter of the social relations within which individuals and groups act" (2002: 9). Difference, dichotomy and categories are included in gender relations, but gender relations are also much more. Gender relations include the processes by which gendered distinctions are made. This is why Garfinkel (1967) refers to gender as an "ongoing accomplishment," Goffman (1977) discusses gender as a social "arrangement" and West and Zimmerman (1987) address the "doing" of gender. Gendered distinctions only make sense within the logic of the fields in which they are made. Connell is also critically concerned with the ways in which power is implicated with gender relations. To discuss power, Connell introduces four concepts: gender regime, gender order, the patriarchal dividend and hegemonic masculinity.

Gender regime is a concept developed to address the issue of field-specificity: why do different contexts have different systems of gender valuation and evaluation? A *gender regime* is a local set of interactional arrangements concerning gender. Elements of gender regimes go above and beyond clothing, intellect, styles of speaking, etc. to the very gender of interactional predispositions, proclivities and preferences toward which individuals are inclined. While gender regimes are internally varied and subject to change as well, Connell argues that changes in regimes tend to be resisted (Connell, 1987, 2002).

Gender regimes are also parts of wider patterns of gender relations that endure over time and space. These wider, more durable patterns are what Connell refers to as the *gender order* (Connell, 1987, 2002). Separate gender regimes may have different degrees of affinity with the gender order.

[. . .]

Hegemonic masculinity is the name that Connell gives to the currently accepted form of masculinity that dominates women and other men (Connell, 1995), subordinating not only femininity, but also other masculinities (Connell, 1987). Hegemonic masculinities vary by gender regime, as gender relations are contextually arranged and continually transforming (Connell, 2002). Counter to this regime-specific conceptualization of hegemonic masculinity, some research has attempted to define it more statically, calling attention to groups of men as upholding the patriarchal order (e.g., Connell, 1990; Gillett and White, 1992; Klein, 1986). However, this denies hegemonic masculinity precisely the transformative capacity that makes it so powerful: it is largely elusive and continually in flux (Connell and Messerschmidt, 2005). Because hegemonic masculinity is negotiated regime-specifically, individuals encounter distinct masculinities occupying the hegemonic position in distinct fields of interaction and historical moments. "'Hegemonic masculinity' is not a fixed character type, always and everywhere the same. It is, rather, a masculinity that occupies the hegemonic position in a given pattern of gender relations, a position always contestable" (Connell, 1995: 76).

[. . .]

Gender capital refers to the knowledge, resources and aspects of identity available—within a given context—that permit access to regime-specific gendered identities. Bodies are not the only source of gender capital, but they are an important source. "A body is a piece of consequential equipment, and its owner is always putting it on the line. Of course, he can bring other capital goods into many of his moments too, but his body is the only one he can never leave behind" (Goffman, 1967: 167). Bodies are integral parts of the social construction of gender. As identities are now more deliberately undertaken than ever before (Giddens, 1991), men have increasingly come to see their bodies as "their responsibility to discipline" (Gill et al., 2005: 55).

Some gender capital maintains similar value across social settings. That is, some forms of gender capital are more trans-situationally "durable" than others. Bourdieu reasons that this is the result of the capital belonging to larger fields, while Connell argues that certain gender capital is a part of the gender order. However, much gender capital varies significantly by context. Individuals employ different aspects of self in different settings to negotiate differently gendered identities (West and Zimmerman, 1987). Above all, "gender capital" [means] what is valued in gender identities may vary widely by context and setting. Gender capital attempts to foreground the independent effect of context on the relative value of gendered presentations of self.

[. . .]

Gender capital also removes some of the difficulties surrounding the use of hegemonic masculinity. For example, gender capital may differ for men and women in certain respects, and overlap in others. In different settings, confidence may be highly valued whether associated with masculinity or femininity. Factors utilized as gender capital by men have changed much throughout history as well and differ by culture. Long hair was a sign of nobility among men when Benjamin Franklin wore it, and while contemporary rock musicians may retain the ability to utilize long hair as "masculine" gender capital, few contemporary politicians are capable of doing the same.

Simply put, the value of bodies is dictated largely by the contexts in which they are presented. . . . Gender capital can exist as practice, knowledge, bodily capital, style, tastes and more: aspects of "self" and social performance that produce gendered statuses within interactional orders.

[. . .]

Gender capital is also defined, employed and evaluated within a patriarchal gender order that values a hierarchical relationship between masculinities and femininities, regardless of contextual distinctions. Thus, domination, subordination, marginalization and complicity remain paramount in discussions of gender capital. Bodybuilders help to underline some key dimensions of gender capital. So let us now turn to an examination of gender and identity in the social world I call Mount Olympus.

The Bodybuilders of Mount Olympus

> This is what guys are supposed to do. Sometimes people think it's because we feel like nobody inside, so we get all big and stuff. . . . But that's not it. . . . Everyone is all about making themselves beautiful. Some of these people do it with, like, clothes or whatever, and expensive jewelry. . . . I don't need to buy anything. I spend time on my body. It's the same thing, just looks different. (Kevin, 220 lb, amateur bodybuilder, 27, bouncer at a club, 7 1/2 years on the bench)

If there is a single recurrent theme that dominates many of the representations and discussions of the bodybuilding world—what Appadurai (1988) refers to as a strong trope—it is undoubtedly *insecurity*. The grunts and groans that typify the gym setting are thought not only to be the guttural sounds of strongmen, but also impassioned pleas for attention and recognition. What sociologists have found most interesting about men's bodybuilding is that it transparently illustrates a sense of insecurity in the development of a masculine self (e.g., Connell, 1990; Gillett and White, 1992; Klein, 1986, 1993; Wiegers, 1998) most illustratively portrayed by Klein's (1993) discussion of bodybuilders as "little big men." Knowing this, I did not expect to find the confident exteriors I first encountered at Mount Olympus.

As the quote above illustrates, Kevin does not perceive himself as any more insecure than other kinds of men (or people for that matter). His quote expresses the belief that everyone is looking for what they perceive to be an adequately gendered self through the use of regime-specific gender capital. While sports cars work for some men, money and occupational prestige for others, bodybuilding is a similar process of acquiring and utilizing gender capital that purchases temporally and contextually contingent gendered identification and status. The regime-specificity of gender capital is explicitly ignored when bodybuilders are thought of only as insecure, rather than—like most people—insecure in certain contexts. While this article is principally concerned with regime-specificity, I will also briefly address issues to do with power and larger gender-political concerns.

Drew started bodybuilding about six years ago. He now works at a nightclub in the evening checking IDs at the door, breaking up fights and ensuring that patrons do not drive home under the influence. The following excerpts from field notes express the ways in which Drew epitomizes the regime-specificity of gender capital.

> A movie theatre is about two blocks from the gym. New action movies are typically a big topic of conversation [at Mount Olympus], particularly debates concerning the body of the star. Having knowledge of the new action movies is a big deal here. It struck me that, although I enjoy action movies, I am clearly less proud of that fact than these men [body-builders]. I walked back from the theatre after a morning workout with Andre, Kevin, and Drew (they all have night jobs and are part-time physical trainers at the gym). . . . Two men walked by us in the opposite direction. As they walked by, they began to laugh and as we looked back at them, they seemed to be laughing at Andre, Kevin and Drew. . . . Drew hung his head, "Fuck, I hate that." "Shake it off man," Kevin consoled him. *Drew would never have let someone get away with that in the gym.* (from author's field notes, emphasis added)

In the gym, Drew was one of the stronger bodybuilders. Although strength does not necessarily have an impact on the size and definition of the body, stronger bodybuilders regularly tease the less strong. Drew's strength was not understood as an asset on our walk back from the movies. But inside the gym, Drew was different.

> Drew finished a set of incline dumb-bell presses [a chest lift] with 130 lb dumb-bells. He was lifting with Johnny. They spot each other [help each other lift]. Drew set his weights down and asked Johnny what weight he wanted to use as Johnny sat down on the bench. "Gimme the 100s." Drew went over and picked up the 100 lb dumb-bells, brought them back over to Johnny and set them down by his feet. [This is typical of lifting buddies so that energy is not expended on carrying the weights over to the bench.] After setting them down, Drew used a lisp to say, "These weights are so cute. Can I get you drink or something? . . . Bitch. 110s on your third [set]?" (from author's field notes)

This is a very different Drew than the one with whom I walked back from the movies. Drew's gender capital purchased a different sort of identification here. His musculature and strength were not laughed at in the gym; he was given high status for his bodily form. Beyond not being laughed at for his physique, he was able to use it to put others down. Typical of bodybuilders in the gym, Drew is extremely confident and believes that he is among the best in the community I studied. As the judging of bodybuilding competitions is often subject to the subjective whims of judges—something often complained about—confidence is understood as an important resource in this setting. This "emotional labor" (Hochschild, 1983) might not alter judges' opinions, but it enables bodybuilders to cope with loss and perceived "negative" evaluations of the gender capital they work so hard to attain. Strength and musculature enable Drew to be confident in the gym, but these resources did not have the same effect outside of the gym. Outside, in a different field, Drew was either less confident in his gender capital, or interactionally aware of the different value his body had in a different setting.

This did not necessitate Drew's conscious awareness of the contextual contingencies of the social status of his gender capital. Rather, he illustrates through his *interactional* awareness that he understands this feature of social life, likely through repeated socialization and subordination. This could be an analogous process to the ways in which children become interactionally aware of topics that we all know about, but no one discusses, what Zerubavel (2006) refers to as "open secrets."

Connell (1987, 1995, 2002) distinguishes intra-gender status relations by referring to hegemonic masculinity as well as marginalized, subordinated, and complicit masculinities. While there are macro-level gender relations, social actors are also uniquely called upon to evaluate individual contexts as they interact with them in different ways—often only making subtle alterations in the performance of their social selves. Drew occupies a hegemonically masculine status in the gym, but his masculinity appeared more subordinate in the interaction outside of the gym. Hence, the reason for talking about gender *relations* in the first place (Connell, 1987, 1995, 2002): *gender is relationally (or interactionally) accomplished.* As a result, local regimes have to negotiate nuanced ways of illustrating the "rules of the game" to newcomers. Humor often plays a distinct role in this socialization process and the reproduction of inequality (Goffman, 1959, 1967).

For example, when Kevin starts to work out with a new bodybuilder, joking is a large part of his socialization. Malik—a young black man who just moved to the city to work out with other competing bodybuilders—works at a storage and loading dock for a large furniture company. Kevin asks him how he likes his "out-of-gym" employment and if he has to lift too much at work, which could hurt Malik's gym performance. He also asks jokingly if the men Malik works with tease him about being a bodybuilder.

Kevin: You work with boys or men?

Malik: Huh?

Kevin: Boys or men. . . . What? Okay, that's when . . . okay, a man respect work. Maybe you get big while he get rich, but you both work. A boy . . . man, a boy tell you . . . a boy is when like, says, like, "You fag" or like, "Pretty boy" this. . . . A boy can't handle a man like you, 'cause you work.

Malik: (laughter) Yeah. Men man, men. Most of these guys [that work with me] are tryin' to get off the street too. I get mine [receive status and respect] for my shit [my dedication to my body]. I'm not tryin' to be a punk [out on the street without a job] (laughter). (field notes taken as soon as possible after the interaction took place)

Kevin is doing two things here. He is asking Malik if he has noticed the contextuality of the gender capital he is accumulating through his work at the gym, and he is instructing him that work environments are available where Malik does not have to be ridiculed for the gender capital in which he has invested time and energy (where he can work with "men"). While these are not always high-status occupations, it is not atypical for individuals to desire to work and play in environments in which their gender capital is considered valuable.

It is likely the case that a great deal of gender capital has regime-specific status. However, it is particularly clear among bodybuilders because of the stark contrast between gym and non-gym settings, and the extreme type of gender capital they possess. Their bodies often go from the height of exaltation and social status to the subject of ridicule (Fussell, 1992; Monaghan, 1999). Some of the bodybuilders in this study were more capable of dealing with contextual contingencies and status distinctions than others, though it was a constant strain for most. In an interview, Chris, an older bodybuilder conscious of regime-specificity, said: "I can't use my street credit anywhere else. This is the only place it works. . . . No one else gets us. We're the freaks to lots of people, but here, we're like gods." While Chris is exaggerating when he states that the gym is the "only place it works," he carefully points out the regime-specificity of gender capital. Chris has also been around long enough to understand and be comfortable with this.

Bodybuilders have many stories in which their gender capital was a source of ridicule and shame. However, most of the bodybuilders I studied also found social spaces where their gender capital purchased high status, like Malik. Bouncers and doormen at bars and clubs were also able to utilize bodybuilder gender capital. Not surprisingly, these were extremely popular jobs. Many bodybuilders worked together both in and outside of the gym. When I first found out that some of the men were bouncers I thought that injuries would be a concern, as they can ill-afford to miss workouts and still compete. However, this is something that bodybuilders do not worry about.

> Jeff and Bruce worked out together today. It was leg day, so both were struggling to enthusiastically engage with their lifts. To pump each other up, they began talking about the night they were about to have together. While they are both bouncers at clubs, they do not typically work together, but tonight they are because Jeff's manager asked for extra guys due to some men leaving, and Jeff was able to recommend Bruce [who would much rather work at Jeff's club than his current location]. This is Bruce's unofficial "tryout" for Jeff's club. "How full will it get tonight?" asked Bruce. Jeff said, "It's all up [all full]. It's always crazy on Fridays, but we just lost like three guys, so we'll be short tonight." "Okay. I can't get hurt though. I only have like two months left [before a competition]," said Bruce. "Look at you son, nobody can get at you. Big mother fucker. Don't trip . . . and don't say that kind of shit around Dave [the manager]." (from author's field notes)

I later asked Jeff if injuries were a concern despite his discussion with Bruce. He laughed. "Would you ever hit Bruce?" "No," I said. "Nobody else would either," said Jeff. He walked away acting as though I had asked a stupid question.

Bouncing is another field in which male bodybuilder gender capital (and bodily capital) often has purchase, although likely in a different way. In the gym, bodybuilders have high status due to their work ethic, strength and the "look" of their bodies. As Chris stated after a long day in the gym, "Props [respect is given] to all those that get in early and get out late." Bars and clubs afford the gender capital of these men a different status: fear and bodies that stand as symbols of violence. Monaghan (2002) had similar findings among doormen in Britain. "[B]odily capital may be transformed into other forms of capital such as income and masculine validating recognition" (Monaghan, 2002: 337). Jeff explained to me the status of bodybuilders as bouncers. "Nobody wants a guy like me on 'em. . . . I scare myself. People respect, but they can't, like, they can't really not. You know?"

Jeff and Bruce are extremely large men, both over 200 pounds. They pat patrons down as they enter the club and check IDs, often muttering "No trouble tonight" to rougher-looking men. In this way, they are also letting people know that they will have to deal with a very large man if they "start trouble." They are symbolically in control of the environment long before they would ever have the need to physically control it. Bruce later reiterated this point in an interview.

> I would actually never get in a fight at work. I wouldn't want to risk, like, getting hurt or something. . . . It doesn't matter though. I never had a situation where I mighta' had to. Most times, if there's trouble, I just walk over and say, like, "Hey, buddy, you need to take it somewhere." . . . The times that someone looks like he might swing on me or something, I got some other guys with me [for assistance]. One time, this one guy's friends pulled him out the bar 'cause, like, they don't want him to try get mixed up either [fight with me]. So, I don't really worry. (Bruce, 235 lb, amateur bodybuilder, 32, bouncer at a club, 10 years on the bench)

However, later in the same interview, Bruce chuckled, "Seems nice, yeah? Try getting out of a speeding ticket with this shit (flexing an arm)." He perceived his gender capital as precluding the possibility of receiving only a warning from a police officer for driving too fast.

Interactions with the police were a popular topic of conversation. Bodybuilders were both proud of and frustrated with the ways in which they understood police as "dealing" with them. Many of the men in my study felt that police seemed to unfairly pick them out of a crowd. Two black bodybuilders at Mount Olympus had the following discussion while taking a lifting break.

> Jerome: "I fucking hate cops. . . . They always follow me around and shit. I'm not tryin' to do nothing [illegal]. Kid, they just can't handle these guns" (flexes a bi [bicep] and grins). Others laugh. Derrick agrees with him and talks about being followed at a grocery store like he was going to steal. Lots of laughter. (from author's field notes)

The police represent a different set of gender relations—or gender regime (and perhaps the gender order)—wherein some people are in charge, not because of their individual gender capital, but because of the power of the positions they occupy. This is also interesting because, in the gym, black bodybuilders are treated and interacted with in much the same ways as white bodybuilders. However, outside of this field, it is likely that huge, muscular black men are interpreted in a qualitatively different way from their white counterparts.

The police symbolize a "masculinity challenge" (Messerschmidt, 2000) among bodybuilders. Messerschmidt (2000) defines masculinity challenges as confrontations between conflicting masculinities. Many bodybuilders understand the police as symbolically representing a masculinity challenge. Though I did not hear of any bodybuilders getting into actual fights or arguments with police, there was another group in the gym that presented similar "challenges": the powerlifters.

The powerlifters at Mount Olympus occupy a separate gender regime, though many aspects overlap with the bodybuilders. Conflict is ever present, but rarely erupts into arguments or fights. While bodybuilders lift for definition and size, powerlifters lift for strength. Connell notes that: "It is common for different groups of men, each pursuing a project of hegemonic masculinity, to come into conflict with each other" (1995: 215). Powerlifters provide a sort of ubiquitous masculinity challenge, serving to both reaffirm distinctions between groups and solidarity among them.

Distinctions between bodybuilders and powerlifters also illustrate the ways in which gender regimes are not always represented as geographically separate in terms of *physical* space. "Different masculinities are [sometimes] produced in the same cultural or institutional setting" (Connell, 1995: 36). Gender regimes represent *social* spaces, or what Goffman (1983) refers to as "interactional orders." An individual can be physically in the middle of a group of individuals who all occupy the same field (or gender regime) while being outside of the field. Think of the experience of "not getting" a joke that everyone else around you seems to understand. In many cases, context, group-specific knowledge and interactional styles preclude your comprehension of the joke, not that you simply missed the punch line.

Based on the jargon, lifting noises and presence in the "heavy weight room," both groups might actually appear more similar than they are. I assumed that powerlifters were bodybuilders when I began my study. I thought that they had more recently begun the process of transforming into a bodybuilder and had not yet attained the same level of definition and size as others. The distinctions between the two subcultures are inscribed into their bodies, and while both are groups of very large men, their bodily and gender capital within the gym setting are different from one another. Gender capital distinctions, particularly when both groups interact with one another, become apparent inside the gym setting. What counts as masculine gender capital differs by group:

> Bodybuilders, powerlifters and individuals who want to "tone up" and "trim down" might each use dumb-bells and bar-bells, for example, and might even do the same exercises (bench press, squat, etc.). However, the way in which they do those exercises will vary. (Crossley, 2005: 12)

As both groups are very vocal, masculinity challenges are a regular feature of the gym's interactional order.

When I asked one of the more seasoned powerlifters—Javier—why powerlifters and bodybuilders tease each other, his response illuminates a popular way in which powerlifters view bodybuilders.

> Because they are gay. . . . I mean, just look at them. Gay! . . . They are always touching each other and checking each other's bodies and stuff. It's nasty. . . . I think they're just all acting like they don't want to get with guys. . . . That's all they talk about though . . . guys' bodies and different parts and stuff. Nasty! . . . We fuck with those guys [tease them] 'cause they act all gay like that. They try to pretend and be all man and all that, but they mostly be shaving their legs and wearing thongs . . . it's just gay. I don't know what else to say. (Javier, powerlifter, 26, 4 1/2 years on the bench)

While I did meet two male bodybuilders who openly identified as homosexual, Javier was not referring to those two. The two homosexual bodybuilders were no different from their heterosexual counterparts in the gym in most respects. Aside from Javier's comments about their sexuality, the rest of his comments are true of bodybuilding subculture. There is a great deal of bodily interaction, they closely examine each others' bodies, they shave their entire bodies (causing razors to be a nearly constant accessory for bodybuilders), and competition requires the use of a very small "posing suit" that would be referred to as a "male thong" in almost any other setting. Much of this "hyper-masculine" behavior is ironically "feminine" in many other contexts. Bodybuilders' gender capital is highly contingent upon context. This is Javier's point. It was not unusual to hear powerlifters calling bodybuilders "gay," "fag," "fairies," etc. Another powerlifter reiterated this point.

> Bodybuilders are mainly a bunch of fuckin' homos [homosexuals]. Serious though . . . I mean those guys are all over each other (laughing). . . . Nobody takes that shit seriously. They're fags. I don't really think they're all manly or whatever. They're girly to me. (Freddie, powerlifter, 27, construction worker, 6 years on the bench)

Bodybuilders have a different way of talking about powerlifters to illustrate distinctions in gender capital. Bodybuilders value definition and size much more than strength. As a result, lifting as much as possible just to lift as much as possible (the powerlifter philosophy) is seen as "immature" among bodybuilders. Kevin jokingly explained how bodybuilders view powerlifters:

Powerlifters are basically a bunch of jocks that never got over leaving high school. They're all like, trying to relive the glory days. . . . I mean, they are just not like us [bodybuilders]. They're like, stupid. They don't lift right and, I'm just sayin', they are some ugly dudes . . . you know? (Kevin, 220 lb, amateur bodybuilder, 27, bouncer at a club, 7 1/2 years on the bench)

Bodybuilders in my study often attributed the "dumb jock" stereotype to powerlifters. From the point of view of a bodybuilder like Kevin, it is difficult to understand why someone would disregard technique solely to display power. Although these two groups occasionally work out together, the gender capital distinctions became clear the more I came to learn.

It is common for bodybuilders to criticize the lifting techniques and movements of power-lifters in the gym. The use of "too much" weight (bodybuilder perspective) does not enable the lifter to maximize the benefit of each lift; rather, it enables the lifter to bear full capacity (powerlifter perspective). Crossley (2005) addresses this by coining reflexive body techniques, which he defines as "those body techniques whose primary purpose is to work back upon the body, so as to modify, maintain or thematize it in some way" (2005: 9). As Crossley (2005) seeks to show in his work, groups that maintain similar reflexive body techniques share much more than only bodily forms. Hence, the ways in which exercises are performed can serve to delineate group boundaries.

[. . .]

Conclusion

It's not like I'm the man wherever I go. . . . People gonna treat you different, if like, well, they treat you different. . . . I mean not everybody out there is like, tryin' to make you feel good. You gotta' do that for yourself. So . . . like, me and these guys [the other bodybuild-ers at Mount Olympus], we hold each other up here [in the gym]. Out there, you hold yourself. That's life. (Malik, 190 lb, aspiring amateur bodybuilder, 25, part-time mover at a furniture warehouse, 4 years on the bench)

Discussions of hegemonic masculinity in the sociology of gender—and perhaps masculinities studies in particular—have yielded diverse meanings and uses. However, when drawing upon practice, . . . an important meaning and intention of hegemonic masculinity is perhaps made more clear. Hegemonic masculinity, like cultural capital, refers to the social value of regime-specific configurations of status, knowledge, body image, performances, etc. While bodybuild-ers are a population that make this distinction viscerally obvious, I suggest that they are perhaps more similar to the rest of us in their negotiation of multiple fields of gendered interac-tion than they are different.

Allowing the meaning and content of gender capital to vary regime-specifically opens up new and interesting questions for sociological and feminist research. What types of interac-tional orders foster hegemonically masculine identifications consistent with the peaceable potential of hegemonic masculinity? How does power operate within gender regimes relative to what is considered "high-status" gender capital? How does power connect gender regimes to larger fields of interaction (e.g., politics, the economy, the gender order)? When is violence a resource and when is it stigmatized? These types of questions are only available to us if we first acknowledge that what "count" as dominant forms of masculinity or femininity (what I am referring to as gender capital) are much more fluid or regime-specific than they are sometimes treated.

Finally, introducing gender capital into our vocabulary for describing gender (and perhaps sexuality as well) allows for a few other contributions. First, both men and women possess gender capital, albeit often different types and in different ways. With the recent academic interest in discussions of the "degendering" of society (e.g., Kimmel, 2007: 339–44; Lorber, 2005)—or what West and Zimmerman (2009) call a society in which gender has been "redone"—it will be increasingly important to develop a vocabulary that allows us to talk about gender without having to address it as *either* masculine *or* feminine. Connell's conceptualization precludes researchers from addressing gender regimes in which androgynous gender capital is valued, other than identifying them as subordinated from a more macrosocial perspective. This is not to argue against the continued use of hegemonic masculinity. In fact, when used as an open concept, I think that this is one of the more powerful conceptual tools sociologists of gender have.

Hegemonic masculinity is a useful term when looking at the ways in which bodybuilders *do* gender. However, it is potentially less useful when attempting to compare the ways in which bodybuilders are doing much the same thing as everyone else, though the value of their presentations of self may be less trans-situationally durable than most. More generally, I suggest that gender capital allows us to compare the gender projects of bodybuilders to those of anyone—not only gender "extremists." Future research should pay close attention to the contextual fluidity of gender capital, as well as the gender-political implications that it resists, expresses or attempts to hide.

[. . .]

References

Appadurai, A. 1988. "Putting Hierarchy in Its Place." *Cultural Anthropology* 3(1):36–49.
Bourdieu, P. 1984. *Distinction*. Cambridge, MA: Harvard University Press.
Bourdieu, P. and J. Passeron. 1977. *Reproduction in Education, Society and Culture*. London, UK: Sage.
Carrigan, T., R. W. Connell, and J. Lee. 1985. "Toward a New Sociology of Masculinity." *Theory and Society* 14:551–602.
Connell, R. W. 1987. *Gender and Power*. Stanford, CA: Stanford University Press.
Connell, R. W. 1990. "An Iron Man: The Body and Some Contradictions of Hegemonic Masculinity." In *Sport, Men and the Gender Order*, edited by M. Messner and D. Sabo. Champaign, IL: Human Kinetic Books.
Connell, R. W. 1995. *Masculinities*. Berkeley, CA: University of California Press.
Connell, R. W. 1998. "Reply." *Gender & Society* 12(4):474–77.
Connell, R. W. 2002. *Gender*. Cambridge, UK: Polity Press.
Connell, R. W. and J. W. Messerschmidt. 2005. "Hegemonic Masculinity: Rethinking the Concept." *Gender & Society* 19(6):829–59.
Crossley, N. 2005. "Mapping Reflexive Body Techniques." *Body & Society* 11(1):1–35.
Fussell, S. W. 1992. *Muscle: Confessions of an Unlikely Bodybuilder*. New York: Harper.
Garfinkel, H. 1967. *Studies in Ethnomethodology*. Cambridge, UK: Polity Press.
Giddens, A. 1991. *Modernity and Self-Identity*. Stanford, CA: Stanford University Press.
Gill, R., K. Henwood, and C. McLean. 2005. "Body Projects and the Regulation of Normative Masculinity." *Body & Society* 11(1):37–62.
Gillett, J. and P. G. White. 1992. "Male Bodybuilding and the Reassertion of Hegemonic Masculinity: A Critical Feminist Perspective." *Play and Culture* 5:358–69.
Goffman, E. 1959. *The Presentation of Self in Everyday Life*. New York: Doubleday.
Goffman, E. 1967. *Interaction Ritual*. New York: Doubleday.

Goffman, E. 1977. "The Arrangement Between the Sexes." *Theory and Society* 4(3):301–31.

Goffman, E. 1983. "The Interaction Order: American Sociological Association, 1982 Presidential Address." *American Sociological Review* 48(1):1–17.

Hochschild, A. 1983. *The Managed Heart.* Berkeley, CA: University of California Press.

Kimmel, M. S. 2007. *Gender and Society.* 3rd ed. New York: Oxford.

Klein, A. 1986. "Pumping Irony: Crisis and Contradiction in Bodybuilding." *Sport Sociology Journal* 3(2):112–33.

Klein, A. 1993. *Little Big Men: Bodybuilding Subculture and Gender Construction.* New York: SUNY Press.

Lorber, J. 2005. *Breaking the Bowls.* New York: W. W. Norton.

Messerschmidt, J. 2000. "Becoming 'Real Men': Adolescent Masculinity Challenges and Sexual Violence." *Men and Masculinities* 2(3):286–307.

Monaghan, L. F. 1999. "Creating 'The Perfect Body': A Variable Project." *Body & Society* 5(2–3):267–90.

Monaghan, L. F. 2001. *Bodybuilding, Drugs and Risk.* London, UK: Routledge.

Monaghan, L. F. 2002. "Hard Men, Shop Boys, and Others: Embodying Competence in a Masculinist Occupation." *Sociological Review* 50(3):334–55.

Shilling, C. 1993. *The Body and Social Theory.* London, UK: Sage.

Wacquant, L. 1995. "Pugs at Work: Bodily Capital and Bodily Labour Among Professional Boxers." *Body & Society* 1(1):65–93.

West, C. and D. Zimmerman. 1987. "Doing Gender." *Gender & Society* 1(2):125–51.

West, C. and D. Zimmerman. 2009. "Accounting for Doing Gender." *Gender & Society* 23(2):112–22.

Wiegers, Y. 1998. "Male Bodybuilding: The Social Construction of a Masculine Identity." *Journal of Popular Culture* 32(2):147–61.

Zerubavel, E. 2006. *The Elephant in the Room: Silence and Denial in Everyday Life.* New York: Oxford University Press.

Body Modification and Trans Men

The Lived Realities of Gender Transition and Partner Intimacy

Katelynn Bishop

> *I think that Michael is sexy not because of the sex organs that he has, [but] because of the way that he talks, and the way that he walks, certain things that he wears . . . how his cologne smells, how he does his hair. I am attracted to Michael sexually, not Michael's body parts. . . . I've realized that [what body parts he has] is just not important to me, intimacy is what's important to me. . . . I feel that when you love someone, you kind of transcend beyond being a lesbian, or a bisexual, or a pansexual, or, whatever, or straight, you know, you just are a couple, and if you have intimacy I believe that you can get through anything together.*

This quote is taken from a YouTube video in which Helen, a 27-year-old woman who appears to be white, discusses her relationship with her partner, a trans man who appears white and similar in age. The video is one of many that Helen has uploaded to a YouTube channel for partners of trans men. In the course of her videos, Helen explains that she identified as a lesbian for several years before meeting Michael and that the two of them were in a committed lesbian relationship for five years before he came out as trans. Helen's privileging of her "intimacy" with Michael over his "body parts" challenges the reduction of trans people and their relationships to body parts in both medical and popular discourses. Yet, Helen does not strictly demarcate the "intimate" as that which is not sexual or embodied, but instead suggests that sexuality and intimacy are entangled. This article delves into the interrelationships between sexuality and intimacy, and bodies and identities, by examining how trans men's changing bodies are experienced by established intimate partners. Drawing on an empirical analysis of partners' narratives in YouTube videos, blogs, and interviews, I explore a number

Katelynn Bishop. 2016. "Body Modification and Trans Men: The Lived Realities of Gender Transition and Partner Intimacy." *Body & Society* 22(1):62–91.

of questions raised by Helen's narrative, including: Do sexual organs simply *not matter* for partners' experiences of intimacy and desire, or do they matter in ways not captured by dominant discourses that conceive of bodies in "parts"? What is the relationship between the materiality of the body and the "person," as experienced by an intimate partner? How does sexual identity matter for attraction to one's intimate partner?

I argue that partners do not experience trans men's bodies as "dumb matter" or generic parts, but instead that partners' intimate bonds with trans men as people are crucial in shaping how they relate to trans men's bodies. Partners report that they are able to sustain an understanding of who trans men are as people through their gender transitions, despite fears about how testosterone might impact trans men's emotions, behavior, or ability to communicate, and in the face of the drastic bodily changes trans men undergo. The process of sustaining an intimate connection to a trans partner—while understood by sociologists within the framework of emotional labor (see Pfeffer, 2010; Ward, 2010)—is also affective and embodied, and partners' narratives about this process work to de-link gender from conceptions of essential personhood. I also find that partners' established intimate relationships with trans men form the context for the emergence of new bodily relations of desire; partners feel desire for bodily changes they might find unattractive in other contexts, and find the process of bodily change itself erotic. Within the context of these intimate partnerships, ideas about which bodies can be viewed and desired as male or masculine are expanded, and the literalness of sexual identity labels is undercut. Thus, the lived realities of gender transition, as they materialize within the context of intimate and embodied relations between trans men and their partners, challenge hegemonic conceptions of gender, sexuality, and desire in a number of ways.

[...]

Rather than scrutinizing these trans men's chosen paths to securing livable embodiments (Salamon, 2010), I aim to document the complex configurations of gender, sexuality, and desire that materialize as their gender transitions are lived out in relation to intimate others.... In addition, I work toward a relational view of how bodies matter, rather than privileging the body subject, or individual trans person.

[...]

Accessing Trans Men's Partners' Experiences: Methods and Data

To address how partners experience trans men's changing bodies, I analyze data from semi-structured, in-depth interviews conducted with 11 partners of trans men, and publicly available YouTube videos and blogs where partners share their experiences with trans men's transitions.

[...]

I conducted the interviews in 2011 as part of a larger study exploring how partners negotiate trans men's transitions. I specifically sought out interviewees who were partnered with trans men through some part of transition, broadly defined. Of the 11 interviewees, all but one met their partner before he came out to others as trans. Thus, the interviewees were generally partnered with trans men as they navigated the personal, social, and embodied aspects of transition.

[...]

When asked to identify their "gender," seven interviewees self-identify simply as "female"; one as "gender-queer/female" and one as "genderqueer/male"; one identifies on the "trans-masculine spectrum"; and one describes herself as a "cisgender, cissexual woman." All are white, most identify as middle-class, and when interviewed their ages ranged between 22 and 42. . . .

I also analyzed videos posted on three YouTube channels devoted specifically to partners of trans men, or FTMs: TmatesFTM, FTMSweethearts, and TransScribersFTM. . . . Contributors typically post 5–10-minute-long videos each week. In most videos, partners of FTMs appear alone, though in some videos the couples appear and speak together.

I reviewed videos on a wide variety of topics; for the purposes of this analysis I draw on videos from weeks covering issues relating specifically to trans men's bodies and body modifications. . . . Almost all appear and/or identify as women, and a few of the women identify themselves as genderqueer. They seem similar in age to interview participants. . . . I collected data from the YouTube channels in 2012 and 2013.

[. . .]

I also collected data from the publicly available blogs of four partners of trans men in 2012 and 2013. . . . The bloggers post with varying frequency and with varying levels of detail, and at the time I collected data had kept their blogs for periods between three months and two years. . . . I do not claim that my sample is representative of those partners who stay with trans men through transition; this sample likely over-represents white, middle-class, young, highly educated, and US located partners of trans men, though my use of multiple forms of data helps to increase the representativeness of the sample. Thus, rather than seeking to produce generalizable findings, I explore how this particular group of partners experience intimacy and desire in relation to trans men's changing bodies.

The Technologies of Transition: T, Surgeries, and Beyond

[. . .]

Nearly all interviewees, YouTube contributors, and bloggers say their trans partners are taking testosterone, which they commonly refer to as T; of the few whose partners are not, most say they plan on using it in the future. Most of the trans men who take T do so through injection, and many partners describe performing the intimate and embodied labor of injecting T into trans men's bodies. Many partners were in relationships with trans men when they first began T, and their trans partners have been using the hormone for periods varying from a few months to a few years. T, as detailed by partners, has a slew of striking material effects, including the growth and thickening of body hair, clitoral enlargement, deepening of the voice, redistribution of body fat, and other changes in the shape of the body and face, such as the broadening of the shoulders and jawline. Partners also point to changes in trans men's mood and personality as potential effects of T. Partners describe the changes effected by T as gradual and often unpredictable, as each man responds to the hormone in a unique way, and on his own timeline.

Many partners also report that T is often trans men's first permanent transition-related body modification, given that doctors often require them to take T for up to two years before obtaining transition surgeries. T is also easier to obtain financially for many trans men, compared to surgeries. Yet, even given this relative accessibility, the prevalence of T usage among these trans men may point to their overwhelming whiteness and affluence, as access to hormonal technologies is stratified by race and class, and various forms of privilege are required to navigate the medical institutions that regulate access to them (Preciado, 2013 [2008]).

Nearly all the trans men have had or plan to have top surgery, or one of a few available procedures for reconstructing the chest. Most partners say that top surgeries are crucial to trans men, as these procedures alleviate the intense dysphoria they commonly experience in relation to their chests, and aid them in attaining recognition as men in their daily encounters. Further, most say that prior to receiving chest surgeries their trans partners routinely used binders to flatten their chests, a practice that can be painful and potentially dangerous, and thus not necessarily sustainable as a long-term practice. Many of the trans men—sometimes with the assistance of their partners—are still raising money to cover the cost of this expensive procedure. Most of these trans men are located in the US, where the procedure is only sometimes covered by private insurance policies; partners from some European countries report that the procedure is covered by state health care plans. One US partner relays the disappointment she and her trans partner suffered when his surgery was cancelled at the last minute, due to changes in his insurance coverage. Whereas T gradually takes effect over months and years, partners describe the difficulties in adjusting to the sudden physical changes resulting from these procedures (though this suddenness is tempered by the years of anticipation preceding these surgeries, along with trans men's alteration of their physique through binding prior to them).

Only a few partners report that their trans partners are planning to have genital surgery, or what is referred to as bottom or lower surgery. Partners describe two available surgical procedures: metoidioplasty, in which surgeons "free" the clitoris from the skin surrounding it, and phalloplasty, in which surgeons construct a penis using skin grafts. These surgeries present greater economic barriers than chest surgeries; one YouTube contributor comments that the prohibitive cost of phalloplasty in particular means asking, "Do you want a house or do you want a penis?" Further, they cite the perceived greater risk of medical complications and their dissatisfaction with the available surgical techniques as reasons for ambivalence about these surgeries. For the most part, the trans men who do intend to obtain bottom surgery plan on having metoidioplasty, which partners say results in a more functional, though smaller, penis. Though most of the trans men do not plan to have bottom surgery, their partners convey that many of them utilize body technologies including packers (prosthetics worn in the underwear for everyday or non-sexual occasions), stand-to-pee devices (devices which allow them to pee while standing up), and prosthetics (for sexual use).

[. . .]

T and (Potential) Changes to Emotions, Behavior, and Communication

Partners commonly express fears about how transition—and particularly the use of T—might change who trans men are "as people." Partners of trans men who have not yet begun to use T, or who are still anticipating its gradual effects, worry that the hormone might alter trans men's emotions, behavior, or ability to communicate, leading to violent outbursts or extreme anger, sexual aggression, or the inability to cry or to communicate emotions effectively. Though most partners ultimately conclude that T does not change the essence of trans men's selves, their fears about how the ingestion of a material agent (T) might affect their trans partners' selves point to the co-constitutive nature of bodies and identities. . . .

A few partners express anxieties about trans men becoming "different people" in ways that reveal how bodily features coded as "masculine" evoke ideas about particular masculine behaviors or emotions. Some partners say they imagined and feared their partners' bodies morphing into monstrous, violent male forms; these images merge the body's contours and the personality. For instance, one video respondent, Helvi, associated growing muscles with aggressive behavior:

> It's really dumb, but I sort of had this concern that him becoming more muscular would change his personality and he would become this person who fights at bars, and gets really aggressive or something, but yeah, I'm really starting to believe that that's not gonna happen.

Lauren, an interviewee, also presents an image of the caricatured masculine body, but connects her fear of her partner becoming a man to past sexual trauma:

> I have a trauma history, specifically with men, so to now be in a relationship with a man in this capacity, it brings things up, and I was terrified of testosterone when he started taking it. I thought it would turn him into the Hulk. I had nightmares for weeks about, you know, him taking a shot and just turning into this big green monster. And obviously that hasn't happened.

Helvi and Lauren are careful to punctuate their narratives by admitting that their fears have not come to pass, and in painting these fears as misguided they arguably perform important supportive work in validating their trans partners' identities and transitions (see Pfeffer, 2010; Ward, 2010).

[. . .]

Other partners point to the work that can be necessary to reconcile trans men's changing bodies with their sense of who their trans partners are as people. This process is exemplified by partners who say that they have had to adjust their own reactions to their trans partners' changing voices, as they have become deeper and, to them, harsher-sounding. Rori, a video respondent, describes communication difficulties that have arisen due to her partner's changing voice:

> [Because] Devon's voice is a lot deeper now; . . . things can come out sounding sharper or angry-sounding. . . . That's come up multiple times for us, where in some situation, I feel like, why are you so mad right now, all of a sudden, and why are you speaking to me that way? And we talk about it, and that's not Devon's intention at all. And so, in those kind of situations, I'm recognizing that I have my own sensitivities, I have my own preconceived notion of what Devon sounds like and now that is different, and so I'm working with recognizing that I have to shift that a little bit, I have to re-learn what their intonation sounds like, and what . . . emphasis Devon's putting on different things means in their voice, and I recognize that I also am a very sensitive person, and so, um, this very quiet super soft-spoken introverted person speaking up in maybe a little bit louder or gruffer way is new to me, and I'm having to recognize that my own sensitivities are playing into our interaction with that as well.

While Rori reacts affectively to Devon's changing tone of voice, this reaction is re-worked by her own efforts to interpret material changes within the social context of their intimate relationship. Rori maintains here that her partner is still the same person despite changes in their tone, yet her stable sense of her partner's self emerges only through social and interpretive processes.

[. . .]

Whereas most of the debate on psychopharmaceuticals has focused solely on the individuals using these drugs, partners' narratives about T demonstrate how intimate relations are constituted through gender technologies, and how notions of core or authentic selves are—far from being essential or pre-social truths—*produced* through intimate interactions.

Changing Bodies and Shifting Desires: Entanglements of Sexuality and Intimacy

Partners' fears about whether T will change trans men as people point to the significance of the intimate contexts in which trans men's transitions take place. In this section, I examine how partners experience desire for trans men as their bodies change. Their connections to trans men as people are central to their narration of these experiences, illustrating the entanglement of sexuality and intimacy. These narratives indicate that neither the desired nor desiring body can be understood as a raw substance or "fleshy materiality" pre-existing social processes. Partners do not simply respond sexually (with their own bodies) to the objectively present material properties of trans men's bodies, but instead, their own embodied experience of and desire for trans men's bodies is inseparable from their intimate bonds with trans men as people. Trans men's "flesh" (as well as the "flesh" of their intimate partners) thus emerges within relations of desire (Merleau-Ponty, 1962).

Some partners describe their desires as shifting along with trans men's changing bodies. These partners say that desire for one's trans partner's body is sensitive to his own self-image, and that desire can be learned and/or re-learned in relation to his self-image. In some cases, partners describe learning desire in relation to a partner's self-image from the beginning of the relationship. One video respondent, Helvi, reflecting on her partner's chest surgery, says:

> I think that now Chris is, well, he's the sexiest he has ever been. And even though he hadn't had the mastectomy [yet] when we got together, I knew from the beginning that those breasts [were] gonna go at some point, and they were not a turn-on for me, they were just there, and it's a great relief that they're gone now.

In contrast, other participants changed their definitions of which parts of the body were erotic, in response to their partner's changing self-image, or their partner's disclosure of his self-image. For example, Vivian, an interviewee, says:

> In the beginning [of our relationship] I remember being really excited about his boobs, but now I could really care less, and I kind of like when he binds. . . . I think as soon as I realized how not interested in his own boobs he is, they became a turn-off. I don't want to be attracted to this body part that he himself thinks is terrible for a lot of reasons, so I kind of switched that off, and now I think my attraction is growing with him, with the image of himself he wants.

Helvi's and Vivian's narratives illustrate how the desired body emerges somewhere between the objectively present body and the shared psychic investments of trans men and their partners. They also suggest that the masculinity of the body is not reducible to parts—or, in this case, to the objective presence or absence of "breasts"—but instead emerges within intimate and sexual relations.

[. . .]

A few partners describe the process of their partners' bodily change as itself erotic, and discuss how these changes impact their sexual practices. Rachel, a video respondent who says she is generally more attracted to female bodies but loves her partner's male body, speaks at length of the excitement she experiences in relation to her partner's changing genitals:

> I am sexually attracted to his dick growth, the more it grows the more I like it. I love exploring his changes, he smells different now, everywhere. And I like exploring it, and seeing how much it changes, because his dick, was you know, obviously like normal-sized for a bio female, as a clitoris, and then, and then it started growing, and you just see these subtle changes, like, all the sudden, it's poking out more and more, um, folds are getting a lot thicker, and when you pull back any kind of skin, like how far back you can see, because now you can actually see like a ridge, it looks like an actual penis, it's really really cool, um, so I do, I find it really really sexy, honestly, I love it.

[. . .]

Emotional intimacy forms the foundation for the continuity of their desire for their trans partners, and also broadens their capacities to experience new bodily relations of desire, and to experience the changing body itself as a source of eroticism. These insights help to specify some of the ways in which relations of sexuality and desire are particular (Merleau-Ponty, 1962). Further, these partners' narratives display a striking openness to and celebration of the shifting forms "dicks" might take, and the varying ways in which trans men's bodies might function sexually. These narratives thus stand in stark contrast to the narrow and phallocentric definitions of sexual function characterizing discourses about masculine bodies in other contexts, including the medical and broader cultural discourses about intersex bodies, and about erectile (dys)function and the use of Viagra (Karzakis, 2008; Loe, 2004; Mamo and Fishman, 2001).

Other partners focus directly on how their attraction to their partners' changing bodies complicates their general patterns of attraction or their understanding of their sexual identities. One video respondent, Cherise, says:

> Considering that I'm a lesbian, I definitely had to be in love with you. . . . I had to be in love with you to love those changes about you, because, had I not known you before, it would have been a little bit more difficult for me to accept those kind of things, 'cause I'm not attracted to men.

And another partner, Shannon, writes on her blog:

> I don't understand how it is that this man, guy, who grabbed my heart and soul and body as a female, is still able to give my butterflies butterflies. His body right now, turns me on. The thought of his body as a male, turns me on. The thought of him covered in hair makes me want to run my hands and my naked body through it. The thought of him waxed or hairless makes me need to shift in my chair. Things that in or on other people do not hold my interest, or make me uncomfortable or I just don't like, when I consider them on him, make me all hot and bothered!

[. . .]

These partners all continue to understand themselves through categories of sexual identity (even as they complicate the meaning of these categories); in this regard, their narratives contrast with Helen, the partner whom I discuss in the introduction and who suggests that intimate couples "transcend" sexual labels. Yet, together these narratives reinforce the idea that intimate bonds serve to open up space for the emergence of new bodily relations of desire, including desire for bodily changes as well as sexual acts one might otherwise find undesirable.

Some partners express concern over whether they will continue to be attracted to their partners as their bodies change. Yet, these partners tend to downplay the relevance of pure sexual attraction to these concerns, and instead frame them as fears about their partners changing as people. In discussing how she is dealing with her partner's recent top surgery, one blogger, Wendy, writes:

> Let's just say [coming to terms with the surgery has] been difficult. It's not that I'm so into breasts that I can't live without them. . . . I think it's more about being with someone who is essentially altering who they are.

[. . .]

Stephanie foregrounds "attraction" in discussing her concerns in a YouTube video, but demonstrates that her attraction to her partner is inseparable from her intimate connection to him as a person. She says:

> My one big concern is the attraction thing. Everyone I've talked to has said that it's not unreasonable of me to be questioning whether or not I'm still gonna be attracted to him once he starts testosterone, and I'm totally nervous for it because I know I'm dating this really sexy, awesome, funny boy, and I'm just scared testosterone's gonna change that. And I don't know if I'm gonna like waking up to some big hairy hormonal boy thing with smelly pee every single morning.

Joanne, an interviewee, says she worried over the possibility of the loss of hearing the voice to which she has grown accustomed say, "I love you." Another interviewee, Megan, says she worried over whether her partner would look like himself if he underwent surgery to masculinize his facial features, though she qualifies this worry by adding that she was *not* worried about losing her attraction for him. These narratives demonstrate how bodily change is never simply reducible to material changes such as the size and contours of body parts, or the pitch of a voice, but always entangled with how the body signifies the self.

Conclusion

Through my analysis of partners' experiences of trans men's changing bodies, this article challenges popular and medical understandings of trans bodies which reduce them to parts. The materiality of trans men's bodies, as experienced by their intimate partners, goes far beyond the presence or absence of particular body parts, and is inseparable from partners' understanding of who trans men are as people. . . .

My findings center on two main aspects of partners' experiences: how partners overcome fears that trans men will change as people as they transition, and how partners experience desire in relation to trans men's changing bodies. Although partners fear that testosterone and other bodily changes might change who trans men are as people, they discover that they are able to continue to understand trans men as essentially the same people through their transitions. The essence of who trans men are as people is not simply given, however, but rather involves partners' social and material efforts to maintain their view of trans men's essential personhood. Partners are also able to sustain or increase their sexual attraction for trans men's bodies as they change, even in the face of bodily changes they might find unattractive in other contexts. Their sexual attraction is not reducible to desire for generic body parts, but is instead responsive to trans men's self-image. The particularity (Merleau-Ponty, 1968; Salamon, 2010) of their intimate bonds and histories with their partners thus allows for the emergence of new bodily relations of desire.

Although these trans men might be positioned as "normative" within some discourses about trans embodiment, their gender transitions, as lived out within their intimate relationships, challenge a number of hegemonic conceptions about gender, sexuality, and desire.

Partners' fears about how testosterone might impact trans men's emotions and ability to communicate are rooted in broader constructs and stereotypes of masculinity, yet partners find that these discourses do not fully determine who trans men become. And in understanding trans men as essentially the same people through transition, they delink conceptions of essential personhood from gender. At the same time, partners find that their sexual identities, or their patterns of attraction, are not predictive of their desires for trans men, but that they are able to enjoy new desires within these established intimate contexts. Partners' narratives also expand ideas about which bodies can be understood as masculine, and disrupt the idea that the masculinity or femininity of the body can be reduced to the presence or absence of generic sex organs. Partners experience breasts as "there but not there" in relation to trans men's own body image, and their narratives expand conceptions of the morphology and functionality of phalluses. These partners' narratives thus challenge the idea that the masculinity of the body is given, instead demonstrating how the masculine body materializes within embodied relations of desire.

[...]

References

Karzakis, K. A. 2008. *Fixing Sex: Intersex, Medical Authority, and Lived Experience.* Durham, NC: Duke University Press.

Loe, M. 2004. *The Rise of Viagra: How the Little Blue Pill Changed Sex in America.* New York: New York University Press.

Mamo, L. and J. R. Fishman. 2001. "Potency in All the Right Places: Viagra as a Technology of the Gendered Body." *Body & Society* 7(4):13–35.

Merleau-Ponty, M. 1962. *The Phenomenology of Perception.* Translated by C. Smith. New York: Humanities Press.

Merleau-Ponty, M. 1968. *The Visible and the Invisible: Followed by Working Notes*, edited by C. Lefort. Translated by A. Lingis. Evanston, IL: Northwestern University Press.

Pfeffer, C. A. 2010. "'Women's Work'? Women Partners of Transgender Men Doing Housework and Emotion Work." *Journal of Marriage and Family* 72:165–83.

Preciado, B. 2013 [2008]. *Testo Junkie: Sex, Drugs, and Biopolitics in the Pharmacopornographic Era.* Translated by B. Benderson. New York: The Feminist Press at the City University of New York.

Salamon, G. 2010. *Assuming a Body: Transgender and Rhetorics of Materiality.* New York: Columbia University Press.

Ward, J. 2010. "Gender Labor: Transmen, Femmes, and Collective Work of Transgression." *Sexualities* 13(2):236–54.

Competing Technologies of Embodiment

Pan-Asian Modernity and Third World Dependency in Vietnam's Contemporary Sex Industry

Kimberly Kay Hoang

T his article illustrates how women in different markets reflect and cater to their clients' distinct perceptions of Vietnam's place in the global imaginary by looking at Vietnam's segmented sex industry, which serves a niche market of local Vietnamese and Asian elites, alongside niche markets that cater to Western businessmen and budget travelers. Sex workers in the niche market where local Vietnamese elite men cement business relationships with their foreign Asian counterparts construct a *pan-Asian modernity* by contesting Western ideals and aspiring to Asian ideals of beauty. These aspirations explicitly represent their nation's progress toward joining the rising "Asian Tiger" economies. Women who cater to Western men embody *Third World dependency*, deliberately capitalizing on their clients' racialized imagination of Vietnam as an impoverished nation where people struggle to find the bare necessities of life, such as adequate shelter, food, and clean water. By comparing niche markets catering to local Vietnamese and transnational Asian elites with those catering to Western businessmen and budget travelers, I illustrate how individual agents living in the developing world actively project their nations' place in the global imaginary through their embodied practices.

Decentering Globalization Through Embodied Modernities

A substantial body of literature deconstructs the binaries of traditional/modern, East/West, and global/local, which were central tropes of early globalization studies (Holtzman 2004;

Kimberly Kay Hoang. 2014. "Competing Technologies of Embodiment: Pan-Asian Modernity and Third World Dependency in Vietnam's Contemporary Sex Industry." *Gender & Society* 28(4):513–36.

Inda and Rosaldo 2002; Manalansan 2004; Robertson 1992; Tsing 2005). This literature high-lights how multiple (Rofel 1999) or alternative modernities reflect diverse local agendas (Chu 2010). While these works question the idea of the unambiguous dominance of Western cultural, political, and economic power within the modern world system, they also make it clear that Western power is still important throughout the globe. As Kelsky (1999) states, "local" modernities opposing homogenizing global forces do not proliferate without some kind of cultural reference to the "originally" modern West. . . .

However, multiple hierarchies emerge that simultaneously inflect the ascending power of East Asia and the simultaneous decline of Western influence. . . .

The economic ascendance of the Asia Pacific region produced a new global economy that is structured by multiple hierarchies in the international division of labor. Urban centers like Singapore, Shanghai, and Hong Kong (instead of New York, London, or Paris) now exemplify distinctive formations of modernity, projecting their collective prominence on a global stage. . . .

By paying attention to shifting fields of economic and cultural power, I analyze how changes in the political economy alter cultural constructions of modernity in everyday life. This study looks at how women's bodies reflect and shape national hierarchies. . . .

Drawing on Foucault (1988), this article introduces the concept of *technologies of embodiment*, which refers to the process through which women produce, transform, or manipulate their bodies through particular kinds of body work that signify divergent imaginations of national progress. These technologies are tools existing outside of the user's body that allow her to manipulate her body or alter her embodied performance of femininity as she interacts with the world around her. Like other technologies, technologies of embodiment are rapidly evolving and quickly consumed and can swiftly respond to evolving standards of beauty to instantly reshape the user. Specific technologies include, but are not limited to, skin lightening creams or tanning lotions/bronzers, natural eye-makeup or heavy makeup, and plastic surgery to alter one's face or chest, as well as clothing that makes one look more modern and fashionable or deliberately impoverished. These technologies of embodiment do not exist in a vacuum; their development and consumption signify and are shaped by a nation's shifting place in the global economy. . . .

By comparing multiple niche markets of HCMC's segmented sex industry, I illustrate how sex workers reflect men clients' different projections of Vietnam's place in the global economy through two competing technologies of embodiment: pan-Asian modernity and Third World dependency. In the case of HCMC's high-end niche market, sex workers help wealthy, elite Vietnamese businessmen attract FDI from Asian investors by constructing themselves as pan-Asian modern subjects whose femininity conveys a deliberately exuberant projection of Vietnam's new position as an emerging economic player within the globalscapes. Vietnamese businessmen's ability to convey a new global configuration hinges on women's well-groomed bodies that adopt a pan-Asian aesthetic ideal as a counterpoint to representations of Western feminine ideals. In contrast, sex workers who cater to Western expatriates and tourists employ different technologies of embodiment that are deeply embedded in discourses of Western paternalism to attract charity capital. These women project Third World dependency by embodying virtuous Third World subjects, holdovers from an era when the "sun never set" on Western dominance. These workers play into their clients' racialized desire to imagine Vietnam as a poverty-stricken Third World country in need of Western help. Sex workers employ competing technologies of embodiment within their distinct niche markets that illustrate how male desire reflects and constructs different national formations in the global imaginary.

Research Methods and Setting

In studying Vietnam's stratified sex industry, I strategically chose to focus on HCMC because it has the greatest concentration of foreign people and capital in the country. Between June 2009 and August 2010, I [worked] as a hostess and bartender to observe relationships among owners, madams, police, clients, and sex workers in bars and clubs. I typically worked a 12-hour shift seven days a week for two to three months in each bar, and I wrote my fieldnotes every morning before returning to the bar.

This article draws on ethnographic data and 130 informal interviews with 65 clients and 65 sex workers distributed across three niche markets of HCMC's sex industry. I prepared and memorized two interview guides, one for clients and one for sex workers. I conducted two to three interviews per night lasting anywhere from two to seven hours. Interviews covered basic background questions and intimate questions about their private lives, including marriage and family life, extramarital affairs, and expectations and anxieties around care and deception. The interviews with the women usually took place backstage during down times as we waited for clients to arrive or to be seated at a table. I interviewed the men in a variety of settings—bars, coffee shops, their offices, and on car rides to development project sites. The participant observation coupled with interview data allowed me to understand the multiple ways that women altered their bodies in these stratified sites.

Progress and Poverty: Divergent Embodied Ideals

Projecting Pan-Asian Modernity Through Sex Workers' Bodies

At Khong Sao Bar, the majority of clients were local Vietnamese and Asian businessmen. In this exclusive bar, an elite group of clients who came from some of Vietnam's top finance, real estate, and trade companies engaged in sex for business purposes (Hoang 2013). Clients usually visited the bar three or four nights a week, spending an average of US$1,000–2,000 per night and US$15,000–20,000 per month. Roughly 25–30 women worked in this bar. Hostesses sat, drank, sang, and danced with clients and would often leave the bar for paid sex. Women earned roughly US$2,000 per month in tips for keeping men company at their tables and US$150–200 for each sexual encounter. All of the hostesses in this niche market came from the same villages as the three "mommies" (the local term for "madam"). They were recruited specifically because they came from poor rural families and would not recognize the high-profile businessmen and political elites who circulated through the bars. . . .

In the milieu of the bars, these [local Vietnamese and Asian] men represented Asia's ascendency in the global economy through their command of economic and symbolic capital. . . .

In addition to the ways in which men wielded capital in the bars, these new configurations hinged on the symbolic etchings of modernity and progress on women's aesthetically desirable bodies (Gal and Kligman 2000; Hanser 2008). . . .

[W]orkers in Khong Sao Bar did not want to look Western. Instead, they wanted to conform to regional Asian standards of beauty by looking like popular icons in Asia. When business was slow, the women sent the bar's men workers to purchase Korean and Japanese magazines from street vendors to study the latest styles. Backstage, women watched Korean soap operas dubbed in Vietnamese on the television and regularly commented on how beautiful the actresses were. Tailors designed dresses like those depicted in the magazines, a combination of long and short gowns similar to what pop stars would wear to a red carpet event. Hostesses saw blonde hair and blue eyes as outmoded desires, believing that, as in the financial world, the global center of beauty was shifting away from the West and toward Asia. Sex workers pointed to the Wonder Girls, a popular group of five women singers from South Korea, as their ideal of femininity. Vy, a 19-year-old sex worker, pointed to a photo of the pop singers and explained, "You see that the women are light-skinned and their makeup looks natural. . . . They do not wear a lot of eye shadow, [but] they accentuate their eyebrows, thicken their eyelashes, and wear blush that highlights their cheekbones."

It is often argued that the body work performed by Asian women—building nose bridges, constructing double eyelids, and lightening their skin—creates changes associated with Western standards of beauty (Lee 2008). Rather than looking to the West for a model of beauty, less developed countries within Asia like Vietnam look toward East Asia to represent modern cultural ideals. However, even as European body features have been integrated into the beauty ideals of Korea and Japan, the resulting beauty standard is not simply white; rather, women choose to highlight "natural" Asian ideal features (Glenn 2008). Furthermore, the meaning that these women ascribe to the resulting appearance is that it is a *modern Asian* look, not a Western look. Nhung, a hostess, explained, "In the past, everyone wanted to look Western, but that is old. Now, the new modern is Asian." In Khong Sao Bar, looking "Western" was not synonymous with looking modern. In fact, the women made it very clear to me that they considered Western and *Viet Kieu* (overseas Vietnamese) women's ideals of beauty unattractive, overweight, and masculine. Ha, a 21-year-old sex worker, said, "Asian women have smaller bones, smaller waistlines, small hips, and boobs that fit their bodies. When you are smaller, you look gentler, softer, more feminine." Dai, a 19-year-old hostess, described skin lightening as an endeavor apart from merely emulating Western whiteness:

> When women use skin lightening creams for the face and body, people think they want to look like white people in America or Europe, but actually, the true skin color of women in Asia is white. When a baby is born in Japan, Korea, or Vietnam, what color is their skin? It is fair and white, right? Dark skin is from going out in the sun a lot. We are just trying to bring out our natural beauty. . . . No one wants to look Western here anymore. People come to Asia for beautiful Asian women, not for women who [want to] look Western.

Dai describes a regional standard of beauty that is much more nuanced than a simple aspiration to Western ideals. Indeed, the tone of Dai's comments illustrates how sex workers use distinctly Asian standards of beauty to resist the ideals of the West. Women's deliberate rejection of Western standards illustrates how local, regional, and global ideals converge in their practices. Sex workers in this niche market engage in practices of bodily modifications where strictly European features are eschewed in favor of a pan-Asian ideal that includes some typically Western features—light skin, eyelid crease/shape—but also serves as a specific East Asian ideal—round face, thinness, and even, un-tanned skin tone. By claiming that skin whiteness is a "natural" Asian feature, sex workers actively contested the racial and aesthetic geographies of beauty in relation to white (Caucasian) women.

Women also focused on the appearance of their breasts. Big breasts were not the primary goal; rather, most women worked to shift their breasts so that they were positioned firmly together. One afternoon, Xinh, one of the mommies, walked into the back room with a bag of new bras. As the women tried them on, Xinh said,

We bring in the richest men in all of Saigon, and you need to look like you are worth a lot of money. There are millions of country girls [*nha que*]—men can go anywhere to get them. They come here to be around women who *look* modern [*mo-den*] and are worth a lot [*sang*]. . . . You do not have to go out and spend a lot of money on expensive dresses all the time. It is about the little things, like the bra and how you wear it.

Breast size did not differentiate urbanites from rural women entering the bar; rather, women in the city distinguished themselves with the knowledge of how to purchase the proper bra and how to position their breasts in the bra for a firm appearance. It was more important for them to appear aesthetically appealing than sexually desirable. Mommies like Hanh relied on workers' ability to portray themselves as modern women whose bodies were worth a lot of money, because that image allowed them to maintain their status as workers at one of the highest-end bars in HCMC. Claiming such a modern subjectivity through consumptive practices displaced a linear understanding of modernity as embodied in the West. Rather, the practices of negotiating, appropriating, and challenging Western beauty ideals reflect the multiple hierarchies signaling Asia's relation to the West.

The highest earners at Khong Sao Bar had subjected their bodies to a great deal of alteration, both because investing in body capital required financial resources and because women who altered their bodies received more attention and bigger tips from men clients. When women began working in the bar, they made aesthetic changes to their bodies by altering their makeup, rubbing whitening creams and powders on their bodies, and learning the right size of bra to purchase and how to walk in six-inch heels. New hostesses turned to more established workers to see what kinds of changes they could anticipate after working in the bar and accumulating enough capital to reinvest in their bodies. According to Hanh, the head mommy, the highest earners were women who "made smart business choices by knowing when to buy new clothes or invest in plastic surgery." As I sat in the back room playing card games, I listened as Hanh advised the women:

When you are new, it's better to invest in cheaper dresses and save your money, because men will bring you to their tables because you are a fresh face. After you've been here for a couple of months, you need to do things to stay fresh [*tuoi*]. . . . You should save your money and use it only if you think that it is going to make you more money. Like with Diem—after four months she saved over 100 million VND [5000 USD]. I told her to take 300 dollars and get a nose job. After she got a nose job, men pulled her into all of their tables. They wanted to see her new face, her change. . . . Men do not come in here to sit next to village girls—they can do that in Kieng Giag or Dong Thap (two villages nearby); they come here to sit next to women with modern styles.

Surgical alterations permanently changed how women looked and enhanced their ability to interact with the clients who came through the bar.

Compared to women in other niches of HCMC's sex industry, the women in Khong Sao Bar underwent the most rapid and pronounced bodily transformations during the course of their employment. The bar had connections with two plastic surgery offices that hired doctors trained in Singapore, Thailand, and South Korea who could perform rhinoplasties that would make the Vietnamese women look like Korean pop stars. These offices often eschewed Western and *Viet Kieu* doctors who botched nose jobs with overexaggerated bridges that looked too Western. They also provided women with free consultations and significant discounts on surgical procedures. I became aware of the extent of women's plastic surgeries one Sunday afternoon when two surgeons came to the bar to provide three of the new girls with free rhinoplasty consultations. All of the women I worked with had undergone rhinoplasty (US$250), and roughly 80 percent of them had double eyelid surgery (US$400)—a type of cosmetic surgery where doctors reshape the skin around the eyes to create an upper-eyelid crease. Fewer than a quarter of the women had saline breast implants, and 20 percent of the women had undergone liposuction. These modifications complicated the women's claims about natural, feminine-looking Asian bodies, as they actively worked to pursue a supposedly innate ideal.

During one of his free consultation visits to the bar, Anh Minh, one of the plastic surgeons, opened a booklet with "before and after" photos of the women who worked at Khong Sao Bar. As I flipped through the booklet, I listened as the women talked about how much they had changed as a result of their work. As the doctor consulted with the women, he often used photos of surgeries he had performed in the past, or of famous models and singers who had their surgeries done in Korea, Japan, or Thailand.

As with makeup styles, models of ideal bodies were taken from photos of women in Asia. Moreover, the women in this niche preferred Korean and Japanese skincare products over Western ones. Anh Minh told the sex workers that products from South Korea "are about 12 years ahead of the U.S. in terms of their skincare technology." South Korea, he said, "has become the new France." These technological developments have enabled women to craft themselves as both modern and distinctly pan-Asian. . . .

For foreign investors making large speculations in Vietnam, women's enhanced bodies provided figurative reassurance that Vietnam was a dynamic market where they could expect to see returns on their investments. Sex workers' altered bodies represented Vietnam as a nation on the move, where even the poorest of the poor were beginning to reap the rewards of economic development. Several clients paid for surgeries as a gift to new women with whom they enjoyed sitting. Gifting such surgeries was not purely altruistic; they enhanced the men's prestige as members of the country these women represent. These bodily modifications, which highlighted the women's malleability, mobility, and modernity, were crucial to local Vietnamese business elites because they signaled the nation's economic development.

Critically, the technologies of embodiment seen in Khong Sao Bar signify the shift in foreign direct investments from the U.S. and Europe to major Asian economic powers that are carefully mapped onto sex workers' embodied practices. The reputation of Khong Sao Bar depended on the hostess's ability to develop and maintain a certain look—one that constructed pan-Asian progress in a global market economy as an embodied ideal. Not all sex workers embodied a pan-Asian modernity, however; as I will describe, Western businessmen and tourists were more interested in imagining Vietnam as an undeveloped nation untouched by flows of global capital. The competing technologies of embodiment employed by women in these two distinct niche markets illustrate the tensions within an emerging market that shaped desire in HCMC's sex industry.

Projecting Third World Dependency Through Sex Workers' Bodies

Unlike in high-end bars, most clients in Naughty Girls were budget tourists looking for cheap adventure. As a result, women practiced technologies of embodiment that were distinct from those of high-end sex workers to cater to their Western clients' desires. Roughly 20 women worked at Naughty Girls. The majority of these women had previously worked in factories or in service jobs where they made less than US$100 per month. Workers were not paid by the bar owner; instead, they earned money from tips and from paid sex. Workers earned US$200–700 per month from paid sex, which was supplemented with occasional cash gifts from regular clients ranging as high as US$50,000, which went toward rebuilding a family home or launching a new business. The clients I studied in these bars were 18–74 years of age, and nearly all of them traveled to Vietnam to experience the culture of a Third World country. When clients walked into the bar, they could order a US$2 beer and expect to have one or two women sit with them. Women immediately handed them wet towels, wiped their faces, and provided them with shoulder massages.

Secrets, a bar geared toward Western, mostly white, expatriates and businessmen, was located in the same district as Naughty Girls. The 20 women working in Secrets were migrant workers from nearby villages who came to the city to work in factories prior to entering into sex work. These workers earned roughly US$100–200 per month in wages and tips and about US$200–700 per month from sex work, which was also supplemented with large cash gifts and remittances from regular clients. The owner, Lilly, a 25-year-old entrepreneur and former sex worker in an area frequented by backpackers, opened Secrets in 2008 in an attempt to differentiate her bar from those frequented by budget travelers, like Naughty Girls. Although the socioeconomic class of the clientele differed between these two bars, sex workers in both Secrets and Naughty Girls shared similar embodiments that distinguished them from the women in Khong Sao Bar. These women altered their bodies to cater to their clients' implicit and explicit racial desires, a proclivity that other scholars have found among sex tourists in the Caribbean (Brennan 2004; Cabezas 2006). Unlike the workers in Khong Sao Bar, the women who catered to Westerners were careful *not* to present themselves as pan-Asian modern subjects. Instead, they capitalized on their embodiment of Third World dependency.

Workers in this niche market made no effort to lighten their skin. In fact, the owners of both bars capitalized on women's darker complexions. During my first several days at work, my coworkers rummaged through my makeup bag and told me what to keep and what to get rid of. Ly, a 24-year-old woman, advised:

> Get rid of the baby powder. It is going to make your skin look too pale, and under the lights in this bar, you are going to look like you are sick. You do not want to look light.... You can't use pink blush in here; it makes you look like those Japanese or Chinese play dolls. You have to go buy a brown, orange, or darker color to use on your cheeks; it will make your face look narrower instead of round.

When I asked the women why they preferred to have darker complexions, Lilly told me, "Men like brown skin, Kim. They like it. I like it, too. Look better." Lilly indeed was darker than all of the women in the bar. She prided herself on her skin color, stating, "Every afternoon around 2:00 P.M., I put on my bathing suit and I go lay on the swing I tied up [on the roof] to make my skin more brown. People laugh. They say, 'Why you look so dark, Lilly?' But I say, 'Because I like it.'" Lilly and Tina, the owners of the expat and tourist bars, respectively, had by far the darkest complexions of the women I studied. While Lilly and Tina both embraced the tan aesthetic that they built their business on, several of the other women working in the bars had more ambivalent feelings about dark skin and used bronzers as part of a costume to play a role. Xuong, a 26-year-old woman working in Naughty Girls, said:

> The men here like darker skin and women who just came up from the village. The girls who just come up from the villages always get the most clients because they look the most innocent and fresh. Men like women with dark skin. They will always touch you and say, "Wow, your skin is so dark and soft."

Altering their skin color was the most notable strategy these women adopted to racialize their bodies in a way that would exaggerate their appearance as poor women in a Third World country. Dark skin provided a narrative of poor, rural labor that could hide women's experiences of factory and service work in HCMC. For many of the workers, their dark complexion was achieved by using a lotion that they applied to their skin for work and then washed off when going about their lives outside of sex work. . . .

The women who worked for Western expatriates and backpackers did not make as much money as the women who catered to elite Asian and Vietnamese businessmen. Therefore, compared to the higher-end niche market, fewer women who catered to Westerners invested in plastic surgery. Those who did opted to have different types of surgical procedures than higher-end women, generally choosing breast implants over nose jobs. Among the 40 women I studied in the two bars catering to Westerners, roughly one third had breast implants, while fewer than 20 percent had nose jobs.

. . . One day, as I was chatting with Yen-Nhi and Mai-Lan in Secrets, I . . . asked, "Do you ever want to get a nose job, double eyelid surgery, or breast implants to look more Western?" Mai-Lan replied, "Western men come to Vietnam because they think that Vietnamese women are beautiful, not because they want women who look Western. The girls who always get picked first in these bars are the ones who just came up from the village or who just started working." This conversation highlighted the racialized and sexualized desires of the clients who frequented Secrets. Both women believed that men would reward them if they could successfully embody a dark aesthetic that conveyed rural authenticity.

Mai-Lan's perceptions of their clients' racialized desires were substantiated during my conversations with several expatriate Westerners. One evening, Alex, a 39-year-old ceramic exporter from France, remarked:

> Stay away from city girls who know how to hustle. If you are an expat in Vietnam and you know better, then you go for the village girls because they are the real deal. . . . They are the real Vietnam. . . . They are not greedy or chasing after this urban lifestyle of consuming new things.

Expats like Alex wanted to be with recent migrants to the city because they felt that rural women provided them with an authentic experience of Vietnam. As his comments suggest, rather than acknowledging that the upwardly mobile urbanite is also authentically Vietnamese, Alex preferred women who represented his vision of a Vietnam where most people were trapped in Third World poverty.

Although most sex workers migrated to the city to experience upward mobility, they were strategic about when and how they displayed their access to foreign capital. All of the women had two cell phones, a cheap Nokia, worth US$20, and another, more expensive phone. Several women had iPhones, which typically sold in the Vietnamese market for US$200–1000, depending on the version. They also purchased fashionable urban clothing that they rarely wore to work. Women who worked in Secrets were required to wear sexier versions of the traditional Vietnamese *Ao dai* [dress], allowing them to embody an ethnically authentic Vietnam. Naughty Girls did not have a dress code, but the women almost always wore jean shorts, tank tops, and plastic high heels to highlight their sexual appeal. Many of these women owned nicer clothing, but they chose outfits that would convey to their clients both overt sexuality and their status as victims of Third World poverty.

I learned of women's strategies to embody Third World poverty through the English lessons I provided at Naughty Girls three afternoons a week. . . .

During the lessons, I helped women translate a series of stock emails, text messages, and phrases that they could use with their clients. I translated phrases in broken English, like "My motorbike broke down. I have to walk to work. Can you help me buy new motorbike?" and "My father very sick and no one in my family help so I have to work. I am from An Giang village. You go to village before?"

I often asked the women why they lied to their clients or why they were careful not to display too much wealth. Diem-Hang explained:

> The men like to meet poor village girls. If you show them that you have nice clothes or new phones, they will start to lecture you about how you should save your money so that you can quit working. If you do not show them what you have, they will feel sorry for you, think that you are poor, and give you money.

Even though the women were more financially secure than family members who worked in the rice fields, in manufacturing, or even as service workers in HCMC, they could not display their new wealth to their clients. Many of the clients thought sex work was acceptable only if the women were flat broke and had no other options. This was very different from the appreciation Vietnamese men had for sex workers in Khong Sao Bar. In the higher-end niche market, clients recognized that women deserved some degree of respect for their skill in attracting foreign capital into the country. In the niche market catering to Westerners, however, women proved their respectability by portraying Vietnam as an impoverished Third World nation, inferior to the wealthy West, and by presenting themselves as innocent victims of that poverty.

To portray an authentically Third World Vietnam, women not only altered their bodies by choosing cheap or traditional clothing and darkening their skin and eyes, they also used trips to villages in the Mekong Delta to provide clients with a visceral experience of Third World poverty and appeal to their generosity as relatively wealthy Westerners. On these trips, women would introduce men to their "families" to tie their own self-presentation to the poverty they witnessed. Often, however, these families were fake. Thuy-Linh explained:

> I am going to Kien Giang tomorrow with one of the guys here because he wants to see my village, but most of my family lives in Saigon now. . . . I am taking him to stay with Vi's family so that he will think that I am really poor and maybe give me money to rebuild the house or help my "family" out.

When the women in the bar first told me about their fake village families and the trips they organized with clients, I was struck by their awareness of their clients' desire to see Vietnam as a developing Third World country rather than as an emerging hotbed of global investment. They organized tours that would portray an "authentic" Vietnam removed from signs of global change, modernization, and capitalism. These men wanted to visit villages where they could walk through rice fields, ride bicycles, and bargain in street markets. More often than not, sex workers were happy to play into their clients' desires because doing so enabled them to ask for large sums of money. Like the women in Frank's (2002) study on strippers in the United States, the women in Naughty Girls and Secrets played on their clients' sympathy for the material inequalities and constraints that might shape a woman's decision to engage in sex work.

Upon their return from these trips to the Mekong Delta, many of the clients explained how they were moved to altruism by the conditions of poverty they had seen. For example, after spending three days in the village with Nhi's family, John, a man in his late 50s to early 60s, commented:

> There are so many things that we in the West take for granted: roofs over our heads, hot water, shoes. . . . When I was with Nhi, I had to shower with buckets of cold water. It was so disgusting because I was brushing my teeth and I didn't realize that the bucket had a bunch of maggots in there. I felt these tiny worms swimming around in my mouth and I had to spit it out.

It is important to note that the women did not buy into the story of Vietnam's inferiority; instead they capitalized on their clients' desires for First World dominance by deliberately placing buckets of maggots in the outdoor shower. Such visceral experiences with poverty allowed workers to ask their clients for a large sum of money. Indeed, John sympathized with Nhi's conditions of poverty, and he gave her family $500 to install a new faucet. Regardless of whether they were real or staged, these visits allowed workers to capitalize on Vietnam's shifting position in the global economy in order to attract charitable gifts from their clients. Men provide women with money to help them escape poverty and improve their standard of living from basic to comfortable. Consequently, even though sex work allowed some women to purchase nicer clothing and expensive cellular phones, they had to hide their wealth and perform poverty because those items symbolized increased access to global capital, mobility, status, and, most importantly, dignity in their work.

Conclusion

This study has important implications for how we understand and theorize the important relationship between new transnational economic flows and intimate life. By linking sex workers' micro-embodied practices to macro-shifts in the global economy in the context of East Asia's recent economic ascendency, I challenge representations that only highlight poverty over the Global South and its oppressed position in relation to the West. As such, this article is as much about sex work as it is about shifting configurations of global capital. . . . This article examined how the complexity of Vietnam's contemporary political economy maps onto sex workers' competing technologies of embodiment and performances of femininity. HCMC's sex industry shaped and was shaped by broader economic forces, such as rapid local development, the global growth of "frontier markets," and the emergence of a homegrown superelite enmeshed in the international political economy. For Vietnamese sex workers, satisfying the needs of their Asian clientele helped cement the growing status of the region. In striving towards new pan-Asian and Third World beauty ideals, which were both distinctly non-Western, women embodied the increasing recognition of previously marginalized countries in the global arena.

   This article highlights how global economic changes map onto women's bodies. Economic change is deeply intertwined with bodywork, racialized discourses, shifting realms of femininity, and complicated terrains of agency. In all three bars discussed in this article, the workers are striving to bring foreign money into the country. High-end workers in Khong Sao Bar work to help attract [foreign investment], while workers in Secrets and Naughty Girls work to attract charity capital. I show how sex workers' competing technologies of embodiment came to represent the changing dynamics of race and nation under globalization. Sex workers' pan-Asian bodies were molded by technologies that reflected Vietnam's striving to emerge as another "rising tiger." However, not all women could secure a foothold in the rapidly developing sectors of the economy, and these women turned to other niche markets and other technologies of embodiment that would appeal to Western men's desires for virtuous Third World dependency. Women across all niches of sex work altered their bodies to fit clients' particular racialized and classed desires, but their divergent technologies of embodiment reflected tensions within Vietnam's gendered landscape. Thus, while men can pay for women's performances of dependency in Secrets and Naughty Girls, the true dependency of the nation on the West is slowly diminishing. Therefore, in this historical moment, Vietnam is rejecting its colonial past and the dependency that comes with it to embrace a vision of the future of global capitalism, with East Asia as a new financial center.

References

Brennan, Denise. 2004. *What's Love Got to Do with It? Transnational Desires and Sex Tourism in the Dominican Republic.* Durham, NC: Duke University Press.

Cabezas, Amalia. 2006. "The Eroticization of Labor in Cuba's All-Inclusive Resorts: Performing Race, Class and Gender in the New Tourist Economy." *Social Identities* 12:507–21.

Chu, Julie. 2010. *Cosmologies of Credit: Transnational Mobility and the Politics of Destination in China.* Durham, NC: Duke University Press.

Foucault, Michel. 1988. "Technologies of the Self." In *Technologies of the Self: A Seminar with Michel Foucault,* edited by L. Martin, H. Gutman, and P. Hutton. Amherst, MA: University of Massachusetts Press.

Frank, Katherine. 2002. *G-Strings and Sympathy: Strip Club Regulars and Male Desire.* Durham, NC: Duke University Press.

Gal, Susan and Gail Kligman. 2000. *The Politics of Gender After Socialism.* Princeton, NJ: Princeton University Press.

Glenn, Evelyn. 2008. "Yearning for Lightness: Transnational Circuits in the Marketing and Consumption of Skin Lighteners." *Gender & Society* 22:281–302.

Hanser, Amy. 2008. *Service Encounters: Class, Gender and the Market for Social Distinction in Urban China.* Stanford, CA: Stanford University Press.

Hoang, Kimberly Kay. 2013. "Vietnam Rising Dragon: Contesting Dominant Western Masculinities in Ho Chi Minh City's Global Sex Industry." *International Journal of Politics, Culture and Society* 26. doi:10.1007/s10767-013-9155-6.

Holtzman, Jon. 2004. "The Local in the Local: Models of Time and Space in Samburu District, Northern Kenya." *Current Anthropology* 45:61–84.

Inda, Jonathan and Renato Rosaldo. 2002. "Introduction: A World in Motion." In *The Anthropology of Globalization: A Reader,* edited by J. Inda and R. Rosaldo. Oxford, UK: Blackwell.

Kelsky, Karen. 1999. "Gender, Modernity, and Eroticized Internationalism in Japan." *Cultural Anthropology* 14:229–55.

Lee, Sharon. 2008. "Lessons from 'Around the World with Oprah': Neoliberalism, Race, and the (Geo) politics of Beauty." *Women and Performance: A Journal of Feminist Theory* 18:25–41.

Manalansan IV, Martin F. 2004. *Global Divas: Filipino Gay Men in the Diaspora.* Durham, NC: Duke University Press.

Robertson, Roland. 1992. *Globalization: Social Theory and Global Culture.* London, UK: Sage.

Rofel, Lisa. 1999. *Other Modernities: Gendered Yearnings in China After Socialism.* Berkeley, CA: University of California Press.

Tsing, Anna. 2005. *Friction: An Ethnography of Global Connection.* Princeton, NJ: Princeton University Press.

PART IV
Culture and Media

Culture refers to things shared by people in a society, including values, beliefs, actions, and even material objects. Institutions such as the media teach and reproduce gender constructs and sexual practices. Social institutions regulate culture but may also assist with transformation and resistance, helping to create social change. In this section, we include central pieces that examine gender and sexuality within the realm of culture and media, through the lens of our four core themes: intersectionality, masculinity, transgender, and global perspective (IMTG) identities and experiences.

In "Hetero-Romantic Love and Heterosexiness in Children's G-Rated Films," Karin Martin and Emily Kazyak examine how media shape children's development of heteronormativity. Through close examination of top-selling G-rated movies produced between 1990 and 2005, the authors find that heterosexual romantic relationships in these movies are presented as powerful and transformative, while relationships outside of these parameters are shown as less serious. Many films, even when they are not centrally about romantic relationships, also present "sexy" content, including ogling women's bodies, while women of color characters are most likely to be depicted as sexy. Media for children can offer powerful messages about gender and sexuality that normalize men's gaze of women's bodies and women's desire for heteroromance, while also resting on racialized and gendered ideals.

Kirsten Firminger's "Is He Boyfriend Material?" continues this analysis of media by looking at how teenage boys are represented in five popular magazines, *Seventeen, YM, CosmoGirl, ELLEgirl,* and *Girls' Life.* About twenty percent of the content focuses on boys, and boys are often depicted in these magazines as another consumer product, like the clothing or makeup being advertised, about which girls need to make good, smart choices. Most boys are presented as having naturally "high" sex drives and being superficial, while girls are expected to find boys who value love and intimacy instead. The magazines use "girl power" language that draws on individualistic rhetoric to point to self-esteem, effort, and constructing identities through consumerism as the barriers preventing girls from heterosexual relationships.

Amy Wilkins's "Masculinity Dilemmas" offers an ethnographic analysis of the masculine subcultural identities of young white Christian and goth men from middle-class backgrounds. Wilkins analyzes how young men in both groups negotiate gender; across groups, they see their masculinity being challenged or marginalized in larger society, even as they access some privileges as white, middle-class men. While goth men remake themselves as sexually adventurous "freaks," Christians remake themselves as "good men," who are abstinent despite being constantly tempted by women. Both groups engage in masculinity projects that disrupt some aspects of hegemonic masculinity, such as abstinence among Christian men or performance of bisexuality among goth men. Yet at the same time, they reinforce gender distinctions and heterosexuality of the broader culture through performing heterosexual temptation among Christians and sexual adventure by goths.

Cheryl Cooky and colleagues' study, "'What Makes a Woman a Woman?' Versus 'Our First Lady of Sport,'" provides a comparative analysis of the media coverage in the United States and

South Africa of the Caster Semenya controversy around her gender identity. Media in the United States and South Africa framed the genetic testing of Caster Semenya in different ways. U.S. coverage framed the process in medicalized terms that justified the investigation as leveling the playing field, ensuring that "men" did not compete against women. On the other hand, the South African coverage argued the process as based in racist and Westernized notions of ideal femininity. Yet both sources reflect essentialized notions of gender that reinforce gender inequality in sport media framing.

In "Cultural and Cosmopolitan," Oluwakemi Balogun demonstrates how particular forms of "beauty" are being marketed through Nigerian beauty pageants, further drawing our attention to how pageants represent gender dynamics. Studying two different pageants, Balogun analyzes how discourses about "true womanhood" or "beauty" differ, even though the body measurements and skin tone of women in the pageants are very similar (and, indeed, the same women compete in both pageants). Yet these pageants evoke different nationalist notions of womanhood in Nigerian society—either emphasizing locally grounded or cosmopolitan gender performances. In one pageant, women need to be able to barter and cook like a "traditional" African woman; in the other pageant, they need to develop competitive skills of assertiveness and self-confidence that will help them win international pageants. In addition to displaying nationalist gender performances, the pageants reflect and reinforce particular ideas about Nigerian femininity.

These pieces emphasize the ways that culture reinforces certain notions of gender and sexuality. Whether through G-rated films aimed at children or magazine articles aimed at teenage girls, traditional ideas about gender and heterosexuality permeate contemporary culture. Media framing of South African athlete Caster Semenya, who had to undergo gender verification testing before returning to competitive sports, also indicates that, despite differences in emphasis, both South African and American articles about the controversy reflect essentialized and binary ideas about gender and gender identity. Subcultures, such as Christian or goth groups, may aim to subvert scripts around gender and sexuality but tend to reinforce gender distinctions and heterosexuality even as they do so. Analysis of two beauty pageants in Nigeria—one reflecting "traditional" Nigerian values and another reflecting "modern" cosmopolitan values—show how nationalism and ideas about femininity come together to inscribe particular notions of womanhood. Culture is a powerful force reflecting and reshaping ideas about gender, gender identity, and sexuality.

Hetero-Romantic Love and Heterosexiness in Children's G-Rated Films

Karin A. Martin and Emily Kazyak

© iStockphoto.com/kali9

Multiple ethnographic studies suggest that by elementary school, children understand the normativity of heterosexuality. That is, by elementary school, children have a heteronormative understanding of the world (Best 1983; Renold 2002, 2005; Thorne 1993). Yet we know little about what children bring with them to the peer cultures these ethnographers describe and how these understandings develop before elementary school. Martin (2009) finds that mothers' conversations with young children normalize heterosexuality, but children's social worlds are larger than the mother-child dyad. Research on adolescence suggests that alongside parents and peers, the media are important in shaping cultural understandings of sexuality (Kim et al. 2007; Ward 1995, 2003). This article provides a beginning step toward understanding the role of the media in the development of children's heteronormativity. We ask, *How* are heteronormativity and heterosexuality constructed in children's top-selling G-rated

Karin A. Martin and Emily Kazyak. 2009. "Hetero-Romantic Love and Heterosexiness in Children's G-Rated Films." *Gender & Society* 23(3):315–36.

movies between 1990 and 2005? . . . [We find] heterosexuality within the context of romantic relationships in G-rated movies is not ordinary or mundane but, rather, is powerful, exceptional, and magical. Outside of romantic relationships, heterosexual desire is much less serious.

Heteronormativity

Heteronormativity includes the multiple, often mundane ways through which heterosexuality overwhelmingly structures and "pervasively and insidiously" orders "everyday existence" (Jackson 2006, 108; Kitzinger 2005). Heteronormativity structures social life so that heterosexuality is always assumed, expected, ordinary, and privileged. Its pervasiveness makes it difficult for people to imagine other ways of life. In part, the assumption and expectation of heterosexuality is linked to its status as natural and biologically necessary for procreation (Lancaster 2003). Anything else is relegated to the nonnormative, unusual, and unexpected and is, thus, in need of explanation. Specifically, within heteronormativity, homosexuality becomes the "other" against which heterosexuality defines itself (Johnson 2005; Rubin 1984).

But not just any kind of heterosexuality is privileged. Heteronormativity regulates those within its boundaries as it marginalizes those outside of it.

According to Jackson (2006), heteronormativity works to define more than normative sexuality, insofar as it also defines normative ways of life in general. Heteronormativity holds people accountable to reproductive procreative sexuality and traditional gendered domestic arrangements of sexual relationships, and it is linked to particular patterns of consumerism and consumption (Ingraham 1999). In other words, while heteronormativity regulates people's sexualities, bodies, and sexual relationships (for both those nonheterosexuals on the "outside" and heterosexuals on the "inside"), it regulates nonsexual aspects of life as well.

Heteronormativity also privileges a particular type of heterosexual. Among those aspects desired in heterosexuals, Rubin (1984) includes being married, monogamous, and procreative. We might also include that heterosexuality is most sanctioned when it is intraracial and that other inequalities, like race and class, intersect and help construct what Rubin calls "the inner charmed circle" in a multitude of complicated ways (e.g., Whose married sex is most sanctioned? Whose reproductive sex is most normal?). Heteronormativity also rests on gender asymmetry, as heterosexuality depends on a particular type of normatively gendered women and men (Jackson 2006). In this article, we examine how children's movies construct heterosexuality to better understand what information is available in media that might contribute to children's heteronormative social worlds.

Children, Media, and Movies

The media are an important avenue of children's sexual socialization because young children are immersed in media-rich worlds. Thirty percent of children under three years old and 43 percent of four- to six-year-olds have a television in their bedrooms, and one-quarter of children under six years old have a VCR/DVD player in their bedrooms (Rideout, Vandewater, and Wartella 2003). . . . [T]o attract young children (and their parents) to films, filmmakers must get their movies a G-rating. Film producers are interested in doing this because the marketing advantages that accompany a successful children's film are enormous (Thomas 2007). The Motion Picture Association of America rates a film G for "General Audience" if the film "contains nothing in theme, language, nudity, sex, violence or other matters that, in the view of the Rating Board, would offend parents whose younger children view the motion picture. . . . No nudity, sex scenes or drug use are present in the motion picture" (Motion Picture Association of America 2009). Thus, a G-rating signals that these films expect young children in their audience.

We examine the top-selling G-rated movies to challenge the idea that these movies are without (much) sexual content and the notion that young children are therefore not exposed to matters relating to sexuality. As theorists of heteronormativity suggest, heterosexuality is pervasive, and we want to examine how it makes its way into films that are by definition devoid of sexuality. If heteronormativity structures social life well beyond the sexual arena, then it is likely at work even in films that announce themselves as free of sexuality. . . .

Enormous numbers of children watch Disney and other G-rated children's movies. In a 2006 survey of more than 600 American mothers of three- to six-year-olds, only 1 percent reported that their child had not seen any of the films we analyze here; half had seen 13 or more (Martin, Luke, and Verduzco-Baker 2007).

Finally, with respect to heterosexuality specifically, there is some evidence that suggests even young children learn from media accounts. Kelley, Buckingham, and Davies (1999) find that six- to eleven-year-old children incorporate what they learn about sexuality on television into their talk and identity work in their peer groups. Martin (2009) finds mothers of children ages three to six years old suggest that children, especially girls, know about heterosexual falling in love, weddings, and marriage from "movies," "princesses," and "Disney." Again, our research cannot address what children take away from their repeated viewings of such movies, but given that the extant research suggests they take something, we analyze what is there for the taking.

. . . [W]e analyze *how* heterosexuality is constructed in children's G-rated films. We ask not how characters might be read as queer but what accounts these films offer of heterosexuality and how such accounts serve heteronormativity. Unpacking the construction of heterosexuality in these films is a first step toward understanding what social-sexual information is available to the children who watch them.

Sample and Method

The data for this study come from all the G-rated movies released (or rereleased) between 1990 and 2005 that grossed more than $100 million in the United States (see Table 18.1). Using this sample of widely viewed films overcomes the limitations of previous analyses of children's, and especially Disney, movies, which often focus on a few particular examples. Here we have tried to examine all the most viewed films within this genre and time period. The films in our sample were extremely successful and widely viewed, as evidenced by their sales numbers in theaters. Home videos/DVDs sales and rentals of these films are also very high (Arnold 2005), including direct-to-video/DVD sequels of many of these films, for example, *Lion King 1.5, Ariel's Beginning,* and *Beauty and the Beast's Enchanted Christmas.* While the audience for these films is broader than children, children are certainly centrally intended as part of the audience. G is the rating given to films that contain nothing that "would offend parents whose younger children view the motion picture" according to the Motion Picture Association of America (2009). Sixteen (80 percent) of these films are animated, and 17 are produced by Disney, a major producer of children's consumption and socialization (Giroux 1997).

After collecting this sample, the first author screened all the films and then trained three research assistants to extract any story lines, images, scenes, songs, or dialogue that depicted anything about sexuality, including depictions of bodies, kissing, jokes, romance, weddings, dating, love, where babies come from, and pregnancy. The research assistants then wrote descriptions of the scenes in which they found material related to sexuality. They described the visuals of the scenes in as vivid detail as possible and transcribed the dialogue verbatim. Two research assistants watched each film and extracted the relevant material. The first author reconciled the minimal differences between what each research assistant included by rescreening the films herself and adding or correcting material. . . .

Table 18.1 Sample: $100 Million G-Rated Movies, 1990–2005

Movie	Year	Produced By	Hetero-Romantic Story Line			Heterosexuality	
			Any Reference	Major Plot	Minor Plot	Sexiness	Ogling of Women's Bodies
Chicken Little	2005	Disney	X		X	X	
The Polar Express	2004	Castle Rock					
Finding Nemo	2003	Disney/Pixar	X				
The Santa Clause 2	2002	Disney	X	X			
Monsters, Inc.	2001	Disney/Pixar	X		X		X
The Princess Diaries	2001	Disney	X	X		X	X
Chicken Run	2000	Dreamworks	X		X		X
Tarzan	1999	Disney	X		X		
Toy Story 2	1999	Disney/Pixar	X			X	X
A Bug's Life	1998	Disney/Pixar	X		X		X
Mulan	1998	Disney	X		X		X
The Rugrats Movie	1998	Nickelodeon					
101 Dalmatians	1996	Disney	X		X		
The Hunchback of Notre Dame	1996	Disney	X	X		X	X
Toy Story	1995	Disney/Pixar	X			X	
Pocahontas	1995/2005	Disney	X	X			
The Lion King	1994/2002	Disney	X	X			
Aladdin	1994	Disney	X	X		X	X
Beauty and the Beast	1991/2002	Disney	X	X		X	X
The Little Mermaid	1989/1997	Disney	X	X		X	X

Results and Discussion

We describe two ways that heterosexuality is constructed in these films. The primary account of heterosexuality in these films is one of hetero-romantic love and its exceptional, magical, transformative power. Secondarily, there are some depictions of heterosexuality outside of this model. Outside of hetero-romantic love, heterosexuality is constructed as men gazing desirously at women's bodies. This construction rests on gendered and racialized bodies and is portrayed as less serious and less powerful than hetero-romantic love.

Magical, Exceptional, Transformative Hetero-Romantic Love

Hetero-romantic love is the account of heterosexuality that is most developed in these films. Only two films have barely detectable or no hetero-romantic references (see Table 18.1). In eight of these films hetero-romance is a major plot line, and in another seven films it is a secondary story line. Those films not made by Disney have much less hetero-romantic content than those made by Disney.

Films where we coded hetero-romantic love as a major plot line are those in which the hetero-romantic story line is central to the overall narrative of the film. In *The Little Mermaid*, for instance, the entire narrative revolves around the romance between Ariel, a mermaid, and Eric, a human.

The same is true of movies like *Beauty and the Beast, Aladdin,* and *Santa Clause 2.* There would be no movie without the hetero-romantic story line for these films. In others, the hetero-romantic story line is secondary. For example, in *Chicken Run* the romance develops between Ginger and Rocky as they help organize the chicken revolt—the heart of the movie—although the movie ends with them coupled, enjoying their freedom in a pasture. While removing the hetero-romantic story line would still leave other stories in place in such films, the romance nonetheless exists. In other movies, like *Toy Story,* references are made to hetero-romance but are not developed into a story line. For instance, this film suggests romantic interest between Woody and Little Bo Peep, but their romance is not woven throughout the film.

While our focus is on the construction of heterosexuality, we recognize that other stories exist in these films. For instance, there are stories about parent-child relationships (e.g., Chicken Little wants his father to be proud of him; Nemo struggles against his overprotective father). Stories about workers, working conditions, and collective revolt also appear, for instance, in *Monsters, Inc.* . . . and *Chicken Run.* . . . Though certainly there is much analysis that could be done around such stories, we do not do so here. Rather, we turn our attention to the hetero-romantic story lines and the work they do in constructing heterosexuality.

Theorists of heteronormativity suggest that the power of heteronormativity is that heterosexuality is assumed, mundane, ordinary, and expected. In contrast, we find that in these films, while it is certainly assumed, heterosexuality is very often not ordinary or mundane. Rather, romantic heterosexual relationships are portrayed as a special, distinct, exceptional form of relationship, different from all others. Characters frequently defy parents, their culture, or their very selves to embrace a hetero-romantic love that is transformative, powerful, and (literally) magical. At the same time, these accounts are sometimes held in tension with or constructed by understandings of the naturalness of heterosexuality. Below, we describe how the films construct these relationships as distinct, set apart, and different from others. We also describe how they are constructed as powerful, transformative, and magical.

These films repeatedly mark relationships between cross-gender lead characters as special and magical by utilizing imagery of love and romance. Characters in love are surrounded by music, flowers, candles, magic, fire, ballrooms, fancy dresses, dim lights, dancing, and elaborate dinners. Fireflies, butterflies, sunsets, wind, and the beauty and power of nature often provide the setting for—and a link to the naturalness of—hetero-romantic love. For example, in *Beauty and the Beast,* the main characters fall in love frolicking in the snow; Aladdin and Jasmine fall in love as they fly through a starlit sky in *Aladdin*; Ariel falls in love as she discovers the beauty of earth in *The Little Mermaid*; Santa and his eventual bride ride in a sleigh on a sparkling snowy night with snow lightly falling over only their heads in *Santa Clause 2*; and *Pocahontas* is full of allusion to water, wind, and trees as a backdrop to the characters falling in love. The characters often say little in these scenes. Instead, the scenes are overlaid with music and song that tells the viewer more abstractly what the characters are feeling. These scenes depicting hetero-romantic love are also paced more slowly with longer shots and with slower and soaring music.

These films also construct the specialness of hetero-romantic love by holding in tension the assertion that hetero-romantic relationships are simultaneously magical and natural. In fact, their naturalness and their connection to "chemistry" and the body further produce their exceptionalness. According to Johnson (2005), love and heterosexuality become interwoven as people articulate the idea that being in love is overpowering and that chemistry or a spark forms the basis for romantic love. These formulations include ideas about reproductive instincts and biology, and they work to naturalize heterosexuality. We see similar constructions at work in these G-rated movies where the natural becomes the magical. These films show that, in the words of Mrs. Pots from *Beauty and the Beast,* if "there's a spark there," then all that needs to be done is to "let nature take its course." However, this adage is usually not spoken. Rather, the portrayal of romantic love as occurring through chemistry or a spark is depicted by two characters gazing into each other's eyes and sometimes stroking each other's faces. The viewer usually sees the two characters up close and in profile as serious and soaring music plays as this romantic chemistry is not explained with words but must be felt and understood via the gazing eye contact between the characters. Disney further marks the falling in love and the triumphs of hetero-romantic love by wrapping the characters in magical swirls of sparks, leaves, or fireworks as they stare into each other's eyes. The music accompanying such scenes is momentous and triumphant.

We asked whether all sorts of relationships might be magical, special, and exceptional in similar ways, as it is possible that many types of relationships have these qualities in these imaginative fantasies where anything is possible. However, we found that romantic heterosexual relationships in G-rated movies are set apart from other types of relationships. This serves to further define them as special and exceptional. All other love relationships are portrayed without the imagery described above. The pacing of friendship scenes is also faster and choppier, and the music is quicker and bouncy. Nor do friendships and familial relationships start with a "spark."

Parent-child relationships are portrayed as restrictive, tedious, and protective. The child is usually escaping these relationships for the exciting adolescent or adult world. Friendships are also set aside as different from romantic love. There are many close friendships and buddies in these stories, and none are portrayed with the imagery of romantic love. Crossgender friends are often literally smaller and a different species or object in the animated films, thus making them off limits for romance. For example, Mulan's friend is Mushoo, a small, red dragon; Pocahontas is friends with many small animals (a raccoon; a hummingbird); Ariel is looked after by Sebastian (a crab) and Flounder (a fish); and Belle is befriended by a range of small household items (teapot, candlestick, broom). Same-sex friendships or buddies are unusual for girls and women unless the friends are maternal (e.g., Willow in *Pocahontas,* Mrs. Pots in *Beauty and the Beast).* The lead male characters, however, often have comical buddies (e.g., Timon in *The Lion King,* Abu in *Aladdin,* the gargoyles in *The Hunchback of Notre Dame, Mike in Monsters, Inc.).* These friendships are often portrayed as funny, silly, gross, and fun but certainly not as serious, special, powerful, important, or natural. For example, in *The Lion King,* Timon (a meerkat), Pumba (a boar), and Simba (a lion) all live a carefree life together in the jungle as the best of friends, but Simba quickly deserts them for Nala, a female lion, once he is an adolescent. Throughout the film, Timon and Pumba provide comic relief from the serious business of the lions falling in (heterosexual) love and saving the kingdom. Thus, the construction of friendships and family relationships reveals that hetero-romantic relationships in contrast are serious, important, and natural.

Furthermore, while friendships provide comic relief and friends and family are portrayed as providing comfort or advice to lead characters, these relationships are not portrayed as transformative, powerful, or magical. Hetero-romantic love is exceptional in these films because it is constructed as incredibly powerful and transformative. Throughout many of these films with a primary plot about hetero-romantic love, such love is depicted as rebellious, magical, defiant, and with a power to transform the world. This is quite different from our understanding of heterosexuality as normative, ordinary, and expected. The hetero-romantic relationships in these films are extraordinary. Falling in heterosexual love can break a spell *(Beauty and the Beast)* or cause one to give up her identity *(The Little Mermaid).* It can save Santa Claus and Christmas *(Santa Clause 2).* It can lead children (e.g., Ariel, Jasmine, Pocahontas, Belle) to disobey their parents and defy the social rules of their culture (e.g., Jasmine, Pocahontas). It can stop a war that is imminent *(Pocahontas)* or change an age-old law *(Aladdin).* . . .

Finally, we observe that hetero-romantic love is not sexually embodied in these films except through kissing. The power of hetero-romantic love is often delivered through a heterosexual kiss. A lot of heterosexual kissing happens in G-rated films. *Princess Diaries,* with its live-action teenage characters, contains the most explicit kissing, as the main character daydreams that a boy kisses her passionately, open-mouthed as she falls back against the lockers smiling and giggling. Most animated kisses are with closed mouths (or the viewer cannot fully see the mouths) and of shorter duration, but they are often even more powerful. Throughout these films, but especially in the animated ones, a heterosexual kiss signifies heterosexual love and in doing so is powerful. Ariel of *The Little Mermaid* must secure a kiss from the prince to retain her voice and her legs. In *The Lion King,* when Nala and Simba kiss (lick and nuzzle) as they are reunited, they not only realize their love, but Simba realizes he must return to his rightful place as king and save his family and the entire kingdom. We often see these powerful kisses first very close-up and in profile and then moving outward to show the wider world that the powerful kisses are transforming. For example, once the Beast is transformed back into a man by Belle's declaration of love, they kiss, and the entire kingdom appears to turn from winter to springtime, flowers bloom, and others who had been damaged by the same spell as the Beast are restored to their personhood.

In one case, the kiss of love initially leads to making the world worse. When Pocahontas kisses John Smith, others see them, and this leads to the death of the man Pocahontas's father wanted her to marry. Eventually, however, their love is what brings peace between the Native Americans and European colonizers. Even this negative transformation brought on by a kiss is different from kisses outside of hetero-romantic love. Take, for example, the only same-gender kiss in these films. In *The Lion King*, Pumba and Timon are eating dinner and sucking on opposite ends of a worm (reminiscent of the classic *Lady and the Tramp* spaghetti vignette). When they reach the middle, their lips touch with a smooch, and they both look toward the camera aghast, seemingly both at the deed (the "kiss") and having been "caught" by the camera. This kiss is treated as humorous and not as serious or powerful as the kisses of hetero-romantic love. Even heterosexual kisses outside of love relationships are not serious, powerful, or transformative. For example, Jasmine kisses the evil Jafar in *Aladdin,* but she does so to trick him. It works as a trick and distraction, but it is not powerful or transformative. Only hetero-romantic kissing is powerful in that it signifies love and in doing so can change the world.

Heterosexiness and the Heterosexual Gaze: Heterosexuality Outside of Love

Thus far, we have described how heterosexuality is constructed through depictions of hetero-romantic love relationships in these films. There is also heterosexuality depicted outside of romantic relationships, though this heterosexuality is quite different and more ordinary. As such, it is depicted not as earnest or transformative but as frivolous, entertaining, and crude. This nonromantic heterosexuality is constructed through the different portrayals of women's and men's bodies, the heterosexiness of the feminine characters, and the heterosexual gaze of the masculine ones.

Heteronormativity requires particular kinds of bodies and interactions between those bodies. Thus, as heterosexuality is constructed in these films, gendered bodies are portrayed quite differently, and we see much more of some bodies than others. Women throughout the animated features in our sample are drawn with cleavage, bare stomachs, and bare legs. Women of color are more likely to be drawn as young women with breasts and hips and white women as delicate girls (Lacroix 2004). Men are occasionally depicted without their shirts, such as in *Tarzan*; or without much of a shirt, as in *Aladdin*; and in one scene in *Mulan,* it is implied that men have been swimming naked. However, having part of the body exposed is more common among the lead women characters and among the women who make up the background of the scenes.

Women's nudity is also often marked as significant through comment or reaction. Women are often "almost caught" naked by men. For example, Mia of the *Princess Diaries* has her dressing area torn down by jealous girls, almost revealing her naked to a group of male photographers. Mulan bathes in a lake when she thinks she is alone, but when male soldiers come to swim, Mushoo refers to her breasts, saying, "There are a couple of things they're bound to notice," and she sneaks away. Similarly, Quasimodo accidentally stumbles into Esmeralda's dressing area, and she quickly covers up with a robe and hunches over so as not to expose herself. She ties up her robe as Quasimodo apologizes again and again and hides his eyes. However, as he exits, he glances back toward her with a smile signifying for the viewer his love for her. A glimpse of her body has made her even more lovable and desirable.

Men's bodies are treated quite differently in these films. Male bodies, to the extent they are commented on at all, are the site of jokes. Men's crotches, genitals, and backsides are funny. For example, in *Hunchback of Notre Dame,* a cork from a bottle of champagne flies between a man's legs and knocks him over and the man yells in pain; later in that movie, during a fight, someone says, "That's hitting a little below the belt," and the woman says, "No, this is!" and aims to strike him in the groin but is deflected by a sword. A boy in *Princess Diaries* is doubled over in pain as a baseball hits him in the groin. This scene is played as funny and the result of another character extracting her vengeance. *The Rugrats Movie* is full of jokes and images of boys' bare bottoms and penises. There are also references in other films to "a limp noodle" *(Mulan)* and "a shrinky winky" *(101 Dalmatians)*. Mushoo in *Mulan* also jokes about male nudity, saying, "I hate biting naked butts." Women's genitals are never mentioned or invoked in any way. Their bodies are not the sites of jokes. Rather, women's bodies become important in the construction of heteronormative sexuality through their "sexiness" at which men gaze.

Much of the sexuality that these gendered bodies engage in has little to do with hetero-sexual sex narrowly defined as intercourse or even behaviors that might lead to it, but rather with cultural signs of a gendered sexuality for women. These signs are found in subplots, musical numbers, humorous scenes, and scenes depicting women's bodies, rather than in the main story lines of hetero-romantic true love. Such scenes contain sexual innuendo based in gesture, movement, tone of voice, and expression. Importantly, in all cases, sexi-ness is depicted as something women possess and use for getting men's attention. Sexiness is more often an attribute of female characters of color (e.g., Esmeralda, Jasmine, Ursula) (Hurley 2005) and is implicitly heterosexual given that the films construct the intended spectator of this sexiness as male (Mulvey 1975).

The best example of the representation of sexiness appears in *The Hunchback of Notre Dame*. Esmeralda, the Gypsy female lead, is drawn with dark hair, big green eyes, a curvy body, cleav-age, and a small waist. She is also drawn with darker skin than other lead Disney characters like Belle *(Beauty and the Beast)* and Ariel *(Little Mermaid)*. Darker skin and hair and "exotic" fea-tures are part of the representation of heterosexual sexiness for women. Moreover, Esmeralda spends much time in this film swaying her hips and dancing "sexily" while men admire her. An early scene in the film resembles a striptease, although all the character's clothes do not come off. The scene begins with the song, "Come one, come all! Hurry, hurry, here's your chance. See the mystery and romance . . . See the finest girl in France . . . Make an entrance to entrance . . . Dance la Esmeralda . . . Dance!" Esmeralda begins to dance. She is dressed seduc-tively, and her dancing is provocative. We then see the men who are watching her. Frollo says, "Look at that disgusting display" to which Captain replies, "YES SIR!" and opens his eyes wider. She perches in front of Frollo and then tosses her scarf around his neck, pulls him in as if she is going to kiss him, puts her lips on his nose, and then pushes his hat over his face. She dances back to the stage where she does a split in front of Quasimodo and gives him a wink. She then steals a large spear from a security guard, stabs it into the stage and begins to swing and twist around the pole. The men in the crowd are all wide-eyed, screaming and cheering, and then they all toss money on stage for her performance.

Not all scenes with the signification of sexiness are so elaborated. . . . Throughout *Aladdin*, especially in fast-paced musical scenes, sexy women prance, preen, bat their eyelashes, shake their hips, and reveal their cleavage. When Genie sings to Aladdin, he produces three women with bare stomachs and bikini-like outfits who dance around him, touch him, bat their eyes at him, and kiss him. He stares at them sometimes unsure, but wide-eyed and smiling. When Prince Ali comes to ask Princess Jasmine for her hand in marriage, his parade to the castle is adorned with writhing, dancing women with bare stomachs and cleavage. Later, Jasmine sees Prince Ali as a fraud and tricks him with similarly sexy moves. Heterosexiness in *Aladdin* is delivered through the bodies of women of color who are exoticized.

There are a few examples of white women depicted as "sexy," although these are more delimited and do not involve the main white women/girl characters. In *Princess Diaries*, a group of teenage friends are shown doing many of the same things as the animated women in *Aladdin*. They dance, shake their hips, make faces with curled and puckered lips and squinting eyes, play with their hair, and slap their hips. In *Beauty and the Beast,* a man is hit on the head for talking to a large-breasted woman with cleavage and much lipstick who moves and speaks in a sexy, flirtatious manner. *Toy Story 2* has a group of singing, dancing, nearly all-white Barbies who are ogled by the masculine toys. These scenes make it clear that women move and adorn their bodies and contort their faces for men.

While the women are being sexy, the (usually white) men are performing a different role as these films construct heterosexuality. As evident from some of the examples above, there is much explicit heterosexual gazing at or ogling of women's bodies in these films. Sometimes such gazing establishes that a woman is worth the pursuit of men and the fight for her that will develop the plot of the film, as in *Beauty and the Beast.* In an early scene in this film, when Belle walks out of a bookshop, three men who had been peering through the window turn around as if to pretend that they had not been staring. The man in the middle is then held up by the other two so that he can stare at Belle's backside as she walks away. All three men stare and then start to sing of her beauty. In other films, sexualized gazing is not so tightly attached to beauty but to the performance of heterosexual masculinity. In one instance in *Chicken Run*, the chickens are "exercising," and Rocky (a chicken) stares at Ginger's (a chicken) backside. She catches him, and he smiles, slyly. . . .

The objectifying gaze at women's bodies is often translated into objectifying, sexist language. Girl/women characters are called doll face, chicks, cuties, baby doll, angel face, sweet cheeks, bodacious, succulent little garden snail, tender oozing blossom, temptress snake, and tramp; and the boys/men say things like "I'll give you a tune up any time" and "give her some slack and reel her in." The desiring gazes, the commentary, and the depictions of them (large eyes, staring, open mouths, sound effects, and anxiousness) are constructed as competitive and conquering or frivolous, in stark contrast to the exceptional, magical, powerful hetero-romantic love described above. These depictions of heterosexual interactions have the effect of normalizing men's objectification of women's bodies and the heterosexual desire it signifies.

Conclusion

Despite the assumption that children's media are free of sexual content, our analyses suggest that these media depict a rich and pervasive heterosexual landscape. We have illustrated two main ways that G-rated films construct heterosexuality. First, heterosexuality is constructed through depictions of hetero-romantic love as exceptional, powerful, transformative, and magical. Second, heterosexuality is also constructed through depictions of interactions between gendered bodies in which the sexiness of feminine characters is subjected to the gaze of masculine characters. These accounts of heterosexuality extend our understandings of heteronormativity.

References

Arnold, Thomas K. 2005. "Kids' DVDs Are in a Growth Spurt." *USA Today* (www.usatoday.com/life/movies/news/2005-04-04-kids-dvds_x.htm).

Best, Raphaela. 1983. *We've All Got Scars: What Boys and Girls Learn in Elementary School.* Bloomington, IN: Indiana University Press.

Giroux, Henry A. 1997. "Are Disney Movies Good for Your Kids?" In *Kinderculture: The Corporate Construction of Childhood,* edited by S. R. Steinberg and J. L. Kincheloe. Boulder, CO: Westview.

Hurley, Dorothy L. 2005. "Seeing White: Children of Color and the Disney Fairy Tale Princess." *Journal of Negro Education* 74:221–32.

Ingraham, Chrys. 1999. *White Weddings: Romancing Heterosexuality in Popular Culture*. New York: Routledge.

Jackson, Stevi. 2006. "Gender, Sexuality and Heterosexuality: The Complexity (and Limits) of Heteronormativity." *Feminist Theory* 7:105–21.

Johnson, Paul. 2005. *Love, Heterosexuality, and Society*. London, UK: Routledge.

Kelley, P., D. Buckingham, and H. Davies. 1999. "Talking Dirty: Sexual Knowledge and Television." *Childhood* 6:221–42.

Kim, J. L., C. L. Sorsoll, K. Collins, and B. A. Zylbergold. 2007. "From Sex to Sexuality: Exposing the Heterosexual Script on Primetime Network Television." *Journal of Sex Research* 44:145.

Kitzinger, Celia. 2005. "Heteronormativity in Action: Reproducing the Heterosexual Nuclear Family in After-hours Medical Calls." *Social Problems* 52:477–98.

Lacroix, Celeste. 2004. "Images of Animated Others: The Orientalization of Disney's Cartoon Heroines from 'The Little Mermaid' to 'The Hunchback of Notre Dame.'" *Popular Communication* 2:213–29.

Lancaster, Roger. 2003. *The Trouble with Nature*. Berkeley, CA: University of California Press.

Martin, Karin A. 2009. "Normalizing Heterosexuality: Mothers' Assumptions, Talk, and Strategies with Young Children." *American Sociological Review* 74:190–207.

Martin, Karin A., Katherine Luke, and Lynn Verduzco-Baker. 2007. "The Sexual Socialization of Young Children: Setting the Agenda for Research." In *Advances in Group Processes*. Vol. 6, *Social Psychology of Gender*, edited by S. Correll. Oxford, UK: Elsevier Science.

Motion Picture Association of America. 2009. "'Film Ratings,' Motion Picture Association of America." (www.mpaa.org/FilmRatings.asp).

Mulvey, Laura. 1975. "Visual Pleasure and Narrative Cinema." *Screen* 16:6–18.

Renold, Emma. 2002. "Presumed Innocence: (Hetero)Sexual, Heterosexist and Homophobic Harassment Among Primary School Girls and Boys." *Childhood* 9:415–34.

Renold, Emma. 2005. *Girls, Boys, and Junior Sexualities: Exploring Children's Gender and Sexual Relations in the Primary School*. London, UK: Routledge Falmer.

Rideout, V., E. A. Vandewater, and E. A. Wartella. 2003. *Zero to Six: Electronic Media in the Lives of Infants, Toddlers, and Preschoolers*. Washington, DC: Henry J. Kaiser Family Foundation.

Rubin, Gayle. 1984. "Thinking Sex: Notes for a Radical Theory of the Politics of Sexuality." In *Pleasure and Danger*, edited by C. Vance. Boston, MA: Routledge.

Thomas, Susan Gregory. 2007. *Buy, Buy, Baby: How Consumer Culture Manipulates Parents*. New York: Houghton Mifflin.

Thorne, Barrie. 1993. *Gender Play: Girls and Boys in School*. New Brunswick, NJ: Rutgers University Press.

Ward, L. Monique. 1995. "Talking About Sex: Common Themes About Sexuality in the Prime-Time Television Programs Children and Adolescents View Most." *Journal of Youth and Adolescence* 24:595–615.

Ward, Monique L. 2003. "Understanding the Role of Entertainment Media in the Sexual Socialization of American Youth: A Review of Empirical Research." *Developmental Review* 23:347–88.

Is He Boyfriend Material?

Representation of Males
in Teenage Girls' Magazines

Kirsten B. Firminger

© iStockphoto.com/wundervisuals

It seems like guys lock up their feelings tighter than Fort Knox, right? Well, here's the key to opening that emotional vault! . . . CG! Epiphany: When a guy finally opens up to you, you'll know he has set you apart from other girls.

—CosmoGirl, All About Guys Section, "Guy Magnet Cheat Sheet"

O n the pages of popular teenage girls' magazines, boys are presented (in)congruently as the providers of potential love, romance, and excitement and as highly sexual, attracted to the superficial, and emotionally inexpressive. The magazines guide female

Kirsten B. Firminger. 2006. "Is He Boyfriend Material? Representation of Males in Teenage Girls' Magazines." *Men and Masculinities* 8(3):298–308.

readers toward avoiding the "bad" male and male behavior (locking up their feelings tighter than Fort Knox) and obtaining the "good" male and male behavior (setting you apart from other girls). Within girls' magazines, success in life and (heterosexual) love is girls' responsibility, tied to their ability to self-regulate, make good choices, and present themselves in the "right" way. The only barriers are girls' own lack of self-esteem or limited effort (Harris 2004). While the "girl power" language of the feminist movement is used, its politics and questioning of patriarchal gender norms are not discussed. Instead, the magazines advocate relentless surveillance of self, boys, and peers. Embarrassing and confessional tales, quizzes, and opportunities to rate and judge boys and girls on the basis of their photos and profiles encourage young women to "fashion" identities through clothes, cosmetics, beauty items, and consumerism.

Popular teenage girls' magazines. In the United States, teenage girls' magazines are read by more than 75 percent of teenage girls (Market Profile: Teenagers 2000). The magazines play an important role in shaping the norms and expectations during a crucial stage of identity and relationship development. Currie (1999) found that some readers consider the magazines' content to be more compelling than their own personal experiences and knowledge. Magazines are in the business of both selling themselves to their audience and selling their audience to advertisers (Kilbourne 1999). Teenage girls are advertised as more loyal to their favorite magazines than to their favorite television programs, with magazines touted as "a sister and a friend rolled into one" (Market Profile: Teenagers 2000). Magazines attract and keep advertisers by providing the right audience for their products and services, suppressing information that might offend the advertiser, and including editorial content saturated in advertiser-friendly advice (Kilbourne 1999).

In this textual environment, consumerist and individualist attitudes and values are promoted to the exclusion of alternative perspectives. Across magazines, one relentless message is clear: "the road to happiness is attracting males for successful heterosexual life by way of physical beautification" (Evans et al. 1991; see also Carpenter 1998, Currie 1999, Signorelli 1997). Given the clarity of this message, little work has been done focusing on the portrayal of males that the girls are supposed to attract. I began my research examining this question: how are males and male behavior portrayed in popular teenage girls' magazines?

Method

To explore these questions, I designed a discursive analysis of a cross-section of adolescent girls' magazines, sampling a variety of magazines and analyzing across them for common portrayals of males. *Seventeen* and *YM* are long-running adolescent girls' magazines. *Seventeen* has a base circulation of 2.4 million while *YM* has a circulation of 2.2 million (*Advertising Age* 74: 21). As a result of the potential of the market, the magazines that are directed at adolescent girls have expanded to include the new *CosmoGirl* (launched in 1999) and *ELLEgirl* (in 2001). Very successful, *CosmoGirl* has a base circulation of 1 million. *ELLEgirl* reports a smaller circulation of 450,000 (*Advertising Age* 74:21). Chosen as an alternative to the other adolescent girls' magazines, *Girls' Life* is directed at a younger female audience and is the winner of the 2000, 1999, and 1996 Parents' Choice Awards Medal and of the 2000 and 1998 Parents' Guide to Children's Media Association Award of Excellence. The magazine reports it is the number one magazine for girls ages 10 to 15, with a circulation of 3 million (http://www.girlslife.com/infopage.php, retrieved May 23, 2004).

I coded two issues each of *Seventeen, YM, CosmoGirl, ELLEgirl,* and *Girls' Life,* for a total of ten issues. . . .

Results

Within the pages of the magazines, articles and photo layouts focus primarily on beauty, fashion, celebrities and entertainment, boys and love, health and sex, and self-development. The magazines specialize, with emphasis more or less on one of these topics over the other: *ELLEGirl* presents itself as more fashion focused, while self-development is the emphasis for *Girls' Life's* younger audience. Within the self-development sections, one can find articles focusing on topics such as activities, school, career aspirations, volunteering, sports, and politics. However, even in these articles, focus is on the social, interpersonal aspects of relationships and on consumption instead of the actual doing and mastery of activities.

Advertising permeates the magazines, accounting for 20.8 percent to 44.8 percent of the pages. Additionally, many of the editorial articles, presumably noncommercial, are written in ways that endorse specific products and services (see Currie 1999, for more information on "advertorials"). For instance, one advice column responded to a reader's inquiry about a first kiss by recommending ". . . [having] the following supplies [handy] for when the magical moment finally arrives: Sugarless mints, yummy flavored lip gloss (I dig Bonne Bell Lip Smackers). . . ."

Male-focused content. On average, 19.7 percent of the pages focused on males, ranging from a minimum of 13.6 percent in *ELLEGirl* to a maximum 26.6 percent in *Seventeen.* Articles on boys delve into boys' culture, points of view, opinions, interests, and hobbies, while articles on girls' activities focus more pointedly on the pursuit of boys. Girls learn "where the boys are," since the "next boyfriend could be right under your nose." They are told,

> Where to go: Minor-league ballparks. Why: Cute guys! . . . Who'll be there: The players are just for gazing at; your targets are the cuties in the stands. And don't forget the muscular types lugging soda trays up and down the aisles. What to say: Ask him what he thinks about designated hitters (they're paid just to bat). He'll be totally impressed that you even brought up the subject.

Males are offered up to readers in several different formats. First we read profiles, then we meet "examples," we are allowed question and answer, we are quizzed, and then we are asked to judge the males. Celebrity features contain in-depth interviews with male celebrities, while personal short profiles of celebrities or "regular" guys include a photo, biographical information, hobbies, interests, and inquiries such as his "three big requirements for a girlfriend" and "his perfect date." *CosmoGirl's* fold-out photo centerfold (see Figure 19.1) informs readers that the first thing 27-year-old Eli notices about a girl is "the way she carries herself," his turn-ons are "Confidence, intelligence, sense of humor, lips, eyes, and a sense of adventure," and his turn-offs are "insecurity, dishonesty, and anything fake." In question-and-answer articles, regular columnists answer selected questions that the readers have submitted. Some columns consistently focus on boys, such as "GL Guys by Bill and Dave" and YM's "Love Q and A," while others focus on a variety of questions, for instance *ELLEgirl's* "Ask Jennifur" profiles of noncelebrity males are presented and judged in rating articles. The magazines publish their criteria for rating boys, via rhetorical devices such as "the magazine staffs' opinions" or the opinion polls of other teenage girls (see Figure 19.1).

Figure 19.1 "The Rating Game" and "All About Eli"

Source: *ELLEGirl* May/June 2003, p. 136, "Fashion Lab," published by Hachette Filipacchi Media, New York, NY.

Ratings include categories such as "his style," "dateable?," and "style factor." For example, in *CosmoGirl*'s Boy-O-Meter article, "Dateable?: I usually go for dark hair, olive skin, and thick eyebrows. But his eyes make me feel like I could confide in him," or *ELLEgirl*'s The Rating Game, "He's cute, but I don't dig the emo look and the hair in the face. It's girlie." Readers can then assess their opinions in relation to those of other girls' and the magazine staff.

Romantic stories and quotes enable readers to witness "real" romance and love and compare their "personal experiences" to those presented in the magazines. For instance, "Then one day I found a note tucked in my locker that said, 'You are different than everyone else. But that is why you are beautiful.' At the bottom of the note it said, 'From Matt—I'm in your science class.' We started dating the next day." These can also be rated, as the magazine staff then responded, "Grade: A. He sounds like a very smart boy."

Finally, the readers can then test their knowledge and experiences through the quizzes in the magazines, such as *Seventeen*'s quiz, "Can your summer love last?", with questions and multiple-choice answers:

As he's leaving for a weeklong road trip with the guys, he: A) tells you at least 10 times how much he's going to miss you. B) promises to call you when he gets a chance. C) can't stop talking about how much fun it will be to "get away" with just his buddies for seven whole days.

Over the pages, boys as a "product" begin to merge with the [other] products and services being sold to girls in "training" as informed consumers, learning to feel "empowered" and make good "choices." While a good boy is a commodity of value, the young women readers learn that relationships with boys should be considered disposable and interchangeable like the other products being sold, "Remember, BFs come and go, but best friends are forever! Is he worth it? Didn't think so."

[. . .]

Representations of males. To assess how males are represented, I coded content across male-focused feature articles and "question and answer" columns. These articles contained the most general statements about boys and their behaviors, motivations, and characteristics (for example, "Guys are a few steps behind girls when it comes to maturity level").

A dominant tension in the representations of boys involves males' splitting of intimacy from sexuality. . . . The magazine advises girls as they negotiate these different behaviors and situations, trying to choose the "right" guy (who will develop an intimate relationship with a girl), reject the "bad" guy (who is focused only on sex), or if possible, change the "bad" guy into the "good" guy (through a girl's decisions and interactions with the male).

> My boyfriend and I were together for 10 months when he said he wanted to take a break—he wasn't sure he was ready for such a commitment. The thought of him seeing other people tore me apart. So every day while we were broken up, I gave him something as a sign of my feelings for him: love sayings cut out from magazines, or cute comics from the paper. Eventually he confessed that he had just been confused and that he loved me more than ever.

As girls are represented as responsible for good shopping, they are represented also as responsible for selecting/changing/shaping male behavior. If girls learn to make the right choices, they can have the right relationship with the right guy, or convert a "bad"/confused boy into a good catch.

The tension is most evident in stories about males' high sex drive, attraction to superficial appearances, emotional inexpressiveness, and fear of rejection and contrasted with those males who are "keepers": who keep their sex drive in check, value more than just girls' appearances, and are able to open up. The articles and advice columns blend the traditional and the feminist; encompassing both new and old meanings and definitions of what it means to be female and male within today's culture (Harris 2004).

The males' sex drive. The "naturally" high sex drive of males rises as the most predominant theme across the magazines. Viewed as normal and unavoidable in teenage boys, girls write to ask for an explanation and advice, and they are told:

> You invited a guy you kind of like up to your room (just to talk!) and he got the wrong idea. This was not your fault. Guys—especially unchaperoned guys on school trips—will interpret any move by a girl as an invitation to get heavy. And I mean any move. You could have sat down next to him at a lab table and he would have taken that as a sign from God that you wanted his body.

When it comes to the topic of sexuality, traditional notions surround "appropriate behavior" for young women and men. Girls learn that males respect and date girls who are able to keep males' sex drive in check and who take time building a relationship. Girls were rarely shown as being highly sexual or interested only in a sexual relationship with a boy. Girls are supposed to avoid potentially dangerous situations (such as being alone with a boy) and draw the line (since the males frequently are unable to do so). If they don't, they can be labeled sluts.

> Don't even make out with someone until you're sure things are exclusive. When you hook up with him too early, you're giving him the message that you are something less than a goddess (because, as you know, a goddess is guarded in a temple, and it's not easy to get to her). Take it from me when I tell you that guys want to be with girls they consider goddesses. So treat your body as a temple—don't let just any one in.

> Most guys would probably assume that a girl who ditches guys after intimacy is slutty. I know, I know—there's a double standard. It seems like the "players" among us can date and dump as frequently as they please, but it's only a social no-no when you girls do it.

> A guy in heat tried to take advantage of you and you wouldn't give in. That's all that matters. You may have kissed him, but, ultimately, the decision to draw the line was yours and you did it. That's nothing to feel slutty about.

Valuing superficial appearances. Driven by sex, males were shown as judging and valuing girls based on their appearance.

> That's bad, but it's scarier when combined with another sad male truth: They're a lot more into looks than we are.

> Okay, I'm the first to admit that guys can be shallow and insipid and *Baywatch* brainwashed to the point where the sight of two balloons on a string will turn them on.

Since males are thought to be interested in the superficial, girls sought advice on how to be most superficially appealing, asking what do guys prefer, including the size of a girl's breasts, hair color, eye color, height, and weight. Girls are portrayed as wanting to know how to present themselves to attract boys, demonstrating an interaction between girls' ideas and understanding of what males want and girls' own choices and behaviors.

Boys are emotionally inexpressive. Across features, readers learn about boys' inability or unwillingness to open up and share their feelings. However, the articles suggest also that if a girl is able to negotiate the relationship correctly, she could get a guy to trust her.

> Let's say you go to the pet store and see a really cute puppy you'd like to pet but, every time you try, he pulls away because he was treated badly in the past. People aren't much different. Move very slowly, and build up trust bit by bit. Show this guy you're into him for real, and he'll warm up to you. Puppy love is worth the wait.

Girls are responsible for doing the emotional work and maintenance and for being change agents in relationships, not allowing room for or even expecting males to take on any of these tasks (see also Chang 2000).

Boys' insecurity and fear of rejection. Boys are displayed as afraid of rejection. Reflecting the neoliberal ideology of "girl power," girls were urged by the magazines to take the initiative in seeking out and approaching boys. This way they are in control of and responsible for their fate, with only lack of confidence, self-esteem, and effort holding them back from finding romance and love.

> So in the next week (why waste more time?), write him a note, pull him aside at a party, or call him up with your best friend by your side for support. Hey, he could be psyched that you took the initiative.

> So I think you may have to do the work. If there's a certain guy you're feelin' and you think he's intimidated by you, make the first move. Say something to relax him, like, "What's up? My name is Chelsea." After that, he'll probably start completing sentences.

Males' potential—the "keepers." "Consider every guy to be on a level playing field—they all have potential." Boys were shown to have "potential" and girls were advised to search out the "right" guys.

> He does indeed sound dreamy. He also sounds like a total gentleman, considering he hasn't attempted to jump your bones yet, so the consensus is: He's a keeper.

> Most guys are actually smarter than you think and are attracted to all sorts of things about the female species. Yes, big boobs definitely have their dedicated fan base, but so do musical taste, brains, a cute laugh, style and the ability to throw a spiral football (to name just a few). What's a turn-on or deal breaker for one guy is a nonevent for another.

> The streets are filled with guys who are nice, hot, smart, fun, and half-naked (joking . . . sort of!) And they all want to spend some time with an unattached pumpkin like you.

These boys become the center of the romantic stories and quotes about love and relationships. Resulting from and sustained by girls' self-regulation, personal responsibility, effort, and good choices (as guided by the tools and advice provided by the magazines), these boys are for keeps.

Discussion

Within the magazines, girls are invited to explore boys as shallow, highly sexual, emotionally inexpressive, and insecure and boys who are potential boyfriends, providing romance, intimacy, and love. Males' high sex drive and interest in superficial appearances are naturalized and left unquestioned in the content of the magazines; within a "girl power" version of compulsory heterosexuality, girls should learn the right way to approach a boy in order to get what they want—"the road to happiness is attracting males for successful heterosexual life by way of physical beautification" (Evans et al. 1991). Girls walk the fine line of taking advantage of males' interest in sex and appearance, without crossing over into being labeled a slut. Socialized to be purchasers of beauty and fashion products that promise to make them attractive to boys, girls are "in charge" of themselves and the boys they "choose." It's a competitive market so they better have the right understanding of boys, as well as the right body and outfit to go with it.

The magazines' portrayals, values, and opinions are shaped by their need to create an advertiser-friendly environment while attracting and appealing to the magazines' audience of teenage girls. Skewing the portrayal of males and females to their target audience, magazine editors, writers, and, though I have not highlighted it here—advertisers take advantage of gender-specific fantasies, myths, and fears (Craig 1993). Boys become another product, status symbol, and identity choice. If girls' happiness requires finding romance and love, girls should learn to be informed consumers of boys. By purchasing the magazines, they have a guide to this process, guaranteed to help them understand "What his mixed signals really mean." In addition, if boys are concerned with superficial appearances, it is to the benefit of girls to buy the advertised products and learn "The best swimsuit for [their] bod[ies]."

As girls survey and judge themselves and others, possessions and consumption become the metric for assessing status (Rohlinger 2002; Salamon 2003), the cultural capital for teenagers in place of work, community, and other activities (Harris 2004). The feminist "girl empowerment" becomes personal, appropriated to sell products. The choice and purchase of products and services sold in the magazines promise recreation and transformation, of not only one's outward appearance but also of one's inner self, leading to happiness, satisfaction, and success (Kilbourne 1999). Money is the underlying driving force in magazine content. However, while the magazines focus on doing good business, girls are being socialized by the magazines' norms and expectations.

"Bottom line: look at dating as a way to sample the menu before picking your entrée. In the end, you'll be much happier with the choice you make! Yum!"

References

Carpenter, L. M. 1998. "From Girls into Women: Scripts for Sexuality and Romance in *Seventeen* Magazine, 1974–1994." *The Journal of Sex Research* 35:158–68.

Chang, J. 2000. "Agony-Resolution Pathways: How Women Perceive American Men in *Cosmopolitan's* Agony (Advice) Column." *The Journal of Men's Studies* 8:285–308.

Craig, S. 1993. "Selling Masculinities, Selling Femininities: Multiple Genders and the Economics of Television." *The Mid-Atlantic Almanack* 2:15–27.

Currie, D. H. 1999. *Girl Talk: Adolescent Magazines and Their Readers*. Toronto, Canada: University of Toronto Press.

Evans, E., J. Rutberg, and C. Sather. 1991. "Content Analysis of Contemporary Teen Magazines for Adolescent Females." *Youth and Society* 23:99–120.

Girls' Life Magazine: About Us. Retrieved May 23, 2004 (www.girlslife.com/infopage.php).

Harris, Anita, ed. 2004. *All About the Girl: Culture, Power, and Identity*. New York: Routledge.

Kilbourne, Jean. 1999. *Deadly Persuasion: Why Women and Girls Must Fight the Addictive Power of Advertising*. New York: Free Press.

Market Profile: Teenagers. 2000. Magazine Publishers of America.

Rohlinger, D. 2002. "Eroticizing Men: Cultural Influences on Advertising and Male Objectification." *Sex Roles: A Journal of Research* 46:61–74.

Salamon, S. 2003. "From Hometown to Nontown: Rural Community Effects of Suburbanization." *Rural Sociology* 68:1–24.

Signorelli, N. 1997. "A Content Analysis: Reflections of Girls in the Media, a Study of Television Shows and Commercials, Movies, Music Videos, and Teen Magazine Articles and Ads." *Children Now and Kaiser Family Foundation Publication*.

Masculinity Dilemmas

*Sexuality and Intimacy Talk
Among Christians and Goths*

Amy C. Wilkins

© iStockphoto.com/Goruppa

I n this article, I compare seemingly antithetical groups of white middle-class young adult men. The first, members of a university-based evangelical organization I call University Unity, engage in a conservative cultural agenda, abstain from partying and sex, and commit themselves to self-discipline and moral cleanliness. The second, goths, self-consciously use dark clothes and dark emotions to transform themselves into self-proclaimed freaks. Apparent boundary transgressors, they adopt elements of gender blending and queer play. Christianity and goth provide distinct ways of navigating the space between adolescence and adulthood, yet their masculinity projects achieve similar things. Both evangelical Christian and goth men attempt to ameliorate some of the more restrictive expectations of masculinity by crafting masculinity projects out of available cultural resources.

Amy C. Wilkins. 2009. "Masculinity Dilemmas: Sexuality and Intimacy Talk Among Christians and Goths." *Signs* 34(2):343–68.

The need to take men's lives seriously is now well established among gender scholars. R. W. Connell defines hegemonic masculinity as "the cultural dynamic by which a group claims and sustains a leading position in social life" (1995, 77). Hegemonic masculinity, then, is a constellation of cultural ideas about "real men" that maintain men's dominance over both women and other men. This cultural ideal creates among men a hierarchy of access to status, power, and esteem, since some men are better able to approximate it than others. No man, however, is able to fully embody it. Thus, the elusive ideal of hegemonic masculinity creates particular gender dilemmas for different boys and men as they struggle to create socially recognized masculinities. The ensuing negotiations over masculinity are embedded in power relations both between men and women and among men.

Heterosexuality and emotional stoicism are central (and often linked) components of hegemonic masculinity. The persistent expectation that boys will be boys mandates and excuses the performance of aggressive heterosexuality among young men. Not only are boys and men assumed to be heterosexual, but they are assumed to be heterosexual in particular ways. For young men especially, heterosexuality is imagined as a relentless drive, endlessly preoccupying and always potentially out of control. Accordingly, men are assumed to be heterosexually predatory and dominant, and more interested in sex than in emotions. Nonetheless, men's heterosexual dominance and emotional stoicism have both come under attack, complicating the cultural terrain of men's dominance (Messner 1993). In this article, I examine the ways in which young men use unconventional sexualities and intimacy talk, an emotional vocabulary associated with a "feminine" style of love, to resolve their masculinity dilemmas.

These young men do not enact gender projects in isolation. Subcultures make alternative gender identities more possible because they provide community and support for practices that might otherwise be isolating. Both the Unity Christian and the goth subcultures create conditions for the staging of alternative heterosexual performances and collectively manipulate dominant meanings of masculinity. In both cases, new collective meanings of heterosexuality and manhood, not the practices themselves, allow participants to manage their masculinities.

Here, I do not attempt to address the question of why each set of young men chose to become Christian or goth. Rather, I am concerned with how they use their subcultural identities to reconstitute their masculinities and with some of the consequences of these reconstitutions. Comparing the two subcultures generates a different kind of analysis than would a discussion of either separately. By examining the similarities and differences between seemingly antithetical masculinities, we can begin to see not just a plurality of ways of being masculine but also patterns among them. Despite striking differences in the gender projects of Unity Christian and goth men, they similarly navigate dilemmas posed by masculine expectations. Each group of men differently renounces components of dominant notions of masculinity, achieving more flexibility in the performance of masculinity. Yet, in the end, both the Christians' conservative project and the goths' gender-blending project fail to challenge gendered power hierarchies.

Thinking About Masculinities

Feminists and other social commentators are concerned about the implications of a masculine culture of aggression and sexual dominance for both boys and girls (Eder 1995), as well as the suppression of "soft" emotionality among boys. William Pollack (1998), for example, worries that the denial of emotions in boys leads to alienation and destructive behaviors. As a result of these concerns, feminists and progressive youth often applaud boys' and men's adoption of unorthodox behaviors. These challenges to definitions of "real" masculinity have opened up some cultural space for the acceptable performance of a wider range of masculine styles (see Schippers 2002; Anderson 2005).

Cultural change is never univocal, however. While some social commentators lament the loss of feelings among boys, others complain that contemporary boys are becoming too soft. Sut Jhally documents an increasing emphasis on masculine toughness in the media (*Tough Guise* 1999). In his research on the families of boys who have been sexually abused, C. Shawn McGuffey (2008) also found that fathers, in part, attribute their sons' abuse to a vulnerability stemming from "softer" parenting strategies. These fathers attempt to cure their sons by deliberately instilling qualities of emotional toughness and heterosexual dominance in them. These examples seem to suggest a cultural struggle in which, on one hand, restrictive notions of masculinity are questioned by progressives while, on the other hand, a conservative backlash reasserts masculine toughness.

But masculinities are more complex than they initially appear. First, masculinities are not static but are contingent and negotiated. Boys and men draw on available resources to actively manage their masculinities (Chen 1999). For example, young men are able to use high-status masculine traits as bargaining chips that allow them to also exhibit lower-status traits (McGuffey and Rich 1999). In a study of a California high school, C. J. Pascoe (2003) found that boys who were athletically successful could exhibit "soft" feelings without consequence but nonathletic boys could not. These examples suggest that high-status boys and men have more flexibility in their gender performances. Because their masculinities are already anchored by investments in high-status dimensions of masculinity (e.g., sports), they are able to play with less manly forms of gender expressions (McGuffey and Rich 1999; Pascoe 2003). But even lower-status boys and men can position themselves as masculine by claiming high-status elements of masculinity. Rather than challenge dominant understandings of masculinity, this maneuvering allows a spectrum of men.

[...]

The Data

This article is based on ethnographic studies of local Christian and goth subcultures. The claims I make in the article are not intended to be generalized to all Christians or goths but instead to document similarities and differences in local projects. I conducted twelve months of participant observation at University Unity meetings as well as at the home church of most of my participants and carried out formal, open-ended interviews with fifteen (six men and nine women) self-identified evangelical Christians. I made my initial contact through a non-Christian student and then recruited the other participants through University Unity networks, on whose organizational material I also draw. In this study, my position as a non-Christian impeded my ability to establish trust. Nevertheless, several of my respondents liked me well enough to connect me with other Christians. In the end, almost all the student leaders of University Unity, as well as many rank-and-file members, had talked to me at some point.

I spent eighteen months in the goth scene, attending the Sanctuary (a local goth club) and private goth events, as well as hanging out with goths in their homes, at bars and coffee shops, and at the mall. I entered the goth scene through a friend of a friend, but my first fruitful contact was with Beth (a pseudonym, like all others used in this article). Beth and I hit it off immediately, and she was able to facilitate my integration into the goth scene, introducing me to the Sanctuary, to a listserv, and to her friends. Once I gained initial access to the goth community,

I found myself easily accepted. This acceptance was perhaps surprising, given goth hostility to "tourists." The reason may be that, in addition to being validated by Beth, I was viewed, I think, as a sympathetic audience.

I conducted in-depth, open-ended interviews with seventeen self-identified goths (seven men and ten women). In addition, I engaged in numerous casual conversations with the interviewees as well as with other goths. Six months of lurking (and some participation) on NetGoth, the Internet community in which local goths participate, yielded reams of additional data. At the time of my participation, NetGoth had approximately eighty members collectively posting up to 150 messages a day. These postings gave me an additional view into the ongoing negotiation of goth identities, since the Web venue was a regular forum for most participants, who used it to engage issues both silly and serious.

[. . .]

Located in the same university community in the Northeast, each subculture draws most of its participants from the university and surrounding colleges. Thus, for both, membership is bounded by the temporal rhythms of the undergraduate experience. The participants in both groups are young adults, ranging in age from eighteen to their late twenties. The area is characterized by its liberal politics and its support for experimental identity projects, particularly among the college-aged population.

The Christians in my study participate in a nondenominational organization that I call University Unity. . . . University Unity claims about forty active members, has a weekly Thursday night meeting, sponsors six different student-led Bible study groups, and coordinates regular trips and events, including fall retreats and evangelizing spring break trips to popular spring break locales. Unlike those in geographical contexts in which conservative Christianity is widespread, the Christians in this study are not normative in their community. Instead, their identity as Christians sets them apart from their peers in significant ways.

The goths in this study are part of a local self-identified goth community, with ties to an international goth scene, which emerged in the early 1980s, and from which they take many of their meanings. In part a music scene, goth nonetheless implies much more than just shared musical taste. These goths come together weekly at a local dance club and maintain daily connections through their prolific community listserv. Although participants interact with nongoths in their daily lives, they think of themselves as part of a distinct community. Goth is defined by its "dark" aesthetic, woven into "freaky" goth fashion and expressed through participants' shared fascination with the macabre. . . .

Masculinity Dilemmas and Subcultural Solutions

Like other men, the men in this study face the central problem of achieving masculinity in the face of a cultural system that denigrates some of their practices as unmasculine. For these men, this problem seems especially pronounced. The particular problem these men face is shaped by their age, race, and class. They are white middle-class men on the cusp of adulthood. Among older boys and young men, toughness, athletic prowess, social visibility, power over others, and heterosexual success are typically key signs of real masculinity (Eder 1995; McGuffey and Rich 1999). Boys and young men who do not meet these criteria often suffer from isolation and/or harassment (Eder 1995).

Accordingly, both groups of men report being marginalized by their peers before becoming evangelical Christians or goths. While some were simply invisible, others were more actively ostracized or picked on. Crow describes himself and other goths as "outcasts," explaining that the "head of the football team" had a "personal vendetta" against him. University Unity men do not tell stories as dramatic as the goths, but they also tell stories about not fitting in, not being able to get a girlfriend, not being good at sports, being too smart or too studious, or having "uncool" interests or concerns (e.g., being interested in gaming or not wanting to drink). Aaron, for example, explains that the people he knew were "immature—they got drunk and stuff. They'd bag on me for not joining in."

As geeks, these young men occupied the lower rungs of youth status hierarchies that are sorted, in part, by gender performance. "If you're a man," Sean, a goth, explains, "it doesn't make your life good to sit down at recess and read rather than play. . . . Doing well in school does not endear you to your peers." However, the development of technological and other academic skills associated with geekiness (even described by goths as "geeking") provides valuable masculine resources in the long run, allowing men to develop the requisite skills for adult careers and thus setting them up for the eventual acquisition of one kind of successful adult masculinity (see Cooper 2000).

This process is tied to race and class. . . . Race and class privilege allow more flexibility in gender performances by anchoring University Unity and goth men to other high-status markers. As with white middle-class young women (see, e.g., Wilkins 2004), race and class privilege also provide University Unity and goth men with the latitude to engage in cultural practices without fear of the historical associations between people of color and "unnatural" sexuality (Collins 1991). Thus, both Christian and goth men occupy the paradoxical position of having low status among youth while benefiting from whiteness, middle-class status, and masculinity more generally, all of which are, however, invisible resources.

Both the University Unity and the goth subcultures provide solutions to young men's dilemmas. Evangelical Christianity and goth culture provide them with community, social support, and tools for thinking about themselves differently. Subcultural participants develop meaningful social ties and find people who are familiar with and sympathetic to their experiences. In both subcultures, participants also learn to think about themselves differently, transforming some of the attributes associated with their marginality into subcultural virtues (Schwalbe and Mason-Schrock 1996). Moreover, evangelical Christianity and goth culture provide participants with the resources to embark on new gender projects. Unity Christians remake themselves as good men. Goths remake themselves as "freaks." In both cases, their new identities are chosen, valorized, and used to make claims about themselves as men.

Sexuality is a principal arena in which both Unity Christians and goths remake their masculinities. In this article, I am concerned not with what Unity and goth men actually do sexually but with how they use sexual practices and rhetoric to reconstitute their masculinities. The sexual performances of Unity and goth men are distinct, even antithetical, yet each violates dominant notions of young men's sexuality as voracious, resolutely heterosexual, sexually dominant, and emotionally shallow. Unity members are sexually abstinent, whereas goths are sexually exploratory and endorse some forms of queer play. Moreover, both sets of men portray sexuality as emotionally intimate and evince concern for women's emotions.

But both Unity and goth men use subcultural resources to salvage their masculinities, in part by packaging their new sexualities as heterosexual enough. These are not identical solutions: queer play notwithstanding, goth men access some elements of heterosexual prowess, but Christian men do not. In both cases, however, their sexual performances manage, rather than jeopardize, their masculinities. Unity and goth sexual performances push against the limits of narrowly defined masculinities, providing young men with more ways to be "real men." Yet even as they create this opening, neither set of men is freed from the need to demonstrate their masculinity.

University Unity Sexual Strategies

University Unity Christians are sexually abstinent. They are universally committed to postponing sex until marriage. In addition, most do not date at all. Abstinence is particularly striking among young men since relentless sexual desire is central to cultural understandings of adolescent and young adult masculinity. . . . At the university, where social rituals are organized around coupling (whether fleeting or sustained), abstinence is altogether strange. However, in contrast to goth practices such as polyamory (explicit and consensual nonmonogamy), Unity men's commitment to abstinence is endorsed by an adult-run international organization and aligns with a popular, conservative-led political agenda that condemns premarital sexual activity. The institutionally structured expectation of abstinence provides resources to protect the masculinity of Unity men. First, the Christian identity provides a reasonable explanation for nonparticipation in heterosexual conquest, hiding other, potentially more gender-discrediting reasons for nonparticipation. Second, ritual attention to "the problem of [hetero]sexual temptation," as a Unity pamphlet put it, allows Unity men to prove themselves sufficiently heterosexual in the absence of actual heterosexual practices.

Before becoming Christians, Unity men were generally not heterosexually successful. Their heterosexual problems took a variety of forms, including the inability to get a girlfriend, a lack of interest in sexuality or dating, and the desire to avoid crushing heartbreak. In an abashed tone, Unity Christian Jon reveals, "I wasn't that popular with girls in high school. It's kind of embarrassing." Kevin expresses disinterest in both dating and sexuality. Aaron regrets that he had sex before becoming a Christian, emphasizing his heartbreak, rather than sin or shame: "Sometimes I think God tells us not to do something because it's just hurtful if we do." For young men, each of these problems is potentially stigmatizing. The inability to capitalize on heterosexual desire, a lack of interest in heterosex, and the expression of emotional vulnerability are all threats to masculinity. For Unity men, the expectation of abstinence provides a way to transform the meaning of their heterosexual experiences. In short, abstinence makes Unity men heterosexual enough. In turn, Unity men use abstinence to emphasize different aspects of masculinity.

Lucas's story is illustrative of the broader pattern in the data. Lucas was harassed in high school. He was raised in a Christian family, but he initially viewed church as a place to seek girls, not God. He explains: "In high school, I was, like, not very popular and I was trying to get a girlfriend. I wasn't very popular and they were all mean to me so I decided to go where there would be nice and good-looking girls: church." Lucas hoped that getting a girlfriend, especially a good-looking one, would ease his humiliation, both because a girlfriend would provide him with intimacy and because she would salvage his masculinity by proving his heterosexual prowess. At church, though, Lucas found something different: "I found my identity in God. It gave me so much joy," he explains. Committing himself to the Christian identity, he abandoned his quest for a girlfriend: "I still haven't had a girlfriend. I made a conscious decision. I just saw people who had girlfriends—they always broke up, and as soon as they broke up, they wanted another girlfriend. Like obsessive. I didn't want that. I wanted to focus on schoolwork and on my relationship with God." Christianity did not make Lucas heterosexually successful. Instead, it transformed the meaning of his heterosexual nonparticipation. Lucas had wanted a girlfriend, but after becoming a Christian, he explains, he chose not to date girls. Once rejected by girls, Lucas is now the rejecter (at least in the abstract): he is choosing not to become romantically or sexually involved. He is making this decision, moreover, not because he is heterosexually uninterested but because the patterns of dating in which his peers participate are "obsessive" and distracting. Thus, he explains his decision not to date in terms of a commitment to self-control. Drawing on University Unity discourse, Lucas neutralizes his heterosexual nonparticipation and turns it into a mark of masculine self-discipline. The Unity group provides Christian men with a label—"abstinence"—and an explanation for heterosexual nonparticipation that allows them to think of themselves not only as sufficiently heterosexual but as better men.

This rationale is not convincing to all audiences, to be sure. Lucas explains that "things didn't get better at school." But it is convincing, at least to him and to other Christians like him. Moreover, for outsiders like me, it provides a cogent explanation, one that deflects attention from his possible heterosexual failure. In sum, then, University Unity men use the expectation and rhetoric of Christian abstinence to transform embarrassing heterosexual records into purposefully chosen sexual identities. Unity men such as Lucas (with the exception of Aaron, whom I discuss later) use Christianity to opt out of not just the sex in heterosexual practice but dating as well. Rather than abandon the centrality of heterosexuality, they temporarily privilege other aspects of masculinity such as self-control; indeed, they claim self-control on the basis of resisting heterosexuality.

In addition, University Unity men perform their heterosexuality collectively, aligning themselves with conventional assumptions about masculinity through the ritual invocation of temptation. . . . Christian temptation talk helps transform heterosexual nonparticipation into abstinence—a moral identity achieved through self-discipline and commitment. But, at the same time, it also maintains the assumptions that heterosexual desire is a central component of masculinity and that Christian men are, in fact, real men.

Temptation talk peppers University Unity materials. The question of why everyone struggles with sexual immorality is a theme addressed in reading materials and by the group leaders. Although the word "everyone" suggests that this is a problem faced by both women and men, Susan told me a story about a University Unity-sponsored summer retreat, for example, that underscored the ways in which temptation talk is gendered. At the retreat, Susan explains, she learned in a conversation with the young men about their struggles with temptation: "I really had no idea, like, for guys, struggling to be sexually pure. They were brutally honest: 'it's a minute by minute thing for us [men] . . . even a spaghetti strap can be hard.' I think girls struggle with different things."

This conversation collectively reaffirmed the masculinity of young University Unity men, allowing them to prove their heterosexuality by talking about it. Instead of bragging about "scoring," they talked about how hard they struggled to be sexually pure. "It's a minute by minute thing" again suggests that sexuality is a constant drive, always on the forefront of men's minds, directed at women, and requiring constant vigilance to be managed; even seeing a woman wearing a tank top with spaghetti (thin) straps creates a difficult temptation. The ritual profession of sexual temptation thus does part of the work of stabilizing the heterosexuality of sexually abstinent men.

Tied as it is to a collective identity, abstinence takes the heat off Christian men, allowing them to deflect not only their own inability to attract women but also imputations of inadequate heterosexual drive that would compromise their masculine identities. Instead, the collective performances allow them to claim masculine heterosexual desire in the absence of heterosexual practice. This strategy minimizes the costs of their unorthodox performances of masculinity, shores up qualities associated with long-term masculine success (such as self-discipline and autonomous decision making), and allows them to think of themselves as real men. As with the goth men described below, this performance is staged primarily for other subcultural participants and for themselves. Although the Unity Christian strategy challenges the assumption that real men are sexually predatory, it does not challenge the assumption that men are naturally more sexual than women.

Goth Sexual Strategies: Reclaiming Heterosexual Prowess

In contrast to University Unity abstinence, the goth scene facilitates heterosexual success. Goths pride themselves on being sexually adventuresome. By fostering a space in which sexuality is encouraged, is public, and is built into community practices, goth men are able to use goth sexual culture to perform a kind of successful masculinity and heterosexuality. The goth scene provides these opportunities by transforming conventionally unattractive men into sexually desirable men (at least within the subculture) and by creating occasions for sexual contact with multiple partners. Thus, goth provides men both with the raw material to make plausible claims to heterosexual success and with an audience for those claims. Despite these conventional forms of success, goth men violate two central assumptions of normative heterosexuality: First, in a reversal of dominant heterosexual courtship norms, goths expect women to be sexually aggressive. Second, goth men engage in elements of queer play.

Like the Christians, goths use talk to establish sexual identities. Instead of talking about sexual temptation, however, they showcase their sexual experiences, sexual knowledge, and comfort with unconventional forms of sex. Goth men participate in forms of sexual boasting associated with men in other contexts. Hunter, for example, told me, "since [his last girlfriend], I've had eighteen partners. I'm a guy. We keep count." Goths also convey their varied sexual repertoire by bragging about their comfort with bondage, group sex, and, as I discuss below, bisexuality.

[...]

The organization and expectations of the goth scene also enable successful heterosexual practice. Many goth men would not be viewed as attractive in other young adult arenas. Some of the men are overweight, others are short or very thin, and many appear effeminate. These men, however, are desirable to goth women. As Jeff explains, "Before the Sanctuary, I didn't feel unattractive, I didn't feel noticed. I think that's the case for a lot of people. Over time, I'm more and more noticed because I get better at it [making himself attractive to other goths]. No one wants to be ugly. It's sort of like a bubble from the outside world." Goth aesthetic expectations redefine desirability in ways that incorporate goth men, and the goth emphasis on creativity means that men can reinvent themselves as desirable. As Siobhan tells me, she "only ever dated freaks." And Hyacinth explains, "Everyone is valued for how they create their appearance, how they create selves, not their physical body." The ideology of performance in the goth scene means that men who do not fit mainstream criteria for attractiveness can feel desirable and are in fact more desirable than "normal" men within the goth scene.

Because of its climate of sexual openness and experimentation, and because the community is organized around weekly dance nights and regular parties, the goth scene provides men with opportunities to add to their sexual coffers. Goth norms discourage monogamy and "vanilla" sex, instead encouraging polyamory, group sex, and "freaky" sexual experimentation. These norms mean that, even when they are in relationships, goth men are able to access sex with a variety of women and are able to frequently fulfill stereotypical male fantasies of sexual encounters with several women at the same time. At the least, they are able to brag about such experiences in a context in which it is conceivable that they are telling the truth.

[...]

Goth norms reverse mainstream courtship scripts. Goth women are expected to be sexually aggressive, and goth men are discouraged from being sexually predatory. This reversal is chiefly achieved through goth etiquette about spatial boundaries. These rules elaborate a set of collective assumptions about appropriate "pick-up" behavior. For example, men are not supposed to approach unknown women. Instead, as I was told, they should arrange an introduction through a mutual friend. These rules help create a space in which women feel freed from the more distasteful aspects of mainstream clubs: overly aggressive men and unsolicited touching. This element of the goth scene is a point of pride among both the women and the men. For example, Lance told me about his shocked reaction to the sexually aggressive tactics of men at a sports bar: "Dude, you can't do that!"

Goth women experience this reversal as empowering. Goth men, however, are not disempowered by it. Instead, men who had little prior experience picking up women can be sexually successful without engaging in behavior that they may also find distasteful, that they are unskilled at, or that runs the risk of rejection and painful humiliation. They are able to see themselves as respectful of women without sacrificing sexual opportunities. For example, as Sean earnestly explains, "I don't really flirt with people first. I don't really try to pick someone up. Mostly from having conversations with women about people flirting with them, it makes them feel bad. I don't want to make anyone's day bad. I know I am not the most nonthreatening person ever. I am not small, not feminine. I am often leathery and spiky." By expecting women to be the sexual aggressors, goth men do not lose out on heterosexual opportunities, but rather, they likely gain them. Because the women from whom they choose their sexual partners think of themselves as egalitarian, men who espouse egalitarian values are more desirable than men who do not.

In addition to assuming the role of sexual catch, goths violate gender boundaries by incorporating some elements of queer play. Regardless of a goth's own sexual predilections, one is expected to demonstrate gothness through tolerance for and familiarity with different kinds of sexual play. Accordingly, many, but not all, goth men "gender blend." Greg comments, "It's hard enough finding clothes for men that are interesting. I am not going to limit myself to men's clothes. It's fun." And Crow says, "Because you can be an individual, some of the things— rules—aren't there. I own skirts, girls' tank tops. I like women's clothing better." In contrast to other contexts, these men's use of feminine accoutrements does not signal a rejection of heterosexuality. Rather, it can increase their heterosexual success with goth women, who confess their attraction to androgynous men and to men in women's clothing. As one goth woman posts, "Men in skirts are yummy!"

In addition, some goth men perform a kind of symbolic bisexuality. Women's bisexuality is increasingly more hip in some circles, but men's bisexuality is less so (e.g., see Schippers 2002; Wilkins 2004). The community in which this study takes place has a large and visible lesbigay population; in addition, both sexual tolerance and sexual experimentation are central to the goth identity. Within this context, goth men situate themselves on the border of bisexuality. Hunter says, "I've kissed men, kissed women. I'm completely straight though; nothing bothers me." Jeff tells me, "There are a lot of guys who I have a close kinship to. It's not sexual, but we are pretty touchy-feely—hug, throw arms around each other's shoulders, kissed a bunch of them." Some goth men, then, talk about homosexual desire and engage in mild sexual play with other men but disavow a bisexual identity.

Goth men are proud of their willingness to experiment physically with other men. Indeed, when they kiss other men, it is public, not private. By flirting with bisexuality, they reinforce their identities as tolerant, enlightened, experimental, and secure in their manhood. At the same time, these men claim to be straight. In the same breath, Crow laments, "Sadly, I'm straight," professes his attraction to men, and explains why he is unwilling to have sex with the men to whom he is attracted. For Crow, behavior, not desire, seems to align with his chosen sexual identity. For other goth men, even bisexual behavior is compatible with being "completely straight." By refusing to relinquish their identities as straight, despite bisexual behavior, goth men are able to maintain the privileges of heterosexuality and to maintain some distance from a potentially discrediting association with gay men. Further, as "completely straight" men, they can experience physical intimacy with other men within the safe confines of the goth scene without worrying about a relationship with another man that could spill over into their outside lives. They can thus avoid the social and political costs of either a gay identity or a relationship with another man. By sidestepping a flexible sexual identity, they also maintain clarity about their core selves; because they think about themselves as coherently straight, they will never have to do any narrative work to realign their stories with the dominant heterosexual script. In short, this strategy makes them hip without making them gay.

Siobhan indicates that these men are at least partially successful: "In my group, there are a few men who are out as bisexual. I really admire them. . . . It's sexy for women to be bisexual but not for men—not as many gay men . . . are considered manly." It's not clear from Siobhan's comment whether being bisexual requires owning the label (as the men I interviewed do not) or just kissing other men in public, as many of these men do. What she does make clear is that the putative added stigma attached to bisexuality for men means that men who dare to explore feelings for other men, or who even suggest that they are open to the possibility, are able to accrue status in a scene that prides itself on its ability to transgress conventional sexual norms, even while they avoid taking on the label "bisexual." Women's bisexuality, because it is considered sexy, does not carry the same status. Critical of the way goth men are able to capitalize on bisexual symbolism, Rory says, "Most men in the goth scene—theoretically bisexuality [*sic*], practice heterosexuality. It's cooler. Chicks dig bisexual guys; it makes them sound open minded."

For goth men, departures from dominant gendered sexual scripts are likely sincere attempts to break down gender and sexual barriers. The quest to be gender alternative, however, does not dismantle the gender status quo. This happens because the goth scene is a space in which men accrue status from being alternative, women are grateful for their freedom from lecherous men, and participants presume that it is harder for men than for women to engage in queer play. Thus, within the goth scene, alternative gendered behavior is a resource that men can use both to increase their heterosexual desirability and to bolster their status in a way that is less available to women (see Wilkins 2004, 2008).

The sexual strategies of the goth men are very different from those of the Christians. Goths remake themselves as heterosexually successful by participating in a subculture in which they have opportunities to have sex. But as with University Unity men, goth subcultural meanings allow goth men to use their unconventional heterosexual strategies as resources to shore up their heterosexuality.

[. . .]

Conclusions

Both Christian and goth men perform heterosexuality in ways that depart from dominant expectations: Christian men are abstinent, whereas goth men flirt with queer symbols. In addition, both eschew a predatory model of male heterosexuality. To be sure, the goth strategies are more radical than those of the Christians; in addition, the Christian strategies enjoy broad cultural and institutional support: abstinence corresponds with a national agenda in a way that men's bisexuality or dress wearing surely does not. But within the northeastern young adult world that these men share, both strategies are significantly at odds with peer expectations. In both cases, the audience for these performances is primarily other subcultural participants; thus, their solutions are enabled by the insularity of their communities.

Nonetheless, what is surprising is that for both the Christian and the goth men, divergent heterosexualities solve, rather than create, problems of masculinity. The recuperation of masculinity occurs because both sets of men connect their divergent sexualities to conventional expectations for masculine heterosexuality. The Christians do this through the rhetoric of sexual temptation and resistance, the goths through the practice and rhetoric of heterosexual achievement. . . . In the cases of both the University Unity Christians' abstinence and the goths' queer play, violations of masculine heterosexual assumptions do not free men from the need to prove their masculinity.

Fissures in contemporary understandings of gender relations provide resources to the young men in this study, who are able to borrow from some of these changes (and from some of the ambivalence they generate) to craft their own masculinity projects. At the same time, these resources advantage them because they remain embedded in enduring gender distinctions. For example, both University Unity Christians and goths seem to construct sexual cultures in which the same behavioral expectations apply to men and women. University Unity Christians expect men to conform to standards of purity typically associated with women; goths expect women to be sexually aggressive in ways that are typically associated with men. Yet in both alternatives, old gender tales persist. Among the Christians, men's abstinence is accompanied by a story about masculine temptation, maintaining the notion that men are innately heterosexually desirous in a way that women are not. Among the goths, the expectation that women should be the aggressors allows goth men to expect women to be heterosexually available to them and allows goth men to perform their own masculine sexual desire. More insidiously perhaps, in both subcultures, comparable sexual behavior means different things depending on who does it. Thus, both a Christian man's abstinence and a goth man's bisexual flirting earn status in ways that women's abstinence and bisexual flirting do not because they occur in contexts that assume that men have more desire than women (Christians) and that men suffer more for violating heterosexual norms (goths). . . . The comparison between University Unity men, who see themselves and are commonly seen as traditional, and the goths who see themselves and are also often seen as alternative, powerfully demonstrates the ways in which masculinity projects are both bound and enabled by the gender rules of the larger culture.

References

Anderson, Eric. 2005. "Orthodox and Inclusive Masculinity: Competing Masculinities Among Heterosexual Men in a Feminized Terrain." *Sociological Perspectives* 48(3):337–55.

Chen, Anthony S. 1999. "Lives at the Center of the Periphery, Lives at the Periphery of the Center: Chinese American Masculinities and Bargaining with Hegemony." *Gender and Society* 13(5):584–607.

Collins, Patricia Hill. 1991. *Black Feminist Thought: Knowledge, Consciousness, and the Politics of Empowerment*. New York: Routledge.

Connell, R. W. 1995. *Masculinities*. Berkeley, CA: University of California Press.

Cooper, Marianne. 2000. "Being the 'Go-to Guy': Fatherhood, Masculinity, and the Organization of Work in Silicon Valley." *Qualitative Sociology* 23(4):379–405.

Eder, Donna. 1995. *School Talk: Gender and Adolescent Culture.* With C. C. Evans and S. Parker. New Brunswick, NJ: Rutgers University Press.

McGuffey, Shawn C. 2008. "'Saving Masculinity': Gender Reaffirmation, Sexuality, Race, and Parental Responses to Male Child Sexual Abuse." *Social Problems* 55(2):216–37.

McGuffey, Shawn C. and B. Lindsay Rich. 1999. "Playing in the Gender Transgression Zone: Race, Class, and Hegemonic Masculinity in Middle Childhood." *Gender and Society* 13(5):608–27.

Messner, Michael. 1993. "'Changing Men' and Feminist Politics in the United States." *Theory and Society* 22(5):723–37.

Pascoe, C. J. 2003. "Multiple Masculinities? Teenage Boys Talk About Jocks and Gender." *American Behavioral Scientist* 46(10):1423–38.

Pollack, William. 1998. *Real Boys: Rescuing Our Sons from the Myths of Boyhood.* New York: Random House.

Schippers, Mimi. 2002. *Rockin' Out of the Box: Gender Maneuvering in Alternative Hard Rock.* New Brunswick, NJ: Rutgers University Press.

Schwalbe, Michael and Douglas Mason-Schrock. 1996. "Identity Work as Group Process." Pp. 113–47 in *Advances in Group Processes.* Vol. 13, edited by B. Markovsky, M. J. Lovaglia, and R. Simon. Greenwich, CT: JAI.

Tough Guise: Violence, Media, and the Crisis in Masculinity. 1999. Directed by S. Jhally. Northampton, MA: Media Education Foundation.

Wilkins, Amy C. 2004. "'So Full of Myself as a Chick': Goth Women, Sexual Independence, and Gender Egalitarianism." *Gender and Society* 18(3):328–49.

Wilkins, Amy C. 2008. *Wannabes, Goths, and Christians: The Boundaries of Sex, Style, and Status.* Chicago, IL: University of Chicago Press.

"What Makes a Woman a Woman?" Versus "Our First Lady of Sport"

A Comparative Analysis of the United States and the South African Media Coverage of Caster Semenya

Cheryl Cooky, Ranissa Dycus, and Shari L. Dworkin

This article examines the tensions associated with sex, gender, race, nation, equality, and oppression as framed by the mainstream news media coverage of Caster Semenya. Semenya is a female track and field athlete from rural Limpopo, South Africa. She underwent gender-verification testing after she won the International Association of Athletics Federations (IAAF) 2009 World Championships in the 800-meter event. Several media accounts claimed the tests were ordered because of her "deep voice, muscular build, and rapid improvement in times" (Associated Press, 2009). We use the media response to her gender-verification testing to explore race, gender, and sexuality injustice in sport. We examine whether and how media frames reinforce or challenge dominant binary notions of sex/gender as well as the ways race, class, and nation intersect to produce culturally specific frames of Semenya and of gender-verification testing. Specifically, we asked how the United States and South African mainstream online and print media (newspapers) framed "gender-verification." We also ask how the United States and South African mainstream online and print media (newspapers) framed the controversy following Semenya's performance at the World Championships. That is, who or what was attributed to the suspicions surrounding Semenya's performance? What, if any, differences are there in the framings between the United States and South African media and what do these differences reflect (and constitute) about each respective context?

Cheryl Cooky, Ranissa Dycus, and Shari L. Dworkin. 2012. "'What Makes a Woman a Woman?' Versus 'Our First Lady of Sport': A Comparative Analysis of the United States and the South African Media Coverage of Caster Semenya." *Journal of Sport & Social Issues* 37(1):31–56.

The IAAF/IOC's historical policies only require sex testing of female athletes and transsexuals and are built on an assumption of categorical female frailty, male superiority, and physical dominance (Birrell & Cole, 1994; Cavanaugh & Sykes, 2006; Cole, 2000; Dworkin & Cooky, 2012; Kane, 1995; Travers, 2008). Similar to other athletes who have undergone sex testing, Caster Semenya was nearly denied the opportunity to participate in sport by having her sex/gender questioned. By holding Semenya's body up for scrutiny and suspecting her for her very success in the 800-meter event, the "sport nexus" legitimated and perpetuated gender injustice (Travers, 2008). Paradoxically, even as gender-verification testing of Caster Semenya reaffirmed the sex/gender binary, this newsworthy event opened the door to rethinking not only the sex/gender binary in sport, but also the ways that race, colonial legacies, and nationalism intersect with and shape understandings of sex testing. As we will argue, the events surrounding the "controversy" also opened the door for envisioning the transformative potential of sport, allowing new avenues for how sport might be restructured and reorganized.

We expected differences in media framings between the United States and South Africa given the relationship each country has to relations of privilege and oppression. Each country's social, political, and cultural context produces unique understandings of gender and of the role of sport in perpetuating or challenging race and gender inequalities (Dworkin, Swarr, & Cooky, 2013). Ostensibly for athletes, spectators, and citizens from the Global North, common sense understandings of gender-verification testing posit testing as an objective, scientific process that ensures a level-playing field and thus, "fairness" in sport competition. For athletes, spectators, and citizens from the Global South, this common sense understanding of the Global North is problematized, given the history of Western scientific knowledge of racial differences to justify and legitimate colonialism, slavery, and the exploitation of colonized peoples (Hoad, 2010; Nyong'o, 2010; Swarr, 2012). Moreover, it is important to acknowledge South Africa's apartheid past and the role that sport played, both materially and symbolically, to reinforce apartheid and to help South Africa partly overcome that history in contemporary terms (Hargreaves, 1997; Pelak, 2005). In this manner, sex testing aligns with past colonialist exploitation and contemporary forms of racial oppression, even in the postapartheid context (see Dworkin, Swarr & Cooky, 2012; Nyong'o, 2010). Thus, for the Global South, Western scientific classifications of raced and gendered bodies are viewed as products of colonialism, European expansionism, and racism, not simply "objective" or "value-free" accounts that ensure equality in sport or in South African society.

We acknowledge these differing historical and sociocultural contexts and situate media framings accordingly. . . . Our analysis reveals conflicting accounts of how womanhood is defined and which bodies are construed as "true" female athletes eligible to compete in international sport competitions. The comparative analysis also illustrates how differing cultural contexts produce contradictory understandings of sex/gender, of gender-verification testing, and of notions of fairness in sport. We conclude the article with a discussion of transformative visions for sport, informed by postcolonial feminism (McClintock, 1995; Mohanty, 2003) and critical feminist sport studies (Cole, 1994; Hall, 1996; Kane, 1995; Messner, 2002), imagining sporting practices as unfettered by the limits of the sex/gender system and by claims of a level-playing field.

Sport, Gender Verification, and the Sex/Gender Binary

Prior to the late 20th century, we could not point to genes in the way we can today to define one's sex. However, the fact that we have knowledge of genetic components of sex identity does not mean we have the "ultimate, necessary, for-all-time answer to what it means to be of a certain sex" (Dreger, 1998, p. 9). Fausto-Sterling's (2000) critique of the binary sex system moves beyond genetic or biological classifications to offer new conceptualizations of sex categories. She states that "a body's sex is too complex. There is no either/or. Rather there are shades of difference" (p. 3). If nature allows for a continuum of sex, as Fausto-Sterling and other feminist theorists suggest, and if sport organizations' policies only accommodate categorical notions of sex alongside a separate-spheres requirement for women and men, then the incorporation and acceptance of bodies into sport that are not easily identifiable as male or female challenges the "cherished aspects" of sex-based forms of social organization in the United States (Kane, 1995; Travers, 2008). Thus, gender-verification tests "constitute one element in a matrix of surveillance and policing practices of the boundaries around gendered bodies" (Cole, 1994, p. 20).

The justification for sex testing/gender verification as a way to uphold and ensure a "level-playing field" (e.g., by identifying and policing women's sport spaces to prevent male "invaders") is built on the assumption that categorically all men are faster, stronger, and better at sport than all women. In this way, sport maintains the myth of absolute categorical sex/gender differences between men and women (Kane, 1995). Rather than viewing the relationship between sport and gender in binary terms, that is, categorically men are faster, stronger, and better at sport than women, Kane (1995) persuasively argued for the acknowledgment of sport performance as a continuum wherein many women outperform men in a range of sports, including traditionally male-dominated sports. Considering Fausto-Sterling's (2000) conceptualization of sex as a continuum furthermore disrupts the material and discursive ways that sport maintains the myth of a sex/gender binary rooted in natural differences as illustrated in and through sex-segregated sport competition. Thus, sex testing/gender verification simultaneously reinforces the myth of a sex/gender binary and the subsequent justification to uphold this binary through sex-segregated sport competition. Ensuring that only "true" women compete with other "true" women, and that this category is distinctly different from "true" men, sex testing clearly constitutes and is constituted by sex segregation in sport.

Preventing women and men from competing with one another—a central role for sex testing—ostensibly ensures that sex-segregated sports are free from "intruders" who are not "real" (i.e., biological) women. As Kane (1995) argues, "This by definition creates the notion that sport is a naturally occurring binary divided along gender lines" (p. 204). However, female athletes who do not fit into traditional Western expectations of femininity are more likely to have their "biological standing as female athletes called into question" (Kane, 1995, p. 210). Cole (1994) adds, "The female athletic body was and remains suspicious because of its apparent masculinization and its position as a border case that challenges the normalized feminine and masculine body" (p. 20). Those female athletes that society views as nonconventionally feminine—that is, those deemed "deviant mutant" (Kane, 1995)—have the most potential to disrupt the sex/gender binary. This is because when "suspicious" athletes are sex tested, the ambiguities of sex and the social processes involved in constituting and reconstituting sex become exposed. This process thus challenges the underlying assumptions that sex/gender difference is inherent, natural, and most of all, can be categorically "known"—all assumptions through which the binary is upheld.

Given that these tests are administered primarily in international/Olympic competitions, and that international sport bodies/federations are responsible for ordering, conducting, and interpreting the tests and for setting the policies for eligibility, the power of these organizations to constitute a singular meaning of sex/gender on a global scale cannot be underestimated. At the same time, international sport organizations are empowered to change policies on sex testing. The pressure from scientific and feminist communities has resulted in some changes, including the abandonment of mandatory testing in international competitions and the IOC's policy regarding the eligibility of transsexuals to participate in international competitions (for a critical analysis of these policies see Cavanaugh & Sykes, 2006; Karkazis, K., B. Jordan-Young, G. Davis, and S. Camporesi, 2012).

[. . .]

Method

Mediated messages (e.g., news media coverage) are not "objective" accounts of events. In other words, news media do not present an unmediated view of what "really happened" during an event. Instead, the media provide cues that encourage readers/viewers to interpret events in particular ways.

[. . .]

What is included in the story and more importantly how it is discussed help "frame" an event for the reader/viewer (Fiske, 1996). As such, we analyzed newspaper articles for what was included inside media frames and what was excluded from the media frames. Examining what is inside and outside media frames provides insights into what Hall (2000) referred to as "preferred meanings" of texts.

[. . .]

Following Hall (2000), it is critical to highlight that media frames, and what is inside the frame and what is left outside the frame, are not only constructed within raced, classed, and gendered hierarchical relations of power but are also read by audiences who are positioned within the same systems of inequality. A combination of content analysis (quantitative counts of media framings) and textual analysis (qualitative examination of media frames) reveals how media create and recreate narratives, which are linked to dominant ideas or ideologies that circulate in wider society (for a detailed explanation of this methodology see Cooky, Wachs, Messner, & Dworkin, 2010).

Using content and textual analysis to locate preferred meanings of texts, we analyzed newspaper coverage of the Caster Semenya controversy in the United States and in South Africa. For the United States sample, we selected major national and regional newspapers. The total sample included 13 newspapers. Four of the top five national U.S. papers were selected based on circulation rates (Audit Bureau of Circulation, 2006): *USA Today,* the *New York Times,* the *Los Angeles Times,* and the *Washington Post.* Ten regional papers were selected using purposive sampling techniques (Patton, 2001) in different regions of the United States (Northeast, Midwest, South, and West) from the top 25 list, which was also based on circulation rates (Audit Bureau of Circulation, 2006). Regional newspapers included *The Star Ledger, Atlanta Journal Constitution, Houston Chronicle, Philadelphia Inquirer, San Francisco Chronicle, Cleveland Plain Dealer, Chicago Tribune, Denver Post, Boston Globe*, and *Seattle Times* (no articles were published on Caster Semenya during the timeframe of the study in the *Chicago Tribune, Denver Post, Boston Globe,* and *Seattle Times).* For the South African sample, we were limited in part by the availability and accessibility of South African newspapers in the United States, as well as the language of the newspaper. As such, three South African print newspapers *Business Day, Sowetan,* and *Mail & Guardian* were analyzed. . . .

Print news articles from the above newspapers were retrieved using Lexis-Nexis database from August 19, 2009, to January 21, 2010, using the search term "Caster Semenya." . . . This search produced a total of 215 articles, 53 from the United States newspapers and 162 from South African newspapers.

[. . .]

Background of the Event

Caster Semenya, aged 18, University of Pretoria student and track athlete competed in the 800-meters event at the World Championships in Berlin on August 19, 2009, and won the event in 1:55.45 (2 s slower than the World record). The silver medal went to Kenyan Janeth Jepkosgei (1:57.90), 2.45 s behind Semenya. Earlier that day, IAAF officials confirmed that Semenya was undergoing "sex-determination testing" to confirm her eligibility to race as a woman (Clarey, 2009). According to a *Los Angeles Times* article that quoted Nick Davies, a spokesperson for the IAAF, the IAAF began to "ask questions about Semenya" on July 31, 2009, when "she ran the fastest time in the world season, 1 minute 56.72 seconds, at the Africa Junior Championships" (Hersh, 2009, C1). By many media accounts, especially in the United States, the IAAF originally suspected doping. However, subsequent media reports confirmed that Semenya had undergone gender-verification tests on the request of the IAAF (Clarey, 2009). Pierre Weiss, general secretary of the IAAF, stated in a press conference that Semenya was undergoing testing because of "ambiguity" and not because the IAAF suspected her of knowingly cheating. Several athletes spoke out immediately after the championships. Elisa Cusma, an Italian runner who finished sixth in the race, said, "These kind of people should not run with us. For me, she is not a woman. She is a man" (Clarey, 2009, p. 13). Russian athlete Mariya Savinova, who finished fifth, told Russian journalists that she did not think Semenya would pass the gender-verification test stating, "Just look at her" (Clarey, 2009, p. 13).

Framings of Suspicion: "Too Fast," "Too Muscular" to Be a Woman Versus Westernized/Racist Definitions of Beauty/Gender

Over one third of our total sample included some discussion of the suspicions surrounding Semenya's performance and/or appearance (see Table 21.1). According to media frames, Semenya's performance raised "suspicions" for several reasons. Media articles framed the suspicions as emerging because of her fast times in the World Championship (i.e., she's too fast to be a "real" woman) or to her fast improvement over the brief course of her running career (the African Junior Championships at the end of July and the World Championships in August). In addition, suspicions were said to emerge because of her "masculine," "muscular," appearance, or because of both her appearance and her performance. Illustrative of the latter frame, for example, journalists in the United States noted that suspicions emerged because of Semenya's "muscular physique and drastic improvement" (Longman, 2009a, p. B10) or her "improved speed and muscular build" (Longman, 2009b, p. D9).

A higher percentage of South African articles framed suspicions regarding Semenya's sex/gender compared to the United States articles. Of the South African articles to discuss the

Table 21.1 Media Frames: Suspicions of Semenya's Sex/Gender

	Too Fast Time (World)	Too Fast Time (Africa Junior Championship)	Appearance (Masculine, Deep Voice)	Both Appearance/ Performance	Too Fast Times (at World and Junior)	Too Fast Increase in Performance
U.S. papers	18% (4)	18% (4)	32% (7)	14% (3)	0% (0)	18% (4)
S.A. papers	25% (14)	7% (4)	11% (6)	36% (20)	2% (1)	20% (11)

Note: Of the articles that had an explicit frame of suspicions.

suspicions surrounding Semenya, most framed suspicions in one of three ways, because of both her appearance and her performance (36%), or because her times were too fast at the World Championship (25%) or because her "performance improved too quickly" (20%; Table 21.1). Of the articles that discussed suspicions in the United States sample, most articles focused on her masculine appearance, deep voice or muscular build (32%) although more than half of the articles (54%) attributed the suspicions to a combination of either her time being "too fast" at the World Championship (18%), or too fast times at the Africa Junior Championships (18%), or that her "performance improved too quickly" (18%). Only a few articles in the United States sample included both frames of appearance and perfor-mance to justify the suspicions. For example, a *New York Times* journalist explained it was because "she improved her times drastically in the 800 and 1500 meters and became the world leader in the 800" (Longman, 2009b). This, along with her "improved speed and muscular build" led to "sex verification testing" (Longman, 2009b).

The United States articles framed the suspicions as objective accounts and very few offered a critical assessment of the validity of the suspicions or the assumptions that undergirded them. In contrast, when mentioning her fast times as a cause for suspicion, South African newspapers were critical of this explanation and implied or stated outright that racism instead was to blame for the suspicions. For example, in an op-ed article published in *Sowetan,* the author wrote, "We all know that her crime is that an African girl outran everybody to clinch the women's 800m final" (Mofokeng, 2009). In a more explicit reference to racism, another *Sowetan* op-ed article con-demned the IAAF stating, "The conduct of the international body was racist and humiliating" ("The IAAF Is a Disgrace," 2009).

Although nearly 46% of the United States articles and 47% of South African articles included some discussion of Semenya's body and appearance as responsible for raising suspicions regarding her sex/gender identity, there are important distinctions across the two regions. The textual analysis revealed that the "appearance" frame in the United States newspapers was often used as justification for the suspicions of other athletes or sport organizations, thus legitimating the need for the IAAF to enact their sex testing policy. For example, the *Los Angeles Times* wrote, "The concerns about whether she met standards to compete as a female athlete were prompted by still and television images of the teenager" that implied it was her appearance that led the IAAF and others to question her eligibility to participate as a female athlete in women's sport events. In a frame that seemed to attempt to explain Semenya's gender expression a jour-nalist for the *Los Angeles Times* explains, "Semenya . . . has grappled with the consequences of looking boyish all her life" (Dixon, 2009, p. A1).

In the South African sample, especially in *Mail & Guardian,* articles were critical of the implication that Semenya's masculine corporeality, strength, or muscularity meant that she was not a "true" woman eligible to compete as a female athlete. Highlighting the linkages among appearance, sex/gender, and race, a *Mail and Guardian* journalist underscored the role that racism plays when Westerners impose White standards of femininity in the global sporting arena. This particular journalist, in a somewhat sarcastic tone, implied that the whole controversy could have been avoided if Semenya had only made "herself appear more girly," and taken "beauty tips from her peers in Berlin," who "glam up for the start with lip gloss, enough gold jewelry to outshine the medals, and even false eye lashes" ("A Better Balance," 2009). Another op-ed article in the *Sowetan* notes that suspicions regarding Semenya's sex "seem to rely on patriarchal sexist stereotyping of women as weak and soft, which Caster does not fit into because she is considered to be too strong and muscular to be a woman" (Langa, 2009). This questioning of a female athlete's gender in the sex/gender binary is not unique to Semenya. Historically, female athletes, especially White, heterosexual, middle-class athletes, must negotiate mutually exclusive constructions of gender whereby muscularity and strength are linked to masculinity, and beauty and glamour are linked to femininity (Cahn, 1994; Dworkin, 2001; Dworkin & Wachs, 2009; Hargreaves, 1994; Heywood & Dworkin, 2003). In mainstream media coverage, female athletes who do not conform to dominant notions of femininity continue to be the subject of ridicule and the targets of racist and sexist commentary (Cooky et al., 2010).

[. . .]

Some articles, in both South Africa and in the United States, provided a discussion of how these standards are "racist" or based on White/Western notions of beauty. An op-ed writer in *Sowetan* noted, "It is very clear that the IAAF used Western stereotypes of what a woman should look like as probable cause, and that is racist and sexist since many of those making the determination are fat and ugly European men" (Anderson, 2009). In addition, the *Mail & Guardian* reported, ". . . although the debate is ostensibly about sex, many in South Africa believe it has a racial dimension. Political leaders have accused Western 'imperialists' of a public lynching . . ." (Smith, 2009). In the United States, articles reported this perspective as the response from South Africa and not necessarily indicative of sentiments in the United States. For example, an article in the main section of the *Los Angeles Times* echoed the South African frame critical of Western standards of beauty and femininity: "Other black South Africans find something more sinister in the controversy erupting around Semenya: another example of demeaning Western attitudes toward black Africans, particularly women" (Dixon, 2009, p. A1).

Of interest, the "appearance" frame in the South African articles that specifically referenced Semenya's "masculine" appearance was used primarily as a physical descriptor of Semenya, and was not invoked to justify the IAAF's gender-verification test, as it was in the United States frames. Nor did the mention of Semenya's masculine appearance necessarily signify that she was not a "girl." In this way, South African media frames simultaneously challenged the sex/gender binary, describing Semenya as masculine, although reaffirming the binary asserting her identity as "our girl" and "golden girl" (Mdlesthe, 2009), a frame we discuss in the following section.

Frames of Semenya's Sex/Gender: "What Makes a Woman a Woman?" Versus "Our First Lady of Sport"

South African media accounts frequently included quotes and images that identified Caster Semenya as "Our Golden Girl," "Our First Lady of Sport," and "Golden Heroine." For example, many articles used these frames in the descriptions of Semenya, "Golden girl Caster Semenya yesterday thanked South Africa for supporting her" (Moeng, Mbamba, & Ratsatsi, 2009). "Caster Semenya is our golden girl," wrote an author in an op-ed in the *Sowetan* ("Semenya is Not a Cheat," 2009). Pictures of the crowd holding signs reading "100% woman" during a rally for Semenya's welcome back to South Africa featured in media articles, intentionally countered questions about Semenya's sex, print media coverage offered confirmation of her sex through quotes from family members, sport fans, and even government officials. A fan awaiting Semenya's arrival home at the airport says, "at the end of the day, she is our hero. She is our African girl and there's no need to question that" (Brooks, 2009). An article appearing in *Sowetan* quoted Semenya's father, "She is my little girl. I raised her and I have never doubted her gender" (Sowetan Reporters, 2009).

Although not a dominant frame, there were several articles in the South African sample that challenged the sex/gender binary by recognizing that having "both male and female characteristics" did not provide evidence that Semenya was not a "girl." An op-ed published in *Business Day* noted, "It is, therefore, not true that we are either male or female, or masculine or feminine. In nature there is more. . . . Unfortunately even good scientific explanations are contaminated by subjective conclusions . . ." (Matshiqi, 2009). The *Mail & Guardian* published an article that questioned the binary and noted how South African politicians' "constant reiteration that she is a woman . . . reinforces the same binary that is the cause of the problem: men have to be men and women have to be women" (Schuhmann, 2009).

It should be noted that the ostensibly celebratory embracement of Semenya's gendered nonconformity by politicians and the public was not representative of South Africa's treatment of transgendered individuals or gender nonconformists. In one of a few articles that raised this issue, Schuhmann (2009) situated the Semenya controversy in the specific historical and cultural context, informing readers that "feminine masculinities and masculine femininities are not normally celebrated so overtly." On the contrary, women who defy gender norms in South Africa are often the targets of hate crimes, "curative" rape, and homophobia. Although in 2009 Semenya earned heroine status in South Africa, in April of 2008, South African Black lesbian football star Eudy Simelane was gang raped and murdered. These "corrective rapes" (a term used by activists and scholars) are intended to punish lesbians for their sexuality and "convert" them to heterosexuality (Dworkin, et al., 2013; Gevisser, 2009; Swarr, 2012).

Moreover, at the same time that South Africa frames focused on the "subjective" aspects of sex although erasing the transphobia and homophobia inherent in their celebration of Semenya as a "true woman," the dominant frame in the United States centered on the "medicalized" aspects of sex/gender. These debates largely took place among scientists and academics on whether or not "sex tests" could identify and verify "real" female athletes. Twenty percent of the United States articles compared to only 7% of South African articles included this frame. We discuss the framing of Semenya's gender-verification test in the following section.

Frames of Semenya's Gender Verification Test: "A Reasoned Choice Among Imperfect Options" Versus "Violation of Human Rights"

The "medicalized" frame acknowledged the scientific limitations of using sex testing/gender verification to determine sex/gender; . . . 35% of articles in the United States sample framed gender-verification testing in this way. Illustrative of this frame, Alice Dreger wrote an article for the *New York Times* that discussed the limitations of gender-verification testing, which included quotes from a professor in human genetics and pediatrics, a pediatric endocrinologist, and a professor of epidemiology on whether or not a process of sex testing, even one that included an interdisciplinary panel (genetics, endocrinology, anatomy, psychology), could determine one's sex in a definitive way that would ensure someone with an "unfair advantage" was not allowed to compete. Although this article, and others like it, provided a critical assessment of the limits of sex testing, rightly acknowledging the complexity of determining an individual's sex, outside the frame was a critical discussion of the legitimacy or purpose for sex testing female athletes (see Table 21.2). This absence left unquestioned the assumptions on which gender-verification tests are based. Thus, the sex/gender binary, and the need for sport to be sex segregated went unchallenged in the United States media frames. One scientist said the "IAAF must acknowledge that all it can do is make a reasoned choice among many imperfect options" (as quoted in Dreger, 2009, SP8).

Surprisingly, inside this frame were quotes from the IAAF and other experts to assure audiences that Semenya's sex/gender would be determined once the testing was complete and the

Table 21.2   Media Frames: Is There a Critical Discussion of Limitations of Sex/Gender Testing to Determine Sex/Gender?

	Yes	No	Total
U.S. papers	15% (8)	85% (45)	53 articles
S.A. papers	7% (12)	93% (150)	162 articles
Total	9% (20)	91% (195)	215 articles

results made public, despite the fact that many of the same articles also acknowledged the limitations of gender-verification testing to determine one's sex. In other words, Semenya's sex and/or her eligibility to compete would be "known" once the IAAF had the results of the test, even though scientists in the articles said the test itself was problematic. As such, the United States articles "medicalized" debates about sex/gender and gender-verification testing, presenting the limitations of assessing male and female bodies and yet were still concerned with how we can determine the "truth" surrounding Semenya's sex/gender. Thus, the United States frames reinforced a binary between male and female sport performances that ultimately served to naturalize sex/gender difference.

Unlike articles in the United States that framed sex testing/gender verification as a scientific process, although one with limitations, the South African media framed gender verification as a lingering artifact of South Africa's apartheid past and the racist history of Global North/Western culture's scientific scrutiny of African women's bodies. . . . More than half the South African sample included a discussion of the process of sex testing as a human rights violation or as racist (although the U.S. newspapers also had human rights and racism as a dominant framing of the process of testing, these articles quoted or referenced the South African response). These articles offered a critique of the policies of sex testing as "sexist and racist" (Brooks, 2009), rather than a scientific attempt to determine true sex/gender. "It is the ghoulish, white-coated scientists of the IAAF who would do well to look into their hearts and ask whether the overwhelming evidence of Caster's life as a girl in South Africa does not count as science" (Brooks, 2009). Such responses are understandable given a long racist and colonial history wherein Black women's bodies were objectified (Dworkin et. al., in press; Ray, 2009).

[. . .]

At the same time that this frame delegitimized scientific claims of Semenya's sex/gender, it also positioned Semenya's family members, coach, teammates, representatives of Athletics South Africa, and South African political leaders and stakeholders as "experts" to verify Semenya's sex, in spite of any pending results of the IAAF's gender-verification tests. Absent from this frame were academic experts or scientists to discuss the validity of gender-verification testing. Instead, articles included quotes from Semenya's mother, father, uncle, grandmother, friends, fans and other members of the community verifying that Semenya was indeed a girl, and as such there was no need to conduct or to await the results of the gender-verification tests. Approximately 12% of the articles in the South African sample (only one article in the United States sample) included this frame. These quotes frequently verified Semenya's gender as a "girl." A *Mail & Guardian* article quoted Semenya's uncle, " 'Caster is a girl'. I am not worried about that too much. I know where she comes from. For myself, I know Caster is a girl" (Brooks, 2009). Semenya's mother, Dorcas Semenya, reflecting on the controversy said, "I cannot comment about the scientists and the professors, all I know is that I gave birth to a girl in 1991" (Moeng, Mbamba, & Ratsatsi, 2009). Thus, in the South African media frames, culturally relevant "local" definitions of gender were inside the frame, whereas scientific determinations and the legitimacy of international sport organizations' policies were dismissed as either violating Semenya's human rights or an example of Western imperialism and racism.

Framings of Semenya: Inside and Simultaneously Outside the Frame

Although every article in our sample was about Caster Semenya, Caster Semenya the athlete and human being was almost always outside the frame. And although she was framed in the South African articles as a "Golden Girl" and "Our First Lady of Sport," which positioned her as a representative of the South African nation-state, this frame constructed only a symbolic representation of South African nationalist identity and largely lacked any substantial discussion of Semenya's experiences from her own voice or perceptions. Semenya's agency was constrained in her silencing by South African political leaders and stakeholders who discouraged her from speaking during press conferences. As a result, in the majority of mainstream print news media coverage of the controversy, her voice, experience, and perspective were outside the frame. Indeed, Semenya was quoted in only 5 (approximately 9%) of United States newspapers and in only 8 (approximately 5%) of South African newspapers.

When Semenya was asked to provide her own perspective on the events, quotes centered on her response immediately after the race, and not on the subsequent controversy: "I took the lead in the 400 meters and I killed them, they couldn't follow. I celebrated the last 200 cause I knew, man" (Bearak, 2009). In a rare example of an article where Semenya's perspective is inside the frame, she was quoted in a *Mail & Guardian* article demonstrating resilience, perseverance, and acceptance, "God made me the way I am and I accept myself. I am who I am and I'm proud of myself" ("Caster is a Cover Girl," 2009). The absence of her voice in mainstream media articles, and the way in which her experience was rendered invisible, served to deny the subjective aspects of her becoming an international phenomenon at the age of 18. She became an international phenomenon not because of her sport performance but as a result of the gender controversy her performance elicited in local and global contexts. Thus, the exclusion of Semenya's voice and her subsequent invisibility deflected any challenge that her perceptions of her own experience would pose to the "controlling images" of Black women (Collins, 1990) that circulate in the mainstream news media (Cooky et. al., 2010).

[. . .]

The controversy surrounding Semenya's performance at the 2009 World Championship provides an analytical framework for a critique of sexism, racism, and homophobia that is embedded in the logic of gender verification. As discussed earlier, Western scientific classifications of raced and gendered bodies are not simply "objective" or "value-free" accounts. Rather than framing the gender-verification tests as a scientific process necessary to "ensure" a level-playing field, as did the United States news media, the South African news media framed the process as racist, a human rights violation, and a product of Westernized standards of femininity and beauty. In the United States' media frames, gender-verification testing and Western definitions of sex/gender were "global" processes by which capitalist, neoliberal notions of fairness, equality, and competition omitted the "local" knowledge of Semenya's sex and gender.

[. . .]

In United States and South African print news media, dominant frames illustrated print media's reinforcement of limiting, binary definitions of sex/gender, although in differing ways.

Moreover, the United States media frames engaged scientific debates regarding Semenya's "real" sex/gender and discussed the science of sex testing. Several newspapers in the United States quoted medical and academic experts who outlined the limitations of existing technology to determine or verify one's sex or gender. Ultimately this medicalized understanding of sex and gender reinforced the sex/gender binary, which allowed the legitimacy of sex testing and the need for sex-segregated sport to remain unquestioned.

Conversely, in South Africa media frames, the sex/gender binary was upheld through nationalist identity claims of Caster Semenya as South Africa's "First Lady of Sport" and a "Golden Girl." Although the South African media framed gender verification as illustrative of the lingering effects of racism, colonialism, and apartheid past, sex segregation in sport remained unquestioned in both countries' news media frames.

Although there were distinctions in the ways that the sex/gender binary was upheld in each context (scientific vs. local definitions), similarities were evident. Outside the news media frames in each country was a discussion of how the sex/gender binary in sport serves to maintain gendered hierarchies and inequalities both within sport and in wider society. Only a few articles in our sample offered any critique of the sex/gender binary or acknowledged that sex and gender are not neatly aligned as dominant cultural and scientific understandings would suggest. Moreover, only three articles (approximately 1%) of the entire sample discussed the possibility or desirability of abandoning sex segregation in sport.

Most of the groups, organizations, and institutions whose representatives were quoted in the news media from both countries were male-dominated and the individuals who were inside the frame were mostly men. In the U.S. context, it was predominantly male scientists and male members of international sport organizations that were framed as "experts" to determine Semenya's identity. In South Africa, it was male political leaders, male sports stakeholders, and family members (male and female) who were framed as "experts" with the right to speak for Semenya. These groups made essential claims to Semenya's identity to support her right to participate in sport as a woman. Indeed, South African politicians suggested that Semenya's human rights had been violated in the process of undergoing gender-verification testing; the President of South Africa, Jacob Zuma, spoke on her behalf, defending her identity and her right to participate in an institution for which women had fought to be included. Yet, outside the frame were Semenya's voice and her own perspectives on her experiences. As the IAAF and Athletics South Africa strongly encouraged Semenya not to speak at press conferences, Semenya's voice remained outside the frame, even though she was discursively positioned as a representative of the South African nation-state.

Transformative Visions

Women athletes throughout history have played a unique role in constituting femininity and national identities through their sport participation (Ritchie, 2003). Caster Semenya is no exception. In South African media frames, Semenya was positioned as a national icon and a representative of the democratic, postapartheid, South African nation-state. Multiple constructions of her femininity and claims of her essential femaleness largely ignored, however, the reality of ambiguities surrounding the boundaries of race, sex, and gender in that nation (Swarr, 2012). The mobilization of nationalist rhetoric in the South African papers and the defense of Semenya's "true womanhood" suggest a reliance on the gender binary to defend what was perceived by many in South Africa as a racist assault.

One might interpret "transforming" sport as a call for recognizing how sports, in their current manifestations, provide a space for transformative visions and new ways to reimagine sporting practices. Reading the Semenya controversy through the lens of postcolonial feminism (Mohanty, 2003), transformative visions come to light that simultaneously allow for and reject the inclusion of the sex/gender binary in sport. Indeed, Caster Semenya, as an agent in the framing of her experience, receded into the background of the story and she was outside the frame. Yet Semenya speaks to us, feminists from both the Global North and the Global South, in and through her sport performance. Semenya, both in her corporeality and in the media framing of her performance, presents a challenge to persisting forms of racism and sexism, both within and outside of sport, in global and local contexts.

[. . .]

References

Anderson, L. 2009. "On What Basis Was Caster Tested?" *Sowetan*, August 24 (www.sowetanlive.co.za/sowetan/archive/2009/08/24/on-what-basis-was-caster-tested).

Associated Press. 2009, September 16. *IAAF: Semenya Decision in November* (http://sports.espn.go.com/oly/trackandfield/news/story?id=4464405).

Audit Bureau of Circulation. 2006 (www.accessabc.com).

Bearak, B. 2009, August 26. "Inquiry About Sprinter's Sex Angers South Africans." *New York Times,* p. A6.

"A Better Balance." 2009, August 21 (http://mg.co.za/article/2009-08-21-a-better-balance).

Birrell, S. and C. L. Cole. 1994. "Double Fault: Renee Richards and the Construction and Naturalization of Difference." Pp. 373–97 in *Women, Sport and Culture*, edited by S. Birrell and C. L. Cole. Champaign, IL: Human Kinetics.

Brooks, C. 2009, August 25. *Warm Welcome Home for Champ Semenya* (http://mg.co.za/article/2009-08-25-warm-welcome-home-for-champ-semenya).

Cahn, S. 1994. *Coming on Strong: Gender and Sexuality in Twentieth Century Women's Sport.* New York, NY: Free Press.

"Caster Is a Cover Girl." 2009, September 8 (www.mg.co.za).

Cavanaugh, S. L. and H. Sykes. 2006. "Transsexual Bodies at the Olympics: The International Olympics Committee's Policy on Transsexual Athletes at the 2004 Athens Summer Games." *Body & Society* 12:75–102.

Clarey, C. 2009. "Gender Test After a Gold Medal Finish." *New York Times*, August 20, p. B13.

Cole, C. L. 1994. "Resisting the Cannon: Feminist Cultural Studies, Sport and Technologies of the Body." Pp. 5–30 in *Women, Sport and Culture*, edited by S. Birrell and C. L. Cole. Champaign, IL: Human Kinetics.

Cole, C. L. 2000. "One Chromosome Too Many?" Pp. 128–46 in *The Olympics at the Millennium: Power, Politics and the Games*, edited by K. Schaffer and S. Smith. New Brunswick, NJ: Rutgers University Press.

Collins, P. H. 1990. *Black Feminist Thought: Knowledge, Consciousness, and the Politics of Empowerment.* New York, NY: Routledge.

Cooky, C., F. L. Wachs, M. A. Messner, and S. L. Dworkin. 2010. "It's Not About the Game: Don Imus, Race, Class, Gender and Sexuality in Contemporary Media." *Sociology of Sport Journal* 27:139–59.

Dixon, R. 2009. "Gender Issue Has Always Chased Her: The African Runner Accused of Being a Man Was Often Teased as a Child." *Los Angeles Times*, August 21, p. A1.

Dreger, A. 2009, October 25. "Seeking Simple Rules in Complex Gender Realities." *New York Times*, p. SP8.

Dreger, A. 1998. *Hermaphrodites and the Medical Invention of Sex.* Cambridge, MA: Harvard University Press.

Dworkin, S. L. 2001. "'Holding Back': Negotiating a Glass Ceiling on Women's Strength." *Sociological Perspectives* 44:333–50.

Dworkin, S. L. and C. Cooky. 2012. "Sport, Sex Segregation, and Sex Testing: Critical Reflections on This Unjust Marriage." *American Journal of Bioethics* 12(7):1–3.

Dworkin, S. L. and F. L. Wachs. 2009. *Body Panic: Gender, Health, and the Selling of Fitness.* New York, NY: New York University Press.

Dworkin, S. L., A. L. Swarr, and C. Cooky. 2013. "(In)Justice in Sport: The Treatment of South African Track Star Caster Semenya." *Feminist Studies* 39(1):40–69.

Dworkin, S. L., A. L. Swarr, and C. Cooky. In press. "Sex and Gender and Racial (In)justice in Sport: The Treatment of South African Track Star Caster Semenya." *Feminist Studies.*

Fausto-Sterling, A. 2000. *Sexing the Body: Gender Politics and the Construction of Sexuality.* New York, NY: Basic Books.

Fiske, J. 1996. *Media Matters: Race and Gender in U.S. Politics.* Minneapolis, MN: University of Minnesota Press.

Gevisser, M. 2009. "Castigated and Celebrated." *Sunday Times,* August 30 (www.timeslive.co.za/sunday times/article34966.ece).

Hall, M. A. 1996. *Feminism and Sporting Bodies: Essays on Theory and Practice.* Champaign, IL: Human Kinetics.

Hall, S. 2000. "Encoding/Decoding." Pp. 51–61 in *Media Studies Reader,* edited by P. Marris and S. Thornham. New York, NY: New York University Press.

Hargreaves, J. 1994. *Sporting Females: Critical Issues in the History and Sociology of Women's Sports.* London, UK: Routledge.

Hargreaves, J. 1997. "Women's Sport, Development and Cultural Diversity: The South African Experience." *Women's Studies International Forum* 20:191–209.

Hersh, P. 2009. "Gender Issues: Others in 800 Meters Raise Questions About Surprise Winner Caster Semenya of South Africa; International Officials Start Inquiry." *Los Angeles Times,* August 20, p. C1.

Heywood, L. and S. L. Dworkin. 2003. *Built to Win: The Female Athlete as Cultural Icon.* Minneapolis, MN: University of Minnesota Press.

Hoad, N. 2010. "'Run, Caster Semenya, Run!' Nativism and the Translations of Gender Variance." *Safundi: The Journal of South African and American Studies* 11:398.

"The IAAF Is a Disgrace." 2009. *Sowetan,* August 24 (www.sowetanlive.co.za/sowetan/archive/2009/08/24/the-iaaf-is-a-disgrace).

Kane, M. J. 1995. "Resistance/Transformation of the Oppositional Binary: Exposing Sport as a Continuum." *Journal of Sport and Social Issues* 19:191–218.

Karkazis, K., B. Jordan-Young, G. Davis, and S. Camporesi. 2012. "Out of Bounds? A Critique of the New Policies on Hyperandro-Genism in Elite Female Athletes." *American Journal of Bioethics* 12(7):3–16.

Langa, M. 2009. "IAAF Decision Sexist and Insulting to Women." *Sowetan,* August 24 (www.sowetanlive.co.za/sowetan/archive/2009/08/24/iaaf-decision-sexist-and-insulting-to-women).

Longman, J. 2009a. "South-African Runner's Sex-Verification Result Won't Be Public." *New York Times,* November 20, p. B10.

Longman, J. 2009b. "A Question of Gender Topples a Track Official." *New York Times,* December 27, p. D9.

Matshiqi, A. 2009. "Finding the Words for Caster Semenya." *Business Day,* August 28 (www.businessday.co.za/articles/Content.aspx?id=799).

McClintock, A. 1995. *Imperial Leather: Race, Gender, and Sexuality in the Colonial Contest.* New York, NY: Columbia University Press.

Mdlesthe, C. 2009. "She Is 'Nice Lovable.'" *Sowetan,* August 24 (www. sowetanlive.co.za/sowetan/archive/2009/08/24/she-is-nice-lovable).

Messner, M. A. 2002. *Taking the Field: Women, Men, and Sports.* Minneapolis, MN: University of Minnesota Press.

Moeng, K., M. Mbamba, and P. Ratsatsi. 2009. "Thanks for All Your Support." *Sowetan,* August 26 (www.sowetanlive.co.za/sowetan/archive/2009/08/26/ thanks-for-all-your-support).

Mofokeng, J. 2009. "Millions Rejoice for Golden Girl." *Sowetan,* August 26 (www.sowetanlive.co.za/sowetan/archive/2009/08/26/millions-rejoice-for-golden-girl).

Mohanty, C. 2003. *Feminism Without Borders: Decolonizing Theory, Practicing Solidarity.* Durham, NC: Duke University Press.

Nyong'o, T. 2010. "The Unforgivable Transgression of Being Caster Semenya." *Women & Performance: A Journal of Feminist Theory* 20:95–100.

Patton, M. Q. 2001. *Qualitative Evaluation and Research Methods.* 3rd ed. Newbury Park, CA: Sage Publications.

Pelak, C. F. 2005. "Negotiating Gender/Race/Class Constraints in the New South Africa: A Case Study of Women's Soccer." *International Review for the Sociology of Sport* 40:53–70.

Ray, C. 2009. "Caster Semenya 21st Century 'Hottentot Venus?'" *New African*, November 4 (http://newafricanmagazine.com/blogs/lest-we-forget/caster-semenya-21st-century-hottentot-venus).

Ritchie, I. 2003. "Sex Tested, Gender Verified: Controlling Female Sexuality in the Age of Containment." *Sport History Review* 34:80–98.

Schuhmann, A. 2009. "Feminine Masculinities, Masculine Femininities." *Mail & Guardian*, August 31 (http://mg.co.za/article/2009-08-31-feminine-masculinities-masculine-femininities).

"Semenya Is Not a Cheat." 2009. *Sowetan*, September 14 (www.sowetan-live.co.za/sowetan/archive/2009/09/14/semenya-is-not-a-cheat)

Smith, D. 2009. "Semenya Sex Row Causes Outrage in SA." *Mail & Guardian*, August 23 (http://mg.co.za/article/2009-08-23-semenya-sex-row-causes-outrage-in-sa).

Sowetan Reporters. 2009. "Leave My Girl Alone, Pleads Caster's Dad." *Sowetan*, August 20 (www.genderlinks.org.za/article/leave-my-girl-alone-pleads-casters-dad-sowetan-2010-02-16).

Swarr, A. 2012. *Sex in Transition: Remaking Gender and Race in South Africa.* New York, NY: SUNY Press.

Travers, A. 2008. "The Sport Nexus and Gender Injustice." *Studies in Social Justice* 2:79–101.

Cultural and Cosmopolitan

Idealized Femininity and Embodied Nationalism in Nigerian Beauty Pageants

Oluwakemi M. Balogun

© iStockphoto.com/PacoRomero

> [Queen Nigeria] is someone Nigerians can easily relate to and identify with in terms of how she is. . . . She has the core values of our people, our culture and our orientation. [Queen Nigeria] is who we are.
>
> —Organizer of Queen Nigeria

> [The Most Beautiful Girl in Nigeria] is a Cosmo girl . . . someone who is trendy, passes time in the U.S. and the UK. . . . Very fashion-forward.
>
> —Fashion Designer for the Most Beautiful Girl in Nigeria

Oluwakemi M. Balogun. 2012. "Cultural and Cosmopolitan: Idealized Femininity and Embodied Nationalism in Nigerian Beauty Pageants." *Gender & Society* 26(3):57–81.

This article examines gendered nationalism through the lens of two national beauty pageants in contemporary Nigeria that, as the two quotes above highlight, engage in different projects of idealized femininity bolstered by separate nationalist claims. Beauty pageants, particularly national ones, provide a unique case for studying how gendered ideals play a role in nation-building discourses since they are tangible sites in the production of gendered national identity (Banet-Weiser 1999). Based on ethnographic research of two Nigerian national pageants, this article asks: How and why are gendered nationalist messages framed differently? This study suggests that beauty pageants perform an important dual role in emerging nations like Nigeria by both creating a unifying vision of Nigerian femininity within Nigeria and a more cosmopolitan vision of femininity that places Nigeria squarely in the international arena.

Women's bodies are often the symbolic sites wherein debates about the trajectory of a nation take form, shaped in part through shifts in the global economy, cultural globalization, and colonial trajectories (Dewey 2008; Hoang 2011; Mani 1998). The woman-as-nation thesis examines how women serve as cultural bearers of tradition through tropes of domesticity, motherhood, and modesty (Chatterjee 1990; Gaitskell and Unterhalter 1989; Hansen 1992; McClintock 1995) and as symbols of modernization through discourses of work, politics, and sexuality (Foucault 1988; Gal and Kligman 2000; Shilling 2003). However, the gender and nation literature does not fully explain why gendered nation-building projects may differ within the context of the same country. I show that gendered national representations—the shared and contested gendered scripts used to characterize a nation—serve multiple purposes and simultaneously target internal and external audiences (Spillman 1997).

[. . .]

Nigeria: Geopolitical Context of an "Emerging Nation"

While all nations must contend with the task of appealing to domestic and international agendas, this process becomes especially heightened in emerging nations who run the risk of pulling the nation apart if they fail to manage these competing interests. By using the term *emerging nation,* I am not referring to newly formed states (i.e., political units) but rather to newly developing nations (i.e., a shared sense of cultural affiliation) which are vying to become major players in the international arena. Nigeria is a useful place to study gendered nationalism, because of the profound economic, political, and cultural changes that the country has witnessed since attaining independence in 1960. As the seventh most populous country and one of the largest oil suppliers in the world, Nigeria's vast human and natural resources highlight Nigeria's potential as a major global player (Apter 2005; Rotberg 2004). Despite its resources, well-known images of corruption, poverty, and communal conflict in Nigeria mar its international reputation and appear to be major roadblocks to nation-building and unity (Obadare 2004; Ukiwo 2003; Watts 1997). These shifts provide a broader context for understanding how Nigeria negotiates the dilemma of staking a claim in the global political economy while remaining attuned to its internal sensibilities.

On the one hand, social divisions such as regional, ethnic, and religious differences within the nation mean that national identities are heavily debated and contested. Although regional/religious splits between a "Muslim" North and a "Christian" South are often invoked as the main source of political tension, these seemingly neat regional divides do not fully capture the highly fragmented religious, ethnic, and regional differences that sometimes erupt into disputes in the country. Nigeria's 36 states and federal capital territory, Abuja, are divided into six geopolitical zones: the Southwest, South-South, South-East, North-Central, Northwest and Northeast. Nigeria has more than 250 ethnic groups, nearly all of which have their own languages and dialects. The nation is almost evenly split between Muslims and Christians, with a minority population that subscribes to traditional spiritual beliefs. With its ethnic and religious diversity, Nigeria requires the creation of joint national symbols like shared language systems (English is the official language), public festivals, sports teams, and national literatures in an attempt to unify the nation.

On the other hand, Nigeria seeks to leverage its position as one of the largest oil producers in the world, to become one of the largest economies of the world, in an attempt to further globalize the nation. Following a series of economic reforms, Nigeria is currently in the process of positioning itself as an emerging market. . . . These markets have been identified, by analysts, as undergoing rapid economic growth and industrialization, as having a growing middle class, and as pivotal in shaping the direction of the international political economy.

. . . Changing class dynamics within the country mean that Nigeria's nationalist visions must support its growing but fragile middle class who can take up the helm of guiding the unification of the nation. At the same time, members of Nigeria's super-elite must tap into international capital to help secure Nigeria's place in the global economic landscape. These class dynamics undergird competing gendered interpretations of nationalism.

Methods and Research Design

I draw from 10 months of fieldwork conducted in Nigeria during the 2009–2010 cycles of both beauty pageants, and use a variety of empirical data including ethnographic observations, interviews, and content analysis of visual and print media. Combining these methods allowed me to focus on the content, structure, and various discourses surrounding these two pageants from a variety of angles, providing insights into how national identities are produced "on the ground" through specific practices as well as symbolically. I spent six months conducting ethnographic observations of the Most Beautiful Girl in Nigeria as an unpaid intern. I also worked as a chaperone at Queen Nigeria for various state-level competitions and at the week-long training sessions leading up to the 2009 Queen Nigeria finale, and observed a week-long "grooming" process of a contestant as she prepared for the 2009 Queen Nigeria national pageant. The grooming process included lessons on poise and etiquette, cat-walking, how to best answer interview questions, diction and accent coaching, and instructions on styling. I was granted access to observe the screening process of selecting contestants to compete, the training period (camp), rehearsals, preliminary competitions, the show and reign (accompanying beauty queens on press interviews, photo shoots, public appearances, and courtesy visits).

[. . .]

I also draw from 35 formal in-depth interviews, with a mix of organizers, producers/groomers, corporate sponsors, reigning and former beauty queens, contestants, and judges. Interviews ranged from 30 minutes to 3 hours, averaging about an hour in length. In order to provide a fuller perspective of the place of beauty pageants in the Nigerian landscape, interview questions focused on the knowledge, understanding, and opinions of (1) the perceived role of beauty pageants in Nigerian society and the world, (2) the broader public's mood toward beauty pageants, and (3) how beauty pageants fit into their own personal experiences and professional positions. . . . I also draw from informal (unrecorded, but included in my field notes) conversations with makeup artists, journalists, production crew, photographers, and fashion designers, as well as analyses of documents such as brochures, websites, video recordings, and newspaper clippings. . . .

Contesting Representations: Tests and Models of Idealized Femininity

This article considers the formation of gendered national representations primarily through the perspective of Nigerian beauty pageant organizers who, as cultural producers, employ a *relational* discourse of idealized femininity (e.g., "true Nigerian womanhood") to bolster their broader nationalist claims. That is, organizers push forward a gendered nationalist vision in direct competition with the rival national pageant. I use the term idealized femininity to highlight the public cultural construction of femininity in these beauty pageants, which emphasizes distinct sets of skills, divergent ways of managing appearance and dress, and varied classed strategies. By looking at how organizers mold competing visions of their contestants, through either a *cultural-nationalist* ideal focused on valuing Nigerian customs and unifying Nigeria's diverse population or a *cosmopolitan-nationalist* paradigm oriented toward highlighting Nigeria's compatibility with a global community, I argue that gendered national identities are produced for specific audiences and constrained by the systems within which they are created.

Although I focus on the discursive differences between cultural and cosmopolitan femininities and their accompanying national ideologies, it is important to point out that there was some crossover among the contestants and would-be contestants for both pageants.

[. . .]

While contestants were aware on some level of the symbolic differences between the two pageants, and readily adapted to the demands and expectations of each contest, it was organizers (who are mostly male) who were the most invested in framing contestants' femininity and their embodied representations of the nation in divergent ways. Contestants approached both pageants from a much more flexible standpoint, stressing a "beauty diplomacy" narrative, which values charity, development, and goodwill in order to connect to everyday Nigerians and promote their own voices and that of the general public in the national arena. In applying this narrative, contestants insisted that all pageants serve as a means of promoting national culture and increasing the nation's standing. For example, while I chatted with a group of three contestants during a brief break at a preshow training session, they all focused on how becoming a beauty queen transformed them into public figures, quickly rattling off the various charity ventures they hoped to pursue during their tenure. All of them had auditioned for, and participated in, a range of pageants, including MBGN and Queen Nigeria. When I asked Doyin, one of the contestants, to describe her motivations behind participating in pageants, she noted how winning a prominent pageant would provide her with a platform in which "everybody will want to listen." During the remainder of our conversation, the contestants also pointed out how beauty pageants had allowed for Nigeria to gain attention abroad, while also "awakening" an appreciation for Nigerian culture among youths. Regardless of the myriad reasons that drove contestants to pursue beauty pageants as an avenue for national recognition, organizers advanced their own gendered visions of the nation.

Serving Up a "Touch" of Africa

A key component integrated into the Queen Nigeria pageant, to show its commitment to producing a "true" Nigerian queen, is a cooking competition. Each contestant is allotted a N1000 ($7) budget to spend on ingredients for a regional dish that represents her state. The judging criteria included speed, cleanliness, taste, and service (e.g., presentation of the dish and interaction with the judges). On the day of the cooking contest, the contestants, the organizers and I gathered outside of the hotel, preparing to head over to the market to buy the necessary ingredients for the upcoming cooking contest to be held later that afternoon. As one of the organizers, Mr. Richard, handed a N1000 note to each contestant, he launched into a lecture. "We are going to be watching you closely," he began. "We are going to be paying attention to how you interact with the sellers. How you bargain. How you choose your ingredients. And, when you're cooking, we will be looking at how clean you keep your station. These are things you all should know. I shouldn't even be telling you this." Mr. Richard's insistence that he should not openly inform the contestants about the judges' expectations signaled that they should already be aware that their assessment extended beyond the flavor and presentation of their meals.

We drove to the small open-air market and tumbled one by one out of the large van. The contestants wandered through the market inspecting goods and haggled over prices at the different wooden stalls filled with fresh meat, peppers, tomatoes, and greens stacked onto small tin plates. Their brightly colored sashes imprinted with the names of their respective states, and the two-man camera crew following close behind them to capture their movements, readily identified the contestants to curious onlookers whose reactions ranged from intense stares to side glances as they continued their own shopping. Some sellers yelled to attract the contestants' attention to their stalls, while others simply continued on with the work of attending to their present customers.

When I asked one of the organizers, Lovett, the rationale behind including a cooking competition into the beauty pageant, she answered:

> Because we are looking for an African woman. We don't just want your shape or your face or just your intelligence, we want to see you do African things; you have to cook African dishes. . . . African women put their skills to work. . . . We want you to know your culture, we'll appreciate it better, we don't have to be Westernized all through, there is a touch of Africa and there is a touch of Nigeria. It must reflect in your cooking etiquette.

Lovett's focus on "cooking etiquette" highlights a set of "skills" that she directly links to African womanhood and an appreciation of Nigerian culture. The contestants received very little guidance as to what recipes would be appropriate and did not get any training in basic cooking skills. Instead, it was assumed that the ability to cook was a skill intrinsic to African women's culture, and that Queen Nigeria would simply be testing this skill.

Queen Nigeria's focus on a culinary test as a symbol of "authentic" Nigerian femininity, taps into a widely held idea outside of the beauty pageant world that conventional markers of domesticity such as cooking Nigerian meals, childrearing, or housekeeping are standard elements of femininity. As such, the cooking competition connected contestants to a recognizable domesticated element of femininity that would resonate with a broad Nigerian audience. Organizers labelled those who could not cook "spoiled" or "out of touch." As Lovett lamented, "It would amaze you that some are 20, 18, and they have never cooked. [The cooking test] is telling them you don't have to depend on mummy and daddy for everything or a fast food joint." Although multinational fast-food franchises like KFC have only recently begun to enter Nigeria, more established homegrown and South African imported fast-food corporations are often viewed as a sign of Westernization and middle-class convenience. By showing off their cooking skills with regards to specific local cuisines and demonstrating their ability to navigate one of the many open-air markets typical of the area, contestants highlighted their cultural competency with Nigerian traditions and also warded off the threat of being seen as spoilt by their parents or overly dependent on Western-derived influences like fast-food joints. As such, Queen Nigeria contestants are presented as the national custodians of Nigerian cultural identity, hedging against foreign influences.

Modeling the Self-Confident Nation

Queen Nigeria's cooking test assumes a preexisting knowledge of traditional African dishes, which highlights access to an intrinsic cultural skill and emphasizes differences from Western culture. In contrast, MBGN's organizers and groomers worked on carefully cultivating skills needed for the modeling segment of their competition, in part through the prism of internationalism. During the show, one contestant would be crowned the "Face of Select Pro," serving as an endorsement ambassador for one of the sponsors of the event, Select Pro Cosmetics, a makeup and styling line. Gina, the African-American producer flown in each year to drill the contestants on poise, etiquette, cat-walking, and posture, spent most of rehearsal periods teaching the choreography needed for the modeling sequence as a Lady Gaga track pulsed in the background. During an interview, she emphasized that international pageants were becoming increasingly focused on modeling and as a result she had to train contestants not only in the mechanics of walking, posing, and grooming but also in gaining self-confidence and professionalism, qualities needed to be successful in the field. When I asked her to describe her ideal candidate, Gina responded forcefully, "Someone really competitive. It's a game they play, and it's about learning to play that game and playing it well."

Learning to "play the game" of self-confidence was woven into the 10-day preshow training and rehearsal period (referred to as "camp"). On the night of the first day of camp, the panel of organizers and groomers sat in a row of chairs facing the 30 contestants. After all the organizers and key members of the production crew were introduced and the national director made his opening remarks, Gina stood up and stated, "I only have one question, which one of you is my queen?" About 5 hands shot up immediately and a couple more were tentatively half-way up in the air. "I only saw a couple of you raise your hands," Gina continued,

> A lot of you seem unsure. We have to work on that. Part of this process is about having confidence. You have to be sure that all of you can say you can be a queen. I'm going to work on instilling that confidence. If you don't want to win, you might as well go home now. I want you all reaching for that crown!

She ended her pep talk with, "Again I want to ask, who's my queen?" This time all hands shot up. Through such tactics, Gina continually instructed contestants on the rules of the game.

The skills contestants were supposed to acquire—especially those promoting self-confidence, professionalism, and competitiveness—were meant to be translated off the stage. One lunchtime discussion revolved around how African contestants are perceived to be at a disadvantage at contests like Miss World or Miss Universe because they lack self-confidence. Eliza, a South

African production specialist, pointed out, "African girls are so soft. They are trained to be quiet and obedient." "Oh, but you know those Latin girls! Watch out. They are so aggressive!" Emeka, a reporter for Silverbird Television, interjected. "They have to be trained to be firm. They can be a lady on the catwalk, but firm off of it," Eliza concluded. Emeka and Eliza's exchange, which draws on an explicit comparison between Nigerian and Latin American women (who are well known for their success at international beauty competitions), highlights the specific transnational poles of feminized gendered ideals that contestants are expected to navigate. While "African" women are conventionally imagined as soft, weak, and dutiful, this clashes with constructions of "modern" women as strong, assertive, and confident. Eliza insists, however, that contestants still can be *trained* to be firm, a process that MBGN directly engages by "grooming" contestants through "international experts" who are thought to provide a competitive edge at subsequent phases of the competition. As agents of internationalism, MBGN contestants were supposed to embody firmness and self-confidence, traits that are expected to signal a cosmopolitan nation.

[. . .]

Challenging and Strategizing Against "International" Beauty Standards

For both competitions, organizers and judges evaluate contestants' bodies based on similar factors such as height, body size, hair style, skin color and texture, and teeth and smile. While Queen Nigeria and MBGN had a fairly similar range of contestants in terms of skin color and negligible differences in body size (the average self-reported bust–waist–hip ratio in inches for Queen Nigeria's 2009 contestants was 33.6"–28.1"–37.8" and 33.6"–27.4"–37.5" for MBGN contestants for the 2009 cycle), they framed their beauty ideals in different ways. Both sets of organizers move away from "traditional" African bodily preferences for voluptuous, heavier set bodies, yet fashioned divergent ways of interpreting the role of "international standards" within beauty contests. Queen Nigeria openly challenged "international standards" noting its Western-based bias and insisting that international standards should be opened up to include a wider variety of appearance ideals. In contrast, MBGN accepted "international standards," choosing to maneuver within these norms in order to position their candidates as competitive within worldwide beauty pageants.

While "international standards" matter to Queen Nigeria organizers, they are critical of Western preferences, insisting that the "international" should be expanded to include more than Western criteria. When I asked one organizer of Queen Nigeria about what specific beauty traits they looked for, he responded: "In Igboland it is someone who is large that is considered beautiful, because it shows she is well taken-care of. But here it doesn't play a role. We are not looking for 'Miss Big and Bold.'" He insisted that international standards of tall and thin beauty queens mattered because organizers had to "move with the trend" within the beauty pageant industry. At the same time, he noted that while MBGN is bound to follow international rules and regulations, if Queen Nigeria were to host an international pageant of their own, other nations would have to abide by Nigerian-derived guidelines, which would directly challenge Western dominance. Another organizer held a similar sentiment, insisting that you could not simply "throw international standards away" but you had to open up international beauty standards to include African ones, in order to reach a kind of "middle ground," noting that "even now you have Western girls who can't fit into those standards. They are becoming bigger, with rounder butts too, so these international standards are changing." His observation that even "Western girls" find it difficult to attain narrow standards of slimness directly calls into question whether or not these ideals are achievable and notes that they are adjusting as a result. Organizers for Queen Nigeria gesture toward a shifting orientation within international standards that must account for, or at least acknowledge, the presence of Nigerian body ideals.

In contrast, MBGN does not openly question these international standards. Gina explained that her involvement in the pageant, which resulted in MBGN (as "Miss Nigeria") winning the Miss World title in 2001, had successfully pushed their standards toward thinner and taller contestants, in line with international criteria. A couple of days before we headed for the auditions, one of the organizers warned, "We don't want any big leg girls. If you have any of those local guys pick the contestants, they will just be looking for girlfriends. We don't want that, so watch out for that." By cautioning screeners to be weary of "big leg girls," his comments suggest a distinction between local-based desirability, against the quest for a candidate that would fit internationally defined notions of attractiveness.

MBGN plays within "international standards," strategizing and picking delegates who tapped into two different kinds of beauties, appealing to niches within international pageantry. MBGN chooses five winners who go on to represent Nigeria at different beauty, modeling, and promotional contests within the country and around the world. The winner and first runner-up continue on to Miss World and Miss Universe respectively. Organizers revealed that for Miss World, a British pageant organized and privately owned by the Morley Family, they chose "a girl next door type" and were a little more flexible with height and body shape. The winner tends to be lighter-skinned. They explained that, since Miss World is focused primarily on raising money for charity events through its "beauty with a purpose" tagline, they pick a fresh-faced, innocent-looking candidate with mass appeal.

In contrast, Miss Universe, owned by the mogul Donald Trump, is viewed as a corporate enterprise focused on integrating the modeling industry into the Trump business empire. As such, MBGN organizers focus on choosing a model-type who is tall, slim, and dark. It was explained to me that dark skin is important for Africans in the international modeling industry because it makes them exotic looking so they stand out. On the one hand, preference for lighter-skin candidates fit in with the commonly accepted paradigm of a Western-dominated media that disseminates such images around the globe. On the other hand, in the case of candidates sent to Miss Universe, MBGN commodifies skin color as a stand-in for difference, without overtly dismissing "international beauty standards" that tend to emphasize height and slimness. In this way, women's bodies stand in for and manage difference in a nonthreatening way (Williamson 1986). Beyond highlighting the social dimensions of skin color (Glenn 2009), by both marketing light skin as a marker of global "mass appeal" and capitalizing on dark skin as a form of desired "exotic beauty," MBGN manages beauty ideals through a global cultural economy, highlighting some flexibility in striving for international legitimacy. . . .

Classed Trajectories: Cultured Beauties and Jetsetters

Nationalist projects are always class-specific. Both contests mold a particular class version of their participants that is shaped by their target audience. Queen Nigeria makes class distinctions based on local references, which promote a cultured middle-class Nigerian woman. In contrast, MBGN focuses on the speedy upward trajectory of their contestants who through winning or even just participating in the pageant gain entrance into an otherwise impossible-to-penetrate jetsetter echelon of Nigerian society who are aligned with transnational capital and culture. These classed paths of nationhood manifest in shifts and varied emphases in the body.

Queen Nigeria organizers specifically targeted college students as ideal candidates and as an unwritten prerequisite for entry, in part to highlight their educated, middle-class trajectories. They also invoked specific tropes of "market women" to create an implicit class distinction between the contestants and other women that they should actively distance themselves from. Late one evening during dance rehearsals, Will, the choreographer, asked the contestants to walk one by one to form two lines for the opening sequence of the dance number. As one contestant walked by he bellowed, pointing at her, "You! Why are you walking like that? You look like a woman carrying firewood on her head. Start over!" Throughout the rehearsal he scolded, "You are all dancing like market women!" Will's repeated statements invoking images of "women carrying firewood on her head" or "market women" were meant to serve as a reference point for women living in rural villages or women working in poor, urban environments. Market women have a long history of trading in urban Nigeria and other areas of West Africa (Byfield 2002; Clark 1994) and as such serve as a recognizable symbolic figure. In the context of beauty pageants, market women are imagined as rough and brash—characteristics that a beauty queen should not exhibit. Instead, contestants were expected to maintain a refined beauty queen stance, maintaining excellent posture in high-heeled stilettos, even while dancing. Women were expected to have skills traditionally associated with Nigerian women that gestured toward an "authentic" African context by showing competency, at traditional cooking for example, but not be *wholly of that* context, allowing Queen Nigeria to construct a class-specific cultural ideal. Jane Collier's (1997) work deals with how an ambivalent stance toward "tradition" features in modernity, in which embracing "traditions" serve as a means of symbolizing region and identity, but the actual way of life is rejected. In this case, rejecting "market women's" embodiment and emphasizing the educated middle-class lifestyles of contestants presents a hierarchy of who can serve as a cultural icon for the nation, elevating the social standing of contestants.

MGBN focuses on signaling the rapid upward mobility of their contestants. The process of "grooming" during camp was noted as having a profound impact on the contestants. "Grooming" contestants focused on changes in both demeanor and physical embodiment, which was directly linked to the class mobility of contestants. People would constantly comment that contestants would change over the course of the 10-day camping (training) period that led up to the finale. I was chatting with one of the chaperones, Ada, as the contestants were having their photographs taken for the brochure. She motioned toward the group of contestants gathered outside the pool of the five-star hotel which served as host for camp, "They will all change. You'll see them next year and you won't even recognize them." With access to hairstylists and makeup artists provided by MBGN and the opportunity to interact with some of the top Nigerian fashion designers, contestants' physical embodiments were expected to change over the course of the contest and beyond.

[. . .]

Conclusion

This article focuses on sets of practices that construct two representations of femininity, and by extension, two visions of national identity. By focusing on differing sets of skills, debates over appearance and dress, and diverging modes of economic mobility, I argue that the two national pageants I studied construct distinct versions of gendered nationhood. Queen Nigeria constructs a *cultural-nationalist* model of femininity that emphasizes *testing* cultural competency, primarily through a cooking contest. This cultural competency test serves as a means of connecting contestants to a broad Nigerian community and showing appreciation for Nigerian culture, with the ultimate aim of unifying the nation. In contrast, by focusing on a modeling competition that emphasizes *cultivating* skills viewed as integral to success at the international phases of the pageant, such as self-confidence, MBGN's *cosmopolitan-nationalist* model stresses Nigeria's compatibility with an international community in order to globalize the nation. I argue that through the cultural production of idealized femininities, contours of the nation—as inclusive of cultural and ethnic diversity for a local audience *and* part of global community for a transnational audience—are consolidated in tandem through the multilayered process of nationalism.

In focusing on the role of globalization in Nigeria, this article counters the conventional conversations about globalization that tend to ignore Africa. I show how Nigeria in particular plays an integral part in broader global processes by highlighting how a postcolonial nation cultivates cultural identity in this present era of increasing globalization. I tease out the complex relationship between the local and the global, detailing how specific versions of gendered national representations are consolidated on national and international stages to serve distinct purposes, adding empirical nuance to the gender and nation literature. Nigeria's broader context of navigating social divisions while attempting to stake a global claim helps us to understand why these two logics must be produced and managed together, as well as the potentially destructive consequences that otherwise threatens to pull the nation apart.

References

Apter, Andrew H. 2005. *The Pan-African Nation: Oil and the Spectacle of Culture in Nigeria.* Chicago, IL: University of Chicago Press.

Banet-Weiser, Sarah. 1999. *The Most Beautiful Girl in the World: Beauty Pageants and National Identity.* Berkeley, CA: University of California Press.

Byfield, Judith. 2002. *A Social and Economic History of Women Dyers in Abeokuta (Nigeria), 1890–1940.* Portsmouth, NH: Heinemann.

Chatterjee, Partha. 1990. "The Nationalist Resolution of the Women's Question." In *Recasting Women: Essays in Indian Colonial History,* edited by K. Sangari and S. Vaid. New Brunswick, NJ: Rutgers University Press.

Clark, Gracia. 1994. *Onions Are My Husband: Survival and Accumulation by West African Market Women.* Chicago, IL: University of Chicago Press.

Collier, Jane Fishburne. 1997. *From Duty to Desire: Remaking Families in a Spanish Village.* Princeton, NJ: Princeton University Press.

Dewey, Susan. 2008. *Making Miss India Miss World: Constructing Gender, Power, and the Nation in Postliberalization India.* Syracuse, NY: Syracuse University Press.

Foucault, Michel. 1988. *The History of Sexuality.* New York: Vintage Books.

Gaitskell, Deborah and Elaine Unterhalter. 1989. "Mothers of the Nation: A Comparative Analysis of Nation, Race and Motherhood in Afrikaner Nationalism and the African National Congress." In *Woman-Nation-State,* edited by N. Yuval-Davis and F. Anthias. New York: St. Martin's.

Gal, Susan and Gail Kligman. 2000. *The Politics of Gender After Socialism: A Comparative-Historical Essay.* Princeton, NJ: Princeton University Press.

Glenn, Evelyn Nakano. 2009. *Shades of Difference: Why Skin Color Matters.* Stanford, CA: Stanford University Press.

Hansen, Karen Tranberg. 1992. "Introduction: Domesticity in Africa." In *African Encounters with Domesticity,* edited by K. T. Hansen. New Brunswick, NJ: Rutgers University Press.

Hoang, Kimberly. 2011. "New Economies of Sex and Intimacy in Vietnam." Ph.D. dissertation, University of California-Berkeley, Berkeley, CA.

Mani, Lata. 1998. *Contentious Traditions: The Debate on Sati in Colonial India*. Berkeley, CA: University of California Press.

McClintock, Anne. 1995. *Imperial Leather: Race, Gender, and Sexuality in the Colonial Contest*. New York: Routledge.

Obadare, Ebenezer. 2004. "In Search of a Public Sphere: The Fundamentalist Challenge to Civil Society in Nigeria." *Patterns of Prejudice* 38(2):177–98.

Rotberg, Robert I. 2004. *Crafting the New Nigeria: Confronting the Challenges*. Boulder, CO: Lynne Rienner.

Shilling, Chris. 2003. *The Body and Social Theory*. London, UK: Sage.

Spillman, Lyn. 1997. *Nation and Commemoration: Creating National Identities in the United States and Australia*. Cambridge, UK: Cambridge University Press.

Ukiwo, Ukoha. 2003. "Politics, Ethno-Religious Conflicts and Democratic Consolidation in Nigeria." *Journal of Modern African Studies* 41(1):115–38.

Watts, Michael. 1997. "Black Gold, White Heat: State Violence, Local Resistance, and the National Question in Nigeria." In *Geographies of Resistance*, edited by S. Pile and M. Keith. London, UK: Routledge.

Williamson, Judith. 1986. "Woman Is an Island: Femininity and Colonization." In *Studies in Entertainment: Critical Approaches to Mass Culture*, edited by T. Modleski. Bloomington, IL: Indiana University Press.

PART V
Religion

In this section, we cover central issues pertaining to gender and sexuality in religion. Religion is a central institution organizing social life and one that overlaps with other primary institutions. Gender scholars have examined the various mechanisms through which inequalities of gender and sexuality surface within the context of a range of religions and religious organizations across time and place. While much attention has been paid to the patriarchal and heterosexist underpinnings of dominant religions, recent scholarship examines how intersecting inequalities within religious spheres are negotiated, resisted, and transformed. We examine gender and sexuality in a variety of religious contexts across the four core themes of the reader: intersectionality, masculinity, transgender, and global (IMTG) perspectives.

In her piece "Women of God," Orit Avishai argues that whether or not religious belief is harmful to women depends a great deal upon the social, cultural, and historical context within which women live. While women may hold traditional gender ideologies, their choices often reflect gender egalitarian practices in negotiating family and work life. Drawing on research done by scholars in a number of locations, Avishai argues that analyzing religion as simplistically "bad" for women, misses the way women actually use religion to navigate their lives. Women may simultaneously experience forms of gender oppression and empowerment through their religion. The piece complicates the role of religion in reproducing gender and sexual inequalities.

Similarly, in "Negotiating Gendered Religious Space," Pamela Prickett examines religious identity negotiations among African American Muslim women. Ethnographic research in a Los Angeles mosque shows how women "do religion" in ways that resist gender and racial inequalities within the mosque, despite men holding access to more resources. Even though women are fewer in numbers, the women in this mosque assert their right to take part in religious observances, policing men and keeping them out of "sisters-only spaces." This is done particularly through women's bonds with each other and their strategic use of physical space. The study demonstrates the intersecting ways that gender and race inequalities are reinforced and resisted within religious spaces.

In "The Stakes of Gender and Heterosexuality," Melanie Heath examines a Christian-based marriage-strengthening program in Oklahoma. Through fieldwork and interviews, she finds the program teaches couples understandings of gender based on essential biological and cultural differences that cannot be changed. At the same time, the curriculum emphasizes hierarchical relationships between men and women, due to women's vulnerability, with instructors modeling "essential" differences between men and women. Instructors emphasize fundamental differences between women and men, even when confronted by a lesbian couple enrolled in the program. Heterosexuality, inscribed as natural and biological, is central to this differentiation. The research shows how the program relies on notions of normative gender practices that reinforce gendered and sexualized hierarchies.

Lynne Gerber examines masculinity within the context of ex-gay ministries in "Grit, Guts, and Vanilla Beans." Ex-gay ministries emphasize gender hierarchies and see homosexuality as resulting from stunted gender development. Gerber finds, though, that these ministries encourage men to practice a "Godly masculinity" that de-emphasizes heterosexual conquest, is relatively inclusive of masculinities, and encourages intimacy with other men. Through these practices, men are able to express masculinity counter to hegemonic masculinity, while simultaneously maintaining the gender order.

Finally, Rachel Rinaldo's piece, "Muslim Women, Moral Visions," considers the politics of gender and religion in Indonesia. Through ethnographic research with Muslim women activists involved in two national organizations, she finds that debates on proposed legislation around pornography play out differently across the organizations. Women in Fatayat use discourses of gender equality to argue against the legislation, noting that its definition of pornography is very wide and would limit women's freedom of expression and support discrimination against women. On the other hand, women in the Prosperous Justice Party (PKS) support the legislation, drawing on Islamic discourses of morality with an aim toward countering Westernized cultural influences on Indonesian society. The piece demonstrates that women activists adapt global discourses of feminism and Islamic revivalism to engage in political debates, showing how global processes are mediated through national and local contexts.

These pieces emphasize the complexity of how gender and religion intersect. As Orit Avishai argues, religion does not simply work in patriarchal ways to limit women's freedom. Women also wield religion to fashion their own strategies and arguments, whether around the politics of space in an American mosque or around the politics of pornography in Indonesian debates. While religiously based marriage promotion programs may emphasize gender hierarchies and heterosexual relationships, same-sex couples disrupt the assumptions of naturally gendered relations. Even ex-gay ministries may incorporate more inclusive forms of masculinity. Religion, like culture more broadly, can be used to support and interpret a variety of approaches and practices to gender and sexuality.

Women of God

Orit Avishai

s God bad for women? Media consumers in North America and Europe are probably familiar with this narrative: conservative and fundamentalist religions—those that take religion seriously and politicize religiosity—are on the rise, and that's bad for women. In France, wearing a headscarf in public spaces is decried as an affront to French notions of citizenship and to women's personhood. In the United States, Afghan women's plight at the hands of the Taliban was used as a justification for American intervention. Since the emancipation of women and the diversification of family forms and sexualities are among the hallmarks of modernity and secularization, and since fundamentalist religious groups tend to hold traditional views on gender, sexuality, and the family, conservative religions are typically viewed as antithetical to women's interests (not to mention modern, democratic ideals of choice and the freedom to chart one's own destiny).

In a sense, conservative religions have *earned* this bad reputation; the historical record is full of instances in which girls and women have been restricted from access to health care, education, and employment in the name of God. Girls' and women's bodies and mobility are regulated, their chastity is "protected," and sometimes they are even maimed or killed as a marker of national or tribal pride, identity, unity, or boundaries. If this is the case, how can we explain women's willingness and motivation to participate in these religions? Some feel the Marxist explanation—religion is the opiate of the people—and its feminist incarnation—women's participation in conservative religions is a form of false consciousness—are sufficient. Others believe women involved in conservative religions are simply oppressed.

Sociologists, anthropologists, historians, and political scientists who study women's experiences in a range of religious traditions in diverse geographical locations have found that the "God is bad for women" formulation provides an impoverished picture of experiences with conservative religions. These studies show that women are simultaneously oppressed *and* empowered by their religion, that their compliance is as much a product of active strategizing as passive compliance, and that religion is as much a site of negotiating traditional gender norms as it is a site of reproducing patriarchal gender relationships. If that's true, it's certainly possible that conservative religions aren't inherently and universally antithetical to women's interests (at least not *all* of the time).

Some commentators make an even more provocative claim: the "God is bad for women" formulation rests on false assumptions about religion and liberal notions of freedom and choice.

Orit Avishai. 2010. "Women of God." *Contexts* 9(4):46–51.

That is, these scholars argue that the trope ignores the similarities between women's complicity with religious regimes and their complicity with other gendered practices like Western beauty norms.

Religion Is Bad for Women

Religion is often viewed as a primary site for the articulation, reproduction, and institutionalization of gender inequality. The combination of male gods, institutions that encode gender inequality (think male-only clergy) and women's subordination (such as Evangelical teachings on male headship), ambivalence toward the female body (think the veil across the Muslim world and a Jewish man's daily prayer with a line that thanks God for not "having made me a woman"), and the belief that gender differences are natural and essential has produced a deep-seated suspicion toward conservative religions among the reform-minded. Elizabeth Cady Stanton captured this spirit in 1885 when she wrote, "History shows that the moral degradation of woman is due more to theological superstitions than to all other influences together." Such sentiments were echoed by many second wave American feminists who viewed religiously inspired ideas about women's work, reproduction, and bodies as detrimental to the women's movement's goals of gender equality and freedom.

This view of religion poses a problem, though: women *are* involved with conservative religions. They join, and they stay. Are these women opposed to equality and freedom? Do they not recognize their complicity in a regime that requires submission? Until the 1980s, the general view was that religion—as an ideology and as an institution—was nothing but a constraint on women's lives, so women's active involvement with conservative religions was viewed as the product of oppression, lack of agency, or false consciousness.

Yet, when researchers turned to study women's *actual* experiences with religion (as opposed to ideologically driven assessments) in the late 1980s, their findings were startling: women—Protestant, Catholic, Jewish, Hindu, and others—are not necessarily oppressed and deprived of free choice by their religion.

[. . .]

Multiple Meanings

When scholars looked past religious dogma to lived experiences, they found discrepancies between ideologies and practices. Women, they saw, don't blindly submit to religious prescriptions; instead, they adapt their religious practices (if not iterations of belief) to the realities of their lives and to dominant gender ideologies. In the process, they sometimes (consciously or unconsciously) subvert and resist official teachings without much fanfare and without explicitly resisting religious gender norms.

This subtlety, though, serves to perpetuate the myth that women are uniformly oppressed by religion. For example, when sociologists Sally Gallagher and Christian Smith (1999) interviewed Evangelical men and women in the U.S. about their family lives, their respondents professed an unwavering support for ideologies such as male headship and women's submission while rejecting egalitarian gender ideologies. Nevertheless, their *real-life* choices about work, family, and child rearing exhibited a de-facto egalitarianism that belied their ideological stance: most of the Evangelical women in their study worked outside the home and routinely participated in domestic decision making. Gallagher and Smith labeled this disjuncture "symbolic traditionalism and pragmatic egalitarianism."

In other cases, researchers have found that what looks like oppression is often a set of strategic choices made to help women navigate gender relations. In a now-classic study, sociologist Lynn Davidman (1991) explored why educated American women might embrace highly patriarchal and conservative strands of Orthodox Judaism. Rather than being duped into an anachronistic religion, these women said that they consciously turned to Orthodox Judaism as a response to problems generated by modern American culture, including its emphasis on careerism, individualism, and gender equality. Caroline Chen (2008), a sociologist who studied the experiences of Taiwanese women who converted to conservative strands of Buddhism and Christianity after immigrating to the U.S., found women used religion to negotiate with patriarchal family structures and to carve out a space of independence and authority. Their newfound religion allowed women to undermine oppressive traditional Taiwanese practices that left them without much power within the family. Gallagher (2003) also saw similar dynamics in her study of low-income Syrian women, who use religious and cultural rationales to improve their access to income and employment while avoiding unattractive employment opportunities. The Syrian women consciously enlist religion to expand their autonomy while simultaneously maintaining a semblance of deference. Defining their economic activities as "not work," for example, means they can contribute to the family economy (sometimes earning up to 40 percent of the family's income) in a society that emphasizes women's primary responsibilities as domestic. The point is: some women achieve progressive ends using traditional, but subversive, means.

So, women aren't oppressed dupes. On the contrary, women like these use religion to make choices and improve their lives; they are strategic actors who appropriate religious traditions and practices to meet the demands of contemporary life, often to further extra-religious ends such as economic opportunities, domestic relations, political ideologies, and cultural affiliation.

Other studies show how seemingly oppressive practices can serve empowering and liberating functions. This is the case with regard to the issue that best symbolizes conservative religion's purported oppression of women: the veil.

In the 1980s, when political scientist Arlene MacLeod (1992) and Turkish sociologist Nilüfer Göle (1996) studied the emergent phenomenon of Muslim women's embrace of veiling in Egypt and Turkey, respectively, each found that context matters. In the Egyptian case, women's embrace of the veil came at a time when economic conditions compelled women to find gainful employment outside the home. Their movement into the workplace was at odds with traditional Egyptian notions of modesty and domesticity. These ideas had discouraged women from venturing into public spaces unaccompanied by men and frowned upon close contact between unrelated men and women. Veiling provided a solution, as it preserved women's modesty and affirmed their domesticity while also providing the mobility to work outside the home. As it opened unprecedented opportunities for women to venture beyond the domestic, the veil became liberating. Macleod terms the veil's liberating potential as "accommodating protest."

In Turkey, Göle found that, to the generation of young, educated, women who embraced the veil on college campuses, veiling symbolized resistance to Western values. Veiling, Göle argues, wasn't imposed on these women, so the act of veiling reveals them to be empowered and strategic political actors. Research on Latin American Pentecostal women reports similar dynamics of women's empowerment through the embrace of religion.

These studies notwithstanding, not all commentators are equally impressed by religion's liberating potential. In her award-winning study of South Korean Evangelical women, sociologist Kelly Chong (2009) writes that conversion to Evangelical Christianity helps some women navigate the forces of modernity while also reinforcing highly patriarchal and non-egalitarian gender dynamics. Further, Chong asserts that religion is *also* a site where the rules of gender relations are constantly being rewritten.

The aggregate message of these studies is that conservative religions are not necessarily oppressive, nor is religion thoroughly anti-modern. Context is extremely important but often lost in popular depictions of conservative religions and their symbols—the veil, men's headship, male-only clergy—as uniformly oppressive. In some instances, the forces of modernity increase the appeal of conservative religion. In others, the embrace of religion helps women cope with and sometimes even challenge preexisting oppressive gender norms and social structures.

Yet, it seems that each study begins with the notion that women's involvement with conservative religions is paradoxical—only to find, time and time again, that this formula provides only a very narrow perspective on the religious experience. More recent research takes issue with the notion that women's complicity and submission are paradoxical, investigating, instead, the assumptions on which this perspective is based.

Past the Paradox

Experts' bewilderment over women's embrace of conservative religions is symptomatic of the broader assumptions about religiosity and modern personhood that have shaped discussions of religion since the Enlightenment. One set of assumptions concerns the incompatibility of religion and modernity. Throughout much of the 20th century, everyone expected the significance of religion would progressively decline. Known as the "secularization thesis," the theory was that modernization and secularization (and, implicitly, westernization) are intrinsically related and that progress—including the emancipation of women from the hold of oppressive religions—follows a uniform and linear (western) trajectory. Religion, in this conception, is incompatible with rational, complex, and individualistic modern societies. When empirical reality proved this theory wrong (conservative and fundamentalist religious movements, for instance, have been on the rise around the world since the 1980s, as evidenced by the 1979 Iranian revolution, the rise of Pentecostalism in Latin America, the increased visibility of Evangelicals in American political life, and the fervor of Orthodox Jewish nationalists), the secularization thesis was replaced by explanations that recognized that *some* aspects of religion were compatible with modernity.

However, a second set of assumptions about the incompatibility of religion with liberal notions of agency, freedom, and choice persists. It is in this set of assumptions that the paradox approach is rooted. The liberal notion of freedom assumes that individuals should strive to be free of commitment and submission to a higher power—thereby precluding many forms of religious devotion. This is why explanations of women's involvement with conservative religion that revolve around strategic choice, the liberatory potential of religion, or passive resistance have been so attractive: women who realize their own economic, political, or intimate interests against the weight of custom and tradition are *redeemed.*

Yet, such explanations ultimately provide binary explanations of religion: either it's a site where women are oppressed and gender inequality is reproduced, or it's a site of empowerment, resistance, strategic planning, and negotiation of gender. What's missing is the possibility that women embrace religious practices such as veiling and male headship in pursuit of religious goals—namely, the cultivation of oneself as a pious *religious* subject.

This is the account that anthropologist Saba Mahmood (2005) provides in her study of Islamic revival and piety among women in Cairo. Starting in the 1990s, many Egyptian women began to attend mosques to teach each other Islamic doctrine. This trend, facilitated by women's increased mobility and education, has subversive potential since scholarly and theological materials had previously been the sole purview of learned men. Yet, these Muslim women were *not* seeking to undermine existing power structures or to resist the secular state, which discouraged their kind of learning and religious piety. Rather, their main motivation was to learn, attain, and uphold Islamic virtues of modesty and docility and reintegrate Islamic knowledge and practices (including those that organize gender relationships) into everyday Egyptian life. For Westerners, it seems impossibly paradoxical: the nature of piety that these women promote depends on subordination to Islamic virtues of femininity that includes modesty and docility and is achieved by teaching the body "modest disciplines" through practices such as veiling and the cultivation of shyness.

It's easy to dismiss something like the cultivation of shyness as oppressive, functional, or a symbol of resistance to the forces of modernity. However, Mahmood presents a different explanation: this practice provides a pathway to achieve piety and to make meaning in the world. Mahmood likens the achievement of piety through submission to the lengthy and painful regime of learning to which musicians or dancers subject themselves as they seek mastery in their field. Like a dancer or musician, the religious woman submits herself to a lifelong regime of ongoing discipline; she becomes a masterful religious woman through daily practice. But, like the dancer or the musician, the religious woman is not oppressed by her regime; rather, her very personhood and agency are predicated upon the ability to be instructed and transformed by submission to her practices.

Mahmood came under fire for positing that the embrace of docility doesn't necessarily amount to oppression and that "freedom" and "choice" aren't universal terms; most discussions of religion, it seems, still spring from the "God is bad for women" formulation. Yet, the most important point that Mahmood makes is that the assumptions that shape discussions of women's experiences with conservative religions are flawed. A shift in perspective opens up new avenues for thinking about religion as a site of identity making. Other commentators approach this question of assumptions from a different perspective by noting the irony of anti-religious fervor among Westerners and citing the similarities between patriarchal regulations emanating from religious dogma and those hailing from cultural norms and standards like the Western beauty ideal.

Church of God, Church of Beauty

Bring up conservative religion and its symbols on any American college campus, and students will immediately point out paradoxes of complicity. With astonishing predictability, they associate compliance with conservative religions with lack of agency, choice, or freedom. Students are usually willing to concede that complicity sometimes masks strategic choices or latent resistance, but arguments such as Mahmood's—that women find meaning through docility—are a hard sell. Students like to point out—triumphantly—that *their* lives in a modern democracy that values women are free of the constraints that characterize the lives of veiled women.

Fatima Mernissi (2001), a Moroccan sociologist who has written extensively about gender and religion in the Middle East, puts these self-satisfied indictments in perspective. In the late 1990s, Mernissi lectured extensively in Europe and the U.S. about her memoir. In it, she recounts her childhood in a typical Moroccan household: a harem. This multi-generational living arrangement housed siblings, families, and parents. The harem limited women's spatial mobility, but was also a site of ongoing power struggles. In the course of her book tour, Mernissi was inundated by questions that exposed the depth of Westerners' ignorance about gender relations in Muslim societies. Westerners, she learned, assumed that Muslims were women-haters and that Muslim women were oppressed, dependent, sex starved, and powerless.

Intrigued by the dissonance between Western perceptions and her own experiences, Mernissi set out on a complementary mission (and wrote a complementary book) to uncover how Westerns represent Muslim gender relations. In the process, Mernissi stumbled upon a revelation: Westerners, too, have their own harem, one that she titles "size 6." Mernissi criticizes Western commentators for feigning ignorance in light of the similarities between the oppressive nature of the Church of God and the oppressive nature of the church of beauty. Recounting her experience in an American department store, where she was deemed "too big" for its elegant selection, Mernissi revealed parallels between the violence of the veil that restricts women's movement and the violence of Western beauty norms that compel women to follow strict diet regimes and undergo dangerous surgeries.

Mernissi's rhetoric is simplistic, but the simplicity helps drive home a more sophisticated claim: the "God is bad for women" formulation is not the truism many believe. Instead, it's a myth that hinges on assumptions about the nature of religion, personhood, freedom, and choice.

Overall, then, *is* God bad for women? Research over the past twenty years has shattered conventional views of conservative religions as monolithic sources of oppression. Social scientists have demonstrated that women can be empowered by their religion, that compliance is often strategic, that religion is a site where gender rules are constantly being rewritten, and that religiosity is produced through acts of devotion. More than anything, these studies show that asking "Is God bad for women?" is misguided, based on ideological assumptions rather than on sound empirical evidence. Ultimately, like most questions about culture and society, the answer can only be "it depends." Context—social, cultural, historical—is paramount, and it's impossible to assess the implications of women's involvement with religion without taking into account the diverse circumstances in which women encounter conservative religions. It's not God, but man, who's detrimental to or affirming of women's interests, both in the practices and behaviors we condemn and condone.

References

Chen, Carolyn. 2008. *Getting Saved in America: Taiwanese Immigration and Religious Experience.* Princeton, NJ: Princeton University Press.

Chong, Kelly H. 2009. *Deliverance and Submission: Evangelical Women and the Negotiation of Patriarchy in South Korea.* Cambridge, MA: Harvard University Press. Explores how women's religious participation constitutes part of their effort to negotiate the dilemmas of contemporary family and gender relations.

Davidman, Lynn. 1991. *Tradition in a Rootless World: Women Turn to Orthodox Judaism.* Berkeley and Los Angeles, CA: University of California Press. A now-classic look at women's embrace of a conservative religion.

Gallagher, Sally K. 2003. *Evangelical Identity and Gendered Family Life.* New Brunswick, NJ: Rutgers University Press. A balanced study of Evangelicals' perspectives on gender, family life, and faith.

Gallagher, Sally K. and Christian Smith. 1999. "Symbolic Traditionalism and Pragmatic Egalitarianism: Contemporary Evangelicals, Families, and Gender." *Gender & Society* 13(2):211–33.

Göle, Nilüfer. 1996. *The Forbidden Modern: Civilization and Veiling*. Ann Arbor, MI: University of Michigan Press.

MacLeod, Arlene Elowe. 1992. "Hegemonic Relations and Gender Resistance: The New Veiling as Accommodating Protest in Cairo." *Signs: Journal of Women in Culture and Society* 17(3):533–57.

Mahmood, Saba. 2005. *Politics of Piety: The Islamic Revival and the Feminist Subject*. Chicago, IL: University of Chicago Press. A study of Islamic revival in Egypt that challenges key assumptions within feminist theory about religious practices.

Mernissi, Fatima. 2001. *Scheherazade Goes West: Different Cultures, Different Harems*. New York: Washington Square Press. Probes representations of Muslim women in Western culture and juxtaposes the relations between men and women in Europe with those in the Muslim world.

Stanton, Elizabeth Cady and J. L. Spalding. 1885. "Has Christianity Benefited Woman?" *The North American Review* 140(1342):389–410.

Negotiating Gendered Religious Space

The Particularities of Patriarchy in an African American Mosque

Pamela J. Prickett

© iStockphoto.com/valeriebarry

A frican American women's participation in men-dominated religious organizations seems to represent a classic paradox of contemporary religious life. Within the popular institution of the Black church, women fill the pews but rarely stand at the pulpits; they serve as "footsoldiers" for clergymen whose concerns often privilege the interests of men over women (Harris 1999), and they appear hesitant to accept women as religious authorities (Putnam and Campbell 2010). The passionate commitment of African American women

Pamela J. Prickett. 2015. "Negotiating Gendered Religious Space: The Particularities of Patriarchy in an African American Mosque." *Gender & Society* 29(1):51–72.

to the Black church has undoubtedly benefited the African American community at large (Carpenter 2003; Gilkes 2001; Higginbotham 1993), but this participation may come at the expense of Black women's gendered interests (Collins 2000, 2004; Grant 1982; Williams 1993). Even the most sensitive portrayals of church involvement among African American women recognize that the presence and commitment of women to the church reflects some "acceptance of male-centered theologies of female subordination" (Frederick 2003, 4).

For African American Muslim women who participate in the mosque, the obstacles may be more cumbersome. They face institutionalized forms of patriarchy as well as find themselves fewer in number than their men counterparts (Bartkowski and Read 2003; Harris 1999; Lincoln and Mamiya 1990). Along with Orthodox Judaism, Islam is one of the only global religious traditions in which men regularly attend worship services in far greater numbers than women (Sullins 2006). For this reason, Sullins argues, Muslim men are more religious than Muslim women, despite Muslim women worldwide reporting higher measures of religiosity (Sullins 2006, 845). Institutionalized gender segregation as well as the exclusion of women from leadership roles contributes to public perceptions of Islam as an innately patriarchal religion that suppresses women's interests (Haddad, Smith, and Moore 2006; Inglehart and Norris 2003; Korteweg 2008; Ong 1995). As Mahmood so eloquently explains, any study of "Muslim women" must at some point engage with "all the assumptions this dubious signifier triggers in the Western imagination concerning Islam's patriarchal and misogynist qualities" (Mahmood 2005, 189; see also Abu-Lughod 2002). Yet, Muslim women demonstrate they are capable of constructing modes of religious being that further their own desired interests (e.g., Read and Bartkowski 2000).

Feminist studies of Islam contribute to a growing body of work on women's engagement of conservative religions that has uncovered an array of surprising and creative ways women benefit from their participation in men-dominated religious traditions (Chong 2008, 133; also Avishai 2008; Bartkowski and Read 2003; Mahmood 2005; Read and Bartkowski 2000; Rinaldo 2013). Avishai argues that the "paradox" approach assumes a false dichotomy "[pitting] agency against compliance," when instead women construct their religious selves through observance and conduct (Avishai 2008, 429). This process, which Avishai terms "doing religion," occurs as women simultaneously negotiate multiple identities (see also Bulanda 2011). In the U.S. context, where Islam is not only a minority religion but one often marginalized in public spheres as misogynistic (Rinaldo 2013, 192), African American Muslim women face the possibility that their religious identity may compound intersecting racial, class, and gender oppressions (Byng 1998). But they also "surrender" to Islam, in part, as a means of resistance to racism and economic exploitation (Rouse 2004, 216), suggesting their negotiation of an Islamic identity may demonstrate a "capacity for action" not captured in conventional framings of Islam and gender (Mahmood 2005, 18).

This study builds on recent insights into religion and women's agency by incorporating feminist theories of space into a "doing religion" framework. I take advantage of data collected over five years in an African American Muslim community to provide an interactionist account of how African American women negotiate spaces in the mosque as a way to perform certain religious and social identities. Religious space matters because to determine its meanings and appropriate uses is to have power over it, along with the symbolic and material resources encoded in such space (Morin and Guelke 2007, xxv).

[. . .]

I analyze the ways in which African American Muslim women's mosque participation constitutes a form of socially engaged religious conduct. In their negotiations of different spaces, at times in direct conflict with men trying to occupy the same spaces, the women reinforced shared gender and racial identities. However, their efforts were not boundless, and the women found themselves with less access to institutional resources than certain men. I discuss how the women leaned further on their network of African American Muslim sisters for support in these struggles, thereby enabling themselves and each other to resist racial, economic, and gender oppressions (Bartkowski and Read 2003; Collins 2000).

[. . .]

Methods

[. . .]

From the street, the mosque—or *masjid*, as members referred to it—was unrecognizable as a place of worship. Surrounded by a wire fence, the lot included a *masalah* (prayer hall), small house, dirt yard, and narrow gravel parking lot. The *masalah* was composed of a simple stucco structure with two sliding glass entrances (one for men, or "brothers," one for women, or "sisters"). Brothers performed *wudu* (ritual cleansing before prayer) at an outdoor sink near a second men's side entrance. For the first three years of the study, sisters used a small powder room inside the house for *wudu*, but they later helped finance the installation of a portable shed next to the house that contained a sink and foot washing station. The small house contained staff offices, kitchen, brothers' bathroom, sisters' powder room, and a bedroom for an elderly brother who lived there.

[. . .]

From May 2008 to August 2013, I gathered data on believers' interactions by participating in and observing a variety of religious and social activities at the *masjid*. I attended *jumah* (Friday community prayer), Islamic classes, fundraising banquets, religious conferences, festivals, and funerals. I volunteered on several planning committees and logged hundreds of hours cooking and cleaning alongside women believers. For thirteen months of the study, I lived four blocks from the *masjid* to better immerse myself in the daily realities of life in a poor urban neighborhood. During this time, I spent two to five nights per week at the *masjid* "hanging out" with a group of longstanding women community members, increasing my visits to nearly every night during the holy month of Ramadan. Over the years, I attended more than 120 community *iftar* dinners, which permitted the most opportunities to study women and men interact outside Friday services.

[. . .]

Negotiating Gendered Spaces

Believers engaged physical spaces at the *masjid* in order to worship, socialize, and acquire support. In analyzing the ways believers constructed and used different spaces at the mosque as well as how these uses varied by gender, we see how control of and access to different spaces accorded women and men different institutional benefits. The sisters had less or often restricted access to certain spaces in the *masjid* but within their maneuverings of individual spaces were able to cultivate strong bonds of sisterhood that aided them outside the mosque. Their actions constitute creative forms of "doing religion" through social interaction, in gender-specific ways.

A Space for Meaningful Worship

Like any religious organization, the *masjid* existed first and foremost as a place of worship (Sullivan 2011), and in this capacity men dominated. Only men served as imams, giving *khutbahs* and leading congregational prayer. Only men performed the *adhan* (call to prayer), a sacred duty of additional symbolic importance in this setting because the first muezzin in Islamic history was a former African slave. And, only men taught official religious classes. While at different times over the five years of the study I observed women form informal religious education classes, coming together to discuss the Qur'an and to give each other lessons about important women in Prophet Muhammad's life, the groups typically waned after a few weeks or months. The groups also failed to gain the authority of being noted in the monthly community bulletin.

This patriarchal division of religious labor was reflected in the spatial layout of the prayer hall. The *masalah* was divided into two sections: the "sisters' side," which measured approximately 400 square feet, and the "brothers' side," roughly 520 square feet (see Figure 24.1). Though I have designated them as separate boxes, in reality this was one open space, with only a half wall where the bold line is indicated.

[. . .]

While the sisters' side was technically smaller, it was surprisingly large given women's lower attendance. On a typical Friday afternoon, between 15 and 20 women sat in the sisters' area, while three or four times that many men clustered in the brothers' portion. Unlike many mosques where women worshippers find themselves praying in basements or hallways (Karim 2009), it was men who sometimes had to make *salat* (prayer) outside on the sidewalk or lawn. With the exception of densely crowded prayers, say on a large holiday like *Eid al-Fitr*, I rarely had to squeeze into the women's space, more often than not getting plenty of room to relax on the floor against a wall. Brothers sat through the *khutbah* with folded legs, their knees or shoulders centimeters from a neighbor.

However, the sisters' disproportionately large spatial representation in the *masalah* did not always improve their ability to participate in elements of the worship experience. Because they worshipped behind the men, facing northwest toward Mecca, they had to look at the backsides of the brothers during *khutbahs* and *salat*. If asked about this, sisters agreed that their positioning should be insignificant, because believers were supposed to focus on their *eeman* (faith) instead of what was happening around them, but I also heard them sometimes complain to each other about having to see men's "cracks" when the latter bent for prostration (see also Karim 2009). The arrangement of women behind men also impeded the sisters' abilities to hear key components of worship services. Poor acoustics inside the *masjid* coupled with the competing sounds of the inner city, such as sirens, helicopters, buses, and booming stereos, frequently drowned out the voice of the speaking imam.

Figure 24.1 Inside of Masjid (sisters' area in white; brothers' area in gray)

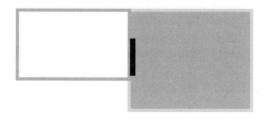

Sisters came to the *masjid* despite these obstacles to worship and, once there, worked to make the prayer hall a sacred space that facilitated women's engagement in processes of religious self-making. The following excerpt illustrates this well:

> The *masalah* is quiet, save for Imam Khalid's soft voice speaking about the importance of *taqwa* (God-consciousness). Although the service started at 1:00, and it is now 1:28 p.m., believers are still trickling into the *masjid,* including one younger non-African American male. As many believers do before they sit for the *khubtah,* he starts to move into *salat* position, bringing his feet together and correcting his posture. Before the man can begin his prayer, a sister sitting in a chair about six feet behind him clears her throat loudly and says, without moving her body an inch, *"As-salaam alaikum,* Brother." The young man turns round, looks at the sister humbly as he lowers his head, and then moves far to the left out of the sister's way. The sister says nothing else, just continues to look forward towards Imam Khalid.

To accommodate the sister, the brother had to wedge himself against a crowded group of men on the north side of the *masjid.* On that day only 15 sisters were in attendance (13 who prayed), while the men's area had at least 60 brothers. The sister's heightened position in a chair would have enabled her to see over the man once he sat down, but she did not wait. She publicly enforced her right to be able to see the imam, an act that demonstrated to anyone watching she was neither subordinate to nor intimidated by the men worshipping ahead of her. . . .

Women's active participation during worship services demonstrates that the *masjid* was "an important performative space" (Chong 2008, 121) where women negotiated multiple social identities. Even though their designated space was smaller, the sisters made it a meaningful place for religious conduct. Individual efforts to enforce the sacredness of the sisters' space benefited the women as a whole, because it furthered every woman's capacity to engage Islam.

A (Safe) Space All Their Own

One evening while I helped a sister clean up the kitchen following a community event, a brother walked in and politely asked us if he could use the sisters' bathroom because the men's was occupied. When he came out, he was drying his hands on an American flag handkerchief and joked, "You don't have any paper towels in there. I have to wipe my hands with the American flag. Blasphemy!" The sister and I laughed, but the joke served as a subtle reminder that for women to have resources—even those as simple as paper towels for their bathroom—they had to fight for them.

Money was a constant source of tension at the *masjid* because there was never enough to cover even basic expenses. These shortages reflected the larger financial insecurity of the community. The ability to spend *masjid* funds rested in the hands of Resident Imam Khalid and his right-hand man, Brother Fareed. These two men decided if, when, and where money would go, often with a lack of transparency that frustrated believers of both genders. Women learned to work within this power system, using informal channels with the men to lobby for money for certain events or activities. They also counted on Imam Khalid's wife to serve as a champion for sisters' causes, a role she relished when heading the annual women's conference or helping her husband decide how to remodel portions of the *masjid.* Women generally did not concern themselves with the quality of men-only spaces, focusing instead on parts of the *masjid* women used, thus reinforcing gender divisions.

When I started my fieldwork, a small group of sisters spearheaded an effort to remodel the bathroom, worn and in need of repair, by getting the *masjid* to install a new sink and toilet. Sisters took turns cleaning it and buying replacement bottles of hand soap that were nicer than the discount-brand the office bought. Not long after the remodel, sisters started "catching" brothers sneaking out of the women's bathroom. Two women, including the imam's wife, put a new lock on the bathroom, keeping the keys away from male staff and taking turns to unlock the door every morning. Although the lock lasted only a few weeks, it sent a message to the brothers that this space belonged to the sisters and indicated to all members that the women were united in their efforts to stop men's appropriation of women's resources.

Women also mobilized to create new gender-specific spaces for intimate religious practices. Like *salat, wudu* (ritual washing before prayer) involves moving and bending the body. Not wanting to do these physical movements in front of men, women relied on the sisters' bathroom as a private space to "make *wudu*." But the bathroom was small and had only one sink. After discussions among the sisters, a concerted effort emerged to install a proper *wudu* station. The women collected money to purchase a storage shed and oversaw its installation. Plumbing for the special sinks for washing feet came later, and although there remains no cooling or heating system, once complete the women were proud of their accomplishment to create a space exclusively designed so sisters could engage more deeply in Islamic practice.

Sisters' efforts to police men's movements in gender-specific spaces grew more extreme after installation of the *wudu* station, which sat next to a popular fig tree. This created tensions between men and women believers, captured in this excerpt from one Ramadan:

> Several sisters are standing outside and talking while *taraweeh* prayer is going on inside. Together we've been watching a brother who the sisters often complain is creepy and crazy because of his physical appearance and odd ramblings. The brother starts to walk towards the sisters' *wudu* station and Lisa says, "What's he doing? No! No! That's not right. He can't be over there!" She decides she's going to rush over there and stop him, with Aisha running after her and shouting that she's coming too! The sisters go up to the man and have some kind of back-and-forth. The brother eventually walks off, away from the *wudu* area. Lisa and Aisha come back to where we're standing, and (imitating a deep male voice and arching her back) Lisa chants, "I want a fig. I want a fig." Then returning to her normal voice and relaxed posture, she says that sisters need to be part of security too, to which another sister mumbles, "We are security."

Even though no sisters were using the shed at the time, the man's trespassing violated a sacred sisters-only space. The irony is that I rarely observed women use the shed, or what one sister mockingly termed "the outhouse." Despite this, the *wudu* station is important because it represented women's abilities to come together to create new, safe spaces for religious ends within the existing institutional structure.

Women's efforts to protect the space exhibited a claim of authority over men, if only for a short time. Following the incident, I pressed Lisa on who she thought has final authority to determine access to the *masjid*. She replied, "No one. The community does." She rejected the idea that only men leaders or security could make those decisions, but her assertion suggests an exaggerated sense of agency in the case of access. Sisters complained repeatedly to Imam Khalid about the brother in the previous excerpt and asked that he be "kicked off the lot," in part because the man failed to observe an appropriate physical distance when he talked to women. Time and time again the sisters complained that they had to be security even though it was the responsibility of the men to protect women.

[. . .]

Conclusion

The African American Muslim women in this study asserted their rights to be engaged pious actors in spite of their smaller numbers and spaces in the *masjid*. Admittedly, the most sacred space in the *masjid* was the most segregated, but the arrangement afforded women a designated space they actively protected. Sisters also exerted power in the community by creating new sisters-only spaces, as establishment of the *wudu* station demonstrated. . . . For these reasons, I hesitate to say Islam is a "patriarchal religion" (cf. Bartkowski and Read 2003). Instead, my analyses suggest there are particular instances in which patriarchy manifests in observable ways.

[. . .]

The particularities of patriarchy in this setting may constrain sisters' abilities to negotiate spaces in certain ways, but they do not stop the women in their goals to engage Islam. Their creative responses to men's maneuverings are further proof that women can "do religion" in institutions led by men. In many ways the actions of African American women in the mosque mirror those of African American women in the church, whose aims are not to feminize leadership but instead work within existing organizations to create stronger communities (Frederick 2003; Higginbotham 1993).

An intersectional frame like the one used here recognizes that religious identity exists alongside other social identities. In negotiating these multiple, competing identities in contested spaces like the mosque, women work to overcome different forms of oppression. In the worship area, the women distinguished their patterns of worship from those of "immigrant" Muslims as one form of resistance. . . . These negotiations are further proof that piety is grounded in everyday observance and conduct (Avishai 2008; Mahmood 2005), to which I add piety is as much a social process intended to engage religion through interaction as it is an achievement of personal conduct (Rinaldo 2013, 92).

By considering how pious women position themselves with respect to others occupying similar spaces, we see that gender is not just a project of understanding the social meanings attached to sexual difference (George 2005, 22). Gender also involves the articulation of racial and class differences that shape one's capacity to act. African American Muslim women may be better able to resist patriarchy, and therefore set their own terms and limits within community life, by performing a distinctly African American Muslim identity positioned against that of "immigrant" Muslims. Such everyday acts of resistance may undermine efforts to create an *ummah* (wider Muslim community) by promoting racial exclusion over gender inclusion (Karim 2009), but my evidence suggests African American Muslims rely on their local communities in distinct ways because they face different oppressions. Research that acknowledges the contours of religious social difference avoids homogenizing religions and the people who identify with them (Korteweg 2008).

Previous research suggests that the majority of U.S. mosques use the most conservative worship arrangement of complete gender segregation during worship (Karim 2009), so the experiences of women in this study may be more the exception than the rule. However, through their microlevel maneuverings of space we see how the dominant "paradox" approach in the sociology of religion, which sees women's participation as a form of submission to patriarchal religious systems, belies a more nuanced and important social phenomenon at play. Religion does not inherently "do" anything to people that practice it—rather, in this case, African American Muslim women and men "do religion" in a context shaped by multiple oppressions.

References

Abu-Lughod, Lila. 2002. "Do Muslim Women Really Need Saving? Anthropological Reflections on Cultural Relativism and Its Others." *American Anthropologist* 104:783–90.

Avishai, Orit. 2008. "'Doing Religion' in a Secular World: Women in Conservative Religions and the Question of Agency." *Gender & Society* 22:409–33.

Bartkowski, John P. and Jen'nan Ghazal Read. 2003. "Veiled Submission: Gender, Power, and Identity Among Evangelical and Muslim Women in the United States." *Qualitative Sociology* 26:71–90.

Bulanda, Jennifer Roebuck. 2011. "Doing Family, Doing Gender, Doing Religion: Structured Ambivalence and the Religion-Family Connection." *Journal of Family Theory & Review* 3:179–97.

Byng, Michelle D. 1998. "Mediating Discrimination: Resisting Oppression Among African-American Muslim Women." *Social Problems* 45:473–87.

Carpenter, Delores C. 2003. "A Time for Honor: A Portrait of African-American Clergywomen." In *How Long This Road: Race, Religion, and the Legacy of C. Eric Lincoln*, edited by A. B. Pollard III and L. H. Whelchel, Jr. New York: Palgrave Macmillan.

Chong, Kelly H. 2008. *Deliverance and Submission: Evangelical Women and the Negotiation of Patriarchy in South Korea*. Cambridge, MA: Harvard University Press.

Collins, Patricia Hill. 2000. *Black Feminist Thought: Knowledge, Consciousness, and the Politics of Empowerment*. 2nd ed. New York: Routledge.

Collins, Patricia Hill. 2004. *Black Sexual Politics: African-Americans, Gender, and the New Racism*. New York: Routledge.

Frederick, Marla. 2003. *Between Sundays: Black Women and Everyday Struggles of Faith*. Berkeley, CA: University of California Press.

George, Sheba Mariam. 2005. *When Women Come First: Gender and Class in Transnational Migration*. Berkeley, CA: University of California Press.

Gilkes, Cheryl. 2001. *If It Wasn't for the Women . . . : Black Women's Experience and Womanist Culture in Church and Community*. Maryknoll, NY: Orbis Books.

Grant, Jacquelyn. 1982. "Black Women and the Church." In *But Some of Us Are Brave*, edited by G. T. Hull, P. B. Scott, and B. Smith. Old Westbury, NY: Feminist Press.

Haddad, Yvonne Yazbeck, Jane I. Smith, and Kathleen M. Moore. 2006. *Muslim Women in America: The Challenge of Islamic Identity Today*. New York: Oxford University Press.

Harris, Frederick C. 1999. *Something Within: Religion in African-American Political Activism*. New York: Oxford University Press.

Higginbotham, Evelyn Brooks. 1993. *Righteous Discontent: The Women's Movement in the Black Baptist Church, 1880–1920*. Cambridge, MA: Harvard University Press.

Inglehart, Ronald and Pippa Norris. 2003. *Rising Tide: Gender Equality and Cultural Change Around the World*. Cambridge, UK: Cambridge University Press.

Karim, Jamillah. 2009. *American Muslim Women: Negotiating Race, Class, and Gender Within the Ummah*. New York: New York University Press.

Korteweg, Anna. 2008. "The Sharia Debate in Ontario: Gender, Islam, and Representations of Muslim Women's Agency." *Gender & Society* 22:434–54.

Lincoln, Eric C. and Lawrence Mamiya. 1990. *The Black Church in the African-American Experience*. Durham, NC: Duke University Press.

Mahmood, Saba. 2005. *Politics of Piety: The Islamic Revival and the Feminist Subject*. Princeton, NJ: Princeton University Press.

Morin, Karen M. and Jeanne Kay Guelke. 2007. "Introduction." In *Women, Religion, & Space: Global Perspectives on Gender and Faith*, edited by K. M. Morin and J. K. Guelke. Syracuse, NY: Syracuse University Press.

Ong, Aihwa. 1995. "State Versus Islam: Malay Families, Women's Bodies, and the Body Politic in Malaysia." In *Bewitching Women, Pious Men: Gender and Body Politics in Southeast Asia*, edited by A. Ong and M. G. Peletz. Berkeley, CA: University of California Press.

Putnam, Robert D. and David E. Campbell. 2010. *American Grace: How Religion Divides and Unites Us*. New York: Simon & Schuster.

Read, Jen'nan Ghazal and John P. Bartkowski. 2000. "To Veil or Not to Veil?: A Case Study of Identity Negotiation Among Muslim Women in Austin, Texas." *Gender & Society* 14:395–417.

Rinaldo, Rachel. 2013. *Mobilizing Piety: Islam and Feminism in Indonesia.* New York: Oxford University Press.

Rouse, Carolyn Moxley. 2004. *Engaged Surrender: African-American Women and Islam.* Berkeley, CA: University of California Press.

Sullins, D. Paul. 2006. "Gender and Religion: Deconstructing Universality, Constructing Complexity." *American Journal of Sociology* 112:838–80.

Sullivan, Susan Crawford. 2011. *Living Faith: Everyday Religion and Mothers in Poverty.* Chicago, IL: University of Chicago Press.

Williams, Delores. 1993. *Sisters in the Wilderness: The Challenge of Womanist God-Talk.* Maryknoll, NY: Orbis Books.

The Stakes of Gender and Heterosexuality

Melanie Heath

© iStockphoto.com/EyeJoy

On a dreary, rainy January day, I attended my first weekend marriage workshop at a church in Oklahoma City that I had located on the marriage initiative's website. After introducing myself as a researcher who was studying Oklahoma's efforts to strengthen marriage to the workshop leader and the two couples present, I was given a workbook. I sat down and tried to hide my astonishment as I read the cover: "'So they are no longer two, but one.' Jesus Christ." This was the Christian version of the Prevention and Relationship Enhancement Program (CPREP), I had read about the secular curriculum before traveling to Oklahoma, but I hadn't realized that the marriage initiative had also adopted a Christian version. Matty, the workshop leader, began by telling the story of Adam and Eve, who were made aware of their nakedness after eating the forbidden fruit, and she continued to deliver a moral message about biblical marriage as part of a Christian curriculum.

Several weeks later, I met with a new surprise. Another rainy March evening at the end of the workday found couples arriving to attend the first of a six-week secular marriage workshop at a

Melanie Heath. 2012. From *One Marriage Under God: The Campaign to Promote Marriage in America*. Chapter 2: "The Stakes of Gender and Heterosexuality," pp. 43–69. New York: New York University Press.

human service agency. Participants took seats around three tables arranged in a U-shape, as the two workshop leaders handed out "All About You" forms for participants to fill out. I counted thirteen couples, and during introductions I learned that ten were married, one engaged, one living together, and one had just begun dating. Four single women attended who—except for me—acted as coaches to the couples during the workshop exercises. The participants were predominantly white, with one interracial couple (African American/white). Just before the class was about to begin, two white women in their late fifties entered the room and took the last two seats across from me. Were they a couple, I wondered? No, I told myself, that's improbable. My speculations gave way as the two workshop leaders began the class. David, a white man in his late fifties, told us that he held a master's degree and had been married for thirty years. Randy, a bit younger and also white, introduced himself as an associate Baptist pastor at a church in town. We then proceeded in a circle, where the male partner at the opposite end of the room set the example by introducing himself and his wife. The two women were last, and the first didn't miss a beat as she said, "Hi, I'm Chris, and this is my life partner, Tammy." There was a moment of silence in the room, and then David mumbled a comment about the diversity of participants.

The presence of Tammy and Chris, along with an additional lesbian couple in the following workshop, troubled the generally seamless teachings on gender and sexuality that dominated the marriage classes. Workshops focused on conservative gender norms in relation to what it means to be a husband or a wife. Referencing the ideal nuclear family, they spoke to a conceptualization of gender that fits the theoretical perspective of the sociologist Talcott Parsons on male and female "roles" and their divergent social functions—the male role being "instrumental" and the female "expressive." Conceptualizing these as complementary, Parsons argued for the necessity of "a clear separation of the sex roles such as to ensure that they do not come in competition with each other" to safeguard "family solidarity."

I examine marriage workshops, attended by predominantly white, middle-class, heterosexual couples, that promote conservative gender norms and often emphasize the Christian principle of the one man and one woman marriage. Workshops focus on the problem of gender relations within an implicit and pervasive heterosexual imperative that is built on the absence of nonheterosexuals and the prohibition of their desire. This lack "haunts" marriage workshops as the unexamined backdrop for teaching about the "opposite sexes," and it organizes an epistemology whose internal logic depends on homosexuality's censure. Workshops teach principles about marriage that rely on commonsense ideas of gender and heterosexuality, ideas that speak to a mythical gendered American family whose predictability is captured by the 1950s sitcom ethos when Dad, after a long day at work, hangs up his coat and proclaims "Honey, I'm home!" In contrast to this predictability, the presence of same-sex couples in the marriage workshops troubled easy assumptions, creating tension and a paradox. No longer an invisible backdrop, heterosexuality was made less stable. The reaction involved boundary work to reaffirm the heterosexual imperative.

Teaching Gender Hierarchy

As the marriage initiative evolved, the primary emphasis focused on facilitating marriage workshops by using the PREP curriculum and its Christian version throughout Oklahoma. . . . The goal has been to train volunteers and state employees to offer marriage workshops in the PREP curriculum. . . . The training is free on the condition that volunteers commit to teach four workshops, free of charge. By April 2004, the initiative reported training 1,072 workshop leaders and offering the workshops to 18,721 individuals.

Leaders selected PREP as the curriculum for these workshops, because of "its strong grounding in research." PREP helps partners "say what they need to say, get to the heart of problems, avoid standoffs and connect with each other instead of pushing each other away." It emphasizes lowering risk factors such as poor communication and negative interaction and raising protective factors such as increasing a couple's awareness of commitment. While PREP's design is based on the tenets of marital therapy, the marriage initiative emphasizes that workshops are not marital counseling or therapy but "marriage education." Taking a PREP workshop involves "coaching very much like learning to play tennis or golf." PREP teaches basic communication skills. Each person attending the workshop receives a "PREP Couples' Manual," a workbook that has writing assignments, blank space in which to take notes, and homework assignments.

[. . .]

The Christian version of PREP combines moral principles with the secular version's thera- peutic language. In CPREP, each new communication or relational skill is followed by a Bible verse, and there is an emphasis throughout on God's design for marriage. The central theme is "Oneness" in marriage, which derives from a key biblical passage (Genesis 2:24) that conserva- tive Christians regularly cite as theological proof of marriage's original union of one man and one woman: "For this reason a man will leave his father and mother and be united to his wife, and they will become one flesh." Oneness involves mystery that is hard to define. It is about "blood kinship as well as spiritual, emotional, psychological, and sexual union between hus- band and wife." The curriculum explains that the "first marriage" represented an absolute, harmonious union of man and woman. In the beginning, Adam and Eve were "naked and unashamed" and there were no barriers to intimacy. The first thing they did after their sin was cover up: "They hid from each other and they hid from God. What had been great intimacy between man and woman, and with God, was shattered." A section titled the "Theology of Marriage" suggests that because God designed marriage to be a perfect union of a man and a woman, marital problems can be traced to original sin. The CPREP curriculum points to an opportunity to achieve a pre-Fall innocence in marital, heterosexual relationships similar to the one possible with God—full of mystery and revelation.

While the Christian curriculum explicitly lays out the tenets of "opposite sex" marriage, it relates to a broader epistemology that equates natural (biological) gendered patterns of hetero- sexual behavior with what it means to be a husband or wife. The pop psychologist John Gray, the keynote speaker for the Saturday luncheon I attended at the Smart Marriages conference in 2004, offered a secular version of this epistemology. . . . Gray utilized the lens of biological essentialism—the idea that men and women are intrinsically different due to an internal, bio- logical essence that differentiates them—to analyze what he sees as a decisive divergence of male and female desires, emotions, and behaviors. He explained these differences in terms of hormones: in contrast to male behavior that is driven by a need to preserve high levels of tes- tosterone, female behavior seeks to raise oxytocin levels. Thus, men feel a need to be right and to be the hero, whereas women need to feel cared for and connected.

For Gray, these differences translate into a gendered hierarchy in marriage. He expressed,

We [men] just want [to be] our little master-of-my-own-kingdom. OK, I'm following everybody's orders at work, they want me to talk a certain amount, I'll do that. I have to wait in line at the airport. I have to follow other people's orders. The king is here, the king is here, the king is here! Give me one place where I'm king, just give me one moment, and that's what a man needs sometimes.

Day, she jumped on the computer to sign them up. When she realized that the dates conflicted with her youngest daughter's bridal shower, she contacted a representative of the marriage initiative who told her about the six-week workshop. She enrolled herself and "a friend." She told me, "I wrote down friend, because I just didn't know if they would screen. I didn't know if I would get a note saying the class is full and whether there would be fallout or repercussions. I just put that down, and we showed up." Chris was a bit apprehensive, but she decided to give it a try since Tammy had been "banging a communication class on my head for ten years." She told Tammy,

> They won't let you in, and if you get in, as soon as they see us, they will probably ask us to leave. . . . Is there anywhere on there that says gays and lesbians welcome? [Tammy] said 'No, but they won't have the guts to throw us out! I will stand up and make such a scene.' I said, 'You? Ha!' But then I just agreed to go. I figured we had a fifty-fifty chance of being allowed to stay.

They were pleasantly surprised that they were accepted in the class.

Similar to presenters at other marriage workshops, David and Randy . . . taught about gender hierarchy as a central feature of marriage. They incorporated sports analogies, for example, to get the men's attention. David introduced the first lesson by skimming over the statistics on divorce and the static and dynamic factors that put a marriage in danger, such as having parents who are divorced. He talked about the tendency for one person to withdraw in an argument, and said, "This is just what men do, withdraw." Randy asked why people withdraw and provided the analogy of playing baseball. When you get hit a few times, you tend to give up. He said this is the same with arguing: sometimes it just feels easier to give up or withdraw. Instead of giving up, what you need to do is practice. David piped in, "Can you do the same analogy with knitting?" and Randy came back with, "I can't, but I'm sure there are those in the audience who can!" Randy described how women have a whole life experience of communication that men don't have. This is why men are more likely to withdraw and avoid. When Randy introduced the listener-speaker technique, he told us that there is one person, usually the female, who wants to talk.

[. . .]

Another lesson looked at filters or the things that get in the way of listening, one being inattention. Randy addressed the male partner of a younger couple, "When you are watching a game on television, what happens if your partner says something to you?" His wife responded for him, "He loses his mind." Randy conjectured that perhaps this happens with women and some television programs. A woman in the audience suggested soap operas, and Randy offered reality shows. He then told the women in the audience, "If you need to say something to your husband, you may need to take his head in your hands to get his attention." One of the men in the audience complained, "Can't it wait until third down?" Randy replied, "That's okay, but whose responsibility is it to ask for that?" Chris spoke up: "The person whose attention is occupied," disrupting the gendered assumption that inattention was a problem specifically relating to men. As it turned out, this had been an issue for Chris and Tammy.

The next lesson examined expectations in marriage. Randy explained that expectations are a problem when they are unconscious, unreasonable, or unspoken. Randy asked for some examples. A woman in the audience said she had an unreasonable expectation about cleanliness because she was a neat freak. One of the men told us that it is unreasonable to think your wife should be a mom. His wife retorted, "You must be really disappointed!" Another woman related that she expects her boyfriend to know when she is upset. Randy remarked, "Gals, if you can train us for twenty years, then maybe we will know. But, otherwise, you have to put it down on the table."

The smooth flow of these gendered illustrations was often disrupted when Tammy or Chris spoke up. Both were very vocal, and their questions and comments often acted as a monkey wrench in the assumptions being made about gender hierarchy and heterosexuality. In one session, David presented a lesson on making "I feel" statements. He described how his wife would yell at him from the other room and get angry when he didn't respond. He had his hearing checked and the physician told him he had some hearing loss but didn't need a hearing aid. He related how the physician told him, "Go to your wife, and tell her that when she has something important she wants to tell you, she should approach you and tell it to your face." At this point, Tammy made a snort and rolled her eyes, suggesting that this has happened with Chris. David continued talking about how it is important to work out these kinds of communication problems. When he finished, Chris said that in her defense, given all the "histrionics" going on next to her (Tammy's snort), "What if one person goes to tell the other something, and it is clear that person is busy and shoos you away." He replied, "Tell her you have something important to say, and it is up to her to listen." Tammy's and Chris's communication problems made the assumption of gendered communication appear incongruous.

The last class covered sensuality and sexuality. David was the presenter and he told the audience how Randy and one of the coaches, Susan, had exchanged emails several times with him about who should give this presentation. David became the default person. He asked, "Why is it we are so uncomfortable talking about sex?" Whereas the presence of the same-sex couple had been more muted by the focus on the emotive aspects of relationships, the topic of sexuality brought the issue of gender and heterosexuality to the forefront. David asked people to share about the way their families of origin dealt with sexuality. I was sitting at the end table with an older couple and Tammy and Chris. David asked the couple at the table opposite from us to begin. One woman said she grew up on a farm, so sexuality was just a fact of life. Another said her mother had given her the book *Our Bodies, Ourselves,* which had been very helpful. David continued around the room but ended with the last person at the table next to mine. Conveniently skipping the table where Tammy and Chris were seated, he related his own experience of how he had found a condom and neither of his parents would discuss it with him.

If the goal was to keep Tammy and Chris from discussing their sexuality, it did not work. When David asked about sensuality and touch, Tammy spoke up, "We assume that what we like the other person likes." Her words drew attention to the fact that her partner is a woman and not a man. While it is probably true that heterosexuals and nonheterosexuals alike make this kind of assumption, her statement stood in bold relief to the dominant message of managing difference in marital (heterosexual) relationships. During this last session on sexuality, Tammy put her arm around Chris. However, even as their presence and comments disrupted the heteronormativity of the marriage workshop, the workshop leaders and participants worked to reintroduce its dominance. Susan, who had declined leading the sexuality session, spoke up after David talked about getting out of ruts and keeping things fresh sexually. She shared what she thought to be a helpful example from Christian PREP—the story of Adam and Eve and their fig leaves. Taking off the leaves was a way to learn to trust each other, and having trust enabled the exploration of sexuality. A little later, David told us that men are from Mars and women are from Venus. Venusians tend to hold a grudge. He talked about how this may be a function of upbringing. Randy remarked that his wife sometimes needed him to understand just how deep the hurt is. He asked, "Is it a man/woman thing?" David responded that, in the case of his wife, he knows sometimes to steer clear because of her hormones. Tammy challenged him, "It is not just about biology or that a woman is on the rag!" Dead silence followed.

On the one hand, the boundary work that focuses on gender within the confines of marital heterosexuality meant an effort to render the same-sex couple's relationship invisible. As the workshop leaders presented the curriculum, no acknowledgment was made of any other relationship outside the heterosexual marriage model. On the other hand, even as the workshop leaders concentrated on the imperatives of gender hierarchy and heterosexuality, these discourses became awkward in the presence of Tammy and Chris. The performance of gendered patterns of marital behavior intrinsic to institutionalized heterosexuality, a generally seamless aspect of the marriage workshops, was rendered more palpable and transparent. This paradox marks the ideological contradictions of what the sociologist Chrys Ingraham refers to as "thinking straight," which requires simultaneous affirmation and negation of same-sex sexuality, at once imbuing meaning to heterosexual identity while at the same time denying the threat of same-sex sexuality to the naturalness and universality of heterosexual desire.

[. . .]

Chris and Tammy were also aware of the focus on conservative gender norms. They were especially annoyed by some of the comments made by David. In fact, Chris said that eventually they'd like to take the class again, but they would be sure that David was not the instructor: "I had a real problem with David. He made three or four comments, statements, remarks during those six weeks, and during that last day, the last one he made—that she's on the rag—I almost leaped out of my chair. So inappropriate!"

On the other hand, Chris expressed that she wanted to listen to everything Randy had to say because he was so open and honest. When I asked Tammy about whether she felt comfortable in the class, she responded:

> You know, it's one of those things that it's interesting to be in a minority group because you learn what you need to swallow. You just learn where to make waves and where to keep quiet. By the second or third week of class, I knew these people wouldn't have said anything to hurt anybody. The fact that they were using the term "marriage," well, that's basically who it was set up for. I did every time on the form, when we had the evaluation, the screening questions asked are you married, and every time, I said, well, what do you mean? Do you mean spiritually, emotionally, yes. Legally, no, of course not. We are not allowed. Maybe the form should be changed. Maybe the law should be changed.

Tammy felt that the heteronormativity displayed in the class didn't necessarily come from animus but more from insensitivity: "You see that when you are in a minority kind of relationship, you see the way the majority thinks differently than you do. It doesn't occur to them that it would be in some way exclusionary if not discrimination. I think it's just insensitive." Their participation made that insensitivity somewhat more visible, even as the workshop leaders and participants conducted themselves as if a lesbian couple were not present.

[. . .]

This chapter has considered the boundary work that took place in workshops over gender hierarchy and heteronormative understandings of marriage. Taken as a whole, the marriage workshops located same-sex couples as outsiders to what constitutes a romantic relationship and dominant conceptions of family. The presence of a lesbian couple palpably uncovered the work necessary to draw a moral boundary of heterosexual marriage based on an understanding of nonheterosexuals as outsiders. Responding to the heightened anxiety about sweeping gender changes of the last fifty years, marriage advocates do work to reaffirm the boundary between the public "male" sphere and the private (domestic) "female" sphere. While these actors often disavow a desire to move back the clock on gender equality, the marriage workshops reference a time past when gender "roles" were clearly defined and were viewed as offering stability to family and nation. Teaching about gender hierarchy in marital heterosexuality acts as a citation to normative conceptions of the white, middle-class, heterosexual family. Generally, marriage workshops rehearse more than ideals of conservative gender norms and marital heterosexuality but speak to an endeavor to define a boundary based on a definition of citizenship steeped in an ideology of family values and the (male) entrepreneurial, Horatio Alger spirit that influences American identity. . . .

Grit, Guts, and Vanilla Beans

*Godly Masculinity in
the Ex-Gay Movement*

Lynne Gerber

G ender theory often conflates conservative religious masculinity with hegemonic
masculinity (Flores and Hondagneu-Sotelo 2013; Robinson and Spivey 2007).
Because conservative religious groups often support gender hierarchy with men
dominant, the forms of masculinity they advocate are confused with the masculinity that
actually dominates a social space and legitimizes the existing hierarchy. Conservative religious masculinities are read as hegemonic and conservatives themselves as hegemonic
masculinity's supporters and defenders.

In this article, I argue that such a conflation is often inaccurate and can obfuscate the
specificity of conservative masculinities and the challenges they can pose to hegemonic masculinity. I use the ex-gay movement as one example of conservative religious masculinity that
problematizes this fusion. Ex-gay ministries are conservative in their gender ideology and
largely endorse gender hierarchy. They seek to secure male privilege for their male members by
legitimizing their masculinity in the evangelical world and in the world at large. Yet they find
many reigning cultural ideals of masculinity problematic. Rather than using hegemonic masculinity as the standard by which their members' masculinity is measured, they criticize it for
falling short of divine intention. Instead, ex-gay leaders and members aspire to godly masculinity, an idealized maleness drawn from evangelical discourse that appropriates some aspects of
hegemonic masculinity while criticizing others. While most believe that godly masculinity
should be hegemonic, they recognize that it is not.

In this article, I show that the discursive structures of godly masculinity as formulated in
the ex-gay movement can challenge the strictures of hegemonic masculinity from a conservative direction, relieving (ex-)gay men from the pressures of heterosexual performance,
expanding the repertoire of legitimate gender expressions, and allowing for a considerable

Lynne Gerber. 2015. "Grit, Guts, and Vanilla Beans: Godly Masculinity in the Ex-Gay Movement."
Gender & Society 29(1):26–50.

degree of male–male intimacy. I argue that this godly masculinity is a queerish masculinity, one that allows a considerable degree of gender experimentation while still maintaining a conservative gender ideology (Gerber, forthcoming; Gerber 2008).

Hegemonic Masculinity and Godly Masculinity

Hegemonic masculinity, as developed by Connell (2005, 77), is the form of masculinity that dominates a given social space and provides the ideological and cultural ground for legitimizing male power and privilege. It exists within a field of multiple masculinities and dominates them all, along with all femininities and all women, by soliciting their complicity, subordinating them, or marginalizing them altogether. It is a structural position as well as a specific form of masculinity. It is generally presumed to be white, heterosexual, and upper class, but its content varies based on cultural context and geographic level of analysis (Connell and Messerschmidt 2005).

Although hegemonic masculinity has proven to be a generative concept, questions regarding its content and significance abound. One tension is between the characteristics of men who actually hold hegemonic power, but who may or may not personally behave in hegemonic ways, versus men who are symbols or exemplars of hegemonic masculinity, but may not themselves be holders of hegemonic power (Connell 2005, 77–78; Elias and Beasley 2009). A related tension is between the models of idealized masculinity struggling for hegemonic power and those that actually have it.

[...]

I demonstrate how one type of conservative, evangelical masculinity can challenge traits that are frequently evoked as emblematic of hegemonic masculinity by gender scholars.

Evangelical Christianity, a largely conservative form of Protestantism founded in Western Europe, developed in the United States, and global in presence, has a complicated relationship to both masculinity and hegemonic masculinity. . . .

In the later half of the twentieth century, evangelicalism was fused in the popular mind with traditional gender hierarchy and political opposition to feminism and gay rights. But recent research has suggested that evangelical thought and practice regarding gender and masculinity is more complex. Gallagher (2003) characterizes contemporary evangelical approaches to gender in marriage as a blend of "symbolic traditionalism and pragmatic egalitarianism." . . . Whereas some aspects of hegemonic masculinity are abundantly evident in contemporary evangelical masculinity projects, for example, an emphasis on sports, others are challenged, for example, the pursuit of wealth and status at the expense of family.

"Godly masculinity" has been used by some scholars to designate masculinity in contemporary evangelicalism (Bartkowski 2004; Gallagher and Wood 2005). I use the term here to denote idealized forms of masculinity that evangelicals use to articulate subculturally specific gender ideals, criticize hegemonic forms of masculinity, and vie for their own hegemonic positioning in the culture at large. Like hegemonic masculinity, godly masculinity is rooted in a binary and hierarchical gender system and advocated by people who support the dominance of masculinity. But it operates by a different set of cultural rules and expectations, generating traits that can differ from those of hegemonic masculinity. It can also generate unintended outcomes that resemble the gender queerness evangelicals ostensibly reject.

The ex-gay movement is one example of an evangelical cultural project grappling with gender and arguing for godly masculinity. Made up of community-based ministries, regional and national organizations, therapists, pastoral counselors, congregations, and evangelical academics, it aims at changing sexual orientation through a mixture of therapeutic and devotional techniques.

[...]

Ex-gay ministries do appeal to a normative, idealized model of masculinity to which their charges aspire. But that ideal, grounded in evangelical models of godly masculinity and the lived experience of homosexually oriented members, looks quite different from hegemonic masculine ideals in contemporary American culture. In this article, I identify and analyze three aspects of godly masculinity that differ from hegemonic masculinity: de-emphasizing heterosexual conquest, inclusivity, and homo-intimacy. In analyzing these features of godly masculinity, I demonstrate that they allow expressions of masculinity and relationships between men that run counter to expectations regarding hegemonic masculinity, the ex-gay project, and opposition to homosexuality.

Methods

My data include participant observation, interviews, and content analysis of ex-gay materials. This research was conducted as part of a larger project that used ex-gay ministries as a comparative case (Gerber 2011). I attended eight public events sponsored by Exodus International, their member ministries, or allied organizations, including two regional Love Won Out conferences, an Exodus International national conference, and local conferences sponsored by Exodus-affiliated ministries. I focused on Exodus because it was the largest ex-gay network, was recognized and respected among evangelicals, and actively sought mainstream recognition. At the time of this research, Exodus was a successful organization with little outward indication of its coming demise.

I also conducted 35 in-depth, semi-structured interviews with then-current members of ex-gay ministries (28) and former (ex-)gays (7). . . . Because interview requests were mediated through ministry leaders, many subjects were highly committed ministry participants. . . . These "true believers" were well-schooled in ex-gay rhetoric and deploying it for persuasive purposes. Respondents ranged in age from early 20s to mid-70s—22 men and 13 women. Two current ministry members and two former members were African American, one current member was Asian American, and the rest of the interview sample was white. Interviews ranged from one to five hours; two were with prominent national leaders. Questions focused on personal experience with faith, sexuality, and the ministries and included questions about their understandings of morality and the change they were pursuing in the ministry. Primary material reviewed included 24 books on homosexuality by Christian authors and endorsed by Exodus, five DVDs promoted by Exodus, three years of Exodus's newsletters, newsletters from Exodus-affiliated ministries gathered at events or online, and websites of ex-gay organizations.

[. . .]

Godly Masculinity in the Ex-Gay Movement

In the ex-gay context, ideals of godly masculinity are developed in conversation with reparative therapy, the major discursive framework ministries use to understand homosexuality.

[. . .]

This theory claims that homosexuality is a disorder resulting from stunted gender development. In this view, men become gay when a disruption in the relationship with the father, either through the father's absence or neglect or the mother's overinvolvement, leads to so-called defensive detachment, alienation from men marked by active dissociation (Moberly 1983; Nicolosi 2004). This relational block causes proto-homosexual men to wrongly identify with women, depriving them of male community within which "proper" masculine identification develops. . . .

This etiology frames homosexuality as a clinical issue, laying the groundwork for a measure of compassion and possible cure. The remedy lies in intensive social exposure to men and masculinity so that identification develops. Sexual desire, the theory goes, is aimed at that which seems different from the self; thus, when a homosexually inclined man stops identifying with women and finds a home among men, desire should "naturally" turn toward his gender other. "The goal is not change as such," Moberly claims, "but fulfillment . . . that would in turn imply change" (1983, 31). This is effected through practices that appear like overt mimesis of hegemonic masculinity: sports activities, information sessions with ever-straights, and other male-male bonding opportunities. But it also works through a critique of hegemonic masculinity and the articulation of new norms.

Like hegemonic masculinity, the content of godly masculinity is vague and somewhat malleable. But its vagueness does not detract from its discursive usefulness in critiquing reigning ideals. Godly masculinity is appealed to as a higher standard from which to evaluate the masculinity that is hegemonic in American culture. . . . In a workshop on masculinity, Andrew Comiskey critiques aspects of hegemonic masculinity, contrasting them to God's vision for men. He advises,

> It doesn't work. Whether it's climbing the corporate ladder, or whether it's prowling for prostitutes, same difference. We just say God, it doesn't work, it doesn't make me more manly, doesn't make anyone love me more. If anything it just brings destruction in its own way. I'm sick of it. So Lord I'm ready for your way. (n.d.)

In this account, sexual prowess and economic achievement, arguably two cornerstones of hegemonic masculinity, are explicitly rejected in favor of a more godly way. Godly masculinity allows ex-gay leaders to critique dominant forms of masculinity in American culture without becoming theologically suspect.

[. . .]

De-Emphasizing Heterosexual Conquest

One distinction between secular and evangelical culture is in attitudes toward extramarital sexual activity. Evangelicals, like many conservative religious people, are deeply suspect of such activity and highly value sexual restraint. The ideal of limiting sexual activity to marriage puts evangelical masculinity at odds with hegemonic formulations prioritizing heterosexual conquest, a tension seen in many evangelical masculinity projects. In an essay on the Promise Keepers, for example, Stoltenberg (1999) notes that participants were urged to confess their sexual mistreatment of women and to recognize the instability of sexual conquest as a foundation for masculinity. E. Glenn Wagner, a Promise Keepers leader, told Stoltenberg:

> What we're trying to tell them is that masculinity, manhood, is not defined by how many people you've slept with, either male or female. And men are finally saying "Oh thank God!" Sexual prowess should have nothing to do with one's personhood or self-esteem, and yet our culture has made it that way. (1999, 97)

This rejection of heterosexual display as a standard for legitimized masculinity reflects the historic suspicion with which Christianity has treated sexuality (Krondorfer 1996). . . . Perhaps the clearest boundary drawn in the ex-gay movement in relation to homosexuality is the prohibition on homosexual sex—genital activity between men is unequivocally regarded as sin.

This rejection of homosexual sex is unsurprising. What is less expected is how de-emphasizing heterosexual conquest as a sign of masculinity reconfigures the terms of the ex-gay project, making its goals more attainable while simultaneously funding a critique of hegemonic masculinity. One of the most tangible effects of this de-emphasis is a reduction in pressure for (ex-)gay men to demonstrate healing through sex with women. Ex-gay ministries often cite the evangelical prohibition on sexual activity outside marriage to discourage (ex-)gay men from proving heterosexuality this way. It also relieves them from doing so. Participants are warned against rushing into heterosexual relationships as symbols of success (Davies and Rentzel 1993, 145; Nicolosi 2004, 202–3), and even marriage is treated with reservation (Dallas 2003, 178). Ex-gay manuals issue cautions on dating and sexuality and try to ease the pressure to perform heterosexually, including on the wedding night (Davies and Rentzel 1993, 156).

[. . .]

(Ex-)gay sexuality is also redeemed by (ex-)gay heterosexuality's likeness to godly sexual norms. As heterosexual partners, (ex-)gay lovers can seem closer to godly ideals because their marital relationships are not contaminated by lust. These marriages are said to be based on personal knowledge, not sheer desire, giving them a more solid foundation. Sexual desires emerge from friendship rather than immediate visual attraction (Davies and Rentzel 1993, 162). For example, Comiskey writes of his marital relationship:

> In spite of glimmers of physical attraction, the catalyst for our relationship in its early stages was not erotic. That surprised me, as my homosexual experiences were fuelled by "high octane" lust that burned out to reveal an emotional immaturity incapable of sustaining a long-term relationship. Annette and I took the reverse path. My erotic feelings for her arose out of a trust and an established emotional and spiritual complementarity. . . . Physical attraction was birthed out of our relationship; it wasn't its overblown starting point, charged with illusion and seductive posturing. (1989, 30–31)

His marriage endures, in this account, precisely because it is not marked by the heterosexual desire that hegemonic masculinity requires. Highly charged heterosexual desire becomes a source of "illusion and seductive posturing" rather than a sign of healing. (Ex-)gay marital relationships can thus realize divine norms regarding lust and friendship in ways that ever-straight ones are rarely able.

(Ex-)gay heterosexual marriages are also considered immune to the threat of other women. Heterosexual desire in an (ex-)gay context is seen as specific to the individuals involved; even the most healed (ex-)gay men tend to fall in love with only one woman. Again, this reality can be interpreted as a sign of healing rather than evidence of its lack. For example, Craig, a West Coast ex-gay leader, told me, "I desire my wife sexually and I'm very glad that I don't have a problem with lust for other women or men. That my focus of my sexual expression can be on her. And her for me. I think that's a much healthier expression." The range of sexual sins that plague heterosexual men is also something that (ex-)gay heterosexual marriages are said to be relieved of:

> A high percentage of heterosexual men in good, loving Christian marriages struggle with attractions to disconnected, impersonal sex: to pornography or maybe to the body of a neighbor woman whom he doesn't even know. This almost never happens to male overcomers with respect to women. This is the reason why I believe that we are actually in a better place than most men. We are closer to God's original intent for our sexuality. (Medinger 2000, 204–5)

In this account, (ex-)gay men become even godlier than ever-straight men because they are not vulnerable to the heterosexual temptations that rend even upstanding Christian marriages. By bracketing the very issue that brings them to ex-gay ministries—homosexual desire—ex-gay discourse redeems (ex-)gay sexuality by depicting its heterosexual expression as exemplary of godly ideals for human relationships.

[...]

Inclusive Masculinity

The ex-gay approach to gender flows directly from its approach to sexuality. The insistence on heterosexuality generates an ideological commitment to a binary system of distinct, opposing, and hierarchically ranked genders. Prohibiting homosexuality enables ex-gay ministries to maintain these key aspects of evangelicalism's conservative gender ideology. In combination with their therapeutic understanding of homosexuality's cause and cure, it also allows a degree of flexibility in terms of gendered tastes, practices, and self-presentation. While other evangelical masculinity projects also allow a certain inclusivity, they are more focused on race and multiculturalism (Bartkowski 2004); in this case, the focus is on inclusivity regarding gender expression.

[...]

(Ex-)gay men are also masculinized in ex-gay discourse. For example, at an Exodus workshop "Breaking the Myth of Masculinity," the (ex-)gay and ever-straight coleaders assured participants that they had a legitimate place in the masculine world. "If you read our description on the website," they told the audience,

> we put a question in there and said do I have what it takes to be masculine? . . . We said if you come to our class that we would answer that question. And the answer to that question is absolutely yes. Because you know what? You were all born male. You were all born men. And everything that you need to be fully masculine is within you. (Goeke and Mayo 2008)

If masculinity is endowed entirely by biology, then men are automatically masculine by virtue of being born male; every person born male has a claim on its attributes and privileges. And because the category of masculinity must include all males, it needs to be inclusive enough for all men to find their place.

As a result, traits, preferences, and dispositions, or what Bridges (2014) terms "sexual aesthetics," can be integrated into godly masculinity that were once the very definition of non-masculinity. Ex-gay ministries work to resignify them as legitimately masculine rather than suspiciously feminine. This labor was evident in the "Breaking the Myth of Masculinity" workshop. There, the leaders talked about their various likes and dislikes. Mike Goeke, the (ex-)gay man, told the audience:

> I love clothes, shopping, I really do, I'm proud of it. . . . I like decorating, I do. Stephanie [his wife] and I love doing that stuff together and I have every bit of a strong opinion on it. I love architecture and art, things that are beautiful. . . . I love to write. . . . I love long dinners, talking about life. I love great conversation, any time where you can sit and talk about stuff, life, relationships.

Jay Mayo, the ever-straight, responded,

> I love UFC [Ultimate Fighting Championship]. It's human cockfighting on . . . Jeeps. I also love love stories. I love chick flicks. I cry at every one. . . . I love to write. I love genuine conversation. I hate BSing. I hate walking into the context of guys and talking about nothing important. It's crap, but I did it most of my life. I love to hug, I love affection. I love candles. And my favorite flavor is vanilla bean. (Goeke and Mayo 2008)

This exchange served, in part, to put the stamp of legitimate masculinity on practices that are frequently used to delegitimize claims to masculinity and especially hegemonic masculinity. Hegemonic masculinity's power is based on the domination of women and has frequently involved the stigmatization of feminized traits in males, especially those who are homosexually oriented (Hennen 2008). But within an inclusive godly masculinity, some feminized traits are reconfigured as valid expressions of masculinity that can even be endorsed by ever-straights with UFC-loving credentials. When successful, these traits become part of a repertoire of legitimate masculinity that even those ever-straights can put into practice without shame (Bridges 2014).

[. . .]

John Hinson (2007), leader of a "Fear of Men and Masculinity" workshop, painted the pursuit of healing as exemplary of masculine courage and endurance:

> I had a feeling about healing. [It's] not going to happen if you're passive. You need to be proactive and do whatever you need to get the kind of healing you want. You need to go do it. I've had four therapists, once when I was in Phoenix, he was in Los Angeles, went every other month and talked on the phone every week. Went to men's weekend in New York, in Florida. Did whatever to get the healing I wanted and needed. [It] takes grit, guts to do this work.

There are few other venues where seeing four different therapists and going to multiple men's weekends evidence the "grit" and "guts" of masculinity. But within godly masculinity, association with feminized activities need not threaten one's claim to male legitimacy; it may even enhance it.

Effeminacy itself can at times be legitimized within godly masculinity. While not always acceptable, being effeminate is sometimes seen as an opportunity for the expression of more essential male traits; at the very least, it is not always interpreted as gender fraud. . . .

Medinger . . . writes of his struggle with feminized characteristics and discusses another ex-gay leader to show that effeminacy need not invalidate claims to godly masculinity:

> Part of [God's] plan for me is that I would manifest more of certain feminine qualities than most men and a few less of the masculine. That's part of what makes me unique, but it doesn't make me less of a man. Sy Rogers is one of the best known leaders in the Exodus International network. . . . For a number of years Sy lived as a woman, and he had the characteristics that enabled him to pull it off quite well. Now, years after his conversion and healing, Sy still bears some feminine characteristics. They are noticeable when you first hear him speak, but after listening to him for a few minutes, you find that these characteristics fade from view. Sy's genuine manhood—something that now dwells at the core of him—starts to emanate with power and masculinity. (2000, 192)

Feminine qualities, in this account, need not discredit masculinity. They are, rather, a unique form of masculinity that should have a place in the godly gender regime. Sy Rogers himself rejects the charge that he is inadequately masculine by invoking the distinction between godly and worldly standards of masculinity:

> Some people think if I was healed I'd be more butch—what standard of butch are we talking about? Which standard of masculinity do you want me to live up to? ... Most [of this] criticism comes from an American market, but [I] belong to a bigger market and to God's market." (2005)

In this case, the defense against a hegemonic masculinity that insists on traits gendered male and the absence of those gendered female is the appeal to godly masculinity that includes even such a man as he, who passed for years as a woman.

Homo-Intimacy

A third distinction between godly masculine ideals and culturally hegemonic ones involves relations between men. Hegemonic masculinity emphasizes individualism, competition, and emotional distance. Godly masculinity, by contrast, advocates homo-intimacy. In ex-gay ministries, as in other gendered evangelical projects, the ideal relationship between men includes an emotional and relational closeness that goes beyond homosocial and flirts with homo-erotic (Sedgwick 1985).

According to reparative therapy, homosexual men become real men when they develop intimate relationships with other men, through mentoring relationships with (ex-)gay men further along in their healing or with ever-straights. These relationships are usually cultivated in church settings, men's groups, or the ministry itself. According to advocates of these relationships—and in contrast to hegemonic assumptions about masculinity—men are happy to support (ex-)gays in their search for masculinity through positive, affirming, supportive processes, not through social trials that consolidate masculine identity by repudiating the abject "fag" (Pascoe 2007).

[...]

In contrast to the hegemonic model, godly masculinity is not produced by isolated men facing obstacles alone and overcoming them through individual strength and social independence. It occurs when the nurturing capacities of the mentor are evoked by a vulnerable man. Homosexuality, in this account, is not the result of too much male-male intimacy, but of too little. "I don't assume that you have never had a healthy relationship with a man," writes Joe Dallas, "but I will assume that you haven't had *enough* intimacy with men" (2003, 160).

Once established, these male-male relationships involve a level of emotional disclosure, intimacy, and closeness that also defy standards for hegemonic male-male relations. According to reparative therapy, men desire homosexual sex as a substitute for the deeper desire for identification and closeness with men. Sex, in this account, will never fill this purpose; only nonsexual male-male relationships can.... In these relationships, men share the details of their lives, express their hopes and fears, and turn to other men for support, caring, and validation. Mark, for example, told me that his ministry participation allowed him to receive positive feedback from men for the first time. While he had received male praise before, in this group he was "able to share on a level that I had never been able to share." Because he knew these men so well, their positive feedback penetrated more deeply. "I was never really able to take in that [earlier] affirmation because they didn't know me. So once I was open and people [in the ministry] kept saying the same thing, then it began to sink in and mean something to help change me." Interpersonal knowledge, personal disclosure, and emotional receptivity are more likely to be derided as feminine than lauded as masculine under the hegemonic regime of masculinity; in the ex-gay context they become fundamental to the masculinization process itself (Medinger 2000, 111).

Physical, albeit nonsexual, intimacy also has a place in healing homosexuality. . . . Alan Chambers (2005) told an audience at the Love Won Out conference about his experience of healing during a five-hour-long hug with men in his church:

> I had a struggle with my relationship with my dad growing up, and . . . in homosexual relationships I always wanted someone who would be that young, affirming, good-looking, wonderful father. Not for the purposes of sex, but I was craving what God intended for me to have, that intimacy and that connection. And I remember one night dealing, it was a couple of years into the process, dealing with this whole issue, praying through these issues and when it was over that night, after I had been hugged for about five hours by this man who was praying for me and another man from the church, I felt like God supernaturally healed my lifelong desire for that type of inappropriate relationship.

In the context of prayer and healing, touch, bodily contact, and the physical expression of closeness with other men become legitimate means of pursuing change rather than suspect expressions of homosexual desire. While this form of homosociality may well be pursued in order to consolidate the dominance of men over women (Sedgwick 1985), it looks strikingly different from the hegemonic form of masculinity that regards physical male-male closeness with suspicion.

Thus, godly masculinity can be marked by a male-male closeness that, in other contexts, may appear to be the homosexuality it is meant to oppose. As long as it is expressed within the confines of godly community, does not include acts deemed sexual, and does not become a rival for communal identification, deep emotional and physical closeness between men need not be problematic. . . . Chad Thompson, for example, writes almost romantically about his experience with other (ex-)gay men, yet is recognized as a movement leader:

> When I first met Lenny [an (ex-)gay mentor] at an Italian restaurant in Chicago, he instantly wrapped his arms around me, looked me in the eye, and told me that he loved me. That moment was the beginning of my healing process, and since then God has put dozens of men in my life to provide the nonsexual love and affirmation that I need in order to change. (2004, 22)

In a different context, the need for love and affirmation expressed by a man would render his masculinity and sexual orientation suspect. Yet in this context it is written without irony as an important move toward the kind of godly masculinity that hegemonic masculinity impedes. Indeed, under the guise of godly masculinity, (ex-)gays are allowed a wide range of emotional intimacies with people of the same gender that may be indistinguishable from, or indeed may be the heart of, homosexual desire.

Conclusion

Ethnographer Tanya Erzen has noted the queer quality of (ex-)gay men's sexual conversions (2006, 14). I would extend that observation to the realm of gender, suggesting that the inclusivity of godly masculinity generates a queerish masculinity, one that effects the kinds of gender blurring that queerness aspires to, without subscribing to the political priorities or critiques that fund more deliberately queer gender experimentation (Gerber 2008; Gerber, forthcoming). In its effort to include those who have been excluded on grounds of gender identity or performance, it runs the risk of including elements that undermine the very meaning of the category. An emphasis on male brokenness, the expression of feeling, and the legitimacy of a wide range of masculine expression would significantly change the terms of hegemonic masculinity and may even have the unintended potential of undermining it. Indeed, it may well have been a factor in Exodus's recent disavowal of sexual reorientation as a legitimate goal of Christian ministry and its dissolution as an organization. If highly feminized traits have a legitimate masculine home, for example, what does masculinity actually mean?

[. . .]

Looking at the discursive strategies within the ex-gay movement provides important reminders to scholars researching religion, sexuality, and gender. The most important, in my view, is the caution not to conflate conservative religious masculinity projects with hegemonic ones. Advocates for the hegemonic positioning of masculinity do not necessarily support the masculinity that is, in fact, hegemonic in a given social space, and there is no reason to think that they should. Godly masculinity is a contender in a field of multiple masculinities vying for hegemonic power. The fact that its advocates believe that gender relations should be hierarchical and that masculinity should be hegemonic does not keep them from advocating for a kind of masculinity that is more reflective of, and advantageous for, their particular position. Conflating the complex gender projects of the ex-gay movement, and evangelical Christianity more generally, with hegemonic masculinity makes it difficult to see the nuanced fault lines on which this project might stand or fall. As Arlene Stein has observed, "Just as we should understand masculinities and femininities in plural rather than singular terms, so are there clearly homophobias in the plural" (Stein 2005, 604). It is critical, I contend, to be specific about the form we are seeing in the ex-gay movement and to be clear about its political possibilities as well as its perils.

References

Bartkowski, John P. 2004. *Promise Keepers: Servants, Soldiers and Godly Men.* New Brunswick, NJ: Rutgers University Press.

Bridges, Tristan. 2014. "A Very 'Gay' Straight: Hybrid Masculinities, Sexual Aesthetics, and the Changing Relationship Between Masculinity and Homophobia." *Gender & Society* 28:58–82.

Chambers, Alan. 2005. "Reaching the Homosexual I: Teaching." Workshop Given at Love Won Out, Seattle, Washington, June 25.

Comiskey, Andrew. 1989. *Pursuing Sexual Wholeness: How Jesus Heals the Homosexual.* Lake Mary, FL: Charisma House.

Comiskey, Andrew. n.d. *Masculinity.* CD. Grandview, MO: Desert Stream Ministries.

Connell, Raewyn. 2005. *Masculinities.* 2nd ed. Berkeley, CA: University of California Press.

Connell, Raewyn and James W. Messerschmidt. 2005. "Hegemonic Masculinity: Rethinking the Concept." *Gender & Society* 19:829–59.

Dallas, Joe. 2003. *Desires in Conflict: Hope for Men Who Struggle with Same Sex Identity*. Rev. ed. Eugene, OR: Harvest House.

Davies, Bob and Lori Rentzel. 1993. *Coming Out of Homosexuality: New Freedom for Men and Women*. Downers Grove, IL: InterVarsity Press.

Elias, Juanita and Christine Beasley. 2009. "Hegemonic Masculinity and Globalization: 'Transnational Business Masculinities' and Beyond." *Globalizations* 6:281–96.

Erzen, Tanya. 2006. *Straight to Jesus: Sexual and Christian Conversions in the Ex-Gay Movement*. Berkeley, CA: University of California Press.

Flores, Edward Orozco and Pierrette Hondagneu-Sotelo. 2013. "Chicano Gang Members in Recovery: The Public Talk of Negotiating Chicano Masculinities." *Social Problems* 60:476–90.

Gallagher, Sally K. 2003. *Evangelical Identity and Gendered Family Life*. New Brunswick, NJ: Rutgers University Press.

Gallagher, Sally K. and Sabrina L. Wood. 2005. "Godly Manhood Going Wild? Transformations in Conservative Protestant Masculinity." *Sociology of Religion* 66:135–60.

Gerber, Lynne. 2008. "The Opposite of Gay: Nature, Creation, and Queerish Ex-Gay Experiments." *Nova Religio* 11:8–30.

Gerber, Lynne. 2011. *Seeking the Straight and Narrow: Weight Loss and Sexual Reorientation in Evangelical America*. Chicago, IL: University of Chicago Press.

Gerber, Lynne. Forthcoming. "'Queerish' Celibacy: Reorienting Marriage in the Ex-Gay Movement." In *Queer Christianities*, edited by M. Larrimore, M. Pettinger, and K. Talvacchia. New York: New York University Press.

Goeke, Mike and Jay Mayo. 2008. "Breaking the Myth of Masculinity." Workshop presented at Exodus International Conference.

Hennen, Peter. 2008. *Faeries, Bears and Leathermen: Men in Community Queering the Masculine*. Chicago, IL: University of Chicago Press.

Hinson, John. 2007. "Fear of Men and Masculinity." Workshop presented at Exodus International Conference.

Krondorfer, Bjorn. 1996. "Introduction." In *Men's Bodies, Men's Gods: Male Identities in a (Post)-Christian Culture*, edited by B. Krondorfer. New York: New York University Press.

Medinger, Alan. 2000. *Growth into Manhood: Resuming the Journey*. New York: Shaw Press/Random House.

Moberly, Elizabeth. 1983. *Homosexuality: A New Christian Ethic*. Cambridge, UK: James Clarke Ltd.

Nicolosi, Joseph. 2004. *Reparative Therapy of the Male Homosexual: A New Clinical Approach*. Lanham, MD: Rowman & Littlefield.

Pascoe, C. J. 2007. *Dude, You're a Fag: Masculinity and Sexuality in High School*. Berkeley, CA: University of California Press.

Robinson, Christine M. and Sue E. Spivey. 2007. "The Politics of Masculinity and the Ex-Gay Movement." *Gender & Society* 21:650–75.

Rogers, Sy. 2005. *One of the Boys Remix: The Sy Rogers Story*. DVD. Fort Lauderdale, FL: Worthy Creations.

Sedgwick, Eve K. 1985. *Between Men: English Literature and Male Homosocial Desire*. New York: Columbia University Press.

Stein, Arlene. 2005. "Make Room for Daddy: Anxious Masculinity and Emergent Homophobias in Neopatriarchal Politics." *Gender & Society* 19:601–20.

Stoltenberg, John. 1999. "Christianity, Feminism and the Manhood Crisis." In *Standing on the Promises: The Promise Keepers and the Revival of Manhood*, edited by D. S. Claussen. Cleveland, OH: Pilgrim Press.

Thompson, Chad. 2004. *Loving Homosexuals as Jesus Would: A Fresh Christian Approach*. Grand Rapids, MI: Brazos Press.

Muslim Women, Moral Visions

Globalization and Gender Controversies in Indonesia

Rachel Rinaldo

[...]

Since 1998, Indonesians have been preoccupied by controversies over issues like pornography, polygamy, Islamic law, abortion, and homosexuality. These debates play out in the mass media, on the internet, in parliament, and on the streets of major cities, where they are the fodder for demonstrations and other forms of collective action. Clearly, Indonesia's democratization has produced intense political struggles. But what do such debates tell us about gender, politics, and globalization?

These debates are complex and entail competing ideas about the family, gender, the relationship between Islam and the state, and the common good. However, the focus of this article is on how these Indonesian moral debates illustrate the ways global processes manifest in local contexts. In particular, this article examines how Muslim *women* activists adapt global discourses to participate in such debates. As we shall see, these controversies not only focus on women but also involve women from across the political spectrum.

Recently, scholars have examined how global discourses of human rights, religion, and sexuality shape identities and local politics (Blackwood 2008; Wyrod 2008; Boellstorff 2005). In addition, the literature on transnational feminism has raised questions of how feminist ideas are transformed in different locales (Davis 2008). Yet there is a need for greater attention to the mechanisms by which transnational processes are manifest in national contexts, and for more detailed accounts of how the global and the national intersect. A key question is: How are national contexts relevant to the ways members of civil society or social movement organizations interpret global discourses?

Rachel Rinaldo. 2011. "Muslim Women, Moral Visions: Globalization and Gender Controversies in Indonesia." *Qualitative Sociology* 34(4):539–60.

Indonesia's moral debates demonstrate an important way in which global discourses are negotiated in national settings. In this article, I examine two global discourses: feminism and ideas tied to the Islamic revival. Indonesia is an ideal setting to study the local manifestations of these discourses. The country has the world's largest Muslim population and in recent years new political freedoms have allowed for vibrant debates in the public sphere. My focus is on how women activists appropriate global discourses as part of their calls for political reforms. Of particular interest is how their activism is shaped by their membership in national organizations, especially the distinct approaches to interpreting Islamic texts that women learn in these national organizations. In the debates, some pious women use discourses of feminism and liberal Islam to argue for women's equality, while others use Islam to call for greater moral regulation of society. My central argument is that global discourses of feminism and Islamic revivalism are mediated through national organizations which shape women's political activism and channel their activism in different directions.

This article focuses on Muslim women from two national organizations—Fatayat Nahdlatul Ulama, and the Prosperous Justice Party—and how they have intervened in debates over pornography. . . . It also examines the more general implications for understanding connections between the global and local. Social scientists who study global processes often imply that individuals simply select from an assortment of ideas that circulate globally or, conversely, that subjectivities are thoroughly molded by global discourses. My analysis suggests that women's political subjectivities are shaped through their involvement in national organizations that structure the ways they engage with global discourses. The Indonesian case shows not only that the national should not be conflated with the local, but also demonstrates the significance of the national context for understanding global processes.

[. . .]

Feminism and Islam in Indonesia

Indonesia has long been influenced by global forces, but the nature and configuration of such forces has changed over time. It is important, therefore, to contextualize the current global discourses of feminism and Islamic revival in Indonesia, to examine the multiple ways women activists are influenced by them, and to consider what they reveal about the current era of globalization. I do not see feminism and Islam as alien to Indonesia; instead, I want to explicate the different ways women activists have engaged with these issues.

Though Indonesian activists don't necessarily use the term feminist to describe themselves, they have a tradition of engagement with ideas of gender equality, as well as a history of mobilizing women. Ideas about women's rights first became prominent in Indonesia in the 1920s in Dutch women's groups. However, they soon spread to nationalist organizations, many of which had women's wings. At that time, women's political equality was often part of nationalist platforms, and Indonesia was no exception (Jayawardena 1986). In the 1920s and 1930s, Indonesian women also became active in Muslim organizations. Yet secular and Muslim women were often divided, especially when it came to issues like polygamy (Robinson 2009).

After independence, the constitution guaranteed equal rights of citizenship to men and women but few women were involved in formal politics. Many women, however, joined the Indonesian Communist Party and by 1957 its women's wing—Gerwani—had 650,000 members. While Gerwani members rarely thought of themselves as feminists, they were inspired by communist ideology, which incorporated ideas of women's equality (Wieringa 2002).

After an attempted coup in 1965 and the violent repression that followed, the Suharto government corralled women into state controlled organizations that emphasized their roles as wives and mothers. Nevertheless, the expansion of the educational system facilitated the emergence of more women who could be active in public life. Bowing to international emphasis on women's rights, the government created the Ministry for Women's Roles in 1978. In 1984, it ratified the "Convention on the Elimination of All Forms of Discrimination Against Women."

Women's independent activism was reignited in the 1980s. Indonesian women who attended the United Nations conferences on women were inspired to establish NGOs (Robinson 2009; Brenner 2005) and some received support from international donors. By the 1990s, a network of women's NGOs was active in Indonesia and the buzzwords of "gender equality" and "feminism" were becoming popular among the growing student movement.

Until the mid-1990s, the stereotypical Indonesian "woman activist" was a secular woman from an elite background (Robinson 2009; Blackburn 2004). There was backlash against feminism, with opponents accusing it of being destructive to religious values. In the last decade, however, discourses of gender equality have been taken up by some Muslim activists. Not only does feminism find fertile ground in Indonesia's national history of women's mobilization, but democracy activism in the 1990s reintroduced many Indonesian women to ideas about equality and rights. This helped to lay the groundwork for the current network of women's organizations, some of which see themselves as part of a transnational women's rights movement.

Transnational Islamic currents have always been influential in Indonesia, but in both the early 20th century and the late 1970s to the present such currents have been especially significant (Ricklefs 2009; Feener and Sevea 2009). Like feminism, these transnational discourses have intersected with national and local imaginings, including more contextual approaches to Islam, an acceptance of some separation between religion and state, and women's involvement in public life.

[. . .]

Global discourses of feminism and Islam, therefore, have long intersected with national imaginations in Indonesia. But these global discourses currently overlap with major shifts at the national level in Indonesia, including the growth of the middle class, democratization, and changes in information technology. While feminism and Islam are tied to transnational networks, they are domesticated by a wide range of Indonesians. Here, I examine how Indonesian Muslim women adapt feminism and Islam to participate in debates on pornography.... The national organizations these women are affiliated with, I argue, play a key role in how these global discourses are interpreted and put into action. In the following section, I provide a brief summary of the history of the two national organizations in this article—Fatayat Nahdlatul Ulama and the Prosperous Justice Party—and then I present the key findings of my research.

Fatayat NU and the Prosperous Justice Party

In this article, I compare women from the Jakarta headquarters of Fatayat Nahdlatul Ulama and the Prosperous Justice Party. I chose these organizations because at the national level the women involved in them are demographically similar but express different views on gender, religion, and politics.

Fatayat, established in 1950, is an organization for NU women between 25 and 45, and has an estimated 3 million members. For decades, women were marginalized within the socially conservative NU and Fatayat was essentially a women's auxiliary. However, the leadership of Fatayat was much affected by the incorporation of ideas about civil society and human rights into the NU's programs (Van Doorn-Harder 2006). For example, in the early 1990s, NU activist Mansour Fakih began doing gender sensitivity trainings for NU staff, including Fatayat. Fatayat leaders also encountered ideas of gender equality through workshops held by the Ford Foundation and the Asia Foundation, and through reading liberal Muslim thinkers. Fatayat now takes a contextual and revisionist approach to Islamic texts and its leaders see women's rights as their mission. Most of the Fatayat staff and volunteers I met were university educated and worked as teachers, and many came from families associated with NU for several generations.

The Prosperous Justice Party (PKS) was founded in 1998 and is one of Indonesia's most successful new political parties. The organization initially called for an Islamic state but after a weak showing in the 1999 elections it was reconstituted with a more moderate platform. It no longer calls for *Shariah* law but advocates for making Islam the source of policy. In the 2009 elections it received nearly 8 percent of the national vote (Indonesian Election Commission 2009).

The women I studied were involved in the Women's Division, though women also participate in other sections of the party. The PKS women I met were mostly university educated, married with children, and many also worked as teachers. However, an important distinction is that most PKS women I met came from families who were not affiliated with NU.

. . . Muslim organizations such as Fatayat and PKS muddy the boundaries between the political and other spheres of life. Another reason to compare these organizations is that their women leaders have much in common. While they emerged from somewhat different Islamic backgrounds, they are all part of the urban middle classes and share a commitment to practicing Islam in all aspects of their lives. Yet the notion of more Islamic society means very different things to these two groups of women (Rinaldo 2008, 2010).

Research Methods

This article draws on a year and a half of ethnographic research with women activists in Indonesia. It is part of a larger study of women activists in four national organizations. The initial research took place in Jakarta from August 2002 to August 2003, with return visits for three months in 2005 and two months in 2008.

My fieldwork primarily involved participant observation. My fieldwork with Fatayat consisted of volunteering in the national office and attending events such as meetings, workshops, and conferences. With PKS I was not able to spend much time in party offices and my interviewees were selected by the head of the women's division. However, I was able to attend events such as the national conference, as well as workshops and demonstrations.

Participant observation was complemented by 48 in-depth interviews, including 8 with members of Fatayat and 12 with PKS members. Follow-up interviews were conducted in 2005 and 2008 with 3 members of Fatayat and 5 members of PKS. Interviews ranged in length from 45 to 90 minutes, and all were conducted in Indonesian.

[. . .]

Women Activists and Moral Debates: Pornography . . .

The pornography bill that was passed in 2008 spurred angry demonstrations and myriad newspaper and magazine articles, as well as heated debates in parliament. Pornography became a topic of increasing concern to many Indonesians with the emergence of a free mass media after 1998. Allen (2009; 2007) notes that interest in new pornography legislation was building through the late 1990s, and Blackwood (2007) argues that momentum for a bill took off after attempts by conservative religious groups to reform national sexuality codes were bogged down in the early 2000s. Older laws providing some forms of censorship remained on the books but some Indonesians began to feel that television shows and magazines were featuring more risqué subject matter, such as previously taboo topics like sex before marriage, or women wearing miniskirts or swimsuits. In an article published in the newsweekly *Tempo,* for example, Syamsul Muarif, the Minister for Communications and Information, said that 60 percent of Indonesians were accessing porn on the internet and other media. "So, because that's what they like, the shows are also being allowed on television," he warned (Sunudyantoro 2003).

Anxiety seemed to center especially on the availability of pornographic DVDs, as well as live TV programs featuring scantily clad female entertainers (Allen 2007). Yet, what counts as pornography also seems to have shifted, much as women's clothing has changed. While Indonesians have long been relatively conservative about clothing, in the 1970s and 1980s younger women often dressed casually in t-shirts or knee-length skirts. Such styles are now rejected by many pious women as too revealing.

The furor that erupted over the singer Inul Daratista in 2002 and 2003 was an indication of this backlash from some Muslims, and also demonstrated the extent to which the presentation of women's bodies was becoming an issue. As Inul became one of the country's most popular entertainers, a moral panic erupted about her signature *goyang ngebor* ("drill dance") and clingy outfits. There was a small television in the Fatayat offices, to which staff occasionally paid attention. It was usually tuned to celebrity magazine shows, and Inul stories were a staple. I can recall one show that claimed Inul's style was influential and showed footage of women in Jakarta malls wearing extremely tight jeans. The women at Fatayat laughed and made jokes about the *goyang.* They took it more seriously when the rival male singer Rhoma Irama, an ostentiously pious Muslim, denounced her. Indonesia's Council of Ulemas (MUI), a quasi-governmental body that rules on matters of Islamic law, also declared her dancing *haram* (forbidden). The issue quieted down after a meeting between Inul and Rhoma, after which she refrained from performing. A few months later, her comeback television performance revealed a new image with a more modest dance routine.

Rhoma's intervention resulted in women activists rising to Inul's defense. As part of a pro-Inul demonstration in May 2003, activists performed *goyang ngebor* in a Jakarta roundabout. Women in Fatayat were somewhat divided; while most were uncomfortable with censorship some lamented the sexualization of entertainment. Others, however, said they enjoyed Inul. One Fatayat member told me: "I say, let her be. Because up till now there is no definition of eroticism or pornography." I asked if she thought that Indonesia's traditional dances were also erotic: "Yes, shaking the hips. Inul, I see as energetic. And she does not aim to arouse people. She is just following the music. It's appropriate, I think. My child can watch this."

In contrast, PKS women considered Inul disgraceful. One PKS cadre explained:

I have seen an Inul video. Inul in the *kampung* [village/low-income neighborhood] is even worse than on the TV. Because there is altogether no censor. This is because of a low level of education, so that their entertainment is more in the direction of self-gratification, not intellectual fulfillment. If their education was good, they would not be too concerned with stuff like this, because they would choose more intellectual fulfillment. If my understanding is good, I think all religions do not permit things that exploit sexuality this way. I think it doesn't lift women's dignity but instead destroys it. So it's very unfortunate because women are being admired only for the curves of their bodies, not for the acuteness of their brains, this is really unfortunate. Very sad.

PKS women felt that Inul was a sign of an increasingly sexualized culture, one in which children were watching pornography at internet cafes and buying counterfeit "blue" movies on the street. It should not be a surprise that the momentum for new legislation on pornography came from within the ranks of PKS.

[. . .]

In February 2006, legislators including PKS members introduced into parliament draft legislation of the bill written in collaboration with MUI and other religious authorities. As originally written, the bill was quite broad and could have outlawed kissing in public and bikinis on beaches. Public outcry forced its return to parliament for revision and it remained stalled there for over a year. At the height of the controversy, Yoyoh Yusroh, a PKS legislator and deputy chairwoman of the special committee deliberating the bill, explained her support for the legislation in an interview with the *Jakarta Post*:

> Our society badly needs the pornography bill. Pornographic acts (on television) and publications, which have so far gone unchecked, have damaged our children's morality, and it has to be stopped. The unchecked availability of pornography has also ruined many marriages. We also disagree that the bill would imperil the right of women to dress as they choose. Having deliberated the bill, we would protect women from becoming victims of globalization. We would protect them from becoming victims of multinational firms that make women "markets" for their (fashion) products. (Suryana 2006)

Finally, in November 2008, a somewhat liberalized version was passed which made exceptions for "sexual materials" as part of traditional culture and fine arts. Legislators who supported the bill also insisted that bikinis at the beach would not fall under its rubric.

As their statements reveal, throughout the debate the arguments PKS women made were infused with Islamic discourses of morality. They called for the protection of women and children and for modesty in the presentation of women's bodies. Most important, they argued that the bill was necessary for creating a moral nation. While their statements also seemed to draw on general concerns about the family and globalization, PKS women made a strong connection between morality and nationalism. Interestingly, men were rarely mentioned in this discourse. This is indicative of how discourses on family and morality are often tied to ideologies of gender that position women as primarily responsible for children, and as requiring moral protection or guidance (Yuval-Davis 1997). But it also should be understood with reference to the party's origins. Inspired by the Muslim Brotherhood's approach to Islam, Indonesian *dakwah* activists emphasized that all aspects of life, including politics, should be infused with Islamic ideals. PKS women's arguments reflected this philosophy, as well as a rather literalist reading of Quranic injunctions to modesty.

Women activists in Indonesia's public sphere found themselves on different sides of the pornography debate (Robinson 2009; Allen 2009; 2007). Women's rights activists, as well as artists and entertainers, opposed it, in contrast to many women in Muslim political parties like PKS who supported it. Although pornography was a divisive issue for the American and Australian feminist movements in the 1980s, this was not the case for women's rights proponents in Indonesia. Both religious and secular women's rights activists in Indonesia opposed the bill because of concerns about censorship and effects on gender equality. While few Indonesian women have advanced the kind of "pro-porn" or "sex positive" positions that emerged in the United States and Australian feminist movements, support for freedom of expression within women's rights organizations led even those who have expressed concern about pornography in the past to oppose the bill.

PKS's interest in pornography reflects the party's wish to reform Indonesia through a very public form of morality. For many women, the organization is not merely a party but a vehicle for instilling Islamic values in society. As one told me, "I hope that politics in Indonesia will be based on Islam, as the majority of the population is Muslim. Islam is believed to be *rahmatan li al-ʿâlamîn,* bringing goodness to the whole world. So, if it is implemented, I am sure Indonesia will progress." Party leaders portrayed the bill as a safeguard for women and children. As an article on the PKS website put it, "The Anti-Pornography Bill protects women from the business of sexual exploitation which is growing in Indonesia" (Heriawan 2006).

PKS women participated in demonstrations supporting the bill, such as a rally organized by Muslim organizations in May 2006 which was attended by an estimated 100,000 people (Ghani 2006). Allen (2009) claims that female supporters of the legislation mobilized under the umbrella of Muslim organizations, while opponents mobilized as part of women's groups or secular organizations. Nevertheless, when I conducted follow-up interviews in early 2008, the PKS women I spoke to were united by their enthusiasm for the legislation. A woman informant explained her view: "Hopefully it will be ratified, because it truly is representative. I mean, once again, it's for the good of women themselves, and also for the common good. Maybe you can imagine that if these things continue to be allowed, future generations of children will consume things that are not appropriate."

Demonstrations against the pornography bill, such as a large march on International Women's Day in 2006, were initiated by women's rights groups who argued that it was an attempt to foist particular ideas of Islamic conduct on all Indonesians (Allen 2007). It was at first unclear whether Muslim women's organizations would oppose or support the legislation. In March 2006, however, Fatayat leaders weighed in with a carefully worded statement opposing the bill because it failed to provide protections for women and children victimized by the sex industry. They also argued that pre-existing legislation could be more effectively implemented. This statement was widely reprinted in the national media and especially on the blogs that sprang up as part of the opposition to the bill. One Fatayat activist explained the group's stance, reiterating the importance of empowering women:

> As for Fatayat, we agree that pornography shouldn't be allowed, but we also don't think these laws should be passed soon. It's not that we agree with pornography, but there are many paragraphs that harm women. . . . For example, women if they go out after midnight must have an escort or they can be arrested. Now what's that for? Meanwhile, it's OK for men, and I think that's unfair. So I think there are a number of items that really harm women, so we rejected it. . . . Yes, there are things that I agree with, but these laws don't empower women, in fact, it's the opposite.

[. . .]

At demonstrations, individual Fatayat leaders expressed more scathing views on the bill. One activist linked it to the recent adoption in several provinces of laws inspired by Islamic *Shariah:* "The phenomena of the anti-pornography bill started with the appearance of bylaws in some of the regions. Although not explicitly packaged as anti-pornography, they have put in place of anti-prostitution laws, morality laws and even Islamic *Shariah* laws. All these laws attempt to force women back into their homes" (Kosoemawiria 2006).

For many women in Fatayat, the debate over pornography was a distraction from more serious problems. When I asked Fatayat members what they considered the most important problems facing women and the country they rarely mentioned morality, unlike women in PKS. Instead, they tended to cite need for political and economic reforms. This accords with Fatayat's interest since the early 1990s in civil society and democratization, as well as the organization's grassroots emphasis. As another Fatayat volunteer explained, "The rich are getting richer, the poor are staying poor, and the poor don't have a strong bargaining position. Civil society in Indonesia is still weak . . . up till now government programs are always top-down, not bottom-up, they don't channel the aspirations of the society."

Fatayat women's arguments against the pornography bill mobilized feminist arguments, questioning whether it empowered women. But they also reveal concerns over individual rights and responsibilities as well as the role of civil society in national politics. In this sense, they bear the marks of liberal discourses of freedom and equality that are often entwined with feminism.

[. . .]

The pornography example demonstrates how concerns related to globalization—in this case the increasing availability of sexualized imagery—are refracted through national issues and concerns and produce gendered moral debates tied to the future of the nation. As the public sphere expanded and became more open in Indonesia, a furor arose over the proliferation of media images of women's bodies. PKS and others blamed globalization for an increase in immorality, in particular what they saw as a spread of a Westernized culture preoccupied with sex. The Islamic revival and the growing power of Muslim organizations also helped to drive growing concern over moral behavior in public spaces. The new interest in modesty was visible in the growing numbers of women adopting Muslim clothing in the early 2000s.

However, while global processes provoked anxieties over pornography, they also stimulated women's participation in this debate. Women on both sides of the issue adapted global discourses, especially Islam and feminism, to make their arguments. They were able to do so because their organizations serve as platforms for different kinds of women's activism and their arguments drew on the ideologies of their established national organizations. Women in PKS used Islamic discourses of modesty and morality to argue that "pornographic" images are a threat to the nation and to emphasize a need for public regulation of morality. Meanwhile opponents of the bill drew on transnational feminism to argue that the bill would contravene progress toward women's empowerment. In particular, women in Fatayat wielded liberal discourses of freedom, civil society, and rights to contend that greater state regulation of expression is not the way to achieve gender equality. And they also drew on their Islamic heritage to question whether one particular interpretation of Islam should guide policy or national development. Importantly, the two divergent ways PKS and Fatayat women interpreted global discourses both had credibility and legitimacy largely *because* they were rooted in the ideologies of their respective national organizations.

[. . .]

Globalization, Moral Debates, and Gender in the Public Sphere

In an ever more inter-connected world, global discourses such as feminism and Islamic revivalism not only shape local identities but are also transformed in different contexts. This article has sought to illuminate these processes through an examination of Indonesian Muslim women's activism in public debates about pornography and polygamy. The case of Indonesia reveals how women activists grapple with distinct but sometimes overlapping global discourses, and it demonstrates the significance of national histories, national organizations, and national imaginations for the ways women adapt these frameworks.

Women in Fatayat NU claim that the pornography bill threatens freedom of expression and discriminates against women, while PKS women supporters of the bill argue that it is necessary to combat national moral degradation and promote Islamic values. . . .

Both of these organizations are rooted in Indonesian political and Islamic traditions. Fatayat draws on a history of complex approaches to Islamic texts, as well as longstanding efforts for women's empowerment, while PKS draws on the heritage of modernist and political Islam. Both groups also capitalize on Indonesia's history of mobilizing women in the public sphere, whether for nationalist purposes or the advancement of women.

The women in these groups adapt global discourses of feminism and Islamic revivalism to intervene in these debates, putting forth very different moral visions for Indonesia's future. Fatayat women use discourses of equality and rights to assert that the pornography bill is discriminatory. They also draw on liberalism, both secular and Islamic, to assert that the por-nography bill instills a narrow interpretation of Islam in the nation-state. PKS women, in contrast, use discourses of modesty and morality, inspired by the Islamic revival, to argue that sexualized images threaten the nation. While Islamic discourses are certainly not new to Indonesia, the women in PKS draw on globalized understandings of Islam that demand greater gender separation and covering of women's bodies.

[. . .]

The Indonesian case sheds light not only on how global processes influence debates in the public sphere but also the ways gender is implicated in such struggles. Women activists are debat-ing over competing moral visions of what kind of nation Indonesia should be, and these visions are intertwined with ideas about women's rights and interpretations of Islamic texts.

Investigating the different ways Indonesian Muslim women adapt discourses of feminism and Islamic revivalism to intervene in the public sphere reveals how political subjectivities are shaped through the national organizations that structure the ways people engage with global discourses. Yet these organizations are also part of a longer national history of engagement with Islamic politics and women's mobilization. Global discourses and national histories intersect in Indonesian Muslim women's activism, demonstrating the relevance of national organizations, contexts, and politics for the study of transnational processes.

[. . .]

References

Allen, P. 2007. "Challenging Diversity? Indonesia's Anti-Pornography Bill." *Asian Studies Review* 31(2):101–15.

Allen, Pam. 2009. "Women, Gendered Activism, and Indonesia's Anti-Pornography Bill." *Intersections: Gender and Sexuality in Asia and the Pacific* 19 (http://intersections.anu.edu.au/issue19/allen .htm#t31).

Blackburn, S. 2004. *Women and the State in Modern Indonesia.* Cambridge, UK: Cambridge University Press.

Blackwood, E. 2008. "Transnational Discourses and Circuits of Queer Knowledge in Indonesia." *Gay & Lesbian Quarterly* 14(4):481–507.

Blackwood, Evelyn. 2007. "Regulation of Sexuality in Indonesian Discourse: Normative Gender, Criminal Law and Shifting Strategies of Control." *Culture Health & Sexuality* 9/3:293–307.

Boellstorff, T. 2005. *The Gay Archipelago: Sexuality and Nation in Indonesia.* Princeton, NJ: Princeton University Press.

Brenner, Suzanne. 2005. "Islam and Gender Politics in Late New Order Indonesia." Pp. 93–118 in *Spirited Politics: Religion and Public Life in Contemporary Southeast Asia*, edited by A. C. Willford and K. M. George. Ithaca, NY: Cornell University Press Southeast Asia Program Publications.

Davis, K. 2008. *The Making of Our Bodies, Ourselves: How Feminism Travels Across Borders*. Durham, NC: Duke University Press.

Feener, M. R. and T. Sevea, eds. 2009. *Islamic Connections: Muslim Societies in South and Southeast Asia*. Singapore: Institute of Southeast Asian Studies.

Ghani, Azhar. 2006. "Indonesia: Anti-Porn Bill Backed by Massive Jakarta March." *Straits Times*, Monday, May 22 (www.asiamedia.ucla.edu/article-southeastasia.asp?parentid=46303).

Heriawan, Ahmad. 2006. "RUU Anti Pornografi Lindungi Perempuan dari Eksploitasi Seks." *PKS Website* (http://pk-sejahtera.org/2006/main.php?op=isi&id=1143).

Indonesian Election Commission. 2009. "Hasil Penghitungan Suara Sah Partai Politik Peserta Pemilu." (http://mediacenter.kpu.go.id/images/mediacenter/berita/SUARA_KPU/HASIL_PENGHITUNGAN_SUARA_SAH.pdf).

Jayawardena, K. 1986. *Feminism and Nationalism in the Third World*. London, UK: Zed Books.

Kosoemawiria, Edith. 2006. "March for Diversity." *Qantara.de: Dialogue with the Islamic World* (http://en.qantara.de/webcom/show_article.php/_c-478/_nr-442/i.html).

Ricklefs, Merle C. 2009. *A History of Modern Indonesia since C. 1300*. 3rd ed. Stanford, CA: Stanford University Press.

Rinaldo, R. 2008. "Envisioning the Nation: Women Activists, Religion, and the Public Sphere in Indonesia." *Social Forces* 86(4):1781–804.

Rinaldo, R. 2010. "The Islamic Revival and Women's Political Subjectivity in Indonesia." *Women's Studies International Forum* 33(4):422–31.

Robinson, K. 2009. *Gender, Islam and Democracy in Indonesia*. London, UK: Routledge.

Sunudyantoro. 2003. "Tayangan Mistik di Televisi tidak ada Nilai Positifnya." *Tempo*, Wednesday, May 14. (www.tempointeraktif.com/hg/nasional/2003/05/14/brk,20030514-15,id.html).

Suryana, Aan. 2006. "Pornography Bill Going Strong in the House." *The Jakarta Post*, Friday, April 7.

Van Doorn-Harder, Pieternella. 2006. *Women Shaping Islam: Reading the Qur'an in Indonesia*. Chicago: University of Illinois Press.

Wieringa, S. 2002. *Sexual Politics in Indonesia*. London/New York: Palgrave Macmillan.

Wyrod, R. 2008. "Between Women's Rights and Men's Authority: Masculinity and Shifting Discourses of Gender Difference in Urban Uganda." *Gender & Society* 22(6):799–823.

Yuval-Davis, N. 1997. *Gender and Nation*. London: University of East London.

PART VI

Families and Intimate Relationships

I n this section, we cover various types of family formations and intimate relationships. Families are fundamental spaces for personal lessons in gender and sexuality. Families to some degree are private organizations in which inequalities are learned, negotiated, and resisted. Scholars have specifically examined how gender inequalities surface in various aspects of family life through interactions, carework, schooling, and workplace schedules, including policies that shape how families form and operate. This section examines gender and sexuality in a variety of family contexts across the core themes of the reader: intersectionality, masculinity, transgender, and global (IMTG) perspectives. These pieces touch on various issues in the field of family such as gender practices between parents and children; divisions of household labor; experiences of lesbian, bisexual, gay, transgender, and queer family formations; and family construction among transnational migrants.

Looking at relationship quality within families, Maria Johnson's "Strength and Respectability" asks how Black daughters' relationships with their fathers influence their ideologies around Black womanhood. This piece investigates how father–daughter relationships are significant in shaping how women navigate heterosexual relationships and notions of Black women's strength and respectability. Based on interviews with women who varied in whether their fathers were supportive or distant, as well as resident or non-resident, Johnson finds involved fathers were formative in shaping daughters' orientation to heterosexual relationships and Black womanhood. On the other hand, those with distant fathers tried to become strong despite their fathers but felt that they had less understanding about how to navigate heterosexual relationships. Johnson argues that understanding Black womanhood requires understanding Black women's relationships with their fathers.

In "'How Could You Do This to Me?'" Katie Acosta examines the strategies sexually nonconforming Latina women use when navigating their families' responses to their sexuality. Acosta's piece complicates the notion of "coming out" by showing the varied ways that Latina women navigate their sexual identity within their families, from parents' rejection to silence or avoidance. Taking an intersectional lens, Acosta argues that it is important to consider migration history, age, and financial dependency in understanding how these processes play out. Yet, all of the strategies have costs for these women; indeed, those who did not disclose same-sex relationships to their families may have been most successful at combining their family lives with their sexual lives (under the guise of "friends"). Despite their efforts, many of these women experience their family and relationship worlds as remaining separate.

Mignon Moore's "Gendered Power Relations Among Women" examines how equitable the distribution of paid work, housework, financial control, and authority over children is within same-gender families. Black lesbian couples are more likely to enact separate finances but also have a clear division of household labor in which biological mothers take more responsibility for stereotypical female-oriented household tasks. Through interviews, observation, and surveys with Black lesbian couples and stepfamilies, Moore shows that a biological mother's greater engagement in household labor relates to her wanting greater control in money management and childrearing. Gender continues to powerfully affect how these families arrange their lives. Stepmothers do not appear to have the same gender advantage and authority that stepfathers might have, but self-defined feminine gender presentation and biological motherhood play a key role in determining who does the housework.

In "Normative Resistance and Inventive Pragmatism," Carla Pfeffer interviews cisgender women who are in partnerships with transgender men to understand how these women negotiate family life. These women often have to navigate being perceived as a member of a cisgender heterosexual couple, when they do not necessarily see themselves that way. Pfeffer finds that some women engaged in "normative resistance," resisting marriage, parenthood, and monogamy and embracing and making visible queer identities. Yet at the same time, some women practice "inventive pragmatism" by strategically navigating social structures to access resources for themselves and their families through legal marriage, legal parenthood, and reproductive technologies. While making decisions about their families, these women and their partners are being shaped by existing ideas about families, including heterosexual and same-sex families, and at the same time are transforming ideas of who families are.

Finally, Rhacel Salazar Parreñas, in "Transnational Fathering," examines the emotional lives of families with fathers who work outside of the country. Interviews with children living in the Philippines, whose fathers do migrant work, show how traditional gender divisions of labor are maintained within the household despite men's distance by their continued status as "pillar of the home." Fathers provide material security but leave daily care and emotional support of children to mothers. Even when fathers are home, children experience a "gap" between themselves and their fathers. While transnational mothers often work to compensate for distance with frequent phone calls, transnational fathers primarily communicate to discipline their children. Even as global economic forces change how families live, the new family forms reproduce gender inequality.

The articles in this section show not only the variation in families but also how family forms are both dynamic and often reproduce gender ideologies and inequalities. Women's relationships with their parents influence how they understand themselves, and their own romantic and sexual relationships, in ways that can be challenging for those with distant fathers or who are in sexually nonconforming relationships. Families headed by Black lesbians, or transgender families, reflect both "traditional" notions of gender and sexuality as well as complicate existing narratives about the organization of families. And even as families are reshaped by global economic forces that create transnational parents, migrant fathers tend to emphasize discipline and maintain patriarchal authority rather than attempt to create closer bonds with their children. While families are changing, they also reflect dominant notions of gender and sexuality.

Strength and Respectability

Black Women's Negotiation of Racialized Gender Ideals and the Role of Daughter–Father Relationships

Maria S. Johnson

© iStockphoto.com/digitalskillet

B lack girls are socialized by their immediate and extended families to be simultaneously strong and respectable in an attempt to prepare them for race-based social and political obstacles (Beauboeuf-Lafontant 2009; Hill 2002; hooks 1992; Ladner 1971; Ward 1996), to respond to stereotypes of black femininity (Collins 2004), and to assume family responsibilities (Beauboeuf-Lafontant 2009; Hill 2002). This model of black femininity sets up contradictory expectations; while the ideal of strength is associated with traits such as independence

Maria S. Johnson. 2013. "Strength and Respectability: Black Women's Negotiation of Racialized Gender Ideals and the Role of Daughter–Father Relationships." *Gender & Society* 27(6):889–912.

and resilience, that of respectability is associated with traits such as submissiveness and domesticity (Hill 2002). Most studies examining how black girls are socialized focus on the role and influence of black mothers, especially how they model and teach their daughters strength and caretaking (Beauboeuf-Lafontant 2009). Less is known about the role and influence of fathers.

Using qualitative data based on 79 in-depth interviews with 40 young black women, I examine daughters' expectations regarding feminine identities linked to strength and respectability. I find that both the quality of the daughter–father relationships and the women's level of exposure to fathers influence the women's self-perceived capability to perform racialized ideals of black femininity, particularly within heterosexual relationships. The study contributes to our understanding of how black women interpret and interact with conflicting expectations of black femininity, and calls for additional examination of daughter–father relationships.

Discourses of Black Femininity

Discourses of strength and respectability dominate the socialization process of black women and girls. These racialized gender discourses operate interracially to reinforce power hierarchies (Beauboeuf-Lafontant 2009; Collins 2004), intraracially to police behavior (Beauboeuf-Lafontant 2009; Moore 2011) and prepare women to respond to societal obstacles (Collins 2004), and individually as strategies for black women's gender performance (Collins 2004; Moore 2011). While discourses of strength and respectability have conflicting expectations, they are essential elements of the racialized gender structure in which black women are seen as fully responsible for their circumstances.

Discourses of strength are rooted in the notion that black women should endure "hardship, caretaking, and selflessness" (Beauboeuf-Lafontant 2009, 75). At work, black women are often expected to burden themselves with extra tasks without complaint (Beauboeuf-Lafontant 2009; Harvey Wingfield 2007). For example, black professional women are required to be "workplace mammies" or "modern mammies" who are willing to forgo personal lives for work (Collins 2004; Omolade 1994) and be "subordinate to white and/or male authority yet maintaining a level of ambition and aggressiveness needed for achievement in middle-class occupations" (Collins 2004, 140). Black women are consequently overworked and undervalued in the workplace. Strength-based expectations extend into family relations as black women "labor" at home with kin-work and household duties (Beauboeuf-Lafontant 2009). Additionally, many black women conceptualize struggle as an essential element of black womanhood (McDonald 2007) and respond to life situations in ways that are aligned with strength rhetoric (Beauboeuf-Lafontant 2009). Expectations of race loyalty compound pressure to be strong because black women are also required to represent their race (Beauboeuf-Lafontant 2009) and to subordinate their gendered experiences (Collins 2004; Combahee River Collective 1986).

Discourses of black respectability, on the other hand, call on black women to conform to the standards of white, middle-class femininity, embracing "piety, purity, submissiveness, and domesticity" (Moore 2011, 10). The roots of black respectability trace back to late nineteenth-century middle-class and church black women and men, who claimed that women were to act beyond reproach in both their public and private lives, with a steadfast commitment to church, civic responsibility, and domesticity (Collins 2000; Higginbotham 1993). Responding to racist stereotypes of black women as sexually promiscuous "jezebels" (Collins 2000; Lubiano 1992), historically, the ideal of respectability has represented a class-based indictment of poor and working-class black women and affirmed their subordination in the domestic sphere (Mitchell 2004). Black respectability was progressive in that it called racist institutions and practices into question, but restrictive in its emphasis on black women's physical presentation and personal decorum (Higginbotham 1993; Mitchell 2004), placing further pressure on women to serve as representatives for the race.

While discourses of strength and respectability prescribe contradictory traits and behaviors (Hill 2002), they are also invoked in complementary ways. Both discourses silence and devalue black women's gender-based experiences and maintain normative value systems that assess black women against dominant femininity standards and intraracial expectations for femininity.

[. . .]

Data and Methods

Between March 2007 and March 2008, I conducted 79 in-depth interviews with 40 college-educated women between the ages of 18 and 22; all of the women identified as either black or African American. Half the women lived with both biological parents for their entire childhood and the other half grew up in single-mother households. The women reported that their biological parents also identified as black or African American. All of the women I interviewed were currently attending a large, public university and were from working- and low-middle-class backgrounds. The women's parents worked in manufacturing, service industries, or in low-middle-class professional positions. All of the women reported only heterosexual experiences. I interviewed the participants twice for an average of 4.5 hours of total interview and contact time, except for one woman who was available only for one interview.

[. . .]

Findings

. . . My findings demonstrate that fathers are influential in shaping how women interpret and interact with notions of black femininity, but how this influence occurs differs according to relationship quality.

To understand relationship quality, I group the women according to their fathers' residence and level of paternal involvement. The four categories that result are supportive resident fathers ($n = 17$), distant resident fathers ($n = 3$), supportive nonresident fathers ($n = 3$), and distant nonresident fathers ($n = 17$).

Supportive resident fathers (SRFs) lived in the same households as their daughters during their childhoods. According to the daughters' descriptions, these fathers were engaged, accessible, responsible, and involved. Most daughters in this category shared numerous examples of their fathers' warmth. *Distant resident fathers* (DRFs) lived in the same households as their daughters but were either emotionally distant or failed to interact with their daughters in ways they found meaningful. Daughters in this category identified their fathers as responsible but expressed discontent with their fathers' warmth and engagement. *Supportive nonresident fathers* (SNRFs) lived in separate households from their daughters but were described by their daughters as warm, engaged, responsible, accessible, and actively involved in their lives. Nonetheless, daughters in this category also felt their fathers' nonresident status limited their opportunities to interact. *Distant nonresident fathers* (DNRFs) lived in separate households from their daughters and had inconsistent contact with them. Daughters in this category reported that their fathers would go months or even years without contacting them. They generally described their fathers' parenting as irresponsible, disengaged, inaccessible, and lacking in involvement.

Women's Identification With Strength and Respectability Ideals

Strength and respectability discourses are central to how the women in this study describe themselves and their aspirations. They want to be independent and excel in professional domains, yet they also report feeling the need to moderate their independence with ideals of feminine respectability. Brenda (SRF) describes her ideal black woman:

> They're still strong, and they still take on roles that are traditionally male . . . being a CEO and taking the lead on decisions. But they still know how to be women and still know how to dress nice and pretty and roll their hair and put on makeup and still be a woman, still be the things that a woman needs to be, like nurturing to her children and caring.

As upwardly mobile women from working-class and lower-middle-class backgrounds, many of whom are also first-generation college students, all of the women in this study articulate strength narratives focused on independence and professional success. In particular, they emphasize obtaining more college education and income than their parents. Although they had not experienced many of the workplace and family burdens outlined in studies of strength discourse (Beauboeuf-Lafontant 2009; Harvey Wingfield 2007; Omolade 1994), the women view strength as an essential strategy for coping with their school-based and personal struggles. Alexandra (DNRF) said the following about ideal black femininity: "I just think that a strong black woman is what every black woman should aspire to be and what every black woman needs to be to live in this world, especially in America."

Despite their support of strength narratives, the women were at times critical of societal expectations that black women be self-sacrificing and long-suffering. Julia, who had a supportive resident father, explained:

> It's good things, but I don't want to be suffering all the time. I don't want to be enduring a lot, but it's your cross to bear. And unfortunately . . . it's interesting the way your gender and the color of your skin automatically, I think, gives you a little bit more of a struggle, or a different struggle. Just because, even if you feel you're not, you know, that's what you have to be.

Like the women in McDonald's (2007) study, Julia identifies struggle as a key component of black women's experiences rooted in both external and self-imposed expectations.

While the women's conceptualizations of strength center on independence, struggle, and perseverance in response to adversity, being respectable means being nurturing and maintaining a feminine appearance, particularly within private spaces and with men. They described respectable public presentations as those that avoided being overtly sexual in appearance or behaving in ways that could be perceived as masculine. They often used the word "lady" to describe appropriate behaviors. For instance, Abigail (DNRF) stated:

> Some of my friends that I hang out with are very, like, masculine or very, like, independent women. I pride myself on being an independent woman too, but they're, like, very masculine with it and they, like, curse and they're not ladylike. And I feel like that's [being ladylike] kind of an important thing to me.

Beth (DNRF) shared Abigail's feelings about being a lady: "I feel like it's important to be ladylike. Not maybe 100 percent aspects, but . . . when girls are going around cussing and all this stuff and dressing like dudes and stuff, I don't think that's womanhood, personally." Like Abigail and Beth, the women I spoke with are hyperaware of how others perceive their femininity. As Brenda explained, "People are constantly judging you. You always want to be on your Ps and Qs." Their expectations are aligned with previous studies that find that upwardly mobile and middle-class black women incorporate discourses of respectability into their gender presentation (Moore 2011), and that newly middle-class black Americans have more traditional gender expectations (Hill 2002).

Although discourses of strength and respectability are contradictory, most of the women endorsed them both as ideal characteristics. This reflects the entrenchment of racialized standards of femininity, but also illuminates the women's quest to access respectability, which is not traditionally or interracially attributed to black women, and to attain the forms of cultural capital (Bourdieu 1984) valued in their families and communities. These women's efforts to meet these ideals should not be dismissed as false consciousness or evidence of indoctrination; rather, their interaction with these discourses reveals an agentic strategy on their part to carve out gender identities that help them to achieve social mobility and respect.

[. . .]

Influence of Fathers on Women's Relationship to the Respectability Ideal

There are two ways that daughter–father relationships shape women's respectability narratives. First, the women often invoke an image of fathers as all-knowing protectors of women's femininity and respectability, though they varied in terms of whether they experienced this as a reality or viewed it as an absent ideal. Second, women in the study cite interactions with fathers and fathers' advice (or lack thereof) as influential in shaping their behavior in heterosexual relationships. However, it is the nature of the daughter–father relationship—whether supportive or distant—that is key in shaping women's specific experiences and strategies. While women with supportive fathers report a direct, positive influence on their ability to meet ideals of respectability, women with distant fathers more often cite their fathers as examples of what to avoid in romantic relationships or as strengthening their investment in respectability as a reaction to their fathers' attitudes toward women.

Women with supportive fathers and distant resident fathers discuss their fathers' efforts to offer physical or symbolic protection, while women with distant nonresident fathers discuss paternal protection as an absent ideal. Where fathers are supportive and actively involved in their daughters' lives, the daughters perceive symbolic protection in the form of adoration, affirmation, and advice. Claire (SRF) described her father's contribution in this way:

He always gave that strong male perspective of telling me my worth and then telling me what I was worthy of . . . in a man and what I shouldn't go for and everything.

Claire and others value their fathers' messages as authentic "male perspectives" on heterosexual relationships and construe their fathers' positive feedback as protection from manipulation and harmful relationships. As Kamilah (SRF) stated, "I would tell him what happened when this dude tried to approach me and we would laugh about it. He'd say, 'Yeah, I used to do that. And if someone does this then [do] this.'" Other times, women described their fathers as protective. Jean, who has a supportive nonresident father, shared that she hesitates to introduce men to her father. She said, "My dad's very protective because I'm, like, his daughter and I'm his only girl and I'm the youngest." These narratives of protection position fathers as defenders against vulnerabilities daughters may experience when interacting with men.

Women with distant resident fathers provide an interesting contrast because they critique their examples of their fathers' efforts to offer advice or protection. For instance, Devin shared, "I think that's his main influence—to make sure we're respected by whoever we're dating and to know that we have the best." However, she later described an instance in which she disagreed with her father's assessment of her friendship with her former partner:

> He just felt like my ex-boyfriend was very disrespectful when he walked in the house— even though my ex-boyfriend said hello to everyone, my father is just like that.

Overall, the narratives of women with distant resident fathers varied, comprising both examples of feeling protected and instances in which they wished their fathers would offer protection in ways that were more affirming.

The women's invocation of dominant imagery of fathers as essential figures and all-knowing protectors makes sense in light of the work by Solebello and Elliott (2011), who find that fathers themselves view protection as a major part of their gender socialization of daughters. Ironically, this imagery is particularly strong when fathers are absent, as studies of black communities find that the prevalence of black fathers who do not live in the same household as their children creates a context in which present black fathers are seen as offering status and protection to girls (Anderson 1989; Kaplan 1997). According to Hill (2005), this role of fathers as protectors is idealized because of the value society places on men-centered households. The women in this study value paternal protection in a context in which the defense of black women and girls is not seen as available to or present among black Americans.

In addition to viewing fathers as actual or potential protectors of daughters' respectability, women also looked to their fathers as guides for how to behave within their personal, heterosexual relationships. Women with supportive fathers, particularly supportive resident fathers, gave multiple examples of how their fathers socialized them to interact with men in respectable ways. Jada (SRF) shared an example of how her father prepared her for dating:

> He'd take us out on dates and, like, show us how guys are supposed to treat girls. He would open the door. Once a month we had dates. We got to pick the place. We got dressed up. And he'd come pick us up from the house, like come ring the doorbell. He'd take us to the place; we'd go to the movie and then . . . out to eat. He'd pay for the bill. Like, all the time . . . this is how a guy should treat you.

Jada's example highlights the direct manner by which some women felt their fathers attempted to influence their private interactions with men. Brittney (SNRF) stated that her father advised her to disagree less with her partner and to defer to her partner's decision making:

> He has this thing about you're supposed to follow the man. I'm not married. He thinks of Brian as my husband. He tells me, "What did Brian say about it?" He tries to tell me not to be so hostile like my mother, not to scream and stuff, to remain calm, things like that.

Brittney's father's advice aligns with normative expectations of femininity, in which women are expected to be quiet and submissive to men. By admonishing her to be less loud and angry, he is telling her to temper her presentation as an angry black woman and acquire a more demure style within the relationship. Far from resisting her father's advice, Brittney finds it to be a valuable insight into her communication style and a way to resist stereotypical presentation as a black woman.

Some women with supportive resident fathers said that they also gleaned information about their fathers' expectations by observing their fathers' interactions with women, particularly their mothers. Women felt these lessons improved their understanding of hetero-relationships and increased their confidence within those settings. These interactions gave them strategies for navigating dominant social norms related to hetero-relationships, but also reinforced dominant expectations of femininity.

Unlike women with supportive fathers, two of the three women with distant resident fathers, Erin and Devin, shared examples of how their fathers' feedback hurt their dating experiences by decreasing their confidence. Erin explained, "I had very low standards because of my relationship with my daddy. He used to call me 'stupid' and 'nothing.' Why would he say that? He didn't want me to be conceited, so this is what he said. So he called me 'ugly' all the time." Erin felt that her father's insults damaged her self-esteem and led her to seek romantic relationships. She said, "I would get my validation from men. I would need to be around them and need their love and affection and feel cared for." Her example demonstrates that some fathers' presence provides continuous opportunities to reinforce damaging messages that subvert daughters' sense of self. Furthermore, the messages communicate that daughters are deviant from traditional standards.

Most of the women with distant nonresident fathers lacked concrete examples of their fathers' socializing advice or activities regarding their feminine development. Instead, their narratives focused on challenges associated with platonic and romantic interactions with men when one's father is absent. Pam (DNRF) explained, "I think that it would be easier for a woman if she can get some type of advice from a man and be able to talk to a man, like a grown man, about certain things that you can't really know—you can't get from a woman." Since Pam had little contact with her biological father, I asked her how she thought she would learn those things. She replied, "I think I got those things from learning what not to do, what not to accept from a man, just from what I've seen done." Like Pam, other women with distant fathers felt that their fathers' lack of involvement hindered their interpersonal skills within hetero-romantic relationships. But, like women with supportive fathers, these women continue to view fathers as possessing a heterosexual knowing that must be "learned"—only, in their case, the opportunity to learn from their fathers is limited.

Many felt that it was more difficult to come of age without some sort of paternal involvement. Tamara described her sexual coming of age without having her (distant nonresident) father in her life: "I was strong in my mind, toward my goals and everything, but I was still lacking in the knowledge of knowing about sexual encounters." Tamara emphasized that her strength did not extend to sexual relationships with men. She reasoned that there are particular ways that women should behave sexually within heterosexual relationships, which was a common belief among the women in the study. Tamara felt that fathers, because of their experiences and mindsets as men, provide unique insight into the dynamics of heterosexual relationships. Tanya (DNRF) explained that she thought uninvolved fathers leave a "void" in their children's lives that cannot be filled by women. She went on to describe the impact of her father's absence:

> I didn't have a father figure growing [up]. I think there is something that I missed out [on]. I'm getting it now, so I'm learning it now. And I see how it would have been useful if I learned it sooner. . . . Like how it is when it comes to guys. Maybe I wouldn't have made that mistake.

The "mistake" is a reference to her first sexual relationship from which she contracted a sexually transmitted infection. Tanya's reflection backs up the women's assertions that fathers who are not involved in their daughters' lives leave voids that render women potentially vulnerable to problematic romantic and sexual relationships.

When Tanya mentioned "she is getting it now," she was referring to advice she received from her pastor, a man she views as a father figure. This tendency to seek a substitute father figure is not uncommon for women with distant nonresident fathers. Indeed, the specter of the (physically and emotionally) absent black father is so prevalent for all of the respondents that even women with supportive, resident fathers talked about how other people deal with it; as Asia (SRF) put it:

> I definitely feel, like, especially in the African American community, that to have a male figure in your life is, like, a big idea. It's almost like if you don't have it, you search for it. . . . I have a lot of friends who just live with their mother, they didn't have dads, and they look for that attention, just approval, and they want this male attention.

What's important here is that, even in the absence of direct influence from or contact with fathers, women continue to look to men and to internalize the male gaze as they seek to perform idealized femininity and respectability.

When women with distant nonresident fathers had contact with their fathers, they were strongly attuned to how their fathers interacted with women. Many women's observations prompted them to strive for respectability in order to avoid attracting men like their fathers. When asked how her father influenced how she thought of herself as a black woman, Abigail (whose nonresident father was in and out of her life) replied:

> I just remember being out with him this past summer for my sister's graduation and there'd be a black woman walk by who was scantily dressed or something. And he was like, "Oh, look at that," or something like that. I knew it was an excuse for him to look [laughs].

While attempting to give Abigail a message about respectable deportment, her father's gaze belied his admonishments and made his desires obvious. Although Abigail laughed as she recounted this event, the remainder of her story demonstrates how she drew an unintended lesson from the encounter:

> I always got to look respectable. Always have to put myself together so that people don't even have that thought. I'm sure people will, but I won't give them another reason to. So he's influenced the way to pull myself together as a black woman, the way that I represent myself as a black woman. Because a lot of times . . . African American women are looked at as sexual objects. He's made me want to be the opposite of that.

Abigail's father reaffirmed for her that black women are seen as predominantly sexual and she hoped to avoid receiving prurient gazes from men. She relied on her father's actions to identify how men may respond to women and decided to pursue what she believed to be respectable deportment in order to avoid being seen as a sexual object.

There were, however, some cases in which women were explicitly critical of their fathers' perspective on how women should behave in relationships. Some women rejected aspects of respectability couched in traditional feminine roles, particularly when they felt their fathers expected them to be subordinate. Jean, who had a supportive nonresident father whom she visited weekly, expressed irritation at her father's behavior:

> Things that bother me, like my stepmother always bring him his plate. Or sometimes I'll be over there and he be, like, "Bring my plate down." I'm, like, [a] grown-assed man—I need you to get up and go fix you a plate. . . . I am not going [to] marry nobody who think I'm going serve them because they will just be SOL [shit out of luck].

Similarly, Asia (SRF) shared an example of her father's views of black women:

> His wife is Filipino and he has this thing that African American, black, women are, like, crazy. He loves them and everything. But he feels like they have this type of attitude and disposition about themselves different from other cultures of women in America. And I always argue with him.

When I asked Asia how he justified this to his own black daughters, she replied:

> [He would say] we're different: "Oh, you guys were raised right and you guys are special." "No," I always tell him, "that is not how that works. No one sees us different. You see us different because we're your daughters, but we're not . . . you just have to open your mind." He raised us one way and the type of woman that he maybe prefers might be different than actually the way he raised us. I think about what he said and I'm, like, no, that's not right. And I try to live actually a way to prove to him that it's not.

Not only did Asia resent her father's subordination of his wife and reject his characterization of black women, she also tried to convince him to change his views and actions. Asia's and Jean's narratives demonstrate that not all fathers' attempts to socialize their daughters into subordinate feminine roles are well received, and are at times resisted.

These women's reports of traditional gender messages raise an interesting question: Are women with distant and uninvolved fathers protected from the normative messaging received by women with more engaged fathers? Could one argue that decreased or no exposure to fathers' gendered expectations is actually better than exposure to the often limiting ideals of femininity and respectability? I would argue no, for even in those cases in which women do not receive daily harmful gender messaging from their fathers, they continue to receive—indeed, are arguably still inundated with—such messages from other people and media. Furthermore, women with distant fathers tend to see themselves as lacking the real and symbolic "protection" of fathers, and describe themselves as deprived of a form of useful knowledge from men regarding dating. Thus, any protection they gain from not receiving patriarchal messages about femininity from their fathers may be mediated by the fact that the women understand themselves as ill prepared for hetero-relations because of that same absence.

These women's interpretations of the quality of their daughter–father relationships are influential in shaping how they both understand and pursue respectability. Even when their interpretations of their individual daughter–father relationships vary, the high value placed on fathers' protection and advice is consistent across categories. And more often than not, the messages that daughters receive from all types of fathers reinforce racialized and traditional gender roles that leave contradictory demands intact to be *both* strong and respectable.

Conclusion

[...]

Previous literature shows that black women's notions of femininity generally stem from daughter–mother interactions and external societal influences, but an interesting theme emerges from this study's data: that the quality of daughter–father relationships influences women's enactment of black femininity. The women I interviewed expected their fathers to help them navigate "within a society that is dominated by men." In many cases, their narratives identified fathers as vital sources of information about heterosexual interactions. Women with supportive fathers, particularly resident ones, described relationships that provided valuable instruction about heterosexual relationships, an important departure from the stereotype of uninvolved black fathers. . . . For women with distant relationships with their fathers, particularly those with nonresident fathers, their daughter–father relationships were sites of struggle that led them to become strong in spite of their fathers. These women, like those with supportive fathers, also sought to perform respectability in their heterosexual relationships, but often felt that their fathers' lack of involvement left them with little understanding of how to navigate those relationships. These narratives strongly suggest that fathers' emotional presence, primarily, and physical presence, secondarily, shapes how women interpret daughter–father relationships and perform black femininity.

The women's embracing of strength and respectability discourses must be understood within the context of the structural inequalities that black women face in public and private spaces. Black women develop strategies to make sense of the obstacles and the gender-related messages they receive. The daughter–father relationship is one, among others, through which daughters glean gendered messages that make them aware of societal, community, and family expectations. Though their efforts often seek to achieve ends we might critique as problematic, it is important to remember that there are community and societal rewards for meeting these expectations. And even when striving to conform to racialized and gendered norms, the women in this study do so in agentic ways, in which their relationships with their fathers are clearly formative (whether positively or negatively).

[...]

Finally, perhaps the most promising contribution of this study is the potential to shift attention away from scrutinizing and critiquing what black women do, to taking seriously the role of men and fathers in either reinforcing or challenging norms that are harmful for women and girls. It also suggests that we focus our attention on the quality of father–child relationships. While resident fathers may provide additional resources within households and contribute to the work of caring for children, the quality of fathers' interactions with their daughters is more important, even if they are living in different spaces. A critical component of supportive fathering involves more than just being present, but also thinking critically about the kinds of messages fathers convey to their daughters regarding the possibilities and paradoxes they will face as women.

References

Anderson, Elijah. 1989. "Sex Codes and Family Life Among Poor Inner-City Youths." *Annals of the American Academy of Political and Social Science* 501:59–78.

Beauboeuf-Lafontant, Tamara. 2009. *Behind the Mask of the Strong Black Woman: Voice and the Embodiment of a Costly Performance.* Philadelphia, PA: Temple University Press.

Bourdieu, Pierre. 1984. *Distinction: A Social Critique of the Judgment of Taste.* Cambridge, MA: Harvard University Press.

Collins, Patricia H. 2000. *Black Feminist Thought: Knowledge, Consciousness, and the Politics of Empowerment.* New York: Routledge.

Collins, Patricia H. 2004. *Black Sexual Politics: African Americans, Gender, and the New Racism.* New York: Routledge.

Combahee River Collective. 1986. *The Combahee River Collective Statement: Black Feminist Organizing in the Seventies and Eighties.* Albany, NY: Kitchen Table: Women of Color Press.

Harvey Wingfield, Adia. 2007. "The Modern Mammy and the Angry Black Man: African American Professionals' Experiences with Gendered Racism in the Workplace." *Race, Gender & Class* 14:196–212.

Higginbotham, Evelyn B. 1993. *Righteous Discontent: The Women's Movement in the Black Baptist Church, 1880–1920.* Cambridge, MA: Harvard University Press.

Hill, Shirley A. 2002. "Teaching and Doing Gender in African American Families." *Sex Roles* 11:493–506.

Hill, Shirley A. 2005. *Black Intimacies: A Gender Perspective on Families and Relationships.* Walnut Creek, CA: AltaMira Press.

hooks, bell. 1992. *Black Looks: Race and Representation.* Boston, MA: South End Press.

Kaplan, Elaine B. 1997. *Not Our Kind of Girl: Unraveling the Myths of Black Teenage Motherhood.* Berkeley, CA: University of California Press.

Ladner, Joyce A. 1971. *Tomorrow's Tomorrow: The Black Woman.* Garden City, NY: Anchor Books.

Lubiano, Wahneema. 1992. "Black Ladies, Welfare Queens, and State Minstrels: Ideological War by Narrative Means." In *Race-ing Justice, En-gendering Power: Essays on Anita Hill, Clarence Thomas, and the Construction of Social Reality*, edited by T. Morrison. New York: Pantheon Books.

McDonald, Katrina Bell. 2007. *Embracing Sisterhood: Class, Identity, and Contemporary Black Women.* Lanham, MD: Rowman & Littlefield.

Mitchell, Michele. 2004. *Righteous Propagation: African Americans and the Politics of Racial Destiny After Reconstruction.* Chapel Hill, NC: University of North Carolina Press.

Moore, Mignon R. 2011. *Invisible Families: Gay Identities, Relationships, and Motherhood Among Black Women.* Berkeley, CA: University of California Press.

Omolade, Barbara. 1994. *The Rising Song of African American Women.* New York: Routledge.

Solebello, Nicholas and Sinikka Elliott. 2011. "We Want Them to Be as Heterosexual as Possible: Fathers Talk About Their Teen Children's Sexuality." *Gender & Society* 3:293–315.

Ward, Janie V. 1996. "Raising Resisters: The Role of Truth Telling in the Psychological Development of African American Girls." In *Urban Girls: Resisting Stereotypes, Creating Identities*, edited by B. J. Ross Leadbeater. New York: New York University Press.

"How Could You Do This to Me?"

How Lesbian, Bisexual, and Queer Latinas Negotiate Sexual Identity With Their Families

Katie Acosta

© iStockphoto.com/DGLimages

Latina/o studies scholars have explored the role of sexuality in Latina/o familial relationships (Espin 1997; Hurtado 2003; Gonzalez-Lopez 2005; Zavella 2003). Yet this work has predominantly focused on familial tensions regarding heterosexual sexuality and virginity. In this article, I explore the unique tensions that sexual nonconformity creates in Latina families by exploring the complex relationships that lesbian, bisexual, and queer (LBQ) Latinas have with their families of origin. I describe how disclosure and nondisclosure of one's sexual identity changes these women's relationships with their families. The questions driving this article are: What strategies do first- and second-generation Latinas use when negotiating sexual nonconformity with their families? How do age, economic autonomy, and geographic location affect these relationships? How do these women minimize the risk of rejection from families?

I propose that sexually nonconforming Latinas' relationships with family cannot be placed into simple categories of acceptance or rejection. I offer three distinct interaction strategies that study participants report engaging in with their families of origin: (1) erasure of nonconformity, (2) sexual silencing, and (3) avoidance after disclosure. Erasure of nonconformity occurs when the respondent discloses her lesbian, bisexual, or queer identity to her family and they in turn try to erase it by using control and manipulation tactics. Sexual silencing is a strategy used by respondents who chose not to disclose their sexuality and instead are complicit with their family members in pretending their relationships with women are platonic friendships. Even though there is no disclosure with the silencing strategy, respondents believe everyone is silently aware of their same-sex relationships. Last, the avoidance after disclosure strategy occurs when the respondents do disclose their lesbian, bisexual, or queer identity to family members and then become complicit with them in rendering the disclosure unheard. With this strategy, families and participants choose to separate the sexual nonconformity completely from family life. This strategy is different from the silencing strategy because it involves direct communication about the sexual nonconformity followed by a clear rejection. This strategy is also distinct from the erasure strategy because with avoidance, the respondents and their families are complicit in separating the lesbian, bisexual, or queer self from family life whereas with the erasure strategy the participants do not have that choice.

[. . .]

This article utilizes a dramaturgical perspective to analyze lesbian, bisexual, and queer Latinas' social interactions with their families. Erving Goffman notes that in our everyday lives we present ourselves to others based on our internalized understandings of cultural values and social expectations in order to gain acceptance from others. In this way, we manage the impressions of ourselves that we give off to others and behave as performers of a role. Others, however, are also engaging in this performance by going along with our presentations and by managing their own impressions (Goffman 1959). The interactional strategies that lesbian, bisexual, and queer Latinas engage in with their families demonstrate this process in action. This article emphasizes the fluidity of these women's identities and the lengths to which they go in order to present themselves as either sexually conforming or as asexual in the front stage. This work further highlights the extent to which family members contribute to one's own presentation of self through these interactional strategies.

This work adds to previous work on sexual disclosure by emphasizing how Latinas'/os' cultural values, their unique histories of migration, their age, and economic dependency shape the value they place on family and how they ultimately come to negotiate familial relationships. These social factors are intertwined in facilitating or hindering acceptance. This article provides an analysis of how Latinas' relationships with their families change, deteriorate, or improve as families struggle to accept their loved one's sexual choices and as sexually nonconforming Latinas come to accept themselves. To the previous work on sexual disclosure, I add an analysis of how first- and second-generation Latinas of different ages and class backgrounds who share similar values regarding the importance of family interact with family in their efforts to minimize rejection. By centering the experiences of women, this article allows for an analysis of the gendered differences in how sexually nonconforming individuals negotiate family and manage the self.

Methods

The data for this study consists of in-depth interviews and participant observations that were carried out between 2006 and 2008. There were forty formal interviews conducted in addition to numerous informal conversations that I engaged in at LGBTQ events as part of the participant-observation process. The interviews were conducted in Massachusetts, Connecticut, New York, and New Jersey, and the participant observation took place primarily in New York City. As of 2000, New York, New Jersey, and Massachusetts were among ten states with the largest Latin American immigrant populations. Massachusetts, Connecticut, New York, and New Jersey are also among the ten U.S. states with the largest Caribbean population (Migration Policy Institute n.d.). The high concentration of immigrants of Latin American or Caribbean descent in this region made it an appropriate area to conduct this research.

All formal interviewees self-identified as lesbian, bisexual, or queer Latinas, were at least eighteen years of age, and lived in the geographic northeast. Participants ranged in age from nineteen to fifty-four. Eighteen of the participants were first-generation Latinas, and twenty-two were second-generation Latinas. Two of the second-generation Latinas were women who were born in a Latin American or Caribbean country but immigrated to the United States as children. These women were included with the second-generation participants because their experiences were more typically of second-generation participants than of first-generation women. The study consisted of eleven Puerto Ricans, seven Dominicans, six Mexicans or Chicanas, six Peruvians, three Colombians, three Nicaraguans, two Cubans, one Guatemalan, and one Ecuadorian. Their class backgrounds varied greatly. The second-generation Latinas were predominantly raised working class although many are currently middle class due to achievements in higher education. In contrast, the first-generation Latinas were predominantly raised middle to upper class in their countries of origin. Half of these women suffered downward social mobility after migrating to the United States; the other half were mostly Puerto Rican migrants whose class level either elevated or remained the same after migration. The first-generation study participants who suffered downward social mobility did so because of their undocumented status, a lack of English fluency, or an inability to work in their studied professions. Thirty of the study participants identified as lesbian, three as queer, and seven as bisexual.

The interviews lasted approximately ninety minutes and were conducted in either English or Spanish based on the participants' preference. For the purpose of this article, all direct quotations used from those respondents who spoke Spanish during their interview have been translated into English. In some instances, words or phrases exist in the original Spanish in order to preserve the meaning of these words. In these instances, the English translations are provided alongside the original Spanish. Interviews were done in a place of the participant's choice, including their homes, cafes, their workplaces, and at LGBTQ community centers.

[...]

Analyses

When I asked the interviewees to tell me about their relationships with their families of origin, they often shared with me their struggles with their mothers. Consistent with previous findings, study participants' mothers were overwhelmingly the major enforcers of sexual morality and heterosexuality in their lives (Gonzalez-Lopez 2005). Study participants report having received more resistance and nonacceptance from their mothers than from any other member in their families. The participants report their mothers reacting to their disclosure with questions like "how could you do this to me?" or "I raised you better than that." The participants believe their mothers saw their sexual nonconformity as a reflection on their parenting and as an outcome to their failure to effectively teach normative sexuality. None of the forty study participants were disowned by family members for their sexual nonconformity. Families were often not accepting of Latinas' same-sex relationships and/or sexual orientations, but they did not rebuke these women entirely. Nonetheless, familial reactions caused guilt in the study participants and led them to engage in the invisible work of appeasing these relationships.

Erasing Nonconformity

The erasure strategy was commonly used by families as a way of rejecting their daughters without disowning them. Erasure of nonconformity predominantly occurred between very young study participants (women between the ages of nineteen and twenty-five) and those who were economically dependent on their families. The participants' young age and financial dependency made them most susceptible to the erasure strategy. Families engaging in the erasure strategy gain leverage against their loved ones because of their lack of autonomy as well as because of their respect for family values. The erasure strategy is premised on hypermanipulation and control, and families engaging in this strategy attempt to force their daughters out of dating other women. When Mariela was sixteen years old, someone caught her kissing her girlfriend Alisa. Her mother confronted her, and thereafter their relationship was greatly compromised. Her experience represents the kind of familial rejection that was common with the erasure strategy. Mariela is a second-generation Colombian. She described her situation in the following ways:

> So my mom approached me about it and said "oh what is this all about? How dare you? How could you do this to me? Haven't I taught you better? I told you she [Alisa] was a bad influence on you." My mom said this is going to end right now. She was in such a shock that all she did was yell and beat me up. But I tried to tell her this is something I chose to do. It's not because I felt influenced by anybody. But she didn't believe me. One of [the] things my mom didn't do is tell my dad. She would never tell him because she thinks he'd commit suicide if he ever found out. So she made me promise her that night that I would never tell him either.

Several years after this altercation with her mother, Mariela has kept her promise to not come out to her father. By saying that her father would commit suicide if he knew about her lesbianism, Mariela's mother is manipulating her daughter's emotions and heightening her control over her on the basis of the secret they share. Mariela's behaviors inside and outside the home are premised on the fact that she promised to keep her lesbian self a secret from her father. Latinas' subjugated position in patriarchal societies has compromised their ability to negotiate sexual nonconformity with family members. Their value on "*no faltar el respeto*" or to not be disrespectful makes them susceptible to hypercontrol as the women in their families enforce patriarchy. Mariela has tried to use college as an opportunity to become independent. However, when she decides not to move back home during the summer, her relationship with her parents worsens as they see her desire for independence as a rejection of their family values.

> When I finished the semester, my mother was very adamant about the fact that I had to move back home. And I told her that that was not what I wanted to do. She just flipped out. Ever since she found out that I'm a lesbian, it's just been a horrible experience being around her. Even though she knows that I am a lesbian, I can't live that lifestyle. My dad was also upset. He said, "how could you do this to us?" He said he lived with his parents up until the time that he got married as did my mom. Because that's what you're supposed to do. And I told him, "I'm sorry dad; I'm not trying to drop you guys, but I want to start living a more independent life."

There are multiple conflicts occurring between Mariela and her parents in this passage. On the one hand, her father feels that she is disregarding familial values by choosing not to live at home. Unbeknownst to him, Mariela's desire not to live at home is fueled by her need to establish her lesbian life away from parental control and disapproval. Mariela's mother, on the other hand, knows why her daughter does not want to move back home. She disapproves of Mariela's desire to stay at college because she associates this with her desire to form relationships with women. Insisting that she come home for the summer is about heightening her control over Mariela and erasing her lesbianism. This experience delineates the way that issues of sexuality can complicate an otherwise typical struggle between second-generation Latinas and their immigrant parents.

Families who used erasure strategies caused major insecurities for some of the study participants. The respondents often questioned their sexuality, their roles as daughters, and their commitment to family. Like most of the study participants, Alexis reported having a very close relationship with her mother. But when she shares with her mother that she is bisexual and in love with Sara, their relationship suffers tremendously. Alexis is a college student who was raised by a single mother with very limited means. She attends a very elite university of which her mother is extremely proud. Alexis is a second-generation Colombian who identifies as bisexual. She describes her experience as follows:

> We were very close not as mother and daughter but as friends. I regret having told her [about her relationship with Sara] without being so sure about myself because anything she told me would affect how I perceived myself. When I told her, she had a fit. She was like, "You're just in the wrong crowd. You're going against God." She said, "You're doing things that animals don't even do." I've never seen my mom in that element ever. It was a very nasty side of her. There was a time that we didn't talk at all. When she would talk to me, she would send me a Bible chapter.

Being rejected by the one person in the world whom she trusted and confided in most made Alexis lose her stable ground. She felt a very strong sense of loss not only because her mother did not accept her relationship but also because she felt as though she failed as a daughter. In an effort to sabotage her relationship with her partner Sara, Alexis started having sex with men.

> This is what made me question my sexuality and made me sleep with men and do all these crazy things to try and figure it out. I wanted to be super straight. I went a little crazy and I had sex with two men in the span of one week. Men that I hadn't really talked to. Men that I know saw me lustfully and not as a person. It was not a pleasant period. It made me feel used and weak and made me see how much sex can be used against me in these male contexts.

Alexis becomes very vulnerable after being so harshly rejected by her mother. This vulnerability results in her later engaging in self-destructive activities. She looks back on this dark period in her life with deep regret and embarrassment. Her actions when trying to be "super straight" have added to Alexis' feeling of failure as she is painfully aware that she let her mother down.

The study participants who engaged in erasure strategies with their parents overwhelmingly report feeling the burden of having to fulfill their parents' dreams. They bear the burden of accomplishing not only their goals but also the goals that their parents could not accomplish on account of a lack of opportunities. They overwhelmingly report taking pride in having always been "good girls" who excelled in school and carried their family's hopes and dreams proudly. Coming out to their families as women who love other women often means shattering the dreams their families had for them in order to pursue their own desires.

[...]

Families engaging in erasure strategies often defer to religion as a way of rationalizing their rejection. This was the case even for families that were not otherwise very religious. In some ways, for families that are uncomfortable with their daughters' choices, religion becomes a shield that protects them from the things that make them uneasy. Kayla, a second-generation Puerto Rican who identifies as a lesbian, met her first female partner while attending college. When Kayla told her mother that she was in a relationship with another woman, her mother immediately pointed her in the direction of the church. Kayla recounts this experience below.

> My mother said you need to go speak to a priest. The next day I went and found where the priest lives on campus. Father John answered the door. And I started crying right there in the doorway. He sits me down in this little area that they have right by the door and asks, "What's the matter?" And I said, "I just told my mom that I'm in a relationship with a woman. I told her that I'm gay." And then he said something that set me free. He said, "You know what, there's nothing wrong with giving your love to another human being, and that's all that you are doing." I asked specifically, "Am I going to be kicked out of the church?" He's like no, no. I said, "Can I tell my mom that?" He said "yes."

Kayla's parents sent her to see a priest because they wanted her to confess her "sin." She went to this church full of anxiety and half expecting to be rejected yet again. Instead, Father John gave her the ammunition she needed to take down her parents' protective shield. By telling her that she was still welcome in the church and that she was not committing a sin, Father John gave Kayla what she needed to confront her parents. In her eyes, they could no longer use religion as an excuse to not accept her.

Respondents whose families engaged in erasure strategies often had self-esteem issues. For these women more so than for any other Latinas in this study, erasure created insecurities, vulnerability, and sometimes internal self-hate. These women were more likely than those in any other group to be manipulated by family members because of their age and financial dependency. Furthermore, they were ill equipped to handle a world without familial support.

Silencing Strategies

Not all the study participants' families engaged in erasure strategies. Some participants engaged in silencing strategies with their families. Among the migrant Latinas, it was common for participants to never have had candid conversations with their parents about their sexual nonconformity. Nor have their parents ever confronted them about it. Rather, both the study participants and their families have taken to silencing this aspect of their lives altogether.

The study participants and their families have found protection in strategies of sexual silence. Sexual silence is a way for families to tacitly accept sexual nonconformity without ever directly acknowledging it. This strategy has also been referred to as "*un secreto a voz*" or an open secret (Zavella 1997). It allows individuals to meet the expectations of normalcy because no one acknowledges or verbalizes the transgressions. Study participants rationalize sexual silencing strategies as their way of remaining respectful of their families. These relationships resemble a tacit agreement in which the families do not meddle in their daughters' personal lives and in return the daughters conduct themselves respectfully and discreetly. Scholars have found that among Latino gay men and men who have sex with men (MSM), "*De eso no se habla*" is a tacit agreement that allows individuals to engage in same-sex behavior outside of the home and away from their families and in return their families turn a blind eye on these activities (Carillo 2002; Lumsden 1996). However, the dynamic taking place between these Latina women who love women and their kin is slightly different. This is not something that occurs away from the home but something that occurs in the home when no one is looking. The families do not pressure their daughters to have relationships with men, to get married, or to have children, and the daughters lead everyone to believe that their female lovers are just "*amigas*" or friends who sleep over on the weekends.

Angelica lived in her parents' home until she immigrated to the United States from the Dominican Republic in her thirties. She had several lovers while living with her parents. She describes the agreement in her home in the following ways.

> They always preferred to think that I was a very studious girl, than to see the reality, which was that I didn't have a boyfriend. That the few people that I brought home were women. What they have always seen in me is female friendships. And they have met my partners without knowing they are my partners. Because the ones that I've had stable relationships with have come to my house. They've met my parents and have established relationships with them. But I've never actually come out and said I'm gay. The partner that I have now, I've been with her for five years. When I lived in Santo Domingo and she lived here [in the United States], she would come on vacation and she would stay in my house. If [my family] didn't see it, it's because they didn't want to see it.

Here, Angelica describes the avoidance strategy she engages in with her family. The difference between this type of sexual silencing and *de eso no se habla* is that Angelica's parents always knew her partners. They developed relationships with these partners and welcomed them into their home as their daughter's "*amigas*" or friends. For them, then, sexual silence is not about keeping same-sex intimacy outside the home but about engaging in such relationships under the guise of platonic friendship.

[. . .]

The utility of sexual silencing strategies is that they allow families to avoid shame in their communities. So long as lesbian, bisexual, and queer Latinas do not openly display their sexual transgression, the families are allowed to save face with the community. For this reason, these families continuously ignore Latinas' intimacy with "amigas" and their lack of interest in men. Family members and study participants are complicit in maintaining sexual silence because it allows them to preserve their familial bond and deflect the tumultuous complications that can come with disclosure. Participants engaging in silencing strategies were fortified by the belief that their families did accept them even if only tacitly, which is something that Latinas engaging in erasure strategies or avoidance strategies did not get.

Even though participants and families engaging in silencing strategies never openly discuss same-sex relationships, participants pointed to subtle comments for validation from their families. These women believed that, although they never spoke of their female lovers, their families knew and accepted these relationships as long as they were discreet. For example, Eileen immigrated to New York City from Peru several years ago. She has no family in New York but speaks to everyone in Peru regularly. She is undocumented and works long hours at a factory in New Jersey. In her spare time, she enjoys a relationship with her lover Ana, whom she met after immigrating. She explained to me that she had introduced her partner to her mother over the phone as her "amiga." Eileen points to their veiled communication tactics as proof that her mother understands these women to be more than friends and that she is accepting of it. Here, Eileen describes the tacit acceptance she receives from her mother: "They like her a lot because she is always with me. And my mother always says she is grateful to her for being by my side. In other words, there are things that you understand that you don't just say to a friend. Those words are a little more profound, especially when it's your mother saying them." This example illustrates the complexity of veiled communication and sexual silence. Here, Eileen describes the implicit meaning in her mother's words. Since Eileen is in the United States alone and without any family, it is meaningful when her mother says that she is glad that Ana is by Eileen's side. Eileen interprets this as being her mother's way of showing acceptance without ever verbally acknowledging that they are lovers.

Sometimes silencing strategies were not just about pretending that participants' lovers were just amigas. In an effort to minimize rejection, sometimes participants took silencing strategies even further by pretending that they were in relationships with men. Some of the sexually nonconforming women who engaged in silencing strategies with their families pretend to have relationships with gay male friends in order to help keep up the ruse. Maritza is an immigrant from Peru. She lived at home with her parents up until she came to the United States. She attended college in Peru and had a professional job that she loved. In Peru, she had a close network of gay and lesbian friends with whom she shared her spare time. Maritza attempted to minimize familial rejection by pretending to date her gay friend:

> By the time I was twenty-four years old, we would pretend that I was their girlfriend and they were my boyfriends for their house and mine. [*Para tapar con la familia.*] To cover with the family. Over there [in Peru] this is very common. So they would always come to weddings and baptisms with me. And I would go to theirs. So, it appeared to my family at least that I had a lot of boyfriends.

This example emphasizes the range of how silencing strategies can be played out between LBQ Latinas and their families. It also emphasizes the extent to which study participants can themselves be complicit in preserving the sexual silence.

The Latinas who held this type of agreement with their families report not wanting to bring them shame. They internalized the importance of maintaining familial honor by being discreet about their transgressions. They were greatly concerned with how their parents would be treated in the community as well as by other family members if the sexual silence was broken. In the event that disclosure did happen, mothers tried to hide this information from other family members and friends. In these instances, however, families sometimes shift from maintaining sexual silence to the avoidance after disclosure strategy.

Avoidance After Disclosure

The third arrangement that study participants reported engaging in with their families is avoidance after disclosure. This strategy can occur when participants disclose or are forced to disclose their sexual nonconformity to families but later choose with their families to render the disclosure unheard altogether. With avoidance after disclosure, it is no longer okay for Latinas to bring *amigas* home. By verbalizing the sexual transgression, new guidelines must be established whereby what Latinas do must remain unknown or out of sight. This is because after verbalization, acceptance is no longer possible.

Study participants and their families can maintain seemingly ordinary relationships by not ever acknowledging their romantic dealings with women and pretending the disclosure never occurred. Diana is a young graduate student at a prestigious university. A second-generation Dominican, she was raised by a single mother in New York City. She lives on her college campus during the school year and comes home to her mother in the summer. When Diana's mother learned she was dating women, she panicked. She entered a state of denial and tried to find a therapist to "cure" her daughter. She convinced herself that her daughter's dealings with women were part of a phase. Since this time, Diana and her mother have found a way to maintain their relationship by never discussing her queer existence. Diana describes this avoidance strategy: "It was tense for a long time. She didn't know who I was. She didn't know who she was dealing with. But we're really, really close so we got back into the swing of things and kind of, you know, we didn't talk about it, didn't really mention it. We are pretending like nothing really exists when it comes to that [the disclosure of her queer identity]." Diana's arrangement with her mother allows her to maintain two separate lives. She has the life that she shares with her lovers and LGBTQ friends and another life that she shares with her family of origin. Because her relationship with her family is contingent upon everyone pretending the disclosure never happened, these two worlds do not coexist or overlap as they do with families utilizing the silencing strategies.

[. . .]

Like all the other strategies, avoidance after disclosure comes at a price. The erasure, silence, or avoidance of Latinas' lesbian, bisexual, or queer selves can often result in their isolation. These Latinas were often raised to keep their problems within the family and to only share their struggles with their parents and siblings and not with friends or psychologists. Given this, when family members render their same-sex relationships unheard or try to erase or silence them, Latinas can be left with no one to turn to in grappling with the difficulties of their same-sex relationships. Gloria always had a wonderful relationship with her mother. Her mother tried to maintain an open line of communication between them regarding sexual experiences and curiosity. However, in college Gloria developed a bisexual identity that her mother did not approve of. After disclosure to her mother, both women engaged in the avoidance after disclosure strategy. A second-generation Mexicana, Gloria recalls the rejection she felt by her mother's reaction and how much she struggled thereafter to maintain separate worlds:

> My mom had always told me don't ever bring your girlfriends home. I would respect that. So I started this relationship with this woman. It was a very ugly relationship. There was a lot of emotional abuse. There was a point when I had a bruise on one arm and one day, my mother said "I've been thinking about the kind of life that you're leading. And I've been thinking about the kind of relationships that you'll be in, and they can be very isolating. Be careful not to fall into an abusive relationship." And that

was a wake-up call for me. I thought, "Shit, my mom who never wants to talk about this called me out." Later, I told her, part of the reason why this relationship lasted this long is because I felt alone. I knew I couldn't talk to her about it. And I didn't know what to do.

Gloria's experience here speaks to the constant tension that mothers and daughters can feel regarding sexual nonconformity. Out of respect, Gloria does not discuss her romantic life with her mother even when she found herself in an abusive relationship and in need of guidance. Still, her mother senses that something is not right, and while she is incapable of verbally articulating her concern about her daughter's same-sex relationship, she provides her with guidance using veiled communication tactics. She does not directly say that she knows Gloria is in an abusive relationship with a woman, but she uses a subtle comment to help redirect her lost daughter. In this way, Gloria's mother reconciles her need to keep her daughter's female relationships unheard with her need to parent.

This experience speaks to how vulnerable these Latinas can be when their families are not fully accepting of their sexual nonconformity. It often leaves these women with no one to turn to in the event of physical or emotional abuse. This familial barrier can leave Latinas exposed as they try to navigate their way through their opposite and conflicting worlds. As women living in the borderlands, they are faced with the task of reconciling these opposing worlds. Their relationships are the byproducts of living in the borderlands and being stuck between the U.S. dominant culture and their own Latina cultures.

Despite the fact that family members try to erase, silence, or avoid an important part of their selves, these women have not given up on their kin. On the contrary, they have rationalized their family's hurtful reactions and healed their own wounds in their efforts to forgive their families. In many ways, they continue to subject themselves to familial abuse because they have such a strong sense that family is central to their happiness. As Luisa states here, "I give opportunities because I was raised that your family is the most important thing. And it wouldn't feel right for me to not have my family around. Even though they are the only ones that cause me pain." The study participants were not judgmental of their families for rejecting them, and they did not turn away from their families even when their families gave them reason to do so. Instead, they have found ways to remain hopeful that their families would eventually move toward acceptance.

Discussion and Conclusions

[...]

The strategies that study participants engaged in cannot be reduced to a narrative of remaining in the closet. One cannot simply look at the closet as something that you are either in or out of. These women negotiate very complex arrangements with their families and lovers. As Decena notes, the closet is a coproduction. The family is just as complicit as the individual in maintaining the strategies described in this article. Arguably, those who had never disclosed and used a silencing strategy were the most successful in combining their sexual lives with their family lives. Those who had engaged in verbal disclosures were less able to combine these two aspects of the self. Therefore, the Western notion of "coming out of the closet" did not really exist for these participants in the way that we presume it does for non-Latinos.

[...]

References

Carillo, Hector. 2002. *The Night Is Young: Sexuality in Mexico in the Time of AIDS*. Chicago, IL: University of Chicago Press.

Espin, Oliva. 1997. *Latina Realities: Essays on Healing, Migration, and Sexuality*. Boulder, CO: Westview.

Goffman, Erving. 1959. *The Presentation of Self in Everyday Life*. New York: Anchor.

Gonzalez-Lopez, Gloria. 2005. *Erotic Journeys: Mexican Immigrants and Their Sex Lives*. Berkeley, CA: University of California Press.

Hurtado, Aida. 2003. *Voicing Chicana Feminism: Young Women Speak Out on Sexuality and Identity*. New York: New York University Press.

Lumsden, Ian. 1996. *Machos, Maricones, and Gays: Cuba and Homosexuality*. Philadelphia, PA: Temple University Press.

Migration Policy Institute. n.d. Retrieved August 3, 2009 (www.migrationpolicy.org).

Zavella, Patricia. 1997. "Playing with Fire: The Gendered Construction of Chicana/Mexicana Sexuality." Pp. 392–410 in *The Gender/Sexuality Reader: Culture, History, Political Economy*, edited by R. Lancaster and M. di Leonardo. New York: Routledge.

Zavella, Patricia. 2003. "Talkin' Sex: Chicanas and Mexicans Theorize About Silences and Sexual Pleasures." Pp. 228–53 in *Chicana Feminisms: A Critical Reader*, edited by G. Arredondo, A. Hurtado, N. Klahn, O. Najera-Ramirez, and P. Zavella. Durham, NC: Duke University Press.

Gendered Power Relations Among Women

A Study of Household Decision Making in Black, Lesbian Stepfamilies

Mignon R. Moore

© iStockphoto.com/Christopher Futcher

The literature on gender and inequality in families commonly concludes that gender ideologies and men's greater earnings are the primary mechanisms through which families define power dynamics and maintain gender stratification (Coltrane 2000; Sorenson and McLanahan 1987; South and Spitze 1994). In the absence of sex differences between partners, however, is there a more equitable distribution of housework, paid work, and childcare? Or, might these couples use some other sorting mechanism to create hierarchies in

Mignon R. Moore. 2008. "Gendered Power Relations Among Women: A Study of Household Decision Making in Black, Lesbian Stepfamilies." *American Sociological Review* 73(2):335–56.

marriage-like relationships? Some research notes that, at least for women, the lack of sex distinctions between partners results in more egalitarian divisions of housework, paid work, and childcare (Patterson 1995; Sullivan 2004).

One limitation to these conclusions lies in the fact that much research centers on the experiences of white, college-educated lesbians who share an ideological commitment to a particular type of egalitarian relationship—an egalitarian relationship defined and encouraged by second-wave feminists of the 1970s women's movement. Studies of peer marriages (Schwartz 1994) and postgender heterosexual couples (Blaisure and Allen 1995; Risman and Johnson-Sumerford 1998) find that when both partners have a commitment to egalitarian distributions of household labor, they produce more equitable marriages. It stands to reason that lesbian couples who espouse this same commitment would similarly produce more equitable marriage-like unions. We do not know, however, whether the tendency toward more egalitarian relationships exists generally among lesbian couples. It may be that prior studies of family process in lesbian households have overrepresented couples who support feminist egalitarian principles.

Conclusions regarding egalitarianism in same-sex couples are further confounded given that the majority of children in lesbian families are from a mother's prior relationship (Morris, Balsam, and Rothblum 2002), making most lesbian households similar in structure to heterosexual stepfamilies. However, data in previous studies have tended to draw from couples who participate in the less common but more egalitarian activity of conceiving children together using alternative insemination methods (e.g., Gartrell et al., 2000, 2005; Patterson 1995). The timing of parenthood and other identity statuses, such as those organized around sexuality, can influence one's construction of motherhood. Women who bear children in heterosexual unions may experience particular gendered understandings of mothering that they then transfer to lesbian relationships. This plausibly has consequences for expectations of household organization and divisions of labor.

In this article, I use a gender relations perspective to frame how lesbian partners produce gendered interactions within a family. Prior work has used this perspective to frame how men and women derive gendered meanings from the performance of household labor (Ferree 1990; Tichenor 2005). Lesbian couples are hardly exempt from the processes that construct gendered selves. A gender relations perspective prods the researcher to delineate how the very creation of and participation in what one defines as "family" encourages preestablished gendered interactions—even in same-sex unions. I take a more critical look at the relationship between non-economic resources and the distribution of authority in families. As the analyses reveal, addressing how the division of household labor, paid work, money management, and childrearing are negotiated among same-sex couples who have developed a lesbian sexuality outside of the feminist egalitarian framework informs sociological understandings of gender construction. It also sheds new theoretical and substantive light on broader issues of gender interaction, power, and hierarchy within familial relationships.

[. . .]

Data Collection and Methods

. . . A Sample of Black Lesbian Families

[. . .]

The larger sample from which I drew the data for this study consists of 100 women who completed and returned a survey about their experiences forming families with other women.

In these households, at least one partner is black, but usually both are. I focus in this article largely on the 32 respondents living in stepfamilies, meaning one partner brought her child or children into a cohabiting relationship with another woman. For data on these households, I draw from the survey responses and approximately 30 months of participant-observation field notes for all 32 women, and in-depth interviews with 22 of them. I also rely on data from a focus group on household decision making. Seven of the ten focus group participants were also part of the stepfamily subsample. As a secondary, comparative analysis to the stepfamily data, I draw on field notes and interview data from eight respondents (four couples) who had at least one child together using alternative insemination methods, as well as 34 respondents who were partnered with no children living in the home.

[. . .]

I conducted four different focus groups on household decision making among couples with children, meanings of gender presentation in lesbian relationships, participation in black gay community life, and religion. The in-depth interviews targeted a sample of respondents who also participated in the survey (about 70 percent of the stepfamily respondents in the survey are also part of the interview sample). The interviews provide detailed information about respondents' childhood experiences with sexuality, forms of gender expression, parenting experiences, how they organize family finances, their experiences in ethnic/racial communities, and how they see their future lives as gay people. These interviews lasted from 45 minutes to two hours. A team of black, female researchers, including myself and four graduate assistants, interviewed partners separately, usually in respondents' homes or my home. We gathered data over approximately three years and followed a nested strategy that began with participant-observation field notes.

[. . .]

Analysis

The analyses highlight three main points. First, they show the importance of economic independence, rather than the egalitarian distribution of household labor, in black lesbian households. Second, they reveal the importance of the status of "mother" in creating hierarchies in lesbian stepfamilies. Third, the analyses and results help delineate how gendered presentations of self in black lesbian relationships are associated with the types of household tasks that partners perform.

Egalitarian Ideologies and Practices in Black Lesbian Stepfamilies

Feminist egalitarian ideologies center on two aspects of family life: women's economic independence and the equal distribution of housework and childcare. These data provide multiple ways to assess the extent and importance of both of these arenas in black lesbian relationships, including the women's experiences with pooling household income and their attitudes toward, and actual distribution of, household labor. Together, the survey, interview, focus group, and observational data suggest that, relative to white women in the literature, black women's relationships contain a stronger emphasis on enactment of economic independence and a weaker practice of feminist egalitarian ideologies vis-à-vis the division of household chores.

Do partners expect to jointly contribute to household finances, an expectation consistent with the literature on lesbian families? The survey data show that both partners in almost all stepfamilies are employed: 30 of the 32 respondents living in stepfamilies are in the labor force and 29 work or attend school full-time. Although all of the respondents report sharing responsibility for household bills, the survey finds that less than half of them (14 women) actually share a bank account. This suggests that partners value self-sufficiency and autonomy. Control over individual finances, particularly for biological mothers, allows both partners to claim a co-provider role even if their incomes are not equal. It also provides an easier way to exit a relationship in case of dissolution.

Consider the experience of Marilyn Richards, president of a national nonprofit organization. When asked whether partners should pool all of their assets in a relationship, she emphatically disagreed:

> We have our own money, our own accounts, and we have household funds that we use to do the lawn, the snow removal. . . . We met as fully-formed adults with other obligations in our lives. I think that we should pool the assets that we want to do together, like a home, a car, which we do, a savings together for things. She is my beneficiary along with my son and I am hers along with her children, so that is pooling out in the afterlife, so to speak. But she doesn't ask me how I spend my money and I don't ask her how she spends hers. She has a job and a very responsible one, and we have our own discretionary income.

This notion of pooling some funds for common goals, but mainly maintaining separate finances, was common throughout the respondents. The survey data show that the women have a strong interest in preserving financial independence, particularly biological mothers. This is true even for women who contribute fewer financial assets than their partners and thus would receive greater economic benefits in combining funds. Relative to their partners, biological mothers are less likely to agree with the statement: "The two mates should pool all their property and financial assets." Responses in the in-depth interviews suggest that this hesitancy stems from the history of relationship transitions they have navigated while raising their children. All of them bore children in past heterosexual relationships, and all spent time as single mothers and sole economic providers for their children prior to cohabiting in a same-sex union. These past experiences influence how they create lesbian stepfamilies and organize household finances.

[. . .]

The emphasis on economic independence is symbolically important because the provider role is more than just the position of breadwinner. It has a strong ideological component of unchallenged authority and is often linked with the male gender, though black heterosexual women have historically been more likely than white women to share the provider role with their partners (Jones 1985; Kessler-Harris 2003). Lesbians raised in black families often have a model of co-provision and an expectation that both partners will contribute financially to the household.

The second component of feminist egalitarian ideologies of the family emphasizes an equal division of household labor. To measure ideological commitment to this philosophy, the survey asked respondents the extent to which they agreed with the statement: "Both mates in a relationship should divide evenly the household tasks (washing dishes, preparing meals, doing laundry, etc.)." Four possible answer choices ranged from strongly agree to strongly disagree. The survey also asked each respondent how often she is responsible for 13 different household chores, relative to her partner, and how many hours per week she and her partner each spend on household chores. Questions in the face-to-face interviews asked respondents how they divide housework

Table 30.1   Division of Labor in Lesbian Stepfamilies (N = 32)

"Certain household tasks are necessary to keep things running smoothly. Who does each of these tasks more often?"

Household Chores	We Do This Equally (percent)	Biological Mother Does This More (percent)	Partner Does This More (percent)
Washes dishes	32	48	20
Does laundry	36	52	13
Cleans bathroom	16	64	16
Cleans floors	6	73	21
Arranges daily meals	23	39	32
Straightens living/family room	16	67	15
Dusts furniture	16	75	8
Shops for groceries	34	24	42
Mixes drinks for company	30	52	18
Takes out trash	25	18	56
Repairs things around house	14	48	37
Cares for pets	20	32	48
Performs yard work	18	32	54

and finances and how satisfied they are with their current arrangements. I supplemented these data with field notes from observations in respondents' homes during birthday celebrations, dinner parties, and other family activities. Data from all of these sources clearly show specialization. Biological mothers perform more of the household organizing tasks and assume more responsibility for making sure chores and activities are implemented smoothly.

[...]

The respondents appear to support egalitarian ideologies regarding the distribution of household labor that are consistent with what research on other lesbian populations has found. In the survey, 27 of the 32 women agreed or strongly agreed with the statement, "Both mates in a relationship should divide evenly the household tasks (washing dishes, preparing meals, doing laundry, etc.)." Yet, while their ideologies are consistent with an equal distribution of labor, they do not actually behave in egalitarian ways. The data suggest that biological mothers have the greater responsibility for completing family chores. Table 30.1 summarizes the responses to the survey question measuring task performance in stepfamilies.

Biological mothers in lesbian stepfamilies tend to perform the time-consuming and stereotypically female household tasks more often than their partners. For example, in 32 percent of the surveys, the respondents report spending equal amounts of time washing dishes. In nearly half of the surveys, however, biological mothers spend more time on this task, and only 20 percent of biological mothers' partners report spending more time washing dishes. In separate surveys, when asked how much time each person spends on household chores, respondents mostly agreed that the biological mother spends much more time on chores relative to her partner. Biological mothers report they spend an average of 11.4 hours per week on household chores, and say their partners spend an average of 5.2 hours per week. The partners say that on average they spend 4.4 hours each week on chores and biological mothers devote about 12.1 hours per week. Interestingly, research on two-earner heterosexual couples shows that husbands tend to undercount the amount of time their wives spend on housework (Ferree 1991). That partners in this study perceive the biological mothers as spending more time on housework than biological mothers report may suggest a greater acknowledgment or respect for stereotypically female household work.

Biological mothers often complain about the imbalance in household work and criticize how their partners complete tasks—tasks they have usually assigned to their partners. For example, Dana Russell's statements are typical of many of the biological mothers:

> Am I happy with it? She don't do nothing! [laughs] But it wasn't an issue. She'll do the laundry or she'll go to the grocery store or take me, which is important, because I can't carry things because I hurt my back. We've always done the laundry together, pretty much. We've always done the food shopping together. Anything around the house, I've got to kind of bitch to get her to do stuff.

Dana, a postal worker and the biological mother of 16-year-old Marina, acknowledged that her partner, police officer Angie Russell, performs less housework. Her comments suggest this is both a problem ("I've got to kind of bitch to get her to do stuff") and something she accepts about the relationship ("She don't do nothing! [laughs] But it wasn't an issue"). This contradiction appears repeatedly in the interview data and observational notes. Biological mothers express frustration about the unequal amounts of time that their partners allot to household chores. A certain acceptance often accompanies this frustration, however, which biological mothers usually follow with a modest boasting of their superior cleaning and organizational skills—a superiority that gives them the final say over the way they run their households.

[. . .]

These findings reflect Tichenor's (2005) work on status reversal couples, as well as Hochschild's (1989) work in *The Second Shift*. Biological mothers devote more time to housework than do their partners, and they assume greater responsibilities in organizing housework and other family tasks, despite both partners' full-time employment. What is the meaning behind this division of labor and how do one person's greater chore responsibilities relate to their labor in other areas of family life? In answering this question, I find that biological mothers accept the greater responsibility for various aspects of household organization not because they like washing dishes or cleaning the living room, but because having control over those areas gives them a stronger say, and sometimes the deciding voice, in other aspects of family life, particularly money management and childrearing.

Money Management, Childrearing Conflicts, and the Strength of the Household Organizer Position

Pahl's (1983) work on the allocation of money shows three distinct points in household finances: control, management, and budgeting of money. At the point where money first enters a family, I find that both partners in lesbian stepfamilies negotiate the money's allocation. This includes how much money they spend on bills and how much of each partner's income will go toward paying bills. Biological mothers, though, usually take the lead in managing these funds. They make sure to pay the bills, and they decide the details of how money will be allotted to each expenditure (e.g., how much to spend on groceries, fuel for the car, or credit card debt).

The biological mother is also usually in charge of budgeting, which includes the more time consuming work of deciding which foods to buy, whether children need sneakers or dress shoes, or whether the family should have premium or standard cable TV.

[. . .]

Consider the Adams family. Anita and Trina Adams share a small two-bedroom apartment in Harlem with Anita's two daughters. Anita did not finish college, while Trina is a college graduate and earns about $12,000 more per year than Anita. They pool their money for household expenses, but Anita writes the checks and makes sure the bills are paid. Anita usually uses her own money to support her daughters. From time to time, she diverts household money to school clothes or holiday gifts, instructing Trina to assume more financial responsibility for the monthly bills. Anita is more likely to factor the children's needs into the family's financial decisions, and she is much more outwardly concerned with how the distribution of finances affects the girls.

When I asked Trina how they divide household chores, she said, "Well, I do the laundry. I cook, I clean up, but it's like I'm very sporadic. Anita will kick my boots or something, or she'll go [makes a sound like she's clearing her throat], and she'll look at the living room and I'll start cleaning it. But she definitely does the chores way more than I do." On separate surveys, both Anita and Trina report that Anita performs more of the daily household tasks, like washing dishes and straightening the rooms, while Trina participates more equally in the less frequent tasks, like grocery shopping and laundry. They both report that Anita spends twice as much time per week on household chores. Looking at the survey data alone might lead one to assume that Trina has more authority in the relationship: She has more education and a higher salary than Anita, fewer family responsibilities, and gets away with doing less housework. Because Anita was a single mother prior to meeting Trina, we might think of her as bringing more baggage into the relationship. The qualitative data, however, reveal a more multidimensional portrait of this family and suggest that the decisions Anita makes actually carry more weight in this union.

Trina moved into Anita's already established household. In this sense, Trina is the "new addition" and must adapt to a structure in which Anita is the leader and organizer. Anita is the money manager and enjoys having this type of authority in the family. In her interview, Anita proudly told me that, "I'm the bill keeper. She [Trina] gives the finances, I stay on the bills. I'm like 'Look, this is due.' And it works out pretty good. We have [a] good little system going on with the bills." Although Anita may want Trina to do more work around the house, she does not want Trina to assume more control over the money or childrearing decisions. Because Anita primarily decides the family expenditures, her decisions play a significant role in how much disposable money Trina has for her own leisure activities. Anita has a full-time job and her family made ends meet before she met Trina. Thus, although Trina is an important co-provider (her income enabled the family to purchase a house approximately eight months after our interview), the knowledge that Anita and her family can survive without her tempers the extent to which Trina's economic contributions influence Anita's decisions.

[. . .]

Unlike in married heterosexual households, where husbands delegate family decision making to their wives, biological mothers in lesbian relationships *want* to take control of this activity—their partners do not assign it to them. The position is seen as important because it directly involves the needs and considerations of the children and biological mothers have a greater motivation to make sure the children are properly cared for. Although doing more housework is not evidence of greater authority or status in a home, for lesbian stepfamilies the returns include a greater say over decisions in other areas of family life.

Motherhood Identity and Gender Construction

[. . .]

In lesbian stepfamilies, one partner has a more clearly defined identity as the mother and primary caregiver. This status also facilitates the performance of a particular gendered identity in her relations with her partner. Controlling certain tasks in the home thus serves as a way to enact social expectations about motherhood, especially when those tasks relate to the children's well-being. In an environment where one's identity as a mother becomes less salient to others since both partners are female, some women may feel compelled to show, both to others and to themselves, that they are good mothers and homemakers in ways that reflect "gendered norms of accountability" (Erickson 2005). Essentialist views of bio-legal motherhood might be particularly salient for women who entered motherhood in a heterosexual context, or who did not initially share parenting responsibilities with a female partner. If a good mother has the greater responsibility for childcare and housework, then performing these duties is paramount to how women construct a gendered sense of self, even women with same-sex desire.

Biological mothers' partners often want more say over childrearing and expect to have some parenting authority as partners, as women, and as adults living in the household. Even when a couple decides at the outset what a partner's responsibility to the children will be (i.e., whether a partner will fulfill a parenting role or merely act as an adult friend to the children), biological mothers always have the option to override these arrangements. . . .

Biological mothers' opinions also carry more weight in lesbian relationships because of the way they form their families. Two-thirds of the stepfamilies in this study share a similar pattern of union formation: the biological mother's partner moved into an existing single-parent household that the biological mother had established. The biological mothers thus often continue parenting and running the households as though they are single mothers; they decide when and how much authority to give to the new cohabiting partner. This kind of union formation makes a partner's place in a family hierarchy less clear, and the uncertainty surrounding her position gives her an initial lower status compared to the biological mother.

In the case of Anita and Trina, Trina does not have an identity as a mother. Yet, as Anita's adult partner, she expects to have a greater say in parenting matters, which Anita will not grant her. Trina said:

> I look at it like [this]: I'm your significant other and I'm not going anywhere and I'm going to be here until you die. Now I have some say because I'm here, you know I pay bills, I help with everything, I'm a mentor to her, to her daughter. . . . Don't get offended if I say something, it is out of care and concern.

In a recent dispute between Trina and Kiyana, Anita's oldest daughter, they called on Anita to decide who was right and who was wrong. Anita did not come down firmly on either person's side and this caused a heated argument with Trina, who believed Anita should have supported her because she is the adult. Anita said she will take Kiyana aside and tell her what she did right and what she did wrong. According to Anita, Trina would rather that Anita "start yelling and screaming in front of Kiyana," but Anita said she cannot do that. She believes that a good mother should "defend her child," and she has a difficult time doing this while simultaneously letting the child know when she is behaving inappropriately. Moreover, as the biological mother, Anita has the decisive authority to determine who is right and wrong in conflicts between her partner and her teenage daughter. Referring to how she settled that dispute, Anita said:

Even if Trina is rebellious and she don't want to hear it, it'll come to a head where she'll say "O.K., now I understand what you're saying." And the same thing with Kiyana. She rebels, after awhile she will see, and it will come to a head.

The language Anita uses ("Trina is rebellious") suggests that she views both her partner and her daughter on the same lower status relative to herself.

[. . .]

Given what we know about family relationships in remarried households, it is not unusual for biological mothers in stepfamilies to have more say in childrearing decisions, nor is it odd when their partners have more distant relationships with the children. Stepparents in heterosexual unions also tend to have less close relationships with their partners' children and may disagree with the biological parents about the best way to parent the children. Stepfathers, however, often bring greater financial resources to a family, which can compensate for a lack of parenting authority. In contrast, lesbian partners do not gain any gender advantage over their partners in the labor market, and thus it is unlikely that they can compensate for their secondary parenting role through greater economic contributions to the household.

Other Family Processes

[. . .]

Do the data from the larger study show any consistencies in union formation and the gender display of partners? In the full survey sample, 74 respondents report an attraction for and tendency to partner with someone who has a physical representation of gender that is different from their own. More specifically, respondents who enact a feminine presentation of gender tend to partner with women who are less feminine in their gender display (Moore 2006). In the

Table 30.2 Division of Labor in Lesbian Couples Without Children (N = 34)

"Certain household tasks are necessary to keep things running smoothly. Who does each of these tasks more often?"

Household Chores	We Do This Equally (percent)	More Feminine Partner Does This More (percent)	Less Feminine Partner Does This More (percent)
Washes dishes	33	38	30
Does laundry	26	33	52
Cleans bathroom	19	35	46
Cleans floors	26	32	42
Arranges daily meals	30	42	27
Straightens living/family room	31	32	36
Dusts furniture	27	40	33
Shops for groceries	59	15	23
Mixes drinks for company	27	40	32
Takes out trash	27	24	48
Repairs things around house	12	36	52
Cares for pets	36	31	32
Performs yard work	0	27	56

stepfamilies, as well as the alternative insemination households, biological mothers tend to have a more feminine gender display relative to their partners.

[. . .]

Among cohabiting couples with no children in the household, the data suggest a relationship between gender presentation and contribution to household chores. Women with a self-defined feminine gender presentation report spending an average of 5.2 hours per week on chores; they report that their partners spend an average of 3.7 hours. In contrast, women with a less feminine gender presentation than their mates report spending a similar amount of time on chores as their partners, an average of 5.9 hours and 5.7 hours per week, respectively. When asked how often they perform certain household tasks, about one-third of the respondents reported spending similar amounts of time as their partners on many chores, including washing dishes, arranging daily meals, and straightening the living room. When these tasks are not equally shared, I did not find any consistent relationship between gender presentation and many of the housework tasks that partners perform. I did find, however, that the less feminine partner was more likely to perform stereotypically male tasks like taking out the trash, making household repairs, and performing yard work. Table 30.2 shows these patterns.

Conclusion

[. . .]

The findings I report suggest that institutional characteristics of the family are quite steeped in traditional gendered relations. Indeed, participating in a "family" results in scripts of actions that, more often than not, carry established gendered meanings. Despite being in a same-sex union, gender continues to profoundly influence the construction of family life. Previously used to explain why individuals in heterosexual relationships find gendered meanings in the performance of household tasks, the gender relations perspective can also account for biological mothers' greater involvement in housework and childcare within lesbian stepfamilies. Although working outside the home is now considered a less gendered activity than in the past, the organization of work within the home remains a process through which individuals construct gendered meanings and identities.

[. . .]

My analyses reveal that without the gender structure of explicit male privilege or the material advantage of high income, lesbian families associate control over some forms of household labor with greater relationship power. Biological mothers want more control over the household because such authority affects the well-being of children—children who biological mothers see as primarily theirs and not their partners. They use the "doing" of housework and authority over childrearing as a tradeoff for control over household finances and organization. This has implications for how we think about the creation of hierarchies and the enactment of power in lesbian couples, of course, but arguably heterosexual couples as well. Heterosexual married women may try to invoke this strategy, but they are mostly defeated by the ideological power of male privilege or male comparative income advantage. Nevertheless, they may garner some vestige of power from the control over household labor, even if their male partners' other kinds of power offset that authority. . . .

This study shows . . . the value of an alternative kind of authority among women—the ability to have the final say over decisions in domestic life. More generally, this work suggests the existence of power differentials—power differentials not centered around income but around other expectations and identities—that are revealed in processes of family formation and interaction.

[. . .]

References

Blaisure, Karen R. and Katherine R. Allen. 1995. "Feminists and the Ideology and Practice of Marital Equality." *Journal of Marriage and the Family* 57(1):5–19.

Coltrane, Scott. 2000. "Research on Household Labor: Modeling and Measuring the Social Embeddedness of Routine Family Work." *Journal of Marriage and the Family* 62(4):1208–33.

Erickson, Rebecca. 2005. "Why Emotion Work Matters: Sex, Gender, and the Division of Household Labor." *Journal of Marriage and the Family* 67(2):337–51.

Ferree, Myra Marx. 1990. "Beyond Separate Spheres: Feminism and Family Research." *Journal of Marriage and the Family* 52(4):866–84.

Ferree, Myra Marx. 1991. "The Gender Division of Labor in Two-Earner Marriages." *Journal of Family Issues* 12(2):158–80.

Gartrell, Nanette, Amy Banks, Nancy Reed, Jean Hamilton, Carla Rodas, and Amalia Deck. 2000. "The National Lesbian Family Study: 3. Interviews with Mothers of Five-Year-Olds." *American Journal of Orthopsychiatry* 70(4):542–48.

Gartrell, Nanette, Amalia Deck, Carla Rodas, and Heidi Peyser. 2005. "The National Lesbian Family Study: 4. Interviews with the 10-Year-Old Children." *American Journal of Orthopsychiatry* 75(4):518–24.

Hochschild, Arlie Russel. 1989. *The Second Shift: Working Parents and the Revolution at Home.* New York: Viking.

Jones, Jacqueline. 1985. *Labor of Love, Labor of Sorrow: Black Women, Work, and the Family, From Slavery to the Present.* New York: Basic Books.

Kessler-Harris, Alice. 2003. *Out to Work: A History of Wage-Earning Women in the United States.* New York: Oxford University Press.

Moore, Mignon R. 2006. "Lipstick or Timberlands? Meanings of Gender Presentation in Black Lesbian Communities." *Signs: Journal of Women in Culture and Society* 32(1):113–39.

Morris, Jessica F., Kimberly F. Balsam, and Esther D. Rothblum. 2002. "Lesbian and Bisexual Mothers and Nonmothers: Demographics and the Coming-Out Process." *Journal of Family Psychology* 16(2):144–56.

Pahl, Jan. 1983. "The Allocation of Money and the Structuring of Inequality Within Marriage." *The Sociological Review* 31(2):237–62.

Patterson, Charolette. 1995. "Families of the Lesbian Baby Boom: Parents' Division of Labor and Children's Adjustment." *Developmental Psychology* 31(1):115–23.

Risman, Barbara J. and Danette Johnson-Sumerford. 1998. "Doing It Fairly: A Study of Feminist Marriages." *Journal of Marriage and the Family* 60:23–40.

Schwartz, Pepper. 1994. *Peer Marriage: How Love Between Equals Really Works.* New York: Free Press.

Sorenson, Annemette and Sara McLanahan. 1987. "Married Women's Economic Dependency: 1940–1980." *American Journal of Sociology* 93(3):957–87.

South, Scott J. and Glenna Spitze. 1994. "Housework in Marital and Nonmarital Households." *American Sociological Review* 59(3):327–47.

Sullivan, Maureen. 2004. *The Family of Woman: Lesbian Mothers, Their Children, and the Undoing of Gender.* Berkeley, CA: University of California Press.

Tichenor, Veronica Jaris. 2005. *Earning More and Getting Less: Why Successful Wives Can't Buy Equality.* New Brunswick, NJ: Rutgers University Press.

Normative Resistance and Inventive Pragmatism

Negotiating Structure and Agency in Transgender Families

Carla A. Pfeffer

© iStockphoto.com/RobertDodge

This empirical work begins by seriously considering (and considering serious) transgender families—something long overdue in sociology. Where do these families *fit* in our existing classificatory systems? What makes a particular couple "same-sex" or "opposite-sex"? Is it the genetic blueprint or karyotype of each partner relative to the other? Unlikely, since most of us will live our entire lives never truly knowing our genetic karyotype,

Carla A. Pfeffer. 2012. "Normative Resistance and Inventive Pragmatism: Negotiating Structure and Agency in Transgender Families." *Gender & Society* 26(4):574–602.

let alone that/those of our partner(s). Is it the relative levels of sex hormones in each partner's body? Hormone replacement and supplemental therapies allow us to control these presumably natural variations—which we now know exhibit greater statistical variation *within* sex categories than *across* them (Fausto-Sterling 2000). Then it must be the genitals, reproductive organs, and secondary sex characteristics of each partner, correct? Yet modern medicine increasingly allows us to alter and (re)construct these somatic features in dizzyingly variable amalgamations (Meyerowitz 2002). Furthermore, most of us go through our everyday lives only *presuming* what lies beneath the clothes and skin of the majority of social others (Garfinkel 1967)—"cultural genitals," as they have been termed (Kessler and McKenna 1978). Then it must be the legal status of each partner—whether there is an "M" or an "F" on their birth certificate, passport, and/or driver's license. Wrong again. In the United States, federal policies on the designation of sex status on legal documents, and state policies on whether or not birth certificates and other legal documents may or may not reflect a literal "sex change," are often inconsistent, as are policies indicating *which* hormonal and/or surgical procedures provide necessary grounds for requesting that such changes be made (Currah, Juang, and Minter 2006; Kirkland 2006).

While these ambiguities and inconsistencies may be perplexing, they also open up possibilities for remarkable social transformation and new family forms that require more focused empirical and theoretical inquiry (Valocchi 2005). For instance, the medical, legal, and social realities of some transgender and transsexual (henceforth "trans") peoples' lives, in this historical moment, may make it possible for one to choose to enter into either a "same-sex/gay" or "opposite-sex/heterosexual" legally recognized marriage or civil union with *the very same partner* in some localities (Robson 2006). Given the complexity of social identity in the context of trans lives and partnerships, it makes sense to further consider the ways in which these identities are both relationally formed and embedded within social contexts, systems, structures, and institutions. As Seidman (1994, 173) writes: "Decisions about identity categories [are] pragmatic, related to concerns of situational advantage, political gain, and conceptual utility."

Furthermore, we might also consider the structural barriers that individuals and couples face as they forge family unions and partnerships that may at first glance seem culturally or legally unintelligible (with multiple overlapping and conflicting gender markers and designations) yet might nevertheless appear quotidian or even normative in everyday social practice. In this article, I draw on empirical data from research with cisgender (henceforth "cis") women partners of transgender and transsexual men to propose two analytic constructs—"normative resistance" and "inventive pragmatism"—for more richly conceptualizing relational processes between agency and structure in the everyday lives of those within trans families.

Toward Theorizing Trans Families

A body of theoretical and empirical sociological scholarship focusing exclusively on trans families does not yet exist. Yet trans individuals and their partners present perplexing sociolegal dilemmas when it comes to conceptualizing and operationalizing the very types or forms of relationships in which they engage. Researchers may be unsure how to classify these research subjects using existing typologies. Are these partnerships gay, lesbian, bisexual, heterosexual, queer, or something entirely new and yet unnamed within the sex/gender/sexuality system (Schilt and Westbrook 2009; Seidman 1995)? Are relationships between trans people and their partners socially assimilationist and normative or counternormative? How might the particular choices or expressions of "agency" made by members of trans families, as embedded within existing social systems, institutions, and structures, trouble existing notions of normativity in ways that may be simultaneously pragmatic, socially destabilizing/transformative, and reinforcing of the status quo? How might choosing to "pass" as unremarkably heterosexual hold both pragmatic and limiting potentials for these couples in terms of mediating social identity group membership and accessing valuable social institutions and resources?

[. . .]

Key to this project is an exploration of normativity in the context of "the family." Normativity has been described as a "charmed circle" within which social privilege, opportunity, and freedom from stigma are conferred to those conforming to particular social rules and regulations (Rubin 1984). Some of these rules and regulations dictate that opposite-sex, normatively gendered individuals monogamously pair (Jackson 2006; Kitzinger 2005). This regulatory social force has been termed "heteronormativity" (Warner 1991), described as "the view that institutionalized heterosexuality constitutes the standard for legitimate and prescriptive sociosexual arrangements" (Ingraham 1994, 204). Heteronormativity has also been cast as "shorthand for the numerous ways in which heterosexual privilege is woven into the fabric of social life, pervasively and insidiously ordering everyday existence" as a key component of social structure (Jackson 2006, 108). Under such social privilege, relational configurations and family forms falling outside of compulsory heteronormative parameters are often rendered invisible (Rich 1980). Kitzinger outlines interactional and institutional processes through which family forms and members that diverge from heteronormative parameters are rendered deviant, thereby instantiating "the family" as a social "categorization device" (2005, 480). As such, heteronormativity exists as a powerful structuring force in our lives and is reflected through numerous social structures and institutions such as marriage, monogamy, and parenting.

Importantly, scholars note that those forming same-sex pairings may also follow proscriptively normative behavioral patterns and support normative social institutions, movements, and structures, described as "homonormativity" (Duggan 2002) or the cultural "normalization" of gay identities (Seidman 2001). These patterns are further evident in contemporary mainstream gay and lesbian politics and social movements, which focus on such "respectably queer" (Ward 2008) topics as legalization of same-sex marriage and same-sex second-parent adoption and elimination of policies excluding "out" gay men and lesbians from military service. Johnson (2002) explores how normativity structures contemporary citizenship, socially compelling gay and lesbian individuals to "pass" as conventional in order to access sociocultural and material benefits. Of critical import to the present study, both heteronormativity and homonormativity are concepts depending on the actual and/or perceived identities (gender and sexual) of social actors in relation to one another (Jackson 2006).

[. . .]

I . . . propose the analytic constructs of "normative resistance" (conscious and active strategies and actions for making life choices *distinct* from those considered most socially expected, celebrated, and sanctioned) and "inventive pragmatism" (active strategies and actions that might be considered clever manipulation of an existing social structure in order to access social and material resources on behalf of oneself or one's family) to articulate processes by which cis women partners of trans men negotiate agency and structure. This study outlines strategies members of one type of trans family deploy as they negotiate social structures and institutions in their everyday lives, to consider how these acts of resisting and accessing regulated social resources carry the potential for social transformation that extends beyond these families or their members alone.

Method

Research participants were recruited using Internet-facilitated social network purposive sampling (Patton 1990) to target the significant others, friends, families, and allies of trans men. Eligible participants included current and former partners of trans men whose relationship(s) were at least three months in reported duration. . . . I conducted audio-recorded, face-to-face interviews with 11 participants and telephone interviews with the rest, lasting from 47 to 150 minutes, averaging just over 100 minutes.

[. . .]

In sum, I interviewed 50 cis women partners of trans men who resided across thirteen states in the United States, three Canadian provinces, and one territory in Australia. . . . Study participants largely self-identified as white (90 percent) and ranged in age from 18 to 51 years, averaging 29 years of age. While most participants were white, nearly 30 percent of cis women reported being in an interracial relationship and only 75 percent of their partners were white. Participants and their trans partners were highly educated, yet reported disproportionately low household incomes for those choosing to report this information. Study participants (52 percent) most often self-identified as "queer" when asked to describe their sexual orientation, and this was the label most often used to describe a trans partner's sexual orientation as well.

. . . More than 80 percent were reporting on a current relationship, and relationship duration ranged from 3 months to more than a decade, with an average of just over 2 years. The majority of relationships involved cohabitation, with partners living together, on average, for about 1.5 years at the point of the interview. About 10 percent of participants were legally married to their trans partner and about 12 percent reported experiences with parenting (while only 4 percent were actively raising children with their trans partner in their home). Participants were in relationships with trans men who were at various stages of sex and gender transition, with most at just over two years into the process. Nearly all of the trans partners were either taking testosterone or planning to do so and had had or planned to have "top surgery," while a minority had had or planned to have "bottom surgery." Study participants reported most often that their trans partner(s) were perceived as male in social situations either "always" or "almost always."

Findings

The following sections outline dimensions of the two major strategic processes that emerged in analyses with regard to cis women's negotiations of agency and structure. I term these strategic processes "normative resistance" and "inventive pragmatism." While the conceptual chart in Figure 31.1 outlines these two strategic processes and their constitutive components, my intention is not to generate a pure typology. Indeed, many cis women in my sample employed strategies of both normative resistance and inventive pragmatism—visually represented in the overlap between the two spheres as trans family negotiations of structure and agency.

In this section, I introduce the concept of "normative resistance" as a set of strategies cis women partners of trans men employed to negotiate social systems, structures, and institutions. "Normative resistance" refers to conscious and active strategies and actions for making life choices *distinct* from those considered most socially expected, celebrated, and sanctioned. Recall that the majority of cis women reported that their trans partner was socially perceived as male most of the time. A considerable minority (30 percent) of cis women I interviewed

Figure 31.1 Sample Participants' Strategies of Normative Resistance and Inventive Pragmatism

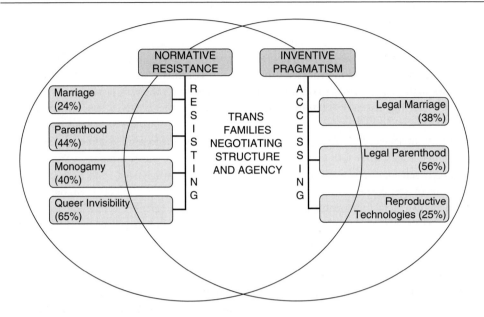

self-identified as "femme," and all of the cis women in my sample reported being perceived by social others as a woman all or most of the time. As such, many cis women reported being frequently misperceived as part of an unremarkably heterosexual couple when in public with their trans partner. This stood in contrast to the self-identification of the majority of cis women in the sample as "queer." Given this tension and discrepancy between personal and political identity and social perceptions, some of the cis women I interviewed described specific strategies for managing and resisting social misrecognition as unremarkably heterosexual and reasserting their identity as "queer" or counternormative. Their strategies for normative resistance spanned across four primary areas. Cis women reported resisting (1) marriage, (2) parenthood, (3) monogamy, and (4) queer invisibility (see Figure 31.1).

Resisting Marriage

"Opposite sex/heterosexual" marriage and parenting are often regarded as primary bastions, symbols, and institutions of heteronormativity, heteronormative practices, and/or heteronormative privilege. Furthermore, "same-sex/gay" marriage rights and parenting have recently taken center stage and become a primary goal of what some consider "homonormative" mainstream politics (see Duggan 2002; Ward 2008). Cis women in partnerships with trans men often face the unique circumstance of being able to choose between "heterosexual/opposite sex marriage," "gay/same-sex" marriage, or no marriage at all with the very same partner (dependent on a trans partner's legal sex status and personal gender identity, and the couple's legal geographic residence). . . . As Tabitha described it: "In a way I think it's kind of an amazing loophole. The Christian right hasn't figured it out yet."

Despite the existence of such a "loophole," nearly one quarter (*n* = 12) of the cis women in this sample expressed antimarriage sentiments, lack of interest in marriage, or situated their support of marriage as far *less* personally or socially important than other issues and causes.

I consider this interface between agency and structure in the lives of cis women partners of trans men one of the forms of "normative resistance" in which they frequently engage. For example, as Trixie stated:

> I'm not really into the idea of gay marriage. If that is something that any gay person wants, I'll definitely support them in that—that they should be able to have whatever they want. It's just not what I want. My idea of living my life successfully has nothing to do with assimilating to that kind of heterosexist ideal of a man and a woman as a unit with children . . . when I think about pressing gay or queer issues, marriage is never one of them. It's not in my agenda to show the public or the world that I'm just like them.

Trixie makes it clear that her notion of what it means to be queer involves anti-assimilation personal life choices, and that accessing marriage would be an assimilationist choice.

Emma articulated another perspective on marriage—that even as it expands to "same-sex/gay" couples, it remains exclusionary in other ways:

> In Canada [same-sex marriage is] legal everywhere, but it's still exclusive in that sometimes people of certain migration can't get married or it's the financial thing and they can't get married and religion plays a lot into marriage. So neither of us wanted to get married in the very traditional sense of going to church or otherwise. We talked about getting married if we wanted the legal benefits with each other . . . [but] we didn't want to play into that because it wasn't where our politics lie.

These expressions of politics and agency centered around resisting, opposing, and decentering marriage are a key component of much queer theory and social activism, which critiques social imperatives to marry and the very linkages between state-sanctioned marriage and regulation of social and material resources (Duggan 1992).

[. . .]

Resisting Parenthood

Participants also expressed normative resistance in the form of eschewing parenthood or expressing the desire to remain childfree. Nearly half (44 percent) of participants I interviewed told me that they were either not interested in becoming a parent now or had no specific plans to become a parent in the future. Among those not expressing a desire or plans to parent, this was conveyed as indifference, conflict, and (in some cases) active resistance to normative ideals and celebration of new possibilities connected to being and remaining childfree.

For example, when I asked Jodi if her decision not to become a parent had been a difficult one for her, she told me, "No. Actually, I celebrated by going and getting a huge tattoo piece. . . . I will not be having babies from this body; it will ruin my tattoo! Part of the symbolism in the tattoo . . . represents an empty womb." Jodi's tattoo exemplifies another critical aspect of normative resistance in transactions between agency and structure—constructing new rituals to signify, and quite literally mark on the body, important life choices that disrupt and diverge from the socially normative and celebrated ideals of having children as key to both womanhood and family. As Tabitha told me, "I'm starting to feel a little bit like an aberration. I'm 33 and I'm not interested in kids. . . . I'm on my own queer path now and that's my focus."

Rachel said, "I know I never want to be pregnant because I think it sounds awful and I also feel really strongly about not further expanding the population. . . . I want to be a professor, so I have a lot of school ahead of me. . . . I don't want to compromise my desire to teach to have a child." The reasons for not desiring to become a parent were varied and included one's own or a partner's infertility, physical and/or mental health problem(s), lack of economic resources, desire to prioritize education and/or career, advancing age, citizenship status, and conflict over reproductive and parenting options.

Resisting Monogamy

Partnering is a social-relational practice that may be particularly "queered" and destabilized when considering the lives and experiences of participants in this study. Participants discussed relationship configurations that differed in striking ways from the monogamous relational structures generally considered emblematic of heteronormativity. For those providing data on intimate relationship structure, 40 percent of the relationships with trans men that participants described were polyamorous (not strictly monogamous) at one point or another over the course of the relationship. This figure does *not* reflect reported infidelities that occurred across the relationships but, instead, captures the proportion of the sample that engaged in consensual, negotiated polyamory/nonmonogamy (or "open relationships").

[. . .]

Queer-identified cis women and cis women younger than 35 years of age were more likely to report practicing nonmonogamy in their relationships than those who identified as lesbian or were older than 35 years of age. For younger, queer-identified cis women in particular, then, forming an open relationship structure with a trans partner may serve as one way in which this group engages in social innovation to keep their relationship counternormative, though they may present the semblance of normativity in the public sphere. Moreover, it may be one strategy of resistance for maintaining a personal and community-based "queer" identity in the context of being perceived by many social others as unremarkably heterosexual.

Robyn discussed that among her community of queer-identified individuals, polyamory is not only common but perhaps even necessary for being "truly" queer: "I know a lot of people who have been in open relationships because it's kind of like people are expected to be in open relationships . . . it's kind of the norm. You're supposed to be in an open relationship because, otherwise, that's like oppressive." Ellia offered a similar perspective: "The more people we meet in life it seems like people are very into open relationships. A lot of the queer community that we've been meeting lately, they all seem to be in open relationships." Study participants discussed numerous types of polyamorous relationship configurations and varying degrees of negotiation between partners regarding the contours of sexual and/or romantic relations with others outside of their primary relationship.

. . . A considerable minority of cis women partners of trans men explicitly discussed their open relationships as a conscious form of resisting normativity (as well as a critical aspect of some queer identities and relationships) and countering others' social (mis)perceptions about the presumed heteronormativity of their relationships. These relationship configurations also parallel emergent trends toward open relationships, even in the context of legal marriage, among other segments of the LGBTQ population (see Green 2008; James 2010). Taken together, these findings challenge assertions that efforts to legalize same-sex marriage reflect simple mimicry of heteronormative relationship configurations and an abdication of a radically queer political agenda, suggesting that it may not be such a simple dichotomy.

Resisting Queer Invisibility

Despite some scholars' claims that sociology might fruitfully move into a "post-queer" era (Green 2002), 52 percent of the cis women I interviewed self-identified as "queer." Furthermore, when offering a label to describe the sort of relationship that they had with their trans partner, 65 percent of these relationships were described by participants as "queer." In the context of others' reported social misperceptions of these cis women as unremarkably heterosexual and/or part of a presumably unremarkable heterosexual couple, however, these queer identities and relationships were often elided. Many cis women described their fears of being perceived as "just like everyone else" by social others. In response, the cis women I interviewed described specific strategies for managing and resisting this (actual and potential) misrecognition and reasserting their own identity as "queer" and/or counternormative.

Participants' narratives also revealed the extent to which some forms of normative resistance highlight sociopolitical and identity divisions *within* LGBTQ communities as well. As Trixie told me:

A lot of my gay male friends and I talk about the difference between just gay people and queer people and, "Don't you hate when gay people are just gay and not queer?" And I guess what we mean by that is just . . . to me I guess it means that . . . someone identifying just as gay wants to assimilate somehow. . . . I know that's not necessarily true and I'm not judging anybody's identification at all. It's totally everyone's own business and I'm so in support of it. But, for me, when I identify as queer, I feel like I'm also putting a message out there that my sexual orientation is not about assimilation to any sort of heterosexist ideal.

Trixie's narrative speaks to many participants' complicated negotiations of LGBTQ identification and disidentification when it comes to resisting normativity. Many strategies of normative resistance that participants described also resonate with Halberstam's (2011, 110–11) discussion of queer as "a mode of critique rather than a new investment in normativity or life or respectability or wholeness or legitimacy."

Narratives like these also emerged as a striking empirical converse to Green (2002), who finds some members of the LGBTQ community identifying as "gay but not queer." These experiences of resisting queer invisibility among cis women in this sample are shared by individuals in another undertheorized and often invisible identity and social group—cissexual (non-trans) "opposite-sex" partnerships wherein one or more partners is bisexual- or queer-identified (Ault 1996a, 1996b; Burrill 2001; Tabatabai and Linders 2011; Wolkomir 2009). Yet trans couples may face challenges that cissexual queer-identified individuals in "opposite-sex" partnerships encounter less frequently, such as accessing legal marriage and having children. Nevertheless, queer invisibility may also hold *pragmatic* potential for some queer social actors in terms of accessing regulated social and material resources, which I detail below.

Strategies of Inventive Pragmatism: Accessing Legal Marriage, Legal Parenthood, and Reproductive Technologies

While normative resistance was one approach cis women described for making their identities and relationships personally and socially intelligible, they also detailed inventive ways in which they sometimes embraced what might seem like normative behaviors and identities for pragmatic purposes. "Inventive pragmatism," as I term it, entails active strategies and actions that might be considered clever manipulation (or "workarounds") of an existing social structure in order to access social and material resources on behalf of oneself or one's family. Recall, once again, that many cis women reported the belief that their relationship with their partner was perceived as unremarkably heterosexual most of the time, which stood in contrast to their majority self-identification as "queer." Despite this discrepancy, some cis women described inventively manipulating such misrecognition in order to access regulated social institutions, resources, and technologies. Cis women's strategies for inventive pragmatism spanned across three primary areas of access: (1) legal marriage, (2) legal parenthood, and (3) reproductive technologies.

Accessing Legal Marriage

Depending on existing laws in their geographic area of residence, the cis women I interviewed often faced the unique circumstance of being able to legally marry a partner after he has engaged in gender transition—something that was often *not* legally possible (in the United States) while the two were legally classified as same-sex. Recall one participant referring to this fact as an "amazing loophole" that "the Christian right hasn't figured . . . out yet." Some participants insisted on the pragmatic importance of having the option to access legal marriage with the hopes of broadening and expanding this institution for a broader diversity of couples. Terry described a contentious interaction she had with another member of the LGBTQ community on announcing her upcoming marriage to her trans partner:

> This one [queer] woman put up this interesting analogy of how she saw getting married as selling out and [asked], "If you could be a member of an exclusive club and go into that club and dine fabulously but your best friend, who is a different ethnicity, could not, how could you live with yourself if you went ahead and went into this club and dined fabulously?" And I said, "You know what? I would expect you to go in there and dine and bring me a plate. Don't be a martyr. . . ." [I think you should] do what's right for you and if you can find a way to reach back and help everybody else, do it.

This analogy parallels the one discussed earlier by Toby; but the analysis and conclusion are starkly different. To Terry, marriage to a trans partner is a move *away from* ideologically motivated, punishing self-interest and may be a move toward LGBTQ community betterment (although she does not explicitly specify how).

Like Terry, a small minority of cis women in the sample (10 percent) reported existing legal "same-sex/gay" ($n = 1$) or "opposite-sex/heterosexual" ($n = 4$) marriages with their partners, while 28 percent ($n = 14$) reported contemplating, discussing, and/or actively planning such legal unions and 22 percent ($n = 11$) reported feeling neutral about the possibility of marriage. Sixteen percent ($n = 8$) of participants did not comment specifically on the topic of marriage. . . . Cis women who self-identified as bisexual were more likely than any other group to report a desire to be legally married. Participants' endorsement of marriage, as a personal goal, increased along with the degree to which one's trans partner was reportedly socially perceived as male—with those reporting that their partner was socially perceived as male "always" or "almost always" most frequently reporting the desire to marry. While only two cis women were actively raising children in their homes with their trans partner at the time of the interview, both were legally married to their trans partner. . . .

Participants' narratives frequently articulated the catch-22 nature of (and personal ambivalence toward) gaining access to an institution to which they may be both politically and ideologically opposed in order to access valuable and regulated economic, legal, and social benefits. Julie, for example, described marriage as "a bad institution" and stated that she thought that marriage should be "abolished." Yet Julie also admitted that she had once contemplated getting married in order to gain citizenship. These narratives frequently attested to the pragmatic concerns often fueling communication and decision making around accessing legal marriage.

Accessing Legal Parenthood

The pressing need for sociologists to consider the paradoxical sociolegal *invisibility* and *hypervisibility* of trans families is particularly highlighted when focusing on the issue of parenting. . . . While only 4 percent *(n = 2)* of participants reported actively raising young children in their homes with their partners at the time of the interview, 8 percent of participants *(n = 4)* reported other current or former personal experiences with parenting, and 44 percent of participants *(n = 22)* discussed intentions (many describing detailed plans) to become a parent in the future.

Participants discussed sociolegal challenges that they and their trans partner may face when considering the options available to them as parents. Rachel told me, "We don't even know if we would be allowed to adopt a kid. He's a transsexual and gay people can't even adopt kids [in some states]. . . . People think trans people are even weirder than gay so who knows if that's even an option." The dilemmas these couples face were sometimes met with frustration and discussion of the privilege that often accompanies non-trans heterosexual relationships. As Samantha stated, "I'm sort of angry that straight people have babies on accident and make it work. It makes me really pissed off. . . . We have to be more responsible because we can't just, like, have that. I'm sure they don't see it as a blessing, but I do."

The narratives of those who were currently parenting at the time of the interview also revealed important and potentially worrisome sociolegal dilemmas. For example, Maya and her partner have a legal, "opposite-sex/heterosexual" marriage in the United States. They are also recognized as the legal mother and father (respectively) of their infant daughter, to whom Maya gave birth. However, as Maya discussed:

> We are legally married . . . as long as no one contests it. . . . He's on the birth certificate and we're legally married [so] he's [our daughter's father by] default. If you're legally married, if something were to happen to me, [our daughter] goes to him automatically. However . . . my mother holds a trump card. In other words, if I were to die, she could conceivably potentially sue for custody, saying that she's the nearest relative, not [my partner]. . . . There's this legal limbo we live in. . . . [In some states] we wouldn't be recognized as being legally married at all. He would never be recognized as [our daughter's father].

Maya's family provides an example of how the marital paternity presumption, which is the legal assumption that children born to a legally married man and woman are that man's biological children, offers a "trans loophole" for accessing legal parentage, but introduces instability insofar as such parentage may face legal challenges (Rosato 2006).

Narratives like these provide striking examples of how the legal rights and privileges conveyed by marriage are often tenuous, at best, for some queer families. While Maya and her family may be considered social innovators, this innovation is dependent on continuing familial and state recognition of both their marriage and their rightful and respective roles as mother and father to their child. As such, accessing legal parentage through legal marriage, legal adoption, and other formal pathways may serve as a pragmatic, though not failproof, safeguard for forming and protecting some trans families.

Accessing Reproductive Technologies

Technological advances in the biomedical sector are making parentage possible for a broader group of people in ways never before imagined (Hare and Skinner 2008; Mamo 2007; Thompson 2005). A considerable number of participants in the sample ($n = 11$; 22 percent) discussed—spontaneously and not under direct prompt—conversations they had with their trans partner about the possibility of retrieving and harvesting his eggs (among those whose trans partner had not had an oophorectomy—removal of the ovaries) for later fertilization and implantation into themselves or a surrogate. While almost all of these participants discussed this possibility as remote because of its present costliness, existing technologies radically shift possibilities for creating and forming families in the twenty-first century. Today, it is possible for cis women partners of trans men to give birth to their trans partner's biological children. While such procedures may not currently be common, they may become increasingly so as these novel reproductive technologies advance and become more affordable to consumers over time.

In the egg harvesting and donation scenario previously described, a trans man who has attained legal status as male might be simultaneously legally classified as a child's "legal father" and "biological mother," depending on local jurisdiction and statutes, which vary widely (see Hare and Skinner 2008; Smith 2009 for an overview of similar legal quandaries for lesbian and gay couples). Were the couple to separate, however, it might also be argued that the trans man was nothing more than an "egg donor," with no existing legal connection or rights to the child at all. Potential sociolegal dilemmas became further complicated as some cis women described their intention to choose a male sperm donor, related to themselves or their partner, in order to maintain a mutual genetic connection to the child. Martha provided a narrative that illustrated many of these complex and new sociolegal possibilities:

> I don't care to birth a child myself at this point in my life. . . . And he really wanted to. So we talked about . . . if he's taking [testosterone] and then stops taking it, will he be able to get pregnant and how? And we would talk about, well, if we'd like a child that comes from both of us, we could use one of my brothers' sperm to impregnate him so we'd have a child that, hopefully, would look like both of us. . . . And then also, how would this play out if he has transitioned further with testosterone and he can get pregnant and he looks very male? How's this gonna work with this person who identifies as male and possibly has had his sex changed on documents coming into a hospital pregnant as a man?

Existing technologies radically shift possibilities for creating and forming families in the twenty-first century. Yet these new possibilities engender complex sociolegal questions regarding who "counts" as a biological and/or social mother, father, and parent.

Conclusion

So why and how does all of this matter? In addition to proposing the theoretical constructs of "normative resistance" and "inventive pragmatism," this work informs and extends existing sociological literature on agency and social structure. Enacting agency may involve strategies virtually *requiring* participation within oppressive social structures and institutions, particularly among those in marginal social positions.

[. . .]

. . . Cis women partners of trans men draw not only from contemporary understandings of what families are or are "supposed" to be, but also resist and reformulate some of these notions as well—if doing so might prove personally and/or socially advantageous. The narratives explored herein detail the ways in which contemporary notions of family *work* and *do not work* in the everyday lives of cis women partners of trans men and their families. Cis women's accounts also reveal the extent to which they actively evaluate and negotiate sociolegal notions and practices of "family," family structure, and family roles in ways that may court pragmatic advantage in the face of systematic structural and institutional barriers.

The cis women described in this study are negotiating new ways of constructing family forms, including those not strictly grounded in normative or nostalgic ideals for families and family life. I find that cis women partners of trans men often serve as social innovators—strategically and pragmatically negotiating system loopholes to access otherwise limited and regulated sociolegal institutions and structures (such as marriage and parentage) for their families that others within the "LGBTQ umbrella" may not be able to similarly access . . . the negotiations of normative resistance and inventive pragmatism that I have outlined hold relevance not only for transgender families headed by cis women and trans men, but for a broad range of queer individuals and queer family types.

[. . .]

References

Ault, Amber. 1996a. "The Dilemma of Identity: Bi Women's Negotiations." In *Queer Theory/Sociology*, edited by S. Seidman. London, UK: Blackwell.

Ault, Amber. 1996b. "Ambiguous Identity in an Unambiguous Sex/Gender Structure: The Case of Bisexual Women." *Sociological Quarterly* 37:449–63.

Burrill, Katkryn G. 2001. "Queering Bisexuality." *Journal of Bisexuality* 2:95–105.

Currah, Paisley, Richard M. Juang, and Shannon P. Minter. 2006. *Transgender Rights*. Minneapolis, MN: University of Minnesota Press.

Duggan, Lisa. 1992. "Making It Perfectly Queer." *Socialist Review* 22:11–31.

Duggan, Lisa. 2002. "The New Homonormativity: The Sexual Politics of Neoliberalism." In *Materializing Democracy: Towards a Revitalized Cultural Politics*, edited by R. Castronovo and D. D. Nelson. Durham, NC: Duke University Press.

Fausto-Sterling, Anne. 2000. *Sexing the Body: Gender Politics and the Construction of Sexuality*. New York: Basic Books.

Garfinkel, Harold. 1967. *Studies in Ethnomethodology*. Englewood Cliffs, NJ: Prentice Hall.

Green, Adam I. 2002. "Gay but Not Queer: Toward a Post-Queer Study of Sociology." *Theory and Society* 31:521–45.

Green, Adam I. 2008. "Same-Sex Marriage: Lesbian and Gay Spouses Marrying Tradition and Change." Paper presented at Annual Meeting, American Sociological Association, Boston, MA.

Halberstam, Judith. 2011. *The Queer Art of Failure*. Durham, NC: Duke University Press.

Hare, Jan and Denise Skinner. 2008. "'Whose Child Is This?' Determining Legal Status for Lesbian Parents Who Use Assisted Reproductive Technologies." *Family Relations* 57:365–75.

Ingraham, Chrys. 1994. "The Heterosexual Imaginary: Feminist Sociology and Theories of Gender." *Sociological Theory* 12:203–19.

Jackson, Stevi. 2006. "Interchanges: Gender, Sexuality and Heterosexuality: The Complexity (and Limits) of Heteronormativity." *Feminist Theory* 7:105–21.

James, Scott. 2010. "Many Successful Gay Marriages Share an Open Secret." *New York Times*, January 28.

Johnson, Carol. 2002. "Heteronormative Citizenship and the Politics of Passing." *Sexualities* 5:317–36.

Kessler, Suzanne J. and Wendy McKenna. 1978. *Gender: An Ethnomethodological Approach.* New York: John Wiley.

Kirkland, Anna. 2006. "What's at Stake in Transgender Discrimination as Sex Discrimination?" *Signs: Journal of Women in Culture and Society* 32:83–111.

Kitzinger, Celia. 2005. "Heteronormativity in Action: Reproducing the Heterosexual Nuclear Family in After-hours Medical Calls." *Social Problems* 52:477–98.

Mamo, Laura. 2007. *Queering Reproduction: Achieving Pregnancy in the Age of Technoscience.* Durham, NC: Duke University Press.

Meyerowitz, Joanne. 2002. *How Sex Changed: A History of Transsexuality in the United States.* Cambridge, MA: Harvard University Press.

Patton, Michael Q. 1990. *Qualitative Evaluation and Research Methods.* Newbury Park, CA: Sage.

Rich, Adrienne. 1980. "Compulsory Heterosexuality and Lesbian Existence." *Signs: Journal of Women in Culture and Society* 5:631–60.

Robson, Ruthann. 2006. "Reinscribing Normality? The Law and Politics of Transgender Marriage." In *Transgender Rights*, edited by P. Currah, R. M. Juang, and S. P. Minter. Minneapolis, MN: University of Minnesota Press.

Rosato, Jennifer L. 2006. "Children of Same-Sex Parents Deserve the Security Blanket of the Parentage Presumption." *Family Court Review* 44:74–86.

Rubin, Gayle S. 1984. "Thinking Sex: Notes for a Radical Theory of the Politics of Sexuality." In *Pleasure and Danger: Exploring Female Sexuality*, edited by C. S. Vance. Boston, MA: Routledge.

Schilt, Kristen and Laurel Westbrook. 2009. "Doing Gender, Doing Heteronormativity: 'Gender Normals,' Transgender People, and the Social Maintenance of Heterosexuality." *Gender & Society* 23:440–64.

Seidman, Steven. 1994. "Queer-ing Sociology, Sociologizing Queer Theory: An Introduction." *Sociological Theory* 12:166–77.

Seidman, Steven. 1995. "Deconstructing Queer Theory or the Under-Theorization of the Social and the Ethical." In *Social Postmodernism: Beyond Identity Politics*, edited by L. Nicholson and S. Seidman. New York: Cambridge University Press.

Seidman, Steven. 2001. "From Identity to Queer Politics: Shifts in Normative Heterosexuality and the Meaning of Citizenship." *Citizenship Studies* 5:321–28.

Smith, Anna Marie. 2009. "Reproductive Technology, Family Law, and the Postwelfare State: The California Same-Sex Parents' Rights 'Victories' of 2005." *Signs: Journal of Women in Culture and Society* 34:827–50.

Tabatabai, Ahoo and Annulla Linders. 2011. "Vanishing Act: Non-Straight Identity Narratives of Women in Relationships with Women and Men." *Qualitative Sociology* 34:583–99.

Thompson, Charis. 2005. *Making Parents: The Ontological Choreography of Reproductive Technologies.* Cambridge, MA: MIT Press.

Valocchi, Stephen. 2005. "Not Yet Queer Enough: The Lessons of Queer Theory for the Sociology of Gender and Sexuality." *Gender & Society* 19:750–70.

Ward, Jane. 2008. *Respectably Queer: Diversity Culture in LGBT Activist Organizations.* Nashville, TN: Vanderbilt University Press.

Warner, Michael. 1991. "Introduction: Fear of a Queer Planet." *Social Text* 29:3–17.

Wolkomir, Michelle. 2009. "Making Heteronormative Reconciliations: The Story of Romantic Love, Sexuality, and Gender in Mixed-Orientation Marriages." *Gender & Society* 23:494–519.

Transnational Fathering

Gendered Conflicts, Distant Disciplining and Emotional Gaps

Rhacel Salazar Parreñas

This article analyses the performance of fathering in Filipino transnational families, whose members are located in two or more nation-states (Parreñas 2001), and looks at intergenerational conflicts engendered by "fathering from a distance." Discussions of transnational fathering remain absent in the literature on migration, despite the multitude of studies on men's migration. This is perhaps because fathering from a distance does not reconstitute "normative gender behaviour" in the family but instead abides by gender-ideological norms such as male breadwinning (Fenstermaker and West 2002). Indeed, migration enables men to better fulfill the traditional responsibility of breadwinning with their access to greater income earning potential abroad (Hondagneu-Sotelo and Messner 2000; Kyle 2000). It also removes fathers from daily interactions in the family and consequently in their absence, even if only inadvertently, further reaffirms the traditional division of labour of a male breadwinner and female homemaker.

In contrast to the lack of research on transnational fathering, studies on transnational mothering abound (Hondagneu-Sotelo and Avila 1997; Gamburd 2000; Parreñas 2001). These studies establish that transnational mothering engenders the reconstitution of gender and mothering to include breadwinning when performing it from a distance. At the same time, researchers carefully note that mothers do not abandon their traditional responsibilities upon migration. Instead, mothers retain their conventional gender responsibility of nurturing when adjusting to the different needs (e.g., greater communication efforts) that the children may have in transnational families.

[. . .]

In the families of migrant men, transnational fathers tend to perform a heightened version of conventional fathering. Transnational fathering is primarily demonstrated through the display of authority and imposition of discipline on children. By projecting authority,

Rhacel Salazar Parreñas, 2008. "Transnational Fathering: Gendered Conflicts, Distant Disciplining and Emotional Gaps." *Journal of Ethnic and Migration Studies* 34(7):1057–72. Reprinted by permission of Taylor & Francis Ltd, www.tandfonline.com

physically distant fathers can project the role of a disciplining "father figure." It is said that men "do gender" (Fenstermaker and West 2002) in the performance of fathering and, by holding on to traditional masculine notions of fathering, transnational fathers not only maintain gender conventions but also hold onto their identity as "fathers," which is threatened by their distance from the family and perhaps questioned by the inclusion of "maternal acts" such as communication in transnational fathering (Ruddick 1982). By holding on to gender traditions, migrant fathers also maintain a gender identity of heightened masculinity. As such, in the reconstitution of their households from nuclear to transnational structures, Filipino migrant men do not transform but instead follow the traditional script of fathering in the Philippines: one that follows the ideology of separate spheres; keeps expressions of emotional ties between children and their fathers to a minimum; and maintains the responsibility of disciplining as gendered masculine (Medina 2001). In this paper, I examine the intergenerational conflicts that arise from the heightened performance of masculine gender conventions in transnational fathering.

[. . .]

Methodology

This article draws from a larger project on the transnational family life of young adult children in the Philippines. For my primary data, I conducted 69 open-ended and tape-recorded interviews with young adult children of migrant parents between January and July 2000. Interviews were one to three hours in length. I limited my interviews with "children" to young adults who spent at least five years of their adolescence in a transnational household and were still in a relationship of economic dependence to a migrant parent. In this way, I interviewed actual members of transnational families.

I conducted interviews with 30 children of migrant mothers, 26 of migrant fathers, and 13 of two migrant parents. For its data, this article draws from the interviews with children of migrant fathers.

[. . .]

The Transnational Household Structure of Migrant Men

The transnational families of migrant men usually mirror modern nuclear households. For instance, unlike those of migrant women, their families hardly rely on the assistance of extended kin. Instead, their families resemble conventional nuclear families. The only difference is the temporal and spatial rearrangement brought by the father's work: instead of the father routinely getting back home to his family at suppertime, he comes back home from work every ten months. Migrant men usually leave their children behind under the custody of stay-at-home wives, who they often discourage from entering the formal labour market. Notably, even if "stay-at-home wives," the wives left behind in the Philippines do not just "stay at home" but instead capitalise on the income earned by the migrant spouse. These mothers run various enterprises including the management of fishponds, poultry or fruit farms. Moreover, slightly less than half of the mothers of children in my sample participate in the labour market, often for the reason of personal fulfillment and not out of financial necessity. Most mothers in the labour force are employed as schoolteachers.

The father-away families in my sample represent the average middle-class household in the Philippines. . . . Most migrant fathers in my study are skilled workers. Twelve are officers and four are crew-members of shipping lines. Of land-based workers, three are professionals, two of them engineers, and seven are manual labourers or low-wage service workers. Most of the 26 young adult children who I had interviewed grew up in comfortable middle-class households. In the Philippines, this means that their family owns a motor vehicle, resides in a cement-structure house, and can afford the private education of children. As members of the middle class, the perspective of my interviewees most likely reflects conventional and mainstream notions of the family in the Philippines and consequently follows traditional "gender ideological frames." Indeed, plenty of them explained the division of labour in their families as conforming to the notion of men as the *haligi ng tahanan* (pillar of the home) and women as the *ilaw ng tahanan* (light of the home).

[. . .]

The gender idioms of men as pillars and women as lights cross class boundaries. As explained to me by my interviewees, including those in both working-class and middle-class families, the metaphorical reference to men as a pillar establishes fathers as breadwinners whose primary duty is to build a home for the family. As a pillar, it is he who makes the home stand and it is he who must literally build a home for his family. This means that the fulfillment of fathering in the Philippines is usually determined primarily by their successful acquisition of a home for the family, whether it is a bamboo hut for the working poor, a modest-sized cement structure for the struggling middle class, or a multi-level unit for upper-income families. As such, I was not surprised when children told me that "to build a home" was a goal of migration for their fathers.

Following traditional ideological views of gender in the Filipino family, we can speculate that the home measures the masculinity of men in the Philippines, with its size considered to be one determining criterion of the successful fulfillment of one's role as the *haligi ng tahanan*. Most families do not immediately but instead slowly acquire the material comfort of owning a cement-structure house. Families would purchase the land in the first few years of migration, then set up the foundational structure of the house, after which they would slowly build the house to completion. Interestingly, the project of building a house never seems to end. There always seems to be a home improvement project for transnational fathers. From a distance, transnational fathers would oversee the completion of the walls of their house, the installation of screens on the windows, the repainting of the home exterior and so on. The process of building the home allows children to witness the mobility that migration affords their families. Moreover, the ongoing project of building the home allows fathers to be symbolically present in the daily activities of transnational household maintenance as it reinforces the breadwinner status of men. In short, the building of the home allows fathers to "be there." Interestingly, in sharp contrast to the transnational family of migrant fathers, the subject of building a home is rarely mentioned in my interviews with the children of migrant mothers and their guardians.

[. . .]

The Gap

What did children mean when they referred to a gap? I repeatedly heard children complain about a gap and I accordingly asked them to describe it. As noted earlier, the gap refers to this sense of discomfort, unease and awkwardness that children feel toward migrant fathers. Additionally, it refers to the inability of young adult children to communicate more openly with their fathers. Finally, it also captures the ambivalence that they feel over the unfamiliarity that has developed in their transnational families.

The children themselves better describe this gap. Embarrassed is one word they frequently use to describe their feelings when it comes to their fathers. For instance, Danica Lavilla, a 20-year-old college student preparing for law school, states:

> I am very grateful that my father has worked hard for us but then it's like something is really lacking. Look at our situation. We are already so grown-up, yet we are still embarrassed around our father.

Danica's father has worked as a seafarer for more than 20 years. This extended length of separation explains why his 24-year-old son and younger daughters, including Danica, still feel quite embarrassed around him. Similarly, Claudio Regala, cannot open up to his father. He explains:

> I tell my mother all of my problems, for instance with my girlfriends, grades, everything.
>
> *How about your father?*
>
> Oh, I am embarrassed.
>
> *Why?*
>
> I am not as close to him as I am to my mother. It's because, well it's because we never get to be together. So we have this gap. We get embarrassed around him.

Like the father of Danica, the father of Claudio has worked as a seafarer for more than 20 years. Children whose fathers have worked outside the country for most of their lives feel a greater sense of emotional distance in the family than those children whose fathers did not leave the Philippines until their early teenage years. This is understandable as a certain level of familiarity gained from the intimacy and routine of daily life would have then developed in the family life of the latter group of children.

Another interviewee, Kiara Billones, grimaced when I asked her to describe her relationship with her father. She then laughed in discomfort before proceeding to explain the distance between her and her father.

> The first time my father went home, it was as if I was really afraid of him. (Laughs.) It is because I was not used to having him around. See every night, I would kiss my mother good night. But when he is around, I am so embarrassed. So when he and my mother are together when I am about to go to sleep, I do not kiss my mother. I get so embarrassed when he is around. My mother of course noticed this. She asked me about it and I told her that I am embarrassed around him. She told me not to be because he is my father. She told me that I should try to be close to my father. So I agreed and I tried, but it is still the same. I am still embarrassed around him. Up to now, I am still very uncomfortable around him.

Kiara's father left the Philippines to work as a seafarer 11 years ago, when Kiara was only seven years old. She has few memories of her father and believes that the "gap" in her family is due to the lack of shared experiences between them. I should note that even the most confident of children feel embarrassed around their fathers. This suggests that we cannot simply attribute the awkwardness that has developed in these families to personality traits (e.g., shyness) of children. For instance, Kenneth Matugas, the student-body president of his university, cringed when I asked why he did not ask his father for advice and responded by saying "Oh, I get embarrassed."

Distance breeds unfamiliarity and this unfamiliarity leads to discomfort. As Leonardo Monfort, another son of a seafarer, explains,

> Love. You can secure it from far away but not that strongly. It is better if your family is physically close. Sometimes, if you are far away and even if you are sincere in your love, your children will feel that it is only money that you can give. If you are there, then you can give more than money. You can give emotional support. You can be there for the emotional problems of your children. You can be there on the phone, but that is not very practical. That is why a gap forms. You develop a tendency to be inhibited. It's because you have not seen each other for years. They become inhibited because they are not used to having them there everyday.

Because distance combined with unfamiliarity imposes a gap of inhibition, children are less likely to share their problems with their fathers.

Unfamiliarity also breeds ambivalence. For instance, Ton-ton Ilano, an 18-year-old college student raised by paternal extended kin who financially depend on the remittances of his father, describes the distance between him and his father.

> Emotional. I do not think I have an emotional connection with my father. It's probably because we are so far away from each other. We are so far apart that I cannot relate myself to him. He also cannot understand me. He also never listens to me. It always has to be his way. He does not even want you to make a comment.

> *Will you ever be close to your father?*

> Never. Maybe, I do not know. Sometimes, it enters my mind to think what will happen when he dies. Would I shed a tear? That enters my mind. With my mother, my grandmother, I would probably cry, but with my father, I do not know if I would or I would not cry at all. Most likely, I will not.

Most children of transnational fathers do not believe that the gap in their relationship is irreparable, but some like Ton-ton do think that the possibility of a closer relationship developing in their families is quite bleak. In the case of Ton-ton's family, the tendency of his father to aggressively discipline him aggravates his feelings of emotional distance. Not unlike other migrant fathers, the father of Ton-ton tends to act like a military commander whenever home and orders his children around as if he were still a chief engineer on board a shipping vessel. Not surprisingly, this tendency to constantly discipline children aggravates the emotional rift that already exists in these families. . . .

Aggravating the Gap

In the Philippines, the gender script of the family relegates the task of implementing order and discipline in the family to fathers (Medina 2001). Similarly, the final authority in the family is legally designated to men, which, whether unintentionally or not, upholds their "macho" image (Medina 2001; Republic of the Philippines 1987). Though the flexibility of gender practices allows men to expand ritual performances of fathering to include traditional women's roles, I found that they still prefer to cling tightly to authoritarian measures of discipline. . . . To be a father seems to require of them what they think fathers should be doing and that is disciplining their children. Unfortunately, as shown in the case of Ton-ton Ilano's family, the practice of holding onto traditional notions of fathering aggravates the gap that strains ties between migrant men and children in the Philippines. Maintaining tradition fails to address the particular needs engendered by geographical separation between fathers and their children.

In the Philippines, child-centred activities of caring are not usually performed by men (Medina 2001). Their intimate involvement with children remains minimal at best, as they usually limit the extent of their nurturing to token bonding rituals between fathers and sons, for instance circumcision in the pre-pubescent stage of life, and other initiations to adulthood. With rare exception, this is for the most part true among migrant fathers. For instance, they rarely communicate with their children. Suzette Doligosa, a 19-year-old college student who lives with her mother in the Philippines, complains:

> It's hard to explain. Honestly, I do not have an easy time approaching him. It's because I am, like, afraid of him. It's just like that. And I am embarrassed around him. . . . My father calls home two times a month. Sometimes we do not talk on the phone. He only talks to my mother. We only get to talk when I happen to be the one to answer the phone and my mom happens not to be there. Sometimes I get so mad. It's because I can't help but wonder why it's like that. Why is that it is just my mom and dad who talk to each other? He should also talk to us. He should ask us how we are doing. Of course it's because that will show you that he really cares.

Does he ever show you that he cares?

> Maybe, when, when he gives me what I want. He will ask me what I want. But my brother and I are the type of children who would not openly tell him what we really want when he asks us. We are embarrassed. We are too embarrassed to ask him to buy things for us.

By maintaining his distance from his children, the father of Suzette technically relegates all of the caring work in the family to his wife. In so doing, he conforms to the most traditional of gender scripts. Not unlike other male migrants, he reduces fathering to the role of the "good provider."

As the "good provider," he completely depends on his stay-at-home wife to take care of the emotional needs of his children. This clear-cut division of labour surely strains intergenerational ties in his family, as his children cannot help but feel emotionally distant from him. This is not to say that Suzette's father is a bad father, but only that his relegation of nurturing tasks to his wife aggravates the emotional strains imposed by the geographical distance in his family. Other children share Suzette's problems, as they often complained about the tendency of migrant fathers to reduce expressions of love to the provision of material goods. The earlier-cited Claudio Regala, for instance, said in a resigned tone with noticeable disappointment, "My dad, he supplies us with our financial needs, but he does not give us anything else."

In contrast to the sporadic communication that embodies relations between migrant men and their children in the Philippines, migrant mothers are ever-present in the lives of their children. Performing their traditional nurturing duties to the family, mothers telephone their children at least once a week. Notably, the frequency of communication is determined by the occupation of the migrant worker. For instance, nurses have more flexibility and resources than domestic workers to call their children. Still, mothers communicate with their children via email, telephone or letter at least once a week regardless of their occupation. We can therefore safely conclude that the families of migrant mothers are not without transnational intimacy.

[. . .]

In sharp contrast to the care practices that embody transnational mothering, transnational fathering practices tend not to include acts of transnational communication with children. . . . In these families, men are "good providers," meaning they provide sufficient material security to their families so as to feel freed and absolved of other obligations to their children and kin. For instance, they carry little sense of responsibility for the emotional work of caring for the family. This typical construction of fatherhood fits the observations of Jesse Bernard, who notes that "good providers" usually become "emotional parasites" as they are likely to expect women to do all of the work required in securing the emotional stability of children in the family (1981: 10).

Fathers rarely communicate with their children and when they do it is not to allay the fears and insecurities of children. Instead, fathers often communicate to discipline their children. To remind children of their authority in the household, migrant fathers frequently reprimand their children from a distance for having low grades, selecting the "wrong" major, or not performing adequately in other school activities. In fact, many children noted that "distance disciplining" is a central part of transnational family childhood. As Ton-ton Ilano complains,

> My father only writes letters to my mother. There he would ask about us and our school grades. Then he asks that my mother photocopy our report cards and send them to him. Then if we have a low grade, he will call immediately and reprimand us. He will spend everything, his entire phone card, on scolding you.

> *How do you feel about this?*

> Nothing. He always says the same thing again and again and again.

Ton-ton long gave up hope of ever achieving close ties with his father. This is despite his recognition of his father's economic contributions to the family. For Ton-ton, these contributions do not override the strains imposed by the gap as well as the fact that Ton-ton's father is an extreme disciplinarian. He actually disciplines not only from afar but also from up close. Whenever home, for instance, he makes a concerted effort to instill work ethics on his children. Complains Ton-ton:

> First, everyone has to work when he is at home. Every single person in the house must work. No one can just sit around in the living room, watching TV, nothing. Everyone has to work. He wakes up and eats breakfast then he starts working. He just works and works. I keep on thinking, doesn't he ever get tired? When he is outside the country, he works. And when he is here, he also works.

> *What does he do?*

> He takes care of his poultry. He cleans everything. He cleans the house, everything. When he is not home, we do not do much. We watch TV. We do not have to cook. We do not clean everything. So I do not like it when he is around. It is very peaceful and quiet when he is not around, quiet for sure.

During our interview, Ton-ton kept on stressing that he would much prefer his incredibly authoritarian father to work permanently outside the country and never come home. He appreciates the monthly remittances that his father sends his family but he would rather not interact with his father at all.

It is not only the father of Ton-ton who feels compelled to impose authority in the household whenever at home in the Philippines. Most other fathers do likewise. They tend to impose themselves as an authority figure over their children. Clara Maria Tantoco, whose father migrated from the Philippines six years ago so as to better provide for his home-based wife and children, gives us another example:

> We get reprimanded more when he is home. See, I am used to walking around the house barefooted and my father does not like that. So he gets mad. He does not like it when I do not wear slippers around the house. He gets very mad. And so he scolds me.

Why do fathers impose their authority as the head of the household? We can speculate that, coupled with the awkwardness of not knowing how to act around their children, fathers may also feel the pressure to act with authority, as that is what they think they ought to be doing to be good fathers. In other words, they assume that they must discipline their children to fulfill their parental duties. Yet, in disciplining, they rarely take into account how children develop set behaviours in their absence. Instead, during their annual visits to the Philippines, they impose disciplinary standards that do not take into consideration the habits already formed by their children. This is illustrated by the case of Clara, who developed the habit of walking barefooted while her father worked outside the country.

Fathers do not abandon their familial duties upon migration. From a distance as well as up close, they try to do what they think they ought to be doing to be good fathers. Accordingly, they provide material security, impose discipline, show authority, and finally enforce order. In short, they are "good providers," as they materially but not emotionally provide for the family and at the same time act as strict disciplinarians. Although children know that their fathers do care, they want them to change the ways that they show this. They would like fathers to cross the gender boundaries of fathering and extend them to include acts of nurturing. While appreciative of the material security afforded by migration, children would also like fathers to try to achieve intimacy with constant transnational communication in the family. In the opinion of children, doing so would ameliorate the gap that plagues their relationships.

Conclusion

[...]

In the transnational families of migrant men, gender boundary crossings are limited at best. However, the crossing of gender boundaries would tremendously ease the emotional tensions incurred by the physical separation between migrant fathers and their children. Efforts of migrant fathers to nurture from a distance, communicate regularly with their children, and reconstitute fathering to not centre on disciplining could enhance intergenerational relationships in transnational families. Yet, performances of transnational fathering usually conform to traditional gender norms of male breadwinning and male authoritarianism. Transnational fathers discipline and impose authority on their children from a distance.

Whether a gap exists or not does not say much about children's attitudes towards transnational families, i.e. whether or not they feel that it is an acceptable household model for raising children. Children with distant fathers such as Ton-ton Ilano would never leave their children in the Philippines. As he states, "I do not want my children to experience what I had experienced. Like with my father, he does not know how to try to understand me. . . . It is hard." Yet, children who pride themselves for having attained close ties with their fathers also hold the same sentiments as Ton-ton. One of these children is the earlier-quoted Erlinda Gaylan. She states, "I do not want to be separated with my children [sic]. Maybe I can be if they are older but not when they are younger. I really do not want it. I will take them with me wherever I go. Me, I do not want to marry a seaman. See, I experienced what it is like to have a father abroad and it is really different if your father is close to you, next to you." The negative sentiments of children tell us that, if given the choice, children would rather not grow up in transnational household arrangements, but instead in households that would allow for greater proximity, time together, intimacy and familiarity. Yet, this view is perhaps one they can afford to express because of their middle-class upbringing. The comforts of class enable them to ignore the economic necessity of migration for many other families or perhaps for even their own parents' strategy of family maintenance.

Regardless of the class-influenced disgruntlements of children, transnational households do form different familial needs for children, specifically the need to reconstitute fathering to include greater emotional care. Thus, only the inclusion of emotional caring work in transnational fathering would begin to address this need among the children left behind by migrant workers in the Philippines.

References

Bernard, J. 1981. "The Good Provider." *American Psychologist* 36(1):1–12.

Fenstermaker, S. and C. West. 2002. "'Doing Difference' Revisited: Problems, Prospects, and the Dialogue in Feminist Theory." Pp. 205–16 in *Doing Gender, Doing Difference: Social Inequality, Power, and Resistance*, edited by S. Fenstermaker and C. West. New York: Routledge.

Gamburd, M. 2000. *A Kitchen Spoon's Handle*. Ithaca, NY: Cornell University Press.

Hondagneu-Sotelo, P. and E. Avila. 1997. "'I'm Here, but I'm There': The Meanings of Latina Transnational Motherhood." *Gender and Society* 11(5):548–71.

Hondagneu-Sotelo, P. and M. Messner. 2000. "Gender Displays and Men's Power: The 'New Man' and the Mexican Immigrant Man." Pp. 200–218 in *Theorizing Masculinities*. 5th ed., edited by H. Brod and M. Kaufman. Thousand Oaks, CA: Sage.

Kyle, D. 2000. *Transnational Peasants: Migrations, Networks, and Ethnicity in Andean Ecuador*. Baltimore, MD: Johns Hopkins University Press.

Medina, B. 2001. *The Filipino Family*. 2nd ed. Quezon City, Philippines: University of the Philippines Press.

Parreñas, R. S. 2001. *Servants of Globalization: Women, Migration, and Domestic Work*. Stanford, CA: Stanford University Press.

Republic of the Philippines. 1987. *The Family Code of the Philippines*. Manila: Republic of the Philippines.

Ruddick, S. 1982. "Maternal Thinking." Pp. 76–94 in *Rethinking the Family: Some Feminist Questions*, edited by B. Thorne with M. Yalom. New York: Longhorn.

PART VII

Education

I n this section, we cover issues in the field of gender that deal with education. Education is a central institution in society and one that individuals engage with across the life course, from childhood through adolescence, young adulthood, and beyond. Gender has influenced the organization of education, including who teaches what and how. Conversely, education maintains and regulates gender norms. In this way, primary, secondary, and higher education are institutional sites of inequality both in terms of who has access and in how they reinforce existing social hierarchies. Gender scholars have examined how gender inequalities surface within educational settings from interactions between peers, teachers, and students to educational policy, pedagogical approaches, and curriculum. This section examines gender and sexuality in a variety of education contexts across the core themes of the reader: intersectionality, masculinity, transgender, and global (IMTG) perspectives.

At a moment when many young people go into significant debt to earn their college degree, Rachel Dwyer and colleagues' "Gender, Debt, and Dropping Out of College" uncovers how levels of debt shape women's and men's college trajectories. Women are more likely to take out educational loans for college than men are. Men also drop out of college at lower levels of debt than women, in part because they recognize that high-school peers can gain relatively well-paying jobs without a college degree. Women who are college dropouts make much less than those who are college graduates; yet men who are dropouts or graduates see no significant differences in earnings at the early stages of their careers. Thus, men resist taking on debt to gain a degree. On the other hand, women see their friends in low-paying jobs, motivating them to stay in school. There are also racial differences, but Black and Hispanic women are also less likely to drop out than co-ethnic men are, given their relatively poor employment prospects. Although women's higher rates of college graduation may suggest that men are disadvantaged in educational settings, this study suggests that, instead, men have greater labor market opportunities than women do, which leads them to take on less debt for a college education.

Gender and race also affect students' experiences at school. In "Gender, Race, and Justifications for Group Exclusion," Simone Ispa-Landa shows how gender, race, and sexuality operate in a racial integration program that busses urban Black students to a predominantly White suburban school. Observation and interviews with students and program coordinators find that bussed students are racially stereotyped in gender-specific ways. White suburban students suggest that the bussed students are not as intelligent or deserving of a high-prestige suburban education. Yet, White students welcome Black boys into suburban social cliques, with acceptance contingent upon their embodiment of Black masculinity stereotypes such as "coolness" and "toughness." On the other hand, White students stereotype Black girls as "aggressive" and too "assertive," excluding them from cliques for not embodying White suburban femininity. While Black boys are popular in the White heterosexual dating scene, Black girls are left out of dating entirely. The study shows the way that racial minority students' gender performance is used as justification for social exclusion and how Black boys' and girls' gender and race performances are read in relation to one another.

Amy Wilkins's "'Not Out to Start a Revolution'" further examines how Black university men manage their emotions on two predominantly White college campuses, distancing themselves from stereotypes of angry Black men as a way to uphold their masculinity. Although racially charged and racist interactions regularly occur, some Black men—particularly athletes—emphasize positive interactions and feel welcome on campus, wheras "regulars" or nonathletes report feeling more invisible. Interviews show how Black college men perform a "moderate Blackness" identity that invokes Black culture to avoid seeming "whitewashed," while showing emotional restraint around racial politics and interactions with their White peers. This allows these students to maintain a positive view of their college experience but pushes the angry Black stereotype onto Black women, reinforcing a racialized gender hierarchy. Once again, Black men's and women's gender and race performance are read in relation to one another.

In "'Now Why Do You Want to Know About That?'" Lorena García investigates how sex education is experienced by Latina youth. Latina girls experience racial stereotyping from teachers and educators that perceived them as "at risk" of pregnancy. By inscribing a good girl/bad girl dichotomy, teachers and sex educators emphasize that girls should not be sexually active and place pressure and responsibility on girls, rather than boys, to avoid sex. Teachers also focus on pregnancy prevention, implying in their narratives that Latina culture is overly sexualized and does not support birth control. Teachers also stress that girls are opposite to boys but should be sexually oriented toward them, promoting heterogender performance and silencing or rendering invisible non-heterosexual desires. The research demonstrates how sex education enforces heteronormative, sexist, and racist discourses that are particularly harmful to Latina youth.

Curricula can work to broaden notions of gender and sexuality, but they can also reinforce particular ideas. Focused on the pressing topic of transgender and genderqueer students, Susan Woolley's "'Boys Over Here, Girls Over There'" observes the routine classroom practices of gender segregation through instruction and course content, even among teachers who mean to be progressive. Despite posters emphasizing inclusivity, teachers and students reinforce a heteronormative binary gender regime, policing bathrooms to ensure that students appear appropriately feminine or masculine and consistently dividing students into groups of "boys" and "girls." Even as teachers mean to be inclusive, their practices can "other" students who do not fall neatly into heteronormative gender binary categories. Students become targets of gender authenticity surveillance by other students and teachers, silencing the experiences of trans and gender nonconforming students and reinforcing the gender binary. Even in spaces marked as "safe" for LGBTQ students, students may feel anything but safe.

Offering a global perspective, Monisha Bajaj's "Un/Doing Gender?" examines the ways that gender transformative educational policies, practices, and pedagogy operate in a nonprofit secondary school in Zambia. Here, as above, boys and girls are separated, but in this case, the curriculum does not even consider LGBTQ students or those who might not fit into gender binaries. Yet, the school works to undo gender by insisting that all students carry out the same tasks—with boys involved in cleaning the school and girls encouraged to do leadership work. Observations, interviews, and surveys with eighth- and ninth-grade students and teachers show how students in the school demonstrate greater understanding and knowledge of gender-specific human rights, as well as an interest in furthering women's rights in the future, than do students at the local government school in the region. Yet students also struggle to navigate the competing gender ideologies between the school and their community and home lives. Bajaj provides an example of how schools attempt to unmake prescribed gender differences, even while reinforcing gender binaries by separating students into boys and girls.

This section shows how education is deeply implicated in upholding and challenging ideas about gender and sexuality. Education is also linked to labor market opportunities and debt, while race and class operate through these institutions as well. In both high schools and colleges, it seems that young Black men and women in predominantly White spaces experience being Black differently, since men are stereotyped as "being cool" and women are stereotyped as "being angry." Latina girls undergoing sex education classes also find themselves reacting to stereotypes of Latinas being sexualized and overly fertile, while same-sex attraction goes unacknowledged. Although educational institutions might work to support change—around trans students or around gender differentiation—these efforts may unintentionally continue to reinforce difference.

Gender, Debt, and Dropping Out of College

Rachel E. Dwyer, Randy Hodson, and Laura McCloud

© iStockphoto.com/sdominick

Higher education was once considered a public good that was a priority for society, but it is increasingly seen as a private good that should be individually financed. One unintended consequence is that many more students have to take on debt to finance a college degree (Baum and McPherson 2008). In this context of heightened borrowing, debt has become integral to educational attainment and the college experience for many young adults. The societal decision to finance higher education with debt shifts the risk of investing in college to individuals, with potentially perverse consequences. While parents and higher education administrators often see the opportunities and risks of taking on student loans as clearly in favor of a college degree—even with debt—there exist real risks to starting adulthood with a substantial burden of debt (Bowen, Chingos, and McPherson 2009; Leicht and Fitzgerald

Rachel E. Dwyer, Randy Hodson, and Laura McCloud. 2013. "Gender, Debt, and Dropping Out of College." *Gender & Society* 27(1):30–55.

2006; Rosenbaum 2001). Personal troubles like job loss, divorce, and illness often cannot be anticipated, and debt can make these difficulties harder to navigate (Drentea 2000; Sullivan, Warren, and Westbrook 2000; McCloud and Dwyer 2011). The transition to adulthood is itself increasingly uncertain, with recent cohorts facing a less clear path into careers, family formation, and home ownership than earlier generations (Bernhardt et al. 2001; Mortimer 2003). These uncertainties make a college degree ever more crucial to securing a place in the middle class, but they also raise the potential risk of carrying debt.

These risks are significantly differentiated by gender, however, as women and men face different material trade-offs and nonmaterial influences on educational attainment and the early career (Aronson 2008). At the same time that higher education has transformed from a quasi-public to a quasi-private good, women have become an increasing majority of college students. The female numeric advantage is even more pronounced at graduation, as men not only enroll in lower numbers than women but drop out in greater numbers (Buchmann and DiPrete 2006). Given this evidence that women and men traverse the terrain of debt-financed higher education differently, it is important to understand gender differences in the role of debt in college attrition. We examine the role of debt in dropping out of college for women and men in order to investigate gender differences in the system of debt-financed higher education. We expect significant gender differences because young women and men face different opportunities and constraints in the uncertain risks and rewards of making their way in a debt-based society.

Financing college is not usually seen as a gendered problem, but once debt is seen as one of the trade-offs young adults make in the course of the transition to adulthood, it becomes clear that gender may shape these calculations. Women and men face different labor market opportunities and so their assessments of whether debt is worth the eventual goal of a college degree can easily differ. Occupational segregation and the gender pay gap for women are especially large among jobs that do not require a college degree, and so women experience a greater relative college premium than men (Bobbitt-Zeher 2007; DiPrete and Buchmann 2006; England 2010). Women may feel more pressured to take on debt to finance college than men because women have fewer options for decent pay in jobs that do not require a college degree. Gender differences in the role of debt in college attainment may arise for reasons other than material trade-offs as well. Women and men differ in many of the nonmaterial influences on college attrition, including academic preparation, family support, and peer networks (Tinto 1987). Institutional support varies by gender even for students enrolled in the same college because of persistent gender differences in majors and extracurricular activities that may create differences in the contacts and contexts for female and male college students (Charles and Bradley 2009; Fox, Sonnert, and Nikiforova 2011). What is less well understood is whether these gender differences in experiences then translate into different likelihoods of taking on debt to complete a college degree. To the extent that this translation occurs, a nonmaterial process becomes a material difference in financial behavior.

The increasing female advantage in college completion shows clear progress for women that represents real improvements in girls' education and family investment in girls (Buchmann and DiPrete 2006). At the same time, women may attend college at higher rates because they have fewer options in the low-education labor market than do men (Bobbitt-Zeher 2007). One unacknowledged consequence may be gender differences in the role of debt in supporting adult attainments. In the analysis that follows, we investigate this process with a two-stage model in which we first consider the effects of carrying debt on graduation probabilities for women and men. Subsequently, we examine the different labor market opportunities facing female and male college graduates and dropouts as a potential lens for understanding gendered debt effects on graduation. This analysis has the potential to shed new light not only on the new debt society, but also on the widely recognized but not fully understood surge in college attendance and completion for women.

[. . .]

Gender and Student Loans

We conceptualize taking on student loan debt to achieve a college degree as an investment, but an investment with risks because of the uncertainties of being able to pay back the debt in the future, risk that we have argued vary by gender. We expect that this double-edged character of debt means that different amounts of debt will have different effects on the likelihood of college completion (Dwyer, McCloud, and Hodson 2012). Educational loans likely reduce the chances of dropping out at lower levels of debt, helping students through difficult periods and serving as a bridge over shortfalls from other sources of funding (Chen and DesJardins 2008; Dwyer, McCloud, and Hodson 2011). As educational debt reaches higher levels, however, it can generate increasing pressure to drop out (Ishitani 2006). Many students enter college relatively uninformed about debt and may take on large amounts of debt without thinking of the consequences until later in their college career as repayment looms (Bowen, Chingos, and McPherson 2009). Indeed, student concern about debt appears to build over the course of college as debt mounts and postcollege realities come into sharper focus—realities that can include negative outcomes like depression and suicidal ideation in addition to dropping out of college (Meltzer et al. 2011). Other students may get into debt because of personal problems or an unexpected decline in family support that makes it difficult to continue in college without extensive borrowing (Christie and Munro 2003). We expect that the gender differences in college experiences and labor market expectations discussed above will affect these mechanisms and the balance between risk and reward in taking on more debt.

Prior research has given almost no attention to gender differences in the role of debt in college attainment. Yet to the extent that women are better prepared and receive greater social support for college, and see more advantages to staying in college compared to dropping out, women should be willing to take on more educational debt to stay in college than men. Young men who see high school friends with relatively well-paying jobs may resist taking on debt to gain a degree with uncertain returns. They may ignore or discount some of the longer-term negatives of traditional male blue-collar jobs, such as the risk of unemployment and industrial decline. At the same time, young women who see friends in low-paying female-dominated jobs, such as retail cashier or day care worker, may be spurred to stay in school, even with debt. The motivation to continue in college in spite of debt is thus likely more pressing for women than for men. We can test these expectations by studying the differential effects of debt on dropping out of college for women and men. . . . We expect that men will drop out at lower levels of debt—because, more often than women, they will make the calculation that higher levels of debt are "not worth it."

[. . .]

Data

We use data from the National Longitudinal Survey of Youth, 1997 Cohort (NLSY97), to examine the effect indebtedness has on young adults' likelihood of graduating from college.

The NLSY97 is an annually administered survey funded by the Bureau of Labor Statistics (BLS) that consists of two subsamples of young adults born between 1980 and 1984; the first subsample is a nationally representative sample of 6,748 young adults and the second subsample oversamples 2,236 Hispanic and Black individuals. The first year of data collection for this NLSY cohort was 1996, and the latest round of data available for our analysis was collected in 2010–2011. At the time of the latest available data, the young adults in our sample range in age from 25 to 31 years old, with a mean of 28 years. The NLSY97 is an optimal data set for our study because it has rich financial data on the cohort of young people who became adults following the democratization of credit in the 1990s.

[. . .]

Results

. . . About 38 percent of those enrolled take on educational loans in a given year. The mean educational loan taken out by debtors in a given year is $4,719. Women are more likely to take out loans than men, with 40 percent of women and 34 percent of men taking out loans on average in each year. These results are certainly suggestive that debt-holding is a gendered experience. The mean *amount* of debt for men and women students who take on debt is quite similar, however, with women holding $4,726 and men holding $4,709. A measure of cumulative debt shows similar patterns, albeit at higher levels of debt, with almost half of all college students carrying debt overall, with a somewhat larger gender differential of women carrying more debt, at $11,133, than men at $10,829. Clearly, educational debt was part of the college experience for many students in the 2000s.

. . . We consider two models of the likelihood of graduating from college, estimated separately for women and men. . . . Higher levels of educational debt increase the chance of graduating (and lower duration to graduating) until a high level of debt is achieved, and then additional debts no longer increase the chances of graduating; in fact, the chances decline a bit compared to moderate levels of debt. . . . Higher amounts of debt produce diminishing returns for college completion, and highlights the worrisome reality that many students leave college with high levels of debt but without a degree.

[. . .]

The gender differences in the effect of debt on college graduation are even more clearly illustrated in Figure 33.1, which graphs the predicted values for the curvilinear effect of educational loans for women and men. . . .

The entire curve tracks higher for women than for men. This is consistent with women's greater graduation probabilities overall, but it also suggests that debt is a greater facilitator of graduation for women than for men. Supporting this interpretation, the curve for men tracks shallower and turns negative at lower levels of debt, indicating that educational loans are less effective at preventing dropping out and that men drop out at lower levels of debt than do women. The gender differential thus increases at higher levels of debt—the gender gap in graduation is less than 0.05 percentage point at zero debt, but close to 1.0 percentage point at the highest levels of debt. This pattern of gender differences supports our expectations that women and men face different pathways through debt-financed higher education, with potentially important consequences for their longer-term financial circumstances above and beyond the effect of college attainment. . . . Lower levels of debt increase the chances of graduating for women more than for men. The curve starts higher for women than men and

Figure 33.1 Estimated Probabilities of Graduating From College by Educational Debt for Women and Men Enrolled in College, Full Model

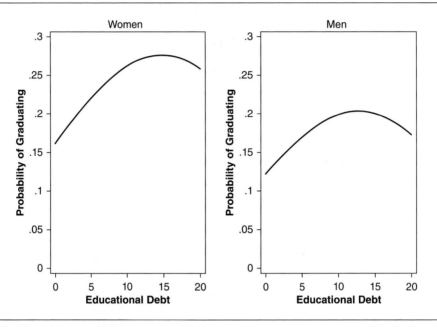

Note: Educational debt is measured in thousands of dollars.

stays higher along the whole curve. At the same time, the curve turns downward at a higher level of debt for women than for men. This supports our expectation . . . in that higher levels of debt are more strongly associated with dropping out of college for men than for women, suggesting that education debt becomes an impediment to completion at lower levels for men than for women.

So far we have highlighted gender differences in debt and graduation, but research on college graduation shows that there are also substantial racial differences in graduation probabilities, and that these interact significantly with gender (Buchmann and DiPrete 2006). We examine racial differences within gender by studying differences in predicted probabilities in college graduation across levels of debt for different racial groups. We find that the curve for Black and Hispanic students tracks lower than the curve for white students for both men and women and that the inflection point occurs at somewhat lower levels as well. At the same time, Black and Hispanic women are more likely to graduate across all levels of debt than are Black and Hispanic men. . . . The perils of dropping out of college without a degree, but with debt, may be particularly serious for minority students who face racial discrimination in the labor market and are more likely to lack family resources to help pay off the debt.

Our analysis sheds light on important realities of gender differences in navigating increasingly debt-financed higher education. Both men and women are vulnerable to getting in over their heads with student loans, and accruing a very large amount of debt without achieving the credential of a higher degree, but men are more deterred from completing by having debt than are women. The resulting debt burden may compound the difficulties faced by young adults as they drop out of college and move more fully into the labor market.

Female and Male College Dropouts in the Early Career

The gender differentials we find support our interpretation that youth face gendered trade-offs in decisions about dropping out or completing college. We have argued that debt affects the likelihood of dropping out differently for women compared to men because of a range of differences in college experience and expectations about postcollege opportunities.... We can investigate the labor market prospects of female and male college dropouts compared to college completers within the early careers of our sample of respondents. This will help us understand not only the material trade-offs faced by young adults as they make decisions about college completion but also gender differences in the implications of leaving college—even if for nonmaterial reasons—with debt but without a degree.

Given prior research that women receive a greater relative wage premium for college than do men, we hypothesized a larger gap between the earnings of women dropouts and graduates than between men dropouts and graduates.... Indeed, this is what we find for this sample of youth in their early careers in regression analyses of earnings for employed women and men.... Employed female dropouts have much lower earnings than female college graduates, making more than $6,500 less even after controlling for demographic factors.... In contrast, men who drop out have similar earnings to male college graduates (at least in the early years after college) with no significant difference in their earnings.... These observed differences are not simply a result of female college dropouts working fewer hours than female college graduates, since differentials exist for hourly wages as well as for annual income. Both female and male college dropouts experience greater unemployment than college graduates, but this difference does not explain the within-gender earnings differentials. As we expected, women experience a much larger immediate economic penalty for not graduating from college than do men. Female dropouts simply face worse job prospects than do male dropouts.

We see evidence in our sample of young adults that the differences in earnings for female and male dropouts and graduates track with persistent gender segregation at the bottom of the labor market.... Figure 33.2 shows the predicted probabilities of employment in different occupational groups for female and male dropouts and graduates.... We group occupations into four categories—service, clerical, professional, and manufacturing, construction, and transportation jobs. Clerical work is highly female dominated and manufacturing highly male dominated, whereas service and professional work reflect more gender balance. The graph clearly illustrates that the occupations of dropouts are more differentiated by gender than are the occupations of graduates. Female dropouts concentrate in service and clerical positions, whereas male dropouts concentrate in manufacturing, construction, and transportation. Female dropouts have an almost 0.30 probability of working in a clerical occupation, whereas the probability of clerical work is less than 0.20 for women college graduates and only 0.10 for male dropouts. Female dropouts also have a more than 10-point higher probability of service work than male dropouts (though male dropouts also have a high probability of working in a service occupation). In contrast, male dropouts have a probability of working in a manufacturing, construction, or transportation occupation of more than 0.30, while for women the probability of being in one of those jobs approaches zero. Manufacturing, construction, and transportation occupations are among the best-paid jobs for those without a college degree, whereas service and clerical jobs are much less well paid (England 2010). Gender occupational segregation thus strongly shapes the occupational experiences of female and male college dropouts.

[...]

Figure 33.2 Predicted Probability of Occupation in Early-Career Female and Male College Dropouts and Graduates

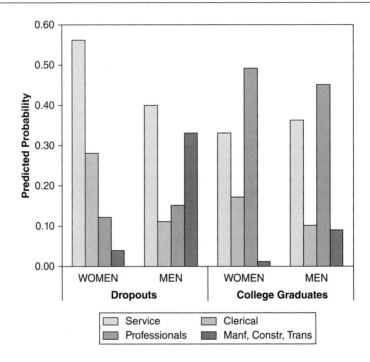

We have argued that these differences in labor market prospects for women and men who drop out of college represent one of the underlying reasons for gender differences in the influence of debt on dropping out of college. Even if the gender differences in the role of debt in dropping out arise out of the nonmaterial influences that we have also discussed, the labor market inequalities suggest that women face even more risk when they do drop out of college with debt for whatever reason. While there has been quite a lot of attention paid to the increasing female advantage in college completion, there has been less consideration of the implications of those differences in a system of higher education that depends heavily on individual indebtedness.

The debt system for financing college creates risks for both women and men. Women are not only at a disadvantage in the low-education labor market, they also face a situation where many gain access to higher levels of achievement only through taking on significant debt. Especially since female college graduates still earn less than male college graduates, debt-financed higher education may hit women harder than men, even as it is more necessary.... On the other hand, men who are lured out of college by the promise of decent pay in manufacturing, construction, and transportation jobs, or who find themselves out of college for other reasons, may face considerable uncertainty in their employment as some of these sectors continue a decades-long contraction, and even the more robust sectors, like construction, are highly sensitive to the business cycle. The short-term earnings benefits of low-education jobs for men may also fade over time, as male college graduates pull ahead of male dropouts in earnings across the life course (Bernhardt et al. 2001).

Conclusions

Our study provides some of the first evidence that debt-financed higher education intersects with the gender system to create differential outcomes for women and men. In a period of high college tuitions and widely available credit, the risks and rewards of taking on debt have become salient issues for many young adults, but scholars have had little to say about these issues. Women and men attempt to make reasonable choices about their finances and college attainment, but these decisions are made within the constraints of a debt system and a gender system that shape opportunities and risks in college, in the labor market, and beyond. We have only begun to understand the role of borrowed resources in the system of gendered status attainment, and future research on the young adults coming of age during the twenty-first century will be critical to understanding how debt effects differentiate by gender. Studying the process by which female and male students move through and exit college, including qualitative work that engages students directly, will be essential in future research on debt and dropping out of college.

[. . .]

As we have argued, there are significant risks to funding higher education with debt, and these risks and rewards differ for women and men. . . . Perhaps debt serves as an effective way to underwrite investment in the next generation's talent—and the positive effects of relatively low levels of educational loans certainly provide some support for this view. The lagging college completion rates are a sign of trouble, however, and we ultimately know very little about how youth manage their debt loads as they move into adulthood. We as educators, and all who work within the system of higher education, are not on the sidelines of this conversation. Just as we defend the core academic values of our institutions, so should we support the value of higher education in an increasingly global world, and the value of *affordable* education without the liability of excessive, even potentially crippling, debt.

[. . .]

References

Aronson, Pamela. 2008. "The Markers and Meanings of Growing Up: Contemporary Young Women's Transition from Adolescence to Adulthood." *Gender & Society* 22:56–82.

Baum, Sandy and Michael McPherson. 2008. "Introduction." In *The Effectiveness of Student Aid Policies: What the Research Tells Us*, edited by S. Baum, M. McPherson, and P. Steele. New York: The College Board.

Bernhardt, Annette, Martina Morris, Mark S. Handcock, and Marc A. Scott. 2001. *Divergent Paths: Economic Mobility in the New American Labor Market*. New York: Russell Sage Foundation.

Bobbitt-Zeher, Donna. 2007. "The Gender Income Gap and the Role of Education." *Sociology of Education* 80:1–22.

Bowen, William G., Matthew M. Chingos, and Michael S. McPherson. 2009. *Crossing the Finish Line: Completing College at America's Public Universities*. Princeton, NJ: Princeton University Press.

Buchmann, Claudia and Thomas A. DiPrete. 2006. "The Growing Female Advantage in College Completion: The Role of Parental Resources and Academic Achievement." *American Sociological Review* 71:515–41.

Charles, Maria and Karen Bradley. 2009. "Indulging Our Gendered Selves: Sex Segregation by Field of Study in 44 Countries." *American Journal of Sociology* 114:924–76.

Chen, Rong and Stephen L. DesJardins. 2008. "Exploring the Effects of Financial Aid on the Gap in Student Dropout Risks by Income Level." *Research in Higher Education* 49:1–18.

Christie, Hazel and Moira Munro. 2003. "The Logic of Loans: Students' Perceptions of the Costs and Benefits of the Student Loan." *British Journal of Sociology of Education* 24:621–36.

DiPrete, Thomas and Claudia Buchmann. 2006. "Gender-Specific Trends in the Value of Education and the Emerging Gender Gap in College Completion." *Demography* 43:1–24.

Drentea, Patricia. 2000. "Age, Debt, and Anxiety." *Journal of Health and Social Behavior* 41:437–50.

Dwyer, Rachel E., Laura McCloud, and Randy Hodson. 2011. "Youth Debt, Mastery, and Self-Esteem: Class-Stratified Effects of Indebtedness on Self-Concept." *Social Science Research* 40:727–41.

Dwyer, Rachel E., Laura McCloud, and Randy Hodson. 2012. "Debt and Graduation from American Universities." *Social Forces* 90:1133–155.

England, Paula. 2010. "The Gender Revolution: Uneven and Stalled." *Gender & Society* 24:149–66.

Fox, Mary Frank, Gerhard Sonnert, and Irina Nikiforova. 2011. "Programs for Undergraduate Women in Science and Engineering: Issues, Problems, and Solutions." *Gender & Society* 25:589–615.

Ishitani, Terry T. 2006. "Studying Attrition and Degree Completion Behavior Among First-Generation College Students in the United States." *Journal of Higher Education* 77:861–85.

Leicht, Kevin and Scott Fitzgerald. 2006. *Postindustrial Peasants: The Illusion of Middle-Class Prosperity.* New York: Worth.

McCloud, Laura and Rachel E. Dwyer. 2011. "The Fragile American: Hardship and Financial Troubles in the 21st Century." *The Sociological Quarterly* 52:13–35.

Meltzer, H., P. Bebbington, T. Brugha, R. Jenkins, S. McManus, and M. S. Dennis. 2011. "Personal Debt and Suicidal Ideation." *Psychological Medicine* 41:771–78.

Mortimer, Jeylan T. 2003. *Working and Growing Up in America.* Cambridge, MA: Harvard University Press.

Rosenbaum, James. 2001. *Beyond College for All: Career Paths for the Forgotten Half.* New York: Russell Sage Foundation.

Sullivan, Theresa A., Elizabeth Warren, and Jay Lawrence Westbrook. 2000. *The Fragile Middle Class: Americans in Debt.* New Haven, CT: Yale University Press.

Tinto, Vincent. 1987. *Leaving College: Rethinking the Causes and Cures of Student Attrition.* Chicago, IL: University of Chicago Press.

Gender, Race, and Justifications for Group Exclusion

Urban Black Students Bussed to Affluent Suburban Schools

Simone Ispa-Landa

© iStockphoto.com/Deborah Cheramine

S cholars have examined how race and class relations shape evaluations of students' gender performances. This research shows that teachers and peers often view ethnic minorities' behavior as gender-inappropriate. Many authors conclude that teachers and students explain the inferior achievement of lower-class and non-white students with references to the

Simone Ispa-Landa. 2013. "Gender, Race, and Justifications for Group Exclusion: Urban Black Students Bussed to Affluent Suburban Schools." *Sociology of Education* 86(3):218–33.

inappropriateness or undesirability of their gender performances (Bettie 2003; Ferguson 2000; Lewis 2003; López 2002; Morris 2007; Pascoe 2007; Schippers 2007; Tyson 2011). However, researchers have yet to theorize the conditions under which dominant groups use subordinate groups' gender performances to maintain race/class hierarchies. Without such an examination, it appears as if the gender performances of *all* individuals belonging to subordinate groups are used against them, all the time. This assumption prevents a more specific understanding of how idealized definitions of masculinity or femininity can serve race/class hierarchies. To address these gaps, I conducted an in-depth study of adolescent culture within a network of affluent, intentionally racially integrated suburban schools. Empirically, the goal was to identify when and how minority participants' gender performances would be used as the rationale for their exclusion from peer cliques. The findings and analysis have broad theoretical implications for the study of gender in racially integrated settings.

The study compares the everyday experiences of male and female black adolescents participating in Diversify, a voluntary urban-to-suburban racial integration program. The Diversify program buses black students from poor and working-class, majority-minority neighborhoods to a participating network of affluent, majority-white suburban schools. Thus, Diversify students are not only ethnically different from their (mostly white) suburban classmates, but also come from a lower class background. Previous research has shown that minority students in such circumstances have a heightened likelihood of experiencing incomplete belonging in majority peer networks (Gaztambide-Fernandez and DiAquoi 2010; Horvat and Antonio 1999). The Diversify students' experiences of peer culture offer an excellent platform for understanding when and how members of a lower-class minority group's gender performance are used as the grounds for its exclusion.

[. . .]

The Idealized Relationship Between Masculinity and Femininity

In a recent article, Schippers (2007) describes how as analysts increasingly focus on multiple masculinities and femininities, they neglect the complementary and hierarchical relation of masculinity vis-à-vis femininity. Critiquing this trend, she writes, "the implicit relationship between genders becomes a taken-for-granted feature of interpersonal relationships, culture, and social structure" (p. 91). In this research, I analyzed the Diversify boys' and girls' seemingly opposite social situations. In so doing, I sought to go beyond an analysis of the Diversify girls' social situation vis-à-vis the femininities deemed desirable within the suburban school. My approach is complementary to, yet distinct from, previous treatments of black girls' "place" within schools (Grant 1984; Morris 2007), which have largely emphasized how black girls may be sanctioned for failing to live up to standards of white femininity. In seeking to understand how the black girls' social position related to the *overall* gender order, I brought a relational gender lens to bear on analysis.

Schippers (2007) emphasizes that the idealized features of masculinity and femininity are those that ensure a complementary and hierarchical relationship between the two. On the masculine side, these include desire for the feminine object, violence, and authority. On the feminine side, these include desire to be the *object* of masculine desire, physical vulnerability, and compliance. Gender is a set of practices, rather than a property of individuals. Thus, women can embody masculine characteristics. However, when they do, these characteristics are constructed as deviant *feminine* characteristics (the bitch, the bad-ass, the slut). For masculinity to remain a legitimate property of men, feminine access to it must be denied. Thus, when a man exhibits hegemonic feminine characteristics—such as desiring to be the object of masculine desire—he is viewed as contaminating social relations. He has violated the idealized relationship between masculinity and femininity. When men enact the quality content of femininity, they are therefore constructed as feminine (the fag, pussy, or mama's boy). Masculinity is superior and desirable. Therefore, masculinity cannot "sustain" stigma and contamination—only femininity can (Schippers 2007).

[. . .]

Moreover, the seeming "gender differences" between women and men within an ethnically or socioeconomically diverse setting are actually race and class differences in *gender performance* or social organization. Race and class differences in gender performance legitimate class and race hierarchies (Schippers 2007:100). For example, the gender performances of those in low-status positions are often constructed as problematic or deviant—as in the well-known tropes about the hyper-sexual "welfare queen" or the black rapist (Collins 2004). Many school ethnographies describe rites, rituals, and patterns of behavior consistent with the basic relational insight that race and class domination hinge, in part, on the ability to deem illegitimate or inappropriate the real or stereotyped gender performances of others.

[. . .]

Contexts, Participants, and Analytic Methods

Background on the Diversify Program and the Suburban Schools

The Diversify program is an urban-to-suburban racial integration program. It busses ethnic minority students from an urban public school district to schools located within a network of 40 suburban school districts. All the participating suburban school districts have voluntarily elected to participate in Diversify, generally with the stated goal of increasing racial diversity within their predominantly white suburban school districts.

[. . .]

Using the Diversify database, I identified and sent letters to the parents/guardians of all black Diversify students ($n = 109$) in Grades 8 through 10 in these affluent suburban school districts. . . .

I formally interviewed all the Diversify students who agreed to be interviewed and turned in consent forms, yielding 38 Diversify students for my sample. . . .

. . . The principal of one of the affluent suburban schools randomly selected for me 30 non-poor eighth-grade students and gave me a list of their names and contact information. I contacted all 30, but only 7 agreed to be interviewed. Several parents of the remaining 23 students told me their children were either not interested or "too busy." . . . I refer to the Diversify and suburban students as either Diversify or suburban students. To reduce the reader's confusion, I call any suburban area either Chilton or Glenfield, rather than providing a pseudonym for each of the 11 suburban school districts. Although the suburban sample is small, it was nonetheless informative, as all the suburban students confirmed that the black girls were generally isolated and marginalized while the black boys tended to be popular and high-status.

. . . I spoke with nine Diversify coordinators, all of whom I initially met at Diversify, Inc. staff meetings.

[. . .]

I observed a school cafeteria and hallway in a Diversify school for two months and attended several ice cream socials aimed at increasing contact between the Diversify and suburban school communities. I also attended a few Diversify Alumni meetings and social events. . . . I used my field notes from these observations as a form of triangulation, examining whether the Diversify students' reports of gender-differentiated friendship and dating patterns were accurate.

[. . .]

Valuing Achievement—A Racialized Context

It is important to know that the suburban schools the Diversify adolescents attend are not only well-funded and largely white, they are also intensely achievement focused. The teachers and white students I talked to put high value on a strong work ethic, excellent grades and test scores, and professional accomplishment. Acceptance at Ivy League colleges was a common goal. Moreover, the white students I talked to felt that their parents "deserved" the right to live in their affluent neighborhoods because they had worked hard. Noah, the white 14-year-old son of two endocrinologists, illustrated this view, adding that the suburban parents had passed their work ethic and motivation to succeed to their children. He went on to say that he felt the Diversify kids had a reputation for not being as hard-working or successful:

I mean most kids that live in Chilton, their parents are successful because it cost a lot of money to live here. So yeah, I'd say the attitude of most kids is obviously to do well and turn out like their parents, or if not, even better. Yeah, there are very few kids that don't care and just give up. . . .

Like Chilton is pretty overwhelming, the amount of work and like the amount of pressure, because there are a lot of smart kids. There's a lot of work and things. . . . But like the Diversify kids, I guess—they're seen as not trying their hardest or just not doing as well academically.

Within this racial and socioeconomic context, the Diversify boys correctly perceived that their suburban classmates saw them as "underachievers" and "troublemakers." For example, Ebo, 15, a high-achieving Diversify freshman, complained about the stereotypes of black students as "troublemakers" and "underachievers" and was very critical of his school's placement policies, saying, "They put the black kids in the stupid classes. Like if you're from the city going to there, they put you in the stupidest classes ever. Like Pre-Algebra I?! Like I can do that stuff, I'm not that stupid!"

Consistent with Diversify students' complaints about race and class stereotyping, the suburban students questioned the Diversify students' presence in the suburban schools, speculating that perhaps they didn't "deserve" the high-quality suburban education they were getting. In so doing, they redefined Diversify as a "scholarship" (rather than a racial integration) program.

Noah, quoted earlier to illustrate the white students' high valuing of achievement, told me that in contrast, the Diversify students were not as hardworking or interested in school. When I asked him how the Diversify program could be improved, he stated that perhaps the Diversify kids could be given an extra "incentive" for working hard:

I think the point of Diversify is . . . to give kids that don't come from the same background and don't have what most kids here have, give them a chance to have a great opportunity to have better teachers and better activities. . . . But I see a lot of kids I know are from Diversify are just skipping class. . . . I don't know what they [school faculty and staff] do to motivate them. . . . I think they . . . need to somehow motivate them more . . . like say, give them like a prize if they do well, or something.

All the suburban students I interviewed liked the *idea* of offering urban minorities spots in "their" schools (Ispa-Landa 2011). However, they felt that suburban schools should try to recruit (in their words) "better," more "hardworking," or "more intelligent" Diversify students. As Joel, another 14-year-old white suburban student, explained, "We need kids who . . . would make more of an effort to make use of their opportunities." Thus, nested within the discourse about the Diversify students' supposed underachievement was another discourse, one that questioned the Diversify students' presence and/or "deservingness" to a suburban education. Further, echoing popular and scholarly concerns about the well-being of affluent youth (e.g., Demerath 2009), Diversify coordinators stated that the suburban students were, if anything, excessively achievement oriented. Thus, achievement (and anxiety about achievement) was racialized, making it seem as though "stress" and "doing well" were suburban (white or Asian) concerns.

Cool and Different: The Social Situation of the Boys

Nonetheless, in a seemingly paradoxical pattern, all the Diversify boys also reported that because they were black and from the city, they had a reputation for being popular. Recall Ebo's complaint about pervasive racial stereotyping about black students as "troublemakers" and "underachievers." Yet, when I asked Ebo if he spends time in the suburbs at friends' houses, he answered, "Well, because I'm black, yeah." He went on to explain, "It's like, if you're a black guy and you're not popular, it's like something must be wrong with you, you know? I don't know what they like about black people, but . . . uh, yeah [they do]." Some Diversify boys reported that they practically "lived in the suburbs." For example, Ronnell, 14, described himself as having like "ten moms" in the suburbs:

Ronnell: I'm always out there.

Interviewer: Oh. Like doing what, what do you do?

Ronnell: Well, it like depends who I'm with . . . with a certain friend, I can probably spend . . . like if it's my best friend, I'll probably spend like two weeks with them, like just stay out there and spend the night. . . . 'Cause so technically I have like ten moms, pretty much. . . . 'Cause like, with my best friend, she [friend's mom] just got like used to me and stuff, . . . like I was her own son. So like I can hang out there, days at a time.

Tough facades. My analysis suggests that the Diversify boys' popularity hinged on their embodiment or exaggeration of stereotypes of black masculinity. For example, some of the Diversify boys consciously exaggerated the perceived differences between themselves and the suburban boys. They tried to appear "street smart" and tough, even as they privately acknowledged (in interviews) that they were not. As 14-year-old Christopher, a black boy in Diversify, explained, being tough is part of Diversify boys' unique social status in the suburbs:

Interviewer: What do the [suburban] kids think of the city kids . . . do you think?

They think we're cool and different. Like we're not the same as them, we come from rougher neighborhoods. And they learn different things from us . . . like different slang. And like since some of these—most of these kids are from Glenfield [a suburb], so they don't like, they don't go for like gangs and stuff like that. So the Diversify kids act tough because they are from the city. Like it helps your coolness to be from a tougher area. For the [city] kids and the suburban kids.

Christopher went on to explain that Diversify boys sometimes fight one another to support their image as tough:

I have been in fights with a couple of people but then we ended up being friends later.

Interviewer: Were they kids in Diversify?

Yeah. Because we all have our differences and like, some of us try to act tough because we're from [the city]. It's like a way of making yourself look better. . . . 'Cause it helps your coolness to be from the tougher areas.

Although Christopher emphasized his toughness in the suburban context, he admitted to me that while suburban kids might think he is tough, he knows that he is not tough by city standards and in fact is afraid of the kids in his own neighborhood. He said that he would be "trying to hide all the time" if he went to his neighborhood school.

Diversify directors also displayed awareness of the unique social position of black Diversify boys in the suburbs. One complained that "a lot of the Diversify guys get headswell. . . . 'Cause out here, they are the big guys, whereas if you put them back in [City] High, they'd just be another guy . . . nothing special." The director went on, "Can you imagine, what it does to the girls (implying it turns them on), to hear their names all over the loudspeaker (from sports wins) all the time? They are like the big guys out here!" The language used in these comments—"big guys"—underscores how the Diversify boys' gender performance was positively evaluated. It could also be an evocation of racial stereotypes about black men's penis size and sexual prowess—stereotypes that reduce black masculinity to bodies and body parts (Collins 2004). Finally, the director's comment about "what it does to the girls" seems to signal the possibility that a "correct" relationship between masculinity and femininity—one of submission/mastery—would be performed.

Sexual politics and dating. Many Diversify boys dated white suburban girls, and being in an interracial, heterosexual dating relationship was seen to raise both parties' status. Tania, 15, an African American girl in Diversify, explained, "It's like fashionable for them [the suburban girls] to be seen dating a Diversify boy, like they'll be like, 'Oh my god, do you hear that so-and-so are dating?!!' and get all excited."

Indeed, interracial dating appeared to offer the suburban girls a set of highly visible opportunities to perform prescribed notions of femininity. Comments from Michael, a 15-year-old black Diversify student, highlighted how the Diversify boys' relationships with suburban girls captured an idealized and complementary relationship between femininity (compliance) and masculinity (goal-seeking). He explained,

Of course we [Diversify boys] are going to be all nice to the white girls, you know . . . like, we are trying to . . . um, get something [sexual] from them. I mean, like, uh, why wouldn't we be? And like, uh, from my side, you know, *they are easier*. No offense [looking at the interviewer, a white woman], but yeah, they [white girls] *are easier to handle*. Just easier, yeah.

Here, it appears that the Diversify boys' enactment of masculinity may have provided an ideal backdrop for the suburban girls to enact a complementary femininity of compliance or sexual submission (being "easy"). These dating dynamics suggest that the Diversify boys were constrained to performing blackness and masculinity in fairly narrow, heterosexual ways—but also that the Diversify boys' social status and popularity hinged on these same hyper-masculine enactments of gender and race. From their perspective as heterosexual males seeking sexual attention from females, the Diversify boys were rewarded for their gender performances.

[. . .]

I observed many boys in my sample showing respect and deference to their mothers, sisters, aunts, and the black Diversify guidance counselors. At the same time, they did not seem to consider the Diversify girls eligible for dating. Perhaps their masculinity was threatened by the specter of the angry black female, who would remove their exclusive access to masculine characteristics (Collins 2004).

In any case, racial stereotypes about black men's intelligence, coupled with the Diversify boys' reluctance to bring their white girlfriends home, seem to undermine the legitimacy of their future masculinity as adult men. . . . As in Pascoe's (2007:5) study, the Diversify boys symbolized "failed, and at the same time, wildly successful men in their heterosexual claim on the girls." Indeed, perhaps the very traits that made the Diversify boys' gender performances attractive within the suburban context also ensured their "place" within the suburbs as failed adult men. Ultimately, their ability to dominate adult women through economic power was questioned. Given that all the suburban students whom I interviewed said that Diversify kids were "troublemakers" and poor students, it is clear that they did not predict that Diversify students would have successful futures.

Isolated and Aggie [Aggravated]: The Social Situation of the Girls

The Diversify girls' evaluations of their social acceptance were different from the boys'. They felt that being black and from the city were social liabilities and, that as a result, they preferred to keep company with one another. Sabrina, 14, lived with her parents in a three-bedroom house they owned in a quiet working-class section of the city. Her comments were typical:

They [suburban kids] know us [Diversify kids] as like . . . loud and obnoxious . . . and I hate that. And like they think that we like wear the same clothes every day and live in an apartment and don't have food every night. . . . I hate it, that's why I try to stay in my own little group [of black Diversify girls].

Even the six Diversify girls in my sample who did spend time in the suburbs complained about the characterizations of blacks as aggressive, overly tough, and poor. For example, Apryl, 15, attended many social events in the suburbs. She was clearly popular with both her Diversify and suburban classmates. Nonetheless, during my interview with her, she complained about racial stereotyping and the constraints it imposed on her behavior, saying, "They [suburban kids] . . . think that black people have to act a certain way. Have to talk a certain way. . . . It's really annoying."

Like the black teenage girls whom Jones (2010) observed in inner-city Philadelphia, the Diversify girls used the folk definitions of both mainstream and black standards of respectability to evaluate and describe themselves. However, the suburban students were unaware of the existence of a "folk category" of strong black woman familiar to the Diversify students—the black middle-class "respectful" or "lady." For the adolescent Diversify girls, like Anderson's

(1999:35) adult participants who characterized the world in terms of "street" versus "decent," "ghetto" and "respectful" represented "two poles of value orientation, two contrasting conceptual categories that structure moral order." The Diversify girls were frustrated and demoralized by the suburban students' use of the term *ghetto* to describe them. Not only did they find it insulting, but it also indicated social and cultural distance between the suburban culture and that of the black students. The suburban students seemed unfamiliar with labels (like "respectful") that the Diversify girls routinely used to describe appropriately feminine behavior within their own communities.

For the Diversify girls and for many Diversify coordinators, being a black "lady" or "respectful" was desirable. This was perhaps most vividly illustrated to me in a conversation with Kathryn, 14, a Diversify student who spoke proudly about her recent evolution from acting "ghetto" to being more "ladylike":

> My dad, he says, well, 'cause I'm loud a lot, or I used to be, and he says I used to be really obnoxious. So he used to tell me stuff like that. And my mom, she would say, I need to lower my voice. She said I need to be more ladylike. So like, I piped down a lot . . . and being obnoxious, like I stopped doing that. And um, I used to be like stubborn a lot and rude, so my maturity level came up a lot on that.

Further, while both suburban and Diversify boys seemed to interpret the Diversify boys' urban clothing styles as "cool," the opposite was true in regards to Diversify girls' clothing. (Almost all the Diversify girls wore some urban styles, like bright sneakers with distinctive shoelaces, and they mostly favored the same hip-hop/athletic clothing brands as the Diversify boys.) Over and over, they told me that people called them, and their clothing, "ghetto" and that they found this characterization to be wrong and insulting. Malika, a 15-year-old student in Diversify, complained:

> They think I'm ghetto, 'cause I'm black. . . . I mean, I mean they think I'm loud, *but I'm not.* And, like, the kind of jewelry that I like, they call me ghetto, 'cause I wear these earrings with my name in it. . . . And like I have the rings that say my name in them across here.

The term *ghetto* clearly has multiple connotations and has—like the broader issue of black girls' loudness—been analyzed before (e.g., Jones 2010). In the suburbs, adjectives like *ghetto* seemed to symbolize not just failure to live up to upper-middle-class white standards of femininity (not being "loud," wearing [discreet] jewelry), but also failure to embody characteristics of femininity that support subordination to *masculinity and whiteness.* In what follows, I show the connection between these adjectives and the ways the Diversify girls posed a symbolic threat to racial privilege and men's exclusive access to aggression.

Diversify girls recognized that they were stigmatized in the suburbs. They, like the white students, attributed this to their conflict management styles, which, importantly, included directly confronting racial insensitivity. Jade, 14, a Diversify student, talked about black girls' unwillingness to be silent when racist remarks are made. She believed that her suburban classmates expected her and other black girls to act "defensive" during conversations about race, as well as in interactions where respect was not sufficiently demonstrated:

> And then there is, "Ohh she lives in The City. She's from the projects." So you are expected to act all loud and stuff. And, um . . . um . . . you're expected to always be defensive. . . . Mostly [about] race, but like, if . . . you are approached the wrong way, you are supposed to get defensive.

Some Diversify girls depicted the suburban girls as "fake," while they were more "upfront." Tellingly, Ranah, 15, a Diversify student, used the term *boyish* to describe the black girls' more direct style of confrontation:

> The Chilton girls . . . they'll talk about you behind your back. . . . Or it's like, "Oh we're going to make up a Facebook group about you and say how much we hate you." But it's never to your face. And City girls, the way we hold ourselves, it's like maybe we're a lot more argumentative, we're more like boyish in a way. We feel like we can fight. . . . We're upfront. . . . 'Cause like, like how we were taught was if you have problem with somebody, say it to their face!

In the end, the Diversify girls did not succeed in promoting a definition of their more aggressive or assertive behavior as "authentic." Thus, the Diversify girls' widespread concern and preoccupation with the *ghetto* label and other pejorative terms reflects the discursive power of the dominant group. In many ways, it was the dominant group's worldviews that were recognized (even by the Diversify girls) as legitimate, something that merited attention and concern.

Out of the dating picture. The Diversify girls reported that neither the white suburban nor the black Diversify boys were interested in dating them. Jade explained that the suburban boys didn't want to get "mixed up" (involved) with the Diversify girls because they were too "aggressive": "The [suburban] boys, they're like, 'Oh, she's a black girl, she has *attitude*,' all that stuff, so they don't want to get mixed up in it." Other Diversify girls said that the suburban boys didn't like the black girls physically, preferring the "Barbie doll" look. Fourteen-year-old Ruth, a Diversify student, explained:

> The boys from the suburbs, they don't pursue the City girls, because . . . they typically prefer blonde hair and blue eyes. . . . Like, the Barbie doll thing. You know? And well, that's just not us, you know—we're ethnic, we have colored skin, we have curly hair, and all that.

For their part, Diversify boys also referred to black girls' assertiveness when explaining why the black girl–white boy dating combination was rare. Jordan, 15, a Diversify boy dating a popular white suburban girl told me, "So you know, most of the white boys, well they just can't handle the black girls. *They just can't handle them.* The black girls, you know, they can be really aggie!" Jordan's comment that the white boys "can't handle" the black girls underscores how the Diversify girls' failure to support masculine dominance—perhaps coupled with Eurocentric beauty standards and the Diversify girls' so-called defensiveness about race—played into their exclusion from the suburban social and dating scene.

The Diversify girls rejected the idea that they could—or would want to—date the black Diversify boys. For the most part, they said they were "too familiar," "too close," or "too much of friends" to date. They reminded me that they had been riding the bus to/from the suburbs together every day since they were small children. As Ruth, quoted earlier, explained, "We're sort of like family . . . it would be kind of like incest or something."

Thus, the Diversify girls felt socially excluded from the suburban social and dating scene, and there are many reasons for their relative isolation. As these data show, one powerful reason is that suburban students and Diversify boys perceived their behavior as threatening to the gender order. In this order, adolescent women's heterosexual desirability is partially predicated on being "easy" for men and boys to "handle." This includes being deferential in many circumstances, including but not limited to racially insensitive and ignorant remarks.

[. . .]

Concluding Thoughts

In this study, interviews and observations with students attending affluent, intentionally racially integrated suburban schools provided a rich set of data for examining when and how an ethnic minority group's gender performance is used as the rationale for social exclusion. Suburban students, Diversify students, and suburban counselors and coordinators agreed that the suburban students generally accepted the African American boys, but not the girls. Diversify boys were included in various suburban social cliques and cast as desirable dating partners. Further, the suburban students seemed to valorize and celebrate the Diversify boys' masculinity, complimenting them for being "cool" and "tough." In stark contrast, suburban students and Diversify boys excluded the Diversify girls from white-dominant social cliques and the suburban dating scene. They justified the Diversify girls' exclusion and social isolation as the natural consequence of Diversify girls' assertiveness and aggression.

A central contribution of this research involves the use of a relational lens to build on the insights of previous scholars who have examined black girls' so-called loudness. Previously, Morris (2007) and other scholars (e.g., Grant 1984) emphasized that teachers may negatively evaluate younger black girls for failing to live up to standards of white femininity. While not rejecting the notion that black adolescent girls in Diversify were penalized by their peers for not living up to white feminine norms, the data presented here suggest it is not the full story.

The African American girls in my study may have been sanctioned and stigmatized in part because they did not embody the same gender performances as their suburban classmates. Critically, however, their gender performance also threatened the boys' exclusive access to the characteristics that provide "cultural insurance" (Schippers 2007:96) for male dominance. This is a plausible explanation for why the white suburban boys disavowed them, making them "invisible." It also suggests a reason why the Diversify boys said the Diversify girls were said to be too "aggie" to date. The Diversify girls' contamination of the gender hierarchy also explains the choice epithet of "ghetto" to describe the Diversify girls. This epithet referred to the girls' loud, obnoxious behavior—behavior that, when embodied by a man, might be interpreted as assertive or confident.

. . . The Diversify girls felt that suburban classmates and black male peers devalued their femininity and blackness, even as the Diversify boys reported that their masculinity was respected. Overall, a framework that focuses on gender differences in friendship patterns can elucidate some aspects of Diversify students' experiences, but I believe that a relational framework provides a more complete fit for these data.

[. . .]

References

Anderson, Elijah. 1999. *Code of the Street: Decency, Violence, and the Moral Life of the Inner City*. New York: W. W. Norton.

Bettie, Julie. 2003. *Women Without Class: Girls, Race, and Identity*. Berkeley, CA: University of California Press.

Collins, Patricia Hill. 2004. *Black Sexual Politics: African Americans, Gender, and the New Racism*. New York: Routledge.

Demerath, Peter. 2009. *Producing Success: The Culture of Personal Advancement in an American High School*. Chicago, IL: University of Chicago Press.

Ferguson, Ann. 2000. *Bad Boys: Public Schools in the Making of Black Masculinity*. Ann Arbor, MI: University of Michigan Press.

Gaztambide-Fernandez, Rubén and Raygine DiAquoi. 2010. "A Part and Apart: Students of Color Negotiating Boundaries at an Elite Boarding School." Pp. 55–78 in *Educating Elites: Class Privilege and Educational Advantage*, edited by A. Howard and R. Gaztambide-Fernandez. Lanham, MD: Rowman.

Grant, Linda. 1984. "Black Females 'Place' in Desegregated Classrooms." *Sociology of Education* 57(2):98–111.

Horvat, Erin and Anthony Antonio. 1999. "'Hey, Those Shoes Are Out of Uniform': African American Girls in an Elite High School and the Importance of Habitus." *Anthropology & Education Quarterly* 30(3):317–42.

Ispa-Landa, Simone. 2011. "The Wealth of Their Neighbors: Understanding Racial Integration as a Gendered Process." Ph.D. dissertation, Department of Sociology, Harvard University, Cambridge, MA.

Jones, Nikki. 2010. *Between Good and Ghetto: African American Girls and Inner-City Violence*. New Brunswick, NJ: Rutgers University Press.

Lewis, Amanda. 2003. *Race in the Schoolyard: Negotiating the Color Line in Classrooms and Communities*. New Brunswick, NJ: Rutgers University Press.

López, Nancy. 2002. *Hopeful Girls, Troubled Boys: Race and Gender Disparity in Urban Education*. New York: Routledge.

Morris, Edward. 2007. "Ladies or Loudies? Perceptions and Experiences of Black Girls in Classrooms." *Youth & Society* 38(4):490–515.

Pascoe, C. J. 2007. *Dude, You're a Fag: Masculinity and Sexuality in High School*. Berkeley, CA: University of California Press.

Schippers, Mimi. 2007. "Recovering the Feminine Other: Masculinity, Femininity, and Gender Hegemony." *Theory and Society* 36(1):85–102.

Tyson, Karolyn. 2011. *Integration Interrupted: Tracking, Black Students, and Acting White After Brown*. New York: Oxford University Press.

"Not Out to Start a Revolution"

Race, Gender, and Emotional Restraint Among Black University Men

Amy Wilkins

© iStockphoto.com/fstop123

[. . .]

Black men face complex emotional dilemmas at the juncture of race, gender, and class. Middle-class black men must avoid being stereotyped as "the angry black man"—"a middle class, educated African American male, who despite his economic and occupational success, perceives racial discrimination everywhere and consequently is enraged"

Amy Wilkins. 2012. "'Not Out to Start a Revolution': Race, Gender, and Emotional Restraint Among Black University Men." *Journal of Contemporary Ethnography* 41(1):34–65.

(Wingfield 2007, 12)—by adhering to "racialized feeling rules" that both strenuously prohibit anger among African American men, and oblige them to deny race-based inequities (Wingfield 2010). Successful participation in dominant institutions, then, requires black men to exhibit extraordinary emotional restraint. Because anger is culturally associated with men, however, suppressing anger also violates masculine expectations. Thus, African American men not only face more difficult emotional expectations but also face emotional dilemmas in which expected emotional displays undermine other identity expectations. In this article, I examine how black men at two predominantly white universities achieve emotional restraint and how they use their emotions to craft and manage their identities as black middle-class men.

[. . .]

Intersectionality and Black Men's Emotional Dilemmas

[. . .]

Because cultural rules about displays of anger also vary by class, class shapes the emotional strategies black men can use to manage their identities. Poor black men may compensate for race and class subordination with displays of anger that accord masculine status in the form of "respect" (Anderson 1999; Bourgois 1995), but these same angry displays are incompatible with middle-class emotional expectations (Stearns 1994). Cultural ideas about masculinity grant dominant men dispensation to display anger. Indeed, white men's situational anger signals and shores up their control, but black men's anger signals their *lack of control.* Thus, when black men display anger, they do not gain power, but instead lose credibility and risk institutional sanctions, including incarceration or termination, at odds with class mobility (Collins 2004; Ferguson 2000). Emotional restraint is not a simple solution to these expectations, however, as it fosters gendered and raced identity dilemmas for black men. On one hand, avoiding the caricature of "the angry black man" requires stringent emotional control. On the other hand, black men's suppression of anger denies them access to masculine privilege and power. The expectation that black men will never express anger contrasts with display rules for white men, and articulates with a history of race relations in which whites demanded that black men perform their subordination through acts of deference (Collins 2004). Thus, avoiding anger can evoke troubling cultural meanings: restrained emotional displays on the part of African American men may seem, not self-controlled, but *deferential.* Thus, when white men display general restraint combined with situational anger, they confirm their position of power, but for black men, both restraint and anger confirm their position of race and gender subordination. To participate in middle-class spaces, then, black men must manage their emotions, but they must do so in a way that allows them to navigate the double binds caused by contradictory gender, race, and class expectations.

. . . I examine the way black university men use emotions to resolve these identity dilemmas. Moderate black men apply cultural ideas about black emotions to solve the problems posed by participation in predominantly white institutions, and to fashion creditable black selves. By crafting emotional distinctions between black men and black women, moderate black men create distinct identities as black men. For these men, the trope of black anger is not only a problem to be managed but a resource used in the construction of identities.

Data and Methods

This study is part of a larger project aimed at investigating the lives of black university students. With the help of a research assistant, I conducted forty-three in-depth open-ended, life history interviews with black or African American–identified undergraduate students or recent graduates (twenty-five women and eighteen men) attending one of two large, predominantly white public universities. Interviews lasted from one to three hours. . . . I supplemented interviews with participant observation at formal and informal campus events, including classes, formal black organization- and Greek-sponsored banquets, talent shows, and picnics, and with multiple, informal conversations. This article focuses on the interviews with the men, but uses the interviews with the women and participant-observation to contextualize and interpret the men's accounts.

[. . .]

Gendered Racism and Campus Life

Richard, a slight, dynamic, nonathlete at Western, exemplifies moderate blackness. He says, "I like to be happy. I don't like being mad." To achieve his good feelings, he maintains an easygoing attitude about race: "I have no problems. I don't let problems get in my way, 'cause I have a purpose. I have things to do with my life. I don't have time to be bitching and complaining about anything, really." Richard presents himself, and comes across as, a naturally happy person, but his emotions require work. He creates and sustains good feelings by discounting the importance of race and racism to his experiences and identity. He uses his good emotions and moderate approach to campus life, in turn, to fashion himself as a particular kind of black person—one who does not "bitch and complain" or let other people "get him down." Richard's talk distances him from the caricature of "the angry black man": he is neither angry nor focused on racial inequality.

Richard claims to be happy, but most men in this study portray themselves, a bit differently, as easygoing people who do not let things, especially racism, bother them. Like happiness, being easygoing is a positive, restrained emotional display embedded in a broader strategy of political moderation. Accordingly, all of the men in this study describe the campus in surprisingly positive terms, making claims like "I feel very embraced by [the campus]," and "my time at college has been one of the greatest experiences" of my life. If one relied on these accounts alone, one might believe that little work is necessary to make campuses welcoming spaces for black students. These characterizations of campus life contradict other research on black experiences in predominantly white universities, which finds persistent social and academic marginalization and everyday racial hostility (e.g., Feagin, Vera, and Imani 1996; Solorzano, Ceja, and Yosso 2000). Like universities in other research, both universities host recurring, well-publicized incidents of antiblack racism. At Western, prominent black students received death threats. White students hold annual anti-affirmative action demonstrations that seem designed deliberately to taunt students of color. At Midwestern, people deface the black cultural center regularly with antiblack symbols. On both campuses, moreover, black women describe ongoing racial hostility and marginalization.

Given the persistence of campus racism, how can we understand men's positive characterization of college life? Perhaps they develop more benign accounts because their experiences are different from black women's experiences. The gendered texture of campus racism insulates some college men more than women. This insulation is uneven among all black men, and is incomplete even for the most well-insulated men. Positive characterizations notwithstanding, these men's accounts reveal gaps and inconsistencies in their experiences of campus life that expose the emotion work required to maintain their easygoing attitudes.

Athletic status organizes campus life for black men. The six athletes in this study, all football players, contend that being an athlete—or being mistaken for an athlete—attenuates racial vulnerability. In this study, they are protected both by the idea that they are big and strong, and by their status, as Dominick notes: "I don't get that—bad experience, if you want to say, because I do play football here. I am looked at as what they say a superstar sometimes." As superstars, athletes are included in white social events and networks. Dennis explains that, "if you play football, you're cool, you know." In addition, many white women pursue athletes as potential sexual and romantic partners. Finally, athletes report good relationships with white teammates, and regular contact with white coaches and team boosters. As Craig says, "They say there's no color in a foxhole. Sports is the same way."

Despite such glowing descriptions of their experiences, being a black athlete has costs. Other campus participants stereotype them as less intelligent and academically unmotivated. I have observed white students roll their eyes when black athletes speak in classes; in informal conversations, faculty members and graduate students characterize athletes as academically unprepared; nonathlete black students in this study dismissed athletes as "not taking their education seriously"; and athletes in this study themselves complain that they are steered away from majors that are considered difficult or time-consuming. Dennis recalls, "I was never encouraged to do anything except to drop engineering. They explicitly told me that I should look at other majors or something like that." David notes:

> I guess I get it twofold, because I'm African American and I'm an athlete. So I think running around this campus there's a very dumb athlete stigma that we're painted with, and then also being African American, they're like, "Jesus, he only got here because he's African American and he's an athlete."

And Dominick says about the dumb, lazy athlete stereotype: "I hear that. I hear that shit all the time." Athletes tend to accentuate the positive and gloss over the negative, but, as these examples show, they are also aware of their complex position in campus life, expressing irritation about the stereotypes that follow them.

In this study, twelve of eighteen men were what black students call "regulars"—that is, they were not rostered as college athletes. Regular black men do not garner the same benefits of black masculine cool, both because they are not athletes and because they often do not conform to its expectations, which include hip hop and/or athletic attire, a kind of swagger, and "being the life of the party." As Tim, a regular, complains, unless he can pass as an athlete, he is not welcomed at predominantly white social events. In contrast to athletes' hypervisibility, regulars are, as Nick confesses, "kinda the invisible ones." Phillip laments, "I'm not seen as something attractive. And I do feel that that's related to, 'Because you're a black male, duh.'" Being a black man but not an athlete is a liability in campus erotic markets. Students, both black and white, often assume that regular black men are gay, as Ekon, a regular, explains: "that is one of the stigmas. . . . Society has it engrained that athletes are supposed to be men . . . and if you're not that . . ." Tim also complains that "everyone says—you gotta be gay, man; you gotta be gay." Thus, regulars do not benefit from stereotypes of black men as "cool," and even incur gender penalties for their failure to live up to its expectations.

. . . Despite different experiences, moderate blackness arises out of the particular identity dilemmas black men share on predominantly white campuses. As upwardly mobile black men, black college men must all navigate the stereotype of the angry black man while also maintaining their gender identities as men. Moderate blackness resolves these problems for them by connecting positive emotions to masculinity. The links between moderate blackness and manhood, in turn, compels all of these men to view the campus in positive terms despite variations in their experiences.

[. . .]

Reframing: Creating Innocent White People

Men's efforts to avoid seeing racism are not always sufficient. Racially charged interactions occur too frequently. Lance admits, "The problem is, though, there are so many of those tiny moments that we just become tired." When forced to recognize them, men use additional strategies to minimize the racial implications of interactions. One way they do this is to discount racially charged incidents as unworthy of their attention. For example, Richard notes that white students routinely question his academic credentials, assuming the only way black men can get to college is through an athletic scholarship, but he says, "I just take everything with a grain of salt and flick it right off because there's no point for me to have a grudge." While Richard, at other times, claims that race does not affect his experiences, here he acknowledges everyday racism but transforms its meaning, reconfiguring it as unimportant to his identity and to his daily life. This strategy works in tandem with his narrow definition of racism; in the absence of physical violence, he is able to view racialized insults as annoying but inconsequential.

More commonly, moderate black men reinterpret motivations. All but one man revealed some version of this strategy. Here, Tim illustrates one way they do this:

> But with the white kids—all my friends were nice. They've never really done anything. They might joke and throw the n-bomb every once in a while just to try to be cool. . . . Cuz they hear it in music videos and stuff and they're like, "Oh man it's cool right, I can call you the n-word . . . and it's like NO!"

Tim is unable to dismiss this interaction as unworthy of his attention, as Richard did, because the perpetrators are not strangers but his friends. To maintain his friendships and defuse the interaction, Tim reinterprets the incident as a "joke" motivated by the desire to be cool. He assigns benign motivations to his "friends"—"nice" people who have "never really done anything." Like white people who manage their discomfort with white racial joking by portraying joke-tellers as "racial innocents" (Picca and Feagin 2007), Tim neutralizes white jokes, preserving both the myth of white racial innocence and his positive view of the campus. . . .

Men also reinterpret motivations by thinking about issues and people as socially complex. Ekon explains that he became "more aware" of racism when he came to the university, but that he also learned that "if you open yourself up and realize that everything is not black and white . . . then you actually enjoy yourself and I did." For Dominick, unkind behavior has nothing to do with race: "I've been around great white people. I've been around shitty ones. I've been around great ones. I've been around shitty black people, I've been around great black people." And Jackson says, "People are just people. Yeah, there's differences because of what's happened historically. . . . But you have to tolerate people." By attributing bad interactions to social causes besides race, or by assuming that race itself is not a "black and white" issue, black men displace antiblack motivations and maintain their good feelings toward their white peers.

By portraying racial barriers as inconsequential, unintentional, or complicated, framing strategies all have the same [e]ffect: they permit men to see white students as racially innocent, well intentioned, and educable, rather than racially hostile, and thus allow them to maintain good feelings toward them. Moreover, men's framing strategies put the burden of change on black people, rather than white. Vincent makes this dynamic most clear when he explained that he holds black people accountable for the diversity of their friendship groups, expecting them to be friends with both black and white students, but does not have similar expectations of white people. When I asked why he did not judge white students for the racial composition of their social networks, he shrugged, "I guess I thought it was okay." Ekon similarly holds black students to higher standards than he holds white students. When I asked him to identify the biggest racial problem on campus, he said, "I think the fact that people aren't educated on it. People don't, like a lot of white students don't know that they have privilege. . . . And I think a lot of black students can be defensive."

Men's emotion strategies are mutually reinforcing. Emotional restraint facilitates a particular interpretation of campus life: seeing interactions as friendly, well-intentioned, or unimportant allows men to avoid anger, while a generally easygoing approach makes possible interpretations of campus as a tolerant, even welcoming place. The emotional restraint men's strategies create likely makes their temperate interpretation of campus racial dynamics *feel* real (Wolkomir 2001), while feelings of ease and happiness make it seem that the campus is indeed an enjoyable, friendly place and that moderate blackness is a sensible approach to racial interactions. These emotion strategies occlude inconsistencies in men's experiences by leading them to accentuate positive, and underplay negative, experiences.

[. . .]

Identity Work

Men's emotion work allows them to distance themselves from "the angry black man," as Ekon makes clear: "I used to have a serious temper and . . . you know I don't want everybody to be afraid of [me]." By managing his emotions, Ekon also managed others' fear. Their emotion work pays off in other ways as well: they report that tamping down their anger makes them feel less "crazy," reduces "tension" in their relationships with white peers, and expands their college social lives. But men's emotion work is also identity work. They don't just use emotions to manage the expectations of college life; they use them to think about themselves as different *kinds* of black people.

Black college men explain who they are, in large part, by explaining who they are *not*: not angry, "not out to start a revolution," "not hung up on slavery," not uncomfortable around white people. Such boundaries are woven throughout their talk. Dominick did not hang out with any "African American people" until his senior year, when he met ones who "aren't trying to start a revolution and whatever. They're just people. They're just acting like people. Not acting like they're being discriminated on." Jeffrey criticizes other black students, for whom, he says, race is "crippling. Race is used as a limit rather than an opportunity for interaction, growth, social change." By emphasizing their treatment of race as an "opportunity for growth [and] social change," rather than for outrage, these men distinguish themselves from the caricature of the angry black man.

When black men orient themselves away from racial inequality, however, they risk being seen, and seeing themselves, as racially inauthentic. Craig notes, black men "don't want to feel guilty that they're not part of BSU [Black Student Union], even though they're black." David laments:

[Town] is a difficult place to navigate as an African American if you don't have a strong sense of you, because there are two ways you can go: You can either become unbelievably pro-black or you can become quote-unquote, and I don't like this term, but I can't think of anything better, "whitewashed." And then obviously, there's no absolutes. There are people who stand somewhere in the middle. But if you don't have a strong sense of identity, those are the two places you're probably gonna go to.

David reveals the racialized identity hazards facing men in white middle-class spaces like these; they could respond to the persistent threat of racism with suspicion and anger or they could respond to it by denying the relevance of race to their identities. The first response leads to racial immoderation (becoming "pro-black"), while the second leads to racial inauthenticity (becoming whitewashed). David presents these problems in racialized terms, but they are also about class. Being pro-black potentially undermines participation in middle-class institutions, but being whitewashed implies that one is a racial "sell-out" who privileges class mobility over racial authenticity. David proposes that only those with "a strong sense of identity" can successfully manage this dilemma, and links this solution to cultural ideas about masculinity; as he says, "we're men." Moderate black men seek to create identities that balance the race and class concerns they face as upwardly middle-class blacks while also maintaining their claim to manhood.

[. . .]

Moderate Blackness and Masculinity

To resolve their race and class dilemmas, black men carve out a middle space—one that is, in David's words, enabled by the "strong sense of self" that accompanies being "men." But David's claim notwithstanding, moderate blackness threatens black university men's claims to masculinity—precisely because it requires them to ignore, trivialize, or reinterpret cross-racial interactions. This emotion work puts black men in the position of changing their reactions and behaviors in order to maintain good relations with whites. In short, it requires them to defer. To maintain their masculinity, then, moderate black men must resignify the meaning of their emotional displays.

To do this, black men define moderation as masculine by inverting the link between anger and gender, portraying anger as a *feminine* emotional response. Black men feminize anger through symbolic boundaries and defensive othering in which they "seek to deflect the stigma they experience as members of a subordinate group" by suggesting that the "angry black" stereotype may apply to black women, but it does not apply to them (Schwalbe et al. 2000, 425). Black university men create these gender boundaries in two ways. First, they typify black women as political and angry, and black men, in both explicit and implicit contrast, as apolitical and easygoing. Second, some men characterize anger and immoderate racial politics as features of black campus political organizations, such as the BSU, and associate these organizations with black women. By feminizing immoderate blackness, they masculinize moderate blackness. Six men directly assigned emotional immoderation to black women by describing them as angry, having an "attitude," or "strong." Dominick comments, "You know and there's the, of course, the stereotype of African American women having an attitude . . . which, there, I've experienced that." And Nick says: "I just feel like they're always—they [black women] kind of always have a bone to pick with white people in general, just about everything." He adds, "Black women, it seems like they are the ones that talk about a lot more issues than what black men do." . . .

Men's attribution of "bitching" and "attitude" to black women draws on both gender and racial stereotypes. The term "bitching" is a racially generic gender stereotype, while "attitude" is a gendered racial stereotype that discounts black women's emotions (Froyum 2010). Thus, men's defensive other-ing not only resists identification with the stereotype of the angry black man by pushing the characterization onto black women but does so by evoking racialized gender stereotypes. The use of gender distances men from black anger, but dismissing women's concerns as "attitude" or as "bitching and complaining" also defines their feelings as unnecessary and incommensurate to the situation, and thus bolsters the legitimacy of men's definitions of racism and of their emotions. But more, by dismissing both black women and, often, black organizations, as immoderate spaces, black men abandon their collective responsibility to fight racial inequality, focusing instead on individual strategies of mobility and leaving the work of fighting racism up to women.

An examination of the three men who do not fully embrace moderate blackness underscores its use as a gender strategy. All men in this study adopted some elements of moderation—and specifically opted out of anger—but three evinced more complex identities. For different reasons, Phillip, Ekon, and Dennis "did" masculinity in different ways than the other men in this study and were thus less reliant on moderate blackness as a gender strategy. Phillip and Ekon both identified as queer, claiming that their sexuality gave them more latitude to embrace feminine qualities, "because," in Ekon's words, "you can kind of do whatever you want and not have to live up to certain stigma." Dennis, the athlete who compared football to slavery, linked himself to a different tradition of black masculine leadership. Thus, alternative ways of doing gender enabled some men to opt out of some of the masculinized expectations of moderate blackness.

Conclusion

In this paper, I have examined emotion work among black university men, both athletes and nonathletes, at two different universities. I find that despite their differences, both kinds of men develop similar emotion strategies and link them to an identity I call moderate blackness. Moderate blackness facilitates membership in institutions in which the white middle class establishes the emotional rules. Black men use moderate blackness to accord with the more general emotional culture and to manage public ideas about (angry) black men. Thus, while moderate blackness is a *racial* strategy, it is compelled by the specific problems black college men face not just as black people but as upwardly mobile black *men*. Ironically, however, while moderate blackness responds to the *gendered* dilemmas facing black university men, it also fosters gender problems. Existing research assumes a consonance between emotions and identity work (Wilkins 2008; Wolkomir 2001), but here, the intersectional lens reveals a more complex relationship, in which emotional restraint and moderate blackness create identity dilemmas that need to be managed through other forms of identity work.

Moderate blackness is a strategy of emotional restraint. Black men control their emotions by learning to ignore, trivialize, and reinterpret everyday racism, and to see white peers as (educable) allies rather than (hostile) enemies. Their strategies are both rewarded and rewarding, as they allow them to see the campus as a friendly place, to enjoy a greater range of campus events, and to maintain working relationships, and potential intimacies, with white people. Although many of the men naturalize their emotion work by attributing it to their experiences growing up in integrated social settings, black men from various backgrounds learn and teach moderation in the context of the university. These strategies may build on preexisting emotional skills for some men, but other men learn strategies of moderate blackness in college. My findings suggest that college provides black men an opportunity to acquire, practice, and share the emotional skills they will need as black middle-class adults. College is a space in which black men learn to play by the racialized emotion rules set by the dominant culture, facilitating their ability to transition into the middle-class workplace.

[. . .]

Moderate blackness relies on two strategies of identity work—"propping up dominants" and "defensive othering" found among other subordinate groups (Schwalbe et al. 2000). Much work on "propping up dominants" examines the ways women endorse men and masculinity (e.g., Ezzell 2009); here, black men's identity work props up racial dominants. In the case at hand, black men do not so much attribute superiority to white people as they simply let them off the hook for their racist behavior by ascribing benign motivations and holding themselves accountable for any racial change. This strategy maintains racial hierarchies by allowing racist dynamics to continue unchecked. "Defensive othering" also maintains racial inequality. By attributing black anger to black women, moderate blackness fails to challenge the links between blackness and (inappropriate) anger. Black men's defensive othering casts black women as not only gender inferiors but as racially inferior: their anger makes them the wrong kind of black people. Thus, men's identity work supports the cultural devaluation of black women on predominantly white campuses, while sustaining the idea that black anger is both real and inappropriate.

[. . .]

References

Anderson, Elijah. 1999. *Code of the Street: Decency, Violence, and the Moral Life of the Inner City.* New York: W. W. Norton.

Bourgois, Phillipe. 1995. *In Search of Respect: Selling Crack in El Barrio.* New York: Cambridge University Press.

Collins, Patricia Hill. 2004. *Black Sexual Politics: African Americans, Gender, and the New Racism.* New York, NY: Routledge.

Ezzell, Matthew B. 2009. "'Barbie Dolls on the Pitch': Identity Work, Defensive Othering, and Inequality in Women's Rugby." *Social Problems* 56:111–13.

Feagin, Joe R., Hernan Vera, and Nikitah Imani. 1996. *The Agony of Education: Black Students and White College and Universities.* New York: Routledge.

Ferguson, Ann Arnett. 2000. *Bad Boys: Public Schools in the Making of Black Masculinity.* Ann Arbor, MI: University of Michigan Press.

Froyum, Carissa. 2010. "The Reproduction of Inequalities Through Emotional Capital: The Case of Socializing Low-Income Black Girls." *Qualitative Sociology* 33(1):37–54.

Picca, Leslie and Joe Feagin. 2007. *Two-Faced Racism: Whites in the Backstage and Frontstage.* New York: Routledge.

Schwalbe, Michael, Sandra Godwin, Daphne Holden, Douglas Schrock, Shealy Thompson, and Michele Wolkomir. 2000. "Generic Processes in the Reproduction of Inequality: An Interactionist Analysis." *Social Forces* 79:419–52.

Solorzano, Daniel, Miguel Ceja, and Tara Yosso. 2000. "Critical Race Theory, Racial Microaggressions, and Campus Racial Climate: The Experiences of African American College Students." *Journal of Negro Education* 69:60–73.

Stearns, Peter. 1994. *American Cool: Constructing a Twentieth-Century Emotional Style.* New York: New York University Press.

Wilkins, Amy C. 2008. "'Happier Than Non-Christians': Collective Emotions and Symbolic Boundaries Among Evangelical Christians." *Social Psychology Quarterly* 71(3):281–301.

Wingfield, Adia Harvey. 2007. "The Modern Mammy and the Angry Black Man: African American Professionals' Experiences with Gendered Racism in the Workplace." *Race, Gender & Class* 14:196–212.

Wingfield, Adia Harvey. 2010. "Are Some Emotions Marked 'Whites Only?' Racialized Feeling Rules in Professional Workplaces." *Social Problems* 57:251–68.

Wolkomir, Michelle. 2001. "Emotion Work, Commitment, and the Authentication of the Self: The Case of Gay and Ex-Gay Support Groups." *Journal of Contemporary Ethnography* 30:305–34.

"Now Why Do You Want to Know About That?"

Heteronormativity, Sexism, and Racism in the Sexual (Mis)education of Latina Youth

Lorena García

© iStockphoto.com/pepifoto

Research on school-based sex education has uncovered the insidious ways in which national and local fears about the instability of racial, gender, class, and sexual hierarchies are articulated within the politics of sex education (Fields 2008; Irvine 2002; Luker 2006; Moran 2000). The implementation of sex education has been guided by the perceived need either to protect the sexual innocence of youth or to protect youth from the dangers of their own sexual curiosity. Scholars have demonstrated that decisions about which objective to pursue

Lorena García. 2009. "'Now Why Do You Want to Know About That?' Heteronormativity, Sexism, and Racism in the Sexual (Mis)education of Latina Youth." *Gender & Society* 23(4):520–41.

are often informed by race/ethnicity (Ericksen and Steffan 1999; Fields 2008; Patton 1996). While middle- to upper-class white youth are often perceived as in need of intervention to guide them through their "normally abnormal" hormone-besieged adolescence, youth of color are constructed as always "at risk" and a source of danger (Patton 1996, 43). Feminist researchers and activists have directed attention to the underlying heterosexism and heteronormativity of sex education, demonstrating how gender and sexual inequalities are (re)produced through its lessons (Fields 2008; Fine 1988; Fine and McClelland 2006; Tolman 1994). Few scholars, however, have examined how heteronormativity, sexism, and racism coalesce in the classroom production of sex education to differentially shape students' experiences. In this article, I focus on the experiences of Latina youth to explore how heteronormativity, sexism, and racism operate together to structure the content and delivery of school-based sex education. Sex education is generally designed to diminish risks for young people, but my findings indicate that sex education also poses risks to Latina youth through its reliance on heterosexualizing lessons that are also gendered and racialized. These lessons may further disadvantage girls already encountering multiple inequalities.

[. . .]

Heteronormative Lessons for Girls in Sex Education

Feminist scholars have drawn attention to the implications of sex education for young women's sexual identities and experiences (Fields 2007; Fine 1988; Risman and Schwartz 2001; Tolman 1994). Fine's (1988) influential study of sex education in an urban New York high school revealed that there is a "missing discourse of desire" in sex education as well as a powerful discourse of victimization and danger that serves to deny young women their sexual subjectivity (Fine 1988; Fine and McClelland 2006). Instead, girls must constantly negotiate the little sexual agency they are permitted within the boundaries of the omnipresent and powerful good (chaste) versus bad (sexual) girl dichotomy (Levy 2005; Schaffner 2006; Tanenbaum 1999; Tolman 1994, 2002). Ingraham's (1994) concept of heterogender, which highlights the intertwined relationship between heterosexuality and gender, is useful for grasping how the maintenance of the good girl/bad girl dichotomy supports compulsory heterosexuality and relies on interdependent social constructions of heterosexuality and gender. Through sex education, girls are taught not only that they are opposite to boys but also that they can be sexually oriented only toward boys (and only within acceptable boundaries) and that sexual identities, practices, and desires outside of these "prescriptive sociosexual arrangements" are abnormal (Ingraham 1994, 204). Binaries such as these are central components of heteronormativity, which are "both those localized practices and those centralized institutions that legitimize and privilege heterosexuality and heterosexual relationships as fundamental and 'natural' within society" (Cohen 1997, 440). Thus, school-based sex education can be understood as a practice that normalizes and enforces heterosexuality within the institution of education.

[. . .]

Research has also demonstrated that race/ethnicity shapes how school authorities respond to students' embodiment of gender and sexuality, finding that Black and Latina/o students' performance of heterosexuality is especially monitored and disciplined within schools. Empirical research has documented how this treatment is informed by perceptions of youth of color as adult-like rather than child or youth-like (Ferguson 2001), as sexually precocious (Fields 2008; Hyams 2006; Morris 2007; Pascoe 2007), and as potential gang members or criminals and teen mothers (Bettie 2003; Ferguson 2001; Lopez 2003; Pérez 2006). This work underscores Cohen's (1997, 451–57) observation that heteronormativity does not evenly assign privilege and power to all individuals categorized as "heterosexual"; instead, a state-sanctioned white middle- and upper-class heterosexuality is most rewarded and used as the reference point to determine how to distribute privilege and power. Given this, Cohen argues that there is a need to attend to an "understanding of race, class, and gender and their roles in how heteronormativity regulates sexual behavior and identities" (451).

[. . .]

For LGBTQ and gender nonconforming youth, school is often a hostile place where it is difficult to find support (Khayatt 1995; Mufioz-Plaza, Quinn, and Rounds 2002; Rofes 1989; G. W. Smith 2005). Although much research remains to be done on the educational experiences of LGBTQ and gender nonconforming students, scholarship on the specific experiences and challenges confronting LGBTQ and gender nonconforming students of color is limited. McCready (2004) asserts that experiences of LGBTQ and gender nonconforming students of color are underexplored because one identity (typically sexuality) is given primacy by researchers while other identities (i.e., race/ethnicity) are just added on. Similarly, Kumashiro (2001, 12) points to the tendency in research to fail and/or refuse to acknowledge the simultaneity of identities, leading him to poignantly ask, "Is there comfort, in other words, in seeing queerness and racial difference as separate and distinct?" LGBTQ scholars of color have challenged the notion that sexual subjectivity and racial subjectivity are mutually exclusive by underscoring how these subjectivities develop interdependently. For example, some scholars have demonstrated that non-white LGBTQ individuals do not necessarily find coming out to be an effective strategy given their dependence on their families and communities as a resource against the racism they encounter in larger society (Guzmán 2006; Rodríguez 2003; Rust 2006). Such work reminds us that it is critically important to recognize that students are negotiating multiple identities inside and outside of schools.

Data and Method

This article is based on a larger study of Latina girls' sexual identity formation conducted in Chicago between September 2002 and November 2004. The study entailed in-depth interviews with Latina youth (and a subset of their mothers), ethnographic fieldwork, and content analysis (García 2006).

[. . .]

I interviewed young women who met the following criteria: self-identified as (a) Mexican or Puerto Rican, (b) sexually active, (c) between the ages of 13 and 18, (d) practicing safe sex, and (e) having no children.

[. . .]

My sample included 40 Latina youth (20 Mexican origin and 20 Puerto Rican girls). Of the young women recruited for this study, 32 self-identified as heterosexual and eight young women self-identified as lesbian. The average age of participants was 16, and the majority were second-generation Mexican-origin and Puerto Rican girls, meaning that they are U.S.-born children of (im)migrants. All of the young women reported having working-class backgrounds. Parents were typically employed in the service sector or in factories. . . .

I conducted two to three in-depth interviews with each girl. . . .

Sex Education and CPS

Presently, sex education curricula are grouped into two broad categories: abstinence-plus (also called comprehensive sexuality education) and abstinence-only-until-marriage (also called abstinence only). Comprehensive sex education does promote abstinence but also teaches about contraception, sexually transmitted diseases, HIV, and abortion. Abstinence-only education promotes abstinence from sex but does not teach about contraception or abortion. When sexually transmitted diseases and HIV are referenced, it is typically to highlight the negative consequences of premarital sex. Study participants reported that they encountered both abstinence-only and comprehensive sex education in middle school; 17 girls reported encountering abstinence-only sex education, and 23 girls reported access to comprehensive sex education.

[. . .]

Learning About Latina Sexuality: Latina Youth as Oversexed and Over-Reproductive

Respondents' narratives reveal that heteronormativity was central to the content and delivery of both types of sex education curricula. In all of the girls' descriptions of their sex education experiences, lessons were crafted around heterosexuality and heterosexual norms. And heterosexuality was most often discussed in relation to masculinity and femininity, that is, masculinity and femininity were given meaning only by heterosexuality, and femininity was tightly linked to the good girl/bad girl dichotomy. However, the institutionalization of heterosexuality via sex education also entailed the incorporation of racialized gender stereotypes to produce specific lessons for Latina youth about how they should engage sex education in the classroom and what sex education information was most relevant to them.

Lessons About Engaging Sex Education in the Classroom

Many of the respondents described interactions with teachers and sex educators in which students were disciplined for their level of engagement with sex education. Quite often, girls reported that boys were scolded or disciplined by teachers for misbehaving during sex education, such as for "acting foolish," "not taking it seriously," or "saying ignorant things." Girls, on the other hand, were reprimanded for their active engagement with sex education in the classroom. In other words, it was possible for female students to be "too interested" in learning about sex. Seventeen-year-old Minerva's experience is evidence of this:

> I raised my hand up and told the [sex educator], "Is it true you can't get pregnant if you take the morning-after pill?" or something like that. Anyways, she was starting to answer me when Ms. Phyllis [her eighth grade teacher] was like, "Now why do you want to know about that, Minerva? You don't got anything to worry about if you're behaving and anyway, we are out of time."

Other respondents narrated similar interactions with their teachers and sex educators, suggesting they were perceived as "knowing girls" (Fields 2007). As other studies have shown, students who display knowledge about sexuality are generally perceived to be sexually active

(Fields 2007, 76–77). Similarly, while all respondents in this study reported that they were invited or expected to ask questions, some of their inquiries were met with suspicion by teachers and sex educators. By publicly questioning Minerva about the motives behind her question, her teacher communicated to students not only that certain questions were invalid but also that such inquiries could shift girls to the wrong side of the good girl/bad girl dichotomy.

The respondents in this study vividly recalled how teachers and sex educators emphasized girls being "good girls" or "young ladies." Most girls described teachers and sex educators as prefacing or following lessons with a statement about the need for girls to be mindful of maintaining their respectability. Seventeen-year-old Imelda recounted how her eighth grade teacher interjected this message during a guest speaker's comprehensive sex education presentation.

> Like the woman [sex educator] was talking about sex as being a personal choice and not letting anyone pressure us, and that when we're ready we should remember to be safe, and all that, you know? And Mrs. Damenzo [teacher] is like, "Yeah, but they shouldn't be doing it, right? They should act like young ladies so that the boys will respect them."

According to girls, these contradictory lessons left them uncertain as to what to do with the information presented to them, as 16-year-old Inez explained: "I don't get it, they tell you all about being safe, then turn around and tell you, 'But you really don't need to know this, unless you a hoochie.'" It is worth noting that in all respondents' interviews, teachers and sex educators were never described as warning boys that their respect was tied to their sexual behavior. These gender-specific messages implicitly communicated to girls not only that they are the intended recipients of sex education but also that there are limits to their sex education given that the knowledge sought should reflect sexual modesty.

Respondents' narratives also suggest that these gender-specific messages were fused with perceptions about them as Latina girls. Teachers and sex educators inscribed the good girl/bad girl dichotomy with racialized sexual stereotypes of Latinas that functioned to specify the kind of "bad girls" they should avoid becoming (e.g., the pregnant Latina teen or the sexually promiscuous Latina). In all, 28 girls reported that teachers and sex educators specifically referred to these "other girls." Seventeen-year-old Olivia's interaction with her seventh grade abstinence-only sex educator serves as an example:

> The lady [sex educator] talking to us was all about how true love waits. Every time I asked a question she didn't like or whatever, she would say, "That is not something someone your age should even be thinking about." . . . I think I was annoying her cause she just said, "Maybe a lot of girls you know are having sex, but you need to be better than that. When you ask things like that, it makes people think you are like those girls."

Similar to Olivia, other respondents reported that teachers and sex educators assumed that they would already "know" or be acquainted with "those girls." Respondents' accounts of their sex education lessons reveal that such girls were perceived to be prevalent in students' neighborhoods, as illustrated in the way 17-year-old Elvia described her eighth grade sex educator's response to her when she questioned her suppositions about Latinas: "She got all embarrassed . . . and just said, 'Well, I'm just telling you how it is. Numbers don't lie, there are a lot of teenagers in your community who are making real poor choices when it comes to sex.'" Olivia and Elvia's teachers' references to "those girls" and "a lot of teenagers" did not mean girls or youth in the general sense but Latina youth specifically.

Latina girls' sex education experiences reveal that their interactions with teachers and sex educators constituted a heterosexualizing process that supported gender inequalities between boys and girls and among girls themselves. Teachers and sex educators not only presumed that all students were heterosexual but also invoked a good girl/bad girl dichotomy that kept boys' sexual behaviors invisible and unchecked. Furthermore, this dichotomy was racialized in that it both drew on and supported the notion that Latinas are culturally predisposed to fall on the "bad" side of feminine sexuality (Fine, Weis, and Roberts 2000).

Lessons About "Latino Culture" and Pregnancy Prevention

A second theme in respondents' accounts of their school-based sex education experiences was the emphasis placed on pregnancy prevention lessons. Despite teachers' and sex educators' warnings to girls about not being like "those girls," respondents' narratives suggest that they were still deemed to be a particular type of girl—a Latina teen always at heightened risk for pregnancy. Minerva articulated her awareness of how this perception of Latinas figured into her sex education:

> Sometimes they come at us like we are these ghetto-ass kids who just make babies and drop out of school . . . like we all have single moms on welfare that don't show us how to be responsible so they talk down to us, like, "OK, we know that in the Hispanic culture it's OK for girls to get pregnant young and become mothers, but not in American culture, OK?"

Minerva, like many other respondents, expressed her criticism of how teachers and sex educators often connected Latina girls' risk for pregnancy to a "Latino culture," whereby Latinas were presumed to be sexually oriented just toward Latino men and gender relations among them were assumed to be shaped by a uniquely Latino machismo oppressive to women. Sixteen-year-old Miriam recounted such a lesson from her seventh grade sex educator: "[She] started talking about Latino culture and saying that because of machismo, guys were always gonna try to control us and tell us how many babies to have, and that they were too macho to wear condoms." Experiences such as Miriam's illustrate how the heterosexual parameters of femininity are maintained through gender and race/ethnicity-specific sex education lessons; such lessons depict Latino boys as sexually manipulative and ignorant about condom use, while Latina girls are taught that their main task as unmarried young women is to develop the skills necessary to effectively fulfill their sexual gatekeeper role (Fine 1988; Thompson 1995; Tolman 2001).

The significance of race and gender stereotypes about Latinas in sex education was particularly evidenced by the ways information about Depo-Provera was provided to girls. Eleven respondents described sex educators spending a considerable amount of time emphasizing the shot as an effective form of birth control. Respondents' narratives suggest that sex educators generously supplied both information and advice about the effectiveness of this particular birth control option. Sixteen-year-old Maritza recounted how a sex educator introduced "the shot" to the young women in Maritza's eighth grade class:

> So this woman [sexuality educator] has the nerve to get up there and say, "I ain't gonna spend too much time on condoms cause you probably won't use them anyway. Guys usually don't wanna wear them cause of all the machismo and stuff. So if you are gonna have sex, and you really shouldn't, then you should wear a condom and at least know about the pill or shot so you won't get pregnant."

Similarly, 15-year-old Martha recounted how the sex educator presented information about Depo-Provera to her eighth grade class:

> She [sex educator] said something like, "Too many Hispanic girls feel that having a baby is no big deal, but don't believe it. . . . The shot is a good way to help you be safe." . . . I felt that she thought we were all *pendejas* [idiots or stupid], like the shot would be easier for us since all we worried was about getting pregnant.

The pregnancy prevention lessons that Latina youth encountered in their sex education are informed by the heteronormative designation of sexual relations and bodies as hetero-sexually reproductive. However, respondents' narratives reveal that while they are assigned heterosexuality, their bodies, read through a racial-gender lens, are interpreted as excessively reproductive and thus nonconforming to idealized heteronormative standards. Historically, racial-gender stereotypes about the reproductive decision making of Latinas in the United States depict them as wanting large families and refusing or being unable to use birth control. However, scholars have asserted that Latinas' sexuality and reproduction have recently received an intense scrutiny that is entrenched in a larger concern about immigrant "invasion" (Chavez 2004; Gutiérrez 2008; Inda 2002). Anti-immigrant discourses and policies have fueled public stereotypes about the "hyperfertility" of Latinas, which, according to Gutiérrez (2008), inform the development of social policies particularly directed at their bodies.

[. . .]

And as girls' narratives indicate, they perceived their sex education to be limited, which they attributed to racial-gender biases, exemplified by Martha when she stated the Depo-Provera shot was emphasized because sex educators assumed that all Latina girls "worried was about getting pregnant." The racialized heteronormative assumption of Latina bodies as potentially over-reproductive often constrained respondents' access to information, particularly the knowledge sought by respondents who were exploring the possibility of non-heterosexual identities in middle school, as I discuss in the next section.

Learning to Conceal Same-Sex Desire

I now focus on the sex education experiences of respondents who identified as lesbians. All of them reported that in middle school they did not yet identify as lesbian. However, they all described an awareness of their emerging sense of sexual identity while in middle school. Several reported having "crushes" on girls at this age. As 18-year-old Margarita put it, "I thought this girl in class was nice, but it was such a crush!" Seventeen-year-old Imelda reflected, "I knew that I liked girls, but I don't think I saw myself as a lesbian at that point." They often described feeling confused about feelings they had for other girls in middle school.

Respondents who identified as lesbian indicated that they did not interpret school-based sex education as a supportive context in which to explore such feelings and related questions. As 18-year-old Christina explained, "I knew I didn't look at guys the way I looked at girls, but hell no, there is no way the teachers were gonna wanna hear that!" With the exception of only one respondent, this group of girls did not report asking questions during sexuality education lessons in middle school. Seventeen-year-old Linda, the only lesbian-identified girl who reported venturing to ask a question (albeit anonymously) while in middle school, described how her teacher reacted to her question:

> She [eighth grade teacher] had us write down our questions . . . so she could pick some to give to the sex ed teacher who was going to be coming to our class the next day. . . . She started yelling, "Who asked this?! Who asked the question about books about lesbian teenagers?!" Shit, I did, but I wasn't gonna say anything! . . . She got more pissed off and was like, "I don't know who did it, but I hope it wasn't one of you girls, because you should know better than to act so immature."

The teacher's response to Linda's anonymous question that the young women in the classroom "should know better" is yet another example of how teachers directed gender-specific comments about acceptable sexual behavior and inquiries exclusively to girls. Such a response can also be interpreted to reflect the expectation that girls will assume "femininized responsibility" for helping maintain order within the classroom (Ferguson 2001). However, the dismissal of Linda's question as "immature" also reflects once again an assumption that all the students were heterosexual while reinforcing the rule that anything outside of heterosexuality is abnormal.

The middle school classroom for this group of girls was not a site in which they felt safe exploring their sexual identity. And while these girls indicated, like Linda, that they were "not gonna say anything" that would draw unwanted attention to same-sex attractions, they reported making efforts to be recognized as "straight" by peers and school authorities. Eighteen-year-old Barbara recounted how and why she performed a heterosexual femininity her eighth grade:

> There was this guy in our class who everyone thought he was gay. . . . Anyway, the guys would always pick on him a lot, calling him *maricón* [queer]. During a workshop, some of the guys were being smart asses and said, "So, Manolo wants to know about having sex with other guys, cause he's a fag." Most of the class laughed and the messed up thing was that the sex educator ended up laughing too, even though she told them to be respectful. I didn't want to be treated that way, so I just acted like I was just a regular girl, you know, saying that I thought this boy and this boy were cute, even though I had a crush on a girl in my classroom.

Barbara's description of the sex educator's laughter at the comments made about Manolo resonates with other studies' findings that teachers support heteronormativity by both their actions and inactions in the presence of homophobia. Like Barbara, other respondents explained that they felt intense pressure to conform to heterosexuality in school to avoid the mistreatment of peers, which they witnessed especially inflicted on gender nonconforming boys. While a couple of these girls described themselves as also being gender nonconforming (i.e., "tomboyish"), they still felt compelled to express desire for boys to deflect their peers' potential suspicion and therefore verbal or physical attacks.

[. . .]

The narratives of respondents who identified as lesbian reveal that same-sex identities, practices, and desires remained unacknowledged, which reinforced heterosexuality as the norm and the assumption that the only significant identity for Latina/o students was a racial/ethnic identity already rooted in heterosexuality (Guzmán 2006; Kumashiro 2001; Rodríguez 2003).

Discussion

In this article, I explored how heteronormativity, racism, and sexism operate together to structure the content and delivery of school-based sex education for Latina girls. In their narratives of middle school sex education, respondents described interactions with teachers and sex educators in which they were provided with heterosexualizing lessons that were not only gendered, but also racialized. In other words, the Latina youth in my sample encountered racialized heterogendered constructions and experiences that limited their access to sex-education-related information and also reinforced inequalities.

Teachers and sex educators invoked a good girl/bad girl discourse to teach girls how to be students of sex education, specifically inscribing racial stereotypes onto the good girl/bad girl dichotomy to indicate what information was most important for Latina youth and to provide girls with a specific example about the kind of Latina girl they needed to avoid becoming (not just a generic bad girl). Yet the students' narratives also reveal that teachers and sex educators still perceived them to be always on the verge of slipping onto the wrong side of the good girl/bad girl divide—the Latina teen who is perpetually at risk for pregnancy because of a "Latino culture." The data indicate that teachers and sex educators infused sex education with their own biases about Latinas/os, reflected in the information that was and was not made available to them, that is, the emphasis placed on the Depo-Provera shot and the failure and/or refusal to include information particularly relevant to LGBTQ students (which is already inadequate in its lack of attention to LGBTQ students of color).

This research shows how heteronormative, racist, and sexist stereotypes and discourses about Latina youth interact within sex education to construct girls as "at risk." The heterosexualizing processes that they encountered through their interactions with teachers and sex educators entailed an emphasis on their racial-gender identities. The interplay of heteronormativity, sexism, and racism in Latina girls' sex education simultaneously reproduced, normalized, and concealed inequalities (Fine 1987). Thus, in this context, Latina youth can be understood to be more broadly "at risk" of these oppressions, which arguably pose greater danger to girls than sex or pregnancy. For instance, one especially troubling lesson that they are taught is to regard the masculinity of young men in their communities as a threat rather than being invited to critically examine the larger societal culture (and not just "Latino culture") that privileges male sexuality. Latina youth are thus taught that they have control of certain things, such as whether they will or will not get pregnant, but they are also taught that they have no control over disrupting gender inequalities. Another risky lesson is that survival inside and outside of their schools necessitates an adherence to heteronormative imperatives and that queer subjectivity is not possible within a Latina/o subjectivity. Together, such lessons contribute to their already vulnerable status as young women of color in this society.

[...]

References

Bettie, Julie. 2003. *Women Without Class: Girls, Race, and Identity.* Berkeley, CA: University of California Press.

Chavez, Leo. 2004. "A Glass Half Empty: Latina Reproduction and Public Discourse." *Human Organization* 4(2):173–88.

Cohen, Cathy. 1997. "Punks, Bulldaggers, and Welfare Queens: The Radical Potential of Queer Politics." *GLQ: A Journal of Lesbian and Gay Studies* 3:437–65.

Ericksen, Julia A. and Sally A. Steffan. 1999. *Kiss and Tell: Surveying Sex in the Twentieth Century.* Cambridge, MA: Harvard University Press.

Ferguson, Ann Arnett. 2001. *Bad Boys: Public Schools in the Making of Black Masculinity.* Ann Arbor, MI: University of Michigan Press.

Fields, Jessica. 2007. "Knowing Girls: Gender and Learning in School-Based Sexuality Education." In *Sexual Inequalities and Social Justice*, edited by N. Teunis and G. Herdt. Berkeley, CA: University of California Press.

Fields, Jessica. 2008. *Risky Lessons: Sex Education and Social Inequality.* New Brunswick, NJ: Rutgers University Press.

Fine, Michelle. 1987. "Silencing in Public Schools." *Language Arts* 64(2):157–74.

Fine, Michelle. 1988. "Sexuality, Schooling, and Adolescent Females: The Missing Discourse Desire." *Harvard Educational Review* 58:29–53.

Fine, Michelle and Sara I. McClelland. 2006. "Sexuality Education and Desire: Still Missing Discourse of Desire." *Harvard Educational Review* 76:297–337.

Fine, Michelle, Lois Weis, and Rosemary Roberts. 2000. "Refusing the Betrayal: Latinas Redefining Gender, Sexuality, Culture and Resistance." *Education/Pedagogy/Cultural Studies* 22:87–119.

García, Lorena. 2006. "Beyond the Latina Virgin/Whore Dichotomy: Investigating Latina Adolescent Sexual Subjectivity." Ph.D. dissertation, University of California, Santa Barbara, CA.

Gutiérrez, Elena R. 2008. *Fertile Matters: The Politics of Mexican-Origin Women's Reproduction.* Austin, TX: University of Texas Press.

Guzmán, Manolo. 2006. *Gay Hegemony/Latino Homosexualities.* New York: Routledge.

Hyams, Melissa. 2006. "La escuela: Young Latina Women Negotiating Identities in School." In *Latina Girls: Voices of Adolescent Strength in the United States*, edited by J. Denner and B. L. Guzmán. New York: New York University Press.

Inda, Jonathan X. 2002. "Biopower, Reproduction and the Migrant Woman's Body." In *Decolonial Voices: Chicana and Chicano Cultural Studies in the 21st Century*, edited by A. J. Aldama and N. Quinonez. Bloomington, IL: University of Indiana Press.

Ingraham, Chrys. 1994. "The Heterosexual Imaginary: Feminist Sociology and Theories of Gender." *Sociological Theory* 12(2):203–19.

Irvine, Janice M. 2002. *Talk About Sex: The Battles Over Sex Education in the United States.* Berkeley, CA: University of California Press.

Khayatt, Didi. 1995. "Compulsory Heterosexuality: Schools and Lesbian Students." In *Knowledge, Experience, and Ruling Relations: Studies in the Social Organization of Knowledge*, edited by M. Campbell and A. Manicom. Toronto: University of Toronto Press.

Kumashiro, Kevin K. 2001. "Queer Students of Color and Antiracist, Antiheterosexist Education: Paradoxes of Identity and Activism." In *Troubling Intersections of Race & Sexuality: Queer Students of Color and Anti-Oppressive Education*, edited by K. K. Kumashiro. Lanham, MD: Rowman & Littlefield.

Levy, Ariel. 2005. *Female Chauvinist Pigs: Women and the Rise of Raunch Culture.* New York: Free Press.

Lopez, Nancy. 2003. *Hopeful Girls, Troubled Boys: Race and Gender Disparity in Urban Education.* New York: Routledge.

Luker, Kristin. 2006. *When Sex Goes to School: Warring Views on Sex and Sex Education Since the Sixties.* New York: Norton.

McCready, Lance Trevor. 2004. "Some Challenges Facing Queer Youth Programs in Urban High Schools: Racial Segregation and De-Normalizing Whiteness." *Journal of Lesbian and Gay Issues in Education* 1(3):37–51.

Moran, Jeffrey. 2000. *Teaching Sex: The Shaping of Adolescence in the 20th Century.* Cambridge, MA: Harvard University Press.

Morris, Edward W. 2007. "'Ladies' or 'Loudies'? Perceptions and Experiences of Black Girls in Classrooms." *Youth & Society* 38:490–515.

Muñoz-Plaza, Corinne, Sandra Crouse Quinn, and Kathleen A. Rounds. 2002. "Lesbian, Gay, Bisexual and Transgender Students: Perceived Social Support in the High School Environment." *High School Journal* 85(4):52–63.

Pascoe, C. J. 2007. *Dude, You're a Fag: Masculinity and Sexuality in High School.* Berkeley, CA: University of California Press.

Patton, Cindy. 1996. *Fatal Advice: How Safe-Sex Education Went Wrong.* Durham, NC: Duke University Press.

Pérez, Gina M. 2006. "How a Scholarship Girl Becomes a Soldier: The Militarization of Latina/o Youth in Chicago Public Schools." *Identities: Global Studies in Culture and Power* 13:53–72.

Risman, Barbara J. and Pepper Schwartz. 2001. "After the Sexual Revolution: Gender Politics in Teen Dating." *Contexts* 1:16–24.

Rodríguez, Juana Maria. 2003. *Queer Latinidad: Identity Practices, Discursive Spaces.* New York: New York University Press.

Rofes, Eric. 1989. "Opening Up the Classroom Closet: Responding to the Educational Needs of Gay and Lesbian Youth." *Harvard Educational Review* 59:444–53.

Rust, Paula C. 2006. "The Impact of Multiple Marginalization." In *Reconstructing Gender: A Multicultural Anthology*, edited by E. Disch. Boston, MA: McGraw-Hill.

Schaffner, Laurie. 2006. *Girls in Trouble with the Law.* New Brunswick, NJ: Rutgers University Press.

Smith, George W. 2005. "The Ideology of 'Fag': The School Experiences of Gay Students." In *Beyond Silenced Voices: Class, Race, and Gender in United States Schools*, edited by L. Weis and M. Fine. Albany: State University of New York Press.

Tanenbaum, Leora. 1999. *Slut! Growing Up Female with a Bad Reputation.* New York: Seven Stories Press.

Thompson, Sharon. 1995. *Going All the Way: Teenage Girls' Tales of Sex, Romance, and Pregnancy.* New York: Hill and Wang

Tolman, Deborah L. 1994. "Doing Desire: Adolescent Girls' Struggles for/with Sexuality." *Gender & Society* 8:324–42.

Tolman, Deborah L. 2001. "Echoes of Sexual Objectification: Listening for One Girl's Erotic Voice." In *From Subjects to Subjectivities: A Handbook of Interpretive and Participatory Methods*, edited by D. L. Tolman and M. Bryndon-Miller. New York: New York University Press.

Tolman, Deborah L. 2002. *Dilemmas of Desire: Teenage Girls Talk About Sexuality.* Cambridge, MA: Harvard University Press.

"Boys Over Here, Girls Over There"

A Critical Literacy of Binary Gender in Schools

Susan W. Woolley

"Y̶ou are forced to *choose* a gender when you go to use a bathroom," Siri explained to me.

Siri self-identified as genderqueer, as neither a boy nor a girl. Like the other transgender and gender-nonconforming students at their high school, Siri chose to leave campus in order to use the public restrooms available at the local YMCA where they could access safe gender-neutral bathrooms. Siri's school, "MacArthur High," was a large urban public high school in northern California, and its lack of gender-neutral bathrooms was not unlike the situation in most public high schools in the United States. Both California state law and MacArthur High School's district's policies aimed to protect LGBTQ students. The California Student Safety and Violence Prevention Act of 2000 protects students from discrimination and harassment based on actual or perceived sexual orientation and gender identity (AB 537 Advisory Task Force 2001). This school district also has an antislur policy in place that includes protections from inappropriate language and insults against one's sex, actual or perceived sexual orientation, gender, and gender identity. Yet, the infrastructure of the building as well as ingrained practices in schooling erases and silences trans identities while simultaneously drawing attention to students' transgressions of binary gender norms. Despite the fact that schools like Siri's are mandated by law to provide LGBTQ students with safe spaces to learn, and despite progressive curricular interventions aimed at addressing gender, sexuality, and LGBTQ issues, gender and sexual inequality are reproduced through students' and teachers' everyday language and social interactions, joking and teasing, and the social production of school spaces. Schooling practices and the built environment reinforce and reproduce binary gender and heteronormativity.

Susan W. Woolley. 2015. "'Boys Over Here, Girls Over There': A Critical Literacy of Binary Gender in Schools." *TSQ: Transgender Studies Quarterly* 2(3):376–94.

While transgender and gender-nonconforming youth and their allies have won important legislative victories in a number of states and jurisdictions (Gay, Lesbian, and Straight Education Network 2014), legal changes have significant limitations if not accompanied by transformations in institutional practices and structures.

Critical Literacy and Reading Gender in Schools

The surveillance of bodies as binarily gendered is taught to young people from the very first days of schooling and continues throughout secondary school as the differences between boys and girls become more and more accentuated (Connell 1996; Ferguson 2001; Goodwin 2006; Martin 1998; Thorne 1993). In schools, the hidden curriculum of gender regulates bodily comportments, practices, and embodiments, making gendered bodies and their movements appear natural and rigidly dichotomous (Martin 1998). Individuals' experiences and subjectivities are constituted to a great extent by school policies, school-level processes, and the identity categories around which educational exclusions and inequalities revolve (Youdell 2006). School structures reinforce heteronormativity and compulsory heterosexuality through rituals of heterosexual performance, regulating binary gender expression, and meting out penalties for crossing gender boundaries (Epstein 1993; Khayatt 1995; Renold 2000, 2005). Moreover, such gendered and sexualized discipline often constructs racialized gendered meanings and subjectivities and reproduces a racial order (Ferguson 2001; McCready 2010). Schools' gender regimes are institutional arrangements that include power relations, divisions of labor, patterns of emotion, and symbolization of gender that work to construct definitions of masculinity and femininity (Connell 1996). A variety of seemingly mundane aspects of schooling govern and reinforce schools' gender regimes, including dress codes, team sports, segregated bathrooms, different entrance lines for boys and girls, typically gender segregated courses like shop and home economics, and heterocentric sex education (Connell 1996).

Dichotomous gender categories consolidate and become the basis of separate collectivities in schools, and when gender boundaries are activated, they are accompanied by stylized forms of action, a sense of performance, and mixed and ambiguous meanings (Thorne 1993). Through processes of *disidentification,* identities are stabilized negatively, such that, for example, to be authentically masculine is to be in opposition to and distant from feminine and feminized versions of masculinity (Mac an Ghaill 1994). In ritualized interactions that demonstrate heterosexuality and dominance along with the repudiation of weakness, heteronormative masculinity is confirmed and, when threatened, rescued through misogyny, the objectification of girls, and homophobic discourses (Pascoe 2007; Renold 2000; Thorne 1993). The specter of homosexuality is evoked to police masculinity, and gendered and sexualized epithets like *sissy, girl,* and *fag* are used to repudiate the "other" and position oneself as occupying normative subject positions (Pascoe 2007; Thorne 1993). The specter of being called a fag operates as a powerful disciplinary mechanism pushing boys to police behaviors that may fail at masculine tasks of competence, heterosexuality, or strength, thus revealing weakness or femininity (Pascoe 2007).

[. . .]

I argue that through language and practice, participants inscribe meaning onto bodies and spaces that reinforces a dominant ideology in society—that of heteronormative binary gender. As Dean Spade suggests in *Normal Life* (2011), inclusive policies guarantee neither the enacting of inclusive practices nor the development of an inclusive gender ethos. In addition to creating policies to protect transgender and gender-variant students, teachers and school administrators need to learn and implement a critical gender literacy that places relations of power at the center of its analysis.

The Study and Researcher Positionality

For three school years, from fall 2007 to spring 2010, I carried out ethnographic research at MacArthur High to examine the ways students and teachers construct, negotiate, and talk about gender and sexuality. This research took place across various sites of inquiry, including the classroom, gay-straight alliance (GSA) meetings, and communal spaces such as hallways and courtyards. I gathered a wide variety of data, including ethnographic field notes, audio-recorded interviews, student questionnaires, cultural artifacts generated by participants in this school, and audio and video recordings of classroom interactions. . . .

Dividing Students: Gender Identification as Definition of Self

Schooling is an important site for learning the possibilities and limitations of gender. It is commonly believed that sex is hard biological fact while gender is a social construction, but the work of biologist Anne Fausto-Sterling (2000) complicates the division of dimorphic sex and points out that biological sex is also a social construction, not simply an innate or essential state of being. . . . Yet, the terms *sex* and *gender* are typically used interchangeably in K–12 schools. Such practice of using *sex* and *gender* interchangeably is evident in the teacher's use of the terms throughout the excerpts presented here. Practices dividing students by gender have been deeply ingrained in the institution of schooling (Connell 1996; Ferguson 2001; Goodwin 2006; Martin 1998; Thorne 1993). Boys and girls routinely queue up in two parallel lines, mirrored binary structures, marching down the hallway to use the sex-segregated bathrooms in early elementary school. Dividing students by gender into working groups in school classrooms reproduces rigid gender binaries. Common practices in education shape the way teachers and administrators think of students as falling neatly into gendered categories of girls and boys, which they expect will match onto the students' assigned sex at birth. Outside this binary imaginary but very present in US public school systems are students who identify as transgender, genderqueer, gender nonconforming, or gender variant, or whose gender presentation and identification may not match onto societal expectations regarding binary gender norms.

Indeed, the structure of the built environment of MacArthur High, which has sex-segregated locker rooms and bathrooms, but no gender-neutral bathrooms, reinforced participants' expectations and conceptions of binary gender. Transgender and gender-nonconforming students at MacArthur High reported being subject to the scrutiny of others when they entered bathrooms at their school—scrutiny that manifested as searching glances up and down their bodies and as declarations of "this is the *girls'* bathroom," implying they must have entered the physical space not designated for their gender. Such scrutiny and surveillance regulated the kinds of bodies and forms of gendered expression and presentation permitted to occupy and use gendered bathroom spaces. As Siri articulated, one must choose a gender in order to use a bathroom at school even if that choice does not reflect their true sense of self. The literacy practice of reading another's body as gendered and sexed, as belonging to one category or another based on the commonplace assumption that gender and sex signifiers are stable and real is a literacy practice that gender-nonconforming and transgender students know intimately. This literacy practice dictates that trans students confront the task of "passing" as masculine male or feminine female in order to be sanctioned users of gendered spaces. Students' attempts at "passing" as cisgender participate in the larger literacy practice of encoding, decoding, and using bodies as texts open for interpretation. . . . Students' occupations of school spaces like gendered bathrooms and locker rooms and their positions in same-gender working groups reinforce the concept of stable binary gender categories. The everyday mundane ways in which binary gender and sex are constructed and reproduced in public schools shape gendered possibilities and boundaries for students. The students' literacy practice of reading school spaces shapes their movement through and presence in spaces like the bathrooms, locker rooms, and classrooms.

Teacher instructions and classroom interactions also play a pivotal role in consolidating the gender binary. In the three classrooms I observed for one year, students were divided into binary gender categories through seemingly small mundane decisions and larger structural principles. "Ms. Green's" freshman social studies course was one of three classes with a unit focused on gender, sexuality, and LGBTQ issues. Ms. Green used a progressive and comprehensive approach to these topics, and as a self-identified lesbian, she made a point to educate her students about LGBTQ experiences. Her classroom bulletin board had many LGBTQ-related posters that indicated her classroom was a safe space to be LGBTQ, marking her as an ally. Yet, the practice of dividing students into gendered groups inadvertently marked transgressions of binary gender norms and positioned certain students as subjects of ridicule. In some moments, Ms. Green's interventions disrupted and challenged difference. Ultimately, however, . . . her instructional practices reinscribed difference and with it systems of power.

One day, when students entered the room, Ms. Green directed the students to divide themselves into sex-segregated groups. Her intention was to deconstruct gendered stereotypes, to examine gendered social expectations, and to reflect on how these expectations made the students feel. Inserted below, excerpt 1 represents a moment of transition in which Ms. Green gave directions and framed biological sex as the delimiting factor for grouping the students. But she did allow students to identify in ways that may not match onto their biological sex. The teacher also described the process of gender identification as being about your definition of self, characterized by truthfulness and honesty.

Excerpt 1. Directions to divide into male and female groups

1 Ms. G.: So, I'm going to put you into—separate you into different sex groups.

2 And again, if you, I'm not going to,

3 if you identify with one sex or another,

4 honestly really identify with a sex that is different from your actual sex,

5 then I'm not going to stand in the way of that,

6 that's really your definition of self,

7 um but other than that we're going to divide along sex male female lines. Okay?

8 Kalil: Males.

9 Ms. G.: So, let me tell you what we're going to do. Um, each group . . .

10 Ryan: Females (in a falsetto voice)

Ms. Green asserted her authority by declaring that they were going to divide along male/female lines anyway. The teacher's announcement that she was not going to "stand in the way" of students' identifying their sex as different from their "actual sex" attached a stigma to those who would do so. Ms. Green allowed some room for student choice, but only if one genuinely identifies this way. The teacher marked those who do "really identify" as the opposite sex as a unique, small group that can step outside the boundaries, but only if they are truthful and honest about their transgression.

In Ms. Green's presentation of trans identities, even as she created space for those whose identity disrupts binary gender, her language also reinforced the stability of gender. She allowed for individual choice and simultaneously undermined that permission by demanding that choice be authentic. Being trans was marked as an option or a choice, which exceptionalized it, and such marking of trans identities was done through the discourse of authenticity. Furthermore, a student's decision to "identify with a sex that is different from [their] actual sex" (line 4) would have been a marked and highly visible choice in the classroom interaction.

Despite Ms. Green's efforts to push her students to think against binary constructions of sex, she lacked the scripts in her lexicon to express the range or continuum of ways people identify themselves beyond binaries. Trans identities were introduced as a third choice only after her initial decision to divide students into male and female groups, but third choices do not necessarily disrupt the stability of binary constructions of sex and gender. . . . The conundrum Ms. Green faced was trying to confront binary categories of sex and gender, while simultaneously working within the limitations of deeply rooted binary frames for gender that structure the English language (e.g., subject pronouns *he* and *she,* object pronouns *him* and *her,* possessive pronouns *his* and *her*), that shape schooling practices of dividing students into groups by systems of categorization (e.g., sex-segregated bathroom and locker room spaces, lining up boys and girls separately), . . . that influence how students interact and move through classroom space.

[. . .]

Ms. Green's directions were operating at two levels: the content of the class and the instructional level. At the instructional level, the message being communicated was a command to follow these directions so the class could proceed with the planned activity. The content, on the other hand, communicated that one could identify their gender in ways that did not match social expectations regarding their biological sex, but this process was riddled with challenges and assessed along lines of honesty and genuineness. This was a moment in which the teacher asked the students to move their bodies in the space of the classroom based on who they were, how they identified themselves, and where they saw themselves in terms of their gender and sex. In this, Ms. Green inadvertently and perhaps even against her own intentions reproduced notions of binary gender and socially constructed boundaries between boys and girls. Her emphasis indicated that sex and gender identification are really about one's definition of self, which is true, but marked as special and worth mention. *Honestly* and *really* modified *identify* and acted as intensifiers and assessments. By using a second redundant modifier, *really,* the teacher marked that this transgression was a problematic or contentious way of identifying oneself that needed to be taken seriously. By emphasizing that this is something one *honestly* really identifies with, Ms. Green indicated that there's some truthfulness and some falsehood, some room for interpretation. Here she marked trans identities as special cases, naturalized through authenticity.

When Ms. Green was done giving instructions, she finished her command with, "Okay, separate. You guys have fifteen minutes, go, separate!" When three students walked into class late, Ms. Green interrupted the lesson to direct the students to join the groups separated by sex. Found below, excerpt 2 shows how trans identities and ambiguous positions in the middle were not only marked as exceptional but also constructed as sites for the exercise of humor. Ms. Green characterized identifying as trans as a path wrought with an entirely different or anomalous set of questions and considerations. This was taken up as a joke when a student echoed her teacher and laughed (line 6). The jokes continued when one student indicated that Anna, one of the latecomers, should sit with the boys, making fun of her gender presentation and transgressions from binary gender norms. Rather than interrupt such teasing or question the meanings and intentions behind such jokes, the teacher was complicit in identifying and marking difference in Anna's, as well as her own, gender presentation. At the end of the excerpt, the teacher further marked trans as special, by highlighting the truthfulness requisite for identifying as trans.

Excerpt 2. There's a bunch of us who are kind of found in the middle.

1 Ms. G.: I'd rather you segregate by sex, not gender, so,

2 boys over here, girls over there,

3 unless you really identify as trans, then,

4 that's a whole other set of questions.

5 (indistinguishable—students talk, yell, and laugh)

6 Gail (laughing): That's a whole other set of questions.

7 Andre (to Anna): Go back, go back over here.

8 (indicating where Anna should sit, motioning toward the circle of boys)

9 Ms. G.: Anna? Yeah, I know.

10 There's a bunch of us who are kind of found in the middle.

11 We could go one way or another based on your sex or gender,

12 unless you're trans,

13 unless you truly identify as trans.

In line 1, Ms. Green directed the students to segregate by biological sex and to situate themselves in the space of the classroom based on this distinction. Her specific instructions for dividing the groups—the boys as belonging "over here" and the girls "over there" (line 2)—spatially indexed their locations in the classroom: "here" and "there" designated positions on either side of her. In these instructions, Ms. Green upheld the stability of binary constructions of biological sex categories, which were able to be segregated spatially and conceptually. In line 3, however, Ms. Green again opened up the possibility for students to not have to choose whether they would join the boys' or the girls' group. Ms. Green qualified the possibility that one might identify as trans as a way out of having to choose to join the boys' or girls' groups. That is, Ms. Green allowed for students to join the group opposite of the biological sex they were assigned at birth or to sit out of the activity and not join either the boys' or girls' groups. Here, Ms. Green used the words *really* (line 3) and *truly* (line 13) to modify and intensify how one identifies as trans, marking the process of identifying as trans as calling on some degree of truthfulness and sincerity and framing such processes of identification through discourses of authenticity.

Andre, as a boy sitting in the circle of boys, called out and characterized Anna's gender presentation as boyish or somewhat masculine for a girl (lines 7 and 8). Andre's reading of Anna's gender as masculine and his preconceived knowledge that Anna was considered to be a girl served as the basis for his joke. His joke operated as follows: Andre's line that Anna belonged back over here with the boys acted as a signifier for an imaginary signified—which, in this case, was also the implied, unspoken punch line—that Anna's biological sex must be male. By indicating that Anna should sit in the circle with the boys, Andre marked her gender presentation as masculine for a girl, so masculine that her biological sex *must* be male.

After clarifying that they were speaking about the same person, Ms. Green claimed knowledge of Anna's gender when she stated, "Anna? Yeah, I know" (line 9). Agreeing that Anna's gender presentation was more boyish than girlish and that she belonged with the boys, Ms. Green signaled her belief that Anna transgressed heteronormative binary gender expectations. The teacher supported the marking and naming of her own and Anna's gender transgressions when she said, "There's a bunch of us who are kind of found in the middle. We could go one way or another based on your sex or gender" (lines 10 and 11). Ms. Green claimed knowledge about gender transgression—both her own and Anna's—and the liminal space their gender presentations occupy, found in the middle of binary gender categories, blending both masculine and feminine elements. . . .

The way Anna reacted to the regulation of her gender differed depending on the context and valence of the situation. At this particular moment at the beginning of the class, Anna remained silent, putting her head down on her desk, not engaging with her classmates or her teacher. Her silence may have been her attempt to ignore their gender policing and teasing. When Andre motioned for Anna to sit in the boys' circle (lines 7 and 8), however, Anna glared at him, frowning and shaking her head. Other times when Anna served as a site for the regulation of gender and sexuality norms, she snapped back with insults, curse words, and sharp looks. Anna claimed that she and others saw her as "a bad girl" because she often got into trouble at school, skipped class, and ran around with a group of boys. She self-identified as an African-American girl who was athletic and loved to play basketball. Anna's athletic identity stood in stark contrast to what she understood as societal pressures for girls to be feminine and sexy. Anna often wore jeans and a baggy hooded sweatshirt, sneakers, and no makeup. Because Anna did not perform femininity in the same ways that social constructions of emphasized femininity called for, she was subjected to her classmates' jokes and teasing about her gender expression and identity, which was at times interpreted by others as more masculine. In a situation such as this, critical gender literacy could have given students the space to unpack how societal expectations manifest in teasing and peer pressure and shape possibilities for sanctioned gender expression.

[. . .]

Whose Claims to Gender Identity?

. . . Ms. Green's students returned to class after their lunch break and found desks to sit in, still separated by sex. Anna sat in a desk against the wall near me, closer to the boys' group than the girls' group, but in neither group, peripheral to the class activity. Anna quietly sat with her head down on her desk—a position she often took in Ms. Green's class. During this class, the students reported what they had discussed in sex-separated groups during the morning's activity. In the afternoon, the students stood as a group and reported on their experiences as girls and boys to the teacher and the group of the opposite sex. Here, the students presented their individual and collective voices, how society expects them to be as boys or girls, and what the social consequences of breaking these expectations look like. As seen in Figure 37.1, the girls presented their findings first, standing toward the front of the room, projecting transparencies on the screen, and facing the boys who were sitting in their desks.

Figure 37.1   Floor Diagram of Ms. Green's Class. Girls Presenting Their Findings. (Image designed by Susan W. Woolley)

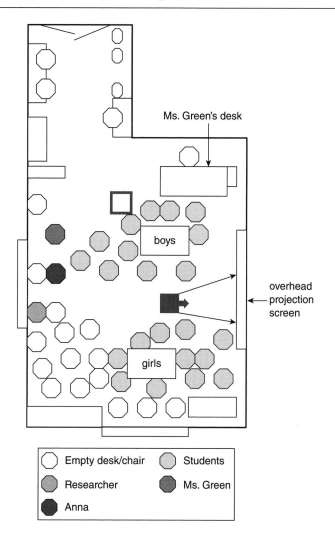

The girls stood together as they read their reflections on gender expectations placed on them. After they presented, the girls fielded questions from the boys and Ms. Green. All the girls were standing on one side of the room, focused around the overhead projector, except for Anna, who was sitting in a desk to the side of the room. Ms. Green, Anna, the boys, and I were sitting in desks facing the girls. Ms. Green interrupted the girls' reporting to the class in order to interrupt a side conversation. On the side, Shavonne had been trying to get Anna to stand up and join the girls at the front of the room. Anna resisted, remaining seated in the desk. In this moment of the teacher's intervention, transcribed below in excerpt 4, two students, Shavonne and Rex, claimed Anna's gender identity for her and the teacher passed over an instance of name calling. Both were friends with Anna—Shavonne was also an African American girl while Rex was a White boy. Their social closeness as friends who joked and teased may have made the following situation in which both Rex and Shavonne claimed Anna's gender identity for her possible. Nevertheless, it was a cisgender male-bodied boy and a cisgender female-bodied girl, both rooted in heteronormative gender presentations and sexuality, who exercised the power to position Anna as a site for gender and sexual regulation.

Excerpt 4. Passing over name calling

1   Ms. G.: Uh, Shavonne! We're listening to one mic.

2   Shavonne: Uh, Anna, you're a girl,

3   get in the group!

4   (indistinguishable student talk)

5   Rex: Anna is trans.

6   (boys laugh)

7   Ms. G.: I can't hear her!

Ms. Green's interruption, "We're listening to one mic" (line 1), told Shavonne that Lisa was the only sanctioned speaker at the moment. Her intention in interjecting was to get Shavonne to stop talking on the side to Anna while Lisa was speaking to the class. Shavonne's claim that Anna was a girl was both an attempt to include Anna and an insistence that Anna physically come join the girls' group, where Shavonne posited that Anna belonged (lines 2 and 3). Rex countered Shavonne's insistence that Anna was a girl by saying, "Anna is trans" (line 5), a comment apparently intended as a denigrating joke and one that garnered laughter from the boys. Here, Rex calling Anna "trans" named and marked her gender transgression while echoing previous jokes (excerpts 2 and 3). A few boys looked at Rex and laughed, some whispering, "whoooah" as if he were going to get into trouble for his comment. Ms. Green exclaimed, "I can't hear her!" (line 7), in an attempt to redirect the students back to Lisa—the sanctioned speaker whom Ms. Green was unable to hear. Instead of addressing the power dynamics at play in this interaction, the name calling, or the politics of claiming another's identity, Ms. Green continued her line of intervention to refocus everybody's attention onto Lisa as the designated speaker in the class activity. Ms. Green did not interrupt Rex's joke that named Anna's gender identity as "trans" and teased her for her gender presentation. Ms. Green's exclamation, "I can't hear her!" (line 7), highlights how difficult it is to hear everything that is going on at the same time in the classroom.

During my time at the school, I had observed that Anna was often called names by her classmates that reflected assumptions about her sexuality—like *dyke* and *lesbo.* During this particular exercise, Anna's classmates utilized a new term they had just learned in this social studies class, and began calling her "trans." *Trans,* like *gay,* as a descriptor is not inherently a derogatory term but here was utilized as a slur in the exercise of power through name calling. While words like *trans* and *gay* should be normalized as part of the everyday language used to describe gender and sexuality, we can see how in the context of teasing and joking such words can carry multivalent meanings and do something different than just describe. Rex's joke buttressed already existing unequal power relations between boys and girls, between White and Black students, and between cisgender and trans people. This event also shaped a classroom context in which jokes may regulate gender or sexual identity, expression, and oppression. Rex's calling Anna "trans" legitimized Anna's choice to remain seated in her desk apart from either group for the duration of the class activity—a choice that the teacher earlier sanctioned. This example demonstrates the ways participants' claims of identity position others, in some cases as interpreted as belonging to a designated kind or group, while in other cases as the punch line for a joke. Anna's classmates' claims to her gender identity left little room for Anna to be a girl, trans, or gendered in any way she may wish. Ms. Green's inaction in interrupting the students' claims coconstructed a social context in this classroom in which declaring another person's gender identity and naming gender transgressions for the purpose of a joke was allowed. Rex's joke, the boys' uptake in the form of laughter, and the teacher's passing over of this name calling socialized classroom participants into relations in which teasing was a sanctioned way to regulate gender and sexuality. Ambiguity opened up spaces for humor to work on regulating gender and sexuality, reinforcing the structure and ideology of binary gender that is durable and difficult to step outside of.

Even in Ms. Green's classroom where the teacher was trying to interrogate and deconstruct binary notions of gender and sexuality, and in a classroom that was marked as a safe space to be LGBTQ, heteronormative binary gender was still being produced and reinforced through participants' joking and teasing the teacher could not control. Furthermore, by pushing students to identify as either masculine male or feminine female, classroom practices such as this run the risk of heightening and drawing awareness to the transgression of heteronormative binary gender norms and identifying as transgender. This pedagogical move worked to reproduce the gender binary and position some people as the site for examination and joking. . . .

Conclusion

As illustrated in the data, the distinction between what Ms. Green says and what she does—or the content of her lesson and how she manages the class maps onto the problem of policy versus practice. Policies are in place, and Ms. Green has the intention of drawing attention to the construction and constraints of binary gender, but everyday practices of categorizing students, joking and name calling, and moving through classroom and gendered spaces reproduce heteronormative binary gender. Challenging such reproduction cannot be done without critical reflection and transformative action aimed at examining and changing dominant power structures. In the quest for a gender equality that includes transgender and gender-nonconforming students, steps are required to bridge policy and practice. Inclusive policies need to be translated into inclusive practices and the development of an inclusive ethos through critical literacy pedagogy. . . .

A critical gender literacy that works to make transgender and gender-nonconforming people equal places at its center the deconstruction of binary gender as it is simultaneously tied to other axes of power such as Whiteness, ability, class, and heteronormativity. Critical gender literacy can be developed and put into practice through concrete changes in the curriculum and instructional practice. The curriculum needs to include the examination of binary gender and how it is constructed and reinforced beginning at a very young age and moving through the lifespan as well as how such meanings are situated contextually. Moreover, an open dialogue about gender variance and the ways people more often operate outside rigid gender expectations than within them helps students to see the diversity of gender expression and identity available. Similarly, the curriculum needs to include the contributions of transgender people to history and society as well as the respected and revered positions transgender people have occupied cross-culturally. . . . This involves a much more expansive scaffolding that requires teachers and students to think deeply about mundane daily practices and incorporate an awareness of those practices into curriculum, instruction, and reflective learning. Through such action and reflection, educators and students can shape social interaction and meaning making aimed at gender equity inclusive of transgender and gender-nonconforming people.

[. . .]

References

AB 537 Advisory Task Force. 2001. *California Student Safety and Violence Prevention Act of 2000*. Retrieved February 13, 2015 (www.cde.ca.gov/ls/ss/se/documents/ab537report.pdf).

Connell, R. W. 1996. "Teaching the Boys: New Research on Masculinity, and Gender Strategies for Schools." *Teachers College Record* 98(2):206–35.

Epstein, Debbie. 1993. "Practising Heterosexuality." *Pedagogy, Culture, and Society* 1(2):275–86.

Fausto-Sterling, Anne. 2000. "The Five Sexes, Revisited." *Sciences* 40(4):18–23.

Ferguson, Ann Arnett. 2001. *Bad Boys: Public Schools in the Making of Black Masculinity*. Ann Arbor, MI: University of Michigan Press.

Gay, Lesbian and Straight Education Network. 2014. "Nondiscrimination Laws Protecting Students by State." Retrieved February 10, 2015 (www.glsen.org/download/file/MjkyNQ).

Goodwin, Marjorie Harness. 2006. *The Hidden Life of Girls*. Malden, MA: Blackwell.

Khayatt, Didi. 1995. "Compulsory Heterosexuality: Schools and Lesbian Students." In *Knowledge, Experience, and Ruling Relations*, edited by M. Campbell and A. Manicom. Toronto: University of Toronto Press.

Mac An Ghaill, Mairtin. 1994. *The Making of Men*. Buckingham, UK: Open University Press.

Martin, Karin A. 1998. "Becoming a Gendered Body: Practices of Preschools." *American Sociological Review* 63(4):494–511.

McCready, Lance. 2010. *Making Space for Diverse Masculinities*. New York: Peter Lang.

Pascoe, C. J. 2007. *Dude, You're a Fag*. Berkeley, CA: University of California Press.

Renold, Emma. 2000. "'Coming Out': Gender, (Hetero)Sexuality, and the Primary School." *Gender and Education* 12(3):309–26.

Renold, Emma. 2005. *Girls, Boys, and Junior Sexualities*. New York: Routledge.

Spade, Dean. 2011. *Normal Life: Administrative Violence, Critical Trans Politics, and the Limits of Law*. Brooklyn, NY: South End.

Thorne, Barrie. 1993. *Gender Play: Girls and Boys in School*. New Brunswick, NJ: Rutgers University Press.

Youdell, Deborah. 2006. *Impossible Bodies, Impossible Selves*. Dordrecht, Netherlands: Springer.

Un/Doing Gender?

A Case Study of School Policy and Practice in Zambia

Monisha Bajaj

Some would say sweeping is a sex role, meaning it's only for women. But in fact, even men can sweep. For example, as it's practiced here, we don't call workers to clean our classrooms or to sweep our surroundings. We do it ourselves. So I would say this has an impact on us . . . (Interview with male student, Umutende School)

That's why you find that at the end of the day, if you observe, most of [the girls] loiter here. They know that "when I go home, there's this and that problem." They don't feel like going home; they want to stay. (Interview with head teacher, Umutende School)

You find that there is this belief especially here in Africa, when you sleep with a teenager or a small child that AIDS will get away from you. As a result, you find that a lot of pupils, especially our girl child[ren], are being attacked such that it has even become dangerous for somebody to leave a child with an uncle, even the real dad, because it's happening in homes. Now, you don't know if he's going to turn into an animal when you are not there. (Parent focus group, Umutende School)

. . . Scholarship on gender in international and comparative education has shifted from primarily addressing women's access to schooling (Prather and Tietjen 1991; Stromquist et al. 2000), to encompassing a broader range of topics, including constructions of masculinity and femininity in and around schools (Mirembe and Davies 2001; Naseem 2004); women's conceptualisations of gendered realities as teachers and students (Adely 2004; Kirk 2004; Stambach 2000); and the role of institutions—such as the state and non-governmental organisations—in formal and non-formal education globally (Stromquist 2004; Vavrus 2005). Literature in the field has also provided information about gendered norms in schooling and assessed innovative "gender education" programmes that have occurred outside of schools in non-governmental organisations, government offices, and other settings (Anderson and Mendoza 2000).

Monisha Bajaj. 2009. "Un/Doing Gender? A Case Study of School Policy and Practice in Zambia." *International Review of Education* 55(5–6):483–502.

Drawing on previous scholarship on gender in international and comparative education, this article offers a glimpse into one Zambian school's unconventional practices through the lens of the "undoing gender" framework (Deutsch 2007). Applying this perspective allows for an exploration of the relationship between educational policies and ideologies at the macro-level, and pedagogies and practices at the micro-level. In particular, the concept of "undoing gender," when examined alongside larger structures of material inequalities, provides a productive starting point for understanding the role of gender and schooling, and the prospects for greater gender equity in global contexts.

Un/Doing Gender

West and Zimmerman (1987) first advanced "doing gender" as a framework for examining gender as the product of social interactions. "Doing gender" foregrounded a relational under-standing of gender, focusing on the reproduction of gendered roles through the practices of daily social life (Deutsch 2007). The theorists argued that gender, as contrasted to a rigid ascription of difference to biological sex, is an *activity* that is constantly undertaken and that varies with regard to the context (West and Zimmerman 1987). Through interactions and rela-tionships, social meanings and dominant roles around gender are typically reproduced, legiti-mated and maintained. In this framework, there is no way to avoid "doing gender" as a category of difference that structures social relations in societies across time and geography, albeit in manifestly different and complex variations (West and Zimmerman 1987). The "doing gender" framework has contributed a conceptual vocabulary—precisely the understanding of gender as a relational, situated, and contextual practice—that can illuminate the experience of gendered human beings engaging systems of education in the context of "developing" societies.

Whereas a "doing gender" framework implies an uncovering of, but a larger conformity to, unequal and gendered realities, the "undoing gender" perspective seeks to examine the resis-tance to and dismantling of gender differences. Deutsch (2007) suggests five areas in which "undoing gender" could expand from simply "documenting the persistence of inequality" to addressing other key issues, such as:

1. When and how social interactions become less gendered, not just differently gendered;

2. The conditions under which gender is irrelevant in social interactions;

3. Whether all gendered interactions reinforce inequality;

4. How the structural (institutional) and interactional levels might work together to pro-duce change; and

5. Interaction as the site of change. (Deutsch 2007: 114)

Although Deutsch does not focus on formal schooling per se, the conceptual resources that she offers are particularly useful for the field of international and comparative education to the extent that they provide a framework for assessing gendered social interactions within and out-side of schools. Deutsch's work also suggests an emphasis on how, through a focus on relational practices, gender inequality may shift, reconstitute and even diminish over time. This article primarily explores schooling as an institution and relational practices around gender, which constitute the fourth and fifth prongs of Deutsch's schema listed above. The sections that follow draw upon her work to examine how gender might be "coming undone" at a small secondary school on the Zambian Copperbelt.

Gender Inequality and Access to Schooling in Zambia

Against the backdrop of economic decline in Zambia, human rights organisations have documented legal and cultural impediments to gender equity that work against women's rights and protections. Domestic violence is a common occurrence: in one study, more than half of the married or previously married women interviewed reported having been beaten by their husbands, while 41% of unmarried women reported having been beaten by a male partner (Kazunga and Chewe 2003). Respondents in my research also reported domestic violence as a common, but often unreported, practice. In a study of attitudes towards domestic violence in Zambia, 85% of women stated that in certain situations, men are justified in beating their wives (HRW 2007). Zambia currently has no law against domestic violence and no legislation that prohibits marital rape (HRW 2007).

[. . .]

A recent Human Development Report (UNDP 2007) ranks Zambia 165th out of 177 nations in its overall gender development index (a composite of statistical factors that elucidate the general situation of women). The index also indicates lower salaries for women, who on average earn only 55% of the salaries of men, and a 17% gap between male (76%) and female (59%) adult literacy (UNDP 2007). The differential in literacy points to historical and current gaps in girls' enrollment in primary and secondary schooling in Zambia.

. . . Girls' enrollment in schooling, however, has steadily increased over the past 40 years, with 89% of girls currently in primary school and 25% of girls in secondary school (compared to 31% of young men) (UNDP 2007; UNESCO 2005). . . . It is in this context of gender inequality in and outside of schools that an alternative, non-governmental school has sought to challenge gender roles through its distinctive school practices.

Methodology

The data presented in this article come from a larger study on youth experiences in Ndola, Zambia, carried out from 2003 to 2004 that included over 500 students, teachers, parents, and administrators. The study utilised mixed methods—quantitative and qualitative—to better understand secondary students' lived realities amidst economic decline and the HIV/AIDS pandemic. The primary methods included interviews, observations, participant observation, focus groups, research diaries and surveys. Interviews were semi-structured and respondents were chosen primarily through random or snowball sampling. Regular observations took place in classes at Umutende School and Ndola government secondary schools during the research period.

[. . .]

The Umutende School

This study examines how one alternative school on the Zambian Copperbelt has attempted to "undo gender," or to resist and transform unequal gender relations, through its educational policies, pedagogy, and practices. The school's intentional effort, as well as students' responses to it, will be presented in order to understand how the "undoing of gender" in this educational institution has occurred amidst economic decline and the HIV/AIDS pandemic, both of which have had an adverse impact on women in Zambia (de Waal and Whiteside 2003).

The Umutende School is a low-cost, non-governmental private school developed in the spirit of pan-Africanist cultural and political ideologies . . . to reflect the values of equity, leadership, non-violence, peace and social justice. . . . This article examines how unequal gender practices are resisted through the school's deliberate attempts, through policy and practice, to "undo gender."

Gender in the Umutende School

Various features of the Umutende School reflect the conscious ways in which gender has been considered in an attempt to disrupt the reproduction of gender inequity through social interactions within the school. The most apparent feature was the separation of the boys and girls into separate campuses across the street from one another. Each campus also had teachers of the same sex in order to provide role-modelling for the students. The decision to have women teachers for the girl's campus was also reportedly based in part on the prevalence of teacher–student sexual relationships in Zambia (BBC 2003), and the school's desire to minimise potential for such occurrences. Thus, girls and boys at the school had separate classrooms, facilities, and teachers, and they carried out assemblies separately each day before instruction started. The decision to have single sex education was explained by one of the school's founders as an opportunity for young women to "develop confidence, speak up and take leadership roles."

In order to better understand the uniqueness of the Umutende School, it is important to clarify certain features *vis-à-vis* those of government schools. Given Umutende's smaller school size . . . there were fewer students in each class (20–40) as compared to government schools where classes I observed were as large as 150 students. The external funding that the NGO school received from international donors also resulted in more timely (albeit not higher) payment for teachers and staff. The Zambian national curriculum was utilised in both government schools and the Umutende School, but the latter had longer hours each day—10 hours compared to 5–6 hours at government schools—and this afforded the school time for community service, human values education, school cleaning, daily assembly and agricultural production periods. During these additional lessons, students were taught about various life skills, including those related to promoting gender equity. . . . Most of the students at Umutende came from families in which some high school education was the highest level of education attained and parents/guardians, if employed, tended to work in small-scale agricultural activities, as teachers, or in low-level positions in the local mining industry.

One noteworthy difference between the Umutende School and government schools was the daily morning assembly period at Umutende that covered a range of topics, some of which explicitly addressed women's rights and realities. In these assemblies, announcements were made, human values lessons were imparted, and role plays and songs were performed; moreover, once a week, boys and girls had a senior administrator give them a 40–50 minute talk on such topics as goal-setting, leadership development, values and social issues. Women's leadership, their equality to young men and their ability to pursue academic and professional pursuits were common topics in these assemblies for young men and women alike.

For young women especially, the morning assemblies provided much opportunity for learning and participation. Given the school's separation of boys and girls, the girls' campus had its own leadership structure, which differed from government schools where boys tended to dominate in leadership positions as well as in classroom discussions. Additionally, morning assemblies started with the students singing and drumming songs in the local language (Bemba); this differed greatly from government secondary schools, where the use of any language other than English was prohibited. At the girls' morning assemblies at Umutende, young women would lead songs, drum, make announcements and participate in role-plays on different issues. Allowing women to drum was a departure not only from government school practice where songs were not sung, but also from the male drumming tradition of the ethnic community to which most students belonged. Similar to men engaging in school cleaning as will be discussed later in this article, young women participating in drumming and school leadership challenged larger social and cultural attitudes around gender.

Specific messages about gender were infused into both the structure and the content of the Umutende School and reflected in its operations. . . . These deliberate attempts and their impact on students suggest that the school was restructuring the ways in which gender roles were understood at institutional and interactional levels, and creating the conditions for greater equity and social change referred to in Deutsch's framework of "undoing gender" discussed earlier in this article.

Disrupting Gender Inequality

School Cleaning

. . . Umutende students were responsible for cleaning their school rather than having hired staff to do so, the common practice in government schools. Given the gendered nature of cleaning work in Zambia, and the separation of the girls' and boys' campuses at Umutende, this meant that young men—in rotation and by classroom, so that everyone was required to participate—had to sweep, clean toilets, wash windows and carry out the many other tasks required for keeping the campus environment clean. Mr Chalwe, a senior teacher at Umutende, explained the practice:

> Here, the pupils are timetabled in each and every classroom to go and clean the toilets. We don't have anyone who has been employed for that. [They are] advised on what good you can derive from doing certain things on your own and not necessarily depending on others to serve your personal needs.

. . . This unusual practice of students cleaning at Umutende was often resisted at first by new male students unaccustomed to it, but, according to teachers, they generally adjusted quickly because entire classes carried out the work together and at an assigned time.

The implementation of activities like school cleaning that disrupted notions about gender differentiation influenced both boys' and girls' expectations of roles within and beyond the school grounds. For many students, this was reported as a notable feature of their schooling experience, particularly because it extended beyond the school to their lives at home. For example, 12th-grader Vincent noted the coupling of formal instruction about gender roles and school practice that impacted his understanding of them:

> I remember in grade eight [at Umutende], we learned the difference between gender roles and sex roles. Gender roles refer to those which do not have a particular sex. Some would say sweeping is a sex role, meaning it's only for women. But in actual sense, they are completely wrong. In fact, even men can sweep. For example, as it's practiced here, we don't call workers to clean our classrooms or to sweep our surroundings. We do it ourselves. So I would say this has an impact on us because even when we reach home,

for me, I don't know about the others, I usually clean my own room and wash my own clothes. I don't ask anyone to do it. I let the ladies do their own thing. I do things on my own. (Interview, 23 June 2004)

This attitude of male students partaking in activities considered to be "women's work" was also noted by several parents in focus group discussions. Mrs. Tembo, the mother of a student in tenth grade at Umutende, offered the following praise for the school in teaching her son to help out around the house:

They sweep the surroundings of the school and the classrooms by themselves. That has helped us as parents because even sweeping the house, these days I don't do it. He comes home [and says], "Mom, I'll do the sweeping. Mom, I'll wash the plates." It's because it has had a beginning from this school. (Parent focus group, 17 April 2004)

From the perspective of many parents, teachers and students, the behaviour of students outside the school was linked to the messages received at school.

The school's cleaning practice has counteracted the reproduction of larger societal messages and practices related to cleaning work on both the institutional levels (school policy) and inter-actional levels (by students and teachers working together to carry out the practice and the ripple effect in students' homes). One aspect of the practice's efficacy was, in part, that it was mandatory and was a regular part of the school schedule. While new students may resist such a practice, their ability to access the benefits of Umutende, such as small classes, caring teachers and a low-cost/high-quality school environment, was contingent on their acceptance of alter-native practices of school cleaning among others.

While boys may have the power to alter their practices without sanction, the transformative potential of school cleaning for girls is less clear in terms of their lives beyond the idyllic school environment. In order to examine the impact of the school's attempts to "undo gender" on girl students, it is important then to look more closely at the broader human values/rights component of the school's curriculum and pedagogical practices.

Human Values and Human Rights

The focus on values such as peace, equity, and social justice by the school—as emphasised through daily interactive lessons, posters, and plays—had a corresponding impact on students' understandings of human rights. As discussed earlier, violations of various gender-specific rights occur throughout Zambia and the most prevalent examples of violations in student accounts of their lives related to domestic violence, rape (known as "defiling") of young women or girl children, and forced or coerced marriages at an early age.

Students of a similar age from Umutende School and a government school were asked in a survey about human rights violations in general, and women's rights issues in particular. The responses to the survey questions about common rights violations demonstrated greater aware-ness about abuses among the students at the Umutende School, who had been exposed to these issues during weekly assemblies, than at Chilemba, a nearby government school. Results from the survey are presented in Table 38.1.

Table 38.1 presents the frequency distribution of responses, and . . . item analysis showed that the mean for each of the items was higher for Umutende students than for Chilemba students of the same age and from the same neighbourhood. This indicates that the respondents

Table 38.1 Student Attitudes Towards Domestic Violence, Rape, and Early Marriage

	Chilemba		Umutende	
	Number	**Percent**	**Number**	**Percent**
A man beating his wife is a human rights violation				
No	24	50.00	16	25.81
Yes	24	50.00	46	74.19
Total	48	100.00	62	100.00
Defilement is a human rights violation				
No	11	25.00	2	3.28
Yes	33	75.00	59	96.72
Total	44	100.00	61	100.00
Early/forced marriage is a human rights violation				
No	11	22.92	1	1.59
Yes	37	77.08	62	98.41
Total	48	100.00	63	100.00

from the Umutende School demonstrated greater knowledge of the women's rights violations listed on the survey as compared to the respondents from the government school. The table above also shows the greater propensity towards understanding and identifying gender specific human rights violations among students attending Umutende.

In addition to identifying violations of rights during surveys, female students at the school often mentioned wanting to become public officials, doctors and leaders of international organisations in order to promote women's rights in the future. For example, seventh-grader Gladys noted that knowing one's rights was an important first step to gender equality, saying, "What men can do, we can also do because we know our rights. Those women who are not educated, they get married [young]. They are beaten up sometimes by their husbands. So we should know our rights . . . so that we can know what's happening" (Interview, 29 April 2004). Awareness of human rights and its influence on a willingness to challenge or "undo gender" norms in a highly unequal context seemed to be based in the school's unique approach.

While difficult to disentangle causality from the data presented above, I argue that the school's structure, content and alternative approach that sought to "undo" the ways students conceived of gender account for the difference in responses from students of similar age at different schools. It would be difficult to point to other variables explaining the significant differences in attitudes. . . . The data are that there is value in the work that the Umutende School is carrying out, namely consistent institutional policy that restructures gender roles, focuses attention on human rights and dignity, and promotes equal treatment with regard to the tasks at school. Examinations of the effects of Umutende School's policy also bear out Deutsch's (2007) charge that studies exploring the ways that structural/institutional and interactional levels might work together to produce change, as well as those examining interactions as the site of change, will offer fruitful testimony to the mutability of difference. Changes in social relations, however complicated and limited, are certainly possible.

. . . Conclusion . . .

The deliberate space for discussing and practicing gender equality created by the Umutende School made it an oasis of safety for young women in a context where sexual violence is rampant (HRW 2002). Going home in the afternoons and graduation from the school both provided a rupture between the alternative norms fostered at Umutende and the larger social norms that students had come to problematise. The head teacher of the Umutende girls' school noted how this was manifested in some of the girls' behaviour:

> When the girls go home, it's difficult for some of them [because] even if they have both parents, maybe the parents are always quarrelling or the father is always drunk. They come back to school, and they tell you, "yesterday when I reached home, daddy beat my mother," and so on. That's why you find that at the end of the day, if you observe, most of them loiter here. They know that "when I go home, there's this and that problem." They don't feel like going home, they want to stay. On half days, we have a lot of problems, especially the older girls, to get them to go home. (Interview, 5 April 2004)

The difficulty students had in reconciling their school-based learnings with the realities they found at home suggests a tension between competing gender ideologies. The relational features of the Umutende School's efforts at "undoing gender" are notable in the young women's preferences to stay at school and interact with people who share their understandings of gender rather than butting up against the unequal, and sometimes violent, gendered realities in their homes and communities.

[. . .]

Despite these limitations, it seems probable that conceptions of gender will be renegotiated by Umutende students in ways that reflect new circumstances and influences after leaving the school. The early instruction in equal relations may manifest itself in diverse attitudes, actions and decisions that reflect gender equity among female and male graduates of the school. Particularly in light of the backdrop of extreme (and gendered) economic uncertainty and the higher prevalence of HIV/AIDS among young women (Fleshman 2004), examining how gender norms might be "undone" offers important insights for scholars and practitioners seeking to use education as a means for social change. Although the future of the young men and women of the Umutende School is uncertain, the unique experience they have undergone in an ideological space vastly different than that of the larger society may impact their future identities, trajectories and actions by giving them the critical tools to engage (if not always to overcome) structures and ideologies of domination.

[. . .]

This article sought to apply the "undoing gender" framework to the exploration of one school's attempts to "undo gender" through its school policies and practices. While not challenging gender inequalities at a macro-level, the students' experiences with reframing notions of masculinity and femininity in the school context offer insights into how schools might participate in incrementally "undoing gender" (Deutsch 2007), particularly in terms of interactions becoming less gendered and how institutions structure interactions that may lead to social change.

[. . .]

References

Adely, Fida. 2004. "The Mixed Effects of Schooling for High School Girls in Jordan: The Case of Tel Yahya." *Comparative Education Review* 48(4): 353–73.

Anderson, Jeanine and Rosa Mendoza. 2000. "Educating About Gender." Pp. 119–50 in *Distant Alliances: Promoting Education for Girls and Women in Latin America,* edited by R. Cortina and N. Stromquist. New York: Routledge.

BBC. 2003. *Teacher-Pupil Sex Blamed for HIV Rise.* Retrieved February 18, 2008 (http://news.bbc.co.uk/1/hi/world/africa/60frica9.stm).

de Waal, Alex and Alan Whiteside. 2003. "'New Variant Famine': AIDS and Food Crisis in Southern Africa." *The Lancet* 362:1234–37.

Deutsch, Francine. 2007. "Undoing Gender." *Gender & Society* 21(1):106–27.

HRW. 2002. *Suffering in Silence: The Links Between Human Rights Abuses and HIV Transmission to Girls in Zambia.* New York: Human Rights Watch.

HRW. 2007. *Hidden in the Mealie Meal: Gender-Based Abuses and Women's HIV Treatment in Zambia.* New York: Human Rights Watch.

Kazunga, Mary and Patrick Chewe. 2003. "Violence Against Women." In *Zambia Demographic and Health Survey 2001–2002.* Lusaka: Central Statistical Office.

Kirk, Jackie. 2004. "Impossible Fictions: The Lived Experiences of Women Teachers in Karachi." *Comparative Education Review* 48(4):374–96.

Mirembe, Robina and Lynn Davies. 2001. "Is Schooling a Risk? Gender, Power Relations, and School Culture in Uganda." *Gender and Education* 13(4):401–16.

Naseem, Muhammad Ayaz. 2004. "State, Education and Citizenship Discourses, and the Construction of Gendered Identities in Pakistan." Pp. 85–106 in *Re-Imagining Comparative Education,* edited by P. Ninnes and S. Mehta. New York and London: Routledge.

Prather, Cynthia and Karen Tietjen. 1991. *Educating Girls: Strategies to Increase Access, Persistence, and Achievement.* Washington, DC: USAID.

Stambach, Amy. 2000. *Lessons from Mount Kilimanjaro: Schooling, Community, and Gender in East Africa.* New York: Routledge.

Stromquist, Nelly. 2004. "Preface to Special Issue on Gender and Comparative Education." *Comparative Education Review* 48(4): iii–v.

Stromquist, Nelly, Steve Klees, and Shirley Miske. 2000. "USAID Efforts to Expand and Improve Girls' Primary Education in Guatemala." Pp. 239–60 in *Distant Alliances,* edited by R. Cortina and N. Stromquist. New York: Routledge Falmer.

UNDP. 2007. *Human Development Report: Zambia.* Retrieved February 5, 2008 (http://hdrstats.undp.org/countries/data_sheets/cty_ds_ZMB.html).

UNESCO. 2005. *Global Rankings Sub-Saharan Africa.* Retrieved March 1, 2008 (http://stats.uis.unesco.org/unesco/TableViewer/document.aspx?ReportId=125&IF_ Language=eng&BR_Fact=NERSM&BR_Region=40540).

Vavrus, Frances. 2005. "Adjusting Inequality: Education and Structural Adjustment Policies in Tanzania." *Harvard Educational Review* 75(2):174–244.

West, Candace and Don Zimmerman. 1987. "Doing Gender." *Gender & Society* 1(2):125–51.

PART VIII

Sport

The arena of sport permeates many aspects of social life, from the individual and interactional levels of athletes, coaches, managers, spectators, and fans to the institutional level of sport teams, organizations, and reporting. Gender scholars have long examined gender and sexuality in the construction of sport as a realm in which multiple inequalities are reproduced and resisted. This section examines gender and sexuality in a range of sporting events across the core themes of the reader: intersectionality, masculinity, transgender, and global (IMTG) perspectives.

Michela Musto's "Athletes in the Pool, Girls and Boys on Deck" examines the gendered dynamics of a coed youth swim team. Interviews and observations with team members show that, although gender differences are de-emphasized and less apparent during structured swim time, during unstructured free time gender differences are emphasized and essentialized. While both boys and girls recognize that girls can be faster than boys and treat gender differences as less central during structured practices and races, during informal time children are more likely to emphasize gender antagonisms and heterosexual teasing. Yet even here, there are not strong gender hierarchies, perhaps because of positive spillover from structured swim time. The study highlights the varied ways that gender is embedded in our everyday lives, but in uneven ways that reflect different contexts.

In "The Female Signifiant in All-Women's Amateur Roller Derby," Jennifer Carlson examines how gender is negotiated in roller derby, a recently popularized high-contact sport. Through participant observation of an all-women's roller derby league, Carlson finds how derby players negotiate femininity through emphasizing aspects of femininity, like wearing short skirts, while critiquing other aspects, as in emphasizing large rear-ends as useful in "booty blocking." Bodies are central to the sport: bruises and injuries serve as badges of honor, and skating ability relates to status. Carlson notes that roller derby women self-referentially engage and revel in contradictions within femininity—celebrating short skirts and aggressive bodies. While roller derby resists some traditional gender ideologies by those practicing the sport, it continues to reinforce other notions and cannot overturn gender inequalities.

Anima Adjepong's "'We're, Like, a Cute Rugby Team'" highlights the ways that women's participation in rugby relies on reproducing White heteronormativity. Drawing from interviews and observation at tournaments, Adjepong shows that even though women's rugby follows the same rules as men's rugby—and may appear to be subverting gender scripts—many of the players highlight gender differences and heteronormativity in these spaces. Many women players attempt to distance women's rugby from stereotypes of being a lesbian sport. At the same time, players' attempts to depict the game as racially diverse tend to essentialize "White bodies" and "Black bodies" in problematic ways. Although some women rugby players experience more acceptance within the sport, Adjepong finds that to do so they normalize women's White heterosexual bodies on the rugby pitch and reinforce existing hierarchies.

In "Transgender Inclusion and the Changing Face of Lesbian Softball Leagues," Ann Travers and Jillian Deri observe the experiences of transgender softball players in lesbian softball leagues with radical trans-inclusion policies. Transgender athletes pose new issues for sporting teams, with inclusion often based on binary understandings of gender that do not transform, but reinforce, gender categories. Based on interviews with athletes on a trans-inclusive league, which includes transwomen and transmen in varied stages of transition as well as non-binary people, Travers and Deri consider how athletes experience this space. Positive encounters were regularly reported among transgender women who felt supported by teammates. Transgender men expressed more ambivalence given experiences of mis-gendering, silencing, and invisibility from team members. Some players, including transwomen, argue that transmen taking testosterone should be excluded from the league because of the potential "edge" testosterone provides. Transmen, who often came out of supportive lesbian communities, remain attached to these communities, even as they are disregarded by some teammates. Trans-inclusion policies appear to be changing the face of softball by disrupting the gender binary boundaries, yet the experiences of trans-players are mixed.

Finally, Inge Claringbould and Johanna Adriaanse's "'Silver Cups Versus Ice Creams'" examines the gendered meanings of parents' involvement in their sons' soccer participation within the context of Dutch club sports. Although both girls and boys play soccer in the Netherlands, boys make up the vast majority of players. Based on interviews with mothers and fathers, as well as on observations of training sessions and matches, Claringbould and Adriaanse map out how children's soccer is gendered. The main field is constructed as masculine and inhabited by fathers and their sons, while the space around the field is constructed as feminine, particularly when their sons are young. As sons grow older, fathers increasingly replace mothers as the sideline spectators, emphasizing competition and performance. Fathers serve as coaches but also as coordinators, referees, and board members, while mothers are more likely to provide snacks. Mothers are constructed as supporting their sons' emotional and social growth, while fathers are constructed as helping them develop skills and competitiveness. When mothers do coach, these experiences are viewed as challenging. The study shows how, even among children's sport, the gendered division of space on and off the field reinforces gender inequality.

Sport may appear to be a venue in which gender inequality has greatly been reduced. There are certainly more women and transgender athletes taking part in sport; yet, gender inequality and heteronormative policing remain fairly omnipresent. Among children, gender processes differ depending on whether athletes are competing or just hanging out, as well as the age of children. These readings also show that attempts to challenge gender hierarchies about men as "better" athletes and coaches may unintentionally or intentionally lead to reinforcing gender differences, heteronormativity, and racial inequalities.

Athletes in the Pool, Girls and Boys on Deck

The Contextual Construction of Gender in Coed Youth Swimming

Michela Musto

© iStockphoto.com/McXas

A
lthough it is only eight o'clock in the morning, the swimming pool at the Sun Valley Aquatics Center is bustling with activity. It is a warm, sunny day in southern California, and 300 kids are participating in a Sun Valley Swim Team (SVST) swim meet. Girls and boys as young as five years old rummage through their swim bags, grabbing goggles and swim caps as they walk toward the starting blocks. Between races, swimmers

Michela Musto. 2014. "Athletes in the Pool, Girls and Boys on Deck: The Contextual Construction of Gender in Coed Youth Swimming." *Gender & Society* 28(3):359–80.

slather their arms with waterproof sunblock, laugh with their friends, and offer each other bites of half-eaten bagels. To my right, three 11-year-old boys, Alex, Kevin, and Andrew, are sitting in a semicircle, scrutinizing a "heat sheet" that lists the names of other boys and girls they are racing against in their upcoming events. Alex notices he is the only boy in his race, sparking the following conversation:

Alex: They're all girls! That's sad.

Kevin: That must suck.

Andrew: I know her [points to a name on the paper]. You're the only male! Have fun! You have the second-fastest time—she's first, you're second.

Alex: What's her time?

Andrew: [Sophia's] really fast. She was in Sharks.

Andrew flips the page, and the boys continue looking at their other events.

Throughout their conversation, Alex, Kevin, and Andrew draw upon multiple and contradictory meanings of gender. Although they agree that it "sucks" to be the "only male" in an "all girls" event, the boys then discuss Sophia's athleticism in a relatively unremarkable manner. Instead of teasing Alex for being slower than a girl, Andrew nonchalantly informs Alex that Sophia is "really fast," something neither Alex nor Kevin contests. How was it possible for gender to simultaneously be of minimal and significant interest to the swimmers?

Because gender is a social structure that is embedded within individual, interactional, and institutional relations, social change toward gender equality is uneven across the gender order (Connell 1987, 2009; Lorber 1994; Martin 2004; Risman 2004). The salience of gender varies across contexts, allowing some contexts to support more equitable patterns of gender relations than others (Britton 2000; Connell 1987; Deutsch 2007; Schippers 2002; Thorne 1993). Within a context, both structural mechanisms and hegemonic beliefs play an important role in determining whether individuals draw on and affirm group boundaries between the genders—what Thorne (1993) calls "borderwork." . . . Although scholars have theorized that alternative patterns of gender relations may shape social relations when gender is less salient (Britton 2000; Connell 1987; Deutsch 2007; Ridgeway 2009; Schippers 2007), few empirical studies have followed a group of individuals across different contexts to understand how gender relations and meanings may change. As the dialogue among the boys on the swim team suggests, because individuals negotiate different systems of accountability as they move from one setting to the next, gender can take on multiple meanings as a result of contextually specific, group-based interactions.

In what follows, I analyze nine months of participant observation research and 15 semi-structured interviews conducted with eight- to 10-year-old swimmers at SVST. I build upon scholarship that examines the contextual salience of gender (Britton 2000; Deutsch 2007; Messner 2000; Morgan and Martin 2006; Thorne 1993; Ridgeway 2009; Ridgeway and Correll 2004), arguing that the variable salience of gender played an important role in shaping the meanings swimmers associated with gender within and across different contexts at the pool. To do so, I outline the "gender geography," or the divisions of space and activity between girls and boys (Thorne 1993), within two contexts at the pool: focused situations when swimmers followed their coach's instructions, and unfocused free time when swimmers had fun with their friends. Within the most focused aspects of practice, gender was less salient and structural mechanisms encouraged the swimmers to interact in ways that undermined hegemonic patterns of gender relations. When the swimmers hung out with their friends before and after practices, however, gender was highly salient and the swimmers engaged in borderwork. In this context, similarities between the genders were obscured and the swimmers affirmed categorical and essentialist—but nonhierarchical—meanings of gender. Because the swimmers associated nonhierarchical meanings with gender across both contexts, I conclude by considering whether more equitable gender meanings and relations can potentially "spill over" from one context to another.

[. . .]

Competitive youth swimming is an ideal setting to examine how gender boundaries and meanings are constructed and negotiated within everyday life (McGuffey and Rich 1999; Messner 2000). Within the United States, sport has historically played a visible role in naturalizing hierarchical, categorical, and essentialist differences between the genders (Kimmel 1996; Lorber 1994; Messner 2011). Because the institutional "center" of sport often affirms hegemonic masculinity (Messner 2002), girls' and boys' interactions within athletic contexts often help strengthen hierarchical and categorical group boundaries between the genders, thus maintaining the power, prestige, and resources boys have over girls (McGuffey and Rich 1999; Messner 2000; Thorne 1993). Yet at the same time, research finds that girls' and women's athleticism is becoming normalized (Ezzell 2009; Heywood and Dworkin 2003; Messner 2011), potentially calling into question hegemonic gender meanings pertaining to athleticism (Kane 1995; Messner 2002). Since it may be easier for individuals to enact alternative patterns of gender relations within contexts that are considered feminine (Finley 2010), the enactment of alternative patterns of gender relations may be especially apparent within competitive youth swimming, a sport that has historically been considered acceptable for white, middle-class girls to participate in (Bier 2011; Cahn 1994).

In this article, I follow a group of eight- to 10-year-old swimmers across different contexts at swim practices, asking: Do the meanings swimmers associate with gender vary as a result of their contextually specific, group-based interactions? If so, what are the conditions that allow swimmers to associate alternative cultural meanings with gender? . . .

Method

From November 2011 to August 2012, I conducted participant observation research with the Sun Valley Swim Team (SVST), a competitive youth swim team in the Los Angeles metropolitan area. Among girls and boys under the age of 10, athletes were separated into three groups based on ability: Dolphins, Piranhas, and Sharks. . . . I chose to study the Sharks group—composed of the fastest "10 and under" swimmers on the team—in order to witness the ways that kids construct and negotiate gender boundaries.

About twice a month, Sharks swimmers attended weekend swim meets, and SVST placed in the top five at several regional and statewide swim meets during the 2011–2012 swimming season. Throughout the nine months I spent at the pool, the Sharks group was composed of 16 girls and six boys. Seven of the girls were white, six were Asian, one was Latina, and two were multiracial (identifying as Asian and white). Three of the boys were white, one was Latino, and two were multiracial (identifying as Asian and white). With the exception of one eight-year-old girl, all the athletes in the Sharks group were nine or 10 years old. The swimmers were from predominately middle- and upper-middle-class backgrounds, and Elizabeth—a white, middle-class former Olympic swimmer in her mid-30s—coached the group.

[. . .]

Between May and July 2012, I conducted 15 semistructured interviews with Sharks swimmers, six boys and nine girls. . . . Because of the athletes' age, the interviews were brief, ranging from 25 to 60 minutes.

[. . .]

The "Gender Geography" of Sun Valley Swim Team

On my first day of research with SVST, Coach Elizabeth started Sharks swim practice with a team meeting. The day before, she explained, she had to "excuse" the athletes from practice early for misbehaving—something she had not done to a group of swimmers in more than three years. While solemnly addressing the swimmers, Elizabeth reminded the athletes that they were the fastest swimmers in their age category; she thus expected more from them than if they were in the Dolphins or Piranhas groups. Elizabeth told the swimmers that while they were at swim practices, "There are a time to listen and a time for fun." When it was "time to listen," Elizabeth stressed that the swimmers should pay attention, remain focused, and follow her instructions. By doing so, they would achieve their goals of becoming faster swimmers.

As Elizabeth's speech suggests, there were two main contexts that organized swimmers' relations at the pool: focused athletic contexts in which swimmers were expected to follow their coach's instructions, and unfocused free time in which swimmers had fun with their friends. As summarized in Figure 39.1, the variable salience of gender at the pool played an important role in shaping the different meanings swimmers associated with gender within and across these contexts. . . . During focused aspects of practice, gender was less salient in this context, and the swimmers interacted in nonantagonistic ways. While doing so, the swimmers regularly witnessed athletic parity between the genders and associated alternative, nonhegemonic meanings pertaining to athleticism. Because the gender meanings changed

Figure 39.1   The "Gender Geography" of Sun Valley Swim Team

	Focused Aspects of Practice	**Unfocused Free Time**
Context	Athletes are expected to listen and follow their coach's instructions	Kids have fun with their friends
Gender Relations	Girls and boys are formally together; gender is less salient	Girls and boys are informally apart; gender is highly salient
Structural Mechanisms	Coaches instruct boys and girls to share lanes, race one another, and compare times	Lack of adult supervision and rules; risk of heterosexual teasing; swimmers enter and exit pool deck through gender-segregated locker rooms
Gender Meanings	Girls and boys undermine opposite and antagonistic group based gender boundaries	Boys and girls affirm opposite and antagonistic group based gender boundaries

across contexts at the pool, however, gender was highly salient during the swimmers' free time. Structural mechanisms instead encouraged the kids to engage in borderwork in this context. Because swimmers tended to interact in antagonistic ways in their free time, similarities between the genders were less visible, ultimately encouraging the swimmers to associate gender with categoricalism and essentialism.

[. . .]

"It's Just, Like, the Same Thing": Alternative Meanings of Gender

Because gender was less salient during focused aspects of Sharks swim practices, the swimmers interacted in ways that allowed them to associate alternative meanings with gender. This became clear when the athletes discussed instances they raced against swimmers of the other gender. Without nervously giggling or averting his eyes, Jon talked about getting "killed" by Sophia when they swam breaststroke. Cody leaned back and shrugged as he told me, "It doesn't matter, . . . it's just, like, the same thing" if he loses to a girl or a boy. When asked who he races during practices, Nick spontaneously compared his times to Sophia's:

> When Brady (11, white) was in the group I always raced against him. Now that he's gone the only one left is Sophia. Which, 200 IMs, no question, she's gonna win because my breaststroke sucks. Butterfly . . . I'll usually [win]—well, most of the time. Backstroke, it's a 50–50 game, and freestyle, 50–50. Breaststroke, no doubt she's in front.

Without a hint of defensiveness about losing to a girl, Nick made detailed comparisons between himself and Sophia. Even in butterfly, his fastest stroke, Nick recognized that he wins only "most of the time." Although boys often have much at stake in maintaining hierarchical and categorical differences between the genders (McGuffey and Rich 1999; Thorne 1993), at SVST the boys instead associated alternative meanings with gender while talking about racing "for times," where athleticism was not associated with hierarchy or difference.

The girls also talked about racing "for times" in ways that suggested they were not inferior or fundamentally different athletes because of their gender. Chelsea, a 10-year-old Asian girl, told me that boys are "not always faster [in swimming], sometimes they can be slower." Similarly, Anna, a 10-year-old white girl, discussed a race she lost to Elijah, a 10-year-old white boy. Instead of justifying defeat by saying that boys are always faster than girls, Anna identified a specific reason why she lost. She explained that when she dove into the water, "I [dove] to the side. It was not a good dive." Even Wendy, a nine-year-old white girl—one of the slowest athletes in the group—told me that because Sophia is as fast as Nick, there was "not really" a difference between the girls' and boys' swimming abilities.

There are two reasons Sharks swim practices were an ideal context for swimmers to enact nonhegemonic patterns of gender relations pertaining to athleticism. First, the Sharks swimmers were the fastest group of "ten and under" swimmers on the team, and highly committed to athletics. Many of the Sharks swimmers told me they attended practice to "get better times" or to "get better" at swimming. Several of the boys and girls expressed a desire to swim in the Olympics one day, and Grace, a 10-year-old white girl, even chose to attend swim practice instead of her best friend's birthday party. Because of the athletes' commitment, the majority of swimmers willingly followed Elizabeth's instructions—even if it meant sharing lanes with swimmers of the other gender. Swimmers in the other "10 and under" groups on the team, however, did not always follow their coaches' instructions as readily. I occasionally noticed girls and boys in the Dolphins and Piranhas group make faces and shriek when instructed to share lanes with swimmers of the other gender—something Sharks swimmers never did while racing "for times." As a result of the Sharks swimmers' commitment to athleticism, acting in accordance with the structural mechanisms instituted by Elizabeth likely mattered more than it did to other "10 and under" athletes.

Additionally, while following Elizabeth's instructions to share lanes and race one another, the swimmers compared times, a relatively transparent measure of ability. If the athletes were playing a team sport like basketball or soccer, where athleticism is assessed through less quantifiable skills, such as dribbling or blocking ability, it may have been easier for the boys to marginalize or masculinize the girls' abilities (McGuffey and Rich 1999; Thorne 1993). Indeed, during interviews, several of the girls and boys discussed instances during recess and physical education classes when boys invoked hierarchical and categorical notions of gender while playing team sports, such as when they refused to play with girls or became upset after losing to girls. During Sharks swim practices, however, the swimmers were frequently provided with specific, quantifiable instances of girls beating boys and boys beating girls. Through these time-based comparisons, it became clear that the girls' and boys' abilities overlapped (Kane 1995). As a result, within a context where swimmers willingly interacted in ways that illuminated similarities between the genders, girls and boys associated nonhegemonic meanings with gender.

Having Fun With Friends: Unsupervised Free Time

The least focused aspects of swimming occurred during the swimmers' free time. Sharks swimmers were never completely unsupervised on the pool deck, but there were times—such as before swim practices or between races at swim meets—when SVST coaches were busy coaching other swimmers. As opposed to focused aspects of practice, which were "hard" and "tiring," unsupervised free time was a chance for the kids to have fun with their friends. David, a 10-year-old Latino boy, explained that before and after swim practice, he and his friends had "lots of fun together." Grace told me, "It's always fun to come here and see [my friends]," and Chelsea similarly said that she had "fun" while "hanging out" with her friends before practices.

The unsupervised aspect of the swimmers' free time played an important role in shaping kids' social interactions with their friends. At the pool, I did not observe patterns of age and racial separation that other scholars have observed among children in schools and summer camps (Lewis 2003; Moore 2001; Perry 2002). In interviews, furthermore, most of the swimmers had a difficult time naming their closest friends on the team, explaining that they were close friends with "everyone" and had "a lot of good friends [on the team]." Despite the ostensive unity among the swimmers, *none* of the swimmers reported being friends with kids of the other gender. For example, Nick, a multiracial nine-year-old, named every male swimmer and male coach he could think of when describing his "good friends":

MM: Who are some of your good friends on the team?

Nick: Let's see, we have . . . Brady (11, white)! It's gonna be a very long, very, very, long list. So beware. Let's see, we have Coach Tom (mid-20s, white)!

MM: He's one of your friends?

Nick: Yeah, we often chat a lot. I have Coach Brad (mid-30s, white), Jayden . . . um . . . Jon (10, multiracial), Andrew (11, Latino), David (10, Latino), Cody (nine, white), Justin (11, white), Derrick (10, white), Dominick (10, white) . . . well, he used to be on the swim team. Let's see, we have . . . Samantha—my sister (eight, multiracial), although she can be very annoying at some times. . . . Let's see . . . um . . . one of the people who works in the café, he gives me a lot of free samples. And he once let me get a discount, so that's pretty good. Zach (11, white) . . . did I say Caleb (11, white)?

Nick's "good friends" range from boys in the Sharks group to one of the men who worked at the pool's café. Like other swimmers in the Sharks group, moreover, Nick developed friendships across racial and age categories. Although the requirements for being Nick's friend are not particularly stringent—you simply needed to "chat a lot" or give him a discount on food—the only girl he mentions is his sister, who can be "very annoying." This is striking because Nick's parents were good friends with the parents of Chelsea, a girl in the Sharks group. On several different occasions, Nick talked about going fishing with Chelsea's family and having her family over for barbecues. Once, he even told me he dreamed about raiding her family's food pantry. Based on Nick's criteria, Chelsea should count as a friend. However, when I asked Nick if he ever "hangs out" with Chelsea, he simply responded, "No." When asked to elaborate, he explained, "I don't hang out with girls."

As Nick's comments suggest, gender was a highly salient category that structured kids' friendships during their free time. Among swimmers in the Sharks group, this gender separation was marked with extensive physical separation. After changing into their swimsuits in sex-segregated locker rooms, the girls would set their swim bags near the right end of the bleachers that lined the length of the pool. The boys would walk past the girls, often without even glancing in their direction, to the far end of the benches, placing their bags almost 50 meters from the girls' space.
[. . .]

"Boys Are Always Wild" and "Girls Are Very Nice and Sweet": Hegemonic Meanings of Gender

Given the high salience of gender boundaries during swimmers' unsupervised free time, the girls' and boys' interactions often strengthened gender-based group boundaries during unsupervised aspects of practice (McGuffey and Rich 1999; Messner 2000; Thorne 1993). Once, before practice, Nick shouted his last name while jumping toward Katie. While mimicking his motion, Katie shouted, "Weirdo!" back at him. Several times, I watched Nick, Brady, and Sophia dump cold water on one another's heads after practice. After a swimming fundraiser, Katie, Jon, and Cody spent 10 minutes hitting and splashing one another with foam swimming "noodles" in the pool. Toward the end of a swim meet, several boys filled their swim caps with water and tried splashing Lesley and Grace. After wrestling the swim caps out of the boys' hands, Grace came over to me and told me that Elijah gave her "cooties."

Although the swimmers tended to interact in antagonistic ways during their free time, borderwork at the pool did not seem to be based on beliefs in male supremacy. Unlike existing research has suggested (McGuffey and Rich 1999; Messner 2000; Thorne 1993), boys did not provoke antagonistic relations more frequently than girls, nor did the boys control more space on the pool deck. Furthermore, the girls never tried to avoid confrontations with the boys, and instead seemed confident in their ability to interact as equals. Once, for example, I was talking with Katie when Amy, an 11-year-old Asian girl, walked over to us. Elijah and Jon were standing several feet away, wearing swimming flippers on their hands. Katie warned Amy that the boys would "smack you with that fin" if Amy got too close. Amy, however, rolled her eyes and told Katie, "I'm not scared." She then punched Katie's arm a couple of times, demonstrating how she would fight if provoked. If the swimmers had believed that boys on the pool deck were stronger than the girls, Amy may have been more cautious about fighting Jon and Elijah. Instead, she confidently proclaimed that she was "not scared" and demonstrated how she would punch them.

Other girls in the Sharks group also seemed confident in their ability to engage in borderwork as equals with the boys. Once, much to the girls' excitement, Katie "pantsed" Elijah at a swim meet. Another time, after Nick dumped what he described as "ice cold" water on Sophia's head, she got "revenge" by pouring red Gatorade on him. If Katie or Sophia had believed the boys were stronger or more powerful than the girls, they may have been afraid to instigate such interactions. Fear of the boys' reactions, however, did not stop Katie from "pantsing" Elijah, or Sophia from dumping a red, sticky drink on Nick's head. Although hegemonic cultural beliefs about gender often become activated when gender is a salient aspect of social interactions (Ridgeway 2011), the swimmers' antagonistic interactions in this context did not appear to be based upon a sense of male supremacy. Instead, they were transformative in the sense that they allowed the girls to occupy space and express agency when interacting as equals with the boys. However, because these interactions continued to affirm categorical and essentialist differences between the genders, they simultaneously undermined and reproduced aspects of hegemonic gender relations.

Furthermore, all the swimmers talked about sharing close physical space with kids of the other gender in ways that were markedly different from how they talked about racing one another. When talking about racing "for times," the swimmers willingly recognized and discussed the overlap between girls' and boys' abilities. However, on a social level, the meanings kids associated with gender were firmly grounded in categorical differences. Perhaps because of the risk of heterosexual teasing (Thorne 1993), boys and girls told me that spending time with athletes of the other gender was "not fun," "awkward," "annoying," "awful," "super uncomfortable," "gross," "kinda weird," and "really bad and really messed up." Furthermore, many of the kids articulated essentialist understandings of gender within these narratives, explaining that "boys are always wild," "girls are very nice and sweet," "girls are more limber," and "boys are more competitive." Notably, however, the swimmers did not include assumptions about male supremacy within these explanations. Instead, as suggested by their patterns of borderwork, the swimmers associated categorical and essentialist—but nonhierarchical—meanings with gender.

As an observer who spent an equal amount of time with the girls and boys, it was puzzling to hear girls and boys make categorical and essentialist distinctions between the genders. If girls were always "more limber" than boys, then how could the swimmers account for the boy from the Sharks group who frequently did the splits before swim practice? If "girls are very nice and sweet," then how could they explain the times when the girls screamed at and hit one another? Although it was easy for me to think of exceptions to the kids' generalizations, whenever I asked kids about these exceptions, my questions were met with shrugs and surprise.

Despite being quite knowledgeable about one another's swimming abilities, the girls and boys were relatively unaware of the other group's social experiences. Because the swimmers tended to provoke antagonistic interactions with one another, similarities between the genders were obscured. . . . The swimmers, however, did not default to enacting *all* aspects of hegemonic gender relations. The swimmers' group-based interactions led the swimmers to associate gender with categorical and essentialist meanings, but the assumption that boys are superior to girls was notably absent from swimmers' interactions during unsupervised free time.

. . . Conclusion

[. . .]

My research contributes to existing literature by exploring how gender meanings and relations change across contexts. By following the same group of individuals across different contexts, I found that the meanings kids associated with a social category such as "gender" did not always align with hegemonic beliefs. Instead, the swimmers' understandings of gender were filtered through group-based interactions and thus varied dramatically depending on the context (Fine 1979; Eliasoph and Lichterman 2003; Swidler 1986). During focused aspects of practice, when swimmers followed their coach's instructions to compare times and race one another, gender was less salient and athletes interacted in nonantagonistic ways. As a result of their group-based interactions in this context, swimmers regularly witnessed athletic parity between the genders, making it difficult to sustain beliefs in categorical gender difference and male superiority (Kane 1995). Because structural mechanisms enabled a different pattern of group-based relations during the swimmers' unsupervised free time, the meanings associated with gender changed across contexts at SVST. During the swimmers' unsupervised free time, gender was highly salient and swimmers interacted in antagonistic ways. As a result, their interactions obscured the similarities between the genders, encouraging the swimmers to associate gender with categorical and essentialist—yet nonhierarchical—meanings.

The fact that swimmers' understandings of gender did not uniformly align with hegemonic cultural beliefs has broader theoretical implications for gender theory. When the salience of gender is low and structural mechanisms allow individuals to interact in ways that illuminate similarities between the genders, it is possible for individuals to associate gender with nonhegemonic beliefs. This study thus provides a glimpse into the types of practices that can potentially enable interactional gender expectations to become less oppressive (Connell 1987; Martin 2004; Ridgeway 2009; Risman 2004). Furthermore, unlike existing research (McGuffey and Rich 1999; Messner 2000; Morgan and Martin 2006; Ridgeway and Correll 2000; Ridgeway 2009; Thorne 1993), the swimmers did not default to enacting *all* aspects of hegemonic gender relations when interacting within a relatively unscripted setting. Beliefs in male supremacy were notably missing from both contexts, highlighting the need to explain the lack of gender hierarchy at the pool.

If individuals enact more equitable gender relations in one context, aspects of these gender relations may "spill over" into other settings within daily life. At SVST, structural mechanisms illuminated the similarities between the genders during focused aspects of practice. While . . . racing one another, time-based comparisons made it clear that girls and boys were equally strong and talented swimmers. Perhaps the embodied strength and confidence girls developed . . . allowed them to be more expansive in their appropriation of space and more confident in their antagonisms with the boys (Hollander 2013; Messner 2011; Travers 2008). The boys' in-pool experiences of losing to the girls may have helped create a baseline of respect for the girls outside of the pool (Anderson 2008; Messner 2011), making the boys less inclined to invade the girls' space and provoke antagonistic relations. As a result, . . . the nonhierarchical aspects of the swimmers' gender relations may have transferred across contexts. The spillover effect likely weakened as the swimmers entered situations further removed from SVST (Ridgeway and Correll 2000), but the swimmers' in-pool experiences appeared to reduce the overall degree of gender inequality at the pool.

[. . .]

References

Anderson, Eric. 2008. "'I Used to Think Women Were Weak': Orthodox Masculinity, Gender Segregation, and Sport." *Sociological Forum* 23:257–80.

Bier, Lisa. 2011. *Fighting the Current: The Rise of American Women's Swimming: 1870–1926.* Jefferson, NC: McFarland.

Britton, Dana M. 2000. "The Epistemology of the Gendered Organization." *Gender & Society* 14:418–34.

Cahn, Susan K. 1994. *Coming on Strong: Gender and Sexuality in Twentieth-Century Women's Sport.* Cambridge, MA: Harvard University Press.

Connell, Raewyn. 1987. *Gender and Power: Society, the Person and Sexual Politics.* Stanford, CA: Stanford University Press.

Connell, Raewyn. 2009. *Short Introductions: Gender.* Malden, MA: Polity Press.

Deutsch, Francine M. 2007. "Undoing Gender." *Gender & Society* 21:106–27.

Eliasoph, Nina and Paul Lichterman. 2003. "Culture in Interaction." *American Journal of Sociology* 108:735–94.

Ezzell, Matthew B. 2009. "'Barbie Dolls' on the Pitch: Identity Work, Defensive Othering, and Inequality in Women's Rugby." *Social Problems* 56:111–31.

Fine, Gary Alan. 1979. "Small Groups and Culture Creation: The Idioculture of Little League Baseball Teams." *American Sociological Review* 44:733–45.

Finley, Nancy J. 2010. "Skating Femininity: Gender Maneuvering in Women's Roller Derby." *Journal of Contemporary Ethnography* 39:359–87.

Heywood, Leslie and Shari L. Dworkin. 2003. *Built to Win: The Female Athlete as Cultural Icon.* Minneapolis, MN: University of Minnesota Press.

Hollander, Jocelyn A. 2013. "'I Demand More of People': Accountability, Interaction, and Gender Change." *Gender & Society* 27:5–29.

Kane, Mary Jo. 1995. "Resistance/Transformation of the Oppositional Binary: Exposing Sport as a Continuum." *Journal of Sport and Social Issues* 19:191–218.

Kimmel, Michael S. 1996. *Manhood in America.* New York: Free Press.

Lewis, Amanda. 2003. *Race in the Schoolyard: Negotiating the Color Line in Classrooms and Communities.* New Brunswick, NJ: Rutgers University Press.

Lorber, Judith. 1994. *Paradoxes of Gender.* New Haven, CT: Yale University Press.

Martin, Patricia Yancey. 2004. "Gender as Social Institution." *Social Forces* 82:1249–73.

McGuffey, Shawn C. and B. Lindsay Rich. 1999. "Playing in the Gender Transgression Zone: Race, Class, and Hegemonic Masculinity in Middle Childhood." *Gender & Society* 13:608–27.

Messner, Michael A. 2000. "Barbie Girls Versus Sea Monsters: Children Constructing Gender." *Gender & Society* 14:765–84.

Messner, Michael A. 2002. *Taking the Field: Men, Women and Sports.* Minneapolis, MN: University of Minnesota Press.

Messner, Michael A. 2011. "Gender Ideologies, Youth Sports, and the Production of Soft Essentialism." *Sociology of Sport Journal* 28:151–70.

Moore, Valerie Ann. 2001. "'Doing' Racialized and Gendered Age to Organize Peer Relations: Observing Kids in Summer Camp." *Gender & Society* 15:835–58.

Morgan, Laurie A. and Karin A. Martin. 2006. "Taking Women Professionals Out of the Office: The Case of Women in Sales." *Gender & Society* 20:108–28.

Perry, Pamela. 2002. *Shades of White: White Kids and Racial Identities in High School.* Durham, NC: Duke University Press.

Ridgeway, Cecilia L. 2009. "Framed Before We Know It: How Gender Shapes Social Relations." *Gender & Society* 23:145–60.

Ridgeway, Cecilia L. 2011. *Framed by Gender: How Gender Inequality Persists in the Modern World.* Oxford, UK: Oxford University Press.

Ridgeway, Cecilia L. and Shelley J. Correll. 2000. "Limiting Inequality Through Interaction: The End(s) of Gender." *Contemporary Sociology* 29:110–20.

Ridgeway, Cecilia L. and Shelley J. Correll. 2004. "Unpacking the Gender System: A Theoretical Perspective on Gender Beliefs and Social Relations." *Gender & Society* 18:510–31.

Risman, Barbara J. 2004. "Gender as a Social Structure: Theory Wrestling with Activism." *Gender & Society* 18:429–50.

Schippers, Mimi. 2002. *Rockin' Out of the Box: Gender Maneuvering in Alternative Hard Rock.* New Brunswick, NJ: Rutgers University Press.

Schippers, Mimi. 2007. "Recovering the Feminine Other: Masculinity, Femininity, and Gender Hegemony." *Theory and Society* 36:85–102.

Swidler, Ann. 1986. "Culture in Action: Symbols and Strategies." *American Sociological Review* 51:273–86.

Thorne, Barrie. 1993. *Gender Play: Girls and Boys in School.* New Brunswick, NJ: Rutgers University Press.

Travers, Ann. 2008. "The Sport Nexus and Gender Injustice." *Studies in Social Justice* 2:79–101.

The Female Signifiant in All-Women's Amateur Roller Derby

Jennifer Carlson

© iStockphoto.com/sumnersgrahpicsinc

I n Drew Barrymore's *Whip It!* (2009), Bliss Cavendar evades her mother's pressure to win the Miss Blue Bonnet beauty pageant by joining a local roller derby league. Cavendar found herself in a world of fast-paced skating, hard hits, tattoos, short skirts, and "bad" attitudes that sharply contrast with the beauty-pageant ideals of femininity she rejects in the film. . . . I argue that real-life roller derby indeed provides an aggressive, high-contact environment in which to interrogate femininity.

Jennifer Carlson. 2010. "The Female Signifiant in All-Women's Amateur Roller Derby." *Sociology of Sport Journal* 27(4):428–40.

Played on indoor oval tracks, derby bouts (or games) draw anywhere from a few hundred to upwards of one thousand spectators and are designed to be fast-paced and hard-hitting. At the beginning of each jam (derby-speak for play), blockers from each team line up to form an eight-person pack; fifteen feet behind them, a jammer from each team lines up. Jammers speed-skate around the track; after their first pass through the pack, jammers gain points every time they pass a member of the opposing team. Blockers, who cannot earn points, assist their jammer through the pack and prevent the opposing jammer from passing. Although fist-fighting and elbowing incur penalties, skaters may move in front of other skaters ("body-" or "booty-blocking") as well as thrust their bodies against other skaters in hopes of knocking them to the floor ("body checking"). Thus, spectators are treated to fastpaced skating, hard hits, and body pile-ups. I argue that this aggressive environment allows skaters to engage in a form of gender critique I call the female signifiant.

I develop the concept of the female signifiant by drawing on Hebdige's (1979) analysis of punk to indicate that in roller derby, norms surrounding femininity and athleticism are cited in ways that draw out tensions within these norms. I first discuss how femininity has been understood in the previous studies on women's sport and then detail my methods before examining how roller derby skaters negotiate femininity.

Emphasized Femininity in Sport and the Female Signifiant

Scholars of gender and sport have examined how female athletes interrogate norms associated with femininity and masculinity through several theoretical perspectives. In this article, I draw specifically on Connell's (1987) concept of emphasized femininity that highlights women's subordinate status relative to men. Emphasized femininity encompasses an idealized version of Western womanhood that posits that women be physically inferior to men, weak, docile, concerned with their appearance, and attentive to enhancing their heterosexual desirability. . . . Feminist sport scholars have employed emphasized femininity to understand the social demands and norms placed on women as well as elaborate ways in which these demands and norms are subverted (e.g., Hargreaves, 1994; Heywood & Dworkin, 2003; Messner, 2002; Messner & Dworkin, 2002).

[. . .]

Castelnuovo and Guthrie (1998) emphasize the liberatory potential of sport while also noting the ways in which (mainstream) sport may continue to constrain women. . . . Though empowered to enter the masculine-marked realm of sports after Title IX, women are also required to engage in body projects such as sports to enhance their heterosexual appeal. Nevertheless, despite these demands, Heywood and Dworkin (2003) have shown that sport continues to provide an opportunity to interrogate emphasized femininity. Rather than viewing gender negotiation in an either/or binary of conformity and resistance, Heywood and Dworkin (2003) articulate sport as encouraging "both individual development and collective action. . . [and] the cultivation of traditionally masculine characteristics as well as traditionally feminine ones" (p. 22). They thus echo previous scholars . . . who claimed sport as a potential source of empowerment for women if they can engage in both masculine and feminine-marked practices in ways that enhance—rather than diminish—their capacity for self-actualization while also acknowledging that sports are not a panacea for addressing systematic gender inequality (or other inequalities, for that matter).

[. . .]

I argue that all-women's amateur roller derby is a space in which a critical engagement of emphasized femininity occurs. However, I expand this previous work by introducing what I call the female signifiant. I adopt the term "signifiant" from Hebdige's (1979) analysis of punk subculture to suggest that skaters engage in practices that do not necessarily abolish norms surrounding gender and athleticism so much as expose their contingency. In his analysis of punk, Hebdige (1979) argues that "punk subculture . . . signified chaos at every level" in such a way that it nevertheless "cohered as a meaningful whole" (p. 112). Following a rule that "if the cap doesn't fit, wear it," members of punk subculture aimed to dramatize and dwell *within* the tentativeness of conventional norms related to dress, language, music, and other cultural practices (Hebdige, 1979, p. 108). Rather than *signifying* a solution to the social contradictions of 1970s Britain, punk of this era was a movement of *signifiance* insofar as it celebrated "the triumph . . . of the signifier over the signified, . . . gestured towards a 'nowhere' and actively *sought* to remain silent, illegible" (Hebdige, 1979, pp. 119, 120). For example, some punks dramatized feminine bourgeois markers such as facial make-up by hyperbolically wearing theatrical blush, eyeliner, and lipstick. As such, hyperbole became a technique with which to engage norms to indicate their flimsiness. Punk thus undermined the link between signifier and signified insofar as punk exposed the signifier's (e.g., make-up) assumed correspondence with the intended signified (e.g., bourgeois femininity) as socially constructed. Thus, punk directly questioned the coherent, socially meaningful relationship between the signifier and signified. In a similar fashion, the subversive edge of roller derby comes from a *signifiance* of femininity. As such, I explore how derby skaters, similar to punks, questioned socially meaningful relationships between the signified (i.e., emphasized femininity) and its different signifiers (namely, clothing, make-up, and sport practice). . . .

Methods of Study

I undertook participant observation (Sands, 2002) with a league I call the Nowhere Roller Girls located in a major metropolitan area in the U.S. Engaging in what Sands (2002) calls "experiential ethnography," I joined the Nowhere Roller Girls and spent four months attending three-times-a-week practices and twice-a-month meetings. During practice, I fully participated in all drills and scrimmages for which I was athletically eligible.

[. . .]

It is also important to note that while I enjoyed the thrill of participating in derby practice, I chose not to actively participate in league meetings to fully observe—rather than become embroiled in—controversial League issues.

[. . .]

The Derby Persona

Skaters interrogate norms surrounding emphasized femininity by presenting a derby self that splices aggression, sexual assertiveness, and femininity in a way that exposes the contradictions inherent in emphasized femininity. Derby skaters call attention to the constructed nature of gender through the citation of feminine norms. They do not eschew femininity entirely but rather productively draw on the tensions of femininity in the context of sports to display themselves as threatening, aggressive, and fearless derby girls. This interrogation of femininity can be observed through the development of a derby persona, evidenced by a new name and costume-like feminine-punk clothing.

[. . .]

One of the most noticeable differences between roller derby and other women's sports is the use of a stage name, known within the League as a derby name. Within a few months of joining the League, each skater is required to invent a derby name for herself. In the Nowhere Roller Girls, skaters refer to each other almost exclusively by their derby names at practice, at bouts (where the public knows them only by their derby names), and outside of practice; most skaters do not know each other's actual names. Derby names are usually playfully aggressive, menacing, raunchy, lewd, and clever, such as A Cup Killer, Chesstosterone, Lolita LeBruise, Brick Shields, West Nile Iris, Lady Pain, Vicious Panties, and Clit Eastwood. They often satirize otherwise feminine names by implying a willingness to take or inflict pain, and in aggregate, they comprise that which should *not* be mentioned over the typically middle-class family dinner table: raw violence, sexuality, and feminine prowess. Just as punks (Hebdige, 1979) threw into relief bourgeois markers by citing them in recognizable (i.e., the markers were understood) but unreadable (i.e., the markers were unexpected, if not incomprehensible) ways, skaters bridge together antithetical notions in their names by presenting themselves as confusingly feminine. By presenting a violent, sexually raw femininity through derby names, they question the emphasized femininity that requires them to be passively sexually available and physically weak without actually eschewing femininity as a whole. Even the term "derby girl" itself demonstrates a charged femininity; skaters embrace the word "girl" only when modified by "derby" or "roller," since "derby" and "roller" presumably conjure up a threatening, aggressive skater. (Note that in other contexts, "girl" is used derogatorily.)

[. . .]

To showcase their derby personas, the three intraleague teams of the Nowhere Roller Girls organize photo sessions that portray skaters as simultaneously aggressive, pain-friendly, and sexy. One team's public photo album includes a photo-roster that features pictures of each member's decaying, decapitated head as well as shots of skaters using chainsaws, whips, and quad skates as weaponry. Another team roster includes pictures of members holding guns while posing in bras and panties. The third team's skaters are dressed in miniskirts against bright, single-color backgrounds; many skaters hold weapons, show off actual bruises and/or wear make-up simulating bloody noses, missing teeth, and other injuries. As with derby names, these photos feature a signifiant self-presentation reminiscent of Hebdige's (1979) analysis of punk. The passiveness usually associated with emphasized femininity is reconstructed. While women marred with bruises and blood are usually represented as victims rather than aggressors, these skaters clearly signify themselves as active participants in their injuries insofar as they brandish weapons. Importantly, skaters are not simply women-turned-Amazons; their mini-skirts, bras, and panties suggest a sexually availability that is belied by the aggression implied by their weaponry and injuries. Thus, emphasized femininity becomes scrambled as skaters juxtapose antithetical attributes, namely, emphasized femininity (indicated by short skirts, bras, and panties) and aggression (i.e., weaponry and injuries).

Bouts become a venue in which to exhibit these derby personas. Although each Nowhere Roller Girls team has uniforms consisting of a dress or a shirt-and-skirt combination, skaters accessorize with fishnets, make-up, and other items. Skaters discuss with each other what they plan to wear and often make special purchases for upcoming bouts to embellish their uniforms, including belts, hot pants, tights, and fishnets. While there is an unspoken feminine-punk dress code to which virtually all skaters conform, *all* skaters—not just those with skinny bodies that fit the mold of mainstream femininity—appear comfortable in exhibiting their bodies.

Through their clothing, skaters give a signifiant nod to norms usually associated with emphasized femininity. The symbolic femininity, for example, of the miniskirt—stereotypically donned by the docile, child-sized, and sexually available female—is subverted in roller derby as it is worn by women of all sizes engaged in full-contact athletics. Moreover, while the uniforms of each League team include either a miniskirt or a mini-dress, hints of aggression signifiantly mark this otherwise sexualized clothing. Fishnets are ripped, uniforms are printed with skaters' menacing names, lifted skirts reveal panties printed with words like "Fuck your mom!" and as per League regulations, all uniforms are accessorized with helmets and knee, elbow, and wrist pads. While traditionally feminine sports "emphasize[] . . . beauty [and] the aesthetic side of athletics" (Cahn, 1995, p. 218) rather than aggression, skaters remake femininity by consciously integrating threatening aggression into feminine dress. Through their engagement in the "masculine" activity of full-contact sports, skaters embrace an aggressive femininity that at once cites and scrambles emphasized femininity.

[. . .]

In addition to displaying aggressive femininity through a derby persona, skaters interrogate the normative assumptions of femininity by actively identifying parts of their bodies with aggressive possibilities. For example, "butts" are both venerated threats and physical weapons rather than a "problem spot" for physical appearance. As a threat, skaters often knock hips with opposing players as they line up for a jam, physically taunting them. In addition, the mere specter of the buttocks can be a debilitating sight, according to one jammer:

> I just get so exhausted skating around and around when I jam. My first jam, I couldn't believe it. And then I had to get around [another skater's] ass—thank god she's on my team this time!

As a weapon, an entire move—the booty block—highlights the use of one's butt to block an opponent. Full body checks are mostly all hip and rear-end; thus, the posterior is responsible for many of the most dramatic moments in derby as well as some of the worst injuries.

In fact, the rear-end is one of the most widely discussed body parts in the League (the other, the elbow, is discussed due to its illegality of use). Skaters talk about their rear-ends in a myriad of ways: how useful they can be when they are big (e.g., "I need a bigger ass block to block her"), how fast they can move (e.g., "Move your ass in front of her!"), how well they block (e.g., "Look at that booty block!"), and how soft they are when skaters fall (e.g., "It's okay [I'm not injured], I just landed on my ass"). As such, skaters resignify butts in terms of how they can be used rather than simply how they look. Moreover, body size in the context of roller derby generally tends to be understood in instrumental terms, that is, with regard to use rather than appearance. The sizes of skater physiques are predominantly discussed with regard to player positions: smaller girls are often pigeonholed as high-speed jammers, while bigger girls are often earmarked as blockers.

In contrast, the size and appearance of bodies in general—and rear-ends in particular—are usually not discussed in normative terms. In fact, I never witnessed skaters expressing consternation regarding how their physiques "should" ideally look. In the rare instances in which skaters discussed size and appearance of their butts, they usually simply express satisfied surprise at their changing bodies. For example, one blocker commented, "thanks to derby, I now have an ass!" Likewise, another skater offered that "I know I have a huge ass . . . derby has just lifted it an inch or two!" While such commentary from skaters suggests that skaters may reference their bodies in normative terms (i.e., they are conscious that plump, lifted butts are a mark of attractiveness), this type of commentary is relatively rare. Thus, derby provides an alternate system of body evaluation based on how bodies move rather than how they look, thereby allowing skaters to experience their bodies in ways beyond the forms of passive embodiment encouraged by emphasized femininity, even if some attentiveness to physical attractiveness (as indicated by skaters' comments on butts) residually remains.

The Limits of the Female Signifiant

Cahn (1995) noted that aggression and intense, rigorous training are often cited as distinguishing characteristics of the "masculine" nature of certain sports such as football or basketball. Other sports perceived to be less rigorous and less aggressive, such as synchronized swimming, are marked as feminine (Cahn, 1995, p. 270). Not only do skaters engage in significant gender practices as discussed above, but they also engage in a hyperbolic rendering of masculine aspects of athleticism. They, thus, hyperbolically highlight the problematic requirements of mainstream athleticism by interrogating aspects of sports participation often categorized as masculine. However, while they question the status of sports as masculine, they continue to stigmatize certain aspects of femininity. Similar to Heywood and Dworkin's (2003) and Castelnuovo and Guthrie's (1998) research, athleticism emerges as a site of both subversion and consolidation of emphasized femininity.

Most prominently, skaters theatrically interrogate sports participation by hyperbolically highlighting injuries and risks associated with athleticism. Although derby leagues require their skaters adhere to a number of safety rules as well as wear protective gear, the sport is often flaunted by skaters as inherently dangerous. As documented with respect to athletes in other sports (Theberge, 1997; Young & Dallaire, 2008), skaters expose the dangers of athleticism by frequently discussing pulled muscles, blood, and fractures as evidence that derby is a legitimate sport. Bruises serve as badges of honor within the derby community, and playing despite injuries represents one's commitment to the sport.

This attention to injured bodies is for both public and private consumption. Publicly-distributed media such as fliers, web site content, and online videos often flaunt injuries. Privately among the Nowhere Roller Girls, injuries are discussed and exhibited, and the League even maintains members-only online photo albums that include pictures of injuries. In addition, the League discussed having a "worst injury" contest. By focusing on injuries, which are the concrete results of aggressive physical contact, skaters fetishize an aggressive physicality that is usually associated with masculine sports.

[. . .]

This risk-taking ethos—namely, that roller derby *is* dangerous and *does* cause injuries—is used as evidence that roller derby is "real." The question "is roller derby fake?" appears on the online FAQ of many leagues, with answers indicating that roller derby is "real" not only because of the danger of injury but also because it is not staged. On their official Web site, the Nowhere Roller Girls connect the "realness" of the sport to "fighting hard." They maintain that the outcomes of bouts are "absolutely not . . . staged. . . . That's why we fight so hard. . . . The fights are real. . . . When we're skating, we can be tough, competitive bitches." With the "unexpected" of competition built into an already-dangerous endeavor, roller derby becomes legitimated as a risky sport. The Nowhere Roller Girls act out the overarching collective project of interrogating femininity—a risky endeavor in itself—by hyperbolically engaging in the risks associated with injuring their physical bodies, a feature often associated with sporting masculinity.

Overall, the Nowhere Roller Girls provide a context in which athleticism can be interrogated, as skaters are able to engage in a hyperbolic fetishization of the risks and injuries associated with contact sports. The obscenity of many athletes' willingness to destroy their bodies for sports (Messner, 2002) is theatrically exposed by skaters as they flaunt their injuries and the risks thereof. Thus, the Nowhere Roller Girls engender an environment in which the problematic aspects of athleticism can be hyperbolically highlighted.

Participation in roller derby allows the double interrogation of norms surrounding both gender and athleticism: women are not supposed to engage in full-contact, physical activity that may mar their bodies with bruises, broken bones, and missing teeth. The price, however, of this interrogation is the stigmatization of certain feminine stereotypes. I observed skaters policing "girly" behaviors, where acting like a "girl" was used frequently as opprobrium against certain behavior. Gossiping, for example, is explicitly discouraged. In addition, skaters derogatively use phrases like "cattiness," "girl drama," and "too much estrogen" to explain disagreements. Furthermore, skaters are discouraged from being "too emotional."

This policing of femininity can be illustrated by a League conflict involving a pregnant skater. The skater was three months pregnant and had obtained permission from her doctor to skate in an upcoming tournament, but the League voted against allowing her to compete, as several skaters were unwilling to play with a pregnant skater out of fear of injuring either the skater or the fetus. One skater recalled attending the meeting in which the pregnant skater's eligibility was determined:

> It was really dramatic. [She] was crying and was hysterical. And then some other girl was yelling at her, telling her she didn't care about her baby. And I just remember this visual image—[she] was sitting in a corner, crying and screaming, and she put her hand out [she demonstrates with her hand out, palm upturned] and yelled "I am NOT a delicate flower!" I mean, it was very Shakespearean and all. Some girls were like, totally shocked, other girls were like [she puts her hand over her mouth, half-laughing], you know, trying not to laugh, because it was so dramatic.

In recounting the story, she sarcastically noted that the pregnant skater's words were so emotionally dramatic as to be "Shakespearean."

If "girls being girls" is derogatory, what should skaters be? "Athletes" seems to be the default response, as illustrated by the social hierarchies in the league. As one skater told me, "there's always that one person that everyone shits on. It's just a huge popularity contest." When I pressed her to find out how this popularity contest is judged, she said that skating ability is paramount: "If you aren't a good skater, no one will listen to you in the meetings." This focus on athleticism and skill seems to belie the professed democratic, grassroots ethos of roller derby and suggests the limits of derby's potential critique of athleticism. Even though women can join the league without much athletic background, their integration into the League depends on the learning curve of their skating abilities. Skaters who join but do not attend enough practices to become recognized as "athletes" are condescendingly referred to being in derby "just for the party," in one skater's words. Real skaters are athletes; bodies matter.

[. . .]

Conclusion

In this article, I have demonstrated that by interrogating emphasized femininity, the Nowhere Roller Girls engage in a critical practice called the female signifiant. Skaters do not cross the boundary between masculinity and femininity but rather self-referentially engage contradictions within femininity. When skaters satirically and hyperbolically splice certain aspects of emphasized femininity (such as sexual availability evidenced by mini-skirts) with elements antithetical to this femininity (such as the valuation of large bodies and aggression), they expose the contingency of emphasized femininity as a coherent system of gender norms.

However, the style of gender negotiation undertaken in roller derby is not without limits. First, certain feminine attributes are stigmatized within derby, such as excessive emotionality. Second, while skaters expose the risks associated with athletics through their theatrical portrayal of injuries, they also use athletic skill as a benchmark by which to discipline other skaters. . . . This suggests the limits of the female signifiant: while exhilarating for the individuals that practice it, it nevertheless appears inadequate on its own to address the broader issues of inequality that—as Connell (1987) notes—perpetuate the emphasized femininity that derby skaters critique.

[. . .]

References

Barrymore, D. (Producer & Director). 2009. *Whip It!* [Motion Picture]. US: Mandate Pictures.

Cahn, S. K. 1995. *Coming on Strong: Gender and Sexuality in Twentieth-Century Women's Sport.* Cambridge, MA: Harvard University Press.

Castelnuovo, S. and S. R. Guthrie. 1998. *Feminism and the Female Body: Liberating the Amazon Within.* Boulder, CO: Lynne Rienner Publishers.

Connell, R. 1987. *Gender and Power: Society, the Person, and Sexual Politics.* Palo Alto, CA: Stanford University Press.

Hargreaves, J. 1994. *Sporting Females: Critical Issues in the History and Sociology of Women's Sports.* New York, NY: Routledge.

Hebdige, D. 1979. *Subculture: The Meaning of Style.* London, UK: Methuen.

Heywood, L. and S. Dworkin. 2003. *Built to Win.* Minneapolis, MN: University of Minnesota Press.

Messner, M. 2002. *Taking the Field: Women, Men and Sports.* Minneapolis, MN: University of Minnesota Press.

Messner, M. and S. Dworkin. 2002. "Just Do . . . What? Sports, Bodies, Gender." Pp. 17–29 in *Gender and Sport: A Reader*, edited by S. Scraton and A. Flintoff. New York, NY: Routledge.

Sands, R. R. 2002. *Sport Ethnography.* Champaign, IL: Human Kinetics.

Theberge, N. 1997. "It's Part of the Game: Physicality and the Production of Gender in Women's Hockey." *Gender & Society* 11:69–87.

Young, A. and C. Dallaire. 2008. "Beware*#! SK8 at Your Own Risk: The Discourses of Young Female Skateboarders." Pp. 235–54 in *Tribal Play*, edited by M. Atkinson and K. Young. Bingley, UK: Emerald Group Publishing.

"We're, Like, a Cute Rugby Team"

How Whiteness and Heterosexuality Shape Women's Sense of Belonging in Rugby

Anima Adjepong

© iStockphoto.com/OSTILL

Sportswriter Jay Caspian King (2012) dubbed the 2012 Summer Olympic Games "the summer of the female athlete," arguing with others (Brown, 2012; Shergold, 2012; Williams, 2012) that these games highlighted a shift in women's access to sport and their representation in popular media. However, Cooky and colleagues (Cooky et al., 2013) found that although more women are participating in sports, coverage is the lowest it has ever been.

Anima Adjepong. 2015. "'We're, Like, a Cute Rugby Team': How Whiteness and Heterosexuality Shape Women's Sense of Belonging in Rugby." *International Review for the Sociology of Sport* 52(2):209–22.

Often, when media covers women's sports, sexualized representations and diminutive narratives reassert sport as a masculine terrain. Furthermore, sportswomen who adhere to normative gender and sexuality may receive more coverage, but through a racialized framework that normalizes whiteness (Bernstein, 2002; McDonald, 2002; Withycombe, 2011) and reproduces the marginalization of women's sports. As Patricia Hill Collins (2005) argues, politics of normative gender and sexuality rely on logics that construct white people as carriers of normative gender. Given the ways in which norms of white heterosexual femininity continue to construct women's sport, how do women who play non-professionally experience their participation? In what ways do these women challenge sports as a masculine space?

In this paper I will argue that although women athletes have the potential to challenge the masculinity of the sporting terrain, their ability to do so relies on the "cash value" (Lipsitz, 2006) of their particular social locations. I begin with a discussion of how access to heterosexual and white privilege may make possible particular challenges to gendered inequality in sport. My case study considers how women rugby players in the United States assert their belonging in a sport characterized by aggressive and violent masculinity (Pringle and Markula, 2005; Schacht, 1996) within a broader context of racism, sexism and heterosexism (Caudwell, 2002; Cooky and McDonald, 2005). In considering how these (predominantly white) women lay claim to their place on the rugby pitch, I discuss the ways in which their privileged positions as white and sometimes heterosexual women shape their sense of belonging in the sport. Additionally, I examine how investments in norms of white heterosexuality may lead to the further marginalization of women's sport.

[. . .]

Women's Rugby and Challenges to Normative Gender

Rugby is a violent and physically aggressive contact sport sometimes referred to as a "white man's game" (Collins, 2009; Spracklen, 2001). Unlike other contact sports, men and women play by the same rules, making it a productive site for examining how gender norms inform women's experiences of the sport. In recent years, the sport has gained popularity among women in the United States. According to a recent study (SGMA Research, 2011) for USA Rugby, the administrative body of rugby in the US, women constitute 32% of all rugby participants, and 20% of those who have played for longer than eight years. Although USA Rugby does not provide information on the race of rugby players, studies of the sport often remark on the fact that the majority of players in the US are white (Broad, 2001; Chase, 2006; Ezzell, 2009). Scholars such as Spracklen (2001), Spracklen and Spracklen (2008), and Long et al. (1997) have examined the ways in which rugby's popularity contributed to an imagined community demarcated by notions of white hegemonic masculinity to the exclusion of women and people of color.

Although women have been playing rugby since at least the 1920s, sport historian Tony Collins (2009: 95) has argued that "women's rugby has offered no challenge to the fundamental masculine nature of the game." Whether played by men or women, the game maintains all the characteristics associated with masculinity—bawdy songs, excessive drinking, and sporting violence. For the most part, scholars who study women's rugby agree with Collins, noting that although women rugby players may fashion themselves as tough and unapologetic, they also reproduce norms of rugby by developing disciplined rugby bodies and participating in rugby culture, including its bawdy songs and excessive drinking (Broad, 2001;

Chase, 2006). At the same time, by playing rugby and (sometimes) refusing to apologize for doing so, these women challenge dominant ideas of what it means to be a respectable heterosexual woman. K. L. Broad's (2001: 89) study characterized women's rugby as a form of queer resistance against "standards of passivity associated with (typically white, middle-class, heterosexual) femininity." But others (Ezzell, 2009; Hardy, 2015) have also shown the ways in which women rugby players may rely on homophobia to distance themselves from the lesbian stereotype associated with the sport.

Previous studies that have examined the ways in which women's rugby is a site for challenging normative gender provide a solid basis for making sense of how women experience this sport characterized by white heterosexual masculinity. However, few of these studies have paid particular attention to how women may experience this sport at the intersections of race, specifically whiteness, and heterosexuality.

[. . .]

Methods

This project is primarily based on in-depth semi-structured interviews with a convenience sample of 15 women rugby players who play at the club level in the southwestern United States. . . .

For this project, I combined my interviews with ethnographic observations at three rugby tournaments and one post-match social. Ethnographic observations provided me with a first hand account of interactions between men and women rugby players, coaches, and fans. . . . To recruit respondents, I attended three tournaments in central Texas and southern California, which I learned about by contacting different teams either through Facebook or email. I also attended one game during the regular spring season in central Texas. During the game and tournaments, I conducted participant observations by volunteering to play with teams that needed additional players. I took this opportunity to build rapport with players and request interviews. At tournaments there were, on average, three men's teams for every woman's team and most players (who also often served as spectators) were white with a few visible Pacific Islanders, Latino/as and black players. Of the 15 women I interviewed, 12 responded as white, one black, and two Latina. They ranged in age from 18 to 36, with the median age being 28. All respondents had at least a bachelor's degree, with the exception of my youngest respondent, who was enrolled in university at the time of our interview. None of my respondents played for the same rugby team and all were still playing at the time of interview.

[. . .]

Findings

[. . .]

The women in my study simultaneously challenged and reproduced essentialist and racialized ideas about women, sexuality, and rugby. Although players sometimes contested the idea that rugby is a man's game, they also agreed with aspects of this construction, a concession I argue is a result of the ways in which the sport culture relies on heterosexuality as an organizing principle. Heterosexual players pushed back against the idea that women rugby players are all lesbians by asserting their teams' collective heterosexual identity (Ezzell, 2009); and all players were ambivalent about the ways in which the sport is racialized. Below, I consider how the white heterosexual space of rugby informs my respondents' sense of belonging in the sport. I follow this discussion with an examination of how whiteness contributed to a sense of racial belonging that mitigated white players' alienation on the pitch.

"Notoriously Straight": Navigating the White Heterosexual Space of the Rugby Pitch

During the summer months, seven-a-side rugby tournaments happen all around the country. As part of my project, I attended three of these tournaments. My observations highlight the ways in which rugby is constructed as a white heterosexual space. The first tournament I attended was in a large park with six playing fields in Central Texas. There were 35 men's teams and 11 women's teams at the tournament. Upon arrival, I saw a group of women sitting under a tent in their jerseys, drinking water and Gatorade while preparing for their game. I learned from this team that all the women's games would be on the same field. Walking along the left bank of the fields I observed several groups of mostly white shirtless men. There were also a few Pacific Islanders and one or two black men. On the sidelines of a women's match, I overheard a white man say to his friends, two tan white women and a black man, that the women's game seemed so dainty compared to the men's game. Looking at the game in question, I found the women's teams to be more inexperienced than dainty. The two men were similarly dressed, in white rugby shorts that came up to their mid-thighs, exposing their muscular quadriceps muscles, and plain tank tops. The women wore short shorts and t-shirts. The men appeared to be trying to impress the women with their knowledge of the game and the women sounded impressed. The white man mentioned that there will be a pub-crawl after the tournament and the players will be dirty. One of the women offered her place for him to take a shower and he responded, "No thanks. Stink and drink, baby." The women cooed in admiration.

Looking around I realized that with the exception of one shirtless woman who wore just a sports bra, most of the other women kept their clothes on at all times, surrounded by mostly shirtless white men. On the other side of the fields in the tents where players were lounging, I heard loud chanting and walked over to see why. A white male player had just completed a Zulu-warrior, a naked jog required of a player who has just scored his or her first try. When he returned to the tents, a group from one of the women's teams called out, "Do it again!" The player's team chanted, "Shoot the boot," asking the "Zulu-warrior" to chug beer from a sweaty boot and the women's teams cheered them on.

The scenes described above are not unlike the other tournaments I attended during my research or as a rugby player for seven years. Within the context of rugby, men and women support one another by cheering at matches, flirting, drinking together and generally being part of rugby culture. Here rugby culture is constructed as ribald, white, and heterosexual. Logics of heterosexuality and normative gender organize the space through the display of naked white male torsos, rhetorical production of women's games as "dainty" compared to supposedly more aggressive men's games, and attractive athletic white women who challenge the stereotype of the butch women's rugby player. Whiteness is central to heterosexuality as an organizing principle within this context. White heterosexuality is safe and as Mary McDonald (2002: 382) has argued, when ascribed to sportswomen it serves as an antidote to the transgression that their athleticism presents to the gender order. Scholars (Cooky and McDonald, 2005; McDonald, 2002) have also noted how the invocation of white heterosexual femininity creates space for sportswomen in different sporting contexts. Furthermore, the ribaldry of rugby culture—chugging beer from sweaty boots, running around naked, and singing raunchy songs—is made safe by the white heterosexuality of the space. In this context, there is nothing gay about taking pleasure in a naked teammate's body as he or she runs up and down the length of the rugby pitch.

Although rugby culture is characterized by white heterosexuality, the stereotype of the lesbian rugby player remains a salient aspect of the sport for women. For many of my respondents, even those who dated women, they responded to this stereotype by "heterosexing" the rugby field. Jayne Caudwell (2002) uses the term "heterosexing" to refer to players' efforts to destabilize the lesbian stereotype that characterizes women's sports. For those women who dated men (and women occasionally), they called attention to their heterosexuality in reaction to the stereotype of the lesbian athlete by affirming that they were different from "those women." My respondents who dated women exclusively did not highlight their sexuality except to note that they felt rugby was a welcoming space for them. I identified three main strategies the women I interviewed who dated men exclusively or both men and women employed to distance themselves from the lesbian stereotype. Respondents: (a) suggested that their team was different from those other lesbian rugby teams; (b) outright rejected the idea that women's rugby was a "lesbian sport"; or (c) highlighted the idea that the stereotype was just that, a stereotype.

Respondents challenged the lesbian label by invoking the respectability of white heterosexual femininity. As one respondent, an 18-year-old white college student who dated men exclusively told me, her team described itself as "notoriously straight" because "we're, like, a cute rugby team." For this player's team, the description "notoriously straight" served to distance them from the lesbian stereotype. Likewise, the use of the word "cute" to describe her rugby team suggests that she sees her team as hetero-sexy. Not only does the hetero-sexy sportswoman not threaten male dominance (Ezzell, 2009; Griffin, 1998), although rarely explicitly noted, she is also often white (De Oca, 2012; Douglas, 2011; Vincent, 2004) and thus acceptable to the sporting hegemony. Although this player called her team notorious for its heterosexuality, she also noted that other teams are just like hers, suggesting that the notoriety her squad asserts as a rugby team of white heterosexual women might be over-emphasized. Several other respondents made mention of the possibility that their teams were unique because most players claimed to be heterosexual. By making claims to the predominant heterosexuality of their rugby teams, my respondents perform the anxieties around rhetorically reproducing women's rugby players as heterosexual and thus conforming to the logics of white heterosexuality that organize rugby in particular and sports in general.

For those women who dated men exclusively or men and women, they called attention to the fact that being a "dyke" is not a sufficient condition to be a rugby player. As one white player who reported dating both men and women explained, "We'll get a lot of girls come out to practice just to try it out that had never played before, and they'll think 'just because I'm gay and just because I'm dyke-y, I'm going to be good at rugby.'" And they're not. They're not athletes and they never come back." This player challenged the idea that rugby is a sport for lesbians by refusing to equate women's athleticism with lesbian sexuality. By doing this, she created space for herself as a rugby player who is not a lesbian. Several respondents repeated this sentiment that being a lesbian was not enough to be a rugby player. For some of my straight respondents, identifying as a woman rugby player was complicated by the stereotype that women rugby players were lesbians. Like the women in Ezzell's (2009) study, some of my respondents relied on their heterosexuality to navigate away from this stereotype. Although these sportswomen did not vilify lesbian rugby players, by defensively constructing themselves as other than the stereotype, they reinforce the glass closet (Griffin, 1998) that queer women rugby players occupy. The strategies these women use to assert their belonging may appear to be individual strategies that focus only on how each player is different from the stereotype. However, I argue that these strategies rely on and reproduce the institutionalization of white heterosexuality in rugby.

"Good Rugby Stock": Asserting Racial Belonging on the Rugby Pitch

Rugby's reputation as a *white* man's game (Collins, 2009; Spracklen, 2001) created a space within which my white respondents could assert some sense of belonging on the pitch regardless of their sexuality. In interviews, I told all my respondents that I was interested in race. White respondents assumed that by race, I did not mean them. Although all respondents insisted on the racial diversity of their teams, non-white respondents remarked on the perception of rugby as a "white game." The only black respondent challenged this perception by calling it a "myth," adding: "It's not hockey. Damn! There's whole continents and countries of black people that play rugby." In a similar vein, when asked to discuss the racial makeup of their teams, some white players said things like, "There's black [or Asian] players on every team [I've played on]," who are "awesome," emphasizing that they were fine with having "others" on their teams. As Sara Ahmed (2012) has argued, the language of diversity can serve to pat institutionalized whiteness on the back for being inclusive and progressive, at the same time that it affirms that whiteness. When my white respondents affirm how awesome players of color are, they mark these players as different from the norm and, as white women, assert their belonging in the space.

At the same time that white players asserted their belonging, they also naturalized some racialized bodies as more suited for the game while marking the pitch as off limits to others (Long et al., 1997). For example, one white respondent disclosed that she's "a little bit jealous" of the "Samoan girls" who are "just really good rugby stock." This player was not the only one to mention Samoans as particularly well suited for rugby. Whereas Samoans were identified as "good rugby stock," other people of color were constructed as not belonging on the rugby pitch. When telling me about an injury she caused another player during a match, another white player described her opponent as "really, really little. She was like, Hispanic or maybe Indian or something." By calling attention to her opponent's non-whiteness—"she was . . . something"— this player may be indicating that certain racialized people do not have the appropriate physiology to be rugby players. The notion that some non-white racial and ethnic groups are better suited for rugby than others engages in the kinds of processes that produce the "fantasy of the 'normal white body'" (Azzarito and Harrison, 2008: 354). Similarly, the Zulu-warrior rugby tradition mentioned in the fieldnote excerpted above is one way in which the predominantly white bodies that comprise rugby culture can affirm their whiteness at the same time that they construct blackness as athletically superior, yet socially powerless. As Ben Carrington (2010) has argued, one part of the racial project of sports is to construct "the black athlete" as a body reduced to physicality and sexuality. The reproduction of this project is seen in the racial bonding over the Zulu-warrior tradition. White athletes put on the mask of animalistic black masculinity in celebration of their prowess on the field, all the while sustaining the normativity of the white body. The ways in which whiteness is privileged on the rugby field are illustrated in how my respondents discussed people of color in the sport.

Conclusion

Like other scholars (Chase, 2006; Collins, 2009), my findings are ambivalent about the extent to which, when women play rugby, they challenge the inherent aggressive masculinity of the sport. Instead, this research highlights the ways in which women's participation in rugby relies on the reproduction of the white heterosexuality of the sport. The normalization of whiteness and the heterosexism that characterizes sports in general means that without a critical self-awareness, players reify the value of these categories in their efforts to assert belonging. Of course this is not to say that white women's inclusion into rugby (and other sports) are not without inequalities including being sexualized and marginalized as athletes (Cooky et al., 2010). Instead, my research highlights the ways in which white women can claim this sporting space by invoking the racial contract, which maintains the white body as the somatic norm (Mills, 1997; Puwar, 2004) on the rugby pitch. This research further demonstrates the ways in which liberal feminism and white privilege (Cooky and McDonald, 2005) characterize the inclusion of white women into a so-called "white man's game" by showing how the racial topography of the sport is demarcated as white. The rhetorical reproduction of the sport in this way allows women players to employ their whiteness as a means of justifying their belonging on the rugby pitch.

Although women may be increasingly welcomed to play stereotypically masculine sports, their acceptance into this terrain is circumscribed by the extent to which they adhere to the rules of a heterosexual (Cahn, 1993; Griffin, 1998; Wright and Clarke, 1999) and racialized (Azzarito and Harrison, 2008; Long and Hylton, 2002; Walton and Butryn, 2006) social hierarchy. Fellows and Razack (1998) have noted the ways in which feminist solidarity politics fail when women refuse to acknowledge their complicity in marginalizing or oppressing others. In the context of women's rugby, heterosexual white women may cash in on their investments in white heterosexuality as a way to affirm how "safe" they are because they do not challenge the white heteropatriarchal hierarchy. By employing competing narratives of how (white) women (lesbian and heterosexual) are marginalized in sport, white women rugby players use their dominant positions to create an imagined community (Cohen, 1985 [2013]) within whose boundaries they can lay claim to the identity of safe (normative, feminine, heterosexual) sportswomen—the kind that can be cultural icons.

[. . .]

References

Ahmed, S. 2012. *On Being Included: Racism and Diversity in Institutional Life*. Durham, NC: Duke University Press.

Azzarito, L. and L. Harrison. 2008. "'White Men Can't Jump': Race, Gender and Natural Athleticism." *International Review for the Sociology of Sport* 43(4):347–64.

Bernstein, A. 2002. "Is It Time for a Victory Lap? Changes in the Media Coverage of Women in Sport." *International Review for the Sociology of Sport* 37(3–4):415–28.

Broad, K. L. 2001. "The Gendered Unapologetic: Queer Resistance in Women's Sport." *Sociology of Sport Journal* 18(2):181–204.

Brown, S. 2012. "London 2012: The Women's Olympics?" *CNN International*, August 10 (http://edition.cnn.com/2012/08/10/sport/london-olympics-women/).

Cahn, S. K. 1993. "From the 'Muscle Moll' to the 'Butch' Ballplayer: Mannishness, Lesbianism, and Homophobia in U.S. Women's Sport." *Feminist Studies* 19(2):343–68.

Carrington, B. 2010. *Race, Sport and Politics: The Sporting Black Diaspora*. London, UK: Sage.

Caudwell, J. 2002. "Women's Experiences of Sexuality Within Football Contexts: A Particular and Located Footballing Epistemology." *Football Studies* 5(1):24–45.

Chase LF. 2006. "(Un)Disciplined Bodies: A Foucauldian Analysis of Women's Rugby." *Sociology of Sport Journal* 23(3):229–47.

Cohen, A. 2013 [1985]. *Symbolic Boundaries of Community*. Hoboken, NJ: Taylor & Francis.

Collins, P. H. 2005. *Black Sexual Politics: African Americans, Gender, and the New Racism*. New York: Routledge.

Collins, T. 2009. *A Social History of English Rugby Union*. London, UK: Routledge.

Cooky, C. and M. G. McDonald. 2005. "'If You Let Me Play': Young Girls' Insider-Other Narratives of Sport." *Sociology of Sport Journal* 22(2):158–77.

Cooky, C., M. Messner, and R. H. Hextrum. 2013. "Women Play Sport, but Not on TV: A Longitudinal Study of Televised News Media." *Communication & Sport* 1(3):203–30.

Cooky, C., F. L. Wachs, M. Messner, et al. 2010. It's Not About the Game: Don Imus, Race, Class, Gender and Sexuality in Contemporary Media." *Sociology of Sport Journal* 27(2):139–59.

De Oca, J. M. 2012. "White Domestic Goddess on a Postmodern Plantation: Charity and Commodity Racism in 'The Blind Side.'" *Sociology of Sport Journal* 29(2):131–50.

Douglas, D. D. 2011. "Venus, Serena, and the Inconspicuous Consumption of Blackness: A Commentary on Surveillance, Race Talk, and New Racism(s)." *Journal of Black Studies* 43(2):127–45.

Ezzell, M. B. 2009. "'Barbie Dolls' on the Pitch: Identity Work, Defensive Othering, and Inequality in Women's Rugby." *Social Problems* 56(1):111–31.

Fellows, M. L. and S. Razack. 1998. "The Race to Innocence: Confronting Hierarchical Relations Among Women." *Journal of Gender, Race and Justice* 1:335–52.

Griffin, P. 1998. *Strong Women, Deep Closets: Lesbians and Homophobia in Sport*. Champaign, IL: Human Kinetics.

Hardy, E. 2015. "The Female 'Apologetic' Behaviour Within Canadian Women's Rugby: Athlete Perceptions and Media Influences." *Sport in Society* 18(2):155–67.

King, J. C. 2012. "The Death of the Anna Kournikova Era: The State of Women's Sports After the Summer of Serena." *Grantland.com*, September 13. Retrieved November 12, 2014 (http://grantland.com/features/from-serena-williams-missy-franklin-gabby-douglas-summer-2012-defined-female-athletes/).

Lipsitz, G. 2006. *The Possessive Investment in Whiteness: How White People Profit from Identity Politics*. Philadelphia, PA: Temple University Press.

Long, J., B. Carrington, and K. Spracklen. 1997. "'Asians Cannot Wear Turbans in the Scrum': Explorations of Racist Discourse Within Professional Rugby League." *Leisure Studies* 16(4):249–59.

Long, J. and K. Hylton. 2002. "Shades of White: An Examination of Whiteness in Sport." *Leisure Studies* 21(2):87–103.

McDonald, M. G. 2002. "Queering Whiteness: The Particular Case of the Women's National Basketball Association." *Sociological Perspectives* 45(4):379–96.

Mills, C. 1997. *The Racial Contract*. Ithaca, NY: Cornell University Press.

Pringle, R. and P. Markula. 2005. "No Pain Is Sane After All: A Foucauldian Analysis of Masculinities and Men's Experiences in Rugby." *Sociology of Sport Journal* 22(4):472–97.

Puwar, N. 2004. *Space Invaders: Race, Gender and Bodies out of Place*. Oxford: Berg Publishers.

Schacht, S. P. 1996. "Misogyny on and off the 'Pitch': The Gendered World of Male Rugby Players." *Gender & Society* 10(5):550–65.

SGMA Research. 2011 "Single Sport Report—2011 Rugby." Report for USA Rugby, Jupiter, FL.

Shergold, A. 2012. "Go Girls! How Team GB's Amazing Women Would Be Seventh in the Olympic Gold Medal Table if They Competed on Their Own." *Daily Mail*, August 10. Retrieved November 10, 2014 (www.dailymail.co.uk/news/article-2186441/Olympics-2012-Go-girls-How-Team-GBs-amazing-women-seventh-Olympic-gold-medal-table-competed-own.html).

Spracklen, K. 2001. "'Black Pearl, Black Diamonds': Exploring Racial Identities in Rugby League." Pp. 70–82 in *Race, Sports and British Society*, edited by B. Carrington and A. McDonald. London, UK: Routledge.

Spracklen, K. and C. Spracklen. 2008. "Negotiations of Being and Becoming: Minority Ethnic Rugby League Players in the Cathar Country of France." *International Review for the Sociology of Sport* 43(2): 201–18.

Vincent, J. 2004. "Game, Sex, and Match: The Construction of Gender in British Newspaper Coverage of the 2000 Wimbledon Championships." *Sociology of Sport Journal* 21(4):435–56.

Walton, T. A. and T. M. Butryn. 2006. "Policing the Race: U.S. Men's Distance Running and the Crisis of Whiteness." *Sociology of Sport Journal* 23(1):1–28.

Williams, R. 2012. "2012: A Truly Remarkable Sporting Year to Be Relished Over and Over." *The Guardian,* December 28. Retrieved November 10, 2014 (www.theguardian.com/sport/blog/2012/dec/28/2012-sporting-year-review).

Withycombe, J. L. 2011. "Intersecting Selves: African American Female Athletes' Experiences of Sport." *Sociology of Sport Journal* 28(4):478–93.

Wright, J. and G. Clarke. 1999. "Sport, the Media, and the Construction of Compulsory Heterosexuality: A Case Study of Women's Rugby Union." *International Review for the Sociology of Sport* 34(3):227–43.

Transgender Inclusion and the Changing Face of Lesbian Softball Leagues

Ann Travers and Jillian Deri

© iStockphoto.com/Anton Donev

T he transgender challenge to the traditional organization of sport on the basis of binary sex categories has had an impact in a series of ways. In mainstream sporting spaces, transsexual women and men have recently won the right to inclusion at the highest levels of sport on the basis of their obtained medical-legal identities: the International Olympic Committee (IOC) arrived at the Stockholm Consensus in 2004 to allow fully (hormonally and surgically) transitioned athletes to compete in their reassigned sex category (Sykes, 2006). This limited level of inclusion reinforces binary-based understandings of sex difference and is consistent with *gender conforming* as opposed to *gender transforming* transgender inclusion (Travers, 2006). The emergence of transmen from within lesbian communities (Dozier, 2005; Noble, 2006), in contrast, has resulted, in some cases, in a queer-identified and hence more radical (binary resistant), gender transforming approach to transinclusion in lesbian softball leagues.

[...]

Ann Travers and Jillian Deri. 2011. "Transgender Inclusion and the Changing Face of Lesbian Softball Leagues." *International Review for the Sociology of Sport* 46(4):488–507.

Our research builds on Travers's (2006) study of transgender inclusion at the policy-level in a sample of North American lesbian softball leagues. . . . At the time of Travers's research (2002–2003), only one league from the sample of approximately 30 lesbian softball leagues studied had adopted what we term a *radical transgender inclusive policy*: a policy designed to include gender transforming participants. This particular league's policy allowed for gender ambiguity by enabling transgender participants to play wherever they felt most comfortable, be that in the open (mixed) division or the women's division. This policy was also unique in that it provided for the inclusion of transgender men who had transitioned *while playing in the league.*

While policy changes "pave the way for greater inclusion and challenges to the gender binary based segregation of sport," Travers states that such policies still "tell us little about the inclusiveness of the environment for transgender participants" (2006: 443). Our research is intended to provide some measure of the socio-cultural context for transgender inclusion: we focus not only on MTF transsexuals (the subject of most social science research relating to transsexual and transgender persons (Dozier, 2005: 300) but add to the "limited research on FTMs" (Dozier, 2005: 300) and make a unique contribution to the limited social science research on relationships between MTF and Female to Male (FTM) transsexuals and transmen.

[. . .]

Gay and Lesbian Sporting Spaces

Gay and lesbian sporting spaces challenge heterosexism and traditional gender roles but they have tended to organize inclusion and participation around binary sex difference (Symons and Hemphill, 2006; Travers, 2006, 2008). In many "mixed-sex" leagues, for example, sex-based criteria for the purposes of registration and/or to ensure various proportions of women and men have persisted, based on the assumption that men naturally have an "unfair advantage" as athletes (Sykes, 2006).

[. . .]

Starting in the late 1970s, lesbian softball leagues emerged to challenge conventional assumptions about women's sexuality, gender expression and athleticism (Gillis et al., 2004). These leagues have a long history as gay positive and women-only social and sporting spaces that offer queer women an alternative to the homophobia of mainstream women's sport and/or the sexism of both gay and straight mixed sporting spaces. . . .

The response of North American lesbian communities to transgender persons to date has been mixed. Some of these communities have been at the forefront of transinclusion, often contributing to the genderqueering of LGBT spaces, while other lesbian and feminist organizations have advocated trans-exclusion and found themselves at odds with transgender persons and the transgender liberation movement. The tensions surrounding transgender inclusion "reveal the political stakes involved in a particular construction of lesbian and transgender identity" (Boyd, 2006: 420). Most of these debates have focused on the inclusion/exclusion of transwomen and ignored issues relating to the inclusion/exclusion of transmen, transgender and genderqueer persons.

[. . .]

Methodology

We explore the extent to which lesbian softball leagues with transinclusive policies are being experienced as inclusive by transgender participants themselves.

[. . .]

Between 2006 and 2008 we interviewed 12 people who self-identified to us as transgender or transsexual—eight FTM transmen, three MTF transsexual women, and one genderqueer/ trans/lesbian—who were participating or had participated within the previous two years in lesbian softball leagues with radical transgender inclusion policies in two North American cities. We draw on these interviews and our own participant observation to establish a measure of the climate—welcoming, neutral or "chilly"—for trans participation in these leagues. We also draw on participant observation and interview data to document the shifts that are taking place in these lesbian softball leagues with regard to gender identities and gender boundaries.

[. . .]

Our subjects participated in lesbian softball leagues with transinclusive policies that go far beyond those of the IOC or even the Gay Games. These radical transinclusive policies include transwomen and transmen of all variations and stages of transition (in terms of surgery and hormones) as well as transgender individuals whose gender identities lie between or outside the gender binary. One league's policy for participation, for example, includes an assertion of lesbian history while at the same time extending a welcome to transsexual and transgender persons of all genders as well as lesbian, bisexual and heterosexual women.

[. . .]

Transinclusion and the Changing Face and Culture of Lesbian Softball Leagues

The changing face and culture of the lesbian leagues our subjects participated in is visible to the observer. Lesbian softball leagues have long been home to gender variant women, but the range of gender expression has increased in the last decade. Ten years ago it was unthinkable—at least in the several leagues that we are familiar with—that a bearded man or a pre-operative transsexual woman would be playing on a lesbian softball team but now, if not exactly commonplace, it is increasingly unremarkable. The presence of transsexual, transgender and genderqueer players on the diamond provides visual evidence of a shift away from dyadic sex boundaries.

The three MTF transsexual women we interviewed reported experiencing participation in their leagues as empowering, talking about feeling a distinctly warm reception from other players. As Cher said, "[the women on my team] that first year were my healing circle." And KD was actively recruited by a co-worker who coaches the team she now plays on:

As soon as Jane found out that I was transitioning, she just took me into the fold and then introduced me to a whole bunch of other women who readily accepted me as another woman.

[. . .]

Every one of our FTM subjects experienced at least some encouragement and support. Brad reported being grateful for team-mates and coaches reminding others to address him with the appropriate pronoun. This made him feel safe and included. And witnessing an increase in trans visibility over time in his league has added to that sense of safety:

I certainly have noticed the visibility of trans players. I know that some of the trans-men who played before used to shave, for example. Now they don't . . . there's no need to be stealthy.

Keanu found his team to be very supportive of his transition:

> They were pretty great about it actually. They were pretty supportive. It's been kind of recent. This is actually the first season I've identified as trans to my team. . . . There have been times when they use my old name or something like that. But they feel bad about it. They've definitely been really supportive; . . . the first game of the season most people came up and said that they support my decision.

[. . .]

Four of the eight transmen we interviewed had experienced negative or hostile responses to their participation by other league members. Nick reported being asked on several occasions by teammates and league participants why he wanted to be treated like a man—referred to as "he"—*and* continue to play in a lesbian league and be included in women-only spaces. Several transmen reported being accused by teammates of transitioning strictly to achieve male privilege. Dean said, "I've had people . . . comment that FTMs are just . . . copping out and they're just leaving their sisters behind for male privilege and stuff." Keanu felt he was punished by lesbians in his league for transitioning:

> When women get hit hard with sexism then they direct that at transmen, and they're like "now you're a traitor, now you're not really on our side, now you're not really with the cause or something." And . . . "why can't you just be a butch lesbian? Why do you have to take on a male identity?"

Two transmen reported experiencing pressure to leave lesbian space; to "complete" their transition by being "man enough" to play in a men's or mixed league. Several league participants challenged their masculinity by suggesting they were not "real men" because they were unwilling to play with non-trans men.

Nick's experiences of inclusion changed as his sex and gender presentation changed:

> When I joined the league I was a butchy dyke. I had no problems. Then I started becoming trans. . . . As soon as my voice started dropping—I didn't even have facial hair . . . it started back then. . . . [We were playing] the Clitcats . . . and . . . we were putting out the bases . . . and they were off on the side and they were making comments about "he shouldn't be here, if he wants to be a man he should get off the field; this is a women's league, get outta here." And we still hear things like that.

The silence of Nick's teammates hurt him almost as much as the transphobic comments themselves. He went on to say:

> You hit the field, comments are made. You go up to bat, comments are made. And it's easier to leave. It usually is just easier to pack up your bag and turn around and walk out.

But Nick is one of the highly visible transmen who not only stayed in the league but let his beard grow. He was one of several transmen we interviewed who reported that the issue of their participation led to a divisive split on their team with anti-trans players breaking away and forming a new team.

River, a trans/queer/lesbian, feels that her genderqueerness shelters her from visibility as a transgender person when boundaries for inclusion or exclusion are on the table. She has used this relative safety to champion transgender inclusion in the league. Nevertheless, the increasing extent of trans visibility in her league sometimes makes her nervous:

> When I see Drew pitching with a full beard, part of me, like my stomach goes whoa . . . that's really out there. Not in games, but in a tournament, because there must be some people who completely don't get it. Let's say they are friends and they come to watch and they see, "there's a guy, like what the fuck?" And it makes me a little nervous, like are we going to get away with this?

"Don't 'Sister Me' Bitch" In/Visibility and Transinclusion

The transsexual women we interviewed desired and valued their experiences of inclusion *as* women, not as transsexuals and for this reason, welcome invisibility. Our transmen participants, in contrast, experienced invisibility negatively—the use of female pronouns in particular was often brought up as an exemplar of an unwelcoming climate. Transmen who do not pass as men in the straight world find it necessary to remind others to call them "he" rather than "she." One might expect that transmen who are able to pass might experience less invisibility but our data suggest that this is not the case. Examples include "being sistered," "she'ing me" or "come on ladies." Without prompting most of our FTM subjects referred to commonplace instances of *transblindness* whereby it was assumed that everyone is a woman in a lesbian league with a radical transinclusive policy, as evidence of unwelcoming climates.

Brad, like several other transmen in our study, has had different experiences on different teams. Most of the players on his last team were from his friendship group: queer-identified, familiar with trans issues, and immersed in social circles comprising dykes, transmen and genderqueers. He recently switched to a more competitive team with less trans awareness.

> There are a lot of new players on this team that don't . . . they just don't really get it. I've been "she'd" a lot by players on my own team, which is kind of annoying for the most part because it is hard to keep correcting. And because it's a new team. When I played for Lavender Menace I had a much easier time. Everybody on the team was totally cool with me being trans and they were very supportive. A lot of them would correct people from other teams if they "she'd" me or whatever. But this team doesn't do that.

Brad tries to be really patient with those who are just being exposed to trans issues through his presence but being addressed by female pronouns hurts.

> Our first practice . . . one of the girls on the team "sistered" me. She was like "right on sister." And I just stared at her. I didn't even know what to do. I was like, "that was worse than you she'ing me." She sistered me and I didn't even know what to do. . . . I try to be really polite about it and not be like "hey bitch, yo, I'm a guy," . . . because I know a lot of people are learning still.

Like Brad, Keanu experiences a lack of "gender consciousness" on his team; team cheers that refer to "ladies" make him uncomfortable. He identifies this kind of atmosphere as being one among several (time commitments and scheduling being others) that are making him consider quitting. But Robert has had fun with his team mates around this issue:

There weren't a lot of first names and every once in a while they would like, "ladies, get your equipment." It was sort of an inside joke. And for me to correct them, and say, "no, no, I'm a gentleman," it was sort of not appropriate because it was a joke anyways. For a while it became "ladies," and then it became, "hey you, pick it up." It was interesting. . . . So it was just me, like I said, changing the pronoun so eventually it became "ladies and boy" when I was up at bat. It was really funny.

The Logic of Testosterone

Concerns about transgender participation in sport tend to crystallize around assumptions about exposure to testosterone—either prior to or as part of transitioning—as conferring an unfair advantage. . . . Testosterone is coded as a male hormone despite its presence in varying degrees in all of our bodies (Fausto-Sterling, 2000). . . . Many of our subjects held the same assumptions about male athletic superiority and testosterone as a performance enhancer. The view of testosterone as a performance enhancing drug is the first "hot spot" our study draws attention to with regard to climates for transgender inclusion.

Comments by many transmen and transwomen exposed assumptions about male strength and the unfair advantage it confers on the playing field. Keanu remarked that, "there's . . . a lot of transwomen who are a lot stronger than bio-female players." And John said that "I can understand why some people might not want FTMs because they are being shot up with T!" Cher too, raises concerns about testosterone injections for FTMS: "he pitches quite fast . . . it would appear that at times his team took advantage of his strength and power from being on that testosterone." Even some of the transfolk we would categorize as gender transformers held onto assumptions about natural male advantage, either pre- or post-transition. KD, for example, said that:

> the minute that somebody identifies as male, and begins that process of transitioning and taking testosterone and having musculature change and all of those things then I think the honorable thing to do would be for that person to step back from a playing position in the league. . . .

Several transmen themselves also identified hormone therapy as the appropriate tipping point for a self-edit from lesbian sporting spaces. According to Robert, "if he was taking hormones and he had male testosterone, the whole playing field [changes]. In this situation it wouldn't be a level playing field."

The transsexual women we interviewed were quick to point to the impact taking "female" hormones had on erasing the advantage testosterone had originally bestowed upon them. Cher recounted the feminizing impact taking female hormones had on her body:

> one of the things that I noticed in that whole process is the lack of muscle mass and body strength for me. So as a [former occupational identity] before taking hormones it was not uncommon for me to be able to do forty to fifty pushups at a set; and leg press eight or nine hundred pounds, and do an awful lot of those typically male types of exercises. So one of the things that I noticed in taking the hormones is that my upper body strength has changed dramatically. I have a hard time doing those pushups now, my leg strength isn't what it used to be.

While Cher described her team and the lesbian league as a whole as her "healing circle," she did share with us that some of the non-trans lesbians in the league had voiced concerns about her hitting power:

the comments I would get in the league at times was about the power of my hitting, and you know hitting the long ball, hitting the homerun, hitting the ball really really hard and in that place there was some concern that I shouldn't be playing in the league because of that power.

From our own observations we know that Cher is definitely one of the better hitters in the league and quite visible as an MTF transsexual through both her appearance and her public advocacy work in the larger community. Cher told us that since her transition she could no longer "hit the ball as hard as [she] used to" and viewed concerns about her strength and power as being based in ignorance about transsexuality. She provided a cultural (male privilege in terms of athletic training) rather than a biological explanation for her high level of skill. She recalled "spending hours and hours and hours in the back yard with my dad on the fielding and pitching stuff."
[. . .]

Transwomen and the Inclusion of Transmen

The transsexual women we interviewed want transinclusive policies that protect them from discrimination—*not* as transwomen but *as* women. And they do not necessarily support the inclusion of transmen or transgender people who do not adhere to a female identity. Two of the three transsexual women in our study expressed the view that FTMs who take testosterone no longer belong in lesbian softball leagues. In stark contrast, none of the transmen we interviewed questioned the appropriateness of MTF participation. This relates to the second "hot spot" we point to in this article—conflicts *among* transsexual and transgender participants about appropriate sex boundaries for participation. This tension emerged as a gendered one in our study but FTMs who have edited themselves out of women's spaces, however, were not part of our sample.

We asked our subjects if they were familiar with the transgender inclusive policy of their softball leagues and followed up this question by reading it to them. Through this process we discovered gaps in knowledge about transgender inclusive policies among trans participants themselves. Cher, for example, was quite surprised to find that her league welcomes transgender people:

Transsexual people? I thought it was transsexual women. . . . The minute that they identify in that way [as a transman] . . . they no longer really belong in the League. Or when it became apparent, in appearance and presentation, that they are clearly male. . . .

KD is pretty much in agreement but feels conflicted about it:

I have quite a few friends that are trans guys, and every time I say this I kind of feel like I'm selling out, when I say that I don't think that trans guys should be in the League because it is a women-only space . . . because they're not women.

Asked where she thinks the line for participating should be drawn, KD responds:

I probably think that once they start showing signs of becoming more male. Like when they start testosterone, their muscles start getting bigger, you know they start getting a lot of facial hair, their voice starts to drop. I think at that point they should kind of review where they're at and ask themselves ok do I at this point belong in a women only space?

Although Cher enjoys the social company of transmen, a softening of the gender binary to include them in lesbian space appears to be threatening to her sense of belonging as a woman in a women-only space. She is not alone among our transsexual female subjects in fearing that too much ambiguity could produce backlash. KD comments on her response to someone she thought was a transwoman who was making an insufficient effort to pass:

> The first time I met Max was after a game and we were shaking hands and I made eye contact with him and he had a five o'clock shadow and he was relatively big and I thought to myself, "shave before you come to the game, you're making me look bad." Because I thought Max was coming the other way. And I thought "Jesus woman, drag a blade across your face for god's sakes."

KD read Max as an MTF transsexual in the early stages of the process; in fact, Max is an FTM who was showing the effects of "male" hormone therapy. KD's anxiety that Max's "sloppy" presentation would create an unwelcoming climate for her and other MTF transsexuals in the league is telling. We speculate that the very presence of transmen and gender transforming transfolk in lesbian softball leagues may actually contribute to a chilly climate for some MTF transsexual women because of the anxiety their presence provokes. Many transsexual women see themselves as having finally come home to the female side of a foundational sex binary and may find disruptions to this binary logic threatening.

Cher expressed a preference for a league policy that is (self-identified) women-only. KD is less resolved. She believes both that transmen should depart from the league and that they should be the ones to make that decision. KD pointed out that she started playing in the league prior to surgery; at least in her mind, this made her technically still a male:

> I still am unresolved because like I said, the loyalty still is with the trans community and I will fight for transinclusion rights wherever I can. But . . . I want an all women's softball league; . . . I know of a trans guy that . . . part of me thinks "you shouldn't be here," but then there's another part of me that says "no that's not fair because [I] could be excluded just as easily." . . . I don't know if my resolve is based in fear or if it's based in loyalty. . . .

KD feels very reluctant to speak up on this issue: partly because she is conflicted but also because she fears it might spark efforts to exclude transsexual women like her.

Transmen Are "Sons of the Movement" . . .

. . . The transmen who participated in our study are "sons of the movement" in this sense in that it is their continued, as opposed to initial, inclusion that is at issue. This places them in a different location than MTFs who seek inclusion on the basis of sex identity coherence. KD speaks to this difference:

> I'm not stereotyping all trans guys—but typically most FTMs came out in a lesbian community and were sort of accepted and encouraged in that community. And it seems that we're on a reverse, so they're coming out of that community, whereas somebody like me [as a transwoman] is going into that community.

[. . .]

. . . All eight of the transmen we interviewed for this study emerged from within the lesbian community. The current re-negotiation of the bases of lesbian affiliation are one site where essentialized versus anti-essentialist understandings of sex, gender and sexual orientation are being re-negotiated. As Noble observes, "It seems that the sex wars are not over at all" (2006: 6). Nick's experience is a powerful example of someone who is deeply imbricated in this re-negotiation:

> How can you ask somebody who's come up in the gay and lesbian community, been nurtured, been looked after, came out as being a lesbian, came out as being a transguy? . . . How can you ask them to give up all that support, all that life experience and . . . go and find your own community now? . . . I don't think it's fair to ask anybody to surrender all that they've gained from that community.

Jennifer, an MTF transsexual, understands why transmen want to stay. Her experience of acceptance and empowerment is something she never wants to give up and this gives her tremendous compassion for the situation of transmen.

> I mean FTMs have often been instrumental in building the league. Like they've played a role in building lesbian communities, they've been part of them. . . . I don't think it's fair to ask anybody to surrender all that they've gained from that community and that's being given to me right now.

Our own observations and interviews with trans subjects indicate that formal and informal membership stipulations are shifting away from the constructed sex binary, at least somewhat, towards inclusion on the basis of cultural affinity. The reasons many transmen continue to play in lesbian leagues has less to do with biological or medical categories of sex and/or sexual orientation, and more to do with cultural history, friendship groups and the sense of belonging to the lesbian community that many of this generation of transmen continue to value. As much as he plays for the sport, for example, Robert also plays lesbian softball for social reasons. . . . Robert remains attached to this community:

> I think I've been acculturated as a lesbian, and so I enjoy being around lesbians. I would miss that tremendously if I played on a gay men's team, even though I am a man. I don't have a lot in common with gay men. It's very strange.

For many transmen, the lesbian community offered a much needed space to express non-traditional gender attributes and queer sexuality. Being a "butch dyke" in the lesbian community may have served as a bridge to an FTM identity (Dozier, 2005).

[. . .]

Some of the transmen in our study, however, experienced great inner conflict. We documented tensions among transmen between the desire to be included in lesbian softball leagues and the dissonance they experience in these spaces over the course of their transition. John and Dean have since edited themselves out of lesbian sporting spaces and are no longer playing softball—anywhere. Brad described his experience of discomfort at a League tournament:

> I had a hard weekend. . . . I didn't expect to anticipate feeling so alone. I don't know how to explain that really. I felt like I was surrounded by a bunch of people who just didn't understand me and it didn't feel good. I was thinking, "can I really do this? Can I really

keep doing this?" . . . So that weekend I just didn't feel comfortable. I'm not a lesbian, what am I doing playing in a lesbian softball league?

But Brad continues to play, at least for now, because:

I totally love them [lesbians]. They're my friends. They are the community that I am usually comfortable with. . . . Most of my friends are in the league. . . . As hard as it may be sometimes I still have a lot of fun.

Asked whether he has considered switching to a men's league, Brad expressed concerns about his invisibility in that context:

I don't think I'd actually get to be really who I am in that kind of atmosphere. . . . I think that because the League is queer it's much easier to—I do identify as male—but I don't deny that I am FTM. So I think that if I played in a men's league that it would be more difficult to do that. I don't feel like the acceptance would really be there. But that's assumptions right, I never really would know.

Several transmen stated that full transinclusion for them would require a rebranding of the space away from lesbian identity. This desire echoes the fears of some of the non-trans women in Travers's (2006) study: that transinclusion might lead to the eradication of the women-only spaces free of men and sexism that they value so much and that have been foundational for lesbian softball leagues.

[. . .]

Conclusion

[. . .]

We suggest that lesbian softball leagues with radical transinclusive policies are providing a window onto a less sex-binary-based sporting future. As such, they provide critics of mainstream sport with, as Travers (2006) suggested they might, a model for organizing sport away from its basis in the two sex system. The two "hot spots" that we identify as obstacles to transgender inclusion in lesbian softball leagues are likely to be mirrored in mainstream sporting spaces as well. The first hot spot we identify—the view of testosterone as a male hormone with implications for improved athletic performance—reflects the powerful culture of sex binary logic in the organization of sport. The second hot spot—the lack of unity among transsexual and transgender participants themselves about appropriate sex boundaries for transgender inclusion—reveals how deeply complicated it is to attempt to re-negotiate sexed boundaries.

Although all their members have yet to catch up to the policies of the leagues they participate in, traditional sex boundaries are being transformed from assumed biological sameness to cultural affinity. Beards and penises are no longer immediate grounds for exclusion in lesbian softball leagues with radical transinclusive policies. The consequences of such cultural re-negotiations of common sense assumptions about sex difference for identity and social organization are impossible to predict. We wonder how shifting criteria will further adapt in the face of transwomen who reject hormonal and surgical alteration. We expect that formerly women-only spaces may be queered and reconfigured in ways that we have yet to imagine.

[. . .]

References

Boyd, N. A. 2006. "Bodies in Motion: Lesbian and Transsexual Histories." Pp. 420–33 in *The Transgender Studies Reader*, edited by S. Stryker and S. Whittle. New York/London: Routledge.

Dozier, R. 2005. "Beards, Breasts and Bodies: Doing Sex in a Gendered World." *Gender and Society* 297–316.

Fausto-Sterling, A. 2000. *Sexing the Body: Gender Politics and the Construction of Sexuality*. New York: Basic Books.

Gillis, S., J. Howie, and R. Munford. 2004. *Third Wave Feminism: A Critical Exploration*. New York: Palgrave.

Noble, J. B. 2006. *Sons of the Movement: FTMS Risking Incoherence on a Post-Queer Cultural Landscape*. Toronto: Women's Press.

Sykes, H. 2006. "Transsexual and Transgender Policies in Sport." *Women in Sport and Physical Activity Journal* 15:3–13.

Symons, C. and D. Hemphill. 2006. "Transgender Sex and Sport in the Gay Games." Pp. 109–28 in *Sport, Sexualities, and Queer/Theory*, edited by J. Caudwell. London/New York: Routledge.

Travers, A. 2006. "Queering Sport: Lesbian Softball Leagues and the Transgender Challenge." *International Review for the Sociology of Sport* 41:431–46.

Travers, A. 2008. "The Sport Nexus and Gender Injustice." *Studies in Social Justice Journal* 2:79–101.

"Silver Cups Versus Ice Creams"

Parental Involvement With the Construction of Gender in the Field of Their Son's Soccer

Inge Claringbould and Johanna Adriaanse

© iStockphoto.com/vgajic

This paper presents findings from a study that explored boys' soccer in the Netherlands as a space for the reproduction of gender by parents, and also as a space for the reproduction of gendered family values. It also examined the way in which parents challenged the construction of soccer as a masculine space. The central question guiding this project was: How do parents construct and negotiate gendered meanings in the

Inge Claringbould and Johanna Adriaanse. 2015. "'Silver Cups Versus Ice Creams': Parental Involvement With the Construction of Gender in the Field of Their Son's Soccer." *Sociology of Sport Journal* 32(2):201–19.

space of their son's soccer? The study is part of a larger investigation into constructions of meaning in the interaction between adults and youth in the space of youth club sport (see Claringbould, 2011; Janssen, 2010).

Soccer was chosen because it is the largest participation sport in the Netherlands (NOC*NSF, 2011). It is also a very male dominated sport, with nearly 1,070,000 male and 120,000 female members. Given that some 531,000 boys play soccer out of a total number of 970,000 boys who participate in a sports club, boys' soccer clearly plays a significant role in the lives of many families (NOC*NSF, 2011). We therefore assumed that the way gender is done in the space of soccer may inform the ideas and attitudes that boys develop toward gender in general.

[. . .]

Methods

Data were collected through 12 semistructured interviews and three observation sessions. Interview participants were six fathers and six mothers, all of whom were white and hetero-sexual. They all had at least one son, aged 8–16 years, who played soccer. . . .

The observations took place at the same soccer clubs where the interviewees were recruited. The first author watched several matches, two of these in the company of two mothers. Only matches were observed, since these were more often watched by parents than were weekly training sessions.

[. . .]

Both the observations and the interviews were conducted in 2010 at two (mostly white and upper to middle class) soccer clubs in the city of Utrecht. With more than 315,000 inhabitants, Utrecht is one of the largest cities in the Netherlands.

[. . .]

The Space: Constructing Borders

Both fathers and mothers acknowledged the different roles they played in the space of their son's soccer play. For example:

> A mother is standing on the sideline, watching a soccer match. She is cheering her 15-year old son. She has supported her son's soccer competition every Saturday for the last seven years. Apart from me (the observer), she is the only woman among 10 or 12 fathers. "That's the way it is, when these boys grow older, the mothers tend to withdraw, while the fathers tend to show up more often," she explains. When the boys were smaller, they even had a small group of "soccer mothers," but nowadays she is generally the only mother watching her son. Further, she explains that her own husband, like most fathers, is invited to act as linesman in matches. "They never ask mothers for these positions but it frees me from any kind of obligation." And, she adds, she would never want to be the only lines (wo)man. (Mother 6, Club 1) *(Fieldnotes, Feb. 2010)*

Other findings confirm the suggestion that, when children are young, mothers generally attend the soccer space more often. At games involving the youngest group of boys (the F-division, children aged 7–8 years), many mothers were present, sometimes even outnumbering fathers. The mothers stood along the sidelines ready to minister to their children with a towel, a banana, or a kiss. Children tended to cross the lines and run to their mothers if they were hurt, sometimes even during the match. Such behavior, however, had to be unlearned. As one father explained:

> I remember [that] mothers accompanied their children during the first years [of his son's membership]. I suppose these mothers felt that their child was still so small and vulnerable that they wanted to be there for them. But they disappeared after the F-division. Anyhow, from then on boys' soccer is concentrated around the fathers and mothers appear only rarely. (Father 1, club 1)

Another father suggested that, when children become older, they no longer need the care and emotional support of their mother.

The "main" play took place within the boundaries of the soccer field. This competition between two sides could be characterized as tough play that needed to be learned. The borders of the soccer field were strictly controlled by the fathers-as-linesmen. Outside these lines, however, was a safe space dominated by meanings about care and support for the boys. Since the borders were relatively easy to cross, these young soccer players could feel somewhat protected. In other words, the space was divided in subspaces by these lines, which represented the boundary between the "main" field and the "serving-the-main" field. These subspaces represented meanings of, respectively, "competitiveness and winning" (in the more important core soccer field) and "care and support" in the surrounding field.

Nonetheless, the "serving-the-main" field changed, since mothers disappeared as spectators when the children grew older:

> I must say, at this age, only very few women attend [their son's] matches, and if they do they are only interested in their own son and not in the team. For me . . . even if my son sits on the bench, I still enjoy the match and love to watch them win. (Father 2, Club 1)

This father is suggesting that the meaning of the "serving-the-main" field is different when the spectators are mostly men, since fathers tend to place more emphasis on the achievements of the whole team. In other words, the presence of the mother may mean that there is a main interest in the son's wellbeing, while the father generally represents interest in the son's or his team's achievements. At the same time, there is a disparaging tone in his voice when he speaks of "only" attending a match for your own son.

Positions in the Space: The "Natural" Gatekeepers

In the two participating soccer clubs, few women occupied positions as linesman, referee, coach or board member (see Table 43.1).

These figures indicate that the "main" field of soccer in these clubs was primarily controlled by men, while canteen work was predominantly done by women. In addition, mothers performed informal club work, such as planning rosters for driving children to away games at other clubs or organizing fundraising activities. These differences in the positions that fathers and mothers took in the space of soccer became visible at competition days.

> At competition days men are more visible than women. They move more, they take different positions, not only as supporter, but as linesmen, referee, coach or board member. You can see it in the ways they move. They literally "control" the field. (Fieldnotes, Feb. 2010)

Table 43.1 Division of Men's and Women's Voluntary Work in Both Clubs

	Soccer Club 1		Soccer Club 2	
	Men	**Women**	**Men**	**Women**
Board members	7	0	6	0
Coordinators/administrators	8	1	11	1
Coaches	41	2	127	16
Referees/linesmen	24	1	unknown	
Canteen personnel	unknown		3	7
Total	80	4	147	14

The habitus of parents naturalized the different positions fathers and mothers take up in the space. As one mother commented: "The role of coaches, referees, etc. is naturally a men's job. Soccer is men's business and men are more ambitious" (Mother 1, Club 2). When the interviewer asked a father why the voluntary positions were divided like this, he reflected: "I think they do not even think about the possibility to ask the mothers for coaching positions" (Father 5, Club 2). Male gate keeping was seen as a normal and enduring situation: "Soccer is a man's world. The coaches are generally fathers and they always like to interfere with the technical aspects of the game. Probably because they have all played the game themselves" (Father 6, Club 2). The field of soccer as a space where men are seen as the natural gatekeepers, however has impact upon the mother's position in the field. When the interviewer asked a woman why she did not want to become a referee, she answered:

In my head I hear them shout "stupid bitch," I don't even know if it is true, since I have never been a referee. But these are returning fears in my head . . . that women do not understand soccer. These notions about the ignorance of women's knowledge about soccer were pumped into my head in one or another way. (Mother 4, Club 1)

However a few women have taken up positions as coach or referee. As a space invader, they may challenge this image of the natural gatekeeper. . . .

. . . Gendered Parental Values

Parents commonly talked about the similarities between themselves and their partner in their support for their son's participation in sport. For example:

We [partner and I] agree on the fact that our son does some kind of sport. We haven't spoken much about it, but we have the same thoughts about it. Of course I arranged it for our son, although my husband would have done it if I hadn't. (Mother 2, Club 2)

At the same time, parents identified important differences between men and women in relation to the sport participation of their child:

Oh yes, there are differences . . . as spectators. If fathers watch the match, they know exactly what the score is and what happens. They naturally know. While mothers are engaged in matters like "how is he feeling" and "how is he developing socially." (Father 6, Club 2)

The fathers were clearly involved in expressing their "knowledge" about the "main" field, not only in the positions they took, but also as a man who has knowledge about soccer. As one father put it: "I try to contribute to the content, to increase my son's performance, because I have the knowledge to do so. And that is a big difference between my wife and me" (Father 2, Club 1).

The image of the knowledgeable father and ignorant mother was often presented by the interviewees. Such an image distinguishes the roles of fathers and mothers, and represents fairly traditional family values.

> Fathers were also said to be more emotionally involved with the performance of their son and/or his team. For example, some parents described how fathers tended to assume a dominant and visible position in the space: "Fathers are excited and heated, and mothers are calm. If the son is successful, a father shouts out loud, and he gets enraged if some of the other players kick his son." (Father 3, Club 1)

In contrast, mothers—if they were involved at all—supported their son's attendance at training and matches and were the ones who cared about the physical and emotional wellbeing of their children. As one father remarked: "If women are chilly they know their son is too. Women know these things, and they put an extra shirt in his bag . . . and I don't feel responsible for these kinds of things, that is his own business" (Father 1, Club 1).

This example also illustrates how the mother's positions are marginalized by fathers. Mothers kept an eye on their son's (emotional) experiences and developments. One mother described how she sometimes tried to "be" there for her son after he lost a match. She related how she tries to put his performance into perspective:

> I express my sympathy and tell him he did a good job anyhow. But he does not want to hear my voice and says "shut up" or something.
>
> Interviewer: How do you feel about that?
>
> Eh . . . let me think, in a way it is a normal situation if a boy of 15 tells his mother, "well what do you know about it?" . . . But he has a different look in his eyes if his father says something, [then] he is more impressed.
>
> Interviewer: Why is that?
>
> I think because his father has played soccer himself. (Mother 2, Club 2)

This exchange illustrates how the son marginalizes his mother's input by dismissing her care because she lacks knowledge about the "main" field. Strikingly, the woman defines her son's derogatory behavior toward her as "normal." In other words, boys in a public and masculine space, such as soccer, may need to withdraw from their mothers.

It is evident that fathers and mothers both privileged the idea of having their son participate in sport, but they embodied a different habitus and took different positions in their involvement with their son's sport. Gendered parental involvement, however, may also interact with gendered characteristics in the space. This is discussed in more detail below.

. . . Meanings Given to Masculinities

Most parents agreed that many fathers believe that soccer is unique in relation to other sports. One mother, for example, remarked:

I don't mind whether he [son] plays tennis or soccer . . . but my husband is crazy about soccer, so he urges my son to participate. . . . It is like . . . he would be very disappointed if Sam played korfball instead. He thinks korfball is nothing, it's a sissy sport. I actually do not understand what's wrong with it. (Mother 4, Club 1)

In other words, this father reproduced the boundary between "real" or dominant versus "sissy" or subordinate masculinities as symbolized by different sports. Here, soccer represents the sport for "real men." The example also shows the commitment of this father to the son's development of a "real" masculinity through soccer. The mother highlighted the consequences for her son's relationship with his father if he did not conform to the desired masculine practice of playing soccer—the father would be "very disappointed." By adopting such a position, fathers may not only increase the pressure on sons to perform as "real" men, but may also create possibilities for parent and child to bond or to drift apart.

A different perspective was provided by some fathers who were quite critical about other fathers' involvement and its possible negative impacts. For example:

Generally speaking, I would say that mothers encourage their sons, while fathers criticize.

Interviewer: Why is that?

Because fathers emphasize performance, they want their son to do better than they have done. They experience their son's failures as their own failures. . . . That is my conclusion, they project their own expectations onto their son, and want him to be better than themselves. (Father 2, Club 1)

The meaning of bonding through soccer as a typical "masculine" value among men was a recurring theme in the interviews. For example: "During a match you need to be tough on each other, but after the match you shake hands. I enjoy that. That is manly" (Father). This father not only defined "fighting" and "bonding" as typical masculine meanings expressed in the space, but he also identified a border between these meanings(before and after the match). In other words appropriate masculinities not only depend on the spatial context, but also on the event taking place in the space.

At times, mothers also loudly cheered for their sons on the field. One mother said she had a strong emotional bond with her son's soccer. She did not, however, focus on her son's achievements but on their shared interest and enthusiasm for the sport.

In contrast to stories about the emotional involvement of fathers (and some mothers) with their son's soccer, parents also described mothers' emotional withdrawal from their son's soccer:

Soccer is the ultimate enemy of feminists and my wife is one. They are disgusted by the language used at the soccer club, the riots and aggression. And she is right, since it is embarrassing and reprehensible sometimes. But in my opinion it's still fun . . . so to her it must be quite horrible to have four men playing soccer in the family. (Father 4, Club 1)

One father even explained that his wife had left the club, due to his behavior: "She dislikes the language I use on the field. She cannot cope with that. I spoil her pleasure, so she prefers to go somewhere else" (Father 3, Club 1). It was not only mothers, however, who tended to withdraw from the hyper masculine behavior of some fathers on the soccer field. Some fathers provided a more critical perspective on the masculinities done in the space of their son's soccer:

> I try to keep some distance from my son's matches, to offer him possibilities to enjoy the match. He plays in a selective team, and other fathers continuously judge the achievements of all the boys, the coach and the referee . . . aloud. . . . This attitude, it makes me feel sick. I see these boys looking at their father, thinking "shut up, you." So, I now distance myself from other fathers and am not involved in these discussions anymore. (Father 4, Club 1)

These examples show that some forms of hyper masculinity continue to dominate in the space of soccer, while femininities and alternative forms of masculinities remain subordinate.

Contested Meanings: Space Invaders

Although most fathers and mothers believed it would be better if the involvement of parents in positions in soccer was more equally divided between men and women, they were convinced that changes would be hard to realize. Nonetheless, a few mothers challenged the stereotypical position taking of men by becoming involved in coaching their son's team. Here we focus on the stories of two such mothers who were interviewed. These mothers coached their son's team, a position they shared with a father. Clearly, such a small sample cannot be taken as representative of women coaches, but they do represent some women in this study and combined with our observations their stories shed valuable light on the experiences of a "space invader." They form an important source of evidence to our understanding of mothers as "insider as outsider" by illustrating how the process of invasion might take place (see Puwar, 2004). The experiences of these mothers are described in two contexts: with their son and with their colleagues.

One mother described her experience in relation to her son:

> My son did not like me being his coach. That had to do with an argument we once had. I was his coach and stood along the sidelines. I shouted that he had to change position from striker to playing in the mid-field. Everyone had to change places now and then, but he didn't want to. He said: "I want to be striker" and I said "You don't get to decide." I felt horrible to have this struggle with my son, openly . . . a mother being in charge. Well, I finally had to take him off the soccer field, because he did not want to listen and that was devastating for him. (Mother 2, Club 2)

This mother observed other signs that her son did not like her being the coach. For example, when she shouted instructions to him or his team he reacted by putting his fingers in his ears, and when she asked him why he acted like that, he responded by saying "after all, this is not funny" and she noticed he then looked very angry. Sometimes he even said "I wish dad was there." The woman went on to explain that she had considered withdrawing from coaching his team for a few years, so her son could develop more freely. In accordance with her "serving" role, in other words, the mother tried to understand her son's position, and from that perspective she intended to withdraw from the space.

This argument between the mother and son reflects a form of dominant masculinity that constructs a hierarchy between men and women. One father alluded to this construction when he stated that he felt quite uncomfortable with the idea of a woman being in charge of him:

Listen, if I were a soccer player and I had to listen to a woman coach, I must admit that I would have problems with that.

Interviewer: Why?

By nature, I don't know why. If I had a women boss . . . after all, I'd have trouble with that too. It's just a feeling. It does not mean they [women] don't have enough sense to do it. . . . I just cannot bear a woman telling me how to play, it won't work. (Father 5, Club 2)

Another mother shared coaching her son's team with a father in the F-division. The mother mentioned that they disagreed on substituting young players when the team was losing. In her opinion, all boys at this level should play the same amount of time regardless of the score. The father, however, preferred not to substitute a boy who was playing well when the team was behind:

He was crazy about it, he insisted on doing it his way and I thought it was ridiculous. So we always disagreed on this point.

Interviewer: Where do you think these differences come from?

Mother: Performance . . . he always wanted to win, and so do the children . . . but he's extremely eager to win. I remember another time . . . after a match we always took penalties, and one time he had bought silver cups for all the players. He likes those kind of heroic awards, while I prefer to spend money on eating ice cream together at the end of the competition. . . . It escalated at a certain moment, he could be very tough on the boys. . . . There was a boy who had just got on the soccer field, he was a bit of a softy and, because he missed a ball, a goal was scored by the opposing team. The father started shouting at the boy and substituted him again which was ridiculous, because he had only just got on. I said: "Look, the boy is eight years old and you yell at him. We had agreed that I would substitute the players and not you." And then, when the boy was in tears, the father said to me: "Why don't you go to him, because I'm not so good at cheering up and talking." So I replied: "I don't think so, this is your job, I'm not going to fix it for you." So now I prefer not to be involved in coaching for a while. That experience really turned me off. (Mother 5, Club 1)

The argument between the mother and her colleague was not primarily about equal playing time; the main issue was that the mother valued this above winning. She insisted on another value system with these young athletes. She prioritized equal opportunity above performance. However, the argument had such an effect on her that, although she had taken a position in a man's space, she decided to (temporarily) withdraw. While this was her decision, it is questionable how "voluntary" her withdrawal was. Although women may be blamed for leaving the space, the situation may also be interpreted as a (conscious or unconscious) strategy to eliminate space invaders who want to change the meaningful order of the positions and habitus.

Discussion and Conclusion

[. . .]

Our study showed that a border divided the "main" field from the "serving-the-main" field. The "main" field was controlled by several formal positions that are generally taken by men.

In the "serving-the-main" field, mothers dominated when their sons were young, but this space changed as the boys grew older. We characterized this space as a place where masculine bodies and positions replaced female bodies and positions. As a result, the boys who play soccer are forced from a relatively safe and caring space into a more insecure space due to "natural" processes of getting older and becoming a man, which includes learning masculinities. Consequently, boys may experience pressure to perform well in the game and play like "a man."

Although fathers replaced mothers in the "serving-the-main" field, they took a different position. They supervised the "main" field by expressing their knowledge and technical insights. In other words, the "serving-the-main" field changed from a supportive to a supervising space, which assumed a different status position toward the "main" field. This suggests a dominant rather than subordinate status position toward the "main" field. While other scholars have found that fathers contribute to the way in which their sons learn masculinities in the space of soccer (see e.g., Kay, 2009; Shaw & Dawson, 2001), our study has emphasized how this process of learning masculinities is maintained and sustained within specific (sub) spaces and positions.

[. . .]

The process whereby boys learn masculinities interacts with the separation between the "main" and the "serving-the-main" field. Learning masculinities involved sons disconnecting from the supportive "serving-the-main" field as represented by mothers. In accordance with their role in "serving-the main" field, mothers withdrew from this public space for the sake of their son's development. In doing so, they reaffirmed the *status quo* of soccer clubs as a space for boys to develop a more traditional masculine habitus.

. . . The alternative scenario—when mothers tried to challenge this habitus by taking a position as a coach—can be interpreted using the notion of a space invader. The few women who had become coaches had only done so at the youngest age groups of their son's soccer. They could be seen as space invaders since they challenged the dominant constructions of the "main" field. As one such mother expressed it, these contrasting meanings can be symbolically represented as "silver cups" versus "ice creams." The few mothers who acted as soccer coaches failed to transform the field, due to the power of the symbolic violence they experienced within the space of their son's soccer. They were viewed as "invaders" which made them feel uncomfortable and therefore they preferred to withdraw from the field.

[. . .]

References

Claringbould, I. 2011. *Sport is geen kinderspel. Een onderzoek naar de betrokkenheid van volwassenen bij jeugdsport in sportverenigingen* (Sport Is Not a Children's Game: The Involvement of Adults in Youth Sports at Sportclubs). Nieuwegein, The Netherlands: W.J.H. Mulier Instituut/Arko Sports Media.

Janssen, M. 2010. "Buitenspel [Offside]." Master thesis, Utrecht University, The Netherlands.

Kay, T. 2009. "Fathers and Sons: Being 'Father Angel.'" Pp. 106–23 in *Fathering Through Sport and Leisure*, edited by T. Kay. New York: Routledge.

NOC*NSF. 2011. *Ledental Rapportage 2010*. Retrieved March 6, 2013 (http://www.nocnsf.nl/cms/showpage.aspx?id=7667).

Puwar, N. 2004. *Space Invaders: Race, Gender and Bodies Out of Place*. Oxford, England: Berg Publishers.

Shaw, S. M. and C. Dawson. 2001. "Purposive Leisure: Examining Parental Discourses on Family Activities." *Leisure Sciences* 23:217–31. doi:10.1080/01490400152809098.

PART IX

Work and Organizations

Workplaces are fundamental spaces in which inequalities are reinforced, negotiated, and resisted. Gender scholars have extensively researched how gender inequalities operate at the individual, interactional, and organizational level in workplaces. This section examines gender and sexuality across the four core themes of the reader: intersectionality, masculinity, transgender, and global (IMTG) perspectives. The pieces touch on a range of issues in the field of work and organizations from gendered practices and negotiations in work and family, to intersections of inequalities across gender-segregated industries, to work involving transnational migration.

Examining gendered practices within workplaces, Joan Acker's "Inequality Regimes" uncovers the various processes and practices that produce and reinforce patterns of inequality in the workplace. Acker defines inequality regimes as "loosely interrelated practices, processes, and meanings that result in and maintain class, gender, and racial inequalities within particular organizations." She considers the bases of inequality and then lays out the organizing processes that produce these inequalities. Acker also highlights possibilities for change, considering successful efforts in the past such as increased representation of all women, men of color in employment opportunities, and pay equity initiatives.

In Sarah Damaske's "A 'Major Career Woman'?" the interview study is conducted with a race- and class-diverse sample of women and examines expectations around work. Damaske finds that women expect to spend much of their adulthood in the workforce. Yet while middle-class women and working-class African American women expect to be employed throughout their adulthood, they differ from White and Latina working-class women who instead view their employment as occasional. Middle-class women—White, Asian, African American, and Latina—describe strong expectations that they will work throughout their lives. African American working-class women also take continual work for granted. Yet, working-class White and Latina women are more likely to imagine working part-time or taking breaks and more likely to see their work as "helping out" rather than as making a substantial contribution to their family income. Class and race intersect in shaping women's expectations about their employment and family prospects.

Adia Harvey Wingfield considers men's experience in a women-dominated field in "Racializing the Glass Escalator." Previous research suggests that men advance more quickly when they are in jobs dominated by women, such as nursing. Yet, based on her in-depth interviews with Black men nurses, Harvey Wingfield finds that while White men in nursing ride the glass escalator in pay and promotions, Black men face "glass barriers" that prevent them from benefiting from these opportunities. Interactions with patients and mostly White female coworkers reinforce inequalities from which Black men do not benefit. Rather than being viewed as competent and deserving of promotion, Black men are misrecognized as janitors. Rather than riding the glass escalator, Harvey Wingfield finds that Black men in nursing face glass barriers to advancement.

Through interviews and observations of employees at a gay adult film studio on the U.S. West Coast, Nathaniel Burke's article, "Hegemonic Masculinity at Work in the Gay Adult Film Industry," shows how intersecting dynamics of gender and sexuality surface within the context of the gay adult film industry. As Burke argues, the "local" hegemonic masculinity in this gay-oriented workplace continues to subordinate femininity as well as reinforce racialized understandings of masculinity. Staff and casting agents categorize models as hirable, or not, based on their perceptions of racialized bodies as potential hires. They police these boundaries by engaging in femophobic discourse, referring to actors viewed as difficult as "she" and "her," or when their bodies are viewed as too old or unattractive. This industry reinforces racially sexualized bodies and particular types of bodies while subordinating femininity, suggesting that even marginalized groups mobilize and bolster hegemonic masculinity.

In their interview study "Do Workplace Gender Transitions Make Gender Trouble?" Kristen Schilt and Catherine Connell find that coworkers of transgender employees who transition at work often reaffirm belief in a rigid gender binary during their attempts to demonstrate acceptance of their transgender colleagues. While it may seem that open transitioning at work would challenge notions of gender hierarchies, in fact, these processes seem instead to shore up existing gender hierarchies. While some transmen and transwomen are relieved when colleagues' gendered expectations change, others note a loss of relationships and distance from coworkers who once shared their gender. Transmen and women also describe an array of reactions and changes in interactions with coworkers, which all tend to highlight and reinscribe gender binaries and inequalities. Through these workplace transitions, transgender people describe gender hierarchy, heteronormativity, and sexism as reinforced rather than troubled by their colleagues.

Finally, in her ethnographic study "Beyond the Industrial Paradigm," Eileen Otis examines the global gendered underpinnings within two luxury hotels in China. Although workers at both hotels are enacting the same corporate template for how to provide good service, their location leads them to perform service differently. In cosmopolitan Beijing, frontline women service workers are trained to perform "virtual personalism," preemptively catering to Western businessmen customer preferences through enacting a form of U.S. middle-class femininity. These workers incorporate extroverted femininity with "giving face" in service interactions, learning to perform deference not as a form of care but as an inauthentic performance that they control. In contrast, in the smaller city of Kunming, workers enact "virtuous professionalism," where they display expertise through performing a more formal and less intimate form of femininity that seeks to distinguish themselves from sex workers and ideas that they are unsophisticated. By comparing the everyday labor practices of workers at these two luxury hotels, the study shows how workers are situated within particular local consumer markets, both of which rely on gendered labor relations that are shaped by the global service industry.

The pieces in this section show how gender, along with other relevant factors such as class, race, sexuality, and location, underlie workplace interactions and inequalities. Even as workplaces change, they continue to support particular notions of gender difference, as when femininity is subordinated in a workplace for gay adult films or coworkers emphasize binary gender differences when workers openly transition. Yet gender shapes interactions differently, depending on context, as when Black men nurses do not benefit from "glass escalators" or Chinese women workers perform service differently based on their specific locality.

Inequality Regimes

Gender, Class, and Race in Organizations

Joan Acker

© iStockphoto.com/Kerkez

M uch of the social and economic inequality in the United States and other industrial countries is created in organizations, in the daily activities of working and organizing the work. Union activists have grounded their demands in this understanding, as have feminist and civil rights reformers. Class analyses, at least since Harry Braverman's 1974 dissection of *Labor and Monopoly Capital* have often examined the doing of work, the labor process, to understand how class inequalities are produced and perpetuated (Burawoy 1979). Feminists have looked at the gendering of organizations and organizational practices to comprehend how inequalities between women and men continue in the face of numerous attempts to erase such inequalities (Acker 1990; Collinson and Hearn 1996; Ferguson 1984; Kanter 1977). Scholars working on race inequality have examined the production in work organizations of racial disparities that contribute to society-wide racial discrimination and disadvantage (Brown et al. 2003; Royster 2003).

Joan Acker. 2006. "Inequality Regimes: Gender, Class, and Race in Organizations." *Gender & Society* 20(4):441–64.

Most studies of the production of class, gender, and racial inequalities in organizations have focused on one or another of these categories, rarely attempting to study them as complex, mutually reinforcing or contradicting processes. But focusing on one category almost inevitably obscures and oversimplifies other interpenetrating realities. Feminist scholars of color have argued for 30 years, with the agreement of most white feminist scholars, that much feminist scholarship was actually about white middle-class women, ignoring the reality that the category gender is fundamentally complicated by class, race/ethnicity, and other differences (Davis 1981; hooks 1984; Joseph 1981). Similar criticisms can be made of much theory and research on race and class questions: "race," even when paired with "ethnicity," encapsulates multiple social realities always inflected through gender and class differences. "Class" is also complicated by multiple gendered and racialized differences. The conclusion to this line of thinking—theory and research on inequality, dominance, and oppression must pay attention to the intersections of, at least, race/ethnicity, gender, and class.

[...]

Inequality Regimes

All organizations have inequality regimes, defined as loosely interrelated practices, processes, actions, and meanings that result in and maintain class, gender, and racial inequalities within particular organizations. The ubiquity of inequality is obvious: Managers, executives, leaders, and department heads have much more power and higher pay than secretaries, production workers, students, or even professors. Even organizations that have explicit egalitarian goals develop inequality regimes over time, as considerable research on egalitarian feminist organizations has shown (Ferree and Martin 1995; Scott 2000).

I define inequality in organizations as systematic disparities between participants in power and control over goals, resources, and outcomes; workplace decisions such as how to organize work; opportunities for promotion and interesting work; security in employment and benefits; pay and other monetary rewards; respect; and pleasures in work and work relations. Organizations vary in the degree to which these disparities are present and in how severe they are. Equality rarely exists in control over goals and resources, while pay and other monetary rewards are usually unequal. Other disparities may be less evident, or a high degree of equality might exist in particular areas, such as employment security and benefits.

Inequality regimes are highly various in other ways; they also tend to be fluid and changing. These regimes are linked to inequality in the surrounding society, its politics, history, and culture. Particular practices and interpretations develop in different organizations and subunits.

[...]

What Varies? The Components of Inequality Regimes

The Bases of Inequality

The bases for inequality in organizations vary, although class, gender, and race processes are usually present. "Class," as I use the term, refers to enduring and systematic differences in access to and control over resources for provisioning and survival (Acker 2006; Nelson 1993). Those resources are primarily monetary in wealthy industrial societies. Some class practices take place as employment occurs and wages are paid. Thus, class is intrinsic to employment and to most organizations. In large organizations, hierarchical positions are congruent with class processes in the wider society. The CEO of the large corporation operates at the top of the national and often global society. In smaller organizations, the class structure may not be so congruent with society-wide class relations, but the owner or the boss still has class power in relations with employees. "Class" is defined by inequality; thus, "class equality" is an oxymoron (Ferguson 1984).

Gender, as socially constructed differences between men and women and the beliefs and identities that support difference and inequality, is also present in all organizations. Gender was, in the not too distant past, almost completely integrated with class in many organizations. That is, managers were almost always men; the lower-level white-collar workers were always women. Class relations in the workplace, such as supervisory practices or wage-setting processes, were shaped by gendered and sexualized attitudes and assumptions. The managerial ranks now contain women in many organizations, but secretaries, clerks, servers, and care providers are still primarily women. Women are beginning to be distributed in organizational class structures in ways that are similar to the distribution of men. Gender and class are no longer so perfectly integrated, but gendered and sexualized assumptions still shape the class situations of women and men in different ways.

"Race" refers to socially defined differences based on physical characteristics, culture, and historical domination and oppression, justified by entrenched beliefs. Ethnicity may accompany race, or stand alone, as a basis for inequality. Race, too, has often been integrated into class hierarchies, but in different patterns than gender. Historically, in the United States, women and men of color were confined to the lowest-level jobs or excluded from all but certain organizations. People of color were totally excluded from the most powerful (white, male) organizations that were central in shaping the racialized and gendered class structure of the larger society. For example, the twentieth-century U.S. military was, until after World War II, a racially segregated organization dominated by white men. Other examples are the elite universities such as Harvard and Yale.

Other differences are sometimes bases for inequality in organizations. The most important, I believe, is sexuality. Heterosexuality is assumed in many organizing processes and in the interactions necessary to these processes. The secretary is or was the "office wife" (Kanter 1977). Homosexuality is disruptive of organizing processes because it flouts the assumptions of heterosexuality. It still carries a stigma that produces disadvantages for lesbians and gays. Other bases of inequality are religion, age, and physical disability. Again, in the not too distant past, having the wrong religion such as being a Jew or a Catholic could activate discriminatory practices. Today, having a Middle Eastern origin or being a Muslim may have similar consequences. Currently, age seems to be a significant basis for inequality, as are certain physical inabilities. I believe that although these other differences are important, they are not, at this time, as thoroughly embedded in organizing processes as are gender, race, and class.

[. . .]

Organizing Processes That Produce Inequality

Organizations vary in the practices and processes that are used to achieve their goals; these practices and processes also produce class, gender, and racial inequalities. Considerable research exists exploring how class or gender inequalities are produced, both formally and informally, as work processes are carried out (Acker 1989, 1990; Burawoy 1979; Cockburn

1985; Willis 1977). Some research also examines the processes that result in continuing racial inequalities. These practices are often guided by textual materials supplied by consultants or developed by managers influenced by information and/or demands from outside the organization. To understand exactly how inequalities are reproduced, it is necessary to examine the details of these textually informed practices.

Organizing the general requirements of work. The general requirements of work in organizations vary among organizations and among organizational levels. In general, work is organized on the image of a white man who is totally dedicated to the work and who has no responsibilities for children or family demands other than earning a living. Eight hours of continuous work away from the living space, arrival on time, total attention to the work, and long hours if requested are all expectations that incorporate the image of the unencumbered worker. Flexibility to bend these expectations is more available to high-level managers, predominantly men, than to lower-level managers (Jacobs and Gerson 2004). Some professionals, such as college professors, seem to have considerable flexibility, although they also work long hours. Lower-level jobs have, on the whole, little flexibility. Some work is organized as part-time, which may help women to combine work and family obligations, but in the United States, such work usually has no benefits such as health care and often has lower pay than full-time work (Mishel, Bernstein, and Boushey 2003). Because women have more obligations outside of work than do men, this gendered organization of work is important in maintaining gender inequality in organizations and, thus, the unequal distribution of women and men in organizational class hierarchies. Thus, gender, race, and class inequalities are simultaneously created in the fundamental construction of the working day and of work obligations.

Organizing class hierarchies. Techniques also vary for organizing class hierarchies inside work organizations. Bureaucratic, textual techniques for ordering positions and people are constructed to reproduce existing class, gender, and racial inequalities (Acker 1989). I have been unable to find much research on these techniques, but I do have my own observations of such techniques in one large job classification system from my study of comparable worth (Acker 1989). Job classification systems describe job tasks and responsibilities and rank jobs hierarchically. Jobs are then assigned to wage categories with jobs of similar rank in the same wage category. Our study found that the bulk of sex-typed women's jobs, which were in the clerical/secretarial area and included thousands of women workers, were described less clearly and with less specificity than the bulk of sex-typed men's jobs, which were spread over a wide range of areas and levels in the organization. The women's jobs were grouped into four large categories at the bottom of the ranking, assigned to the lowest wage ranges; the men's jobs were in many more categories extending over a much wider range of wage levels. Our new evaluation of the clerical/secretarial categories showed that many different jobs with different tasks and responsibilities, some highly skilled and responsible, had been lumped together. The result was, we argued, an unjustified gender wage gap: Although women's wages were in general lower than those of men, women's skilled jobs were paid much less than men's skilled jobs, reducing even further the average pay for women when compared with the average pay for men. . . .

In the past 30 years, many organizations have removed some layers of middle management and relocated some decision making to lower organizational levels. These changes have been described as getting rid of the inefficiencies of old bureaucracies, reducing hierarchy and inequality, and empowering lower-level employees. This happened in two of the organizations

I have studied—Swedish banks in the late 1980s (Acker 1991) . . . and the Oregon Department of Adult and Family Services, responsible for administration of Temporary Assistance to Needy Families and welfare reform (Morgen, Acker, and Weigt n.d.). In both cases, the decision-making responsibilities of frontline workers were greatly increased, and their jobs became more demanding and more interesting. In the welfare agency, ordinary workers had increased participation in decisions about their local operations. But the larger hierarchy did not change in either case. The frontline employees were still on the bottom; they had more responsibility, but not higher salaries. And they had no increased control over their job security. In both cases, the workers liked the changes in the content of their jobs, but the hierarchy was still inviolate.

In sum, class hierarchies in organizations, with their embedded gender and racial patterns, are constantly created and renewed through organizing practices. Gender and sometimes race, in the form of restricted opportunities and particular expectations for behavior, are reproduced as different degrees of organizational class hierarchy and are also reproduced in everyday interactions and bureaucratic decision making.

Recruitment and hiring. Recruitment and hiring is a process of finding the worker most suited for a particular position. From the perspectives of employers, the gender and race of existing jobholders at least partially define who is suitable, although prospective coworkers may also do such defining (Enarson 1984). Images of appropriate gendered and racialized bodies influence perceptions and hiring. White bodies are often preferred, as a great deal of research shows (Royster 2003). Female bodies are appropriate for some jobs; male bodies for other jobs.

A distinction should be made between the gendered organization of work and the gender and racial characteristics of the ideal worker. Although work is organized on the model of the unencumbered (white) man, and both women and men are expected to perform according to this model, men are not necessarily the ideal workers for all jobs. The ideal worker for many jobs is a woman, particularly a woman who, employers believe, is compliant, who will accept orders and low wages (Salzinger 2003). This is often a woman of color; immigrant women are sometimes even more desirable (Hossfeld 1994).

Hiring through social networks is one of the ways in which gender and racial inequalities are maintained in organizations. Affirmative action programs altered hiring practices in many organizations, requiring open advertising for positions and selection based on gender- and race-neutral criteria of competence, rather than selection based on an old boy (white) network. These changes in hiring practices contributed to the increasing proportions of white women and people of color in a variety of occupations. However, criteria of competence do not automatically translate into gender- and race-neutral selection decisions. "Competence" involves judgment: The race and gender of both the applicant and the decision makers can affect that judgment, resulting in decisions that white males are the more competent, more suited to the job than are others. Thus, gender and race as a basis for hiring or a basis for exclusion have not been eliminated in many organizations, as continuing patterns of segregation attest.

Wage setting and supervisory practices. Wage setting and supervision are class practices. They determine the division of surplus between workers and management and control the work process and workers. Gender and race affect assumptions about skill, responsibility, and a fair wage for jobs and workers, helping to produce wage differences (Figart, Mutari, and Power 2002).

Wage setting is often a bureaucratic organizational process, integrated into the processes of creating hierarchy, as I described above. Many different wagesetting systems exist, many of them producing gender and race differences in pay. Differential gender-based evaluations may be embedded in even the most egalitarian-appearing systems. For example, in my study of Swedish banks in the 1980s, a pay gap between women and men was increasing within job categories in spite of gender equality in wage agreements between the union and employers (Acker 1991). Our research revealed that the gap was increasing because the wage agreement allowed a small proportion of negotiated increases to be allocated by local managers to reward particularly high-performing workers. These small increments went primarily to men; over time, the increases produced a growing gender gap. In interviews we learned that male employees were more visible to male managers than were female employees. I suspected that the male managers also felt that a fair wage for men was actually higher than a fair wage for women. I drew two implications from these findings: first, that individualized wage-setting produces inequality, and second, that to understand wage inequality it is necessary to delve into the details of wage-setting systems.

Supervisory practices also vary across organizations. Supervisory relations may be affected by the gender and race of both supervisor and subordinate, in some cases preserving or reproducing gender or race inequalities. For example, above I described how women and men in the same aspiranter job classification in Swedish banks were assigned to different duties by their supervisors. Supervisors probably shape their behaviors with subordinates in terms of race and gender in many other work situations, influencing in subtle ways the existing patterns of inequality. Much of this can be observed in the informal interactions of workplaces.

Informal interactions while "doing the work." A large literature exists on the reproduction of gender in interactions in organizations (Reskin 2003; Ridgeway 1997). The production of racial inequalities in workplace interactions has not been studied so frequently (Vallas 2003), while the reproduction of class relations in the daily life of organizations has been studied in the labor process tradition, as I noted above. The informal interactions and practices in which class, race, and gender inequalities are created in mutually reinforcing processes have not so often been documented, although class processes are usually implicit in studies of gendered or racialized inequalities.

As women and men go about their everyday work, they routinely use gender-, race-, and class-based assumptions about those with whom they interact, as I briefly noted above in regard to wage setting. Body differences provide clues to the appropriate assumptions, followed by appropriate behaviors. What is appropriate varies, of course, in relation to the situation, the organizational culture and history, and the standpoints of the people judging appropriateness. For example, managers may expect a certain class deference or respect for authority that varies with the race and gender of the subordinate; subordinates may assume that their positions require deference and respect but also find these demands demeaning or oppressive. Jennifer Pierce (1995), in a study of two law firms, showed how both gendered and racialized interactions shaped the organizations' class relations: Women paralegals were put in the role of supportive, mothering aides, while men paralegals were cast as junior partners in the firms' business. African American employees, primarily women in secretarial positions, were acutely aware of the ways in which they were routinely categorized and subordinated in interactions with both paralegals and attorneys. The interaction practices that re-create gender and racial inequalities are often subtle and unspoken, thus difficult to document. White men may devalue and exclude white women and people of color by not listening to them in meetings, by not inviting them to join a group going out for a drink after work, by not seeking their opinions on workplace problems. Other practices, such as sexual harassment, are open and obvious to the victim, but not so obvious to others. In some organizations, such as those in the travel and hospitality industry, assumptions about good job performance may be sexualized: Women employees may be expected to behave and dress as sexually attractive women, particularly with male customers (Adkins 1995).

[...]

Can Inequality Regimes Change?

Inequality regimes can be challenged and changed. However, change is difficult and change efforts often fail. One reason is that owner and managerial class interests and the power those interests can mobilize usually outweigh the class, gender, and race interests of those who suffer inequality. Even where no obvious economic interests are threatened by changes, men managers and lower-level employees often insist on maintaining ongoing organizing patterns that perpetuate inequalities. For example, white masculine identity may be tied to small relative advantages in workplace power and income. Advantage is hard to give up: Increasing equality with devalued groups can be seen and felt as an assault on dignity and masculinity. Several studies have shown that these complicated motives on the part of white men, in particular, can scuttle efforts at organizational change, even when top management is supporting such change. For example, Cynthia Cockburn (1991) analyzed the multiple ways that men resisted equality efforts in four British organizations in spite of top-level support for these efforts. In the Oregon pay equity project (Acker 1989), some male unionists could not believe that women's work might be as skilled as theirs and thus deserve higher pay. The men maintained this objection even though their own wages would not be lowered if the women's wages were increased. It was as though their masculine self-respect depended, to a degree, on the differences in pay between women and men, not the actual level of pay.

Successful change projects seem to have had a number of common characteristics. First, change efforts that target a limited set of inequality-producing mechanisms seem to be the most successful. In addition, successful efforts appear to have combined social movement and legislative support outside the organization with active support from insiders. In addition, successful efforts often involve coercion or threat of loss. Both affirmative action and pay equity campaigns had these characteristics. Affirmative action programs sought to increase the employment opportunities for women of all races and men of color in organizations and jobs in which they had very low representation. The federal legislation required such programs, and similar equality efforts, in organizations that received government funds. Employers who did not follow the law were vulnerable to loss of funds. Pay equity projects, intended to erase wage inequality between women-predominant jobs and men-predominant jobs of equal value, were authorized primarily by state and local legislation and took place primarily in public-sector organizations. In both types of efforts, the mobilization of civil rights and women's movement groups was essential to success.

When the political climate changed, beginning in the 1980s, pressures against such equality-producing initiatives grew. By 2006, affirmative action programs had become mere bureaucratic paper shuffling in most organizations, undermined by a lack of outside enforcement and inside activism and by legal attacks by white men claiming reverse discrimination. Pay equity efforts were undermined by industrial restructuring, attacks on labor unions, delegitimation of the public sector, and legal attacks. Industrial restructuring began to undermine blue-collar, well-paid, male employment and to turn unions away from pay equity to the problems of their white male members and the defense of unions themselves against employer attacks. Unions had been prime actors in the pay equity movement; their relative weakening undermined the movement. Furthermore, government organizations came under attack in the era of private-sector, free market celebration, and funds for various programs including wage reforms were cut. When pay equity campaigns succeeded, wage gains were often modest, as, for example, the Oregon case showed (Acker 1989). The modest gains that did occur resulted from political compromise to keep costs down: The potential costs of raising clerical and other service workers' pay to comparable levels with skilled blue-collar workers or the pay of female-typed professions to the pay of male-typed professions were enormous. These potential costs were, I believe, the underlying reasons for legal challenges to pay equity (Nelson and Bridges 1999). Real pay equity extending into the private sector would have imposed huge increases in labor costs at the very time that employers were cutting their workforces, turning to temporary workers, outsourcing, and off-shoring jobs to save on labor costs.

The history of pay equity projects reveals a fundamental contradiction facing many efforts to reform inequality regimes: The goals of inequality reduction or elimination are the opposite of some of the goals of employing organizations, particularly in the United States at the beginning of the twenty-first century. In the private sector, management wants to reduce costs, increase profit, and distribute as much as possible of the profit to top management and shareholders. In the public sector, management wants to reduce costs and minimize taxes. Reducing costs involves reducing wages, not raising them, as pay equity would require. While wage inequality is not the only form of inequality, eliminating that inequality may be basic to dealing with other forms as well.

Another lesson of this history is that a focus on delimited areas of inequality, such as gender and racial imbalance in job categories or pay gaps between female and male jobs of equal value, do nothing to address underlying organizational class inequality. Both of these models of intervention work within the organizational class structure: Affirmative action intends to remove racial and gender barriers to entry into existing hierarchical positions; pay equity efforts compare male and female jobs and sometimes white predominant jobs and other-than-white predominant jobs within organizational class levels, not across those levels.

These interventions also fail to address other underlying processes of inequality regimes: the male model of organizing or the persistent gendering and racialization of interactions in the workplace. Family-friendly policies provide only temporary relief for some people from the male model of organizing. The use of family-friendly policies, primarily by women when they have young children, or the use of part-time work, again primarily involving women, may increase gender inequalities in organizations (Glass 2004). Such measures may reinforce, not undermine, the male model of organizing by defining those who conform to it as serious, committed workers and those who do not as rather peripheral and probably unworthy of promotions and pay increases (Hochschild 1997).

Diversity programs and policies seem to be often aimed at some of the more subtle discriminatory processes dividing organizational participants along lines of race/ethnicity and sometimes gender through education and consciousness raising. Diversity programs replaced, in many organizations, the affirmative action programs that came under attack. As Kelly and Dobbin (1998) point out, diversity programs lack the timetables, goals, and other proactive measures of affirmative action and may be more acceptable to management for that reason. But that may also be a reason that diversity training will not basically alter assumptions and actions that are rooted in the legitimation of systems of organizational power and reward that favor whites, particularly white men. The legitimacy of inequality, fear of retaliation, and cynicism limit support for change. The invisibility of inequality to those with privilege does not give way easily to entreaties to see what is going on. The intimate entwining of privilege with gendered and racialized identity makes privilege particularly difficult to unsettle.

Change projects focused on gendered behaviors that are dysfunctional for the organization provide examples of the almost unshakable fusion of gendered identities and workplace organizing practices. For example, Robin Ely and Debra Meyerson (2000) describe a change project aimed at discovering why a company had difficulty retaining high-level women managers and difficulty increasing the proportion of women in upper management. The researcher/change agents documented a culture and organizing practices at the executive level that rewarded stereotypical "heroic" male problem-solving behaviors, tended to denigrate women who attempted to be heroes, and failed to reward the mundane organization building most often done by women. Although members of the management group could see that these ways of behaving were dysfunctional for the organization, they did not make the links between these organizing practices, gender, and the underrepresentation of women. In their eyes, the low representation of women in top jobs was still due to the failure of individual women, not to system processes.

[. . .]

Conclusion

. . . I have suggested the idea of inequality regimes, interlinked organizing processes that produce patterns of complex inequalities. These processes and patterns vary in different organizations; the severity of inequalities, their visibility and legitimacy, and the possibilities for change toward less inequality also vary from organization to organization. In the United States at the present time, almost all organizations have two characteristics that rarely vary: Class inequality, inflected through gendered and racialized beliefs and practices, is the normal and natural bedrock of organizing, and white men are the normal and natural top leaders.

My second goal was to better understand why so many organizational equality projects have had only modest success or have failed altogether. Looking at organizations as inequality regimes may give some clues about why change projects designed to increase equality are so often less than successful. Change toward greater equality is possible, but difficult, because of entrenched economic (class) interests, the legitimacy of class interests, and allegiances to gendered and racialized identities and advantages. When class identities and interests are integrated with gender and racial identities and interests, opposition may be most virulent to any moves to alter the combined advantages. However, top male executives who are secure in their multiple advantages and privileges may be more supportive of reducing inequalities than male middle managers who may lose proportionately more through equality organizing.

Greater equality inside organizations is difficult to achieve during a period, such as the early years of the twenty-first century, in which employers are pushing for more inequality in pay, medical care, and retirement benefits and are using various tactics, such as downsizing and outsourcing, to reduce labor costs. Another major impediment to change within inequality regimes is the absence of broad social movements outside organizations agitating for such changes. In spite of all these difficulties, efforts at reducing inequality continue. Government regulatory agencies, the Equal Employment Opportunity Commission in particular, are still enforcing antidiscrimination laws that prohibit discrimination against specific individuals (see www.eeoc.gov/stats/). . . . The visibility of inequality seems to be increasing, and its legitimacy decreasing. Perhaps this is the opening move in a much larger, energetic attack on inequality regimes.

References

Acker, Joan. 1989. *Doing Comparable Worth: Gender, Class and Pay Equity.* Philadelphia, PA: Temple University Press.

Acker, Joan. 1990. "Hierarchies, Jobs, and Bodies: A Theory of Gendered Organizations." *Gender & Society* 4:139–58.

Acker, Joan. 1991. "Thinking About Wages: The Gendered Wage Gap in Swedish Banks." *Gender & Society* 5:390–407.

Acker, Joan. 2006. *Class Questions: Feminist Answers.* Lanham, MD: Rowman & Littlefield.

Adkins, Lisa. 1995. *Gendered Work.* Buckingham, UK: Open University Press.

Brown, M. K., M. Carnoy, E. Currie, T. Duster, D. B. Oppenheimer, M. M. Shultz, and D. Wellman. 2003. *White-Washing Race: The Myth of a Color-Blind Society.* Berkeley, CA: University of California Press.

Burawoy, Michael. 1979. *Manufacturing Consent.* Chicago, IL: University of Chicago Press.

Cockburn, Cynthia. 1985. *Machinery of Dominance.* London, UK: Pluto.

Cockburn, Cynthia. 1991. *In the Way of Women: Men's Resistance to Sex Equality in Organizations.* Ithaca, NY: ILR Press.

Collinson, David L. and Jeff Hearn, eds. 1996. *Men as Managers, Managers as Men.* London, UK: Sage.

Davis, Angela Y. 1981. *Women, Race & Class.* New York: Vintage.

Ely, Robin J. and Debra E. Meyerson. 2000. "Advancing Gender Equity in Organizations: The Challenge and Importance of Maintaining a Gender Narrative." *Organization* 7:589–608.

Enarson, Elaine. 1984. *Woods-Working Women: Sexual Integration in the U.S. Forest Service.* Tuscaloosa, AL: University of Alabama Press.

Ferguson, Kathy E. 1984. *The Feminist Case Against Bureaucracy.* Philadelphia, PA: Temple University Press.

Ferree, Myra Max and Patricia Yancey Martin, eds. 1995. *Feminist Organizations.* Philadelphia, PA: Temple University Press.

Figart, D. M., E. Mutari, and M. Power. 2002. *Living Wages, Equal Wages.* London, UK: Routledge.

Glass, Jennifer. 2004. "Blessing or Curse? Work-Family Policies and Mother's Wage Growth Over Time." *Work and Occupations* 31:367–94.

Hochschild, Arlie Russell. 1997. *The Time Bind: When Work Becomes Home & Home Becomes Work.* New York: Metropolitan Books.

hooks, bell. 1984. *Feminist Theory: From Margin to Center.* Boston, MA: South End.

Hossfeld, Karen J. 1994. "Hiring Immigrant Women: Silicon Valley's 'Simple Formula.'" In *Women of Color in U.S. Society,* edited by M. B. Zinn and B. T. Dill. Philadelphia, PA: Temple University Press.

Jacobs, Jerry A. and Kathleen Gerson. 2004. *The Time Divide: Work, Family, and Gender Inequality.* Cambridge, MA: Harvard University Press.

Joseph, Gloria. 1981. "The Incompatible Ménage á Trois: Marxism, Feminism and Racism." In *Women and Revolution: The Unhappy Marriage of Marxism and Feminism,* edited by L. Sargent. Boston, MA: South End.

Kanter, Rosabeth Moss. 1977. *Men and Women of the Corporation.* New York: Basic Books.

Kelly, Erin and Frank Dobbin. 1998. "How Affirmative Action Became Diversity Management: Employer Response to Antidiscrimination Law, 1961 to 1996." *American Behavioral Scientist* 41:960–85.

Mishel, L., J. Bernstein, and H. Boushey. 2003. *The State of Working America 2002/2003.* Ithaca, NY: Cornell University Press.

Morgen, S., J. Acker, and J. Weigt. n.d. *Neo-Liberalism on the Ground: Practising Welfare Reform.*

Nelson, Julie A. 1993. "The Study of Choice or the Study of Provisioning? Gender and the Definition of Economics." In *Beyond Economic Man: Feminist Theory and Economics,* edited by M. A. Ferber and J. A. Nelson. Chicago, IL: University of Chicago Press.

Nelson, Robert L. and William P. Bridges. 1999. *Legalizing Gender Inequality: Courts, Markets, and Unequal Pay for Women in America.* Cambridge, UK: Cambridge University Press.

Pierce, Jennifer L. 1995. *Gender Trials: Emotional Lives in Contemporary Law Firms.* Berkeley, CA: University of California Press.

Reskin, Barbara. 2003. "Including Mechanisms in Our Models of Ascriptive Inequality." *American Sociological Review* 68:1–21.

Ridgeway, Cecilia. 1997. "Interaction and the Conservation of Gender Inequality." *American Sociological Review* 62:218–35.

Royster, Deirdre A. 2003. *Race and the Invisible Hand: How White Networks Exclude Black Men from Blue-Collar Jobs*. Berkeley, CA: University of California Press.

Salzinger, Leslie. 2003. *Genders in Production: Making Workers in Mexico's Global Factories*. Berkeley, CA: University of California Press.

Scott, Ellen. 2000. "Everyone Against Racism: Agency and the Production of Meaning in the Antiracism Practices of Two Feminist Organizations." *Theory and Society* 29:785–819.

Vallas, Steven P. 2003. "Why Teamwork Fails: Obstacles to Workplace Change in Four Manufacturing Plants." *American Sociological Review* 68:223–50.

Willis, Paul. 1977. *Learning to Labor*. Farnborough, UK: Saxon House.

A "Major Career Woman"?

*How Women Develop Early
Expectations About Work*

Sarah Damaske

© iStockphoto.com/freemixer

nderstanding why some women spend the majority of their adult lives in the paid labor market, while other women perform work largely outside of the paid workforce, as homemakers and caregivers, long has been a central topic of gender scholarship (Blair-Loy 2003; Gerson 1985).

Sociologists have investigated the determinants of paid labor force participation from several perspectives, including opportunities available in the workforce (England 1992; Gerson 1985; Roth 2006), support that women receive at home (Blair-Loy 2003; Hochschild 1989; Stone 2007), and women's gender ideologies, particularly expectations about work formed during adolescence (Davis and Greenstein 2009; Moen, Erickson, and Dempster-McClain 1997;

Sarah Damaske. 2011. "A 'Major Career Woman'? How Women Develop Early Expectations About Work." *Gender & Society* 25(4):409–30.

Risman 1998). Young adulthood is a significant transitional period in women's work lives and early ideas about working influence future paid workforce participation and potential earnings as well as educational attainment and workforce skills (Goldin 2006; Risman, Atkinson, and Blackwelder 1999; Stickney and Konrad 2007). Since early expectations appear to influence a wide variety of outcomes, this article, using an intersectional approach, returns to the question of *how* women develop expectations about their future in the workforce.

Intersectional perspectives have greatly shaped the discussion of gender and work in recent years, as scholars criticized earlier research that tended to privilege white middle-class women (Collins 1991; Hansen 2005; Higginbotham 2001). Despite the growing consensus that gender interacts with class and race (Glauber 2008; McCall 2011), few studies have explored how race and class shape women's early work expectations or their experiences with work across the life course (Bettie 2003; Vespa 2009). Since there are lifelong economic consequences to participating in full-time versus part-time work (Spivey 2005) and working-class women, as well as women of color, have greater gaps in full-time employment during their lives than do their white middle-class counterparts, particularly at crucial early workforce stages (Alon and Haberfeld 2007; England, Ross, and Garcia-Beaulieu 2004), it is important to understand how gender, class, and race intersect in women's formation of their work expectations.

Using data from 80 in-depth qualitative interviews with women randomly sampled from New York City, I build on prior research on women's workforce participation by focusing on the intersection of gender, race, and class in the formation of women's early expectations about work. Specifically, I consider how women develop expectations about their future workforce participation. My primary goal is to understand women's perceptions of the labor market when they were at an age at which they first contemplated entering it, the intersection of gender, race, and class in shaping these perceptions, and how early experiences help form women's expectations of their own workforce participation.

[...]

Gender Ideologies and Expectations About Work

Gender ideologies are sets of beliefs that may guide marital decisions, workforce participation, and family formation; they are not static, but flexible and responsive to life changes, such as job opportunities and marital and parenthood status (Fan and Marini 2000; Hochschild 1989; Risman 1998; Vespa 2009). Since gender ideologies change across the life course, there is particular benefit in investigating gender ideologies at crucial transitional periods (Moen, Erickson, and Dempster-McClain 1997; Moen 2001). The transition to young adulthood is one such pivotal moment during which young adults make decisions (or anticipate making decisions) about "continuation of education, movement into and out of the labor force, entry into marriage, and becoming a parent" (Elder 1995; Fan and Marini 2000, 258).

Prevailing cultural gender schemas can bias people's expectations about women's ability to participate in paid work and can negatively influence a woman's expectations about her own abilities (Ridgeway and Correll 2004, 518). Women's expectations about the way that they will work may be shaped by the opportunities that they perceive will be available to them (or the constraints they expect to face) and their expectations about their own abilities (Baird 2007; Risman, Atkinson, and Blackwelder 1999).

[...]

For women, the decision to stay at home is only available to those who have another adult in the household who can fulfill the breadwinning role, typically a division of labor found only in heteronormative family formations in which a husband is the primary breadwinner and the wife the primary caregiver (Hansen 2005; Townsend 2002). Historically, gay and lesbian, working-class, and African American or Latino households have had less access to this gendered division of private and public spheres (Collins 1991; Garey 1999; Williams 2010). . . .

Structural inequalities that prevented men from earning family wages excluded many working-class families of all racial groups from this family norm (Hansen 2005; Higginbotham 2001). Historically, class has intersected with race in complicated ways to shape women's expectations of paid work. Since Black men historically earned much less than their white counterparts, African American communities depended on working mothers and never embraced motherhood as an acceptable alternative to full-time paid employment (Collins 1991; Landry 2000). . . . Research consistently finds that Black women grow up expecting to work and to support themselves through their own employment (Higginbotham 2001; Taylor 2000).

. . . Today, working-class white and Latino men are more likely to be viewed by employers as potential breadwinners and working fathers than their Black counterparts (Hamer 2001). . . .

Working-class white women also live in households in which women are expected to work and to weave workforce participation with caring for family (Garey 1999). . . . Moreover, although working-class white women were historically more likely to work than white middle-class women (Garey 1999), this trend has changed in recent years (England, Ross, and Garcia-Beaulieu 2004). . . .

These changing trends may mean that middle-class women have higher expectations about the opportunities available to them in the paid workforce and raised occupational aspirations as a result (Baird 2007; Bettie 2003).

Even though there is evidence that work and family experiences differ across race and class, there is a less well developed understanding of how differences in gender ideologies about work emerge. . . . Building an intersectional perspective into this question, we must also ask how working-class women and women of color develop frames to evaluate what their own workforce options will be and whom they consider similarly situated others.

Methods

From 2006 to 2007, I conducted in-depth qualitative interviews with 80 women selected in New York City (NYC) from the NYC Voter Registration database (NYCVRD). The NYCVRD is updated several times a year and includes contact and demographic information, including age, sex, and race. Eighty-seven percent of the eligible population in NYC is registered to vote (U.S. Census of the Bureau 2006). I used data from the 2000 U.S. Census to identify tracts most similar to the national population in terms of several key factors including race, gender, and women's workforce participation. I then used a combined ranking of income and education level to identify the tracts by class quartile, selecting one tract per quartile. Finally, I randomly selected women born between 1966 and 1976 living in the four tracts from the NYCVRD, using an electronic copy available for purchase.

I sent letters describing the study and inviting participation in the study and followed this with a phone call that screened for ineligible participants. I then made appointments with those who agreed to. . . . On average, the interviews lasted two to three hours, with the shortest at one hour and the longest at six. The vast majority of the interviews were conducted in the women's homes, allowing for the collection of some observational data.

[. . .]

The women were a diverse group: nine were African American, nine were Latina, five were Asian, and 57 were white. While 23 percent had never married, just fewer than 10 percent were currently divorced and 68 percent were currently married; 75 percent had at least one child. At the time of the interviews, half of the sample lived in middle-class households and the remaining half lived in working-class households. The women ranged in age from 32 to 42 and the average age was 38. Seventy-nine of the 80 participants identified as heterosexual.

[. . .]

Early Expectations About Work

Most women now expect to spend at least some part of their adult lives in the paid workforce (Gerson 2010). This was true for all of the women I interviewed. On the verge of adulthood, 64 percent expected they would work full-time throughout their adult lives, while the remaining 36 percent expected that they would work more occasionally in the paid labor market.

[. . .]

While the factors that motivated women to be continual workers were shared across class and race, the factors that motivated women to be occasional workers were far more likely to be found in white and Latino working-class families. African American working-class women were quite distinct from their white and Latino working-class counterparts and developed expectations in a manner that was much more similar to white, Asian and African American middle-class women—they expected to work continuously.

[. . .]

Middle-Class Privileges

The white, Asian, African American and Latino women raised in middle-class families almost unanimously reported that their parents promoted the importance of education and future professional employment to their daughters. Eighty-one percent of women from middle-class homes expected continual work, including all but one of the six middle-class women of color and 12 of the 15 white women; the only exceptions were three white women and one Asian woman from families with religious objections towards women's paid work. Women raised in middle-class families are often brought up to achieve excellence in the classroom and the workforce (Goldin 2006; Stone 2007), and often hold high expectations about future labor market participation, regardless of their mothers' workforce participation (see Moen, Erickson, and Dempster-McClain 1997; Gerson 1985).

Parents' expectations created an atmosphere in which the middle-class women believed long-term employment was the normative experience for all women. Lila, an Asian American middle-class woman, recalled that her parents:

Wanted [their children] to get the most education that we possibly could in order to do what we wanted. And, of course, they stressed thing like—*what most families would stress*—like, try to get into the medical field or go into something that's going to land you a job that's going to provide for you, in medical field or engineering.

Jodi, a white middle-class woman, felt her parents were not explicit about their expectations that she would excel in school and enter the workforce, but this was because they took both steps for granted: "[the expectations] weren't vocalized, but I was expected to go to school and do well in school. And it was just a given that I would be going to college and then to work. There was nothing more to it than that." Sheila, a white middle-class woman, agreed: "Oh, it was just—it was without question."

Middle-class families stressed the connection between paid work and financial independence. . . . Aisha, a middle-class African American woman, said that not only was continued workforce participation assumed, but success in the workplace was as well: "I think for the most part, success wasn't an option for me or for any of us, it was more something that we knew was tangible, that we would just work for, that we would get." Indeed, for most of the middle-class women, there was simply the expectation that they would excel in school, enter the workforce, and work continually.

There were some exceptions to the general focus on continued education and work in middle-class families. The only women from middle-class origins to expect occasional work lived in homes in which their parents held more traditional religious and cultural beliefs. Regina, a white middle-class woman, explained that her Catholic father made it clear that "they were not paying for college" for a daughter. Her parents had helped her older brothers, but expected Regina to marry. Gurneet, an Asian middle-class woman, expected to work rarely. Her family's expectation that she would marry and raise a family were very clear: "No, I was not expected to work, no. Just to get an education, that was the expectation . . . my parents only wanted me to get married. And then it's your husband's responsibility." Strong family objections to workforce participation made it difficult for Gurneet to imagine continual work. Both Regina and Gurneet were encouraged to focus on marriage and starting families—an expectation of a traditional family form that depended on their heterosexuality (and ability to find a spouse).

Working-Class Women Who Look to Full-Time Work

I found the working-class white and Latina women evenly divided in their expectations about work. As Table 45.1 shows, 58 percent of the women from working-class backgrounds expected continual work, including half of the white and Latina women. The African

Table 45.1 Early Work Expectations by Class of Origin and Race

	Continual (%)	Occasional (%)	Total (n)
Working-class origins	58	42	59
White	50	50	42
Asian	100	0	1
African American	100	0	8
Latina	50	50	8
Middle-class origins	81	19	21
White	80	20	15
Asian	75	25	4
African American	100	0	1
Latina	100	0	1
Total	64	36	80

American working-class women, on the other hand, were united in their expectation that they would work continually. Working-class white and Latina women formed hopes for good paid work when their parents encouraged it as the best way to be financially secure. Working-class African American women grew up in households in which women's work was taken for granted.

Many working-class women's parents encouraged them to focus on continual workforce participation. Some women from working-class origins were inspired by their mother's work. Maria, a Latina from a working-class family, felt she should match her mother's continued workforce participation:

> It was nice to see that my mother works. It gave me the inspiration to work myself as a kid. I have always worked because I saw it as important for a woman to work and have their own bank account.

Like half of the working-class Latina women, Maria expected to work continually. Financial insecurity during childhood led some women to focus on full-time work. Amy grew up the daughter of Asian, working-class immigrants who owned a corner store. There were a lot of "ups and downs" for her family and this financial instability led Amy to want to never "worry about money. To be able to make sure that my kids have everything they needed." Ambitions for upward mobility may drive women's expectations of continual work and encourage them to gain greater skills to enter the workforce (Goldin 2006).

Although only half of the white and Latina working-class women I interviewed held expectations of continuous work, all of the working-class African American women did. These women described growing up in households in which women worked full-time and in which they were expected to as well. All of the African American women grew up in homes in which their mothers and the other mothers that they knew worked full-time. Cameron, an African American woman, was puzzled when I asked her if her mother had ever considered leaving the workforce:

> I don't know, not work at all? I don't know; that's sort of complicated. She liked her job. [Might she have wanted to] do something different? I'm not sure; she just said she liked her job because it fit the needs of the family.

Her mother's job inspired Cameron's own work pathway: "it influenced me to do what I am now, an occupational therapist, and she works in the rehab department, so that's how I was introduced to it." Tina, an African American woman, discussed her mother's continued workforce participation: "I mean, everyone around me, their parents worked; so it wasn't like there were people who had stay-home mom's they were—generally everybody worked. . . . It was normal."

Partly because there were few Black homemaker mothers, African American women's continued workforce participation was presumed. . . . Not all working-class Black women had mothers who enjoyed their work. Lauren, a working-class Black woman, explained about her mother's job, "Working in a factory is like a slave job, so I definitely did not want that." Her mother's experience led Lauren to recognize that she wanted a better job than her mother had had, but not that she did not want to work. A strong community orientation toward women's paid work meant that negative images of women's work in the larger culture did not dissuade Black women from expectations of continual work. The normalization of continual work for

Black women led their daughters to expect that they, too, would work. Like their African American, white, Asian, and Latino middle-class counterparts, working-class Black women took continual workforce participation for granted.

[. . .]

When Work Is Likely to Disappoint

Hopes about work were tempered by the doubts raised by the very real constraints white and Latina working-class women saw around them. Women who saw that their mothers did not have good workforce opportunities did not want these same poor workforce options for themselves. Virginia, a white working-class woman, explained that after her parents divorced, her mother started to work even longer hours: "She was always cleaning; . . . she always worked that 4–1 shift." Virginia's mother told her what would happen if she didn't go to college, "'If you don't go, well, you are just going to be a cleaner.' So, it's like if you go, then you advance or you stay where you are and do what she did." But since Virginia "didn't like school," she feared that full-time work would be in a job like her mother's. Janice, a white working-class woman, had a mother who worked odds-and-ends jobs part-time. "I think she went back to work when I was maybe five or six—waitressing. It was like off and on—then she had side jobs cleaning apartments or like little here and there—she cleaned a dentist's office." This painted a picture of women's paid work that was unstable and these women developed expectations of occasional work for themselves.

Working-class white women described mothers who went back to work to help out the family, but whose work was characterized as secondary. Audra, a white working-class woman, explained: "She went back to work, like I said, when my brother was in junior high school. . . . That's when you start finding out that everything costs money." Although her mother stayed in the workforce long after the family's financial strains were less pronounced, Audra explained that her mother worked to "help out" her dad. Working-class mothers' work was often considered "help" or not real work. Wanda, a white working-class woman, explained:

> She never had an actual job . . . she cleaned houses. She was, like, a maid. [For] people in the neighborhood, like, and she made some extra pocket money for herself . . . and she'd go into the beach club because there was a beach club close by, she'd clean their bungalows and cottages.

Although Wanda remembered that her mother cleaned houses and also worked for the local beach club as a maid, she also explained that her mother "never had an actual job." Paid work that is done in the home is often characterized by poor wages and low status (Folbre 2001), suggesting that such "women's work" is not particularly worthwhile, or even, as in Wanda's mother's case, not recognized as real work.

[. . .]

Conclusion

[. . .]

This article shows how women's class and race intersects with gender to influence the processes through which women form opinions about their future work. The majority of white,

Asian, African American, and Latina middle-class women described a process in which expectations that they would enter the workforce were so strong that they gave little consideration to other options. Similarly, African American working-class women described growing up in communities in which women's continual work was taken for granted. On the other hand, the vast majority of white and Latina working-class women described a process in which they considered the possibility of working fulltime or part-time and half expected to work occasionally while the other half expected to work continually.

The women who grew up in white, Asian, African American, and Latina middle-class families, with very rare exceptions, were focused on continual workforce participation from a young age, regardless of whether their mothers worked. As norms have changed about women's work, women's attitudes about work have changed, too, and, regardless of their own workforce participation levels, mothers hold different expectations for their daughters than they did for themselves (Moen, Erickson, and Dempster-McClain 1997). . . . The middle-class women I interviewed were able to delay the consideration of work-family conflict and form early expectations of continual workforce participation, which led them to gain important work skills.

Unlike their middle-class peers, women from white and Latina working-class homes grew up with conflicting pictures of their potential workforce participation. The structural pushes and pulls of workforce opportunities and constraints and the continuing prevalence of the traditional division of work and family spheres was much more present in their lives. Many had parents who emphasized long-term workforce participation as the key to economic success and independence. On the other hand, their mothers' paid work was often classified as "help" and not crucial income for the family. Some white and Latina working-class mothers worked in low-status, low-paying jobs that they found unsatisfactory. These contradictions left white and Latina women who grew up in working-class homes more divided about their future workforce possibilities than their middle-class peers and their African American working-class contemporaries.

Class and race influenced not only women's expectations about paid work but also the process through which these expectations developed. The vast majority of women from middle-class origins, regardless of race, did not question their desire to be continual workers. In fact, when I asked them about this, many of the women from middle-class homes seemed puzzled that there could have been an alternative to continual work. Just as white, Asian, Latina and African American middle-class women rarely questioned the possibility that they would work continually, African American working-class women similarly believed that they would work continually throughout their adult lives. On the other hand, the majority of white and Latina working-class felt that at a young age, they needed to choose whether or not they would work continually as adults. The women who articulated a conscious calculation of continual versus occasional work were white and Latina working-class women.

[. . .]

Since the 1970s, women have made great strides in the labor market, but these changes have been incomplete, leaving many working-class women on the margins of the labor market and in some of the most vulnerable social positions. Although prior research suggests that early expectations are particularly influential for skill building and early work entrances (Goldin 2006; Risman 1998; Stickney and Konrad 2007), it is necessary to investigate the intersections between early expectations, race, gender, and class, and subsequent workforce participation. At the turn of the 21st century, much social progress has been made in advancing women's rights. Yet gendered, raced, and classed cultural norms about work remain resilient as well.

References

Alon, Sigal and Yitchak Haberfeld. 2007. "Labor Force Attachment and the Evolving Wage Gap Between White, Black, and Hispanic Young Women." *Work and Occupations* 34:369–98.

Baird, Chardie. 2007. "The Importance of Community Context for Young Women's Occupational Aspirations." *Sex Roles* 58:208–21.

Bettie, Julie. 2003. *Women Without Class: Girls, Race, and Identity.* Berkeley, CA: University of California Press.

Blair-Loy, Mary. 2003. *Competing Devotions: Career and Family Among Women Executives.* Cambridge, MA: Harvard University Press.

Collins, Patricia Hill. 1991. *Black Feminist Thought: Knowledge, Consciousness, and the Politics of Empowerment.* New York: Routledge.

Davis, Shannon and Theodore Greenstein. 2009. "Gender Ideology: Components, Predictors, and Consequences." *Annual Review of Sociology* 35:87–105.

Elder, Glen H. 1995. "The Life Course Paradigm: Social Change and Individual Development." In *Examining Lives in Context: Perspectives on the Ecology of Human Development.* Washington, DC: American Psychological Association.

England, Paula. 1992. *Comparable Worth: Theories and Evidence.* New York: Aldine de Gruyter.

England, Paula, Mary Ross, and Carmen Garcia-Beaulieu. 2004. "Women's Employment Among Blacks, White and Three Groups of Latinas." *Gender & Society* 18:494–509.

Fan, Pi-Ling and Margaret Mooney Marini. 2000. "Influences on Gender-Role Attitudes During the Transition to Adulthood." *Social Science Research* 29:258–83.

Folbre, Nancy. 2001. *The Invisible Heart: Economics and Family Values.* New York: New Press.

Garey, Anita Ilta. 1999. *Weaving Work and Motherhood.* Philadelphia, PA: Temple University Press.

Gerson, Kathleen. 1985. *Hard Choices: How Women Decide About Work, Career, and Motherhood.* Berkeley, CA: University of California Press.

Gerson, Kathleen. 2010. *The Unfinished Revolution: How a New Generation Is Reshaping Family, Work and Gender in America.* New York: Oxford University Press.

Glauber, Rebecca. 2008. "Race and Gender in Families and at Work." *Gender & Society* 22:8–30.

Goldin, Claudia. 2006. "The Quiet Revolution That Transformed Women's Employment, Education, and Family." *American Economic Review* 96:1–21.

Hamer, Jennifer. 2001. *What It Means to Be Daddy: Fatherhood for Black Men Living Away From Their Children.* New York: Columbia University Press.

Hansen, Karen V. 2005. *Not-So-Nuclear Families: Class, Gender, and Networks of Care.* New Brunswick, NJ: Rutgers University Press.

Higginbotham, Elizabeth. 2001. *Too Much to Ask: Black Women in the Era of Integration.* Chapel Hill, NC: University of North Carolina Press.

Hochschild, Arlie Russell. 1989. *The Second Shift: Working Parents and the Revolution at Home.* New York: Viking.

Landry, Bart. 2000. *Black Working Wives: Pioneers of the American Family Revolution.* Berkeley, CA: University of California Press.

McCall, Leslie. 2011. "Women and Men as Class and Race Actors: Comment on England." *Gender & Society* 25:94–100.

Moen, Phyllis. 2001. "The Gendered Life Course." In *Handbook of Aging and the Social Sciences,* edited by L. George and R. Binstock. San Diego, CA: Academic Press.

Moen, Phyllis, Mary Ann Erickson, and Donna Dempster-McClain. 1997. "Their Mother's Daughters?" *Journal of Marriage and the Family* 59:281–93.

Ridgeway, Cecilia and Shelley Correll. 2004. "Unpacking the Gender System: A Theoretical Perspective on Gender Beliefs and Social Relations." *Gender & Society* 18:510–31.

Risman, Barbara. 1998. *Gender Vertigo: American Families in Transition.* New Haven, CT: Yale University Press.

Risman, Barbara, Maxine Atkinson, and Stephen Blackwelder. 1999. "Understanding the Juggling Act: Gendered Preferences and Social Structural Constraints." *Sociological Forum* 14:319–44.

Roth, Louise. 2006. *Selling Women Short: Gender Inequality on Wall Street*. Princeton, NJ: Princeton University Press.

Spivey, Christy. 2005. "Time off at What Price? The Effects of Career Interruptions on Earnings." *Industrial and Labor Relations Review* 59:119–40.

Stickney, Lisa and Alison Konrad. 2007. "Gender-Role Attitudes and Earnings." *Sex Roles* 57:801–11.

Stone, Pamela. 2007. *Opting Out? Why Women Really Quit Careers and Head Home*. Berkeley, CA: University of California Press.

Taylor, Ronald. 2000. "Diversity Within African American Families." In *Handbook of Family Diversity*, edited by D. H. Demo, K. R. Allen, and M. A. Fine. New York: Oxford University Press.

Townsend, Nicholas. 2002. *The Package Deal: Marriage, Work, and Fatherhood in Men's Lives*. Philadelphia, PA: Temple University Press.

U.S. Census of the Bureau. 2006. "Current Population Survey" (www.census.gov/programs-surveys/cps.html).

Vespa, Jonathan. 2009. "Gender Ideology Construction: A Life Course and Intersectional Approach." *Gender & Society* 23:363–87.

Williams, Joan C. 2010. *Reshaping the Work-Family Debate: Why Men and Class Matter*. Cambridge, MA: Harvard University Press.

Racializing the Glass Escalator

Reconsidering Men's Experiences With Women's Work

Adia Harvey Wingfield

© iStockphoto.com/shironosov

Sociologists who study work have long noted that jobs are sex segregated and that this segregation creates different occupational experiences for men and women (Charles and Grusky 2004). Jobs predominantly filled by women often require "feminine" traits such as nurturing, caring, and empathy, a fact that means men confront perceptions that they are unsuited for the requirements of these jobs. Rather than having an adverse effect on their

Adia Harvey Wingfield. 2009. "Racializing the Glass Escalator: Reconsidering Men's Experiences With Women's Work." *Gender & Society* 23(1):5–26.

occupational experiences, however, these assumptions facilitate men's entry into better paying, higher status positions, creating what Williams (1995) labels a "glass escalator" effect.

The glass escalator model has been an influential paradigm in understanding the experiences of men who do women's work. Researchers have identified this process among men nurses, social workers, paralegals, and librarians and have cited its pervasiveness as evidence of men's consistent advantage in the workplace, such that even in jobs where men are numerical minorities they are likely to enjoy higher wages and faster promotions (Floge and Merrill 1986; Heikes 1991; Pierce 1995; Williams 1989, 1995). Most of these studies implicitly assume a racial homogenization of men workers in women's professions, but this supposition is problematic for several reasons. For one, minority men are not only present but are actually overrepresented in certain areas of reproductive work that have historically been dominated by white women (Duffy 2007). Thus, research that focuses primarily on white men in women's professions ignores a key segment of men who perform this type of labor. Second, and perhaps more important, conclusions based on the experiences of white men tend to overlook the ways that intersections of race and gender create different experiences for different men. While extensive work has documented the fact that white men in women's professions encounter a glass escalator effect that aids their occupational mobility (for an exception, see Snyder and Green 2008), few studies, if any, have considered how this effect is a function not only of gendered advantage but of racial privilege as well.

In this article, I examine the implications of race–gender intersections for minority men employed in a female-dominated, feminized occupation, specifically focusing on Black men in nursing. Their experiences doing "women's work" demonstrate that the glass escalator is a racialized as well as gendered concept.

[. . .]

The concept of the glass escalator provides an important and useful framework for addressing men's experiences in women's occupations, but so far research in this vein has neglected to examine whether the glass escalator is experienced among all men in an identical manner. Are the processes that facilitate a ride on the glass escalator available to minority men? Or does race intersect with gender to affect the extent to which the glass escalator offers men opportunities in women's professions? In the next section, I examine whether and how the mechanisms that facilitate a ride on the glass escalator might be unavailable to Black men in nursing.

Relationships With Colleagues and Supervisors

[. . .]

The congenial relationship with colleagues and gendered bonds with supervisors are crucial to riding the glass escalator. Women colleagues often take a primary role in casting these men into leadership or supervisory positions. In their study of men and women tokens in a hospital setting, Floge and Merrill (1986) cite cases where women nurses promoted men colleagues to the position of charge nurse, even when the job had already been assigned to a woman. In addition to these close ties with women colleagues, men are also able to capitalize on gendered bonds with (mostly men) supervisors in ways that engender upward mobility. Many men supervisors informally socialize with men workers in women's jobs and are thus able to trade on their personal friendships for upward mobility. Williams (1995) describes a case where a nurse with mediocre performance reviews received a promotion to a more prestigious specialty area because of his friendship with the (male) doctor in charge. According to the literature, building strong relationships with colleagues and supervisors often happens relatively easily for men in women's professions and pays off in their occupational advancement.

For Black men in nursing, however, gendered racism may limit the extent to which they establish bonds with their colleagues and supervisors. The concept of gendered racism suggests that racial stereotypes, images, and beliefs are grounded in gendered ideals (Collins 1990, 2004; Espiritu 2000; Essed 1991; Harvey Wingfield 2007). Gendered racist stereotypes of Black men in particular emphasize the dangerous, threatening attributes associated with Black men and Black masculinity, framing Black men as threats to white women, prone to criminal behavior, and especially violent. Collins (2004) argues that these stereotypes serve to legitimize Black men's treatment in the criminal justice system through methods such as racial profiling and incarceration, but they may also hinder Black men's attempts to enter and advance in various occupational fields.

For Black men nurses, gendered racist images may have particular consequences for their relationships with women colleagues, who may view Black men nurses through the lens of controlling images and gendered racist stereotypes that emphasize the danger they pose to women. This may take on a heightened significance for white women nurses, given stereotypes that suggest that Black men are especially predisposed to raping white women. Rather than experiencing the congenial bonds with colleagues that white men nurses describe, Black men nurses may find themselves facing a much cooler reception from their women coworkers.

Gendered racism may also play into the encounters Black men nurses have with supervisors. In cases where supervisors are white men, Black men nurses may still find that higher-ups treat them in ways that reflect prevailing stereotypes about threatening Black masculinity. Supervisors may feel uneasy about forming close relationships with Black men or may encourage their separation from white women nurses. In addition, broader, less gender-specific racial stereotypes could also shape the experiences Black men nurses have with white men bosses. Whites often perceive Blacks, regardless of gender, as less intelligent, hardworking, ethical, and moral than other racial groups (Feagin 2006). Black men nurses may find that in addition to being influenced by gendered racist stereotypes, supervisors also view them as less capable and qualified for promotion, thus negating or minimizing the glass escalator effect.

Suitability for Nursing and Higher-Status Work

The perception that men are not really suited to do women's work also contributes to the glass escalator effect. In encounters with patients, doctors, and other staff, men nurses frequently confront others who do not expect to see them doing "a woman's job." Sometimes this perception means that patients mistake men nurses for doctors; ultimately, the sense that men do not really belong in nursing contributes to a push *"out* of the most feminine-identified areas and *up* to those regarded as more legitimate for men" (Williams 1995, 104). The sense that men are better suited for more masculine jobs means that men workers are often assumed to be more able and skilled than their women counterparts. As Williams writes (1995, 106), "Masculinity is often associated with competence and mastery," and this implicit definition stays with men even when they work in feminized fields. Thus, part of the perception that men do not belong in these jobs is rooted in the sense that, as men, they are more capable and accomplished than women and thus belong in jobs that reflect this. Consequently, men nurses are mistaken for doctors and are granted more authority and responsibility than their women counterparts, reflecting the idea that, as men, they are inherently more competent (Heikes 1991; Williams 1995).

Black men nurses, however, may not face the presumptions of expertise or the resulting assumption that they belong in higher-status jobs. Black professionals, both men and women, are often assumed to be less capable and less qualified than their white counterparts. In some cases, these negative stereotypes hold even when Black workers outperform white colleagues (Feagin and Sikes 1994). The belief that Blacks are inherently less competent than whites means that, despite advanced education, training, and skill, Black professionals often confront the lingering perception that they are better suited for lower-level service work (Feagin and Sikes 1994). Black men in fact often fare better than white women in blue-collar jobs such as policing and corrections work (Britton 1995), and this may be, in part, because they are viewed as more appropriately suited for these types of positions.

For Black men nurses, then, the issue of perception may play out in different ways than it does for white men nurses. While white men nurses enjoy the automatic assumption that they are qualified, capable, and suited for "better" work, the experiences of Black professionals suggest that Black men nurses may not encounter these reactions. They may, like their white counterparts, face the perception that they do not belong in nursing. Unlike their white counterparts, Black men nurses may be seen as inherently less capable and therefore better suited for low-wage labor than a professional, feminized occupation such as nursing. This perception of being less qualified means that they also may not be immediately assumed to be better suited for the higher-level, more masculinized jobs within the medical field.

As minority women address issues of both race and gender to negotiate a sense of belonging in masculine settings (Ong 2005), minority men may also face a comparable challenge in feminized fields. They may have to address the unspoken racialization implicit in the assumption that masculinity equals competence. Simultaneously, they may find that the racial stereotype that Blackness equals lower qualifications, standards, and competence clouds the sense that men are inherently more capable and adept in any field, including the feminized ones.

[. . .]

Data Collection and Method

I collected data through semistructured interviews with 17 men nurses who identified as Black or African American. Nurses ranged in age from 30 to 51 and lived in the southeastern United States. Six worked in suburban hospitals adjacent to major cities, six were located in major metropolitan urban care centers, and the remaining five worked in rural hospitals or clinics. All were registered nurses or licensed practical nurses.

[. . .]

Six identified their specialty as oncology, four were bedside nurses, two were in intensive care, one managed an acute dialysis program, one was an orthopedic nurse, one was in ambulatory care, one was in emergency, and one was in surgery. The least experienced nurse had worked in the field for five years; the most experienced had been a nurse for 26 years.

[. . .]

The average interview lasted about an hour.

[. . .]

Findings

[. . .]

Reception From Colleagues and Supervisors

When women welcome men into "their" professions, they often push men into leadership roles that ease their advancement into upper-level positions. Thus, a positive reaction from colleagues is critical to riding the glass escalator. Unlike white men nurses, however, Black men do not describe encountering a warm reception from women colleagues (Heikes 1991). Instead, the men I interviewed find that they often have unpleasant interactions with women coworkers who treat them rather coldly and attempt to keep them at bay. Chris is a 51-year-old oncology nurse who describes one white nurse's attempt to isolate him from other white women nurses as he attempted to get his instructions for that day's shift:

> She turned and ushered me to the door, and said for me to wait out here, a nurse will come out and give you your report. I stared at her hand on my arm, and then at her, and said, "Why? Where do you go to get your reports?" She said, "I get them in there." I said, "Right. Unhand me." I went right back in there, sat down, and started writing down my reports.

Kenny, a 47-year-old nurse with 23 years of nursing experience, describes a similarly and particularly painful experience he had in a previous job where he was the only Black person on staff:

> [The staff] had nothing to do with me, and they didn't even want me to sit at the same area where they were charting in to take a break. They wanted me to sit somewhere else. . . . They wouldn't even sit at a table with me! When I came and sat down, everybody got up and left.

These experiences with colleagues are starkly different from those described by white men in professions dominated by women (see Pierce 1995; Williams 1989). Though the men in these studies sometimes chose to segregate themselves, women never systematically excluded them. Though I have no way of knowing why the women nurses in Chris's and Kenny's workplaces physically segregated themselves, the pervasiveness of gendered racist images that emphasize white women's vulnerability to dangerous Black men may play an important role. For these nurses, their masculinity is not a guarantee that they will be welcomed, much less pushed into leadership roles. As Ryan, a 37-year-old intensive care nurse says, "[Black men] have to go further to prove ourselves. This involves proving our capabilities, *proving to colleagues that you can lead*, be on the forefront" (emphasis added). The warm welcome and subsequent opportunities for leadership cannot be taken for granted. In contrast, these men describe great challenges in forming congenial relationships with coworkers who, they believe, do not truly want them there.

In addition, these men often describe tense, if not blatantly discriminatory, relationships with supervisors. While Williams (1995) suggests that men supervisors can be allies for men in women's professions by facilitating promotions and upward mobility, Black men nurses describe incidents of being overlooked by supervisors when it comes time for promotions.

Ryan, who has worked at his current job for 11 years, believes that these barriers block upward mobility within the profession:

> The hardest part is dealing with people who don't understand minority nurses. People with their biases, who don't identify you as ripe for promotion. I know the policy and procedure, I'm familiar with past history. So you can't tell me I can't move forward if others did. [How did you deal with this?] By knowing the chain of command, who my supervisors were. Things were subtle. I just had to be better. I got this mostly from other nurses and supervisors. I was paid to deal with patients, so I could deal with [racism] from them. I'm not paid to deal with this from colleagues.

Kenny offers a similar example. Employed as an orthopedic nurse in a predominantly white environment, he describes great difficulty getting promoted, which he primarily attributes to racial biases:

> It's almost like you have to, um, take your ideas and give them to somebody else and then let them present them for you and you get no credit for it. I've applied for several promotions there and, you know, I didn't get them. . . . When you look around to the, um, the percentage of African Americans who are actually in executive leadership is almost zero percent. Because it's less than one percent of the total population of people that are in leadership, and it's almost like they'll go outside of the system just to try to find a Caucasian to fill a position. Not that I'm not qualified, because I've been master's prepared for 12 years and I'm working on my doctorate.

According to Ryan and Kenny, supervisors' racial biases mean limited opportunities for promotion and upward mobility. This interpretation is consistent with research that suggests that even with stellar performance and solid work histories, Black workers may receive mediocre evaluations from white supervisors that limit their advancement (Feagin 2006; Feagin and Sikes 1994). For Black men nurses, their race may signal to supervisors that they are unworthy of promotion and thus create a different experience with the glass escalator.

Strong relationships with colleagues and supervisors are a key mechanism of the glass escalator effect. For Black men nurses, however, these relationships are experienced differently from those described by their white men colleagues. Black men nurses do not speak of warm and congenial relationships with women nurses or see these relationships as facilitating a move into leadership roles. Nor do they suggest that they share gendered bonds with men supervisors that serve to ease their mobility into higher-status administrative jobs. In contrast, they sense that racial bias makes it difficult to develop ties with coworkers and makes superiors unwilling to promote them. Black men nurses thus experience this aspect of the glass escalator differently from their white men colleagues. They find that relationships with colleagues and supervisors stifle, rather than facilitate, their upward mobility.

Perceptions of Suitability

Like their white counterparts, Black men nurses also experience challenges from clients who are unaccustomed to seeing men in fields typically dominated by women. As with white men nurses, Black men encounter this in surprised or quizzical reactions from patients who seem to expect to be treated by white women nurses. Ray, a 36-year-old oncology nurse with 10 years of experience, states,

> Nursing, historically, has been a white female's job [so] being a Black male it's a weird position to be in. . . . I've, several times, gone into a room and a male patient, a white male patient has, you know, they'll say, "Where's the pretty nurse? Where's the pretty nurse? Where's the blonde nurse?" . . . "You don't have one. I'm the nurse."

Yet while patients rarely expect to be treated by men nurses of any race, white men encounter statements and behaviors that suggest patients expect them to be doctors, supervisors, or other higher-status, more masculine positions (Williams 1989, 1995). In part, this expectation accelerates their ride on the glass escalator, helping to push them into the positions for which they are seen as more appropriately suited.

(White) men, by virtue of their masculinity, are assumed to be more competent and capable and thus better situated in (nonfeminized) jobs that are perceived to require greater skill and proficiency. Black men, in contrast, rarely encounter patients (or colleagues and supervisors) who immediately expect that they are doctors or administrators. Instead, many respondents find that even after displaying their credentials, sharing their nursing experience, and, in one case, dispensing care, they are still mistaken for janitors or service workers. Ray's experience is typical:

> I've even given patients their medicines, explained their care to them, and then they'll say to me, "Well, can you send the nurse in?"

Chris describes a somewhat similar encounter of being misidentified by a white woman patient:

> I come [to work] in my white uniform, that's what I wear—being a Black man, I know they won't look at me the same, so I dress the part—I said good evening, my name's Chris, and I'm going to be your nurse. She says to me, "Are you from housekeeping?" . . . I've had other cases. I've walked in and had a lady look at me and ask if I'm the janitor.

Chris recognizes that this patient is evoking racial stereotypes that Blacks are there to perform menial service work. He attempts to circumvent this very perception through careful self-presentation, wearing the white uniform to indicate his position as a nurse. His efforts, however, are nonetheless met with a racial stereotype that as a Black man he should be there to clean up rather than to provide medical care.

Black men in nursing encounter challenges from customers that reinforce the idea that men are not suited for a "feminized" profession such as nursing. However, these assumptions are racialized as well as gendered. Unlike white men nurses who are assumed to be doctors (see Williams 1992), Black men in nursing are quickly taken for janitors or housekeeping staff. These men do not simply describe a gendered process where perceptions and stereotypes about men serve to aid their mobility into higher-status jobs. More specifically, they describe interactions that are simultaneously raced *and* gendered in ways that reproduce stereotypes of Black men as best suited for certain blue-collar, unskilled labor.

These negative stereotypes can affect Black men nurses' efforts to treat patients as well. The men I interviewed find that masculinity does not automatically endow them with an aura of competency. In fact, they often describe interactions with white women patients that suggest that their race minimizes whatever assumptions of capability might accompany being men. They describe several cases in which white women patients completely refused treatment. Ray says,

> With older white women, it's tricky sometimes because they will come right out and tell you they don't want you to treat them, or can they see someone else.

Ray frames this as an issue specifically with older white women, though other nurses in the sample described similar issues with white women of all ages. Cyril, a 40-year-old nurse with 17 years of nursing experience, describes a slightly different twist on this story:

> I had a white lady that I had to give a shot, and she was fine with it and I was fine with it. But her husband, when she told him, he said to me, I don't have any problem with you as a Black man, but I don't want you giving her a shot.

While white men nurses report some apprehension about treating women patients, in all likelihood this experience is compounded for Black men (Williams 1989). Historically, interactions between Black men and white women have been fraught with complexity and tension, as Black men have been represented in the cultural imagination as potential rapists and threats to white women's security and safety—and, implicitly, as a threat to white patriarchal stability (Davis 1981; Giddings 1984). In Cyril's case, it may be particularly significant that the Black man is charged with giving a shot and therefore literally penetrating the white wife's body, a fact that may heighten the husband's desire to shield his wife from this interaction. White men nurses may describe hesitation or awkwardness that accompanies treating women patients, but their experiences are not shaped by a pervasive racial imagery that suggests that they are potential threats to their women patients' safety.

This dynamic, described primarily among white women patients and their families, presents a picture of how Black men's interactions with clients are shaped in specifically raced and gendered ways that suggest they are less rather than more capable. These interactions do not send the message that Black men, because they are men, are too competent for nursing and really belong in higher-status jobs. Instead, these men face patients who mistake them for lower-status service workers and encounter white women patients (and their husbands) who simply refuse treatment or are visibly uncomfortable with the prospect. These interactions do not situate Black men nurses in a prime position for upward mobility. Rather, they suggest that the experience of Black men nurses with this particular mechanism of the glass escalator is the manifestation of the expectation that they should be in lower-status positions more appropriate to their race and gender.

[. . .]

Conclusions

Existing research on the glass escalator cannot explain these men's experiences. As men who do women's work, they should be channeled into positions as charge nurses or nursing administrators and should find themselves virtually pushed into the upper ranks of the nursing profession. But without exception, this is not the experience these Black men nurses describe. Instead of benefiting from the basic mechanisms of the glass escalator, they face tense relationships with colleagues, supervisors' biases in achieving promotion, patient stereotypes that inhibit caregiving, and a sense of comfort with some of the feminized aspects of their jobs. These "glass barriers" suggest that the glass escalator is a racialized concept as well as a gendered one. The main contribution of this study is the finding that race and gender intersect to determine which men will ride the glass escalator. The proposition that men who do women's work encounter undue opportunities and advantages appears to be unequivocally true only if the men in question are white.

[. . .]

It is also especially interesting to consider how men describe the role of women in facilitating—or denying—access to the glass escalator. Research on white men nurses includes accounts of ways white women welcome them and facilitate their advancement by pushing them toward leadership positions (Floge and Merrill 1986; Heikes 1991; Williams 1992, 1995). In contrast, Black men nurses in this study discuss white women who do not seem eager to work with them, much less aid their upward mobility. These different responses indicate that shared racial status is important in determining who rides the glass escalator. If that is the case, then future research should consider whether Black men nurses who work in predominantly Black settings are more likely to encounter the glass escalator effect. In these settings, Black men nurses' experiences might more closely resemble those of white men nurses.

References

Britton, Dana. 1995. *At Work in the Iron Cage.* New York: New York University Press.

Charles, Maria and David Grusky. 2004. *Occupational Ghettos: The Worldwide Segregation of Women and Men.* Palo Alto, CA: Stanford University Press.

Collins, Patricia Hill. 1990. *Black Feminist Thought.* New York: Routledge.

Collins, Patricia Hill. 2004. *Black Sexual Politics.* New York: Routledge.

Davis, Angela. 1981. *Women, Race, and Class.* New York: Vintage.

Duffy, Mignon. 2007. "Doing the Dirty Work: Gender, Race, and Reproductive Labor in Historical Perspective." *Gender & Society* 21:313–36.

Espiritu, Yen Le. 2000. *Asian American Women and Men: Labor, Laws, and Love.* Walnut Creek, CA: AltaMira.

Essed, Philomena. 1991. *Understanding Everyday Racism.* New York: Russell Sage.

Feagin, Joe. 2006. *Systemic Racism.* New York: Routledge.

Feagin, Joe and Melvin Sikes. 1994. *Living with Racism.* Boston, MA: Beacon Hill Press.

Floge, Liliane and Deborah M. Merrill. 1986. "Tokenism Reconsidered: Male Nurses and Female Physicians in a Hospital Setting." *Social Forces* 64:925–47.

Giddings, Paula. 1984. *When and Where I Enter: The Impact of Black Women on Race and Sex in America.* New York: HarperCollins.

Harvey Wingfield, Adia. 2007. "The Modern Mammy and the Angry Black Man: African American Professionals' Experiences with Gendered Racism in the Workplace." *Race, Gender, and Class* 14(2):196–212.

Heikes, E. Joel. 1991. "When Men Are the Minority: The Case of Men in Nursing." *Sociological Quarterly* 32:389–401.

Ong, Maria. 2005. "Body Projects of Young Women of Color in Physics: Intersections of Race, Gender, and Science." *Social Problems* 52(4):593–617.

Pierce, Jennifer. 1995. *Gender Trials: Emotional Lives in Contemporary Law Firms.* Berkeley, CA: University of California Press.

Snyder, Karrie Ann and Adam Isaiah Green. 2008. "Revisiting the Glass Escalator: The Case of Gender Segregation in a Female Dominated Occupation." *Social Problems* 55(2):271–99.

Williams, Christine. 1989. *Gender Differences at Work: Women and Men in Nontraditional Occupations.* Berkeley, CA: University of California Press.

Williams, Christine. 1992. "The Glass Escalator: Hidden Advantages for Men in the 'Female' Professions." *Social Problems* 39(3):253–67.

Williams, Christine. 1995. *Still a Man's World: Men Who Do Women's Work.* Berkeley, CA: University of California Press.

Hegemonic Masculinity at Work in the Gay Adult Film Industry

Nathaniel B. Burke

At the height of its success, the combined revenue of the adult film industry has been estimated at close to 14 billion dollars annually (L Williams, 2004), a sum greater than the combined revenue of major league baseball, football, and basketball. More recent estimates place it closer to 6 billion dollars annually—an approximately 30–50% reduction (Fritz, 2009)—though even at this more conservative estimate, the adult industry still has a tremendous societal presence. . . . The majority of academic research in the adult film industry has historically been feminist scholarship which . . . debated whether the industry and its content may exploit and perpetuate a subordinate image of women (Dworkin, 1985, 1987; Kipnis, 1996; MacKinnon, 1989; MacKinnon and Dworkin, 1998) . . . or emphasized the complexities of pleasure and agency obtained from or displayed in adult content (Echols, 1984; Rubin, 1993; Vance, 1984).

While the debates over the morality and effects of pornography still occupy a great deal of academic discussion, what has received comparably little attention are studies of the industry as a workplace. This is understandable given the challenges of entering a very private and often stigmatized industry, as well as the modest academic aversion toward studying sex for sale. The fact that gay pornography, however, has received comparably little scholarly attention is surprising given that it is estimated to account for a disproportionately large amount of the industry's revenue at approximately 25% (Thomas, 2000) and approximately 10% of web traffic on popular content sharing sites (Reddit, 2013). The adult industry not only reaches mass amounts of consumers, but employs countless people whose labor is insufficiently understood, and occurs within patterns of labor that remain unexplored. Studying the adult industry can therefore tell us a great deal not only about desire, but also about the social structures which generate the products of consumption, and how sexuality, race, class, gender, and the body are mechanisms of organizing power in their creation.

Nathaniel B. Burke. 2016. "Hegemonic Masculinity at Work in the Gay Adult Film Industry." *Sexualities* 19(5–6):587–607.

The high rates of employment and attrition in the adult film industry call for greater attention to the hierarchies of power and privilege that may influence its workings (Williams, 2004). This study draws on eleven months of participant observation in a gay adult film studio to provide a window into the labor aspects of the industry, their relation to overarching patterns of hegemonic masculinity, race, and gender and their connection to systems of inequality. Through analysis of discourses that police the boundaries of masculinity, I offer an outline of a local hegemonic masculinity produced within the gay adult film industry that continues to legitimate the subordination of femininity, and discuss this local form's relationship to regional hegemonic masculinity.

[. . .]

In the past 30 years, gender scholars have engaged in tremendous theoretical and methodological development of the study of masculinities, arguing that we cannot speak of "masculinity" in the singular form as masculinities are not essential, but are instead socially constructed and plural (Connell, 1987; Kimmel, 2004; Kimmel and Messner, 2012). A significant portion of the work on masculinities has utilized the theoretical concept of hegemonic masculinity, which Connell defines as the practices that "institutionalize men's dominance over women" and men of subordinated masculinities (1987: 185). Drawing upon Gramsci's concept of hegemony (1971), this framework acknowledges that domination is perpetuated not only by force, but also by consent with, and the perpetuation of the values and ideals of those in privileged positions. Hegemonic masculinity is reinforced through the embeddedness of practices, beliefs, and values in the given society, and simultaneously affords dominant groups numerous privileges while constituting subordinated groups as less or non-masculine, thereby partitioning their social access.

[. . .]

While most men do not meet the "ideals" of hegemonic masculinity, many, including women and subordinated men—whether by race, class, sexuality, or ability—are complicit in sustaining it (Chen, 1999; Wingfield, 2009; Yeung et al., 2006). Within the broader gender order, gay men may be targeted because of stereotyped feminine behavior (Lusher and Robins, 2007), yet even within gay male settings, studies have demonstrated gay men's adherence to practices that reinforce men's superiority over women (Johnson and Samdahl, 2005; Lanzieri and Hildebrandt, 2011) and the devaluation and abjection of femininity in other gay men (Levine, 1998; Lewis, 2009; Mercer, 2012; Taywaditep, 2001). Within the framework of hegemonic masculinity, these two processes have been formulated as "external hegemony"—that which reinforces men's superiority over women—and "internal hegemony," power over subordinated masculinities (Demetriou, 2001). This dynamic approach to hegemonic masculinity acknowledges that it is not only practices by those who hold positions of power that bolster patriarchy; diverse and marginalized persons or groups may also engage in practices that reinforce hierarchies of masculinities (Yeung et al., 2006). Indeed, it is within such settings that hegemonic masculinity may prove a valuable framework to understand the maintenance of patriarchy, as marginalized men may deceptively present what appears to be counter-hegemonic, but is actually "an instrument of . . . patriarchal reproduction" (Demetriou, 2001: 355). Thus, in a setting in which a group of men—in this study, gay men who produce homosexual erotic content—do not "measure up" to hegemonically masculine ideals, we might expect to see processes which actively challenge the existing gender order, yet may in fact bolster it (Chen, 1999).

[. . .]

How these elements play out in a market-driven industry—in this case the adult film industry—and how this valuation reflects and (re)constitutes the desires of presumably gay men consumers requires further exploration. Gay men view pornographic content at over twice the rate of heterosexual men (Thomas, 2000), and because of its prevalence and legitimation of homoeroticism, pornography has become a vehicle through which a gay personal identity can be asserted (Escoffier, 2009). This study . . . explores the connection between labor practices and the products of the gay adult film industry to elucidate the relationship between local and regional hegemonic masculinities.

[. . .]

By utilizing a framework of hegemonic masculinity to explore men's labor-force experience, we can attend to the dynamics of racial, class, and sexual inequalities, and their interconnections. Studies of the workplace have demonstrated that workers who best exemplify valued traits are likely to receive greater organizational rewards (Hodges and Budig, 2010). Male sex workers, for example, have a great deal to gain by advertising qualities associated with hegemonic masculinity. Logan (2010) finds that men who advertise stereotypical masculine attributes are able to charge significantly more than those with less masculine attributes (at a differential of approximately 17%). The racialized nature of masculinity again emerges and complicates these dynamics—Black, Latino and white men each receive substantial pay increases for "top" attributes, while Asian men do not. Conversely, the penalty for "bottom" attributes is significantly greater for Black men (at 30% income reduction), indicating that failing to conform to racialized stereotypes of masculinity incurs significant penalties.

The impact of the political natures of desire (i.e. the hierarchical presence of race, class, and gender performance) upon the adult film industry continues to emphasize the privileging of hegemonic forms of beauty, for instance, the labor marginalization of Black women performers in pornography (Miller-Young, 2010). While there is a wealth of research on the relationship between race and sexuality in adult film (Bernardi, 2006; Forna, 2001; Gardener, 1980; Shimizu, 2007), such research that explores the politics of desire with regard to labor in adult film is sparse. This study addresses this deficiency through the exploration of labor practices in gay adult film, and connects it with the literature on hegemonic masculinity. By doing so, this work contributes to better understandings of how the structural gender order is upheld by marginalized men through the relationship between local hegemonic masculine forms and the cultural products that are taken up in the construction of regional hegemonic masculinities.

Methodology

[. . .]

The findings from this study are drawn from participant-observation over the period of 11 months during 2012 and 2013 at *From Behind Films*, a gay adult film studio located on the West Coast of the USA. At the time of my study, *From Behind Films* had been in business for approximately 15 years and employed some of the most prominent, award-winning performers in the gay adult film industry. . . . *From Behind Films* produces online and DVD video content for three websites: The first website, which I refer to as *Bottoms Up*, features a single performer who is featured in all of the films produced for that website, and engages in sexual activity with an assortment of other models. The second website provides what the staff refer to as "mainstream" gay adult films, in that they feature primarily young (18 to roughly 30-year-old), muscular, well-endowed, and primarily white performers, a subsidiary which I term *Stock Cocks. From Behind Films*' third website, *Boi Toys*, features an older/younger scene partner pairing. Each website costs consumers approximately US$35 for a 30-day subscription, with a discount offered to those who sign up for automatic monthly membership renewal.

[. . .]

From Behind Films employs six full-time staff: the owner (Steve), his partner who manages financial aspects of the business, a web designer, a video editor, a casting director (Samuel), and a video director (Bobby). All staff were between the ages of 25 and 50 at the time of my field-work, self-identified as gay men, and white, with the exception of Samuel who is Latino. My primary interactions were with Bobby, Samuel, and Steve, in addition to many adult film models hired by the studio for shoots. The studio has employed "exclusive" contracted performers in the past, though at the time of my observation there were no contracted performers, but instead a pool of 10 to 20 models who appeared every few months for the websites, while the remaining positions were filled by a cadre of approximately 200 performers, many of whom were employed 1–3 times on average by my estimation. As the majority of models were also white, race often went interactionally "unmarked" during my time at *From Behind Films*.

[. . .]

Defining Local Hegemonic Masculinity in Gay Adult Film

The ways in which the staff at *From Behind Films* construct desirable masculinity for the gay adult film industry occur both in discussions during casting and through the direction given to performers during filming. In casting, the staff primarily discuss the bodies of the models that they employ or plan to employ. While Samuel, the casting director, and I were reviewing submissions together during a visit, he pulled up a photograph of a relatively lithe, young white man, and stated, "He doesn't really have much muscle mass, and that's the thing, he's really cute, but he's not like . . . porn." The ability to say that one is *not* porn relies on the premise that they know what porn *is*. Samuel, Bobby, and Steve all routinely agreed on who was hirable and desirable for gay pornography, indicating a shared understanding of the requirements for this category of masculinity.

During one field visit, the owner, Steve, described to me a performer who was coming in later that day for a shoot:

> Today's shoot is a performer named Griffin who they had shot content with for a straight website a number of years ago. Steve goes on to say that back then, he was "fine, nothing special," that he was "kind of slim," but that he has since put on a lot of muscle and is "6'4", with a shaved head [pauses] Really hot."

From this excerpt, we can see that being considered valuable enough to hire is contingent upon a certain amount of muscle mass; models need to be "jockish" to be considered for hire, even when they are looking for performers for *Boi Toys*, as Samuel educated me through the review of two performers' submissions which were rejected:

> Samuel continued reviewing performer submissions, and said, "Nineteen, so that's good he's young . . . 5'7, 125 pounds . . . really skinny . . . even if we're looking for *Bois*, we want them to be a little built." Bobby added, "more jockish," to which Samuel replied, "that's the perfect word." Later during the visit, Samuel pulled up a submission and said, "See, this guy, he's kinda just skinny . . . he's got no body . . ." and closed out the submission.

These kinds of conversation begin to elucidate what is appropriate, desirable and employable masculinity for the gay adult film industry, but it is through discussion of the penis that the necessary attributes become overt. . . .

The value of a large penis became evident during casting sessions, and is explicitly evident in the following fieldnote excerpt that describes an interaction between the casting director and studio owner:

> Steve entered the casting office and he and Samuel began discussing a model for an upcoming scene. Steve instructed Samuel to negotiate with the performer. Samuel replied, "He's gonna want like $1400 for that," and Steve said, "Yeah he's not getting that." Samuel replied, "The thing is for that scene he's gonna get notoriety. Those are two well known guys." Steve said, "I don't know that he wants that," and explained that his manager just wants him to get work and nothing more. Samuel asked, "So where can I go? Like what's my ceiling? [for negotiating]." Steve replied, "I don't even know. . . . He's got a huge dick . . . remember it's a three-way, he is going to be doing more work, he is going to be sucking two dicks . . . I don't know, maybe it shouldn't be a three-way . . . $1200 . . . if he wants more, come talk to me."

In this interaction, Steve, the owner, is taking the size of the model's penis into consideration when determining how much money they are willing to offer him for the scene. Both the amount of work he will have to do during the scene as well as his body are monetized by the studio, and in turn serve as bargaining chips for the performer. In another visit, toward the end of the year when business is slowest and Samuel had some free time, I had the opportunity to ask him to train me in the process of casting models. I asked questions about what they were looking for while reviewing submissions, and he stated:

> "This guy is 23, but he looks a little old for [Boi Toys] . . . he could work for Stock Cocks . . . he's got a nice thick dick, that always helps. A big dick is always a plus, never a negative, it's never a point against someone."

The size of a model's penis is routinely used to determine the appropriate sexual role in the films (either insertive or receptive). When reviewing performer submissions, statements about performers such as "he has a huge one" or "he's got a huge cock" are made specifically in reference to performers that they want to bring in for filming. A large penis, as Samuel had informed me, is best used for insertive purposes; a model with a large penis who bottoms is seen as "a waste." When contrasted with an example where a model was cast as a bottom, we can see that this logic also impacts the model's agency.

> When Samuel and I reviewed model submissions, he showed Bobby a photograph of a potential performer and said, "Oh *he's* a bottom," Bobby replied, "Yeah, he doesn't have much of a cock." Samuel paused and then said, in a somewhat derisive tone, "Oh yeah, *there* it is."

Here we can again see the association between penis size, attractiveness, and appropriate role on the part of the performer. The performer's penis was judged to be rather small, and therefore the appropriate role for him was that of bottom. This is in contrast to models with large penises who possess the agency to elect their desired role. It is also worth noting that the lines of valuation go beyond penis size and also have racial components:

> Samuel and I returned to reviewing submissions and Samuel pulled up a submission from an Asian performer, and said, "Asians don't do well, they're not big sellers . . . Asians, Black guys, they do better in niche sites."

[. . .]

The reliance on racialized tropes in the casting process makes explicit the racialized nature of desirable gay masculinity for the adult film industry. Asian performers are feminized and rendered undesirable as they cannot "be dominant" and it is assumed that they will be anally receptive, and therefore do not "sell well." By contrast, the racial component of this masculinity requires that Black men be dominant and anally penetrative, underlined for me when Samuel then showed me a photograph of a Black former "studio exclusive" they had employed, who was very large, muscular, and well-endowed. The racialized elements of this local form of hegemonic masculinity within the gay adult film industry rest on tropes of Black hypermasculinity and hypersexuality as well as the emasculation of Asian men. Thus, because Black men are able to be seen or portrayed as "dominant" in a way that Asian men are not, Black men appear to be moderately less disadvantaged within the gay adult film industry.

Policing the Borders—the Femiphobic Discourse

All of the performers employed by *From Behind Films* are male, however the use of female gender pronouns such as "she" and "her" are key mechanisms by which the staff police the borders of the local form of hegemonic masculinity they seek to produce. Female gender pronouns are often utilized when a model causes difficulty for the studio staff. In the studio there is a corkboard, which I refer to as "the casting board," on which the staff post 4 × 6 photographs of the performers for scheduled scenes. During one visit to the studio, I noticed that a photograph that had previously been paired with another performer's 4 × 6 was suddenly absent from beside a scene partner.

> I asked, "Did you lose a scene partner for Eli?" Bobby replied that they didn't have one, but Samuel corrected, "No we lost him." Bobby turned around and asked who the partner was, and Samuel responded, "Trevor Smith, but he suddenly retired." Bobby replied, "Yeah, she's retired, until her rent's due."

In this situation, the porn star had suddenly decided to leave the industry only days before the scheduled shoot, creating the challenge for the studio to scramble to find a new scene partner for the shoot. The subject of retired porn stars had come up in previous visits, but the use of a female gender pronoun had not been used until this point. The male pronoun in the foregoing interaction between Bobby and Samuel was used when it was stated that they had "lost him," but once it was revealed that the model had suddenly decided to retire and that this had impacted the studio, the model was feminized ("she's retired, until her rent's due"). The use of female gender pronouns in this situation is connected with the dependability of the performer, thus while there are explicit bodily requirements for desirable masculinity, there are performative and interactive attributes, such as dependability, that are required as well. The model must also be polite and respectful, as indicated during another visit when Samuel said that he did not want to hire a performer again because "she yelled at me on the phone."

When the studio staff wishes to disparage a performer or their actions, they utilize female gender pronouns in order to do so. The aforementioned acts of disparagement occurred specifically when the model had caused difficulty for the studio or to the staff, but this is not the only instance in which female gender pronouns are utilized. In cases where a performer is viewed simply as not a good fit because of his appearance, he is frequently feminized by the staff:

Samuel was reviewing 4×6 photographs for potential scene partners and suggested a pairing to Bobby, who stated that the model was too old. Samuel asked, "Well, he can't be for *Stock Cocks?*" Bobby replied "He's 45." and Samuel asked, "She's got some city miles on her?"

This example highlights how the femiphobic discourse is deployed not only to police a performer's behavior, but also his body. It is implied that the model is "rough" or "overused" for his age—in the manner of a car only driven in the city—and thus is undesirable for employment. The use of a female gender pronoun in this instance implies a negative, ageist connotation of undesirability. During my time at *From Behind Films,* the staff did not ever use "she" or "her" in a positive manner, it was always associated with the negative: too old, too difficult, unattractive (too skinny, too small, not sufficiently endowed), or too demanding.

[. . .]

Through the use of female gender pronouns, the staff at *From Behind Films* define models who are of no value or lesser value to the studio: those who are difficult to work with, those who are too old or unattractive, and while "bottom" performers are employable, my observations suggest they are less valuable than penetrative performers. . . .

Discussion—From Local to Regional

Mechanisms of gender policing are nuanced, historically and geographically specific, and diverse in the ways that they define hegemonic and subordinated masculinities (Messerschmidt, 2012). The use of a femiphobic discourse at *From Behind Films* indicates that it is the spectre of femininity that regulates the local hegemonic masculinity constructed through their production of gay adult film. These adult film producers, during both casting and directing, engage in symbolic boundary work (Lamont and Molnár, 2002) through discussion of "appropriate" masculine bodies for gay pornography and the deployment of a femiphobic discourse. These mechanisms construct a local hegemonic masculinity that privileges professionalism, reliability, dominance, muscularity, men between 20 and 35 years of age who are "jockish," well-endowed, and white. These processes determine who gets hired as a performer, who receives more work, and who gets paid more money. Men who are viewed as conventionally masculine and as tops receive the benefits of this gender hierarchy, while those who do not are devalued or precluded from hire. This is racialized in complicated but demonstrable ways. White performers experience the most workplace privilege as they are the clear first choice during casting. Latino men occupy a secondary position, though they are routinely considered for hire. Black men may very rarely be considered, while Asian performers are categorically excluded.

[. . .]

Where Pascoe's (2005) high school boys used the fag discourse to reinforce their own masculine identity at the expense of another's, the staff at *From Behind Films* use female gender pronouns to construct the category of a devalued, or unhirable performer. This symbolic boundary work of exclusion at the interactional level ultimately results in social boundaries that maintain unequal access to material resources and opportunities for those who work in the gay adult film industry. This devaluation occurs not only to models who cause difficulty for the studio, but along lines of race and of sexual role. Asian men are feminized, they "cannot be dominant," and are rarely considered for hire, and then only as bottoms. While the studio does not consider Asian men for hire, Black men appear to marginally profit from hypersexual tropes to obtain work. Through these symbolic and social boundaries the staff create hierarchical categories of difference, resulting in discriminatory hiring practices which are then justified as a result of "market demand." Steve explained to me during one fieldsite visit that they "know what sells" through metrics that track view counts on specific videos, the number of times people list a video as a favorite or download it, and through comments they submit. They use these metrics to justify the gender and racial hierarchy constructed through their hiring practices.

The findings in this study continue to provide support for the arguments of previous researchers who identify homophobia as an essential mechanism for defining contemporary masculinity (Burn, 2000; Kimmel, 2003; Pascoe, 2005, 2007; Plummer, 2001) yet the complexities of how gender is regulated in all-gay contexts complicates this framework. The femiphobic discourses in homosocial and homosexual spaces extends theories of the homophobic "fag" discourse by pulling apart the stratum of meanings and mechanisms that can be deployed in abjection; men of subordinated masculinities (in this instance, the producers in the gay adult film industry) further "other" those already scorned by the larger cultural fag discourse. Through this discourse the gender hierarchy is reconstituted; feminine men (and by extension, women) are devalued in much the same way that they are in heterosexual contexts.

[. . .]

References

Bernardi, D. 2006. "Interracial Joysticks: Pornography's Web of Racist Attractions." Pp. 220–43 in *Pornography: Film and Culture*, edited by P. Lehman. New Brunswick, NJ: Rutgers University Press.

Burn, S. M. 2000. "'Heterosexuals' Use of 'Fag' and 'Queer' to Deride One Another: A Contributor to Heterosexism and Stigma." *Journal of Homosexuality* 40(2):1–11.

Chen, A. S. 1999. "Lives at the Center of the Periphery, Lives at the Periphery of the Center: Chinese American Masculinities and Bargaining with Hegemony." *Gender and Society* 13(5):584–607.

Connell, R. W. 1987. *Gender and Power*. Cambridge, UK: Polity Press.

Demetriou, D. Z. 2001. "Connell's Concept of Hegemonic Masculinity: A Critique." *Theory and Society* 30(3):337–61.

Dworkin, A. 1985. "Against the Male Flood: Censorship, Pornography, and Equality." *Harvard Women's Law Journal* 8:1–29.

Dworkin, A. 1987. "Pornography Is a Civil Rights Issue for Women." *University of Michigan Journal of Law Reform* 21(1–2):55–67.

Echols, A. 1984. "The Taming of the ID: Feminist Sexual Politics 1968–1983." Pp. 1–28 in *Pleasure and Danger: Exploring Female Sexuality*, edited by C. S. Vance. Boston, MA: Routledge.

Escoffier, J. 2009. *Bigger Than Life: The History of Gay Porn Cinema From Beefcake to Hardcore.* Philadelphia, PA: Running Press Book Publishers.

Forna, A. 2001. "Pornography and Racism: Sexualizing Oppression and Inciting Hatred." Pp. 102–12 in *Pornography: Women, Violence and Civil Liberties*, edited by C. Itzin. New York: Oxford University Press.

Fritz, B. 2009. "Tough Times in the Porn Industry." *Los Angeles Times*, August 10. Retrieved April 17, 2013 (http://articles.latimes.com/2009/aug/10/business/fi-ct-porn10).

Gardener, T. A. 1980. "Racism in Pornography and the Women's Movement." Pp. 94–101 in *Take Back the Night: Women on Pornography*, edited by L. Lederer. New York: William Morrow.

Gramsci, A. 1971. *Selections from the Prison Notebooks*. Translated by Q. Hoare and G. N. Smith. New York: International Publishers Co.

Hodges, M. J. and M. J. Budig. 2010. "Who Gets the Daddy Bonus? Organizational Hegemonic Masculinity and the Impact of Fatherhood on Earnings." *Gender and Society* 24(6):717–45.

Johnson, C. W. and D. M. Samdahl. 2005. "'The Night They Took Over': Misogyny in a Country-Western Gay Bar." *Leisure Sciences* 27(4):331–48.

Kimmel, M. 2003. "Adolescent Masculinity, Homophobia, and Violence: Random School Shootings 1982–2001." *American Behavioral Scientist* 46(10):1439–58.

Kimmel, M. 2004. "Masculinity as Homophobia: Fear, Shame and Silence in the Construction of Gender Identity." Pp. 182–99 in *Feminism & Masculinities*, edited by P. F. Murphy. Oxford/New York: Oxford University Press.

Kimmel, M. and M. A. Messner, eds. 2012. *Men's Lives*. 9th ed. Boston, MA: Pearson.

Kipnis, L. 1996. *Bound and Gagged: Pornography and the Politics of Fantasy in America*. Durham, NC: Duke University Press.

Lamont, M. and V. Molnár. 2002. "Cultivating Differences: Symbolic Boundaries and the Making of Inequality." *Annual Review of Sociology* 28(1):167–95.

Lanzieri, N. and T. Hildebrandt. 2011. "Using Hegemonic Masculinity to Explain Gay Male Attraction to Muscular and Athletic Men." *Journal of Homosexuality* 58(2):275–93.

Levine, M. P. 1998. *Gay Macho: The Life and Death of the Homosexual Clone*. New York: New York University Press.

Lewis, V. 2009. "When 'Macho' Bodies Fail: Spectacles of Corporeality and the Limits of the Homosocial/Sexual in Mexican Cinema." Pp. 177–92 in *Mysterious Skin: Male Bodies in Contemporary Cinema*, edited by S. Fouz-Hernandez. New York: I.B. Tauris & Co.

Logan, T. D. 2010. "Personal Characteristics, Sexual Behaviors, and Male Sex Work: A Quantitative Approach." *American Sociological Review* 75(5):679–704.

Lusher, D. and G. Robins. 2007. "Hegemonic and Other Masculinities in Local Social Contexts." *Men and Masculinities* 11(4):387–423.

MacKinnon, C. A. 1989. "Pornography: On Morality and Politics." Pp. 195–214 in *Toward a Feminist Theory of the State*, edited by C. A. MacKinnon. Cambridge, MA: Harvard University Press.

MacKinnon, C. A. and A. Dworkin. 1998. *In Harm's Way: The Pornography Civil Rights Hearings*. Cambridge, MA: Harvard University Press.

Mercer, J. 2012. "Coming of Age: Problematizing Gay Porn and the Eroticized Older Man." *Journal of Gender Studies* 21(3):313–26.

Messerschmidt, J. W. 2012. "Engendering Gendered Knowledge: Assessing the Academic Appropriation of Hegemonic Masculinity." *Men and Masculinities* 15(1):56–76.

Miller-Young, M. 2010. "Putting Hypersexuality to Work: Black Women and Illicit Eroticism in Pornography." *Sexualities* 13(2):219–35.

Pascoe, C. J. 2005. "'Dude, You're a Fag': Adolescent Masculinity and the Fag Discourse." *Sexualities* 8(3):329–46.

Pascoe, C. J. 2007. *Dude, You're A Fag: Masculinity and Sexuality in High School*. Berkeley, CA: University of California Press.

Plummer, D. C. 2001. "The Quest for Modern Manhood: Masculine Stereotypes, Peer Culture and the Social Significance of Homophobia." *Journal of Adolescence* 24(1):15–23.

Reddit. 2013. *We Are the Pornhub Team. Ask Us Anything*. Retrieved January 21, 2014 (http://www.red-dit.com/r/IAmA/comments/1un3wn/we_are_the_pornhub_team_ask_us_anything).

Rubin, G. 1993. "Misguided, Dangerous and Wrong: An Analysis of Anti-Pornography Politics." Pp. 18–40 in *Bad Girls and Dirty Pictures: The Challenge to Reclaim Feminism*, edited by A. Assiter and A. Carol. Boulder, CO: Pluto Press.

Shimizu, C. P. 2007. *The Hypersexuality of Race: Performing Asian/American Women on Screen and Scene*. Durham, NC: Duke University Press.

Taywaditep, K. J. 2001. "Marginalization Among the Marginalized: Gay Men's Anti-Effeminacy Attitudes." *Journal of Homosexuality* 42(1):1–28.

Thomas, J. A. 2000. "Gay Male Pornography Since Stonewall." Pp. 67–90 in *Sex for Sale: Prostitution, Pornography, and the Sex Industry*, edited by R. Weitzer. New York: Routledge.

Vance, C. S. 1984. "Pleasure and Danger: Toward a Politics of Sexuality." Pp. 1–28 in *Pleasure and Danger: Exploring Female Sexuality*, edited by C. S. Vance. Boston, MA: Routledge.

Williams, L. 2004. *Porn Studies*. Durham, NC: Duke University Press.

Wingfield, A. H. 2009. "Racializing the Glass Escalator: Reconsidering Men's Experiences with Women's Work." *Gender and Society* 23(1):5–26.

Yeung, K-T, M. Stombler, and R. Wharton. 2006. "Making Men in Gay Fraternities: Resisting and Reproducing Multiple Dimensions of Hegemonic Masculinity." *Gender and Society* 20(1):5–31.

Do Workplace Gender Transitions Make Gender Trouble?

Kristen Schilt and Catherine Connell

Gendered expectations for workers are deeply embedded in workplace structures (Acker, 1990; Britton, 2004; Gherardi, 1995; Padavic and Reskin, 2002; Valian, 1999; Williams, 1995). Employers often bring their gender schemas about men and women's abilities to bear on hiring and promotion decisions, leading men and women to face very different relationships to employment and advancement (Acker, 1990; Britton, 2004; Valian, 1999; Williams, 1995). However, when an employer hires a man to do a "man's job," he or she typically does not expect this man to announce that he intends to become a woman and remain in the same job. Open workplace gender transitions—situations in which an employee undergoes a "sex change" and remains in the same job—present an interesting challenge to this gendered division of labour. While the varied mechanisms that hold occupational sex segregation in place often are hidden, gender transitions can throw them into high relief. Becoming women at work, for example, can mean that transwomen lose high powered positions they are seen as no longer suited for (Griggs, 1998). On the other hand, becoming men can make transmen more valued workers than they were as women (Schilt, 2006). Beyond illuminating deeply naturalized gendered workplace hierarchies, however, these open transitions also have the potential to make workplace "gender trouble" (Butler, 1990), as transsexual/transgender people denaturalize the assumed connection between gender identity, genitals and chromosomal makeup when they "cross over" at work.

This article considers the impact of open gender transitions on binary conceptions of gender within the context of the workplace. Drawing on in-depth interviews, we illustrate how transsexual/transgender people and their co-workers socially negotiate gender identity during the transformative process of open workplace transitions. As gendered behavioural expectations for men and women can vary greatly depending on organizational cultures and occupational contexts (Britton, 2004; Connell, 1995; Salzinger, 2003), transmen and transwomen must develop a sense of how to facilitate same-gender and cross-gender interactions as new men or

Kristen Schilt and Catherine Connell. 2007. "Do Workplace Gender Transitions Make Gender Trouble?" *Gender, Work & Organization* 14(6):596–618.

new women in their specific workplaces. In this renegotiation process, some of the interviewees in our study adopt what can be termed "alternative" femininities and masculinities—gender identities that strive to combat gender and sexual inequality. However, regardless of their personal commitments to addressing sexism in the workplace, many transmen and transwomen are enlisted post-transition into workplace interactions that reproduce deeply held cultural beliefs about men and women's "natural" abilities and interests. We argue that the strength of these enlistments, and the lack of viable alternative interactional scripts in the context of the workplace, limit the political possibilities of open workplace transitions. Rather than "undoing gender" (Butler, 2004) in the workplace, then, individuals who cross over at work find themselves either anchored to their birth gender through challenges to the authenticity of their destination gender, or firmly repatriated into "the other side" of the gender binary.

[. . .]

Putting our focus on the context of the workplace, we examine how our interviewees negotiate cross-gender and same-gender workplace interactions after their open workplace transitions. Rather than causing gender trouble, transmen and transwomen report that their co-workers either hold them accountable to their birth gender, or repatriate them into the "other side" of the gender binary. Even when our interviewees want to challenge this rigid binary thinking about gender, they can feel pressured to downplay their opposition because of their need to maintain steady employment. . . .

Methods

This research was conducted with 28 transsexual/transgender people in Los Angeles, California and Austin, Texas between 2003 and 2005. Both cities have vibrant transgender communities, as well as recently adopted citywide employment protections for transgender workers. Seventeen interviewees came from the first author's study of the workplace experiences of transmen in southern California and 11 interviewees came from the second author's study of transwomen's workplace experiences in Austin, Texas. . . .

The interviews ranged from two to four hours.

[. . .]

Analysis

Workplaces are not gender-neutral locations filled with bodies, but rather complex sites in which gender expectations are embedded in workplace structures and reproduced in interactions (Acker, 1990; Britton, 2004; Williams, 1995). Gendered behavioural expectations for men and women vary greatly depending on organizational cultures and occupational contexts (Connell, 1995; Salzinger, 2003). While there is always some personal leeway in how to do gender, workers face pressures to conform to specific gender expectations for their workplaces. Not meeting these expectations can result in gender harassment, ostracization and loss of advancement possibilities (Miller, 1997; Rhode, 1997; Talbot, 2002; Valian, 1999).

In undertaking an open workplace transition, transgender people face the task of doing gender in their new social identity in a way that fits with both gendered workplace expectations and their personal gender ideologies. In the next two sections, we outline how interviewees see their transitions impacting on cross-gender interactions, interactions with co-workers who do not share their destination gender, and same-gender interactions, interactions with co-workers who do share their destination gender. Rather than challenging binary views on gender, we demonstrate that these renegotiations often push transmen and transwomen towards reproducing workplace gender hierarchies that privilege masculinity and devalue femininity, thereby reaffirming their co-workers' belief in the naturalness of the gender binary in the workplace.

Negotiating Cross-Gender Interactions

[...]

New gender boundaries. After the public announcement of their gender transition in the workplace, both transmen and transwomen describe the erection of new cross-gender boundaries in workplace interactions. As transmen increasingly develop a masculine appearance, many find that they are less frequently included in "girl talk" at work—generally conversations about appearance and dress, menstruation and romantic interests. For transmen who describe themselves as "always already men" (Rubin, 2003) despite being born with a female body, these new boundaries are a relief. Illustrating this type of reaction, Aaron says:

> Even when I was living as a female, I never did get the way women interacted. And I was always on the outside of that, so I never really felt like one of them.

For Paul, who transitioned while working in one of the "women's professions" (nursing and teaching), these new boundaries signaled a welcomed end to being held accountable to stereotypical feminine interactional expectations, such as noticing new hairstyles or offering compliments about hair and clothing—interactions he describes as not coming to him naturally.

Some transwomen also express relief about the cessation of gendered expectations to participate in stereotypically masculine interactions. Laura, who transitioned in a professional job, notes that her actual interactions with men changed little with her transition. When working as a man, he—at the time—had removed himself from "guy talk"; generally conversations about cars, sports, and the sexual objectification of women, as participating in these types of interactions did not fit with his personal sense of being a woman, despite having a male body. Now that she has made her feminine identity public at work, she feels that men in her workplace have a new interpretative frame for understanding these boundaries. "I think they understand a little more why I could have cared less who won the football game!"

Rather than challenging their ideas about the permanency of gender, interviewees felt that co-workers reincorporated their pre-transition interactions into an understanding of "being transgender" and the innateness of gendered interests. In other words, Laura's lack of interest in football and Paul's lack of participation in the feminine niceties were re-evaluated as proof that transgender people are somehow trapped in the wrong body, a situation that is made right through a gender transition.

Not all interviewees felt a sense of relief at the creation or sudden acceptance of cross-gender boundaries. For some transmen who formerly identified as queer, bisexual or lesbian women, these new boundaries create a sense of sadness and exclusion. Describing this feeling, Elliott, who transitioned in a retail job, says:

> It's just like a little bit more of a wall there [with women] because I am not one of the girls anymore.... Like [women] have to get to know me better before they can be really relaxed with me.... I grew up surrounded by women and now to have women be kind of leery of me, it's a very strange thing.

Transmen who are saddened by their perceptions of a new distance between themselves and women in the workplace still try to be respectful of these boundaries. This acceptance, however, does little to challenge notions of the gender binary; rather, conceding a loss of participation in "women's space" reifies divisions between men and women as natural. Yet, showing the importance of context in theorizing the potential of gender crossing to undo gender, transmen who seek to have masculine social identities at work have few other options, as most workplaces do not provide accepted interactional scripts for men who want to be just one of the girls. In order to keep social relationships smooth during the turmoil of an open workplace transition, then, transsexual/transgender people can hesitate to create additional challenges to gendered workplace expectations, as they desire to retain steady and comfortable employment.

In some cases, these new cross-gender boundaries can translate into workplace penalties. Agape, who transitioned in a high-tech company, remembers her boss worrying that taking estrogen would adversely affect her programming abilities. She says:

> I think he just doesn't really have that high of an opinion of women. I think it's just he, he thinks fire and aggression is what gets things done. . . . And I guess he sees women as being more passive, and was worried my productivity would decrease.

Lana faced a similar situation. As a man, Lana co-owned a professional business, a company she describes as a "real boys' club," with three other men. While they began their business as close friends, the friendship did not survive the announcement that Lana—he at the time—intended to become a woman. Moving from being a hegemonically masculine man who did not outwardly acknowledge his inner feminine gender identity, Lana's transition disrupted the homosocial bonds of the company's power elite. After multiple expressions of their discomfort about both the transition and having a woman as a business partner, Lana was forced out of the company. Underscoring the gendered aspect of these drastic new boundaries, she recalls that during the negotiations to buy her shares of the company:

> The only thing I remember [my business partner] saying in the entire three days was, "How can you expect to run a company when all you're going to be thinking about is nail polish?"

As this comment suggests, Lana's partners locate their challenge to her in terms of gendered expectations that women cannot be serious business partners because they are too concerned with frivolities of appearance. Her transition does not undo gendered expectations, but rather is reincorporated into a workplace gender hierarchy that disadvantages and devalues women and femininity.

Interactional styles. Open workplace gender transitions reveal the gender dynamics behind what are considered workplace-appropriate cross-gender interactions. Both transmen and transwomen recount their sudden realization that changing gender at work requires a renegotiation of once comfortable interactional styles. In some cases, transmen and transwomen make personal decisions about changing cross-gender interactions in an effort to meet their personal ideals of how men and women should act—such as the case of Preston, who transitioned from woman to man in a blue-collar job. When working as a woman, Preston—who publicly identified as a lesbian—describes frequently engaging in joking, sexualized banter with both men and women in her dyke-friendly workplace. However, after his transition, he suddenly felt uncomfortable engaging in similar conversations:

> I used to flirt a lot as a lesbian! It was easy for me to flirt. . . . Since I have transitioned, a lot of the stuff that I could say as a dyke is so inappropriate! [laughs]. There is this one woman at work . . . she is just really straight. Very much. I used to tease her about . . . switching sides. . . . And if I say that now [as a man], it is just like so fucking inappropriate. There is no way for me to find a justification for that, even though that is the history of our relationship. It is the history of how we have interacted with one another. . . . [It] could be perceived wrong. Even though my motive for it hasn't changed, but it is still inappropriate.

Preston's sense of discomfort with this interactional style translates into adopting a policing role toward sexualized banter at work. His co-workers were surprised at his behavioural changes, as he used to engage in the same type of behaviour he now critiques. However, for him, this type of behavioural change was necessary, as he did not want to enact a form of masculinity that can be construed as sexist. As he gains cultural competency in the variety of ways men and women interact, he might feel more leeway to adopt different interactional styles, as some men in his workplace did engage in sexualized banter with women. At the onset of transition, however, many transmen err on the side of caution by policing their behaviour, as—even with legal protections for gender identity in the workplace—they can feel vulnerable as openly transgender employees.

Other changes to cross-gender interactional styles can be a result of implicit or explicit pressure from co-workers. Ellen, who transitioned from man to woman in a customer service job, describes implicit pressure to tone down stereotypically masculine styles of interaction:

> There is one thing that really drives me crazy—when I'm asked for my opinion on a subject [from men], I have to remember—"Do not express it as firmly as I actually believe."

While she personally does not wish to change, she realizes that muting opinions and emotions is the predominant interactional style for women in her workplace. She continues:

> At work I tend not to trumpet my own horn very much, and the workplace environment demands that [women keep quiet]. I don't know if that's anything about me as transgender. I think that's just being a woman.

While this change to her interactional style does reproduce men doing dominance and women doing deference (West and Zimmerman, 1987), Ellen, like Preston, feels she needs to make these concessions in order to gain a feminine social identity at work and to keep friendly relationships with her co-workers.

Pressures to change cross-gender interactional styles also can be explicit. Several transmen describe women in their workplaces enlisting them into what can be termed "gender rituals" (Goffman, 1977), stereotypical interactions that are typically played out between heterosexual men and women. After the announcement of their transition from woman to man, transmen recount women raising expectations that they will now, as men, do any requisite heavy lifting around the workplace, such as changing office water bottles, moving furniture, or carrying heavy boxes. Interestingly, this change in behavioural expectations occurs almost immediately after the transition announcement. The change was so rapid that many transmen were, at first, not sure how to make sense of these new expectations. Kelly, who transitioned in a semi-professional job, notes:

Before [transition] no one ever asked me to do anything really and then [after], this one teacher, she's like, "Can you hang this up? Can you move this for me?" . . . Like if anything needed to be done in this room, it was me. Like she was just, "Male—okay, you do it." That took some adjusting. I thought she was picking on me for a while. And then I realized that she just, she just assumes that I'm gonna do all that stuff.

Ken describes a similar experience in his semi-professional workplace. While his co-workers were slow to adopt masculine pronouns with him, women did enlist him in performing masculine-coded duties in the workplace immediately after his transition announcement, such as carrying heavy items to the basement and unloading boxes.

For some transmen, being enlisted into these masculine gender rituals is exciting, as it gives them access to chivalrous behaviour they were sanctioned for when they performed them as masculine women. For others, this enlistment is viewed as blatant sexism. Describing this reaction, Trevor says:

[In one job] I had a supervisor who kept asking me to move fucking furniture and to do electronic equipment. And I would have to explain to her all the time. This would happen several times a day because it was a new program and we were setting up the office. There was furniture that needed to be moved but I have a hand disability, so I can't do it. I had already told her that like four or five times. And in the meanwhile, there were a couple of big, strong women who were much bigger and stronger than I was. But [my supervisor] asked me. I am kind of a little guy! I pointed out to her [assuming a man should do heavy lifting] is a really sexist assumption.

While this enlisting signals a certain level of social validation for his masculine social identity, it conflicts with his physical abilities as well as his personal gender ideology. Trevor's frustration comes from this supervisor's constant slippage into gender rituals that position women as frail and men as able. Even when he challenges what he sees as a sexism assumption, however, she continues to make the requests, illustrating how gendered workplace assumptions come to be naturalized. In other words, his attempt to undo this kind of gendered interaction has little impact on workplace ideas about what tasks are appropriate for men and women.

Challenges to authenticity. A small number of both transmen and transwomen experienced explicit challenges to the authenticity of their destination gender in cross-gender interactions. Kirsten transitioned from man to woman in a retail setting that was predominantly staffed by women and gay men. She found that once she began to transition, her friendly relationship with a colleague, a gay man, ended: "We used to laugh and joke together on the floor all the time. But he totally changed." As a drag performer, her colleague appeared to be threatened by Kirsten's decision to become a woman. Kirsten notes that while her co-worker had adopted facial surgery and had breast augmentation to enhance his drag performances, he thought transition "was wrong, and [said] he would never do that." He began to critique her appearance and behaviour after her transition.

[He would say], "Sometimes you look a little thrown together, and I think you need to work on that . . . and you need to build relationships with [co-workers] at the counter because they're saying that you're real bossy."

This co-worker's response is unsurprising—there is a history of competitive border wars between gay men who do drag and transwomen (Perkins, 1983; Rupp and Taylor, 2004). In the case of Kirsten, her co-worker's animosity precludes her from becoming a woman at work, as he is continually referencing her birth gender. Additionally, he challenges her feminine authenticity by suggesting she retains too many masculine traits—assertiveness that is suddenly labelled as "bossy" once she gains a feminine social identity. Located within this challenge, again, is explicit pressure for Kirsten to conform to a particular type of femininity to fit into her specific workplace.

For transmen, challenges to the authenticity of their masculinity were less explicit. Typically, it came in the form of feminine advice. Jake, who transitioned in a professional job, recounts his irritation at a woman he worked with who began to offer unsolicited advice about hysterectomies after he announced his transition. While this advice might have been well intentioned, he read it as an attempt to connect with him on a level of bodily sameness, a move that disregarded his transman identity. In this context, this type of advice can take on a mother/daughter dynamic that is uncomfortable and unwanted by many transmen.

Paul encountered similar advice at work from women who were concerned about his decision to pursue chest surgery—a procedure that requires a complete mastectomy. Attempting to relate to him as a woman, these colleagues encouraged him not to "cut off his breasts," a decision they saw as mutilation of healthy tissue. This type of reaction from women appears to be located in body identity, as these women co-workers make sense of transmen's surgical choices through the lens of something shared—a female body by birth.

Women, then, react with consternation to transgender body modification from their own position of feeling "appropriately" gendered, or not trapped in the wrong body. However, while these reactions from women negate transmen's masculine social identities on some level, they also keep them anchored in a binary view of gender: transmen are still women rather than really men.

Negotiating Same-Gender Interactions

[. . .]

Interactional styles. Open workplace transitions bring with them opportunities for engaging in same-gender interactions as new men or new women. In describing their relationships with other women in the workplace posttransition, transwomen express a new sense of freedom. When they were working as men, many transwomen had very stereotypically masculine workplace personas, as do many pre-transition transwomen (Griggs, 1998). Achieving these personas meant that they did not acknowledge their personal sense of relating more to women and "women's interests" than to men and "men's interests." As women, however, they now are able to openly express interest in feminine things that they often denied when they were working as men. Describing this new freedom, Laura, who transitioned in a professional job, notes:

> I got a bigger field of friends in this building. And of course, they're all female, because we all have lots of talk about. You know, I have grandchildren that range from two and up, so you know, we can talk about kids, we can talk about babies, you know, just about anything any other woman would talk about is what I'm knowledgeable and like to talk about. I like to cook, I like to sew. So it makes it pretty easy.

Prior to her transition, she did not, as a man, attempt the same types of interactions with women, as she worried these interactions would be seen as inappropriate, or she would be labelled as an atypical or gay man.

Illustrating the greater leeway for women to admit interest in activities coded as masculine (Thorne, 1993), transmen do not recount having to hide their preference for masculinity—indeed, most transmen in this study describe themselves as embodying this preference in their personal appearance. Yet, many transmen recount men explicitly engaging them in "guy talk" immediately after their announcement of their impending transition. Kelly, who transitioned in a semi-professional workplace where men were the minority, says:

> I definitely notice that the guys . . . they will say stuff to me that I know they wouldn't have said before [when I was working as a woman]. . . . And like one guy, he never talked to me before. I think he was uncomfortable [that I was a lesbian]. . . . Recently we were talking and he was talking about his girlfriend and he's like, "I go home and work it [have sex] for exercise." And I know he would never have said that to me before.

Jake describes a similar enlisting into what can be described as masculine gender rituals. In his professional workplace, he recounts making few changes in his interactional style with men in his workplace. However, he notes:

> One of the funny things that happened that was gender specific was that a lot of my male colleagues, at least at first, started kind of like slapping me on the back [laughs]. But I think it was with more force than they probably slapped each other on the back. . . . And it was not that I had gained access to "male privilege" but they were trying to affirm to me that they saw me as a male. . . . That they were going to try to be supportive and that was the way they were going to be supportive of me as a guy, or something of the sort [laughs]. Slapping me on the back.

As he remarks, he does not take this backslapping as a signal that these men have forgotten his birth gender. Rather, he interprets these actions as a kind of social validation performance his colleagues are acting out in an attempt to signal acceptance. The awkwardness of these back-slaps illustrates his colleagues' own hyperawareness of trying to casually do gender man to man. As Jake actively cultivates a transman identity, he, like Kelly, is uncomfortable with this incorporation, as he perceives it as intended to gloss over his life history. Yet, while he is able to disrupt this incorporation momentarily by mentioning things from his life as a woman, such as when he was a Girl Scout, he notes that men in his workplace appear more comfortable trying to relate to him as "just a guy" rather than a transman with a female history.

Gender apprenticing. Rather than challenging the authenticity of transmen and transwomen's destination gender, some same-gender colleagues took their transitioning colleague on as what can be described as a gender apprentice. For transmen, this form of apprenticing typically came from heterosexual men who sought to socialize them into how to be a man. Colin, who transitioned in a professional workplace, remembers being stopped by the director of his office the first day he came to work in a tie. "He's like, 'Oh no, no, no. That's not a good tie. Come here!' And he showed me how to tie a Windsor knot." In this situation, his older colleague adopts Colin as a younger protégé, teaching him "masculine" knowledge—how to tie a Windsor knot—that typically is handed down from father to son.

Simon, who transitioned in the "women's professions," also encountered apprenticing from the father of one of the children he worked with, as well as from his brother-in-law. While some transmen appreciate this form of apprenticing, others chafe at it, as it coerces them into hegemonic performances of masculinity that do not fit with their personal identity projects. This pressure from men in the workplace to do gender as men in the "right" way suggests, as well, that co-workers may have more anxiety about appropriate gender performances than the person who is actually transitioning.

While transwomen describe less frequent occurrences of gender apprenticing, they are, in contrast to transmen, typically appreciative of these apprenticing efforts of women they work with. This gender difference in reactions may be a result of the different reactions to gender crossing. In other words, as women, pre-transition transmen have more leeway for adopting masculine appearances and behaviour, which gives them more experience with masculinity when they transition. As men, on the other hand, pretransition transwomen face severe social sanctions for expressing interest in feminine styles and behaviour. This difference, an adult version of the "tomboy/sissy" dynamic (Thorne, 1993), means that transwomen have little experience with how to do femininity once they become women, and are appreciative of women's efforts to socialize them. Describing this reaction, Laura, who transitioned in a professional job, recounts how moved she was when a woman at her work took her shopping for make-up:

> I've had other women here help me with make-up. . . . There's a lady here who said, "Oh, let me do it! I can show you simple things." I said, "Ok!" and we went shopping, that kind of thing. . . . I forgot how it was brought up—but somebody said, "You know, Crystal loves to do makeup." And I said, "I'm gonna have to get a hold of her and see what her ideas are." And that is how it began. And so—I paid for lunch and we ran out to Target or someplace and picked out a few things that would work. And she taught me how to put it on.

Laura initiates her own apprenticing by directly approaching her colleague for make-up advice. This apprenticing allows her to develop more confidence in her feminine appearance. While other transwomen describe being "allowed" to engage in "girl talk" about children, romance, and fashion, they do not recount such strong incorporation into their destination gender by women as transmen do from men. As with the previous examples in this section, men appear more invested in including transmen as just one of the guys than women are in incorporating transwomen into the world of women at work. In both cases, however, this kind of gender apprenticing reinforces strongly held cultural beliefs about how men and women should act and look. Even when transmen attempt to create new ways to be a man at work, they often are socially repatriated into the gender binary as men—showing again the difficulty of undoing gender in the context of the workplace.

Discussion

In this article we consider the impact of open gender transitions on binary conceptions of gender in the context of the workplace. While transsexuals often are represented as being gender overachievers (Garfinkel, 1967; Kando, 1973; Raymond, 1979), this article shows that in open workplace transitions, co-workers, rather than transmen and transwomen, can overdo and reinforce gender. This over-doing of gender typically occurs when co-workers attempt to demonstrate their acceptance of their transitioning colleague. Men slap transmen on the back and engage them in "guy talk," while women begin to ask transmen to do heavy lifting. Co-workers also try to teach transmen how to be men, or begin to hold transwomen accountable to restrictive standards of appropriate work femininity.

As everyone re-negotiates the meaning of gender and sexual difference made visible by open workplace transitions, binary thinking about gender is often upheld and the resulting gender hierarchies interwoven with heteronormativity and sexism are reproduced. Transmen and transwomen can be frustrated by the rigid gender expectations placed upon them by co-workers. For some transwomen, facing the devaluation of femininity in the workplace is detrimental to their careers, as they are rejected from powerful homosocial men's networks or classified as less able workers. The reactions transmen and transwomen describe to their gender transitions suggest that co-workers may face more anxieties about how to properly do gender in open workplace transitions than their transitioning colleague. Rather than causing gender trouble, however, these anxieties result in a reinforcement of binary views on gender through the reproduction of gendered hierarchies that disadvantage women and rigid adherence to the "right" way to do gender.

[. . .]

In open workplace transitions, co-workers, transmen and transwomen all are renegotiating and managing gender and sexual difference. Yet, within this identity work, these data suggest there is little initial challenge in the workplace to naturalized attitudes about the immutability of gender, binary views about the compl[e]mentary nature of masculinity and femininity, or gendered workplace hierarchies. In other words, the mere introduction of a visibly transgender subject does not result in an undoing of gender or the creation of gender alternatives, such as a third gender category or a gender continuum (Bornstein, 1994; Garber, 1992).

[. . .]

Transgender workers—a vulnerable population economically—must balance political desires to shake up gender with job security. Retaining job security can mean participating in existing workplace gender structures of doing dominance for men and doing deference for women. As transgender workers settle into their new gender at work, they may have more leeway for creating gender trouble. However, organizational cultures are slow to change, even with direct confrontation or legal reforms, making the documentation of this type of workplace transformation difficult.

In conclusion, we suggest that theoretical conceptions about the transformative potential of gender performances that are not in line with birth gender (Butler, 1990, 2004) should pay close attention to context, as well as the way in which these performances are socially interpreted. While intentional gender trouble performances can have political possibilities, such as in certain drag performances (Rupp and Taylor, 2004), they also can—as in the context of the workplace—be repatriated into a binary, or dismissed as inauthentic.

References

Acker, Joan. 1990. "Hierarchies, Jobs, Bodies: A Theory of Gendered Organizations." *Gender & Society* 4(2):139–58.

Bornstein, Kate. 1994. *Gender Outlaw: On Men, Women, and the Rest of Us.* New York: Routledge.

Britton, Dana. 2004. *At Work in the Iron Cage: The Prison as Gendered Organization.* New York: New York University Press.

Butler, Judith. 1990. *Gender Trouble: Feminism and the Subversion of Identity.* New York: Routledge.

Butler, Judith. 2004. *Undoing Gender.* New York: Routledge.

Connell, Robert. 1995. *Masculinities.* Berkeley, CA: University of California Press.

Garber, Marjorie. 1992. *Vested Interests: Cross-dressing and Cultural Anxiety.* New York: Routledge.

Garfinkel, Harold. 1967. *Studies in Ethnomethodology.* Englewood Cliffs, NJ: Prentice-Hall.

Gherardi, Sylvia. 1995. *Gender, Symbolism and Organizational Cultures.* London: Sage.

Goffman, Erving. 1977. "The Arrangement Between the Sexes." *Theory and Society* 4(3):301–31.

Griggs, Claudine. 1998. *S/he: Changing Sex and Changing Clothes.* New York: Berg.

Kando, Thomas. 1973. *Sex Change: The Achievement of Gender Identity Among Feminized Transsexuals.* Springfield, IL: Charles C. Thomas.

Miller, Laura. 1997. "Not Just Weapons of the Weak: Gender Harassment as a Form of Protest for Army Men." *Social Psychology Quarterly* 60(1):32–51.

Padavic, Irene and Barbara Reskin. 2002. *Women and Men at Work.* 2nd ed. Thousand Oaks, CA: Pine Forge Press.

Perkins, Roberta. 1983. *The "Drag Queen" Scene: Transsexuals in Kings Cross.* Sydney, Australia: George Allen & Unwin.

Raymond, Janice. 1979. *The Transsexual Empire: The Making of a She-Male.* London, UK: Women's Press.

Rhode, Deborah L. 1997. *Speaking of Sex: The Denial of Gender Inequality.* Cambridge, MA: Harvard University Press.

Rubin, Henry. 2003. *Self Made Men: Identity and Embodiment Among Transsexual Men.* Nashville, TN: Vanderbilt University Press.

Rupp, Leila and Verta Taylor. 2004. *Drag Queens at the 801 Cabaret.* Chicago, IL: University of Chicago Press.

Salzinger, Leslie. 2003. *Genders in Production: Making Workers in Mexico's Global Factories.* Berkeley, CA: University of California Press.

Schilt, Kristen. 2006. "Just One of the Guys? How Transmen Make Gender Visible at Work." *Gender & Society* 20(4):465–90.

Talbot, Margaret. 2002. "Men Behaving Badly: When Men Harass Men, Is It Sexual Harassment?" *New York Times Magazine,* October 13, p. 11.

Thorne, Barrie. 1993. *Gender Play: Girls and Boys in School.* New Brunswick, NJ: Rutgers University Press.

Valian, Virginia. 1999. *Why So Slow? The Advancement of Women.* Cambridge, MA: MIT Press.

West, Candace and Don Zimmerman. 1987. "Doing Gender." *Gender & Society* 1(1):125–51.

Williams, Christine. 1995. *Still a Man's World: Men Who Do "Women's" Work.* Berkeley, CA: University of California Press.

Beyond the Industrial Paradigm

Market-Embedded Labor and the Gender Organization of Global Service Work in China

Eileen M. Otis

Service sector employment has grown prodigiously in recent decades, driven in large part by economic globalization. Globalization of commerce creates demand for highly-paid professionals to travel across national boundaries, and these professionals spend generously on consumer services in host countries (Sassen 2000). Vastly expanded global travel brings service-hungry visitors to previously pristine locations. Globalization of markets, particularly in once-socialist economies, facilitates the development of new consumer service industries (Davis 1999).

[. . .]

To illuminate the relationship between new gender norms and labor control, I compare ethnographic case studies of work in luxury hotels in two Chinese cities. Both hotels import the organizational template of the same U.S.-based lodging conglomerate and recruit same-aged and similarly-educated female workers. The first Transluxury hotel is located in Beijing, a northern metropolis, and it is directly linked to Galaxy, a U.S.-based corporation that manages hundreds of properties and employs more than 100,000 people in about 80 countries. The second hotel is located in Kunming, a southwestern metropolis. The Kunming Transluxury hotel has no direct organizational link to Galaxy: it recruits experienced Chinese Transluxury managers to implement the firm's template and protocols. Despite the common organizational heritage, distinctive patterns of control emerge among managers, female workers, and customers.

Workers in Beijing enact "virtual personalism," catering preemptively to customer preferences using feminized practices imported from the United States. As part of this enactment, they use local constructs of "face" to maintain interactive distance from customers, even while

Eileen M. Otis. 2008. "Beyond the Industrial Paradigm: Market-Embedded Labor and the Gender Organization of Global Service Work in China." *American Sociological Review* 73(1):15–36.

acting as if they know the customers intimately. In Kunming, the workers perform "virtuous professionalism," displaying service expertise to establish control over customers who might otherwise mistake them for sex workers. They are more formal and less intimate than their Beijing counterparts. Why is the interactive labor of women in service workplaces so different despite the single corporate-organizational template? The answer lies in the work process in service firms that, unlike manufacturing firms, is embedded in the local consumer market. The embeddedness in local consumer markets leads to the influence of region-specific work legacies and cultural practices on the work process of service labor.

[. . .]

Research Setting and Methods

Hotels were the first global service industry to enter China during the reform era. In 1978, there were a mere 203 hotels in the country (Sun 1992). By 2000, more than 7,000 hotels served a booming tourist economy, employing over 1.2 million workers (*China Labor Statistical Yearbook* 2001:119). For this study, I observed frontline work at two Transluxury Hotels, one in Beijing and the other in Kunming.

While both Beijing and Kunming are highly urbanized metropolises, Beijing, located in the North China macroregion, is one of the two most economically advanced metropolises in the country. In contrast, Kunming is one of the least developed metropolises, located in the impoverished Yungui macroregion (Skinner et al. 2000). Beijing receives far more foreign direct investments and hosts substantially more foreign travelers. Kunming, on the other hand, is a magnet for male domestic tourists drawn by the appeal of the region's ethnic minority populations, which add exoticism to the city's reputation as a no-holds-barred, red-light district (He and Qiao 1995). Throughout urban China, it is common for service outlets to double as brothels, and service work sometimes carries the taint of association with the illegal sex industry. To protect the reputation of its clientele, the Beijing Transluxury (hereafter BT) deploys a video surveillance system and security staff to obstruct prostitution. In contrast, the Kunming Transluxury (hereafter KT) organizes escort services for its pleasure-seeking clientele. Differences between the two hotels emerge from the very distinctive sets of clientele and the institutionally and culturally embedded strategies that local actors developed to manage customers.

. . . Typical of many service industries, men occupy the higher managerial strata; almost all executive management positions are held by men (men compose approximately three-quarters of midlevel management at both hotels). Women fill the vast majority of frontline staff and supervisor positions.

. . . Most frontline workers are female high school graduates who live with their parents and range in age from 17 to 28 years. They sign two-year labor contracts and receive comparable wages after adjusting for the higher cost of living in Beijing (*China Labor Statistical Yearbook* 2001). Workers wear similarly sexualized uniforms, including French maid outfits and brocaded, thigh-revealing *qipaos*. In each Transluxury site, workers purvey goods and services they cannot personally afford. For example, a basic room in each hotel costs about one month of the average frontline worker's salary.

[. . .]

I conducted semistructured interviews with 55 individuals attached to the Beijing Transluxury and 60 attached to the Kunming Transluxury from 1999 to 2000. I interviewed frontline staff from the bars and restaurants, housekeeping, security, and concierge. . . . Interviews lasted between 45 minutes and two hours. . . . I also spoke with employees and managers informally during lunches in the staff canteen. I shadowed waitresses, butlers, hostesses, housekeepers, and middle managers as they worked. I also participated in multiple training seminars, meetings, informal outings, and departmental parties.

Virtual Personalism at the Beijing Transluxury

A Masculine "Global" Consumer Market

"Who is he sleeping with? . . . the [Transluxury] Hotel," reads the tagline on a Beijing Transluxury (BT) advertisement. Equating the intimacy of a sexual encounter with the choice of hotel, the advertisement features a man of European origin slumbering (alone) in a Transluxury hotel bed. This is no one-night stand. Another advertisement reads: "We know you intimately."

The BT seeks a monogamous relationship with its well-heeled, globetrotting clientele, courting their commitment with discreet attentiveness in an atmosphere designed to appeal to the sensibilities of Western, male, luxury-seeking clients. As the capital of the fastest growing economy in the world, Beijing draws global executives, professionals, and officials accustomed to the trappings of a modern aristocratic lifestyle, at least when they travel. These amenities include butlers, maids, chauffeurs, and a cigar room. The hotel's lobby is a spectacle of elegance with Italian marble floors, silk-upholstered furniture, and towering palm trees; live quartet music wafts down from the balcony.

[. . .]

To serve this market, the BT offers individualized service delivered by a frontline staff made up almost exclusively of carefully-selected young women trained in Western-imported, middle-class feminine deference to appeal to the clientele. ("Men like to be served by young women," reasoned the BT's lounge manager.) The BT General Manager told me, "We focus on a niche market segment, which is high yield and less price sensitive." With access to guest preference data stored on computer files, staff members tailor services to the specific sensibilities of Western, affluent, and predominantly male consumers who patronize the hotel. I call this labor regime "virtual personalism" because it mimics the service the hotel's customers would receive from their personal staff.

[. . .]

Staff-Management Relations

With a substructure of material support as the foundation for worker goodwill, local, midlevel managers spin a fabric of trust with employees that permits them to comment on the intimate details of hygiene, comportment, facial expressions, and even morality. Indeed, the hotel evaluates managers on how effectively they coach and build employee confidence. Many managers frame their role as assisting workers in navigating the rite of passage into adulthood. I observed managers using social events to build a foundation of sentiment, granting their young protégés personal time and attention outside of work hours. One manager told me, "I'm teaching them to become human beings."

Flattened organizational hierarchies narrow functional distance, permitting managers to observe, advise, and even work alongside their staff members. One manager explained,

"I'm their supervisor and their assistant." Restaurant managers tote drink orders to guests and dispatch dirty ashtrays to the dishwasher. Managers often dine with workers at the canteen, where they commiserate over irascible customers. During these occasions, managers act like surrogate parents, inquiring into staff members' sex lives, home lives, and futures; they know the dating status of workers and regularly offer relationship advice. Many meet with workers' parents, occasionally intervening in family affairs to assure workplace commitment. One manager told a waitress's mother, "Work at the hotel is hard and tiring . . . the child can't do a lot around the house."

. . . Overall, workers welcome gestures of managerial care, calling managers "older sister" or "older brother." One waitress said, "Our manager is so amiable, she's like my old mother."

[. . .]

From the first day a female job applicant steps into the hotel, managers screen her for stature, youth, and sexual modesty. After one job interview, a manager soberly told me, "I will hire her for her body." Management rejects women who look to be of "questionable morality." For example, a personnel director rejected one applicant because she thought she was too sexy: her "wild long hair and big earrings" made her look like a "fox fairy," the mythical seductress of Chinese folk tales. On the other hand, management rejects women who are "too short" or past their late twenties because they are not considered sufficiently attractive.

Once hired, managers consider workers "blank sheets of paper." As inexperienced, live-at-home adolescents, managers view staff members as impressionable and pliable. Through continual training, managers expect to mold them into refined servers who attend to the minutiae of customer preferences, preferences that the customers themselves might not be consciously aware of. During intensive training sessions, managers attempt to inculcate a deep consciousness of seemingly minor variations in taste. . . .

Employees are prompted to notice if customers prefer, for example, Perrier or Evian water, Fuji or Macintosh apples, Styrofoam or feather pillows. If a customer makes his preferences explicit, particularly in the form of a complaint, employees should demonstrate empathy, inquire into the details of the problem, and solve it with dispatch.

In addition to adopting a micro-focus on customer preferences, workers learn new bodily practices. Before each work shift, workers stand at attention as managers inspect fingernails and makeup. They incite workers to smile, make eye contact with customers, and "walk like ladies," chastising those who "walk like men." For example, the male manager of the hotel's Chinese restaurant personally demonstrated how to walk like "ladies," pointing out the slight sway of his hips, his upright neck and shoulders, and his tightrope-treading gait. He then contrasted it with the "back-and-forth" swagger of a man.

The employee handbook precisely prescribes workers' behavior in public areas of service: "Do not lean or squat, do not place hands in your pockets, do not pick your nose, do not spit, do not talk loudly or shout, do not hold hands, do not clear your throat, do not scratch any part of your body." The topic of women's hair merits 19 handbook guidelines. Women's fingernails are not to exceed ".5 centimeters beyond the fingertip," and earrings may not be larger than 1.5 centimeters. Watches are to be of a "conservative style." Makeup is to "create a natural appearance." Lip liner, tattoos, and second earrings are prohibited. Managers lecture about appropriate underwear, daily sock changes, dandruff prevention, and teeth brushing techniques. They even encourage workers to sniff out other employees emanating unpleasant smells. A manager censured a waitress in a good-natured but still firm tone, "Your breath stinks like garlic! Don't you brush your teeth?" Another used humor to convey an equally pointed criticism: "Some of your hair looks so messy that I could sweep the floor with it."

In general, managers craft workers' self-presentation so employees appear familiar to Western clientele, even giving them English names, embossed on their badges, which they are required to use on the service floor. The directive for staff members to make direct and positive eye contact with customers is especially challenging for many female employees whose parents taught them to avoid eye contact with unfamiliar men. Managers use all manner of appeals to train their protégés to smile while looking directly at the customer. One manager emphasized that "if you speak with a smile, you'll look prettier." Another explained to a hostess that "you are the hostess because you are pretty. But it won't do much good if you don't smile.... A beautiful smile is a good start. Also you should take the initiative to speak with the guests. When they are at the door, greet them." Emphasizing the profitability of smiling was a common theme. A manager explained, "Why do we smile? To give guests self-esteem. They are paying for self-esteem and respect.... More than 50 percent of our profits come from your smiles."

Instead of enacting femininity through a reserved bearing and by avoiding eye contact with men—the predisposition engendered by the women's upbringing—management requires extroversion. New rules for when and how to smile proved nonintuitive to employees so managers dissected them. An assistant manager described the appropriate technique:

> If you have eye contact with a guest then you have to smile. Of course, don't always smile. If they have a complaint, don't smile.... Listen to the guest attentively and think about how to use your smile flexibly. Your smile is a tool.

[...]

Managers implicitly link such modes of emotional expression to a norm of femininity that emphasizes extroversion, new rules for facial expression, microscopic attention to others' needs, and regimented comportment and hygiene. Workers would be averse to adopting such nonintuitive directives were it not for kinlike relations with managers. The ample material and social supports that the work unit supplies fosters these amiable relations. Once on the service floor, workers inventively combine Western-imported repertoires with their own schemas of interaction.

Staff-Customer Interactions: Embeddedness in Local Meanings

Despite conceiving of workers as *tabula rasa,* management does not completely expunge local dispositions. Frontline workers develop their own interactive solutions to dilemmas consistently confronted in the consumer market. By combining imported, middle-class femininity with the local cultural schema of "face," frontline workers adapt luxury service protocols and gain a modicum of service-floor control and autonomy. This amalgam of practices, however, fosters assent to customer control.

Trainers tutor workers to respond to the nuances of customers' consumption habits. The hotel uses the knowledge employees glean from interactions to build customer computer records containing lists of preferences that amount to, in some cases, 50 pages of information. Each worker tailors her activity to individual guests' likes and dislikes, though the intensity of customer interaction varies by department and service. Room cleaners, for example, interact with customers during turndown service. Like detectives, they take note of where each guest leaves the television remote, wastebasket, and shaver, placing the items accordingly on each visit. Hostesses and cocktail and restaurant waitresses have more intense customer interactions; they memorize the names and titles of guests, their partners, and children. If a customer looks confused or disoriented, workers often resolve the problem before he utters a word. A customer bobbing his head or craning his neck produces a server with the desired item: a missing spoon, extra cream, or more water. When a customer drops a napkin a new one appears immediately.

Thrown into an alien luxury environment, surrounded by the appraising eyes of managers, customers, and security staff behind surveillance cameras, the young girls often experience deep anxiety. One waitress recalled, "When I first saw the restaurant . . . I didn't dare touch a thing, the cups are crystal, the ashtrays are crystal, the cutlery is silver . . . I felt nervous. I didn't want to go anywhere in the hotel. I feared I would do something wrong."

[. . .]

Workers use two tactics to navigate the luxury environment. First, they use specific performances of femininity to manage difficult interactions with customers. Most staff members feel that the new feminine repertoire they learn carries with it an aptitude for handling customers with subtle expressions of disapproval that are meaningful because they emanate from an overt, middle-class, feminine sensibility. A waitress offered this example: "Today, there was a guest who seemed rich. He made a mess . . . cigarettes everywhere. I put a clean ashtray in front of him, so that he knows. It's very subtle."

[. . .]

A cocktail waitress responded to a customer's request for a date by smiling and saying, "May I bring my boyfriend?" Workers also gently guide customers who are ordering unfamiliar foods and fumbling with chopsticks in the hotel's Chinese restaurant. . . . Many workers subtly enforce etiquette among customers, strategically using feminine charm in the process. A cocktail waitress's polite disdain for customers epitomizes the strategic use of femininity: "The quality of the guest's manner doesn't have anything to do with me. . . . I try to teach them through my smile, so that they can improve their breeding." As a class display, this femininity illustrates female workers' sophistication and therefore legitimates an assertion of control over the customer. In other words, this small exercise of control is softened and made palatable because it is delivered through the middle-class, Western-imported, feminine disposition.

[. . .]

The second tactic deployed by the workers involves modifying service protocols to conform to local repertoires of interaction. Workers draw on the cultural schema of "face-giving" to keep customers at arm's length. "Giving face" refers to a conferral of status and honor involving semiritualized, culturally encoded acts of deference. "Face" is a hierarchical model of interaction (Yang 2002). The workers construe virtual personalism as so many ways of giving face. For example, when a particular guest enters the hotel's Italian restaurant, the hostess always greets him by name and looks him in the eye with a smile of recognition. She then escorts him to his preferred table where she hands him over to the waitress. Describing this process, a waitress said: "This man . . . doesn't need to say a thing, we bring him an ashtray, a glass of Tsingtao. They then prepare his usual dish, saffron risotto, the information is stored on the computer . . . for the friends he brings this gives him face. 'Look at me, I come to this five-star restaurant and everyone recognizes me.'"

Construing virtual personalism as face-giving exposes the link between emotion work and revenue. This link is often concealed when emotion work is considered an authentic expression of femininity. The wide and ritualized status difference produced by face-giving creates a realm of emotional autonomy for the worker through the manufacture of status difference. As a form of emotion work (Hochschild 1983), "giving face" is not conditioned by an underlying notion of individual authenticity. Workers do not conceive of giving face as giving care or nurture. Instead, they view it as a method of tapping into customer wealth, as the device that justifies the unseemly amounts of money guests spend at the hotel. . . .

Because the workers do not strive for authenticity in interactions, they have greater scope to interact strategically, to exploit their own construction of customer status, and to acknowledge the centrality of their status-giving to revenue. For example, most staff members are initially reluctant to apologize when customers complain, out of fear that an apology will be taken as an admission of responsibility for which they might be punished. By reinterpreting contrition as face-giving, though, workers shift the definition of the interaction from recognizing to manufacturing customer status. Face-giving, unlike servility, suggests that status is not inherent but is produced through performances of deference by workers. Face-giving fosters social hierarchy, but it also makes the worker, not the customer, the active agent in sustaining that hierarchy.

Despite immersion in customer needs, workers exploit the interactive space created by virtual personalism to carve out a small arena of interactive autonomy. Giving workers the resources they need to minimize indignities fosters assent to inequalities between customers and workers. By strategically combining femininity with face-giving, workers appropriate and temper service protocols, both manufacturing and coping with stark service-floor inequalities.

Virtuous Professionalism: The Kunming Transluxury Hotel

A Masculine Domestic Elite Consumer Market

Housed within a modernist glass and concrete structure, the Kunming Transluxury (KT) stands amid Yunnan's tourist complex. The perennial Kunming sunshine floods the lobby through wall-sized windows. The hotel resembles Beijing's five-star hotels, save for semi-erotic paintings and statues of ethnic minority women. An advertisement posted in the hotel elevators features a young European woman wrapped in a small towel luxuriating in the hotel's sauna. The immodest picture broadcasts a clarion message: sex is for sale. A hotel manager used professional parlance to describe the phenomenon: "Every hotel has this kind of service program. It's a way to attract guests, because men are like that. When they go out they want to have a good time."

[. . .]

The organization of sexual services on the hotel premises places workers at risk of misidentification as escorts. In this context, professionalism becomes an essential shield. It establishes the workers in a legitimate industry and deters customers' advances. Workers thus adopt professional protocols with a severe bearing, very different from the virtually intimate style created at the BT. Several factors influence the strong sales consciousness that emerges as a central feature of their work: scarce benefits, fragmented employee relations, punitive bureaucratic measures, and manager-worker antagonism. I call this labor regime "virtuous professionalism."

[. . .]

Staff-Management Relations

Unlike the BT managers, who handle infractions informally, KT managers use punitive measures to enforce discipline. The employee handbook meticulously describes 70 infractions for which management may levy monetary penalties. For such minor infractions as eating in the locker room, punching in late or leaving early, making inappropriate noises in the hotel, or failing to wear nametags, 20 percent of a worker's salary is docked. Management exacts a 40 percent penalty against workers who defy their orders, act impolitely toward customers, or slack off in their duties. Grave offenses such as fighting (with customers, fellow workers, or management), stealing hotel property, or trafficking in prostitution result in an 80 percent wage penalty and sometimes dismissal, which entails confiscation of the work deposit (the equivalent of about $60). Transgressions are recorded in worker dossiers, which follow workers to new employment throughout their lives.

Unlike the congenial manner of supervision adopted at the BT, the KT executive team complements their harsh penalties with a harsh supervisory style that includes assailing the dignity of workers as a form of discipline. At daily pre-shift meetings, managers publicly castigate workers for such mistakes as diverting customer requests to other departments rather than directly responding to them. Vicious comments, and orders issued with implicit or explicit threats, are common. During a pre-shift meeting at the hotel's Chinese restaurant, a manager praised one worker while scolding another, "Li sold the most steamed bird's nest last night. Tremendous. Everyone should follow her example, especially Ming who did not sell a single featured entrée. This is the third night you performed poorly? It's an embarrassment." . . . On two occasions, workers broke down in tears during interviews as they described public shaming by managers.

Unlike the BT executives, who view their workers as innocents ready to absorb American culture, the managers at the KT openly express disdain for the "backwardness" of local workers. They link the workers' lack of cultural sophistication to Yunnan's peripheral economic status and its ethnic minority population. One manager complained that "they don't know what it's like to really work." Another asserted that "they are loose and inattentive. They are not used to competition." A third declared, "These local workers don't have the consciousness or the feelings for this. No one ever taught me these things but I feel that I just know how to act."

Management focuses customer service on selling hotel services to guests who typically use the competitive market to negotiate relatively low-cost accommodations. The hotel seeks to recoup this loss with additional services and consumption. Instead of immersion in customer preferences, frontline workers invest their energy in developing nuanced knowledge of the food and services KT provides and mastering the aggressive, suggestive sales techniques designed by management to mine clients' expense accounts. The KT service regime emphasizes knowledge of the product over knowledge of the guest. The hotel's cost-cutting efforts prohibit investment in an extensive computer network, which the BT requires to record customer preferences. Whereas the BT management designs service to be invisible, service at the KT is deliberately on display to maximize sales.

At the KT, staff training emphasizes the use of product knowledge to maximize customer expenditures. Management requires staff to spend at least two hours in training each week reviewing procedures and hotel products. The daily pre-shift meetings at the restaurants, for example, feature role-playing in which waitresses recite in mouthwatering detail the manifold ingredients and style of preparation of the gourmet dishes served at the restaurants. They learn the names, descriptions, and origins of the rare sea life in the nine large tanks, which house the menu's selection of fresh fish. Cocktail waitresses memorize the descriptions, as well as the English and Chinese names, of dozens of Western beverages offered in the nightclub and lounges. Waitresses are expected to promote drink and appetizer specials every night. A mantra of pre-shift meetings in the cocktail lounge is: "Before you do anything else, ask them to try the featured drinks."

In addition to scarce benefits, an absence of workplace community, manager-worker antagonism, and punitive bureaucratic measures, management's integration of paid sex work into the hotel's daily routine further shapes the character of work for staff members. Though not formally attached to the hotel, escorts are recruited through informal channels to work in the sauna and karaoke bar. They enter the hotel as guests and frequent public locations. As a result, customers routinely confuse formal workers for sex workers. In response, formal workers adopt a specific style of professionalism that deemphasizes sexuality to avoid harassment on the service floor.

Staff-Customer Relations: Embeddedness in Local Meaning Systems

At the KT, the respectability of women workers is constantly at risk. Faced with a double indictment—"backwardness" by managers and sexual promiscuity by customers—staff members wield virtuous professionalism as a weapon to assert their sophistication and respectability while deemphasizing their sexuality. The omnipresence of escorts, profitable precisely for their transgression of social norms of feminine virtue and legal codes, creates an imperative for employees to signal that their bodies are not for sale. They must make this clear to both stave off customer predations and accomplish appointed tasks. Workers use professional protocols, learned in the workplace, to refigure local meanings imposed on them by customers.

At the BT, workers encounter difficult-to-negotiate foreign languages and have to overcome class insecurity to function appropriately in the luxury hotel environment. At the KT, workers fret over a very different kind of fault line with customers: they report uncomfortable, frightening, and even dangerous encounters with guests that threaten their respectability and physical safety. A female restaurant supervisor voiced the general complaint that "[guests] look down on us.... They feel that it's best for girls to be working in a factory or a school, or to be a nurse.... They imagine the service sector... is illicit and related to 'that' type of work." Customers often proposition staff members and touch them inappropriately. A waitress described a typical incident: "Men will tell me I'm beautiful and ask me to join them for a drink. Last night a Japanese tourist rubbed my hand when I served his drink.... Sometimes I'm afraid they will be waiting for me after work. I showed him my nametag, that I am a waitress—and don't provide *that* kind of service." A room-service waitress described a more frightening experience: "A guest locked me in and asked, 'Do you have any *xiaojie* (prostitutes) here?' I said, I'm not a *xiaojie*. You have to go to the nightclub to find a *xiaojie*." ...

... Compared to the smiling staff at the BT, KT workers seem more like soldiers on a battlefield, ready to manage any service contingency with a serious bearing and a calculated distancing strategy. One waitress captured the KT workers' typical orientation: "I'm not empathizing with people.... If I encounter some problem I can calmly consider it rather than act impulsively." Instead of proactively "giving face," as BT employees do, KT staff maintain an impassive bearing, often avoiding eye contact and smiling only occasionally.

Frontline workers set the tone of their interactions with customers using elaborate, rapid-fire, and often aggressive sales pitches about special drinks and foods. Given the ample local delicacies, workers act as gatekeepers to the world of Yunnan cuisine. Instead of the silent service that BT patrons experience, guests at the KT face an opening salvo of detail about food items that leaves them little opportunity to alter the tone of the exchange. For example, during a typical exchange I observed, a waitress greeted a patron with: "Good evening, welcome to the [Ocean Empress] restaurant. Would you like to try our salmon? It is from our fresh tanks. It's made with *hongsu* sauce and wrapped inside a papaya. It's 220 *yuan* each person [$27]. Perhaps you'd also like to try shark fin; it's nutritious and quite rare ... we boil it for 10 hours, then we peel off the skin and extract the filling." Sometimes waitresses embark on monologues before customers utter a word, adopting a professional tone with little trace of affect in their voices.

Cocktail waitresses enact similar routines, pressuring guests to order specialty cocktails. If customers objectify female staff members as sexual objects, workers reciprocate by objectifying customers as walking wallets.

Frequently misidentified as escorts, KT workers mobilize symbols of professionalism to signal their formal attachment to the hotel. A hostess in a bar, eager to clarify the distinction between the "informal" sex workers and "formal" hotel workers, described the sharp contrast in self-presentation: "They wear sexy street clothes . . . we have formal nametags and uniforms." She added, "they're casual," a euphemism for carelessness of demeanor and moral laxity. When workers encounter unwanted customer advances, they point to their name badges and uniforms, which signal formal attachment to the hotel. To make the distinction less subtle, they wear light makeup and simple hairstyles that contrast dramatically with the elaborately-coiffed escorts adorned with dark lipstick, eyeliner, false eyelashes, hair attachments, and dyed red and blond hair. Although the KT management does not set guidelines for hygiene and personal appearance, workers must engage in self-surveillance to ensure their physical and moral distinction from the escorts.

[. . .]

The link between professionalism and virtue helps explain why managerial despotism does not produce surly service workers. Workers adopt a professional bearing to reclaim respectability and self-respect. Instead of displacing irritability onto customers or openly rebelling against management, workers often complain to one another about managers, pilfer small guest amenities like soaps and shampoos, and quietly break other hotel policies.

KT workers use professional protocols to navigate the structural constraints of adapting a Western service template to an elite, masculine domestic market with regional work legacies. Virtuous professionalism, to a great extent self-created, enables workers to both distinguish themselves from sex workers and fend off managerial accusations of backwardness. Virtuous professionalism, based on a distinctive form of femininity that contrasts dramatically with the form cultivated at the BT, constitutes a resource for gaining respectability.

Conclusion

[. . .]

The labor strategies used by each of the hotels to institutionalize different luxury consumer markets illustrate two types of market-embedded labor. In the BT, managers developed a labor regime of virtual personalism: imported, U.S. middle-class femininity is used as a model to train workers to care about, notice, record, and preemptively cater to a consumer market comprised of affluent, Western businessmen, understood by the firm as having elaborate preferences in need of attention. Flattened work hierarchies permit middle managers to transform workers into a refracted version of U.S. middle-class femininity. In turn, this fosters thorough, if invisible, control of workers' actions by customers. In contrast, the KT developed a labor regime of virtuous professionalism. Instead of creating virtual intimacy, KT workers struggle for recognition as service professionals from domestic businessmen who are entertaining clients and seeking to experience haute cuisine and high spirits. Instead of understanding consumption preferences as already formulated—as at the BT—the KT uses workers to cultivate the tastes of customers. The workers are trained to focus customer attention on high-profit products to maximize patron spending. Underwritten by myriad bureaucratic penalties, managerial relationships with workers are coercive and hierarchical.

[. . .]

In both locations, workers develop a synthetic service-floor meaning system in response to persistent dilemmas that their respective consumer markets create, modifying the prescribed repertoires to enhance their interactive autonomy and control. BT's employees, frequently intimidated by the extreme demands of the intense interaction with clients, develop a style of extroverted femininity to claim class status and exert some control over customers. Yet they also temper enactments of femininity with ritualistic displays of "face" that keep customers at arm's length.

KT workers, on the other hand, face moral and physical risks as women in the tourist industry. While the BT service floor fosters status anxiety, the KT service floor engenders moral trepidation. Whereas in Beijing workers import local meanings into an unfamiliar setting, Kunming workers use professional protocols to refigure local meanings imposed by their customers. KT workers adopt professionalism as a technique for deemphasizing sexuality, to place limits on the ways in which their bodies and selves are consumed. By adopting professionalism, women workers turn their class exclusion into a gender virtue in labor markets that restrict their mobility and present the risk of misidentification as sex workers. For both hotels, adaptations of professional protocols ultimately facilitate interactive service labor, preserving the dignity of workers without posing fundamental challenges to the inequalities of the service floor.

[. . .]

References

China Labor Statistical Yearbook. 2001. Beijing, China: China Statistics Press.

Davis, Deborah S. 1999. "Introduction: A Revolution in Consumption." Pp. 1–24 in *The Consumer Revolution in Urban China*, edited by D. S. Davis. Berkeley, CA: University of California Press.

He, Zhonghua and Hengrei Qiao. 1995. *Yunnan Nongcun Funu Xianzhuang Yanjiu* (Research on the Current State of Women in Yunnan). Kunming, China: Yunnan Education Press.

Hochschild, Arlie Russell. 1983. *The Managed Heart: Commercialization of Human Feeling.* Berkeley, CA: University of California Press.

Sassen, Saskia. 2000. *Cities in a World Economy.* Thousand Oaks, CA: Pine Forge Press.

Skinner, William G., Mark Henderson, and Jianhua Yuan. 2000. "China's Fertility Transition Through Regional Space: Using GIS and Census Data for a Spatial Analysis of Historical Demography." *Social Science History* 24:613–52.

Sun, Shangqing, ed. 1992. *Ershi Shiji de Xuanze: Fazhan Zhongguo Liuyou de Shouduan* (Choices in the 21st Century: China's Tourism Development Strategies). Beijing, China: People's Publishing House.

Yang, Mayfair Mei-hui. 2002. "The Resilience of Guanxi and Its New Deployments." *China Quarterly* 170:459–76.

PART X

Violence, Crime, and Incarceration

This section examines the ways that gender and sexuality operate across various institutions in which crime, violence, incarceration, and social control surface. Gender scholars have extensively researched how gender inequalities are maintained, reproduced, and resisted at the individual, interactional, and organizational level within the criminal justice system. This section examines gender and sexuality across the core themes of the reader: intersectionality, masculinity, transgender, and global (IMTG) perspectives.

In "Normalizing Sexual Violence," Heather Hlavka examines young women's experiences of sexual violence. Analyzing audiotaped interviews with racially diverse girls, Hlavka attempts to understand how girls experience sexual violence. Respondents view everyday harassment and sexual violence through gendered and heteronormative scripts. Rather than seeing boys' and men's objectification, harassment, and abuse as criminal, they tend to normalize it, seeing it as natural. Girls try to avoid being attacked and tend to accept responsibility when forced to have sex or "do things" rather than blame their attacker. The findings show how young women understand their experiences and sexual identities via a lens of compulsory heterosexuality and a naturalization of boys' and men's violence.

"Rehabilitating Criminal Selves" by Jessica Wyse uses mixed methods to examine how rehabilitation officers use gendered constructions of the criminal self in their rehabilitative strategies. Through observation, records, and interview data, she finds that community correctional officers construct men as underdeveloped, flawed selves. In contrast, women are seen as permeable selves who lack boundaries. Correctional officers try to motivate men toward goals of getting a good job that will make them financially independent. On the other hand, their conversations with women are primarily focused on relationships, often discouraging romantic entanglements. The result is that rehabilitation programs and officers shape the gendered subjectivities of criminals—women in relational and emotional terms, and men in economic terms—demonstrating gendered disparate opportunities in their treatment.

In Victor Rios's ethnographic and interview study, "The Consequences of the Criminal Justice Pipeline on Black and Latino Masculinity," he observes the day-to-day experiences of Black and Latino boys. Law enforcement surveillance of these youth in their daily activities at school and in the community construct them as criminals. In response, boys develop a tough front that uses hypermasculinity to manage these experiences. Rios observes these processes through interactions in school, in neighborhoods with the police, in jail or prison, and on probation. If the boys or men resist hypermasculinity, they are branded soft, passive, and unable to succeed, leaving them with little opportunity other than enacting hypermasculinity. The study uncovers the way the criminal justice system uses contradictory reform mechanisms focused around hypermasculinity that end up reinforcing gendered racial inequality.

In "'We're Like Community,'" Lori Sexton and Valerie Jenness describe the gendered experiences of transgender women in prisons for men. Sexton and Jenness use both survey and interview data with over 300 very diverse respondents. While men's prisons are a challenging and dangerous place for transgender women, many communicate a strong sense of community with one another, with some referring to fellow transgender inmates as "family" and many reflecting that they share similarities with non-trans prisoners as well, since they are all inmates. Transgender women express a greater sense of collective-efficacy when they have developed trusting friendships within their community; they do not always develop these relationships, though, citing drama and competition between transgender inmates. Yet, transgender identity is quite meaningful to these inmates even though they are often mis-identified by prison personnel as gay men.

Daniela Jauk's ethnographic study, "Gender Violence Revisited," examines gendered violence toward transgender communities. Transgender individuals experience interactional and institutional violence. Many trans people face serious risk of physical violence, as well as discriminatory behavior, harassment, and verbal assaults. Heightened risk of experiencing violence surfaces during periods of gender transition when respondents describe "looking trans," while transwomen reported experiencing more sexualized violence. Most trans people in Jauk's study suggest that police will not protect them if they are being attacked, or may add to the harassment and violence they face. Trans people actively address this violence by making choices about how they present themselves as they navigate space, portraying themselves as potentially violent to hostile neighbours, building community, and creating art. These findings demonstrate how gender-based violence is used to patrol the gender binary, driven by underlying transphobia, misogyny, and homophobia.

Finally, "Gendered Violence, Cultural Otherness, and Honour Crimes in Canadian National Logics," by Dana Olwan, examines the media's construction of honor-based violence as seen within the mainstream Canadian press. Honor killings are defined as killing women to regain honor; the media views honor killings as different from, for example, killings that result from intimate partner violence. The findings show how the media constructs stories about these killings in ways that bolster boundaries of superiority around culture and nation. The media emphasizes the West as focused around gender equality and nonviolence, but the Muslim East as focused around gender oppression and violence, with little attention given to feminist activism around violence against women. This reinforces stereotypical gendered notions of Canadians from particular nationalities, undermining multiculturalism and venerating Canada as a space otherwise free of gendered violence. The study demonstrates how this type of media coverage reproduces gendered and racist discourses rather than recognizing that violence against women is a broader societal problem.

Gender, sexuality, gender identity, race, and nationality are deeply embedded in systems of violence and the criminal justice system. While it appears that all girls and women learn to view men's sexual violence as natural, the press can bolster and emphasize the idea that certain nationalities or cultures are particularly violent and oppressive. Trans people face unusually high rates of violence and harassment, though they act to address and avoid this violence. Within prison, transwomen can create community with one another, as well as with inmates. Yet it is critical to recognize how police and correctional officers reinforce particular notions of gender identity, sexuality, femininity, masculinity, and hypermasculinity as they engage with the community, prisoners, and parolees.

Normalizing Sexual Violence

Young Women Account for Harassment and Abuse

Heather R. Hlavka

oming up against "the wall of patriarchy" (Gilligan 1990, 503), early adolescence is a defining period for young women. Many regard harassment and violence to be a normal part of everyday life in middle and high schools (Fineran and Bennett 1999), yet most of these crimes go unreported. A 2011 American Association of University Women (AAUW 2011) study found that almost half (48 percent) of the 1,965 students surveyed experienced harassment, but only 9 percent reported the incident to an authority figure. Girls were sexually harassed more than boys (56 percent vs. 40 percent); they were more likely to be pressured for a date, pressured into sexual activity, and verbally harassed (AAUW 2001; Fineran and Bennett 1999).

According to prevalence studies, reported violence in adolescent dating relationships ranges between 8.8 and 40 percent (Sousa 1999). Data from the Youth Risk Behavior Survey (YRBS) show that almost 20 percent of girls experience physical and sexual violence from dating partners (Silverman et al. 2001), and sexual assault accounts for one-third of preteen victimization (Finkelhor and Ormrod 2000). It is tempting to ask: Why do so few young women formally report their victimization experiences? Assuming that peer sexual harassment and assault is an instrument that creates and maintains gendered and sexed hierarchies (e.g., MacKinnon 1979; Phillips 2000; Tolman et al. 2003), attention instead must turn toward understanding how and why these violent acts are produced, maintained, and normalized in the first place. Despite the considerable body of research that shows high rates of gendered violence among youth, there has been little discussion of its instruments and operations.

[. . .]

This study addresses how girls negotiate their lived experiences in ways that are often ignored by law and policy. This work aims to re-cast youth as agentic, having intentions,

Heather R. Hlavka. 2014. "Normalizing Sexual Violence: Young Women Account for Harassment and Abuse." *Gender & Society* 28(3):337–59.

desires, and standpoints (Corsaro 1997; Hlavka 2010; Lee 2001), rather than as passive objects. The study is situated within feminist research and practices that embody the legitimacy of patriarchy, including sexual harassment and violence, sexual subjectivity, and heteronormativity (Gavey 1992). The narrative data come from a larger study on child sexual abuse in which youth were interviewed by specialized forensic interviewers following reports of sexual victimization. I situate the analysis to show how girls make use of culturally available discourses to explain their experiences. The findings complicate studies on the formal underreporting of sexual assault and provide a nuanced understanding of how violence is woven into youths' sexed and gendered relationships from very young ages (Phillips 2000; Tolman et al. 2003).

Feminist Perspectives and Hetero-Relational Discourses

[. . .]

Young people are socialized into a patriarchal culture that normalizes and often encourages male power and aggression, particularly within the context of heterosexual relationships (Fineran and Bennett 1999; Tolman et al. 2003). As men's heterosexual violence is viewed as customary, so too is women's endurance of it (Stanko 1985). For example, Messerschmidt (1986) has argued that "normative heterosexuality" involves a "presumption that men have a special and overwhelming 'urge' or 'drive' toward heterosexual intercourse." Women come to be justifiable objects of sexual exploitation. These discourses shape embodied experiences (Crawley, Foley, and Shehan 2008; Lorber and Moore 2007), normalizing the presumption that men's sexual aggression is simply "boys being boys" (Connell 1987; French 2003; Messerschmidt 2012). Stanko (1985, 73) argued that "women learn, often at a very early age, that their sexuality is not their own and that maleness can at any point intrude into it." Girls are thus expected to endure aggression by men because that is *part* of man. Coupled with the presumption that women are the gatekeepers of male desire (Fine 1988; Tolman 1991), heteronormative discourses have allowed for men's limited accountability for aggressive, harassing, and criminal sexual conduct. Indeed, dominant notions of gender and heterosexuality underscore much of young people's identity work; they are subject to the pressures of heteronormativity from an early age. Youth negotiate and maintain gendered hierarchies and hegemonies, both within and between genders (Butler 1999). Young women's subjective understandings of gender, sexuality, and violence are thus critical sites for the reproduction of inequality on which feminist scholarship has much to offer.

[. . .]

Methods

The data for this study include audio-videotaped interviews of youths seen by forensic interviewers for reported cases of sexual abuse between 1995 and 2004. The interviews come from the nonprofit Children's Advocacy Center (CAC) located in an urban Midwest community. The CAC provides investigative interviews and medical examinations for youths who may have been sexually or physically assaulted or witnessed a violent crime. Interviews take place between one forensic interviewer and one child referred to the CAC by law enforcement or Child Protection Services (CPS). Youths were brought to the CAC for an interview because they reported sexual abuse to someone, someone else witnessed or reported the abuse to authorities, or the offender confessed to the abuse.

. . . Protocol components include first establishing rapport and, next, obtaining details about sexual abuse only if the child first verbally discloses victimization to the interviewer. The two then discuss the circumstances surrounding the abuse using nonsuggestive, largely open-ended, questions. So, while the interview is set up to investigate whether or not abuse occurred, youths were consistently allowed to raise and discuss subjects important to them in response to questions such as "What happened? Did you tell anyone? How did they respond? How did you feel about that? Are you worried about anything?" This format allows for rich narrative data that do not rely solely on retrospective reports common in most sexual abuse studies. The interviews were video recorded and varied in length and scope, primarily based on age. The average interview length was 40 minutes for children between ages three and eight; 70 minutes for youths between ages nine and 14; and 110 minutes for youths between ages 15 and 17. Following the interview, CAC team members participated in a postinterview meeting to make one of three findings: abuse occurred, did not occur, or is inconclusive. Findings are based only on what the child is capable of communicating during the interview rather than on outside reports from law enforcement or CPS.

[. . .]

The study subsample includes 23 racially diverse young women (13 white girls, six black girls, and four Latina girls) between 11 and 16 years of age. The reported offenders were known to the girls, either as acquaintances or intimate others (intrafamilial abuse was more common in the larger study sample). Accounts were unpacked as everyday violence, instruments of coercion, and accounts of consent. These categories illuminate the heteronormative cultures within which girls accounted for sexual violence and negotiated what happened, how it happened, and why.

[. . .]

Everyday Violence

Objectification, sexual harassment, and abuse appear to be part of the fabric of young women's lives (Orenstein 1994). They had few available safe spaces; girls were harassed and assaulted at parties, in school, on the playground, on buses, and in cars. Young women overwhelmingly depicted boys and men as *natural* sexual aggressors, pointing to one of the main tenets of compulsory heterosexuality. Incorporating male sexual drive discourse (Phillips 2000), they described men as unable to control their sexual desires. Male power and privilege and female acquiescence were reified in descriptions of "routine" and "normal" sexualized interactions (Fineran and Bennett 1999; French 2003). Assaultive behaviors were often justified, especially when characterized as indiscriminate. For example, Patricia (age 13, white) told the interviewer: "They grab you, touch your butt and try to, like, touch you in the front, and run away, but it's okay, I mean . . . I never think it's a big thing because they do it to everyone." Referring to boys at school, Patricia described unwelcome touching and grabbing as normal, commonplace behaviors.

Compulsory heterosexuality highlights how conventional norms of heterosexual relations produce and often require male dominance and female subordination (Phillips 2000; Tolman et al. 2003). Young women like Patricia described sexually aggressive behaviors as customary: "It just happens," and "They're boys—that's what they do." Similarly, Kelly (age 13, white) told the forensic interviewer about her experiences with 20-year-old Eric:

> [He] would follow me around all the time, tell me I was beautiful and stuff, that he could have me when he wanted to. He did that all the time, like, would touch me and say, "Am I making you wet, do you want me?" when he wanted. I think that's just . . . like, that's what he does, it's just, like, how it goes on and everyone knows it, no one says nothing.

Kelly trivializes her experiences of sexual harassment by a man seven years older, telling the interviewer of this ordinary and allowable "masculine" practice. Her description of ongoing harassment also confounds romance and aggression, because Eric's harassment was fused with courting, compliments, and sexual desire (Phillips 2000).

Girls' characterizations of everyday violence paralleled both their assessments that "boys will be boys" and their understanding of harassment as a normal adolescent rite of passage. Sexual harassment is an instrument that maintains a gendered hierarchy (MacKinnon 1979), and girls described the many ways they protected themselves against expected sexual aggression, at the expense of their own feelings. Carla (age 14, white), for example, cast assault and threats as expected because they were typical. In this passage, she described chronic harassment by a young man as they rode the school bus. He often threatened to "come over to [her] house and rape [her]":

Carla: Like, on the bus, like when I'll sit, he'll try and sit next to me and then slide his hand under my butt.

Interviewer: Okay, does he say anything?

Carla: No, he just kinda has this look on his face. And then I'll, like, shove him out of the seat and then he'll get mad.

Interviewer: What happens when he gets mad?

Carla: He just kinda doesn't talk. He gets, like, his face gets red and he doesn't talk. And he, I guess he feels rejected, but I don't care. He told me . . . he was like, "I'm gonna come over to your house and rape you." And then, I know he's just joking, but that can be a little weird to hear.

Interviewer: Yeah, so when did he tell you that?

Carla: He tells me it all the time, like the last time I talked to him. He just says that he's gonna come to my house and rape me since I won't do anything with him. And, I mean, I think . . . I'm . . . I know he's joking, it's just hard to, like, why would he say that?

Threats were used for compliance, becoming more persistent and coercive over time. Unsure of whether to take the threats seriously, Carla names her experience "weird" while normalizing the young man's behavior as understandable within a male sexual drive discourse ("I guess he feels rejected"), and trivializes his threats twice, saying, "I know he's just joking." Harassment was dangerously constructed as romance and flirting. These discourses often entitle young men to violate the bodies of young women (Connell 1995; Messerschmidt 2012). Prior to the forensic interview, Carla had not told anyone about these experiences, considering them an everyday hazard of riding the bus.

Given expectations of, and experiences with, male aggression, young women were charged with self-protection by reading and responding to potentially dangerous situations. While some girls attempted to "ignore" the behavior, others had to make additional maneuvers. In her interview, Lana (age 15, white) explained how 18-year-old Mike "tries to bring [girls] downstairs in the [school] basement and, like, try and force 'em to like make out with him and stuff." She said Mike tried to force her to go downstairs on numerous occasions and he would "get mad when [she'd] say no." In response, Lana altered her behavior by avoiding being alone in the school hallways, at her locker, or in the bathroom. Young women responded to harassment with a barrage of maneuvers, like avoidance and diverting attention. These tactics did not always work, however. In Lana's case, Mike was eventually "able to catch [her] off-guard":

> I was going to the bathroom and he wouldn't let me go in. He put his foot in front of [the door], and he's a really strong person, so I didn't really, like, I couldn't open the door. And he said, "I'll let you in if you give me a kiss," and I said, "No." And I was going back to the classroom and he pinned me against the wall and tried to, like, lift up my shirt. And, like, touched me, and then I . . . I got up . . . I started to scream, and I guess someone heard, 'cause then, um, someone started coming. So he got away from me, I just went back in the classroom and forgot about it. I just didn't think it was really anything.

Girls in this study said they did not want to make a "big deal" out of their experiences and rarely reported these incidents to persons in authority. Most questioned whether anyone would care about the behavior; if it was not "rape" it was not serious enough to warrant others' involvement. "Real" assault was narrowly defined and contingent on various conditions that were rarely met (Phillips 2000; Stanko 1985).

Young women constructed classic boundaries between "real rapes" and everyday violence or "little rapes." Terri (age 11, black) was interviewed at the CAC because she told a friend she was forced to perform oral sex on a 17-year-old neighbor boy: "He forced me, he, uh, he grabbed me tighter, and he said if I didn't do it he was gonna rape me." For Terri, rape was only intercourse, as she candidly explained: "They always say they gonna rape you, if you don't do what they want, they say they'll rape you." Terri's mother also cautioned her about male sexual drives, warning her to expect aggression and to protect herself. Sitting in her apartment stairwell alone that day, Terri assumed responsibility for her own assault. Terri's experience demonstrates that if girls do not acquiesce to the pressure to have sex, they risk being raped. She did not tell her mother, because "I shouldn't have been there, my mom said I should've been home anyway, but I didn't want to get raped so I had to."

Instruments of Coercion

The normalization of violence was intensified in peer groups and assault was often perpetrated by one older man. Peers communicated a specialized sense of sexual acceptability largely based on the perception of women as sexual gatekeepers. Gatekeeping occurred in a variety of ways, including allocation of resources, such as food, alcohol, or a space away from adult others. Janice (age 14, white), for example, told the interviewer that 30-something-year-old Matt touched her and four girlfriends on a regular basis:

> He does, like, touch us, you know? Like, he like rubs my leg, the thigh, but none of us told him, told him to stop, you know? But I . . . I always moved away when he did it. He'd just rub my leg and touch my boobs. And one time when I was over at his house, I asked him for something to eat and he goes, "Not unless I can touch your boobs."

Via access to resources, Matt presented Janice with a "gatekeeping choice" that deflected responsibility. Janice later told the interviewer that Matt had also touched her vagina, commenting, "He does it to everyone, you know, it just happens sometimes," and justified Matt's behavior by placing responsibility on the group: "But none of us told him to stop." Matt's actions were minimized because they were customary and something they "just dealt with."

[. . .]

Overwhelmingly described as "normal stuff" that "guys do" or tolerating what "just happens," young women's sexual desire and consent are largely absent (Martin 1996; Tolman 1994). Sex was understood as something done to them and agency was discursively attributed only to gatekeeping. Abby (age 12, white) presents an ideal example of the highly prescriptive norms of heterosexual practice. Like others, Abby's peer group normalized the sexual interactions between her and 19-year-old Glen. According to Abby, many of her friends had been "hit on" by Glen, knew about how he "moved from girl to girl" in the group, or were sexually active with him. Abby was referred for a forensic interview after her mother overheard her talking to Glen about "having sex." Abby recounted her experience, making use of particular culturally available discourses of gender, heterosexuality, and power:

Interviewer: What didn't you like about [Glen]?

Abby: The way he used a lot of people, the way he moved from girl to girl, the way that . . . he thought that he was the ruler of everybody, he was really commanding, he always had to be in control, and he was rough, and just, you know.

Interviewer: What kind of stuff did he do that was rough or commanding?

Abby: I don't know, he'd just order me around, and be like, "Oh, do this for me," or, I don't know, he'd ask me to do certain things to him and he'd take my hands and put em' . . . I don't know, he'd just . . . he'd make me do things.

Interviewer: When he would, like, take your hands and make you do things, was it stuff that you didn't want to do?

Abby: Sometimes, and then I'd stop and he'd be fine with it, but after a while he'd, like, start it up again and he'd keep trying.

Interviewer: You said he was rough—did he ever hurt you?

Abby: No, but, like, he was just . . . I don't know, he was just . . . I don't know how to explain it, he was just . . . he'd pull my hair [laughs], so I don't know what he did, he'd like, he'd grab my hair and he'd pull me closer and he'd just, like, pull my hair backward, push my head or somethin' like that and it'd be weird. I don't know what he did.

Interviewer: Okay, did he ever hit you or anything?

Abby: He was very controlling.

Interviewer: Can you give me examples of that?

Abby: Basically he thought I was his maid, or, like, a toy with him that he could just, like, wind up and use whenever he wanted me to, and then he'd just, like, you know, like you have a Barbie doll and you can, like, use it whenever you want to and then you, like, throw it in the back and then you pick it up, how you have, like, a maid or butler, and you can just order them around if you don't get what you want you get mad at them and then you keep trying, he'd just . . . he'd do that, but I wasn't really . . . I think he thought I wanted it—but part of me did, but I knew it was wrong that he . . . that I didn't really care for it, and I knew that he'd just leave anyways since he was nineteen.

In this powerful sequence, Abby links sex with male power and female passivity. She positions herself as "acted upon" and Glen as the "actor" in sexual encounters. In response to the interviewer, she describes how Glen was controlling and rough and would "make" her do things. Analogous to "working a 'yes' out" (Sanday 1990), Abby twice told the interviewer ". . . he'd, like, start it up again and he'd keep trying" despite her resistance. Juxtaposed with Glen's pulling and pushing of her head, when asked if he ever hurt her, Abby responds, "No . . . I don't know how to explain it. . . . It'd be weird. I don't know what he did." She positions herself within particular social hierarchies, describing feeling like a "Barbie doll," a "maid," or a "toy" that could be used and thrown away. Abby reflexively identified with particular cultural positions, simultaneously perceiving herself as object but also as subject, holding herself responsible for Glen's actions.

With all its complexity, Abby interprets her experience far outside of victim/agent, passive/active dichotomies. Positioned in a social landscape of gendered power and sex, Abby struggles to account for consent and desire ("I think he thought I wanted it—but part of me did . . .") and responsibility ("but I knew it was wrong that he . . . that I didn't really care for it, and I knew that he'd just leave anyways since he was nineteen"). These shifts in blame uncover the power of heteronormative discourses that support a sexually unconstrained, emotionally detached male, but a "relational" female. Embedded in the dilemmas and double standards of heterosexual practice (Phillips 2000), Abby silences her own feelings and desires (Thorne 1993) and questions whether a sexual relationship was acceptable if "he'd just leave anyways."

Accounts of Consent

The links between everyday harassment and violence were further reproduced through attributions of blame. Girls criticized each other for not successfully maneuvering men's normalized aggressive behavior. Even when maneuvers "failed," concessions were made. For example, Lily (age 14, Latina) was raped by a 17-year-old school acquaintance in a park as she walked home from school. The offender quickly spread rumors and she was labeled "sexually active" and a "slut" by her classmates: "There's rumors about me already, that aren't even true . . . that I want, that I want to, and I let him do that . . . and it wasn't even true." Cast as promiscuous, she was deemed complicit in her rape. On the rare occasion that rape was reported to an adult or authority figure, young women described feeling suspect. Kiley (age 14, black) was raped by a 27-year-old family friend at his home. She provided details about the assault, including how he held her down and covered her mouth to muffle her cries:

I didn't want to but he did, you know, and I don't know, [sex] just happened. I thought he was just a friend and that's it. . . . He was calling me names, he was calling me a "ho" and a "slut" and all this kind of stuff, and that I gave him a lap dance and everything. That I was, I can't . . . I took all my clothes off and that I was, like, asking him for it. That I wanted to be with him, and everyone believed him.

Sexual reputation mattered to girls (Van Roosmalen 2000) and the threat of being labeled a "ho" or a "slut" loomed large. The threat of sexualization and social derogation was often a barrier to rape reporting; it was connected with accusations of exaggeration through which peers decided whether and how to include, label, and ostracize. This finding is consistent with prior studies (Phillips 2000) that find young women are under pressure to manage their sexuality and sexual reputations. This is a confusing endeavor, of course, as girls may gain cultural capital among peers for being desired and pursued but not for sexual agency.

The precarious balancing act of attaining sexual status and avoiding the "slander of the slut" (Schalet 2010) proved powerful. Some girls belittled others' experiences, holding them responsible for their victimizations. Obligated to set limits for sexual behavior (Orenstein 1994), it was girls' duty to be prepared to say "no" (Tolman 1994) and to police each other. When asked about her friend who had reported sexual assault by a mutual acquaintance, Jacki (age 15, white) said, "I don't know why she's making such a big deal out of it anyway. He does it to everyone, so I say, well, 'Just back off,' I say 'No'—so she should if she don't want it, but she probably wants it anyway." Jacki worked to discursively separate herself from her friend as she spoke of sexual desire and exaggeration.

[. . .]

Girls were also aware of double standards and traditional sexual scripts. They claimed "guys get away with everything" and "they can do anything and not get in trouble." This critique stopped short of attributions of sexual responsibility, however; girls self-framed as active subjects by labeling others as passive objects. In this way, the complexities of naming sexual aggression was premised on behavior comparisons. April (age 13, white) reported that her 13-year-old friend "had sex" with Sean, a 22-year-old man. During her interview, she described her friend as passive and naïve:

> I've heard rumors about that he's had sex with girls, and I know Sara has had sex with him, she came out and told me . . . she said that he came over and he was telling her that she was gorgeous and that he loved her and that he wanted to have her baby and all this stuff, and I guess it just happened, and that's what she said, it just happened, and I was like, "Oh, okay" [laughs], you know, which didn't surprise me, 'cause Sara, she'll be mad at him and then she'll go back to him, like, two days later.

April characterized sexual intercourse ("it") as something men do "to" women. She further interpreted Sean's manipulative tactics ("telling her that she was gorgeous and that he loved her and that he wanted to have her baby") as successful because "it [intercourse] just happened." April said similar ploys did not work on her: "First of all, he asked me, 'Would you . . . would you ever go out with me?' and I said, 'No' . . . and he's like, 'Well, would you ever have sex with me?' and I was like, 'No.'"

Despite April's resistance, Sean put his hands under her shirt, and tried to put her hands in his pants and her head on his penis. April told the interviewer: "I told him to stop and he didn't and he got to, like, right here, you know, he was tryin' to lift up my bra and I was like, 'No, stop!'" Further couched in rumors and reputation, April differentiated herself from Sara: "There's rumors going around saying that Sara had sex with him and so did I and that [she's] a slut and all this stuff." April insisted the rumors about her were untrue because, unlike Sara who let "it just happen," she "said no." As Nelson and Oliver (1998, 573) state, "Under these rules, any girl who permits herself to be persuaded into sexual activity is weak and to blame, as is a girl who voluntarily enters a situation where she can be raped."

Conclusion

Research on sexual violence has long asked why victims do not report these incidents. Studies with adults have examined how women account for and "name" their experiences, yet adolescents remain largely outside the scope of this work. Exploring sexual violence via the lens of compulsory heterosexuality highlights the relational dynamics at play in this naming process. . . .

Descriptions of assault here are concerning, having much to do with heteronormativity and compulsory heterosexuality. Sex was "something they [men and boys] do," or "something he wanted," and sexual assault was a "weird" threat, something "they just say," or "something she let happen." When resistance was voiced, as in April's case, it was couched in sexual refusal and used to establish boundaries. In their policing of each other, young women often held themselves and their peers responsible for acting as gatekeepers of men's behaviors; they were responsible for being coerced, for accepting gifts and other resources, for not fending off or resisting men's sexual advances, for miscommunication, or, in Abby's words, for engaging in sexual activity she "didn't really care for." The discourses offer insight into how some young women talked about their sexual selves and relationships as they navigated a world ordered by gendered binaries and heterosexual frameworks (Butler 1999).

[. . .]

. . . The sexual scripts culturally available to girls largely exclude sexual desire and pleasure, representing girls as victims in need of protection against boys' desires (Fine 1988). Placing responsibility on women and girls to "just say no" and excusing boys and men as they "work a 'yes' out" works to erase institutional and structural responsibilities. The lack of safe, supportive space for girls is palpable. We can thus better understand why young women in this study felt they were expected to protect themselves from everyday violence with little help from others, including those in authority positions. . . .

References

AAUW (American Association of University Women). 2001. *Hostile Hallways II: Bullying, Teasing and Sexual Harassment in School.* Washington, DC: AAUW.

AAUW (American Association of University Women). 2011. *Crossing the Line: Sexual Harassment at School.* Washington, DC: Catherine Hill and Holly Kearl.

Butler, Judith. 1999. *Gender Trouble.* New York: Routledge.

Connell, Raewyn. 1987. *Gender and Power.* Cambridge, UK: Polity Press.

Connell, Raewyn. 1995. *Masculinities.* Berkeley, CA: University of California Press.

Corsaro, William. 1997. *The Sociology of Childhood.* Thousand Oaks, CA: Pine Forge.

Crawley, Sara, Lara Foley, and Constance Shehan. 2008. *Gendering Bodies.* Lanham, MD: Rowman & Littlefield.

Fine, Michelle. 1988. "Sexuality, Schooling, and Adolescent Females: The Missing Discourse of Desire." *Harvard Educational Review* 58:29–53.

Fineran, Susan and Larry Bennett. 1999. "Gender and Power Issues of Peer Sexual Harassment Among Teenagers." *Journal of Interpersonal Violence* 14:626–41.

Finkelhor, David and Richard Ormrod. 2000. *Characteristics of Crimes Against Juveniles.* Washington, DC: U.S. Department of Justice, Office of Justice Programs.

French, Sandra L. 2003. "Reflections on Healing: Framing Strategies Utilized by Acquaintance Rape Survivors." *Journal of Applied Communication Research* 31:298–319.

Gavey, Nicola. 1992. "Technologies and Effects of Heterosexual Coercion." *Feminism & Psychology* 2:325–51.

Gilligan, Carol. 1990. "Joining the Resistance: Psychology, Politics, Girls and Women." *Michigan Quarterly Review* 29:501–26.

Hlavka, Heather. 2010. "Child Sexual Abuse and Embodiment." *Sociological Studies of Children and Youth* 13:131–65.

Lee, Nick. 2001. *Children and Society: Growing Up in an Age of Uncertainty.* New York: Open University Press.

Lorber, Judith and Lisa Moore. 2007. *Gendered Bodies: Feminist Perspectives.* Los Angeles, CA: Roxbury.

MacKinnon, Catherine. 1979. *Sexual Harassment of Working Women.* New Haven, CT: Yale University Press.

Martin, Karin. 1996. *Puberty, Sexuality, and the Self.* New York: Routledge.

Messerschmidt, James. 1986. *Capitalism, Patriarchy, and Crime.* Totowa, NJ: Rowman & Littlefield.

Messerschmidt, James. 2012. *Gender, Heterosexuality, and Youth Violence: The Struggle for Recognition.* New York: Rowman & Littlefield.

Nelson, Andrea and Pamela Oliver. 1998. "Gender and the Construction of Consent in Child-Adult Sexual Contact: Beyond Gender Neutrality and Male Monopoly." *Gender & Society* 12:554–77.

Orenstein, Peggy. 1994. *Schoolgirls: Young Women, Self-Esteem, and the Confidence Gap.* New York: Doubleday.

Phillips, Lynn M. 2000. *Flirting with Danger: Young Women's Reflections on Sexuality and Domination.* New York: New York University Press.

Sanday, Peggy Reeves. 1990. *Fraternity Gang Rape: Sex, Brotherhood, and Privilege on Campus.* New York: New York University Press.

Schalet, Amy. 2010. "Sexual Subjectivity Revisited: The Significance of Relationships in Dutch and American Girls' Experiences of Sexuality." *Gender & Society* 24:304–29.

Silverman, Jay, Anita Raj, Lorelei Mucci, and Jeanne Hathaway. 2001. "Dating Violence Against Adolescent Girls and Associated Substance Use, Unhealthy Weight Control, Sexual Risk Behavior, Pregnancy, and Suicidality." *Journal of the American Medical Association* 286:572–79.

Sousa, Carole A. 1999. "Teen Dating Violence: The Hidden Epidemic." *Family and Conciliation Courts Review* 37:356–74.

Stanko, Elizabeth. 1985. *Intimate Intrusions: Women's Experience of Male Violence.* London, UK: Routledge and Kegan Paul.

Thorne, Barrie. 1993. *Gender Play: Girls and Boys in School.* New Brunswick, NJ: Rutgers University Press.

Tolman, Deborah. 1991. "Adolescent Girls, Women and Sexuality: Discerning Dilemmas of Desire." In *Women, Girls and Psychotherapy: Reframing Resistance,* edited by C. Gilligan, A. Rogers, and D. Tolman. New York: Haworth.

Tolman, Deborah. 1994. "Doing Desire: Adolescent Girls' Struggles for/with Sexuality." *Gender & Society* 8:324–42.

Tolman, Deborah, Renée Spencer, Myra Rosen-Reynosa, and Michelle Porche. 2003. "Sowing the Seeds of Violence in Heterosexual Relationships: Early Adolescents Narrate Compulsory Heterosexuality." *Journal of Social Issues* 59:159–78.

Van Roosmalen, Erica. 2000. "Forces of Patriarchy: Adolescent Experiences of Sexuality and Conceptions of Relationships." *Youth & Society* 32:202–27.

Rehabilitating Criminal Selves

Gendered Strategies in Community Corrections

Jessica J. B. Wyse

T he increasingly punitive nature of the American penal system and its rapid expansion have been well documented (Chesney-Lind and Pasko 2004; Travis 2005; Western 2006). Though a less frequent topic of research, these changes have also affected community supervision, where one of every 48 American adults is currently on probation or parole (Glaze and Bonczar 2011). As resources dwindle and legislators strive to appear "tough on crime," community supervision has moved away from rehabilitation as traditionally conceived and towards a strategy of containment, risk management, and efforts to enlist offenders in their own regulation (Feeley and Simon 1992; Garland 2001). . . .

[. . .]

In this article, I explore how contemporary supervision is structured in response to offenders' gender. I uncover the gendered beliefs and strategies officers rely on as they aim to rehabilitate criminal men and women, and in so doing shape their (gendered) subjectivity, and extend the research on offender management, suggesting ways in which distinct concepts of the criminal self contribute to gender disparities in treatment.

[. . .]

Using mixed methodology that draws on observational, interview, and case note data collected within the probation/parole systems of a western U.S. state, I suggest that both officers' conceptualizations of the criminal self and the rehabilitative strategies they employ are gendered. I find that officers view the male self as flawed or underdeveloped and the female as permeable and amorphous, that is, lacking firm boundaries by which to contain emotions and function independently of others. In response to these constructions, officers' rehabilitative efforts with men emphasize economic roles and responsibilities, while for women, officers aim to solidify boundaries: encouraging emotional containment and discouraging relationship

Jessica J. B. Wyse. 2013. "Rehabilitating Criminal Selves: Gendered Strategies in Community Corrections." *Gender & Society* 27(2):231–55.

formation. Qualitative data illustrate officers' gendered beliefs and supervision strategies, while quantitative data confirm that these accounts are representative.

[. . .]

Data and Methods

The analyses that follow draw on interviews with community correctional officers, observations of meetings between officers and their clients, and quantitative analyses of a sample of officers' case notes, all collected within a western U.S. state. In "Western State," while community corrections is operated semiautonomously at the county level, offenders' administrative records are maintained by the state's Department of Corrections (WDOC). I thus pursued access to the quantitative data and field sites independently. After reaching out to WDOC's research division, I was granted access to administrative records containing basic demographic, criminal, and supervision history information for all offenders on probation and parole supervision within the state. From these data, I drew a sample of offenders whose case notes I would review. The interview and observational data were drawn from two county community corrections systems within Western State. I initially contacted several counties across the state by letter, explaining the goals of my research and inquiring as to their interest in participating. Within days I received responses from the counties I refer to as Greendale and Riverside.

[. . .]

I interviewed 26 officers and staff in the sole county office in Greendale and 24 officers and staff across the five offices in Riverside. Interviews averaged between 45 minutes and one hour and addressed a variety of topics, from beliefs about the causes of crime, to the personal mission of the job, to what gender-specific treatment meant in practice. . . .

In Greendale, I also observed more than 50 meetings between community corrections officers and their clients, after obtaining consent from the officers. These meetings averaged between 15 and 45 minutes.

[. . .]

Supervision Meetings: A Site for Gendering the Criminal Subject

In supervision meetings with both men and women, officers discussed alcohol and drug treatment, housing, and access to transportation, and encouraged conventional behaviors. Despite these similarities, gender differences were substantial, reflecting differences in officers' primary goals for men and women. With men, officers focused on the formal rules of supervision, including abstaining from crime, obtaining employment, and paying fees, suggesting that officers view a rehabilitated man as having exchanged criminality for a role in the marketplace. With women, officers focused on social networks (particularly romantic relationships) and emotions, suggesting that officers view a rehabilitated woman as socially independent and emotionally contained.

Constructing Men

Within the context of the supervisory meeting, officers worked with offenders to identify conventional long-term goals and encouraged men to take initial steps along a noncriminal path.

Officers used a technique known as motivational interviewing that is designed to lower client resistance and strengthen commitment to personal change (Miller and Rollnick 2002). Bill, a white officer supervising a generic caseload, explains how he uses the technique:

> I try and find out . . . what they want out of life and from that ask them how they expect to get it . . . whether it's having a good job or having a car or having a house or having a family. . . . I work with them to figure out how they can attain those things in a legal way so they don't have to worry about losing it. . . . If it's one thing at a time, whether it's the shirt on their back . . . and work up from there.

For Bill, work with men entails reframing both the goals the offender is striving toward and the strategies used to meet these goals. The officer encourages men to conceive of an alternative reality, in which criminal choices are passed over in favor of conventional adult responsibilities.

For officers, conventional responsibility seemed largely to entail men's assumption of an economic role. Indeed, discussion of employment (job search, work hours, wages) was often the central focus of meetings with men, regardless of whether the offender voiced other significant needs or faced substantial barriers to obtaining employment. This was exemplified in one meeting I observed between one young offender and his white supervising officer, Debra.

The offender had recently been released from prison and was homeless. As the meeting began, he informed the officer that without family or friends to offer him a place to stay, he had no place to go. Rather than responding to this question, the officer asked the offender what he had done to seek out a job and whether he had a résumé, and informed him of a help wanted sign she had seen posted nearby. The client and officer then discussed how he should best present the crime for which he was incarcerated, a serious beating of another teenager, when future employers inquired about it. Only then did she inform him of a counselor he could speak with to get help finding both employment and housing. At the end of the meeting, the officer encouraged the offender, noting that he was smart and presented well (not like her other clients), and that she was sure he would be able to get a job. This client's homelessness and adjustment from prison to the community receded into the background in comparison to the primary focus: employment.

Another example of this approach can be seen in an excerpt from my field notes, recorded following the observation of a meeting between Jerry, a black officer supervising a generic caseload, and his client:

> Young Mexican American man. Looks down, says little. Reports that he recently got a job in a local factory. . . . Correctional Officer (CO) is very pleased, tells him so repeatedly. How did he get that job? Are they still hiring? He just kept calling. He works five days a week but will soon be working seven days a week at minimum wage. Has he finished up his community service hours? He . . . [is] not quite done. CO states that he must get those hours done before [he] starts working seven days a week. Agrees to do so. CO asks how things are going at home? Much better now that he has a job. [CO informs me after the meeting that his crime was meth related.]

The offender's employment status dominates this conversation, almost as if employment in a conventional job has rectified his criminal status. Of secondary importance, the officer inquires about his community service, in recognition that full-time employment may clash with other supervision conditions. Finally, the offender's family relationships are inquired after

Table 51.1 Negative Binomial Regressions of Counts of Case Notes: Crime, Employment, Fee Payment, Timeliness, Sanction, and Romantic Relationships

Independent Variables	Crime (1)	Employment (2)	Fee Payment (3)	Timeliness (4)	Sanction (5)	Romantic Relationships (6)
Male offender	2.02***	1.28*	1.44**	1.24	0.90	0.66†
Male officer	0.70	1.43**	1.40	1.46†	0.92	1.57*
Age	1.00	1.00	1.02**	1.04***	1.01	1.01
Race	1.05	0.75*	0.96	1.03	1.10	0.67
Urban county	2.62***	0.87	0.68	2.07***	1.61*	1.18
Number of offenders	100	100	100	100	100	100

†$p < .10$; *$p < .05$; **$p < .01$; ***$p < .001$.

(in a way that implies that something had been problematic in the past), but are clearly not of central importance to the conversation.

While both male and female officers emphasized employment when talking with men, this was particularly true of male officers. Indeed, quantitative analysis of the case notes reveals that male officers are significantly more likely to mention employment and timeliness than are female officers. Results are displayed in Table 51.1, models 2 and 4. As shown in model 2, male officers' case notes have 1.43 times as many comments referencing employment and 1.46 times as many comments referencing timeliness as do the case notes recorded by female officers. The focus on employment may reflect the central role that work tends to play in men's self-concepts more generally (Lamont 2000; Thompson and Walker 1989). The focus on timeliness may reflect a similar belief about the importance of employment, as showing up on time is a prerequisite for maintaining a job.

Such an interpretation was suggested by my interview with Jerry, when he explained that as an African American man who experienced racism both on and off the job, he identified with the frustrations and hopelessness his clients often expressed. Nevertheless, he stuck with his job, deriving a sense of purpose and masculine identity from it: "If I didn't feel like I made a difference with my clients I wouldn't be here. There's been days when I . . . wanted to bag it, but I'm a fighter." He worked to instill a similar positive identification in his clients as a substitute for the hopelessness that he believed fueled criminality:

Teaching guys how to be responsible fathers, making better choices, understanding that, okay, we live in a society that is not really set up for us to win, but how do you survive, how do you make the best of it? You do that by getting an education . . . getting into a job at the entry level but working your way up through the system. Being a responsible person, being a law-abiding person, drugs aren't going to get you there.

He encouraged offenders to persevere, as he had.

Closely linked with the focus on employment was officers' attention to fee payment. In meetings, officers often began the conversation by asking whether men were up-to-date on their payment and stressed the importance of paying fees. Barriers to payment were frequently discounted. As Carol noted, "They can find money for what's important to them . . . maybe 75 percent of our cases, they're smokers, if we made it to their homes they'd have big-screen TVs and they all have cell phones." Some officers stressed the importance of paying fees whether the client was employed or not. I observed one officer counseling an undocumented worker who was having trouble finding a job to pick up cans by the side of the road in order to pay his fees. I observed another officer mention that, given the offender's recent payment, he would rescind the warrant he had issued. Although the offender had not obtained a job, the officer did not inquire as to where he had obtained this money. It was the fulfillment of economic obligations that mattered to many officers, and not the social relationships or circumstances that made this possible.

This focus on economic responsibilities was also evident in my examination of the case notes, where I also found greater attention to men's crimes. Table 51.1 shows the main results. Displayed in models 1 through 3, I find that men's case notes showed more frequent discussions of crime, employment, and fee payment than did the case notes of female offenders. Specifically, being male increases the number of comments about crime by a factor of 2, comments about employment increase by 1.28 times, and comments referencing fee payment increase by 1.44 times. Thus, officers' work with men seems more focused on criminal behaviors and economic roles and responsibilities than is their work with women. However, gender differences are not evident in two related areas: discussion of timeliness of arrival to supervision appointments and comments about sanctions imposed (models 4 and 5). Regarding timeliness, this lack of difference may reflect officers' views of the supervision meeting as a crucial aspect of their work with both male and female offenders. The equal number of comments about sanctions is more understandable when informed by my observations, which suggest that differences in sanctioning between men and women are not those of frequency, but of type of sanction imposed.

The emphasis on normative behaviors and responsibilities was also reflected in officers' style of interaction with men. Officers aimed to forge a respectful, officious rapport, as Scott, a white supervisor of a generic caseload, explained: "The rapport is based on just a basic level of trust and respect, that I'm gonna treat you as a human being, and I expect to be treated the same. And as long as we don't violate that, then we have somewhere to work from." If the offender trusted the officer, the officer could then "start to hold up the mirror a little bit and maybe create a little cognitive dissonance," opening up the possibility for cognitive shifts away from criminal thought patterns and identities, and toward conventional goals. This approach also tells the offender that the officer considers him a mature adult, albeit one whose behavior has gone astray.

In contrast to work with women, rapport was not built on engagement with men's emotions or traumas. Rather, officers described their quite limited attempts to work through traumatic histories and engage in therapeutic discourse. Men would generally be allowed to unload feelings of anger and frustration for a short time, but were quickly encouraged to move on to other issues. Erin, a white supervisor of a domestic violence caseload, explains:

> I let them . . . talk about how frustrated they are or why they shouldn't be here: "I've seen worse things, I mean, there's other guys that do worse than I do." . . . Let them get that all out . . . but if it continues to be really unuseful . . . I can say, "Okay, you're here now, let's focus on what you need to do here. Can't change that."

In other words, listening was intended as a starting point to forge a positive working relationship with men, but generally not as a mini-therapy session. Deborah, a white officer supervising a generic caseload, noted that she was careful not to delve too deeply into clients' personal lives:

> I want to make sure that we address the problems that are important to them, but . . . whatever can of worms you open in a session you have to be able to close, you can't let them walk out this door raw. . . . I try to keep it a little more superficial because . . . our job is not as counselors.

I was able to observe several meetings between this officer and her male clients and confirmed that although some men seemed to be seeking a connection with her, she largely stuck to the script, focusing on the formal conditions of supervision. A field note excerpt reveals her approach:

> He comes in looking for love. He's exhausted, working two jobs, a swing shift and regular day shift. Short blond hair, sort of a frat-boy look . . . slumped in his chair. Towards the end of the meeting . . . he gives her a speech about how different things are this time, he didn't really see the light before, he was still blaming other people, but now he realizes it is all him. . . . She doesn't really respond. . . . She is quite reserved, telling him he has to go to aftercare, and giving him the list with the options, etc.

In spite of his attempts to elicit sympathy from her and forge a connection, she maintained a business-like style that left little space for talk of emotions or relationships.

As men's criminality resulted not from emotional or relational problems, but rather developmental deficits, officers' rehabilitative efforts encouraged men to assume economic roles and responsibilities, markers of a conventional, masculine self.

Constructing Women

Within supervisory meetings, officers aimed to harness women's emotional disorder, build self-esteem, and monitor their relationships. Officers addressed these goals by probing, often deeply, into women's emotional lives and attachments. While officers also inquired after women's progress in meeting the formal goals of supervision, it was these socioemotional aspects of women's lives that seemed to be at the heart of the supervisory relationship. This focus on emotions was revealed in the following meeting I observed between Leslie, a white officer who supervised primarily women, and a young woman on the cusp of completing supervision:

> Blue-tipped nails, tapping on the table. CO asks her if she's excited, how she's feeling. She says she's really excited, but really nervous too. What are you nervous about? Everything. What are you going to do about those feelings? Who are you going to talk to about things? She says she has [a friend], going to group, there are girls in the house, but [her eyes fill with tears] what makes her upset is that people she thought were her friends turned out not to be, she didn't know that could happen even in recovery. CO asks if she has other friends and she says that she does. Asks what is her plan? How much longer is she in school?

As in many meetings with women, discussion of women's housing, employment, and long-term plan is only part of the conversation, while the emotions that are understood to drive women's criminality are central.

Female offenders' perceived self-esteem deficits were also a key area of concern for officers. Officers working with women saw the meeting as an opportunity to address and begin to work through these emotional needs. Rita, an African American officer supervising a caseload of women, explains:

And I have to tell my clients every day, you have to work on your self-esteem. Every day you have to work on your self-worth, and when you start feeling that low self-esteem and low self-worth, go in the backyard, dig it outta the dumpster, put it back on, and keep pushing.

One way, Rita explained, that she helped women build self-esteem was by discouraging her clients from using language like "babymama" to describe themselves; another was to encourage her clients to wear less revealing clothing. In contrast, officers working with men worried that men's self-esteem was already too high, that their criminality resulted from a narcissistic personality. Because narcissism is one feature of "criminal thinking," these officers believed that building men's self-esteem could then prove counterproductive.

For some officers, women's emotional lives were seen as so central that the meeting took on the character of a therapy session. As Gloria, a Latina officer supervising a generic caseload, explains:

Finally, I built a relationship with her enough that it's, like, "Come on . . . I know your pattern. You're dating these men because of your father." Her father abandoned her when she was a young child, and she's always had this wanting to find a man.

Discussion of women's problematic personal patterns becomes an integral part of court-ordered supervision.

Officers' intense focus on women's emotional lives was also evidenced in the tone of the supervisory meeting. While officers working with men aimed for a respectful but emotionally contained relationship, officers working with women believed that women required empathetic, emotionally responsive treatment in order to engage in processes of personal change.

Melinda, a white officer supervising a caseload of women, explains:

Women are much more into sharing, and they wanna know they can trust you. . . . They love to talk, so it's a lot of listening and relationship building. They wanna know that you know their kids' names; they need that connection. Men, not so much.

Without such a reception, these psychologically troubled women would continue to "self-medicate" with drugs or unhealthy, "addictive" relationships.

Officers forged this emotional connection by interacting informally with offenders, engaging in a chatty style that minimized social distance, and remarking on successes at work or school and changes to appearance, like a new haircut or color. One particularly engaged female officer on a women's team spent time on the weekends and evenings with her clients, texting, taking them out to dinner, and even overseeing a family visit at the zoo. Another officer on a women's team led a knitting class for her clients once a week. Officers felt that this was an important aspect of working with women, in part, because their clients had so few positive relationships in their lives. The criminal activity that led to supervision thus availed women of one person (their corrections officer) whom they could rely on. Lisa, a white officer supervising a women's team, explains:

> I've had people use me as a reference on jobs, as the emergency contact number on applications. . . . Sometimes there's no one else left, so I'm like this authoritative, responsible person they actually have a relationship with that they can refer other people to.

Jenny, a white officer supervising a women's team, concurs: "I don't mind them needing a hug at the end. I don't mind being the one person they call if I'm the one person they have right now." Of course, like male officers' focus on employment, female officers' emotional engagement with women may not be just a reaction to offenders' gender but also a way for officers to do gender themselves, aligning supervisory style with normative conceptions of femininity. Building a relationship with women was also seen as important because of the widespread assumption that the other relationships in women's lives, particularly those with men, were a fundamental cause of women's criminality.

Indeed, only one domain was noted more frequently in female offenders' case notes: romantic relationships (model 6), which show a marginally significant difference. Specifically, being male decreases the number of mentions of romantic relationships by a factor of 0.66. This suggests that officers' work with women focuses less on women's own behaviors, and more with the potentially negative influence of those with whom a woman becomes involved.

In the relationship model, officer gender also has a significant effect, with male officers more likely to mention relationships. Though counterintuitive, this may be explained by differences in the gender pairing of officer and offender. Although small sample size prohibits testing for the significance of cross-gender pairings, the raw numbers suggest that, while both male and female officers frequently mentioned female offenders' relationships, female officers paired with men rarely mentioned relationships and male officers paired with men fell somewhere in the middle. Thus, as a whole, male officers discussed relationships with greater frequency. Because male offenders occasionally propositioned female officers, it could be that female officers avoid discussion of relationships in order to maintain a professional distance.

In contrast, romantic relationships were a big part of the discussion with female offenders, and inquiring about boyfriends and partners was routine. Officers tried to discover whether women were romantically involved with male friends or associates they mentioned in passing, and commonly asked whether men they were in relationships with were also on supervision or had a substance abuse problem. Lisa explained that officers generally assumed that the men criminal women were involved with were problematic: "I mean, what we call it here is that their picker is broken . . . that part of the brain that picks the man you're attracted to, that picker is broken and you only pick bad men, either abusive or addicted or all of the above." Officers focused on the men in women's lives because of the widely held belief that men had led women into criminality initially, and were likely to do so again. Thus, involvement in relationships posed a threat to women's rehabilitation.

In one meeting, Lisa inquired initially about the offender's housing and job search. Yet, both of these questions led to further inquiries about the nature of relationships. On hearing that the offender planned to reside with her father, the officer asked about the history of the relationship. She was interested not just *that* the offender had secured housing, but in the emotional implications this residence might have. Similarly, when the offender noted that she had obtained a job at a pizza parlor through a friend, the following conversation ensued:

> CO [Correctional Officer] asks, who is this friend? An old friend [offender replies]. She worked there [at the parlor] in the past. He saw her go through the whole bad cycle of doing well and then falling apart. . . . CO asks if he is interested in a relationship with her—"He was!"—but the client explains that she straightened him out, she doesn't want a relationship with him ever, and not with anybody right now.

Later, the officer brings up relationships again:

> CO asks if she is looking for a boyfriend right now. "No way. I'm not looking for that at all, not for at least a year." CO asks why. "I just have really bad taste in boyfriends. . . ." CO highlights that not getting involved in relationships is a good choice right now.

Lisa makes it clear to the offender that staying out of relationships is important to her success on supervision. Notably, this offender had already secured a job and housing and was attending Narcotics Anonymous meetings twice weekly, achievements that, for men, often meant there was little else to discuss.

In the case notes not just the frequency, but how relationships were discussed differed as well. For male offenders, relationships seemed to signal progress towards conventional goals: "O [offender] moved in with his GF, working at McDonalds, wants to go to college! Overall I am very impressed w/O's progress, by all appearances doing very well." Officers generally assumed that partnership for men was positive. In contrast, notes about women's relationships were largely negative. While the resources boyfriends offered were mentioned, boyfriends' drug use, supervision histories, and roles in encouraging the female offender's own criminality were also frequently noted:

> Told O that she could not live with a male who is also on supervision due to her relapses in the past. I reviewed O's past relapses with her, how she gets lost in relationships w/males who have criminal history and then she relapses.

> PO told O that any contact with husband [who continues to sell marijuana] would result in loss of custody of child.

> Admits she is still with Jake, states he drinks but no law enforcement involvement.

In these quotes, it is not imminent danger posed by the male partner that the officer seems to be concerned with; rather, involvement in a relationship itself seems to run counter to officers' conceptions of proper female rehabilitation.

Because women's criminality is believed to result from insufficient boundaries, officers' rehabilitative efforts center on policing these boundaries, encouraging emotional independence, and discouraging romantic relationships.

Conclusion

As the carceral net has expanded, drawing an astonishing number of men and women under criminal justice supervision, often for years at a time, it has become increasingly important to understand how such governance is both shaped by and constitutive of particular notions of men and women as criminal subjects. Building on past literature, which finds that criminal women are viewed as emotionally and psychologically damaged, I suggest that the criminal woman's self is understood to lack firm boundaries, what I characterize as a permeable or amorphous self. Women's crime is understood to occur in reaction to her current social context: when she is overcome by emotions and influenced by relationships with criminal others. While the particularly gendered nature of men's subjectivity has received less attention, I diverge from that which suggests that men's criminality is a rational choice made by a whole self. Rather, I find that officers view the criminal male self as flawed and underdeveloped and understand this self to be emergent from patterns learned in childhood. As an adult, these criminal thought processes and self-concepts lead men to criminal choices. In addition to describing the root causes of criminality, these gendered typologies contribute to distinct goals in work with men and women.

While it has been established that contemporary supervision aims primarily to govern offenders by guiding their choices (choices for which they are seen as ultimately responsible), this article suggests ways in which such responsibilizing practices are gendered. I find that while officers' efforts to normalize men aim to encourage the assumption of economic roles and responsibilities, viewed as the counterpoint to criminal engagement, efforts to normalize women aim to solidify boundaries: discouraging romantic engagements and containing women's emotions. Thus, beliefs about the context in which criminal choices are made, and the rehabilitative response needed to encourage conventional choices, are distinctly gendered.

[. . .]

This study suggests that, for women, whose needs are defined largely in relational and emotional terms, community supervision extends far beyond the presumed objectives of preventing crime and protecting public safety to bring officers' powers of social control to bear on deeply personal aspects of women's lives. While there may be truth to officers' beliefs about women, for instance in the role relationships play in women's criminality (Daly 1994; Richie 1996), it remains important to consider whether such regulation should be a central goal of criminal justice supervision. Though it may be that women are reliant on problematic romantic partners and lacking in self-esteem, if women have no source of income and no place to stay (other than with this partner), self-esteem building alone will not translate into real independence for women. In contrast, for men, whose needs are defined largely in economic terms, officers often fail to consider the barriers men may face in fulfilling supervision conditions, as well as how men's social and emotional lives influence their success or failure. While men's lives face less scrutiny, ignoring the very real obstacles men encounter in attempts to obtain employment, secure housing, and pay fees may then prove discouraging to male offenders, and even hold the potential to spark a reinitiation of substance abuse and/or criminal offending. Although the gendered attributions I have identified are not unique to this setting, their significance is: while officers view themselves more as social workers than correctional officers, their words are backed by the threat of force. These gendered strategies may then have significant implications, as offenders, responding to the power officers hold over their lives, shape their conduct in response to officers' expectations.

References

Chesney-Lind, Meda and Lisa Pasko. 2004. *The Female Offender: Girls, Women, and Crime.* Thousand Oaks, CA: Sage.

Daly, Kathleen. 1994. *Gender, Crime, and Punishment.* New Haven, CT: Yale University Press.

Feeley, Malcolm and Jonathan Simon. 1992. "The New Penology: Notes on the Emerging Strategy of Corrections and Its Implications." *Criminology* 30:449–74.

Garland, David. 2001. *The Culture of Control.* Chicago, IL: University of Chicago Press.

Glaze, Lauren and Thomas Bonczar. 2011. *Probation and Parole in the United States, 2010.* Washington, DC: U.S. Department of Justice.

Lamont, Michelle. 2000. *The Dignity of Working Men: Morality and the Boundaries of Race, Class, and Immigration.* New York: Russell Sage Foundation.

Miller, William and Stephen Rollnick. 2002. *Motivational Interviewing: Preparing People for Change.* New York: Guilford.

Richie, Beth. 1996. *Compelled to Crime: The Gender Entrapment of Battered Black Women.* New York: Routledge.

Thompson, Linda and Alexis Walker. 1989. "Gender in Families: Women and Men in Marriage, Work, and Parenthood." *Journal of Marriage and the Family* 51:845–71.

Travis, Jeremy. 2005. *But They All Come Back: Facing the Challenges of Prisoner Reentry.* Washington, DC: Urban Institute.

Western, Bruce. 2006. *Punishment and Inequality in America.* New York: Russell Sage Foundation.

The Consequences of the Criminal Justice Pipeline on Black and Latino Masculinity

Victor M. Rios

© iStockphoto.com/innovatedcaptures

Black and Latino youth are overrepresented in every major component in the juvenile justice system (Kupchik 2006; Leiber 2002). Some researchers have called this "cumulative disadvantage," as the overrepresentation increases from the time of arrest through the final point in the system, imprisonment (National Council on Crime and Delinquency [NCCD] 2007, 4). It is noteworthy that nearly 75 percent of juveniles admitted to adult state prisons in 2002 were youth of color (Kupchik 2006; NCCD 2007), although only 30 percent of juveniles arrested in this country are persons of color (NCCD 2007).

Mauer and Chesney-Lind (2004) have argued that the disproportionate incarceration of people of color has had unintended consequences in poor communities. They contend that such punishment not only adversely affects confined individuals but also extends to negative effects on families, communities, and the future livelihoods of those who come into contact

Victor M. Rios. 2009. "The Consequences of the Criminal Justice Pipeline on Black and Latino Masculinity." *The Annals of the American Academy of Political and Social Science* 623(1):150–62.

with the criminal justice system. Among the collateral consequences of punitive criminal justice treatment of young adults in the inner city are constant surveillance and stigma imposed by schools, community centers, and families (Rios 2006); permanent criminal credentials that exclude black males from the labor market (Pager 2003); and a sense of mistrust and resentment toward police and the rest of the criminal justice system (Brunson and Miller 2006; Fine and Weiss 1998). In this article, I argue that an additional consequence of enhanced policing, surveillance, and punitive treatment of youth of color is the development of a specific set of gendered practices, heavily influenced by interactions with police, detention facilities, and probation officers. This criminal justice pipeline provides young men with meanings of masculinity that ultimately influence their decisions to commit crime and engage in violence. While race affects how a young person is treated in the criminal justice pipeline, masculinity plays a role in how young men desist or recidivate as they pass through the system. One of the outcomes of pervasive criminal justice contact for young black and Latino men is the production of a hypermasculinity that obstructs desistance and social mobility.

Harris (2000, 785) defines hypermasculinity as the "exaggerated exhibition of physical strength and personal aggression" that is often a response to a gender threat "expressed through physical and sexual domination of others." Drawing on this definition, I contend that the criminal justice pipeline encourages expressions of hypermasculinity by threatening and confusing young men's masculinity. This, in turn, leads the young men to rely on domination through violence, crime, and a school and criminal justice counterculture. Multiple points in the criminal justice pipeline may be salient for producing hypermasculinity, including three that are examined here: policing, incarceration, and probation. Detrimental forms of masculinity are partly developed through a youth's interaction with these institutions of criminal justice.

Messerschmidt (1993, 1997, 2000) has argued that crime is a resource for "doing" race and gender (see also West and Fenstermaker 1995; West and Zimmerman 1987). He contends that "crime is employed to produce and sustain a specific race and class masculine identity" (1997, 41). In other words, crime is one of the avenues that men turn to in developing, demonstrating, and communicating their manhood. Indeed, criminal activity constitutes a gendered practice that can be used to communicate the parameters of manhood. As such, crime is more likely when men need to prove themselves and when they are held accountable to a strict set of expectations (Messerschmidt 1997). Furthermore, West and Fenstemaker (1995) contend that this accountability—the gendered actions that people develop in response to what they perceive others will expect of them—is encountered in interactions between individuals and institutions:

> While individuals are the ones who do gender, the process of rendering something accountable is both interactional and institutional in character. . . . Gender is . . . a mechanism whereby situated social action contributes to the reproduction of social structure. (P. 21)

Here, I expand on Messerschmidt's notion of crime as a masculinity-making resource and on West and Fenstermaker's understanding of gender as a mechanism by which social structure is created and reproduced. Conceptualizing gender as structured action, a social process that changes based on interactions with specific types of institutions, in turn, allows us to explore how the criminal justice system shapes the development of specific forms of masculinity.

Masculinity, Crime, and Crime Control

Individuals shape their behavior according to gendered expectations and are subject to a system of accountability that is gendered, raced, and classed (Fenstermaker and West 2002; West and Fenstermaker 1995). Youth of color are inculcated into a set of hypermasculine expectations that often lead them to behaviors that conflict with the structures of dominant institutions. For example, Ferguson (2000) demonstrated that schools participate in the making of black masculinity in children as young as ten years old. Masculinity-making is heavily responsible for the deviance and punishment that takes place in the classroom and later in the criminal justice system.

To be assigned "real man" status by relevant others and institutions, young men must pass multiple litmus tests among peers, family, and other institutions. These masculinity tests, or codes, were identified by sociologists as early as the 1920s. In 1924, Edwin Sutherland discussed how boys are taught to be rough and tough, rendering them more likely than girls to become delinquent (cited in Sutherland and Cressey 1955).

[. . .]

Contemporary urban ethnographers also emphasize this point. For example, Anderson (1999) describes "young male syndrome" as the perceived, expected, and often necessary pressure to perform a tough, violent, and deviant manhood to receive and maintain respect (see also Dance 2002; Duneier 1999). Pyke (1996) found that masculinity is expressed differently by men of varied class positions. While wealthy men can prove their masculinity through the ability to earn money and consume products that make them manly, poor young men have to use toughness, violence, and survival as the means of proving their masculinity and resilience. Toughness, dominance, and the willingness to resort to violence to resolve interpersonal conflicts are central characteristics of masculine identity (Anderson 1999; Messerschmidt 1993). Such studies also explore how masculinity is central to the perpetuation of crime, but they do not examine how the criminal justice system is involved in the masculinity-making process.

[. . .]

Kimmel and Mahler (2003, 1440) move beyond an emphasis on crime, arguing that violent youth are not psychopaths but, rather, "overconformists to a particular normative construction of masculinity." I contend that these overconforming violent and delinquent youth give us clues as to how masculinity is developed in relation to institutional constructions of manhood. Mainstream society and the criminal justice system expect a masculine conformity that emphasizes hard work, law abidance, and an acceptance of subordinate social positions. Some young men attempt to embrace this masculinity as a means to reform. However, when they attempt to follow these expectations, they come to realize that doing so does not allow for survival on the streets, a place to which they can always expect to return.

In attempts to deal with young men's criminality, institutions develop practices heavily influenced by masculinity. In turn, inner-city males become socialized to specific meanings of manhood that are diametrically opposed to those expected by dominant institutions of control. Thus, gendered interactions with the criminal justice system place young men of color in a double bind. Most buy into the system's ideals of reform by being "hardworking men." However, frustration with the lack of viable employment and guidance opportunities leads many young men to what seems to be the only alternative: hypermasculinity, or the exaggerated exhibition of physical and personal aggression. The stories and actions of young men in this study provide insight into how this double bind is partially generated by the criminal justice system itself.

Method

This investigation is based on ethnography involving in-depth interviews with forty black and Latino male adolescents living in Oakland, California. The study was conducted from 2002 to 2005. The sample includes twenty black males and twenty Latino males, ranging from ages fourteen to eighteen. Participants were recruited from two organizations that worked with "at-promise" youth and were selected through convenience and snowball sampling. Interviews were conducted either at the sites of the two community organizations or at a public space where the youth felt comfortable. Throughout this article I use pseudonyms for participants, organizations, schools, and gangs. Thirty of the forty participants had recently been incarcerated. The remaining ten youth had not come into contact with the criminal justice system. Most of the offenses committed by the delinquent boys were nonviolent. All forty youth reported having persistent contact with police officers while growing up. The thirty formerly arrested youth had all spent at least a week in juvenile facilities, and twenty-four had been assigned a probation officer.

I shadowed these young men, with permission from them and their parents, as they walked the streets, attended court, and participated in community center. . . . Shadowing allowed me to see and analyze routine practices and how these fit in with the full range of participants' activities.

[. . .]

Masculinity Versus Criminalization

Junior, a sixteen-year-old Chicano from Oakland, California, attended continuation school, which is a small campus where delinquent, truant, and other problem students are sent to do their course work as a final alternative to expulsion. I often shadowed Junior, walking with him to and from school, places of leisure, and home. One morning, as I walked with him to school, I counted six police cars patrolling his usual route, which is used by most teenagers from the poorer side of the neighborhood to get to school. Each patrol car slowed to stare us down as they spotted him. To buy a snack, Junior had to wait outside the neighborhood store for a few minutes because of store policy clearly stated on a sign reading, "only two kids allowed in store at one time."

Junior's school was located in the middle-class part of town, about five miles uphill from his home. As we approached the school's neighborhood, the residents who had previously called the police on Junior for sitting on their steps stared with suspicion. As he entered the school, he passed by the school-stationed officer. The officer asked him, "What kind of trouble are you going to give me today?" We parted ways as I left him at the foot of the school entrance and watched him enter under the eye of the surveillance camera. He later told me that his teacher reported him to the school-based police officer for sleeping in class. All of this policing happened in a one-hour span, from 7:45 to 8:45 a.m. on a typical Monday morning.

These day-to-day interactions fostered a sense of criminalization, that is, being viewed as a criminal when simply going about routine practices, and they forced Junior to wonder whether he would ever be seen as a normal person or only as a criminal:

> I mean, I mean, you know, I try hard but I get messed with all the time even if I'm trying to keep it cool. It's like when I keep it cool is when they fuck with me the most. . . . I might as well be hard and let them know that they ain't gonna fuck with me.

As a reaction to such treatment, Junior developed a tough front (Dance 2002) that used hypermasculinity as a form of coping, survival, and resistance. Junior's criminalization intensified his conflicts over manhood and ran a collision course with the criminal justice system's demands of passivity, compliance, and conformity to a subjugated racialized social status. Expectations of passivity and compliance, unaccompanied by change in social conditions, engender hopelessness and an inability to function both in mainstream institutions and on the street, where survival skills are intricately connected to hypermasculinity. Criminalization, policing, and the justice system's pressures on young men force them to make a choice: comply or become hard. When they comply, they fail on the street because they have to become passive and nondeviant, while at the same time they are unable to obtain employment or eliminate the criminal stigma marked on them by the system. On the other hand, when they fail to comply, they are likely to be harassed or arrested. Like Junior, the rest of the young men in this study encountered criminalization through gendered interactions as they entered the system. The first point of contact with hypermasculinity through criminal justice is with the police.

[. . .]

Police

Police officers are themselves embedded in an environment that embraces masculinity. Indeed, academies train officers to practice a rogue and hostile masculinity. Prokos and Padavic (2002, 442) note that male officers "equate men and masculinity with guns, crime-fighting, a combative personality . . . and a desire to work in high crime areas." This positioning reverberates in the inner city as "police officers in poor minority neighborhoods may come to see themselves as law enforcers in a community of savages, as outposts of the law in a jungle" (Harris 2000, 798). In this context, punitive police treatment of men of color is not only racial violence; it is also gender violence: "Violent acts committed by men, whether these acts break the law or are designed to uphold it, are often a way of demonstrating the perpetrator's manhood. I call this kind of violence 'gender violence' and assert that men as well as women may be its victims" (Harris 2000, 783).

Young people in Oakland encounter this gender violence regularly by police on the street, at school, at community centers, and in front of their apartment complexes. The boys often become victims in the course of police officers' attempts to uphold the law. Officers want to "teach" young men lessons by feminizing them. They manhandle them, constantly call them "little bitches," humiliate them in front of female peers, challenge them to fights, and otherwise brutalize them. The following interchange is illustrative of how the young men respond:

Castro: Dude [the officer] was pointing his gun. "I give up, I give up." He hit him with stick and broke his arm and this other fool had his knee on my neck. All 'cause we were smoking some weed . . . they beat us down and call us "little bitches."

Rafa: They lack your ass, pistol whip you even try to kill you . . . them bust'as just trying to prove themselves you feel me? They trying to prove they are more manly than us but if they didn't have guns or jails they would end up being the bitches.

Gendered police interactions and gendered violence begin at an early age (see Brunson and Miller 2006; Ferguson 2000). Slick's story illustrates this phenomenon. He lives in the heart of a neighborhood that is home to one of Oakland's largest gangs, "La Nueve" (the East

9th Street Gang). In his childhood, Slick expected police to protect him from violent gang members. Then one day he realized that police saw him as "the enemy." Slick was eleven years old when he was first brutalized by the police, the same officers who had policed his neighborhood from the time that he was a small child:

> One time we were at St. Anthony's [park] . . . the police out of nowhere started talking shit to me. And I uh, uh I pulled up my pants, I just pulled up my pants and he just grabbed me and slammed me on the ground and hit me with the club. He was like, he was like "Oh you look like you was gonna' pull up your pants and do something." I was, I was pullin' up my pants 'cause I be sagging my pants sometimes.

Slick tried to pull up his pants to appear more formal and to signify to the officer that he was complying with the law. He figured if he pulled up his pants, the cop might see him as a "good kid," by explaining, "He tried to tell me not to sag my pants anymore so he wouldn't have to think I was a criminal." Eventually, Slick would develop coping strategies that helped him deal with the animosity he felt around police: he acted tough and put on a menacing performance when police came around. Slick cursed at police and gave them "dirty" looks when they drove by or pulled up next to us; his hypermasculinity became a resource for keeping the police at bay. This strategy often worked, which led officers to call in backup when they decided to approach us. During my shadowing in Oakland, officers often approached preadolescent boys in only one patrol car. However, once the boys reached adolescence and commanded a certain bravado, officers always showed up in at least two patrol cars. The boys' "hardcore" behavior—developed through negative interactions with police officers—may have signaled to officers that they were armed and dangerous, and officers treated them as such.

On various occasions, the boys and I were "roughed up" by groups of police officers who drove up in multiple patrol cars. We were harassed, humiliated, and sometimes beaten. During these dozen or so times over the three years, I learned that officers use a brutal masculinity that inculcates a tough-toughness, a manly-manliness, and a hypermasculinity. This model often leads young men to perpetrate crime and violence, and it may sanction police to brutalize and arrest them, which leads youth to the next gate in the justice pipeline: incarceration. Once in confinement, these young men adopt a masculinity that would protect them not only from the streets and police but also from violence in confinement.

Incarceration

While incarcerated, young men are forced to overemphasize their masculinity. The story of Big Rob, an African American sixteen-year-old from Oakland, illustrates this point. He had been arrested for driving a "G-ride" (i.e., a stolen car). Rob's specialty was stealing cars and selling them to "chop shops," car shops that dismantle the cars and sell them for parts. At the time of the arrest, Rob was driving in a 1987 Buick Grand National. He was stripped and cavity-searched upon arrival at "one-hundred-and-fiftieth," the county's juvenile justice facility. His possessions were confiscated, and he was provided a dark blue jumpsuit with the words "property of Alameda County" printed on it.

> The guard told me "take a shower and make sure you don't drop the soap, boy!" I didn't know what he was talking about. It wasn't until I asked some dude that I figured out what he meant.

"Don't drop the soap" is a reference to rape by other inmates in detention showers. Rob was placed in a cafeteria where about twenty or so youth congregated. They stared Rob down, giving him dirty looks. A few boys walked up to him and asked, "Where you from?" Rob told them, "Dirty thirties." They responded with the names of their turfs. "I had to act hard. I balled up my fist and was ready to knock a nigga' out." Rob eventually got into a fight, protecting himself from an attack. He was sent to "solitary," only allowed outside of his tiny cell with a cement bed to take a shower and call home. The officer who supervised his cell commented "you gonna' learn how to be a man the hard way." Once released, Rob and other young men like him bring this repertoire to the streets. "Man! They think I got better. Mothafucka's just taught me how to be more violent, steal tighter rides [nicer cars]. . . . I even ended up with more bitch-ass enemies."

Probation

Probation practices subject boys' ideas of manhood to strict evaluation. As agents of reform, probation officers attempt to teach young men how to be "real men" by demanding that they work toward a societally acceptable form of masculinity: acquire an education, attain a job, and support a family. They are told to get a job, do well in school, and stay out of trouble. The likelihood of failure is high since most avenues of legitimate success are out of reach. Kimmel (2006) argues that in the contemporary era,

> Deindustrialization made men's hold on the successful demonstration of masculinity increasingly tenuous; there are fewer and fewer self-made successes and far more self-blaming failures. (p. 216)

When these youth fail, they abandon the false expectations of obtaining a job; instead of becoming passive and hopeless, they adopt a hypermasculine ideal of survival.

[. . .]

For example, José, a fifteen-year-old who had been arrested for selling marijuana, lived in a state of confusion when it came to masculinity. His description highlights the contradiction he confronted:

> They [probation officers] tell us to be "real men," to show respect but they don't see that if we show respect we'll get treated like punk . . . being a man out here is different. It means smashing on a scrub [beating an enemy up] if he breaks your respect . . . it means handling your business in order to get paid . . . not being a bitch and shit, it means going to jail if you have to.

From José's perspective, and those of many other youth I interviewed, it was extremely self-defeating for probation officers trying to reform them to attempt to do so by teaching them how a real man should act. These messages did not provide youth with tools to navigate the streets, to do well at home and in school, or to succeed at a job and make an income. Instead, youth saw two extreme worlds of manhood where only one was accessible—hypermasculinity. It is at this point where male youth made their decisions to affirm, develop, and demonstrate a manhood that appears to offer respect, economic gain, and social status (Anderson 1999; Jones 2004) instead of hopelessness.

The ideal of manhood that probation officers try to inculcate is also one of responsibility. For these officials, the responsibility of a young man is to follow his "program" and not be rear-rested. The message becomes, "a real man does not belong in jail." Once a male enters jail or prison, he is at risk of becoming emasculated as his life is run by a system outside of himself. According to José, his probation officer, Mr. Bryan, explained the condition of men in containment through associations with feminization, by playing upon the fear and dread associated with men being treated like women:

> You want to go to prison where everybody is gonna pimp you? The guards are gonna run you like a little bitch. The murderers and rapists [will] make you bend over, they gonna treat you like somebody's wife.

While probation officers, and the community, attempt to instill young men with positive notions of manhood, the street contradicts this masculinity—one demands law abidance, the other contempt for the law. In trying to teach a dominant masculinity as a set of ideals, probation officers unintentionally push young men of color further into hypermasculinity.

Discussion and Conclusion

After being arrested and placed on probation, unable to continue selling drugs or stealing cars for income, and unable to secure a job because of his record, T, a sixteen-year-old African American from Oakland, resorted to using women as a central source of income. When asked, "Where do you get money from?" T replied,

> Pimp a bitch you know, let that bitch come out her pocket . . . act like I like her so she'll give me money and shit . . . most bitches will give me whatever I need . . . shoes, shirts, food, bus pass, whatever . . . or make her sell shit for me.

T made the decision to no longer commit crime. However, his solution was to fully embrace hypermasculinity and dominate women to accomplish what the criminal justice system expected of him—to desist from committing crime.

As a result, inner-city men come to embrace gendered practices that further limit their futures and harm those around them. The youth in this study reported trying to be "good men," following the criminal justice system's ideals of manhood by being passive, trying to do well in school, or looking for work. However, these strategies often placed them in a double bind such that they were unable to succeed both at work and in the streets. When the strategies fail, a seductive alternative surfaces in times of crisis—hypermasculinity.

As the criminal justice system perpetuates gender violence on young men to "teach them a lesson," young men develop a hypermasculinity that symbolically attacks the system. They also embrace domination of others as a way to compensate for having their masculinity threatened. As adolescent boys make masculinity on the street, the institutions of control that manage them also generate meanings of manhood that correlate with the damaging identities these youth form on the street.

Both gender and race simultaneously shape the life course of inner-city men in the criminal justice system. Gender, like race, is always determined by specific contexts. In this case, the criminalization of black and Latino males and the criminal justice system's expectations of masculinity provide young men with gender resources that often limit their life chances and channel them deeper into the racialized and gendered criminal justice system. The gender ideals purveyed by police, probation officers, and others do not translate adequately into the realities of the youth's lives. In this context, hypermasculinity serves both as resistance and as a resource for self-affirmation. The criminal justice pipeline, in its attempt to reform racialized youth, imposes gender practices fraught with failure and insolvable contradictions. Provided with the options of hypermasculinity or hopelessness by the criminal justice system and the streets, marginalized boys end up choosing to become "real men," to embrace hypermasculinity. While hypermasculinity may attract disrepute, it makes its practitioners feel self-fulfilled. This survival strategy, in turn, impedes desistance and social mobility and entitles the system to further punish racialized and gendered youth. In essence, then, gender is one of the processes by which the criminal justice system is involved in the reproduction of racial inequality.

References

Anderson, Elijah. 1999. *Code of the Street: Decency, Violence, and Moral Life of the Inner City*. New York: Norton.

Brunson, Rod K. and Jody Miller. 2006. "Gender, Race, and Urban Policing: The Experience of African American Youth." *Gender & Society* 20:531–52.

Dance, Lory Janelle. 2002. *Tough Fronts: The Impact of Street Culture on Schooling*. London, UK: Routledge.

Duneier, Mitchell. 1999. *Sidewalk*. New York: Farrar, Straus and Giroux.

Fenstermaker, Sarah and Candace West. 2002. *Doing Gender, Doing Difference: Inequality, Power, and Institutional Change*. New York: Routledge.

Ferguson, Anne A. 2000. *Bad Boys: Public Schools in the Making of Black Masculinity*. Ann Arbor, MI: University of Michigan Press.

Fine, Michelle and Lois Weiss. 1998. *The Unknown City: Lives of Poor and Working-Class Young Adults*. Boston, MA: Beacon.

Harris, Angela P. 2000. "Gender, Violence, Race, and Criminal Justice." *Stanford Law Review* 52:777–807.

Jones, Nikki. 2004. "'It's Not Where You Live, It's How You Live': How Young Women Negotiate Conflict and Violence in the Inner City." *The Annals of the American Academy of Political and Social Science* 595:49–62.

Kimmel, Michael S. 2006. *Manhood in America: A Cultural History*. New York: Oxford University Press.

Kimmel, Michael and Matthew Mahler. 2003. "Adolescent Masculinity, Homophobia, and Violence." *American Behavioral Scientist* 46:1439–58.

Kupchik, Aaron. 2006. *Judging Juveniles: Prosecuting Adolescents in Adult and Juvenile Courts*. New York: New York University Press.

Leiber, Michael J. 2002. "Disproportionate Minority Confinement (DMC) of Youth: An Analysis of State and Federal Efforts to Address the Issue." *Crime and Delinquency* 48:3–45.

Mauer, Marc and Meda Chesney-Lind, eds. 2004. *Invisible Punishment: The Collateral Consequences of Mass Imprisonment*. New York: New Press.

Messerschmidt, James W. 1993. *Masculinities and Crime: Critique and Reconceptualization of Theory*. Lanham, MD: Rowman & Littlefield.

Messerschmidt, James W. 1997. *Crime as Structured Action: Gender, Race, Class and Crime in the Making*. Thousand Oaks, CA: Sage.

Messerschmidt, James W. 2000. *Nine Lives: Adolescent Masculinities, the Body, and Violence*. Boulder, CO: Westview.

National Council on Crime and Delinquency. 2007. *And Justice for Some: Differential Treatment of Youth of Color in the Juvenile System*. Retrieved April 10, 2008 (www.nccd-crc.org/nccd/pubs/2007jan_justice_for_some.pdf).

Pager, Devah. 2003. "The Mark of a Criminal Record." *American Journal of Sociology* 108:937–75.

Prokos, Anastasia and Irene Padavic. 2002. "'There Oughtta Be a Law Against Bitches': Masculinity Lessons in Police Academy Training." *Gender, Work and Organization* 9:439–59.

Pyke, Karen D. 1996. "Class-Based Masculinities: The Interdependence of Gender, Class, and Interpersonal Power." *Gender & Society* 10:527–49.

Rios, Victor. 2006. "The Hyper-Criminalization of Black and Latino Male Youth in the Era of Mass Incarceration." *Souls* 8:40–54.

Sutherland, Edwin H. and Donald R. Cressey. 1955. *Principles of Criminology*. Philadelphia, PA: J. B. Lippincott.

West, Candace and Sarah Fenstermaker. 1995. "Doing Difference." *Gender & Society* 9:8–37.

West, Candace and Don Zimmerman. 1987. "Doing Gender." *Gender & Society* 1:125–51.

"We're Like Community"

Collective Identity and Collective Efficacy Among Transgender Women in Prisons for Men

Lori Sexton and Valerie Jenness

A considerable body of research paints a complex picture of prison life by focusing empirical attention on the diversity of prison populations, the subjective experience of prisoners, the multifaceted nature of prison communities, and the myriad ways prisons are structured. . . .

The robust literature on prisoner life yields a paradoxical picture of prisons. On the one hand, prisons are generally understood to be harsh environments, full of potential problems and conflicts born of the deprivations inherent to such confinement. . . .

Coincident with this picture of prisons as uniformly harsh, the prison literature also reveals the myriad ways carceral environments are organized around cooperation and collaboration based on institutionally recognized shared identities and subjectivities. Despite—or perhaps as a result of—being confined in institutions characterized by harshness and laden with conflict and coercion, inmates operate in a highly structured social environment with mutual expectations of loyalty and allegiance born of community-level expectations. . . . It is commonly accepted that, within prison walls, there is a cohesive inmate culture characterized by group-shared (and enforced) norms (Clemmer, 1940; Hayner and Ash, 1940; Sykes, 1958; Sykes and Messinger, 1960), including norms that define a stratification order particular to prison life.

[. . .]

Donaldson's (1993) classic work, as well as Dolovich's (2011), Robinson's (2011) and Jenness and Fenstermaker's (2014, 2016) more recent work, reveal how markers of gender and sexuality organize prisoners' lives in carceral environments designed for men. Prisons are, in the first instance, sex segregated institutions (Britton, 2003) organized around heteronormative understandings that produce a consequential stratification order among inmates (Fleisher and Krienert, 2009; Kunzel, 2008). This stratification order positions sex offenders and those with

Lori Sexton and Valerie Jenness. 2016. "'We're Like Community': Collective Identity and Collective Efficacy Among Transgender Women in Prisons for Men." *Punishment & Society* 18(5):544–77.

non-normative gender identities and sexualities near the bottom of that order and consequently renders them fair game as prey for other prisoners (Clemmer, 1940; Ireland, 2002; Knopp, 1984; Leddy and O'Connell, 2002; Schwaebe, 2005; Vaughn and Sapp, 1989). This is especially true for transgender women in prisons for men (Jenness, 2010a; Jenness and Fenstermaker, 2014, 2016; Jenness et al., 2011; Sexton et al., 2010).

[. . .]

Given the complex structure of inmate communities in prisons in the United States, the tension between solidarity and affiliation, on the one hand, and self-interest and disaffiliation on the other, merits empirical interrogation. This tension is complicated precisely because prison environments are simultaneously characterized by harshness, deprivation, and distrust as well as inter- and intragroup loyalties and commitments that organize prison life and undergird prisoner communities. Modern day prisons provide a unique setting in which to examine the intricacies of allegiance to one's own kind in a closed social system with finite resources for managing a particularly harsh, degrading, and disempowering social environment.

[. . .]

Transgender Women Prisoners

Until very recently, very little social science research had been published on transgender prisoners—prisoners whose gender identity and/or presentation are different from their sex as assigned by the institution. In 2005, Tewksbury and Potter (2005) deemed transgender prisoners a "forgotten group." Four years later, Sexton et al. (2010: 860), published the first demographic profile of transgender women in prison and concluded that they are exceptionally marginalized both inside and outside of prison.

Prior to this landmark publication, previous studies portrayed transgender inmates as minor characters in the cast of the early literature on prison culture—as "punks" or "queens" among the more normative "Men." In one of the most illuminating articles on the topic, Donaldson (1993) vividly describes distinctions between a jocker, a punk, a queen, a bootybandit, a Daddy, and a Man. However, he does not address the social status, identity, behavioral repertoire, or efficacy of this particular group of prisoners. . . . What we do know is that transgender women prisoners have much in common with other prisoners in prisons for men. Most notably, they experience many of the same pains of imprisonment as other prisoners (Crewe, 2009; Jenness et al., 2013; Kruttschnitt and Gartner, 2004; Sexton, 2014; Sumner, 2009; Sumner et al., 2015; Sykes, 1958).

Transgender women in prison for men are also distinct from other prisoners in consequential ways. They embrace non-normative gender identities and/or display non-normative gender presentations in a rigidly gendered carceral setting that assumes males—and only males—as inhabitants. In this sense, they occupy a minority status in prison that renders them vulnerable and marginalized. With regard to vulnerability, for example, transgender prisoners are 13 *times* more likely than their nontransgender counterparts to be sexually assaulted in prison (Jenness et al., 2007; Jenness, 2010a, 2014; see also Jenness and Fenstermaker, 2016). When examined along the lines of previous employment, marital status, mental health, substance abuse, HIV status, homelessness, sex work, and victimization, transgender women prisoners in men's prisons are comparatively disadvantaged and marginalized (Sexton et al., 2009).

As a uniquely situated group within the larger prison culture in prisons for men, transgender women in prisons for men are bound by a common social location within prison and commonality of experience that flows from it. At the same time, however, as a population of prisoners they are distinct and display considerable diversity among themselves. For example, they report a range of sexual and gender identities, attractions, sexual orientations, and presentation of self modalities. These and sources of diversity such as race/ethnicity, educational attainment and other sources of social capital, mark transgender prisoners as a heterogeneous group of inmates (Jenness et al., 2011, 2013). Transgender women prisoners in prisons for men simultaneously share with their nontransgender counterparts the fact that they are, in the first instance, prisoners—even as they are situated as a distinct subpopulation of prisoners with a unique relationship to life in prisons for men and display considerable diversity among themselves as a distinct subpopulation that routinely violates the gender order.

[. . .]

A key question for this work is whether transgender women in prisons for men report perceptions of collective identity and collective efficacy as a distinct subpopulation of prisoners, as prisoners in a generic sense, or as both.

[. . .]

Recent qualitative analyses of transgender women in men's prisons reveal a friendly yet fierce competition among transgender women prisoners for the attention and affection of "real men" in prison. As Jenness and Fenstermaker (2014: 29) explain:

> Transgender prisoners in men's prisons express a desire to secure standing as a "real girl" or "the best girl" possible in a men's prison. This desire translates into expressions of situated gendered practices that embrace male dominance, heteronormativity, classed and raced gender ideals, and a daily acceptance of inequality. To succeed in being "close enough" to "the real deal" requires a particular type of participation in a male-dominated system that can dole out a modicum of privilege and respect.

Transgender prisoners accomplish these goals to varying degrees through the enactment of hyper-femininity in a demonstrably hyper-masculine environment. The result is a culture of competition among transgender prisoners—a competition with a clear prize at the end ("real men") and strategies to achieve this prize (the accomplishment of femininity)—that could mitigate the development of a collective identity and the perception of collective efficacy associated with being a transgender woman prisoner in an alpha male environment. In short, extant work suggests that transgender women in prisons for men can be seen as both a subculture and as strategic competitors within the prison arena. Their similarity as transgender women is a possible anchoring point for a subculture (Sumner, 2009; Sumner and Sexton, 2014), while their competition for the attention of men and other valuable resources can render them adversaries (Jenness and Fenstermaker, 2014).

In this context, we . . . focus on whether and to what extent transgender inmates express a sense of collective identity and perceptions of collective efficacy with two prison communities to which they belong: the transgender inmate community and the larger inmate community.

[. . .]

Data and Method of Analysis

[. . .]

When data collection began in April 2008, California was home to over 300 transgender inmates in prisons for men (Jenness et al., 2011, 2013). The 315 transgender women we interviewed and collected official data on were housed in 27 of California's 30 prisons for men. Recognizing that distinct types of gender variant people may or may not identify as transgender (Valentine, 2007), for the purposes of this work transgender prisoners were delineated by deploying four specific criteria. A transgender inmate is a prisoner in a men's prison who: (a) self-identifies as transgender (or something analogous); (b) presents as female, transgender, or feminine in prison or outside of prison; (c) receives any kind of medical treatment (physical or psychological) for something related to how she presents herself or thinks about herself in terms of gender, including taking hormones to initiate and sustain the development of secondary sex characteristics to enhance femininity; or (d) participates in groups for transgender inmates. Meeting any one of these criteria qualified an inmate for inclusion in the larger study from which this article derives (Jenness et al., 2011).

Inmates in California prisons who met the eligibility criteria described above were invited to participate in the study, and almost all of them agreed to be interviewed. A team of eight interviewers traveled to 27 prisons for adult men in California, met face-to-face with over 500 inmates identified by the California Department of Corrections and Rehabilitation (CDCR) as potentially transgender, and completed interviews with 315 transgender inmates. The shortest interview was less than a half an hour (19 minutes), while the longest extended to just under three hours (two hours and 55 minutes). The mean duration for interviews was slightly less than one hour (56 minutes). The total amount of live interview time approached 300 hours (294 hours and six minutes). The overall response rate was 95 percent, which leads us to conclude that the findings reported below are not biased by refusals to participate in the study.

[. . .]

Transgender women inmates are . . . diverse in terms of how they think about their gender, sexual orientation, and attractions. For example, the vast majority (76.1%) identify as female when asked about their gender identity, with considerably fewer identifying as "both male and female" (14%). About a third (33.3%) identify as "homosexual," while 19.4% identify their sexual orientation as "transgender," 18.1% identify as heterosexual, 11.3% identify as bisexual, and the remaining 17.8% identify as something else. The vast majority report that they are sexually attracted to men while in prison (81.9%). A small minority indicated being attracted to both men and women in prison (15.6%); and a majority (75.8%) report being attracted to men both outside of prison and inside prison. Transgender prisoners also vary in terms of continuity of gender presentation, with over three-fourths (76.7%) of transgender inmates reporting presenting themselves as female outside of prison and anticipating presenting as female if/when they are released from prison. They display consistency between their gender presentation and their status as transgender both inside and outside of prison. This finding challenges the commonly held notion that prisoners adopt transgender identities as an adaptation to being in a sex segregated environment organized around masculinity and its many displays; in fact, transgender women in prisons for men report perceiving themselves as more feminine after being incarcerated than before being incarcerated, despite the fact that "man up" is a commonly heard refrain in prison (Jenness, 2015).

Despite considerable diversity in the transgender inmate population and the fact that, at the time of data collection, they were dispersed across 27 prisons in California, transgender inmates report relatively high levels of both collective identity and perceived collective efficacy. . . . These differences indicate that transgender inmates affiliate more strongly with other transgender inmates than they do with the larger inmate population, in both a generalized and a targeted sense: they are committed to the notion of a transgender community and report a stronger affective commitment to their fellow transgender inmates who comprise this community. In other words, neither their diversity as a subgroup of prisoners nor their geographical dispersion across 27 different prisons prevents them from embracing a "shared sense of 'oneness' or 'we-ness' anchored in real or imagined shared attributes and experiences" (Snow, 2001: 2213). Rather, they perceive themselves as part of a larger group of transgender prisoners, regardless of other individual characteristics or physical location.

Transgender women in prisons for men identify primarily, but not exclusively, with other transgender women in prisons for men. They frequently refer to other transgender prisoners not just as "community," but also as "family." With regard to the former, a transgender prisoner described it this way: "The transgenders are all in one group. We get along. We're like community. We have to stick together in here." Going further, a young Hispanic transgender prisoner who identified as Catholic and reported being raped in prison while drunk explained that she would like to be placed in a particular housing unit "because there are so many family—so many transgenders there." When asked why she wanted to live with other "transgenders," she elaborated: "I consider them family. I don't have much family on the streets. With lots of transgenders in here, it feels like one big family" (ID#10). Commensurate with a broader discourse on "families we choose" (Weston, 1997), the transgender women in this study embrace this kind of meaning and easily deploy it when asked about their location and community in prison.

Our interviewees distinguished themselves from other transgender prisoners in another way, too. They often expressed pride in being who they are and, above all else, being "true to oneself" rather than being what they call a "fabricator." For example, an HIV-positive African American transgender prisoner serving time for fraud described how she grew breasts with hormones, wears wigs and weaves, applies make-up on most days, and "does a bunch of other things to look like a lady" (ID#5). Later in the interview, she said, simply and with pride, "I'm not much of a fabricator" and described how efforts to look feminine reveal her true self and a willingness to be public about who she is, what she is, and how she is in the world, both inside and outside of prison. Another transgender prisoner corroborated this view when she said "people respect people for being who they are, not who they pretend to be. No one respects a fabricator" (#ID10). This respect is hard-earned insofar as being who you are is not an easy task for some transgender prisoners. As a final comment at the end of her interview, one transgender prisoner explained it this way:

> It's very hard to be transgender in prison because you don't identify with the gender of the people you're incarcerated with. You're sexually vulnerable all the time. It's exhausting. Because you feel like you can't be yourself. Like most people, we just want to be ourselves and express ourselves (ID#10).

For many transgender prisoners, being true to oneself as a woman is a source of identity pride, often expressed in defiance of acknowledged stigma and despite the many hassles and harms that they recognize accompany doing so in a prison for men. Designed to advance a decidedly authentic self, these kinds of expressions implicate other transgender prisoners as less than authentic, thus a distinction between transgender women in prison is rendered legible.

Many transgender prisoners reported a keen awareness of how nontransgender prisoners perceived them in derogatory ways. A middle-aged, white transgender prisoner explained the following when asked about getting respect from other prisoners: "Most transgenders on this yard, well, they get called 'cum buckets'. The guys here have no respect for them and they have no respect for themselves. Do you know what I mean by cum bucket? I hope it's obvious" (ID #8). An African American transgender prisoner from another state who described herself as a "crack whore" outside of prison explained it this way: "They think I'm a slut because I have breasts. We're prison whores. That's how we're seen, especially if we have breasts" (ID #3). These and other comments reveal that transgender prisoners, while often having pride in their distinct identity, are nonetheless aware of a stratification order in prison that does not serve them well insofar as they are situated near the bottom of the ladder (Sumner, 2009)—a "reject among rejects," to quote one transgender prisoner. Interestingly, these kinds of reports are often coupled with a preemptive articulation of how the transgender woman being interviewed is not at all like the image of transgender women in prison, even as other transgender women fit the bill.

Transgender women in prisons for men clearly see themselves as different from other prisoners and identify with that difference, albeit not always on the same grounds and in the same ways. This does not preclude them from also seeing their humanity and status as a prisoner as sources of commonality with non-transgender prisoners. For example, a transgender prisoner who reported that she "just broke up with my cellmate [who was also her institutional husband]" and felt the need for less drama and a "calmer existence" proclaimed the following when asked what she thought people on the outside should know about transgender prisoners: "It's all about humanity. All of us—races and genders—civil rights, women's rights, all rights. We're human. Live and let live. Can we all get along?" (ID#5). From this point of view, there is no more powerful common denominator among prisoners than being human; the rest is secondary.

Likewise, many transgender prisoners noted that everyone in prison is a criminal and that being a criminal constitutes the overarching commonality among all prisoners. As an African American transgender prisoner who distinguished herself from other transgender prisoners and nontransgender prisoners alike said: "We're all criminals and convicts of one type or another—rapists, thieves, murders. I did fraud. If we were trustworthy, we wouldn't be here. We're convicts" (ID#5). Less dramatically, a white transgender prisoner who reported being raped in prison, attempting suicide in prison, and struggling with mental health issues in prison concluded in her final comment during the interview: "We're no different than any other person, except we're criminals" (ID#17). A similar sentiment was expressed by a young, Hispanic transgender inmate in her closing remarks. She opted for the term "inmate" over "criminal," but nonetheless emphasized the common humanity of those who share her identity: "Consider us a human. Don't discriminate. Treat us as every other inmate" (ID#44). Perhaps the most vivid example of "sameness" came in the form of a transgender prisoner who very much identified as a woman and was living as a woman in prison while serving on the Men's Advisory Council, which is charged with bringing concerns from inmates to the attention of the prison administration. After the interview, she took great pride in explaining how she was on the *men's* advisory council while commenting on how she was helping "us" (referencing all prisoners) in so many important ways.

. . . Transgender inmates express a sense of collective identity and collective efficacy with both the transgender community and the general inmate community, but they affiliate more strongly with the transgender community in prison. Given these findings, the question becomes: What predicts varying levels of collective identity and collective efficacy, as perceived by transgender women in prison? Further, are the same factors predictive of perceptions of collective identity and collective efficacy across reference groups? . . .

Individual Characteristics

[. . .]

We found that social interaction with members of a reference group—rather than mere physical proximity—is associated with a stronger collective identity with that group. . . . Specifically, the higher the proportion of one's friends in prison that were transgender, the higher her collective identity with this reference group. . . .

When friendships in prison were examined not just in terms of their presence or absence, but with regard to their strength and meaning, the picture changes. Measures of trust in transgender friends and assessments of the degree to which transgender friends care were not significantly associated with collective identity, but were significantly positively related to . . . perceived collective efficacy. . . . In other words, the presence of transgender prisoner friends who are perceived to be trustable and who genuinely care makes the difference between commitment to a group and a belief that members of the group will act in one's own best interest.

These . . . findings are corroborated by qualitative data that reveal transgender prisoners' complicated view of friendship. On the one hand, when asked about their preferences for living environments, they often report wanting to be around other transgender women prisoners for support, "girl talk," and protection. A white transgender prisoner from a middle class family in an affluent part of California explained, simply, "I'm a girl, so I'd rather be around other girls. For sociability" (ID#10). Likewise, a Hispanic transgender prisoner who was in a holding cage awaiting placement in administrative segregation during the interview explained that having other transgender friends in prison is important because "we could talk about girl stuff. . . . We can talk about feelings together and get a break from the madness" (ID#4). A transgender prisoner who spent over twenty years working as a prostitute in Los Angeles, during which time she churned in and out of prison routinely, explained in response to a question about whether she wants to be housed with other transgender prisoners: "I never thought about it. It's hard. I want the company of men, but I feel safe around transgenders. I like women friends" (ID#1). Our data reveal that transgender women in prisons for men desire the presence of other transgender women in their living environment; however, that desire is mitigated by other concerns.

Transgender women in prison for men also commented on the problematic nature of friendships with other transgender prisoners by referencing drama, competition, and distrust in ways that can effectively preclude meaningful friendships between transgender prisoners. A transgender prisoner with a BA in a social science discipline who is serving her ninth term and has been in the system for over 20 years explained that she would welcome more transgender prisoners in her dorm, "but not too many because a lot of transgenders cause too much drama. They like to compete. I'm more passive. I'd like friends, but not drama" (ID #13). A middle aged transgender prisoner who identifies as Mexican was more emphatic in her response to a question about friendships with other transgender prisoners when she said "everything is cutthroat over here" and "a lot of transgenders are filled with hatred toward other transgenders because they compete. It's ugly" (ID#12). . . .

In this context, it is telling that some transgender prisoners found our questions about friendships with other transgender prisoners naive at best and laughable at worst; in fact, they sometimes responded to questions about friendships by equivocating about what is meant by "friend" and concluding that no one has real friends in prison; they have "associates" (i.e., people you engage with in a friendly way and might even rely upon, but do not necessarily trust). A transgender prisoner explained it this way: "My mother said a friend is someone who will take a bullet for you. Well, I don't have those kind of friends, but I have friends. Just regular friends" (ID#3). Our data reveal that, in the main, "regular friends" for transgender prisoners are not necessarily friends who will intervene on their behalf in prison precisely because the prison environment encourages "trusting no one," even those with whom they identify. As an African American transgender prisoner who has been presenting as female since she was 17, was close to 30 at the time of the interview, and enjoys attending transgender support groups in prison explained: "There's a lot of backstabbing, drama, and gossip [among transgender prisoners]. You can't trust people like that" (ID#25). . . . Another transgender prisoner summed the situation up quite persuasively when she said: "Girl, you want them other girls and need them other girls and they are the last thing you really want or need. Drama. Gossip. Shit. It never ends well, and you need to stop it before it gets too far. You try to stay out of it, but you can't really" (ID#105).

Interestingly, while the presence of transgender friends in prison is significantly associated with higher levels of perceived collective identity with the transgender inmate community, no such relationship is found among transgender inmates with regard to the general inmate community. . . . The greater transgender inmates' exposure to other transgender inmates, the less they identify with the larger inmate population. Thus, it appears that exposure to transgender friends in prison strengthens affiliation with the transgender inmate community, while exposure to transgender inmates—quite apart from friendship—diminishes affiliation with the inmate community writ large. This provides strong evidence or the presence of a subculture among transgender prisoners, at least at the level of self-reported identity and affiliation.

[. . .]

Discussion and Conclusion

[. . .]

Transgender women in prisons for men present the opportunity for us to explore both diversity and commonality among prisoners. They are exemplary of the myriad ways in which a unique subset of inmates both fits within the confines of the overall prisoner community and is distinct as a smaller subset of prisoners identifiable by their common identity(ies) and shared experience as "girls among men" in an alpha male environment (Jenness and Fenstermaker, 2014). . . .

. . . Transgender inmates' sense of collective identity with the larger inmate population is evidence that they "buy in" to the institutional imputation and affiliate with others who are similarly marked and socially situated. The label "transgender inmate," in contrast, is seldom ascribed by the institution to prisoners who identify or present as female—not because their often noticeable differences from the larger inmate population are ignored by institutional personnel, but rather because they are frequently (and often erroneously) categorized as homosexual (Jenness, 2010a, 2010b, 2014; Robinson, 2011). This conflation of gender identity and sexual orientation is continually reproduced by both prison staff and the larger inmate population (Jenness, 2010a, 2010b; Robinson, 2011). Consequently, the adoption of a transgender inmate identity, and the attendant affiliation with this group, finds its source within the community more so than being imposed from without.

The extent to which transgender women inmates in prisons for men feel a sense of belonging with the transgender community is predicted by the presence of transgender friends more so than shared personal characteristics or characteristics of the physical environments in which they find themselves in prisons. Transgender inmates who are friends with similarly situated others affiliate more strongly (i.e., express a stronger sense of collective identity) with the transgender inmate community. . . . A sense of belonging to the transgender inmate community is translated into affective commitment to community members and an expectation of intervention when the relationships among community members are stronger and marked by trust and mutual caring—qualities often in short supply in prison.

The findings presented in this article throw into stark relief the tension between competition and cooperation in carceral contexts. The social allocation of allegiance among transgender inmates is quite telling in this regard. Two specific findings—that transgender inmates' sense of collective identity and perceived collective efficacy is higher with the transgender inmate community than with the larger prison community, and that their affiliation and allegiance are predicted by the presence and strength of friendships that transgender inmates have with others in their community—reveal that significant competition among this group does not preclude demonstrable allegiance and presumed cooperation. The "friendly competition among ladies" that Jenness and Fenstermaker (2014) report is aptly described: despite being engaged in a very real competition for a host of desirable winnings—the achievement of femininity, the attention and affection of men, increased social status—our findings reveal that transgender inmates engage in these contests in ways that acknowledge commonality of experience and identity and ultimately reaffirm their place in the transgender community.

[. . .]

References

Britton, D. 2003. *At Work in the Iron Cage*. New York: NYU Press.

Clemmer, D. 1940. *Prison Community*. Boston, MA: Christopher.

Crewe, B. 2009. *The Prisoner Society: Power, Adaptation and Social Life in an English Prison*. Oxford, UK: Oxford University Press.

Dolovich, S. 2011. "Strategic Segregation in the Modern Prison." *American Criminal Law Review* 48:1–110.

Donaldson, S. 1993. "A Million Jockers, Punks, and Queens, Stop Prisoner Rape: Sex Among American Male Prisoners and Its Implications for Concepts of Sexual Orientation." Retrieved January 26, 2013 (http://spr.igc.org/en/stephendonaldson/doc_01_lecture.html).

Fleisher, M. S. and J. L. Krienert. 2009. *The Myth of Prison Rape: Sexual Culture in American Prisons*. Lanham, MD: Rowman & Littlefield.

Hayner, N. S. and E. Ash. 1940. "The Prison as a Community." *American Sociological Review* 5(4): 577–83.

Ireland, J. 2002. *Bullying Among Prisoners: Evidence, Research and Intervention Strategies*. New York: Brunner-Routledge.

Jenness, V. 2010a. "From Policy to Prisoners to People: A 'Soft Mixed Methods' Approach to Studying Transgender Prisoners." *Journal of Contemporary Ethnography* 39(5):517–53.

Jenness, V. 2010b. "Getting to Know 'the Girls' in an 'Alpha-Male Community': Notes on Fieldwork on Transgender Inmates in California Prisons." In *Sociologists Backstage: Answers to 10 Questions About What They Do*, edited by S. Fenstermaker and N. Jones. New York: Routledge.

Jenness, V. 2014. "Pesticides, Prisoners, and Policy: Complexity and Praxis in Research on Transgender Prisoners and Beyond." *Sociological Perspectives* 57(1):6–26.

Jenness, V. 2015. "The Feminization of Transgender Women in Prisoners for Men: How an Alpha Male Total Institution Shapes Gender." To be presented at the Annual Meeting of the American Sociological Association in Chicago, IL.

Jenness, V. and S. Fenstermaker. 2014. "Agnes Goes to Prison: Gender Authenticity, Transgender Inmates in Prisons for Men, and the Pursuit of the 'Real Deal.'" *Gender & Society* 28(1):5–31.

Jenness, V. and S. Fenstermaker. 2016. "Forty Years After Brownmiller: Prisons for Men, Transgender Inmates, and the Rape of the Feminine." *Gender & Society* 30(1):14–29.

Jenness, V., C. L. Maxson, K. N. Matsuda, et al. 2007. "Violence in California Correctional Facilities: An Empirical Examination of Sexual Assault." Report to the California Department of Corrections and Rehabilitation. University of California, Irvine, CA.

Jenness, V., L. Sexton, and J. Sumner. 2011. "Transgender Inmates in California Prisons: An Empirical Study of a Vulnerable Population." Report to the California Department of Corrections and Rehabilitation. University of California, Irvine, CA.

Jenness, V., J. Sumner, L. Sexton, et al. 2013. "Cinderella, Wilma Flintstone, and Xena the Warrior Princess: Capturing Diversity Among Transgender Women in Men's Prisons." In *Understanding Diversity: Celebrating Difference, Challenging Inequality,* edited by C. Renzetti and K. Bergen. Upper Saddle River, NJ: Allyn & Bacon.

Knopp, F. H. 1984. *Retraining Sex Offenders: Methods and Models.* Orwell, VT: Safer Society.

Kruttschnitt, C. and R. Gartner. 2004. *Marking Time in the Golden State: Women's Imprisonment in California.* Cambridge: Cambridge University Press.

Kunzel, R. 2008. *Criminal Intimacy: Prison and the Uneven History of Modern American Sexuality.* Chicago, IL: University of Chicago Press.

Leddy, J. and M. O'Connell. 2002. "The Prevalence, Nature and Psychological Correlates of Bullying in Irish Prisons." *Legal and Criminological Psychology* 7:131–40.

Robinson, R. K. 2011. "Masculinity as Prison: Sexual Identity, Race, and Incarceration." *California Law Review* 99:1309–408.

Schwaebe, C. 2005. "Learning to Pass: Sex Offenders' Strategies for Establishing a Viable Identity in the Prison General Population." *International Journal of Offender Therapy and Comparative Criminology* 49(6):614–25.

Sexton, L. 2014. "Penal Subjectivities: Developing a Theoretical Framework for Penal Consciousness." *Punishment & Society* 16(5):114–36.

Sexton, L., V. Jenness and J. M. Sumner. 2010. "Where the Margins Meet: A Demographic Assessment of Transgender Inmates in Men's Prisons." *Justice Quarterly* 27(6):835–66.

Snow, D. 2001. "Collective Identity and Expressive Forms." Pp. 2212–19 in *International Encyclopedia of the Social and Behavioral Sciences,* edited by N. J. Smelser and P. B. Bates. Oxford, UK: Pergamon Press.

Sumner, J. 2009. "Keeping House: Understanding the Transgender Inmate Code of Conduct Through Prison Policies, Environments, and Culture." Ph.D. dissertation, Criminology, Law and Society, University of California, Irvine, CA.

Sumner, J. and L. Sexton. 2014. "Lost in Translation: Looking for Transgender Identity in Women's Prisons and Locating Aggressors in Prisoner Culture." *Critical Criminology* 23(1):1–20.

Sumner, J., L. Sexton, V. Jenness, et al. 2015. "The (Pink) Elephant in the Room: The Structure and Experience of Race and Violence in the Lives of Transgender Inmates in California Prisons." In *The International Handbook of Race, Class, and Gender,* edited by S. A. Jackson. London, UK: Routledge.

Sykes, G. M. 1958. *The Society of Captives: A Study of a Maximum Security Prison.* Princeton, NJ: Princeton University Press.

Sykes, G. M. and S. L. Messinger. 1960. "The Inmate Social System." Pp. 6–10 in *Theoretical Studies in the Social Organization of the Prison,* edited by R. Cloward, D. R. Cressey, G. H. Grosser, et al. New York: Social Science Research Council.

Tewksbury, R. and R. H. Potter. 2005. "Transgender Prisoners: A Forgotten Group." In *Managing Special Populations in Jails and Prisons,* edited by S. Stojkovic. New York: Civic Research Institution.

Valentine, D. 2007. *Imagining Transgender: An Ethnography of a Category.* Durham, NC: Duke University Press.

Vaughn, M. S. and A. D. Sapp. 1989. "Less than Utopian: Sex Offender Treatment in a Milieu of Power Struggles, Status Positioning, and Inmate Manipulation in State Correctional Institutions." *The Prison Journal* 69:73–89.

Weston, K. 1997. *Families We Choose: Lesbians, Gays, Kinship.* New York: Columbia University Press.

Gender Violence Revisited

Lessons From Violent Victimization of Transgender Identified Individuals

Daniela Jauk

© iStockphoto.com/Mari

"**A**s transgender you have to take care" says Sylvia, an approximately 60-year-old transwoman referring to her lifetime experiences of harassment and violence. Morgan, a 53-year-old transwoman, nods and says "Yeah, I am observing constantly, I am always aware of my surroundings." Jeff, a 37-year-old transman, laughs and says "Us guys have it easier!" I sit in a haphazard circle together with 26 transgender identified individuals in a transgender support group meeting hosted by a local LGBT Center. It is a late Saturday afternoon in Belt-town, a medium-sized Midwestern town, in 2009. The group was founded in the mid 1990s when transgender identity politics hit the public policy stage in the USA and created virtual and physical space for a transgender movement. Since the 1990s the category transgender has bound together an abundance of diverse gender identity expressions

Daniela Jauk. 2013. "Gender Violence Revisited: Lessons From Violent Victimization of Transgender Identified Individuals." *Sexualities* 16(7):807–25.

by a collective transgender rights and community and social service movement in the USA (Broad, 2002; Stone, 2009; Stryker, 2008). Transgender, also referred to as "trans," denotes an array of individuals whose gender identities do not match their assumed genders based on sex categories assigned at birth. This includes persons who identify as the "opposite" birth-sex but also individuals who identify as gender-variant beyond the binary gender order who may permanently or temporarily change or bend their gender presentation, with or without surgical or chemical help. Yet transgender is not in itself an identity term, nor a label for a new "minority with special needs," but a descriptive label for being differently gendered that illuminates the complexity of gender for everybody (Currah et al., 2008; Elliot, 2009; May, 2002).

The goal of this article is to give voice to transgender individuals who have experienced violence. By addressing physical violence in a politically repressive environment, my research responds to the call for more materiality in sociological transgender studies (Hines and Sanger, 2010). It also illuminates notions of transphobia, genderism and genderbashing (Hill, 2003).

[. . .]

Violent abuse and its mental health consequences are serious, frequent, and lifelong experiences in the majority of transgender-identified populations (Kidd and Witten, 2007; Witten and Eyler, 1999). In the USA, approximately two individuals are murdered every month because they act or look trans. Between 2008 and March 2011 alone, 38 transphobic homicides have been documented in the USA, which means an increase in documented transphobic homicide from previous years (TDOR, 2011; TMM, 2011). Transgender people are often stereotyped as "deserving" of violence (Merry, 2006), which makes them a group particularly prone to gender policing through harassment and interpersonal violence perpetrated by "gender defenders" (Bornstein, 1994). Compared to victimization patterns of the general population, violence against transgender people can be particularly brutal (Bettcher, 2007; Lynch, 2005). It is twice as likely to cause injury and four times as likely to cause hospitalization (Lynch, 2005). Lombardi et al. (2001) found that 60% of their transgender sample ($n = 402$) had experienced either violence or harassment and 26% had experienced a violent incident.

[. . .]

Given the severity and high prevalence of anti-trans violence, we need to understand the meanings of violence in transgender lives. This community has largely been ignored in the gender violence literature and in public policy. With few exceptions (Namaste, 2000; Valentine, 2007) most of the existing research has been conducted in metropolitan areas using quantitative measures. My study adds to the literature on (trans)gender violence by employing an inductive research design in a Midwestern area that is characterized by large rural areas and midsized cities. In order to understand the conditions under which transgender violence occurs and how individuals react to it, we need to examine the untold stories behind the statistics and explore the experiences and priorities of the trans population.

Methods

To unpack the meanings of violence in the lives of transgender individuals, I conducted ethnographic field research in transgender communities in three differently sized Midwestern cities (River Falls has 200,000; Belt-town has 430,000; Half Heaven Hills has more than 700,000 inhabitants). From October 2007 to December 2010, I engaged in participatory observation of support groups at transgender related events such as symposia, movie screenings, social networking gatherings, and annual Transgender Day of Remembrance activities amounting to approximately 800 hours of fieldwork. . . . My fieldnotes and 15 recorded interviews with transgender identified individuals (average interview length = 90 minutes) were transcribed into digital word-processing files.

[...]

All of the participants in my study identify as "trans" or "transgender." All of them participate in the transgender community by attending transgender support groups, volunteering for transgender organizations, or performing on stage as drag queens, drag kings or genderqueer performers. Most of them identify as working class, yet the majority are unemployed and struggle to make ends meet. An essential limitation, that equally constitutes a finding, is that the transgender support group meetings I attended in the Midwestern area under consideration attract almost exclusively white individuals. . . .

Findings

"People like me need to be destroyed" (Shawn, 32, MTF, Belt-town. From fieldnotes on *transphobia, genderbashing, and the state)*

Because many trans people are visually transgressing gender norms, they often attract rage reserved for people who are perceived as queer, homosexual (Namaste, 1996) or otherwise different from gendered norms. Thus, genderbashing serves as a warning to the entire queer community. This became evident in a meeting sparked by multiple robberies in a "gayborhood" on the Westside of Belt-town. The emergency meeting in the local LGBT center attracted about 30 concerned participants from the queer community. They discussed the interrelatedness of homophobia and transphobia. Lauren (52, MTF, Belt-town resident), for instance, said "One guy in a bar called me tranny faggot. But I'm not gay! If you gonna be ignorant be an educated ignorant!" . . .

Belt-town had been struck by an epidemic of hate crime incidents against the queer community. The monthly support group meetings repeatedly highlighted an increasing amount of violent assaults and incidents. A hate crime meeting between LGBT activists and city hall representatives did not yield any effective strategies, because legal federal and state protections for transgender populations were nonexistent. The absence of legal protection is meaningful for individuals, because it leaves them feeling helpless and demoralized. A middle-aged couple attended the support group meeting for the first time. One week earlier, they were the victims of a violent property crime. As the woman told their story, her partner, MTF, sat beside her and held her shaking hand. In only four days, several cars on their street were set on fire and several neighborhood gay bars were broken into. She said: "[The state] has no hate crime laws. [The state] sucks. It feels pretty hateful, they really just want our community to go away. Matthew Sheppard was not that long ago" the woman said as she cried. . . .

An overwhelming majority of respondents in my study reported experiencing verbal harassment at least once in their lifetime because of their gender expression. . . . There are several possible explanations. First, the Midwestern area where I conducted my research might be a particularly repressive environment. The Bible-belt notion is referenced frequently in interviews as in this one: "This one guy just wanted to kick my ass. Because I was to him, sick, I was a sick motherfucker. And people like me need to be destroyed. The Bible says so. And we are in the Bible belt. All right?!" (Shawn, 32, MTF, Belt-town). Second, the sample consists of individuals who actively participate in transgender support contexts. That means that they have sought out help because they encountered difficulties—such as violence—in their lives. It also means that these persons are creating advocacy oriented networks and, consequently, have a heightened sensitivity for violence. These participants developed a vocabulary to talk about their experiences, empowered by others who did so before them. Third, many trans individuals are not connected to awareness raising support contexts and/or do not name their experiences as violence.... Verbal harassment might not be reported as violence, as Jeff (FTM, 37), facilitator of transgender support groups in Half Heaven Hills, explained: "They call me a freak, they make me an 'it,' that is dehumanizing. We experience daily verbal violence and we get used to it. We don't call it violence."

Narratives of participants clearly reveal the embeddedness of physical violence in a social system that structurally discriminates.... If one lives their desired gender, discrimination, medicalization, and violent victimization are often the price to pay; conforming to normative gender expectations, however, often results in individual distress, depression and suicidal ideation. Almost all of the trans persons I met in the field face economic hardship, employment and housing discrimination, and problems accessing medical services.... Clara attended the support group and in her introduction shared that when she started transitioning she lost her job in Belt-town. She tried to move to Florida and get a job, she had been a security service worker before. She did not get the job in Florida because she was transgender and ended up homeless. She had no money to buy hormones and thought she might find a job as a man, so she went without hormones, with the effect that she ended up in a special "crazy hospital," because she was suicidal and depressed....

Police harassment epitomizes the transgender Catch 22 and lays bare the intersection of individual victimization and institutionalized transphobia at the state level. The state ... does not allow citizens to change the gender marker on their birth certificates. That means that if one chooses to live as a different gender, the ID documents cannot be matched to actual gender identity and expression. This creates problems when dealing with insurance agencies, health institutions, and the justice system. Lilly also addressed her fear of transphobia in the criminal justice system, which leads to her perception of police as a huge threat to her personal safety. She explained:

> If something happens to me, if I get raped, murdered, anything like that, the cops will care less.... Just one more piece of crap off the street.... I mean, the average person goes out and hopes they don't blow a stop sign ... that is nice and dandy, I wish I had those problems. My fear is getting stopped and shot by a cop. My fear is getting pulled over, 'cause I even look like a transsexual. And then they see my driver's license and it is over and out. The cop taking me into the jail, just screw with me, and beat the crap out of me or somth'n. Okay ... ahm ... getting in jail I'd surely be raped. Most transsexuals go to prison, usually in the diamond prison, due to the fact they are raped and beaten. All right. And usually not by their fellow inmates, but by the officers. (Lilly, MTF, 43, River Falls)

Over the course of about seven years of living out as trans, Lilly has learned that her visual transgression of gender norms puts her at higher risk for assaults. She has been pulled over by the police who ridiculed her. She has never been in prison herself but she is friends with several transwomen who have been jailed for solicitation and shared with her experiences of sexual violence (see Jenness, 2009 and SRLP, 2007 for prison experiences of transgender populations).

Jeremy (FTM, 41, River Falls) is the elected chairperson of a transgender support group and knows about the problems his friends have with the police. For years he has been fighting for a policy change in the state that would at least make possible a change of gender categorization on the driver's license. In his role as a service and advocacy person, he always "pushes the people to make police reports, but many of them do not want to be identified and outed. Also, if police reports are made, they are often not followed up by the police because transgender people are seen as freaks and wackos. Many stories remain untold." Jeremy shared with me one of these "untold stories" of four transwomen in Belt-town, as we take the 40-minute ride from River Falls to a support group meeting in Belt-town together. Hannah (28, MTF, Belt-town), whom I met later that night, and her friends were leaving a gay bar and intended to go to the car, which was a block away. Four men were hanging out in front of the bar and kept yelling at them—"We don't want freaks!" They followed and attacked the transwomen, kicking, beating, and stabbing them. Although the police were called, they never arrived. However, the victims were not out as trans and thus did not want to file a police report anyway (Fieldnotes 5 October 2009, Belt-town, support group).

. . . Almost half of the respondents (46%) reported being uncomfortable seeking police assistance and almost one-third (29%) of respondents reported harassment and disrespect by police. . . . Transgender and gender nonconforming people may have higher levels of interaction with police. They are more likely to be victims of violent crime and they may work more often in the underground economy due to lack of formal employment. Some face harassment and arrest simply because they are out in public, which is referred to as "Walking While Transgender"(Grant et al., 2011: 158), like Mona: "When I dressed up the first time as Mona—I was 16 at the time—and went out, the police arrested me for solicitation on the street. I wasn't out to my parents then, it was horrible" (29, FTM, Half Heaven Hills). Mona was arrested because she displayed what was interpreted by police officers as exaggerated femininity. The experience of femininity as a threat to personal safety is an experience many transwomen share with her.

"Us Guys Have It Easier"—(Trans)Gender Violence Revisited

The narratives of individuals in my sample provide clear evidence for heightened victimization risk in periods when individuals "transition" or are read as gender-ambiguous. Female to male transgender individuals (FTM) find it easier to "blend in" and "pass" as male. Male gender markers, such as the adam's apple and a large physical build, are less easy to hide. Lillith, a tall, blond, young woman who considers herself a "perfect pass" nowadays, shared her experience of early transitioning and stated that ". . . when I started transitioning I got people yelling at me, and that was tough, you know, scary at times. I had some incidents then, of people insulting me as I walked down the street, or when I was in a bar" (Lillith, MTF, 25, Half Heaven Hills). For Morgan, who started transitioning in her late 30s and at times struggles to afford hormones, passing as a woman is more difficult. She is often read as a non-normative gender rather than as a woman. When I first met her she worked in a gas station with high customer frequency in what she considers a "seedy" neighborhood: "I get at least five remarks a day during work. I also have to take care off work in public, every minute a car could come by and shoot me" (Morgan, MTF, 53, River Falls). One morning Morgan called me and said "You wanna know about transphobia, right?" She was still upset when she shared that while she was working the night before, a man pulled up to the gas station, walked up to the window, and when he realized she was transgender while she handed him some items, he "threw all the stuff on the floor and screamed: 'oh you are a sick motherfucker, I am coming back here no more, you need to be killed, I am taking your ass, when you come outside!' And this is not the only one; stuff like this happens all the time!" (. . . Morgan, MTF, 53, River Falls).

The perpetrators the participants in my study encountered are exclusively male (as Wilchins and Taylor, 2008 point out as well), and all participants report a higher risk for assault because they "look trans," indicating violence as gender border patrol (Lynch, 2005) based in genderism (Hill, 2003). But transgender individuals also have a unique social location to experience shifts in victimization patterns as they change their gender presentation. Their stories offer valuable insights into gender violence more broadly. Transgender individuals, some of whom pass as their preferred gender perfectly (as seen from a heteronormative perspective), are prone to physical and structural violence as well. This is especially true for transwomen, Lillith explained, as men are a threat to her differently than before her transition:

> Maybe I can explain. When walking down the street now, by myself, no matter where I am, and I see a group of guys, even if there are girls with them. As I walk and pass them I kinda tense up. . . . I am ready for them to say something to me, insulting, insulting me as a woman . . . and that is completely different from when before I transitioned. Before that, like, I would not think about that at all. You know. I wouldn't think to get worried, you know, by men. And so, yeah, all the people who have been insulting me have been men, you know. So its like, ahm, it would be stupid to kind of not pick up on that and realize that men are a threat to me in a way that they weren't before. (Lillith, MTF, 25, Half Heaven Hills)

Many transwomen in my sample told me that they are more exposed to sexualized harassment such as men grabbing their butt in bars, and yelling sexual slurs at them in public spaces. . . . Serano (2007), a transgender woman and activist, stated that most of the anti-trans discrimination she faces is probably better described as misogyny. Transgender women face disadvantage because they choose to be feminine in a world in which women and men devalue femininity (Connell, 2002; Serano, 2007). Indeed, the transmen I spoke to would often say "us guys have it easier": their exposure to interpersonal violence decreases and perceptions of personal safety increases. This shift has its flipsides and complexities, as a conversation with Nathan, a 27-year-old transman in Half Heaven Hills, shows. He said he feels a lot safer as a male, because he is male but also because he blends in perfectly now. People take him more seriously as a male. As a woman he was very butch and got lots of remarks, which have stopped completely now. But he also thinks "it is more complicated" and not always easier as a man, since "the likelihood that you get attacked on the street if you get into an argument is higher if you are a guy. Also it has the flipside that women change street sides if they see you, a guy, coming across. This is a new experience."

[. . .]

"As Transgender You Have to Take Care"— Responses to Genderism and Genderbashing Between Resignation and Resistance

Trans individuals are not only passive receivers of violence but also agents that actively cope with the transphobia, genderism and genderbashing to which they are exposed. In my sample I find coping strategies and reactions based in resignation, like self-imposed constraints of mobility and limited gender presentation. I also find proactive resistance such as self-policing and intimidation, community building, and resistance to violence through creative arts.

Constraints of mobility and gender presentation. My data confirm that spatial mobility of trans individuals is limited in daily life. . . . Morgan for instance stopped traveling long distances completely, and does not drive her car after 9 p.m., because she does not know the night shift of the local police and is afraid of getting harassed. She has gone "back and forth" between male and female gender presentation for several years because she felt safer as a man. Also Tara (45, MTF, Belt-town) changes into male presentation by wearing hoodies, hats, and no make up whenever she has to travel on the highway for more than 50 miles. Tara feels not only unsafe in her car but also in her home. She started transitioning in 2009 and was considering moving from River Falls to Half Heaven Hills at the time of the interview because she felt threatened by her male neighbors since she began dressing as female:

> In the last 6 months, since I am going out as Tara, I am constantly getting harassed on my street. People yell at me and laugh, they behave like little boys. My house got broken into twice and I have been living in this hood since 10 years with no incident! I cannot take this anymore! I am totally broke, but I need to get outta here. (Tara, MTF, 47, River Falls)

Low social class exacerbates the problem of trans violence because transgender individuals with more resources can choose to live in safer neighborhoods and can afford facial surgeries for enhanced visual conformity (Keisling, 2004). The participants in my study do not have the money for facial surgery or gated neighborhoods. Despite the lack of material resources to enhance personal safety, I encountered several individuals who practiced active resistance to verbal and physical assault.

Self-policing. Lacking the opportunity to move, getting dogs and guns for self protection are strategies most frequently reported by the participants in my study. Sofia smiled confidently while she shared how she solved "the neighbor problem":

> First moved in, bought this house. Fixed things up. In the meantime it was starting the summer, so neighbors did see me. And of course, long hair, blahblahblahblah, the style I dressed, the way I acted . . . I got a lot of crap from the kids and from neighbors. Not all of them. I have had threats, my windows started getting busted. My car started being vandalized. This kept costing me thousands of dollars. Okay . . . I let it be known around the neighborhood that . . . ah . . . several weapons were purchased . . . there is ways to let people know without telling them . . . that several weapons have been purchased, and that that I have also gotten out of prison. I purposely did this. It is not true, but . . . I said I just got out of prison for murder. Somebody gave me some shit, so I shot 'em. Since then it is calmer. (Sofia, MTF, 65, River Falls)

Sofia's strategy to intimidate her neighbors suggests that she voluntarily self-imposed the stigma of being a convicted murderer to outweigh the stigma of being a gender transgressor. Kate (MTF, 48, Half Heaven Hills) resorted to martial arts since being beaten up by four men— "because cowards always run in groups." Her male voice, which is not trained or hormonally altered, is a gender cue that does not match a feminine outfit, which puts her at heightened risk for violence as described earlier. But Kate continues to actively fight (back) in order to protect her identity because she'd "rather have somebody beat the shit out of me than not recognizing myself in the mirror. It is a battle with yourself every day, be who you are or be at risk that you might get beat up. The one is a 'might' but the other is a definite." Sandi does not practice martial arts but considers herself a "big girl." She is a stocky, blond, energetic woman who laughs a lot and often cheers up the support group circle with her humor and positive attitude. She also giggled during the interview sharing that she had to actively fight off aggressors twice:

> I was getting out of a bar with a friend and there was this drunk. He was outside waiting, and asked us for a ride. I said "Listen, my friend is gay and I am trans" and he said "Fuck, OK." So we gave him a ride home, but as he gets out of the car he jumps on the front seat, and shouts "you want to be a woman? I make you one!" But I am a big girl, I jumped on him and I broke my nail in his cheek (laughs loud). . . . The other time a guy attempted to rape me in his apartment, I kicked holes in his wall. I finally told him "it is dirty, let me wash it" and called the police in the bathroom. The police was nice, but I hadn't changed my name yet, so I was afraid to press charges. (Sandi, MTF, 35, River Falls)

Sandi was a singular example in that she reported a positive experience with the police although the documentation issue discussed earlier hindered her from reporting a crime. Rather than perceiving the criminal justice system as support, the transgender individuals in my study feel oppressed by the state, and that evokes anger against structures that need to be changed.

Building community. Lillith funnels her frustration and anger into communal support. She "decided to use my head in activism, you know, and in many situations I need to . . . to . . . hold my anger inside me, you know. But, in activism, I lay it out in other sorts of ways" (Lillith, MTF, 25, Half Heaven Hills). Her friend Jeremy (FTM, 41, River Falls) has organized and maintained transgender support groups in several cities and also serves on the board of a state-wide transgender advocacy organization. For more than 10 years Jeremy has tirelessly lobbied politicians and fought to include gender identity in anti-discrimination ordinances of city councils. He has brought back national advocacy information to support groups and given hundreds of classes, workshops, and lectures for the broader public and service providers. Community building as resistance to violence and discrimination are most important strategies to him, yet he encounters a lack of trans people who want to volunteer time and energy for the local transgender movement: "The fact that people want to blend in, don't come out, leave the support group once transition is done is especially bad for young guys. They have no one to talk to." Together with other activists, Jeremy has been successful in his long struggle and eliminated one of many risk factors for violent victimization. In late 2009, a statewide policy was put into effect by the state's Bureau of Motor Vehicles to enable individuals to change their gender marker on the driver's license which has enhanced the livelihood and increased the safety of several hundreds of transpeople so far. Still, there is a long way to go on the road to full quality of life for transgender persons in the American Midwest. . . .

Art as resistance. Art and performance are creative coping strategies that are shared and spark communication and awareness in the transgender community. In an autobiographical silent performance at TDOR in 2010 in Belt-town, Adam, an FTM drag king, walked onto stage. He turned his back to the audience and removed his nightgown. Next he pulled out silver duct tape and began "binding" his breasts in order to flatten them. He proceeded to put on blue jeans and a shirt, and then walked to a mirror and fixed his mustache. When his transformation was complete, he grabbed a stack of posters. One by one, he revealed the posters, and his experiences, to his audience (excerpted as transcribed from photographic material):

I should have been careful what I asked for

This is what my family sees me as (with a photo of a girl)

Even though this is me I don't recognize her (with a photo of a girl)

I am an actor and artist I've been a drag king for 11 years I am stranger than you might think I am not afraid to die A bullet just missed my head I am human

I've been stabbed and beaten with crowbars, bats, and wood I have always hated looking in the mirror because I was born in the wrong body I have a big heart

There are days where it just hurts to walk after all the abuse my body has taken

I have been raped

The police said I deserve it

Yet I am glad I was raised female, and I won't forget it, because it helps me being a good man

(Performance, TDOR, 2010, Adam Apple, FTM, 32, Belt-town)

In a compelling, creative, and concise way Adam sums up the transgender experience of violent victimization. Being about 5 feet 4 inches tall, and of lean stature, he often did not pass as male (this performance took place before he started hormonal therapy) but as "too masculine for a girl." He—as many others in my study—did not find support in the criminal justice system, and has suffered from depression for long periods in his life. He lived below the poverty line when I met him, generating income from occasional painting and construction jobs. He still struggles to make ends meet but, after periods of resignation, has resorted to art and community building as strategies of resistance against state and social structures that have caused him so much harm. Adam's performances, and the narratives of the portrayed trans persons in this article, tell a story of gender violence that differs from the "violence against women" paradigm. These stories urge us to rethink both the concept of violence and the concept of gender violence. The lived trans experiences suggest that our understanding of violence needs to move beyond interpersonal violence to include institutional, legal and state-perpetrated discrimination. They also suggest that gender violence as a concept needs to be radically revisited in order to include gender-variant populations.

Conclusion

Findings from my ethnographic research in a Midwestern state in a transgender support group context show that violent victimization of transgender individuals is a severe threat to public health and quality of life. Transphobic violence is clearly perceived as a hate crime and gender-bashing exists in the lives of trans individuals as both a daily potentiality and a vivid memory. Transgender is also a strategic research site to illuminate dynamics of gender violence, as the narratives of the predominantly white working- and lower-class study participants show that gender violence is more than violence against women. We must broaden our view and understand gender violence not only as violence against women, but as violence that targets victims because of their real or perceived gender, gender identity, or gender expression (Hill, 2003). . . . The dichotomous gender order, and the policing of the boundaries between the boxes "men" and "women" have been identified as main causes of transphobic violence and discrimination (Bornstein, 1994; Hill, 2003; Kidd and Witten, 2007; Lynch, 2005).

[. . .]

References

Bettcher, T. M. 2007. "Evil Deceivers and Make-Believers: On Transphobic Violence and the Politics of Illusion." *Hypatia* 22(3):43–65.

Bornstein, K. 1994. *Gender Outlaw: On Men, Women, and the Rest of Us.* New York: Routledge.

Broad, K. L. 2002. "GLB + T? Gender/Sexuality Movements and Transgender Collective Identity (De) Constructions." *International Journal of Sexuality and Gender Studies* 7(4):241–64.

Connell, R. 2002. *Gender.* Cambridge: Polity and Malden, MA: Blackwell Publishers.

Currah, P., J. Green, and S. Stryker. 2008. *The State of Transgender Rights in the United States of America.* San Francisco, CA: San Francisco State University. Retrieved April 10, 2008 (http://nsrc.sfsu.edu/ sites/default/files/Trans%20Rights%20in%20the%20USA_10APR08-Final_12-19-08-2.pdf).

Elliot, P. 2009. "Engaging Trans Debates on Gender Variance: A Feminist Analysis." *Sexualities* 12(1):5–32.

Grant, J. M., L. A. Mottet, J. D. Justin Tanis, et al. 2011. *Injustice at Every Turn: A Report of the National Transgender Discrimination Survey.* Washington, DC: The National Gay and Lesbian Task Force and National Center for Transgender Equality. Retrieved March 5, 2011 (www.thetaskforce.org/reports_ and_research/ntds).

Hill, D. B. 2003. "Genderism, Transphobia, and Genderbashing: A Framework for Interpreting Anti-transgender Violence." Pp. 113–36 in *Understanding and Dealing with Violence: A Multicultural Approach*, edited by B. C. Wallace and R. T. Carter. Thousand Oaks, CA: SAGE.

Hines, S. and T. Sanger. 2010. *Transgender Identities: Towards a Social Analysis of Gender Diversity.* New York: Routledge.

Jenness, V. 2009. "Transgender Inmates in California's Prisons." In *California's Department of Correction and Rehabilitation Wardens Meeting*, April 8, 2009. Retrieved April 17, 2010 (http://nicic.gov/ Library/023832).

Keisling, M. 2004. "Trans Mission. Interview with Mara Keisling." *Metro Weekly*, August 19, 2004. Retrieved August 28, 2013 (www.metroweekly.com/feature/?ak=1194).

Kidd, J. D. and T. M. Witten. 2007. "Transgender and Trans Sexual Identities: The Next Strange Fruit— Hate Crimes, Violence and Genocide Against the Global Trans-Communities." *Journal of Hate Studies* 6(1):31–63.

Lombardi, E. L., R. A. Wilchins, et al. 2001. "Gender Violence: Transgender Experiences with Violence and Discrimination." *Journal of Homosexuality* 42(1):89–101.

Lynch, A. M. 2005. "Hate Crime as a Tool of the Gender Border Patrol: The Importance of Gender as a Protected Category." Pp. 19–21 in *When Women Gain, So Does the World, IWPR's Eighth International Women's Policy Research Conference*. Washington, DC.

May, K. 2002. "Becoming Women: Transgendered Identities, Psychosexual Therapy and the Challenge of Metamorphosis." *Sexualities* 5(4):449–64.

Merry, S. E. 2006. *Human Rights and Gender Violence: Translating International Law into Local Justice.* Chicago Series in Law and Society. Chicago, IL: University of Chicago Press.

Namaste, K. 1996. "Genderbashing: Sexuality, Gender, and the Regulation of Public Space." *Environment and Planning D: Society and Space* 14(2):221–40.

Namaste, V. K. 2000. *Invisible Lives: The Erasure of Transsexual and Transgender People.* Chicago, IL: University of Chicago Press.

Serano, J. 2007. *Whipping Girl: A Transsexual Woman on Sexism and the Scapegoating of Femininity.* Emeryville, CA: Seal Press.

SRLP. 2007. "It's War in Here": A Report on the Treatment of Transgender and Intersex People in New York State Men's Prisons.* The Sylvia Rivera Law Project, New York. Retrieved April 17, 2007 (http://srlp .org/files/warinhere.pdf).

Stone, A. L. 2009. "More Than Adding a T: American Lesbian and Gay Activists' Attitudes Towards Transgender Inclusion." *Sexualities* 12(3):334–54.

Stryker, S. 2008. *Transgender History.* Berkeley, CA: Seal Press.

TDOR. 2011. *Statistics 2000–2010.* Retrieved February 3, 2011 (http://www.transgenderdor.org/?page_ id=192).

TMM. 2011. *Trans Murder Monitoring.* Retrieved February 3, 2011 (http://www.tgeu.org/node/53).

Valentine, D. 2007. *Imagining Transgender: An Ethnography of a Category.* Durham, NC: Duke University Press.

Wilchins, R. A. and T. Taylor. 2008. *50 Under 30. Masculinity and the War on America's Youth. A Human Rights Report.* New York: Gender Public Advocacy Coalition (GenderPAC).

Witten, T. M. and E. A. Eyler. 1999. "Hate Crimes and Violence Against the Transgendered." *Peace Review* 11(3):461–68.

Gendered Violence, Cultural Otherness, and Honour Crimes in Canadian National Logics

Dana M. Olwan

© iStockphoto.com/PaulMcKinnon

In the early morning hours of June 30, 2009, the bodies of four women were discovered in a submerged car in the Rideau Canal in Kingston, Ontario. Shortly after, the Kingston Police released the names and ages of the victims to Canadian media and press. The four victims were identified as Zainab Shafia (age 19), Sahar Shafia (age 17), Geeti Shafia (age 13), and Rona Amir Mohammad (age 50). The three victims were biological sisters while the fourth victim, initially identified as the girls' aunt, was later determined to be the first wife of Mohammad Shafia. The women, reports explained, had drowned while driving to their home in a Montreal suburb from a trip in southern Ontario. Following a swift investigation, the Kingston Chief of Police, Stephen Tanner, ordered the arraignment and charging of Mohammed Shafia, Tooba Mohammad Yahya, and Hamed Shafia with four counts of conspiracy to commit

Dana M. Olwan. 2013. "Gendered Violence, Cultural Otherness, and Honour Crimes in Canadian National Logics." *Canadian Journal of Sociology* 38(4):533–55.

murder. On January 29, 2012, the Shafia trial—also known as the Canadian honour killing trial—ended with the jury finding all three guilty of four counts of first degree murder. In Canada, a first degree murder charge carries with it a life sentence, without possibility of parole for 25 years. It is the maximum sentence possible under Canadian law for a murder crime.

Drawing on the Shafia murders, and the national controversies it brought to the fore, this article maps what the honour crime label reveals about the national politics of race and racism in multicultural Canada today. It begins by providing a general definition of the honour crime as articulated by feminist scholars and international agencies, including the UN and Amnesty International. This work asks two interrelated questions: What ideas about racialized, gendered, and sexual violence does the honour killing label disseminate and construct in the Canadian context? How does the mobilization of the term shape national discourses and racial realities in Canada? This article examines the ways that major English-language Canadian dailies and Canadian state officials have deployed the honour crime discourse while shedding light on the various political projects and racial logics underpinning national investments in this crime. Drawing on what Lila Abu-Lughod (2011:26) describes as the "political work" of the honour crime, I examine how this crime was transported from a transnational and foreign geography to a domestic and racialized context of violence against women.

[. . .]

Narrating Foreign Geographies of Violence

Defined by various feminist scholars and international human rights organizations as the killing of a woman for the purposes of sexual control and social management, honour crimes are also "marked as a culturally specific form of violence, distinct from other widespread domestic or intimate partner violence, including the more familiar passion crime" (Abu Lughod 2011:17). Honour crimes are described as the killing of a woman to recover wounded, damaged, or lost patriarchal honour. As Aisha Gill (2006:1) reminds us, "killing is not the only crime committed in the name of honour, but simply the most violent." Understood as a crime that is distinct in form and practice from other forms of gendered violence, international bodies like the United Nations Entity for Gender Equality and the Empowerment of Women (n.d.) describe honour related crimes as "violence stemming from a perception to safeguard family 'honour'" which includes "sexual, familial and social roles and expectations assigned to women and as prescribed by traditional ideology." In providing a definition of these crimes, Amnesty International (2012) states that "so-called honor killings are based on the deeply rooted belief that women are objects and commodities, not human beings entitled to dignity and rights equal to those of men." These definitions demonstrate that acts of gendered violence—and especially the honour crime—do not occur singularly but often go hand in hand with psychological and emotional harm, social and sexual control, and physical violence (Shalhoub-Kevorkian 2002). While the meanings of gendered violence that these definitions disseminate are not singular, they are collectively underpinned by an assumption of honour as a "predetermined concept," rooted in traditional cultures and ideologies (Grewal 2013:15).

Although the honour killing term has been used to describe certain eastern acts of violence against women (Abu Odeh 1997), the term has a relatively nascent history in Canadian mainstream and national parlance. In the immediate period before 2001, mainstream Canadian daily newspapers such as *The Globe and Mail,* the *National Post,* and the *Toronto Star* made frequent references to crimes known as "honour killings." Editorials covering these crimes focused mostly on their occurrence in Muslim states such as Pakistan, Turkey, Palestine, and

Jordan. Invested in exposing the transnational aspect of these crimes, editorials often cited the United Nations Population Fund's (UNFPA's) widely circulated estimate that 5,000 women are murdered per year in honour related violence world-wide. Cleaved from a broader discussion of local manifestations of gendered and sexual violence, such quantitative evidence helps reify the idea that women in Canada live in relative safety, freed from the threat of violence. These works confirm the role that cultural geographers ascribe to media in constructing "a symbolic geography" of space and place (Mahtani 2009:258).

An article on honour killings in Pakistan by Meriel Beattie (1999), published in *The Globe and Mail* exemplifies this discursive style and politicized retelling:

> *Lahore*—When Sarnia Imran walked up the stairs to her lawyer's office, it was in the hope of finalizing arrangements for a divorce.

> When she came down, she was a corpse on a stretcher—shot through the head by a gunman who came to the office with Mrs. Imran's own mother and uncle. The killing has further inflamed a social and political debate about "honour killings"—when families kill a female relative considered to have shamed the household—even though Mrs. Imran's family members deny that they ordered her death.

> The debate turns on the way Pakistani women are treated by the family and the state in a society where feudal power mixes with tribal customs and Islamic practice.

With a single word for her opening, the author transports her audiences to Lahore, Pakistan, where they become privy to the selective details of the life and death of Samia Imran. Her death, the author asserts, is a result of an "honour killing." Without providing much detail about the circumstances surrounding the crime, the author insinuates that Samia was punished for her desire to divorce her husband. The treatment of Pakistani women who live in a "feudal" society—as opposed to modern nation-states—is also briefly explored but only to signify the diminished capacities of the state when faced with a "society where feudal power mixes with tribal customs and Islamic practice" (Beattie 1999). Without discussing her position as a correspondent writing for a western daily, and without making clear her political investment in the details of this particular case, the author inserts Sarnia's death into a laden civilizational context where "modem, enlightened, secular peoples must protect themselves from pre-modern, religious peoples whose loyalty to tribe and community reign over their commitment to the rule of law" (Razack 2008:9-10).

Through this article and other media reports on foreign honour killings appearing in Canadian mainstream dailies immediately prior to 2001, the Canadian citizen becomes ideally situated to lament the fate of women from third world contexts (Cohn 1999; Farrukh 1999; Jehl 1999; Turgut 1998). Leaving unexplored the contexts of resistance to this example of gendered violence, readers are left to assume that violence against women remains largely accepted and unchallenged in Muslim majority states. Yet, as evidence from the local context of feminist organizing in Pakistan shows, Samia's murder became a rallying call for local feminist and human rights activists who pushed the state to take a tougher stance against state legislations that sanction violence against women (Hussain 2006). As Amina Jamal demonstrates in her work on feminist discursive practices and strategies in Pakistan, Samia's murder led to

> a huge outcry in the country, especially over the failure of police to make any arrests and the hesitation of the state to provide security for human rights lawyers Asma Jahangir and Hina Jilani, who were threatened by supporters of Samia's family. (2005:73)

While the success of these campaigns has been limited, local evidence of activism and resistance trump dominant narratives of female victims, unsung individual feminist heroes, and overwhelming societal approval for the violation of women's lives—seductive narratives underpinning the stories circulated in many western editorials on the honour crime (Abu Lughod 2011).

[. . .]

Domestic Horrors: Honour Killings in National Media Narratives

[. . .]

This section provides a textual analysis of a number of print media articles appearing in major English language Canadian dailies from 2009–2012. I located these articles by conducting a search of ProQuest Canadian Newsstand, a database containing texts of major newspaper dailies in Canada. While there were more than 3,500 articles printed on the topic of honour killings in Canadian newspapers in the three years between the murder and the trial, I focus on a small sample to highlight prevailing framings of the honour crime. . . .

To understand how the Shafia murders were first naturalized in Canadian media as a foreign, exceptional, and racialized occurrence, I will turn to the press conference held in Kingston by Chief Stephen Tanner shortly after the arraignment of Mohammed and Hamid Shafia and Tooba Mohammad Yahya. This conference was crucial in popularizing a culturalized understanding of the murders. After calling a moment of silence for the victims of the murders, Tanner announced to various Canadian media representatives:

> In our Canadian society, we value the cultural values of everyone that makes up this great country, and some us have different core beliefs, different family values, different set of rules. . . . Certainly, these individuals—in particular, the three teenagers—were Canadian teenagers who have all the freedom and rights of expression of all Canadians. (quoted in Proudfoot 2009)
>
> . . . [They] all shared rights within our great country to live without fear, to enjoy safety and security, and to exercise freedom of choice and expression and yet had their lives cut short by members of their own family. (quoted in Chung and Dale 2009)

Tanner's assumption that the murders were motivated by a cultural and civilizational difference in "core values" and beliefs between Muslim Canadians and Canadian society is evident. He thus notes the collective deprivation of the women's right to life, a right enjoyed by Canadian citizens of all genders.

In his brief speech, Tanner appears moved by the loss of life and highlights in particular the murder of the three Canadian sisters. This focus on the three sisters resonated in Canadian media as well, especially as stories of the eldest sister's "rebellious" nature began to surface. Echoing the story of the young Aqsa Parvez, who, Canadian media argued, was killed for wanting to lead a "normal" life of a Canadian teenager, stories of Zaineb Shafia's desire for a Canadian life helped reify the assumption that the three sisters were killed because of the fundamental incongruity of Islam with modernity (Haque 2010; Zine 2009). Notably absent from Tanner's lament, however, was the adult female victim in the Shafia murders. As the first wife of a polygamous man, Rona Amir Mohammad's body cannot be represented in the same way as the bodies of innocent, young, and female Canadian teenagers because it is tainted by the "cultural differences" which Tanner considers to be the motive for murder. Rona's body cannot be used as an altar for Canadian ideals and cultural values because it had already broken them through its participation in the illegal practice of polygamy. In life, Rona's body accepts the conditions of polygamy, an affront to all women, and thus, in death, she cannot be contained within the heteronormative nuclear family ideal. Unable to recuperate Rona's body through the liberal feminist saviour trope, Tanner focuses his attention on the lost lives of young women, wanting the promise of a Canadian life. Tanner's statement, released shortly after the discovery of the crimes, raises the spectre of the honour crime, providing Canadian dailies license to present this act of violence against women as an exceptional occurrence.

Overwhelmingly, media responses to Tanner's speech were positive, affirming his assumption of the family's guilt and conceding the cultural divide argument he invoked. In *The Globe and Mail*, Ann Hui (2010) lauded Tanner for relieving Canadians of "the 'honour killing' taboo." Drawing on Wendy Brown's work on multicultural states, this "taboo" of honour killing can be understood as an example of tolerance at work. Brown writes that tolerance towards objects is a method of racial management and control and that "designated objects of tolerance are invariably marked as undesirable and marginal" (2006:28). The so-called lifting of the taboo on honour killings in Canada is an indication of a break with the discourse of tolerance and a failure of "tolerance . . . to repress or override . . . hostility or repugnance in the name of civility, peace, or progress" (Brown 2006:28). This failure to curb hostilities and disgust cannot simply be confined to an individual act or an independent breach in the Canadian discourse of civility. Rather, it reveals the fractures occurring in the veneer of multicultural civility surrounding discussions of honour related violence before September 11, 2001.

[. . .]

With few exceptions, the extensive coverage of the Shafia trial also replicated the same civilizational logic characterizing the first few weeks of discovery of the crimes. Because the judge presiding over the Shafia trial placed a publication ban on media preventing the reporting of evidence presented at the preliminary hearings, journalists who attended the trial such as Christie Blatchford of the *National Post* and the *Toronto Star's* Rosie DiManno gained particular importance in shaping public understanding of the murders. As an indication of the popularity of her work on the trial, Blatchford's articles have also been collected in an e-book entitled *Killed Because They Were Girls: The Complete Coverage of the Shafia Trials* (2012). In her various court reports, Blatchford reminded readers that the Shafia sisters lived under the power of a patriarchal, temperamental, and violent man. Their household was governed by lies that were perhaps sanctioned by the religion, language, and culture from other and their familial relationships were inherently premodern. In describing their family arrangements, for example, Blatchford routinely referred to the Shafias as a "sprawling clan," reinforcing the assumption that the Shafias were unusual, foreign, and even primitive (2012).

Expressing her anger and frustration at the murders, Rosie DiManno (2011) asserted that the murders were an atrocious tragedy that was "spawned by punitive cultural traditions transplanted to Canada." She wrote,

> There's a reason why the Justice Lady is blindfolded. It depicts objectivity—fairness and equality for all before the law. A disregarded concept in Afghanistan; a core value in the Canadian court system. Let us state the obvious: Canada isn't Afghanistan. That culture is not our culture and their attitudes towards females are totally alien to ours.

Central to the national hierarchy reproduced in DiManno's work is a belief in the egalitarian conception and application of the law. While Afghanistan is seen as a place of inequality and lawlessness, Canadian courts are imagined as spaces of objectivity where notions of "fairness and equality for all" guarantee justice for victims. What remains absent from this representation is recognition of how the legacies of genocide and colonialism have shaped the operations of the law against victims of gender and sexual violence. As scholars have shown, legal justice remains a difficult feat for indigenous women and racial others in the Canadian state (Razack 1998, 2012; Fournier et al. 2012). Contesting the trial of serial murderer Robert Pickton and the state inquiry that followed, indigenous groups fighting for justice for missing and murdered Native women have shown how the law and the courts are complicit in concealing and enabling violence against indigenous women. While DiManno's work continues to gain mass circulation, stories that trouble legal and cultural innocence remain absent from her analysis. At their core, racialized and indigenous people's encounters with Canadian courts dislodge assumptions of national, racial, and moral superiority and innocence—assumptions that buttress the popularity of the writing of DiManno and others on the Shafia trial in particular and the honour crime in general.

What do such framings suggest? How do they reproduce civilizational thinking and reinforce the borders of the nation-state? What roles do they play in both representing and creating the reality of differential belonging for racialized others in multicultural Canada? What do they tell us about the status of Canadian national belonging and unbelonging? . . .

Discover Canada: No Barbarians Allowed

. . . On July 12, 2010, then Minister of Status of Women Canada, Rona Ambrose, . . . speaking to a gathering of journalists and community members at the Punjabi Community Centre in Mississauga, Ontario, . . . condemned honour related violence against women, making clear that such crimes have no place in Canadian society and that their perpetrators would be prosecuted to the full extent of the law. Arguing against the appeal to culturally relativist positions and ideas, the minister proclaimed Canada a nation vehemently opposed to violence against women and asserted the state's commitment to the human rights and dignity of all persons.

Labelling the honour crime a "serious problem" plaguing Canada, Ambrose went on to denounce the murder of family members:

> People come to this country to enjoy and embrace the values and opportunities that Canada provides, and as a nation we are proud of the contributions made by our diverse cultural communities. . . . However, killing or mutilating anyone, least of all a family member, is utterly unacceptable under all circumstances and will be prosecuted to the full extent of the law. (Status of Women Canada 2010a)

By focusing on immigrant victims who have arrived in Canada "to embrace the values and opportunities that Canada provides," Ambrose makes gendered violence appear exceptional, placing it squarely in the daily practices of Canada's cultural others. The juxtaposition between good immigrants who make contributions to Canada and bad ones who kill and mutilate is stark and makes a connection between cultural practices and acts of gendered and sexual violence. In this way, Ambrose can render fact the speculative charge of cultural violence without questioning the cultural basis of gendered violence in Canadian society at large.

Of course, this is neither a new or particularly original strategy. Its power to inscribe Canadian national superiority and underwrite the cultural inferiority of Canada's racial others cannot be underestimated, however.

. . . In Ambrose's speech, Canada is cast as a country of opportunity, a welcoming and safe home that is distinctively superior to "places around the world where violence against women is formally endorsed and employed" (Status of Women Canada 2010b). Popular narratives of such stature, while enduring, are repeatedly being replenished through the state's exclusive focus on the honour crime.

[. . .]

In its different announcements and initiatives that target a version of violence cleaved from the broader continuum of violence against women, the Canadian government shows that the bodies of dead Muslim women killed by Muslim men can be used to strengthen exclusionary narratives of national belonging. In fact, it is on the murdered bodies of Muslim women that myths of national and cultural superiority and racial and historical innocence are repeatedly inscribed. It is precisely this narrative that allows the Canadian nation state to commit over $2.8 million to community projects targeting honour related violence while simultaneously stripping Native women's associations from funding crucial for their work. The 2010 defunding of Sisters of Spirit, an organization that has dedicated its energies to exposing and ending violence against Native women, is one example of the ostensibly contradictory discourses at work in the intensified focus on the honour crime. As Sedef Arat-Koç notes, the "key to this seeming paradox is that the hyper-visibility of 'other' women helps *normalize* and *naturalize* the gender order in the larger society" (2012:9; emphasis in original). Through their focus on the honour crime, Canadian state officials perpetuate a national order that willfully ignores evidence of violence, sexism, and inequity in Canadian society at large. This historical moment, rather than advancing the cause of women or securing their rights, often fractures their communities and undercuts the possibility of feminist solidarities.

Conclusion

In recounting events leading up to the Shafia trial, this article has attempted to show how the mobilization of honour killing discourse has shaped media representations of gendered crimes of violence and the practices of the Canadian state. Examined through the lens of race, I have argued that the interplay between media and state focus on the honour killing label delimits the lives of racialized Canadians. In reading media and state responses to the honour crime, I have shown how the discourse codified acts of gendered violence in ways that targeted racialized communities. This paper argued that the selective focus on honour crimes has inspired "culturalist (and racist) discourses and policy approaches" that hide systemic and institutionalized forms of violence, including the violence of racism (Arat-Koç 2012:9).

To understand why the honour crime occupies a central place in national discourses, one needs to place this heightened interest in a historical context in which the bodies of dead Muslim women are used to assert national superiority and extend techniques of border management and control (Thobani 2007). Rather than view these mobilizations primarily at the discursive or affective levels, I argue that the selective state interest in acts of gendered violence has already charted a new Canadian racial landscape that is most clearly evidenced in migration policies and practices. In 2011, for example, the *Toronto Star* reported a 25 percent decrease in the number of immigrants admitted to Canada in the first quarter of the year

(Keung 2011). This measure has been accompanied by the increased shift from permanent settlement to precarious and temporary belonging. As migration justice groups have shown, the Conservative government has adopted harsher family reunification measures, and introduced a two-year "conditional" permanent resident status for the sponsored partners and spouses of immigrants and Canadian citizens. Under the guise of fiscal responsibility, the government has also cut federal health refugee programs and lowered the salaries of temporary migrant workers (*Star* editorials 2011; Cohen 2012; Keung 2012). Together these migration policies do not simply usher new or unusually precarious forms of belonging but enshrine, instead, racial differences at the national level.

. . . Efforts to confront gendered and sexual violence under the rubric of honour killings buttress the claim of the crime's rise and singularity. Without attention to the larger contexts of gendered and sexual violence, they can play a dangerous role in furthering exclusionary politics and realities. Powerfully wielded by state officials and dominant media, the current manifestations of the honour killing discourse conceal—rather than disrupt—the conditions that reproduce gendered violence within Canadian society. This includes the violence of migration and the unresolved tensions of citizenship. My concern with honour killing discourse is not simply the condemnation of state or media practices. Instead, I am invested in thinking about the possibilities of feminist solidarity and alliance in combating gendered violence. Envisioning radical feminist solidarities against the intricacies and intersectionalities of gendered violence requires challenging the exclusionary and dangerous contours of Canadian national logics.

References

Abu Lughod, Lila. 2011. "Seductions of the 'Honour Crime.'" *Differences* 22(1):17–63.

Abu Odeh, Lama. 1997. "Comparatively Speaking: The 'Honor' of the 'East' and the 'Passion' of the 'West.'" *Utah Law Review* 20(2):287–307.

Amnesty International. 2012. "Cultures of Discrimination: A Fact Sheet on 'Honour' Killings." Retrieved May 26, 2013 (www.amnestvusa.org/sites/.../honor killings_fact_sheet_final_2012.do).

Arat-Koç, Sedef. 2012. "Invisibilized, Individualized, and Culturalized: Paradoxical Invisibility and Hyper-Invisibility of Gender in Policy Making and Policy Discourse in Neoliberal Canada." *Canadian Woman Studies* 29(3):6–17.

Beattie, Meriel. 1999. "Honour Killings Continue to Punish Pakistani Women." *Globe and Mail*, June 3, Toronto: A13.

Blatchford, Christie. 2012. "No Honour in Cold-Blooded, Shameless Murder of Sha-Fia Girls." *National Post.* Retrieved July 25, 2010 (http://firllcomment.nationalpost.com/2012/01/29/iurv-reaches-verdict-in-shafia-tiial/).

Blatchford, Christie and the *National Post.* 2012. *Killed Because They Were Girls: The Complete Coverage of the Shafia Trials.* Ottawa: *National Post.*

Brown, Wendy. 2006. *Regulating Aversion: Tolerance in the Age of Identity and Empire.* Princeton, NJ: Princeton University Press.

Chung, Andrew and Daniel Dale. 2009. "Were Deaths of 4 Women a Matter of 'Honour'?" *Toronto Star.* Retrieved October 10, 2010 (www.thestar.com/news/ontario/2009/Q7/24/were_deaths_of_4_women_a_matter_of_honour.html).

Cohen, Tobi. 2012. "Immigration Marriage Fraud Crackdown Raising Concerns About Domestic Abuse." *Vancouver Sun.* Retrieved May 26, 2013 (www.vancouversun.com/news/Immigration+marriage+fraud+crackdown+raising+concerns+about/6919226/storv.html).

Cohn, Martin. 1999. "They Kill Their Own in the Name of Honour." *Toronto Star*, August 1:1.

DiManno, Rosie. 2011. "Cultural Questions Posed in Kingston Quadruple-Murder Trial." *Toronto Star.* Retrieved March 5, 2012 (www.tfaestar.com/news/canada/article/1085652–dimanno-cultural-questions-posed-in-kingston-quadruple-murder-trial).

Farrukh, Saleem. 1999. "The Shame of 'Honour Killings': In Male-Dominated Pakistan, Some Families Get Away with Murdering or Maiming Women Who Try to Escape Abusive Husbands." *Vancouver Sun*, September 17:A21.

Fournier, Pascale, Pascal McDougall, and Anna R. Dekker. 2012. "Dishonour, Provocation, and Culture: Through the Beholder's Eye?" *Canadian Criminal Law Review* 16:161–93.

Gill, Aisha. 2006. "Patriarchal Violence in the Name of 'Honour.'" *International Journal of Criminal Justice Sciences* 1(1):1–12.

Grewal, Inderpal. 2013. "Outsourcing Patriarchy: Feminist Encounters, Transnational Mediations and the Crime of 'Honour Killings.'" *International Feminist Journal of Politics* 15(1):1–19.

Haque, Eve. 2010. "Homegrown, Muslim and Other: Tolerance, Secularism and the Limits of Multiculturalism." *Social Identities* 16(1):79–101.

Hui, Ann. 2010. "Confronting the 'Honour Killing' Taboo." *Globe and Mail*. Retrieved December 13, 2011 (www.theglobeandmail.com/news/toronto/confronting-the-honour-killing-taboo/articlel387273/).

Hussain, Mazna. 2006. "'Take My Riches, Give Me Justice': A Contextual Analysis of Pakistan's Honour Crime Legislation." *Harvard Journal of Law and Gender* 29:223–46.

Jamal, Amina. 2005. "Transnational Feminism as Critical Practice: A Reading of Feminist Discourses in Pakistan." *Meridians: Feminism, Race, Transnationalism* 5(2):57–82.

Jehl, Douglas. 1999. "A Killing for Honour: In Some Parts of the Arab World Where a Woman's Chastity Is Everyone's Business, the Price of Family Honour Is Paid in a Daughter's Blood." *Edmonton Journal*, June 27:Fl/Front.

Keung, Nicholas. 2011. "Immigration Down 25 Percent for This Year: Fewer Permanent Visas Were Issued in the Quarter of 2011." *Toronto Star*, July 18:A4.

Keung, Nicholas. 2012. "Wage Cuts for Foreign Workers in Canada Discriminatory, Critics Say." *The Star*. Retrieved May 26, 2013 (www.thestar.com/news/gta/2012/05/24/wage_cuts_for_foreign_workers_in_Canada_discriminatory_critics_say.html).

Mahtani, Minelle. 2009. "The Racialized Geographies of News Consumption and Production: Contaminated Memories and Racialized Silences." *GeoJournal* 74:257–64.

Proudfoot, Shannon. 2009. "Up to a Dozen 'Honour Killings' in Canada in Past Decade." *Vancouver Sun*, July 24:B.l.

Razack, Sherene. 1998. *Looking White People in the Eye: Gender, Race, and Culture in Courtrooms and Classrooms*. Toronto, Canada: University of Toronto Press.

Razack, Sherene. 2008. *Casting Out: The Eviction of Muslims from Western Law and Politics*. Toronto, Canada: University of Toronto Press.

Razack, Sherene. 2012. "Memorializing Colonial Power: The Death of Paul Frank." *Law and Social Inquiry* 37(4):908–32.

Shalhoub-Kevorkian, Nadera. 2002. "Reexamining Femicide: Breaking the Silence and Crossing 'Scientific' Borders." *Signs: Journal of Women in Culture and Society* 22(2):582–608.

Star Editorials. 2011. "The Conservative Record: Immigrants See a Harsher Canada." *The Star*. Retrieved May 26, 2013 (www.thestar.com/opinion/editorials/2011/02/19/ the conservative record immigrants see a harsher canada.html).

Status of Women Canada. 2010a. *Minister Ambrose Calls for Community Action to Help End "Honour Crimes."* Retrieved May 26, 2013 (www.ronaambrose.com/media_/in-the-news2/breaking-the-silence-on-acts-of-violence-commiUed-m-the-name-of-honour).

Status of Women Canada. 2010b. *Speaking Notes for the Honourable Rona Ambrose*. Retrieved August 10, 2010 (www.ronaambrose.com/media_/in-the-news2/breaking-the-silence-on-acts-of-violence-committed-in-the-name-of-honour).

Thobani, Sunera. 2007. *Exalted Subjects: Studies in the Making of Race and Nation in Canada*. Toronto, Canada: University of Toronto Press.

Turgut, Pelin. 1998. "For the Family's Honour: Any Defilement of a Young Woman's Virtue, or Suspicion of an Illicit Liaison, Can Mean Death at Her Family's Hands." *The Gazette*, May 4:B6.

United Nations Entity for Gender Equality and the Empowerment of Women. n.d. "Defining 'Honour' Crimes and 'Honour' Killings." *End Violence Now*. Retrieved May 26, 2013 (www.endvawnow.org/en/articles/731-defining-honourcrimes-and-honour-killings.html).

Zine, Jasmin. 2009. "Unsettling the Nation: Gender, Race, and Muslim Cultural Politics in Canada." *Studies in Ethnicity and Nationalism* 9(1):146–63.

PART XI
Politics, Activism, and Social Movements

In this section, we cover central issues in the realm of politics, activism, and social movements. Scholars have examined the various mechanisms through which inequalities of gender and sexuality surface within the context of politics, activism, and social movements at the local, national, and global level. This section examines gender and sexuality in a variety of political contexts across the core themes of the reader: intersectionality, masculinity, transgender, and global (IMTG) perspectives.

In "The International Women's Movement and Women's Political Representation, 1893–2003," Pamela Paxton and colleagues examine women's participation in formal politics across time and place. The authors test hypotheses about how the international women's movement has impacted women's political representation, including women's suffrage, women's representation in parliament, and attaining 10, 20, and 30 percent women in the national legislature. Global pressures regarding women's representation have become stronger over time. The institutionalization of international women's movements appears to have had a significant effect on women's representation, including on women's suffrage and in attaining 10 percent of women in the national legislatures. Yet the international women's movement has not been successful in institutionalizing a discourse supporting high (e.g., 30 percent) representation for women. This piece shows how historical international contexts around gender have shaped women's participation in formal politics.

Mieke Verloo's "Multiple Inequalities, Intersectionality and the European Union" examines the importance of an intersectional lens in addressing gender inequalities, using the European Union as an example. Verloo considers how gender, race/ethnicity, sexuality, and class are generally understood or constructed, and where and how inequality is located for these groups. She then relates political structures with these identities, such as how gender, race/ethnicity, sexuality, and class are institutionalized in unions, parties, or ministries, as well as their political claims and struggles. This leads to identifying how inequalities differ in how they map onto policy problems, which affect how political strategies might be designed. Assuming gender inequalities are "the same" in their operation as class, race/ethnicity, and sexual orientation is insufficient for effectively addressing these inequalities at the political and structural levels. More complex political models are necessary.

Masculinity can also be mobilized through politics and movements. "'Don't Deport Our Daddies,'" Monisha Das Gupta's ethnographic study of a New York–based organization that advocates for deportees and their families, shows how state deportation policies and practices are gendered in their targeting of immigrant men. These processes of criminalization are a central mechanism shaping the organization of immigrant families' daily lives. Analyzing *testimonios*, Das Gupta shows how activists organizing against "crimmigration" highlight men's roles as caregivers, rather than simply as economic providers, in an attempt to highlight their roles as caring, involved family members deserving of rights and to counter assumptions that immigrant men are undeserving criminals. The findings reflect the way that, through activism, these families resist policies and practices that reproduce racialized, gendered, and sexual norms of immigrant communities.

Poulami Roychowdhury's "Brothers and Others" examines the organizing practices and logics of a very diverse group of New York City street vendors. Ethnographic and interview data show how New York City street vendors organize by engaging in gendered boundary work meant to unite men who differ by race, ethnicity, nationality, religion, and language. One rhetoric of brotherhood emphasizes equality and independence, another militancy and aggression, and a third responsibility and care. These three different rhetorics made it difficult to communicate, silenced women, and alienated less privileged groups of men. The findings demonstrate how organizing can be undermined by focusing on rigid notions of masculinity, suggesting the importance of receptive communication to build successful political strategies.

Abigail Andrews and Nazanin Shahrokni's study "Patriarchal Accommodations" highlights the paradox of women's mobility as linked to exclusionary policies. While patriarchal policies such as gender-segregated bussing or limiting women's political rights might reduce women's power, they can also have unexpected effects. Based on ethnographic, interview, survey, and archival data, the findings examine women's public transportation participation in urban Tehran, Iran, and women's predominance in emigration to the United States from rural San Pedro, Mexico. Segregated buses in Tehran may have emphasized gender difference, but they also facilitated women's mobility, allowing more women to engage in paid labor and encouraging women to see these spaces as reflecting their "rights." Excluding women from politics in San Pedro may have limited their voice, but it also stimulated women's migration for work, since men needed to stay home to staff village government. The study shows how globalization can foster women's movement into new realms even in the face of patriarchal policies.

These articles emphasize how assumptions about gender and sexuality shape politics and social movements. Women's movements play a key role in mobilizing for women's political representation. Yet women can also gain some increased freedoms in response to patriarchal policies that emphasize differences between men and women. Masculinity also matters to politics, as when immigrant rights groups emphasize caregiving men to address assumptions about criminal men, or when narrow definitions of masculinity limit solidarity within a social movement. Political processes need to recognize differences by not only gender but also race/ethnicity, class, and sexuality, as these inequalities are embedded in political structures and policies.

The International Women's Movement and Women's Political Representation, 1893–2003

Pamela Paxton, Melanie M. Hughes, and Jennifer L. Green

© iStockphoto.com/CrushRush

W omen's participation in politics has increased dramatically over the past 100 years. In 1890, women did not have the right to vote anywhere in the world. Currently, only one country, Saudi Arabia, denies women the right to vote. In 1907, Finland became the first country to elect a female member of parliament. Currently, women make up almost 50 percent of the national legislature in countries such as Sweden and Rwanda. The first country to reach 10 percent women in its national legislature was the Union of Soviet Socialist Republics (USSR), in 1946. In 2005, 60 percent of countries had at least 10 percent women in their national legislatures. Although women still are substantially underrepresented in politics in most countries of the world (Inter-Parliamentary Union 2006), they certainly have made remarkable gains over time.

What forces drove these remarkable changes in the political incorporation of women? Crossnational research on women's political representation has previously focused mainly on

Pamela Paxton, Melanie M. Hughes, and Jennifer L. Green. 2006. "The International Women's Movement and Women's Political Representation, 1893–2003." *American Sociological Review* 71(6):898–920.

domestic factors, examining internal features of countries such as their political institutions or electoral system (Caul 1999; Kenworthy and Malami 1999; Kunovich and Paxton 2005; Matland 1998; Paxton 1997; Rule 1981). Less often has research on women's political representation considered the role and power of *international* actors (Gray, Kittilson, and Sandholtz 2006; Hughes 2004; Ramirez, Soysal, and Shanahan 1997).

Did, for example, the growth and discourse of the international women's movement encourage global expansion of women's political participation? The international women's movement grew substantially over time (D'Itri 1999; Rupp and Taylor 1999). From just a few organizations in Western nations during the late 1800s, the international women's movement ultimately grew to encompass more than 40,000 women and men from more than 180 countries who came together in Beijing for the Fourth Global Conference on Women in 1995 (Dutt 1996). More important, the movement increasingly cooperated with the agents of world society, such as the United Nations (UN) and international nongovernmental organizations (INGOs), which act to diffuse global norms to nation states (Boli and Thomas 1997; Meyer et al. 1997). Thus, through this global expansion and collaboration, the international women's movement was increasingly able to transmit a discourse of substantial gender inclusion to nation-states over time (Berkovitch 1999b; Ramirez et al. 1997; True and Mintrom 2001).

But the messages and goals of the international women's movement regarding women's political incorporation also have changed and evolved (D'Itri 1999). In the early years of the movement, pressure on states centered on the provision of political citizenship to women (Rupp and Taylor 1999). Later, as suffrage became a taken-for-granted component of national sovereignty, the international women's movement began to call for positive discrimination policies to increase women's political representation (Jayawardena 1986). Pressure on states to incorporate women was therefore "ratcheted up" over time as gains in initial political representation for women were solidified.

Did this increasing pressure and the changing discourse of the international women's movement have an effect on women's political incorporation in a diverse array of countries? To answer this question, we address women's political representation in more than 150 countries over 110 years (1893–2003). We consider multiple political outcomes: female suffrage, first female parliamentarian, and achievement of 10, 20, and 30 percent women in a country's national legislature. We test whether increasing global pressure for the inclusion of women in international politics and the changing discourse of the international women's movement explain women's acquisition of these multiple political outcomes. We also consider whether the national-level political, social structural, and cultural characteristics typical in previous literature on women in politics act in conjunction with or in opposition to these global pressures.

[. . .]

Theoretical Background

The Global Institutionalization of Women's Equality

[. . .]

The mere existence of a transnational network capable of diffusing global norms does not ensure that this network will benefit women or even address their concerns. But, as Berkovitch (1999b) has shown, working through the world polity, the international women's movement has actively promoted a discourse of gender inclusion, ensuring that norms about female

rights, equality, and participation in economics and politics are transmitted to
Since the early days of the international women's movement, a major component
discourse has been the claim that women are entitled to equal rights, including p
broadly defined (Chafetz and Dworkin 1986; D'Itri 1999; Rupp and Taylor 1999)

Although women's movements at the national level are highly variable, subject to the structural and cultural constraints of nation-states, the international women's movement has been
steadily increasing in size and strength (Berkovitch 1999a). For example, international conferences, which bring disparate women together to exchange ideas, show substantial growth in
movement activity over time. In 1878, the first international women's congress convened in
Paris, attended by 11 foreign countries and 16 organizations (Rupp and Taylor 1999). By 1975,
the first UN World Conference on Women in Mexico City was attended by 133 national delega-
tions. And in 1995, 189 countries attended the Fourth World Conference in Beijing. Similarly,
during the past century, women increasingly created their own "women's" international non-
governmental organizations (WINGOS). From 1885 to 1970, WINGOs were founded steadily
except for breaks during wartime. But the number of WINGOs exploded in the 1970s, changing from steady to exponential growth (Berkovitch 1999a).

Since their founding, international women's organizations have used the institutions and agents
of world society—the UN, INGOs, and so forth—to make their claims (Berkovitch 1999b)....

The international women's movement continued to pressure the UN to address women's
concerns throughout the century. Motivated by the demands of the Women's International
Democratic Federation, the UN declared an International Women's Year in 1975 and declared
the Decade for Women (1975–1985). In the ensuing decade, the UN hosted two additional
World Conferences, in Copenhagen (1980) and Nairobi (1985).

[...]

Thanks to WINGOs and the international women's movement, the political rights of women
were kept on the agenda of the UN and its conferences. For example, one of 34 resolutions
adopted at the First World Conference in Mexico in 1975 called on governments to "pay special
attention to political rights of women" (UN 2000). At the outset of the second conference in
Copenhagen, conference delegates suggested that one of the obstacles preventing attainment of
the goals set out in Mexico was that too few women held decision-making positions. And at the
1985 nongovernmental organization (NGO) forum in Nairobi, the most heavily attended
workshop was "If Women Ruled the World," at which 18 female parliamentarians from around
the world discussed women's contribution as political leaders and the struggle to gain support,
even from female voters, for women's political representation (UN 2000).

Does this international activity make a difference to states?

[...]

Indeed, international agents work to influence states sometimes in the absence of significant
mobilization by local women's movements. For instance, in 1997, the male-dominated legislature of Peru approved gender quotas "without prior pressure from domestic women's organizations and with minimal debate, presumably because then-president Alberto Fujimori had
sensed the advantages of such a measure" (Towns 2004:214). Government leaders may introduce measures supporting the political advancement of women to increase state power or the
flow of resources, regardless of the levels of internal pressure from domestic women's movements. For example, ... the UNDP provided training to 144 female candidates in Viet Nam,
likely contributing to a rise in women's representation in the national legislature from 18 to 26
percent (UNDP 2000:97). And in the very recent past, the international community has used
periods of reconstruction to jump-start women's representation in countries such as Afghanistan
and Iraq (Dahlerup and Nordlund 2004).

One way that international and transnational forces influence states is by framing women's political empowerment in terms of modernity, which carries expectations not only of improved status in the world, but also of financial rewards (Towns 2004). States that pass quotas and elect higher numbers of women are characterized as modern, whereas states relying on traditional electoral practices are stigmatized as backward. . . .

In summary, the international women's movement both grew over time and became increasingly intertwined with carriers of global culture such as the UN. The existence of an increasingly powerful network of international organizations means that states have experienced increasing pressure over time to incorporate women into politics (Meyer et al. 1997; Ramirez et al. 1997). This pressure is general, influencing all states through agents of world society. These statements lead to our first hypothesis:

Hypothesis 1: As the international women's movement institutionalized women's equality in world society, it generated increasing pressure on countries to allow women access to the political sphere. This pressure is universal, having an impact on all countries and all political milestones for women.

The Changing Discourse of the International Women's Movement

We have argued that pressure on countries to incorporate women has generally increased over time. *But what counts as appropriate incorporation has changed over time.* Around the world, the women's movement proceeded in two distinct waves. First, during the latter half of the 19th and early 20th centuries, women struggled to achieve suffrage and eliminate barriers in education, employment, and property ownership (Ferree and Mueller 2004:584). During this first wave of the women's movement, pressure on states to incorporate women into politics centered on the provision of political *citizenship* to women (Chafetz and Dworkin 1986; Kelber 1994). National women's movements and WINGOs united in the goal of getting women the vote.

The language used by WINGOs and adopted by the world polity during this period focused on "political rights" for women. For example, the founding principles of the International Woman Suffrage Alliance state: "Women should be vested with all political rights and privileges of electors" (International Alliance of Women 2005). Likewise, the 1953 UN Convention on the Political Rights of Women used the following language: "desiring to implement the principle of equality of rights for men and women . . . and desiring to equalize . . . political rights."

During the 1970s, a second wave of the women's movement emerged, contesting women's status on a broader scale and emphasizing women's liberation, reproductive rights, and the contestation of patriarchy. As the women's liberation movement began, women were becoming more aware of the substantial inequality that existed between men and women in all areas of life (Freeman 1973). Building on these themes, in the realm of politics, the international women's movement began to call for policies to increase women's *representation*. The discourse of the second wave thus focused on the "inclusion" of women. And over time, language at the UN shifted from "political rights" to "women in political decision making" (Galey 1995:23). The change is evident by the 1980 UN Second World Conference on Women, which documented concerns about "too few women in decision-making positions" (UN 2000).

Beginning in the 1990s, the discourse of WINGOs and the world polity changed once more to emphasize specific thresholds or *targets* for women in political decision-making positions. The discourse continued to concern "inclusion," but now phrases such as "critical mass," "gender quotas," and even "gender balance" were stressed by women's groups and incorporated into the world polity message. It was argued that 30 percent women in parliament was the critical mass, or necessary threshold, that countries needed for women to have a visible impact on the style and content of politics and policy. For example, the UN Commission on the Status of Women now judges member-state progress on women's political incorporation using the critical mass yardstick: "Equitable participation remains a challenge . . . and only eleven Member States have reached the critical mass of 30 percent of women in parliament" (Division for the Advancement of Women 2005). The notion of critical mass dovetailed well with the rise of a new policy recommendation for states: gender quotas. States were encouraged to institute laws requiring that women make up a certain percentage of a candidate list, a parliamentary assembly, a committee, or a government. Since the 1990s, more than 40 states have implemented gender quotas for women in politics (International Institute of Democracy and Electoral Assistance [IDEA] 2006).

In the language of world polity theory, the international women's movement emphasized different "policy scripts" over time, focusing on suffrage in early years and high levels of political representation in later years. Thus, depending on *when* a country first encountered this international pressure, it was exposed to a different message from the international women's movement. Theories of state formation suggest that a country is at highest risk of absorbing a prevailing international norm during the period surrounding its acquisition of national independence—when it becomes sovereign (Ramirez et al. 1997). When Bolivia became sovereign in 1825, women's political incorporation was not yet on the international agenda (no country granted women the right to vote until New Zealand did so in 1893). When Norway became sovereign in 1905, the prevailing message from the international women's movement concerned women's suffrage. Currently, the international women's movement touts gender quotas and other affirmative action measures for enhancing women's political representation (Dahlerup and Friedenvall 2005; Krook 2003). Thus, Eritrea, which became sovereign in 1993, was subject to a different message about the appropriate level of women's representation. These changes in prevailing norms suggest that the time of a country's transition to sovereignty (pre-1893; pre-World War II; World War II to 1970; 1970 to 1990; post-1990) exposed it to one of several dominant models of women's incorporation in politics (no expectation, little expectation, expectation of suffrage, expectation of representation, expectation of high representation).

Hypothesis 2:   The changing discourse of the international women's movement emphasized different policy scripts related to women's incorporation into politics over time. Countries becoming sovereign under each period of discourse were subjected to different expectations of incorporation.

[. . .]

Data and Methods

Data on 151 independent countries begin in 1893, when New Zealand grants suffrage to women, and continues 110 years, through 2003. Independent nations recognized by the UN with populations exceeding 1 million enter the analysis at time of sovereignty, determined using a number of sources (*CIA Factbook* 2005; IPU 1995; U.S. Department of State 2005).

. . . We predict five sequential dependent variables: attainment of female suffrage, first female parliamentarian, and country achievement of 10, 20, and 30 percent women in its national legislature.

[. . .]

To measure the global institutionalization of women's equality in world society, we combined three world-level indicators: (1) cumulative foundings of WINGOs (updated from Berkovitch 1999b to include organizations founded between 1985 and 2003); (2) the cumulative count of international conferences, UN treaties, and UN groups related to women; and (3) the cumulative count of countries ratifying the International Labor Organization (ILO) 1919 Maternity Protection Convention. Each indicator captures a different aspect of the global institutionalization of the women's movement: women's organizing in the international arena, UN activity related to women, and ratification rates of a convention representing an early precursor to modern progressive maternity benefits.

[. . .]

Results

Worldwide trends in milestone achievement across all countries between 1893 and 2003 are represented in Figure 56.1. This graph demonstrates an increase in milestone achievement across time for all political outcomes, but the timing of milestone achievement differs. Gains were made in female suffrage in the early 1900s and increased steadily until the 1970s. By that time, nearly all (94 percent) of sovereign countries had granted suffrage to women. The number of countries with at least one female parliamentarian began to rise in the mid-1910s, increased slowly until 1945, then grew steadily after World War II. Like suffrage, initial female representation in politics is nearly universal in the contemporary period.

Figure 56.1   Percent of Sovereign Nations Achieving Political Milestones, 1893–2003

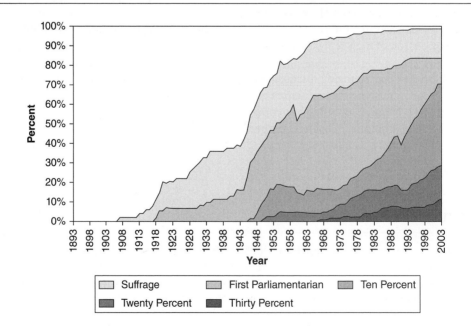

The first country to achieve 10 percent women in parliament was the USSR, in 1946. The percentage of sovereign countries that had achieved 10 percent women in their legislatures increased to 70 percent in 2003, with faster gains occurring after the 1970s. The number of countries reaching the 20 and 30 percent milestones also increases over time, but these countries begin later (the German Democratic Republic hit 20 percent in 1950 and 30 percent in 1967) and follow a more linear pattern of growth. By 2003, 29 percent of sovereign countries had achieved 20 percent women in parliament and 12 percent had achieved 30 percent.

Table 56.1 provides another view of milestone achievement, this time demarcated by achievement during the independence period (within three years of sovereignty year). To begin, Table 56.1 demonstrates that, consistent with prior research (e.g., Jayawardena 1986; Ramirez et al. 1997), the pressure for countries to treat women and men as equal citizens increased sharply after World War II. Whereas only about 26 percent of countries sovereign between 1893 and 1944 granted universal suffrage within three years of independence, 83 percent of countries sovereign from 1945 to 1969 and almost 88 percent of countries sovereign from 1970 to 1989 incorporated women into the citizenry of their newly formed states. By the fall of the Soviet Union, new membership in the international system clearly entailed allowing women to cast their votes alongside men.

Moving beyond political citizenship to initial political representation, we see that the election of a woman within three years of sovereignty rises almost 34 percent when the sovereignty periods before and after World War II are compared. Yet women's election to office is even more common in countries sovereign after the rise of the second wave of the international feminist movement. Three-fourths of countries independent between 1970 and 1989 elect a female member to parliament within three years of sovereignty. By 1990, women's political representation is an institutionalized part of nationhood, as 100 percent of countries independent in 1990 or after elect a woman to parliament within three years.

The pattern of milestone achievement over time is rather different when we consider higher levels of women's representation. There, instead of a pre-/post-World War II demarcation, the importance of 1970 and the advent of the second wave of the women's movement stand out. Of countries sovereign in periods before 1970, at most 1 in 20 elected 10 percent women to parliament within three years of independence. In sovereignty periods after 1970, more than 1 in 3 countries reached this same threshold. Countries reaching independence during the second wave more often reached 20 percent women in parliament soon after independence, but this figure drops from 13 to 4 percent for countries sovereign during or after 1990. Finally, although the international women's movement has recently begun to pressure countries to reach 30 percent

Table 56.1 Achievement of Milestones Within Three Years of Sovereignty

	Pre-1893	1893–1944	1945–1969	1970–1989	1990 On
Suffrage	0%	26.1%	83.1%	87.5%	100%
First Parliamentarian[a]	0%	17.4%	50.9%	75%	100%
10 Percent	0%	0%	5.1%	37.5%	37.5%
20 Percent	0%	0%	1.7%	12.5%	4.2%
30 Percent	0%	0%	0%	0%	0%
N	40	23	59	8	24

Note: [a]For five countries (Libya, Nigeria, Sierra Leone, Tanzania, and Latvia) the date of First Parliamentarian is unknown, and they are therefore not included in any calculations for this measure.

women in their national legislature, not a single country in the world system elected 30 percent women to parliament within three years of independence. The pattern of the results in Table 56.1 provides initial support for Hypothesis 2, but multivariate tests are also needed.

Table 56.2 shows the estimation results of the discrete-event history model for each of the five dependent variables. The second row of Table 56.2 shows positive and significant effects of the institutionalization of the international women's movement on the first four political outcomes. The likelihood of suffrage, first member of parliament, and 10 and 20 percent women in national legislatures all increase as the international women's movement established the principles of women's equality in world society. Furthermore, the institutionalization of the women's movement variable also significantly increases the likelihood of attaining 30 percent women in parliament if prior milestone (20 percent) is not included in the model. Hypothesis 1 is therefore generally supported: as the international women's movement institutionalized women's equality in world society, it generated increasing pressure on countries to allow women access to the political sphere.

Transforming the coefficients from this logistic regression into predicted probabilities aids in understanding effect sizes. . . . For example, a 10-year increase in the institutionalization of the women's movement is expected to result in a 13 percent increase in the predicted probability of suffrage attainment (from 2.1 to 14.8 percent).

It takes a longer time for 10 percent women in parliament (column 3) to be affected by the international women's movement variable. A 10-year increase in the institutionalization of the women's movement marginally increases the predicted probability of attaining 10 percent women from .2 to .7 percent. But moving to the midway point, 1948, increases the probability of attaining 10 percent women to 29 percent. Across all models, the effect sizes indicate that the global institutionalization of women's equality powerfully affects country-level attainment of political power for women.

The next five rows examine Hypothesis 2—that countries becoming sovereign under periods of distinct discourse were subjected to different expectations about the incorporation of women. The results for suffrage, first MP, and 10 percent women in parliament strongly support Hypothesis 2. Countries attaining sovereignty during the 1893–1944 period are at higher risk of attaining suffrage than countries sovereign before 1893: 30 percent compared with the original 15 percent. But countries attaining sovereignty after World War II have a *significantly* higher probability of attaining suffrage than the pre-1893 countries, with the chance of suffrage increasing to 92 percent. These results are consistent with the dominant discourse of the women's movement during those periods. Before 1945, the international women's movement was struggling in national battles and provided only weak and inconsistent pressure on nations to incorporate women as voting citizens. After 1945, suffrage was a taken-for-granted feature of national sovereignty. The results for first MP are similar. Although with first MP, increased pressure to incorporate women as elected representatives occurs only in countries sovereign after World War II.

The period results for attainment of 10 percent women in national legislatures are equally supportive of Hypothesis 2. Indeed, the results are striking. They show no difference in the probability of attaining 10 percent women across the pre-1893, 1893–1945, and 1945–1969 periods. Instead, it is in countries sovereign after the discourse shifted from "political rights" to "women in political decision making" that we see an increased probability of this level of attainment. Countries sovereign during 1970 to 1989 have a 27 percent chance of attaining 10 percent women in a given year, compared to a probability of 5 percent in earlier periods. Countries sovereign after 1990 increase their probability of attaining 10 percent women in a given year to 34 percent.

Table 56.2   Discrete Time Event History Models of Women's Political Milestone Achievement[b]

	Suffrage	First MP	10 Percent	20 Percent	30 Percent
Intercept	−3.85***	−2.37***	−6.19***	−12.59***	−22.63***
	(.61)	(.53)	(.86)	(1.85)	(5.98)
Global Influences					
Inst of international	.21***	.13*	.13*	.34**	.35
women's movement	(.05)	(.06)	(.06)	(.11)	(.24)
1893–1944	.89*	.42	.48	1.06^	−.60
	(.39)	(.38)	(.43)	(.58)	(.86)
1945–1969	4.15***	2.69***	.58	−1.68*	2.47
	(.62)	(.59)	(.57)	(.83)	(1.87)
1970–1989			1.94*	−.53	
			(.80)	(1.21)	
1970 on	4.46***	4.02***			1.52
	(.79)	(.80)			(2.13)
1990 on	ACA[a]	ACA[a]	2.26**	1.22	NCA[b]
			(.77)	(1.06)	
Domestic Influences					
Cultural					
British colony	−2.06***	−1.71***	−1.10*	.05	−2.99
	(.51)	(.46)	(.51)	(.80)	(1.98)
Portuguese colony	−1.17	−1.82*	−1.28[A]	−.59	3.39*
	(.85)	(.77)	(.70)	(1.41)	(1.68)
Spanish colony	−.90*	−.95*	−.23	.13	2.59^
	(.41)	(.42)	(.46)	(.82)	(1.37)
Belgian colony	−3.00**	−3.35***	.48	.83	3.55
	(.96)	(.84)	(.92)	(1.54)	(3.08)
French colony	−2.19***	−1 92***	−.64	1.23	NCA[b]
	(.59)	(.54)	(.57)	(1.01)	
Other colony	−1.52*	−.67	.03	.92	NCA[b]
	(.72)	(.66)	(.61)	(.89)	
Muslim	−1.49**	−3.47***	−1.59***	−1.95*	.96
	(.49)	(.48)	(.45)	(.79)	(2.01)
Catholic	−.63	−1.75***	−1.15**	−1.40*	−3.90***
	(.56)	(.47)	(.42)	(.68)	(1.15)
Orthodox	−1.51*	−2.25***	−2.62***	−3.08**	−2.37^
	(.71)	(.63)	(.62)	(1.09)	(1.30)
Other religion	−1.28*	−2.52***	−1.25**	−.68	−4.32**
	(.50)	(.43)	(.42)	(.58)	(1.44)

(Continued)

Table 56.2 (Continued)

	Suffrage	First MP	10 Percent	20 Percent	30 Percent
Structural					
Industrialization	−1.16***	−.48*	.32^	−.07	2.14**
	(.23)	(.22)	(.17)	(.37)	(.71)
Political					
Democracy	.09***	.03	−.05^	.00	.01
	(.02)	(.02)	(.03)	(.06)	(.16)
Marxist-Leninist	2.89***	.59	3.11***	2.40**	5.62**
	(.69)	(.59)	(.47)	(.77)	(1.81)
PR			1.32***	.72	5.47*
			(.35)	(.74)	(2.50)
Mixed			.22	−1.10	NCA[b]
			(.46)	(1.23)	
Other			−.33	1.41	3.66
			(.41)	(.95)	(2.68)
Linkages to World Society					
WINGO memberships	.09	.18**	.11**	.12[a]	.30*
	(.07)	(.07)	(.04)	(.06)	(.14)
CEDAW ratification			.40	−1.39*	−.55
			(.35)	(.66)	(.93)
Prior Achievement					
Previous milestone		.06	−.01	.24***	.36**
		(.04)	(.02)	(.06)	(.11)
Previous milestone^2		.00	.00	−.005*	−.01**
		(.00)	(.00)	(.00)	(.00)
N, *country years*	2178	2360	4206	5478	5786
N, *countries*	151	146	151	151	151

Note: WINGO = women's international nongovernmental organizations; CEDAW = Convention on the Elimination of All Forms of Discrimination against Women; MP = member of parliament.

[a]All Cases Achieved—cannot estimate coefficient because all cases achieved outcome in first year of observation.

[b]No Cases Achieved—cannot estimate coefficient because no case in this category achieved outcome.

*p ≤ .05, **p ≤ .01, ***p ≤ .001 (two-tailed test); ^p < .05 (one-tailed test).

The period effects in the final two columns of Table 56.2 are not supportive of Hypothesis 2. There, period of sovereignty does not generally have an impact on attainment of milestones. No period effects are significant for the 30 percent model, and for 20 percent, the patterning of coefficients is unexpected. While countries sovereign between 1893 and 1944 have a greater probability of attaining 20 percent women in their national legislatures than those sovereign before 1893, countries sovereign between 1945 and 1970 have a significantly negative coefficient.

The combination of the discourse period effects for 20 and 30 percent and the lack of a significant international women's movement effect for 30 percent suggests that the international women's movement has been less successful during later periods in fully institutionalizing a discourse of high representation for women. Although pressure to incorporate women has grown over time, 30 percent women in parliament is a fairly new and fairly ambitious goal. Indeed, of the 18 countries that have reached 30 percent women in parliament, almost half did so after 1994. It may therefore take more time and international pressure for a substantial body of countries to accept 30 percent women as an appropriate goal for their parliaments.

[. . .]

Conclusion

Women's political representation, once considered unacceptable by politicians and their publics, is now actively encouraged by powerful international actors. . . .

We find that as the international women's movement worked to institutionalize women's equality in world society, it generated global pressure on nation states to incorporate women. Thus, the international women's movement did help women attain political power over the past century, one of its primary goals. The international women's movement was largely responsible for getting the world community to consider the issue of women's political disenfranchisement, and later for setting standards governing women's incorporation. Through INGOs, WINGOs, IGOs, and conferences, the movement spread these messages around the globe and used the strong voice of the world polity to turn the ears of individual nations. The effectiveness of this approach is evidenced by the increasingly demanding discourse of the women's movement and the corresponding increases in women's political participation. Throughout the 20th century, arguments about female suffrage, for example, moved from "acceptable" in a nation-state, to "encouraged," to "unequivocally required." As the women's movement worked to institutionalize women's inclusion in politics in the world polity, nations responded by increasing women's representation over time.

However, the international women's movement also changed its discourse over time, and this changed the nature of the pressure experienced by states. Early transnational pressure centered simply on the provision of political citizenship to women (the right to vote). But the women's movement eventually turned to more ambitious demands. In the 1970s, the second wave of the women's movement emphasized that representation, rather than formal equality, was important. In recent periods, international pressure has encouraged particular targets such as 30 percent women in the legislature as appropriate levels of representation. Pressure on states to incorporate women was therefore "ratcheted up" over time as gains in initial political representation for women were solidified.

[. . .]

References

Berkovitch, Nitza. 1999a. "The Emergence and Transformation of the International Women's Movement." Pp. 100–126 in *Constructing World Culture: International Nongovernmental Organizations Since 1875*, edited by J. Boli and G. M. Thomas. Stanford, CA: Stanford University Press.

Berkovitch, Nitza. 1999b. *From Motherhood to Citizenship: Women's Rights and International Organizations*. Baltimore, MD: The Johns Hopkins University Press.

Boli, John and George M. Thomas. 1997. "World Culture in the World Polity: A Century of International Non-Governmental Organization." *American Sociological Review* 62(2):171–90.

Caul, Miki. 1999. "Women's Representation in Parliament: The Role of Political Parties." *Party Politics* 5(1):79–98.

Chafetz, Janet S. and Anthony Gary Dworkin. 1986. *Female Revolt: Women's Movements in World and Historical Perspective.* Totowa, NJ: Rowman and Allanheld.

CIA Factbook. 2005. "Central Intelligence Agency, Office of Public Affairs." Retrieved February 5, 2005 (http://www.cia.gov/cia/publications/ factbook/index.html).

Dahlerup, Drude and Lenita Freidenvall. 2005. "Quotas as a 'Fast Track' to Equal Representation for Women: Why Scandinavia Is No Longer the Model." *International Feminist Journal of Politics* 7(1):26–48.

Dahlerup, Drude and Anja Taarup Nordlund. 2004. "Gender Quotas: A Key to Equality? A Case Study of Iraq and Afghanistan." *European Political Science* 3:91–98.

D'Itri, Patricia Ward. 1999. *Cross Currents in the International Women's Movement, 1848–1948.* Bowling Green, OH: Bowling Green University Popular Press.

Division for the Advancement of Women (DAW). 2005. "Equal Participation of Women and Men in Decision-Making Processes, with Particular Emphasis on Political Participation and Leadership." *Expert Group Meeting,* October 24–27.

Dutt, Mallika. 1996. "Global Feminism After Beijing: Some Reflections on U.S. Women of Color and the United Nations Fourth World Conference on Women and NGO Forum in Beijing, China." *Feminist Studies* 22(3):519–28.

Ferree, Myra Marx and Carol Mueller. 2004. "Feminism and the Women's Movements: A Global Perspective." Pp. 576–607 in *The Blackwell Companion to Social Movements,* edited by D. A. Snow, S. A. Soule, and H. Kriesi. Oxford, UK: Blackwell.

Freeman, Jo. 1973. "The Origins of the Women's Liberation Movement." *American Journal of Sociology* 78:792–811.

Galey, Margaret E. 1995. "Women Find a Place." Pp. 11–28 in *Women, Politics, and the United Nations,* edited by A. Winslow. Westport, CT: Greenwood Press.

Gray, Mark M., Miki Caul Kittilson, and Wayne Sandholtz. 2006. "Women and Globalization: A Study of 180 Countries, 1975–2000." *International Organization* 60:293–333.

Hughes, Melanie. 2004. "Another Road to Power? Armed Conflict, International Linkages, and Women's Parliamentary Representation in Developing Nations." Master's thesis, Department of Sociology, the Ohio State University, Columbus, Ohio.

International Alliance of Women (IAW). 2005. *Declaration of Principles.* Retrieved January 12, 2006 (www.womenalliance.com/declare.html).

International Institute of Democracy and Electoral Assistance (IDEA). 2006. Retrieved April 2, 2006 (http://www.idea.int/).

Inter-Parliamentary Union (IPU). 1995. *Women in Parliaments 1945–1995: A World Statistical Survey.* Geneva: IPU.

Inter-Parliamentary Union (IPU). 2006. *PARLINE Database.* Retrieved August 1, 2006 (http://www.ipu .org/parline-e/parlinesearch.asp).

Jayawardena, Kumari. 1986. *Feminism and Nationalism in the Third World.* London, UK: Zed Books.

Kelber, Mim. 1994. *Women and Government: New Ways to Political Power.* Westport, CT: Praeger.

Kenworthy, Lane and Melissa Malami. 1999. "Gender Inequality in Political Representation: A Worldwide Comparative Analysis." *Social Forces* 78(1):235–68.

Krook, Mona. 2003. "Not All Quotas Are Created Equal: Trajectories of Reform to Increase Women's Political Representation." Paper presented at the Midwest Political Science Association National Conference, April 3–6, 2003, Chicago, IL.

Kunovich, Sherri and Pamela Paxton. 2005. "Pathways to Power: The Role of Political Parties in Women's National Political Representation." *American Journal of Sociology* 111:505–52.

Matland, Richard E. 1998. "Women's Representation in National Legislatures: Developed and Developing Countries." *Legislative Studies Quarterly* 23(1):109–25.

Meyer, John W., John Boli, George M. Thomas, and Francisco O. Ramirez. 1997. "World Society and the Nation State." *The American Journal of Sociology* 103(1):144–81.

Paxton, Pamela. 1997. "Women in National Legislatures: A Cross-National Analysis." *Social Science Research* 26:442–64.

Ramirez, Francisco O., Yasemin Soysal, and Suzanne Shanahan. 1997. "The Changing Logic of Political Citizenship: Cross-National Acquisition of Women's Suffrage Rights, 1890 to 1990." *American Sociological Review* 62(5):735–45.

Rule, Wilma. 1981. "Why Women Don't Run: The Critical Contextual Factors in Women's Legislative Recruitment." *Western Political Quarterly* 34:60–77.

Rupp, Leila J. and Verta Taylor. 1999. "Forging Feminist Identity in an International Movement: A Collective Identity Approach to Twentieth-Century Feminism." *Signs* 24(2):363–86.

Towns, Ann. 2004. "Norms and Inequality in International Society: Global Politics of Women and the State." Doctoral dissertation, University of Minnesota.

True, Jacqui and Michael Mintrom. 2001. "Transnational Networks and Policy Diffusion: The Case of Gender Mainstreaming." *International Studies Quarterly* 45(1):27–57.

United Nations (UN). 2000. *Women Go Global.* CDROM. New York: United Nations.

United Nations Development Programme (UNDP). 2000. *Women's Political Participation and Good Governance: 21st Century Challenges.* New York: UNDP.

U.S. Department of State. 2005. *Background Notes.* Retrieved February 6, 2005 (www. state.gov/r/pa/ei/bgn/).

Multiple Inequalities, Intersectionality and the European Union

Mieke Verloo

W hile the concept of intersectionality is increasingly used in gender studies, sociology and economics . . . political and policy practice in Europe has seldom referred to intersectionality when trying to deal with multiple inequalities.

After three decades of creating a considerable body of European legislation to address inequality between women and men, attention to inequality has in the last 10 years or so been broadened to include discrimination on a range of additional grounds. The Treaty of Amsterdam (1997) introduced a broader anti-discrimination provision in Article 13, involving appropriate action to combat discrimination based on sex, racial or ethnic origin, religion or belief, disability, age or sexual orientation. The Charter of Fundamental Rights (2000: Article 21) provided further initiatives to tackle discrimination on these different grounds.

Mieke Verloo. 2006. "Multiple Inequalities, Intersectionality and the European Union." *European Journal of Women's Studies* 13(3):211–28.

In the proposed Constitution, these initiatives are to be consolidated. In 2000, the Council unanimously adopted the Racial Equality Directive (2000/43/EC) and the Employment Equality Directive (2000/78/EC). The Racial Equality Directive implements the principle of equal treatment between people irrespective of racial or ethnic origin and gives protection against discrimination in fields of employment and training, education, social security, healthcare and access to goods and services. The Employment Equality Directive implements the principle of equal treatment in employment and training irrespective of religion or belief, sexual orientation and age. It includes identical provisions to the Racial Equality Directive and also requires employers to accommodate, within reason, the needs of a disabled person qualified to fill the position in question. The EU sees these recent initiatives to combat discrimination and to promote equal treatment as major achievements (Green Paper; European Commission, 2004). In the next few years, the Stop Discrimination campaign can be expected to further promote these EU activities.

[. . .]

Intersections: A Closer Look at the Complexity of Multiple Inequalities

Crenshaw introduced the concept of intersectionality as an escape from the problems of identity politics, to "denote the various ways in which race and gender interact to shape the multiple dimensions of Black women's employment experiences" (Crenshaw, 1989: 139). She distinguishes between structural intersectionality and political intersectionality (Crenshaw, 1994). *Structural intersectionality* occurs when inequalities and their intersections are directly relevant to the experiences of people in society. Structural intersectionality can help to explain why a black woman is not considered for one job because she is black since the "norm employee" is a white woman, while other jobs are also unavailable to her since the jobs available to black persons in that context are predominantly male jobs. It addresses the fact that heteronormativity is part and parcel of gender inequality, which means that the position of lesbians is very different from the position of heterosexual women. Crucial questions in analysing structural intersectionality are: How and when does racism amplify sexism? How and when does class exploitation reinforce homophobia? How and when does homophobia amplify racism?

Crenshaw uses *political intersectionality* to indicate how inequalities and their intersections are relevant to political strategies. Political differences are most relevant here, as strategies on one axis of inequality are mostly not neutral towards other axes. She uses an example of the unavailability of statistics on domestic violence police interventions broken down by Los Angeles district, which, given the racial segregation in this city, could provide information she needed on arrests differentiated by race. She found that this information was blocked (by domestic violence activists in and outside the police department) because of fears that it might be abused to reinforce racial stereotypes about some groups being pathologically violent. She argues that these concerns, while well-founded, are also potentially against the interests of women of colour since they do not help to "break the silence" within the respective communities, thus hindering broad mobilization against domestic violence in these communities. Crucial questions in analysing political intersectionality are: How and where does feminism marginalize ethnic minorities or disabled women? How and where do measures on sexual equality or on racism marginalize women? How and where do gender equality policies marginalize lesbians?

[. . .]

Questioning Assumed Similarities

Through comparing specific sets of inequalities, . . . I address the notion of assumed similarity underlying the appeal of, or the ambition for, consistent policies on multiple inequalities. This might also shed some light as to where and how intersections might be relevant. The comparisons made will necessarily be exploratory, as they are intended solely to demonstrate how we could start to articulate the similarities and differences between multiple inequalities. Obviously, such a comparison would need to be time- and place-specific, so I focus here on the EU and its old member states in the last decade.

All inequalities relevant to the new European anti-discrimination regulations can be seen as connected to social groups or categories, to distinctions made in interactions and institutions by people themselves or others. The comparison will focus on four social categories strongly connected to inequalities: gender, race or ethnicity, sexual orientation and class. The first two are chosen from the categories prominent in current European anti-discrimination policy. Gender and race/ethnicity are categories addressed by comparatively well-developed equality policies in the EU. Sexual orientation is added as a category specific to European policy, and social class as the most prominent example of a social category that is strongly connected to inequalities, yet not currently included in the European equality agenda.

The first comparison presented here uses five dimensions: the range of positions in each category; the common understanding of the origin of the social category; the possible location of the inequalities connected to it; the possible mechanisms producing them; and the norm against which this social category seems to be compared. Table 57.1 presents an understanding of how these four social categories are commonly (presented as being) linked to inequalities in public debates and in the strategies of social movements and organizations dedicated to the abolition of these inequalities. I am well aware that there is a wide variety of political and theoretical positions on all these points, but in order to outline why various social categories cannot be treated as linked to inequalities in equivalent ways, I have roughly mapped out what are widely recognized positions. Table 57.1 summarizes this first comparison.

The table shows differences in the first two dimensions, in the range of positions commonly recognized in the social category and in the perceived origin of the category. Gender is the most limited category of the four, commonly seen as having two positions that are perceived as originating in nature, in biology. While this perception of biological origin is contested, and gender is often defined as a socially constructed set of interpretations, norms, symbols, behaviours, institutions and identities, only postmodern gender theory includes biology in this social construction and this understanding is hardly ever part of gender equality policies or integrated in the demands of feminist organizations. Class, while being similarly dichotomous (the working class vs the owners of production), is a very different kind of category because it combines this dichotomy with a strong representation of its origin as "nurture," as the result of historical patterns of education, ownership and exploitation. Comparing gender categories with class positions thus shows that gendered social identities are to a large extent fixed in two positions, while class identities are represented as positions that can be overcome or lost. In contrast to gender and class, sexual orientation has a wider, if still limited, range of positions. It is quite common to see a presentation of three positions (as in the Flemish "holebi" label that wraps them as *ho*mosexual, *le*sbian, *bi*sexual). It is also quite common to see four to five positions, as in the US organizations for LBGT, referring to Lesbians, Bisexuals, Gay and Transgender or Transsexuals. When we turn to race/ethnicity, it becomes clear that the range is even wider, and that what counts as "race" or as "ethnicity" is much more contextually constructed and contestable than

Table 57.1 Comparing Four Social Categories That Are Linked to Inequalities

Representations of Social Categories in Terms of:	Gender	Race/Ethnicity	Sexual Orientation	Class
Range of positions	Dichotomous	Multiple	Three/four or more	Dichotomous
Origin of social category	Contested: Nature/nurture	Contested: Nature/culture	Nature [constructed]	Socioeconomic construct
Location of inequality	Organization of labour, intimacy and citizenship	Organization of citizenship and labour [intimacy]	Mostly organization of intimacy and citizenship	Organization of labour
Mechanisms (re)producing inequality	Material (resources) Discursive (norms) (Sexist) Violence	Discursive (norms) Material (resources) (Racist) violence	Discursive (norms) [material, violence]	Material (resources)
Norm	[White heterosexual middle-class] man	White [heterosexual middle-class man]	[White] heterosexual [middle-class man]	[White heterosexual] middle-class [man]

gender, sexual orientation or class. The label "race" seems to be constructed as more closely linked to nature, to biology, to being born as belonging to a certain category, while the label "ethnicity" is constructed as linked more closely to nurture, to culture and geographical roots, but both labels overlap. We see differences along a dimension of essentialism vs constructionism, where class is recognized widely as social, while race/ethnicity is often still seen as essentialist, as having a natural, objectively physical origin.

Further differences come to the fore when we compare what are commonly articulated to be the most important locations of the inequalities connected to these social categories. The problem of inequality of sexual orientation is primarily located in the organization of intimacy and citizenship. In contrast, gender inequality is connected to at least three sociopolitical realms. Gender, while primarily linked to the division of labour in many policy texts, is also connected strongly to the organization of citizenship and the organization of intimacy. While social, sexual and parenting relations are racialized or ethnicized, race/ethnicity, like class, but contrary to gender and sexual orientation, are not seen as located predominantly or even partly in the sphere of personal relationships and intimacy; they are not seen to be "a private problem" in that sense, their public character is widely acknowledged. Compared to gender and sexual orientation, class and race/ethnicity are represented more as firmly located in the public sphere, in the spheres of citizenship and employment. Class is seen to originate in how labour is organized, while race/ethnicity inequality is seen to derive from the way we organize citizenship (who belongs to "us"? who is the outsider?).

Differences also occur when analysing the variation in conceptualizations of how inequalities connected to these social categories are (re)produced. While addressing both material and discursive mechanisms is often an obvious recourse in policies concerning gender and race/ethnicity inequality, class inequality is represented as predominantly a problem of the distribution of resources (including educational resources), while sexual orientation inequality is articulated mostly as a discursive problem, a lack of recognition and a problem of stereotyping.

One cannot help but remark that all four social categories are confronted with the same dominant and privileged norm citizen, with slight differences in accent: for gender categories the norm citizen is first of all male, followed by white, heterosexual and middle class. In sexual orientation categories the norm citizen is predominantly heterosexual and then male, white and middle class. The norm class citizen is predominantly middle class, then male, white and heterosexual. For race/ethnicity categories, the norm citizen is first of all white, followed by male, heterosexual and middle class.

My evocation of conceptualizations of how social categories are connected to inequalities is necessarily simplistic. One could question to what extent the differences rendered here result from my poor depiction of common representations, to what extent they result from poor articulations of the link between social categories and inequalities, or to what extent there actually are "real" underlying differences here. My intention is to question and debate what the framing of social categories, and the way they are seen as linked to inequalities, means for social movement and policy strategies.

Table 57.2, then, presents a comparison of five other dimensions that show differences in political and policy activities connected to the social categories under scrutiny here. This table examines whether the social categories are articulated as political cleavages, whether they are institutionalized, and what are the predominant goals, claims and strategies used to deal with the inequalities connected to them.

First of all, the social categories chosen are all defined as political cleavages as the result of active agitation and articulation by social movements. For the category of class, this articulation has developed from workers' movements into the heart of the political party landscape. In this sense, class is a cleavage that has found its way into the centre of parliamentary politics. . . . This is not the case for the other categories. There are a small number of women's parties or parties based upon ethnicity, but this is rare in Europe. There are no parties based upon sexual orientation.

There are also important differences in the degree of institutionalization of the social categories; the extent to which politically relevant and recognized institutions have been installed to address the inequalities assigned to them. Class has a very high degree of institutionalized representation across Europe as a politically recognized dimension of inequality (as such, class is represented in political parties, in trade unions and in corporatist systems), whereas race/ethnicity is just starting to achieve some—limited—representation. Gender is much more institutionalized, not only in bureaucracies (departments for equal opportunities) but also within governments (ministers for gender equality). Sexual orientation is rarely institutionalized as an inequality category.

Furthermore, differences appear in the presentation and common acceptance of political goals connected to these inequalities. Multiple goals can be identified for sexual orientation and gender at the level of political movements. At times equality is the advocated goal, sometimes difference, and occasionally the goal seems to be the deconstruction of the categories. Even if such political differences often lead to heated debates within the respective movements, this results in a wide variety of goals, from same-sex marriage or quotas (forms of inclusion) to extended maternity leave (forms of reversal) and queer thinking (displacement). For the categories of race/ethnicity and class, this is different. While the abolition of class differentials is a respected political goal, the issue of whether the goal of equality with regards to race/ethnicity should be assimilation, integration or multiculturalism is hotly debated.

The main struggles and claims differ as well, with the main struggles for sexual orientation being about recognition and equal treatment (opening of the institution of marriage), or about the right to be different (gay pride). There are not many voices addressing the lesbian/gay pay

Table 57.2 Comparing Political and Policy Activities as Connected to Four Social Categories

Representations of Social Categories in Terms of:	Gender	Race/Ethnicity	Sexual Orientation	Class
Political cleavage	Social movement	Social movement	Social movement	Political parties
Institutional mechanisms	Many	Growing	Few	Many
Goals	Equality, difference and deconstruction: multiple goals	Equality; assimilation vs multiculturalism is a hot topic	Equality, difference and deconstruction: multiple goals	Accepting abolition of class differentials as a goal
Claims	Redistribution and recognition	Redistribution and recognition	Recognition	Redistribution
Political strategies	Struggle for equal treatment, positive action, mainstreaming	Struggle for equal treatment, positive action, mainstreaming	Struggle for equal treatment	Redistribution, some positive action

gap, although there is increasing attention to discrimination in the labour market. The struggles around gender and race/ethnicity are about both redistribution (equal pay, discrimination in the labour market) and recognition (revaluing care and cultural differences).

Current political strategies show a threefold comprehensive approach to gender issues, but a singular focus on equal treatment and a strategy of inclusion when it comes to sexual orientation. For class and race/ethnicity, there are, in addition, some cases of positive action. The calls for diversity mainstreaming parallel to gender mainstreaming are very recent and seem to be connected mostly to race/ethnicity (as well as to categories not taken into consideration here, such as age and disability).

More comparisons of other sets of social categories linked to inequalities would probably only add similar patterns. Without playing down the similarities that are found, I hope the two tables illustrate the case I make here: different inequalities are dissimilar because they are differently framed to be relevant as policy problems. This does, and should, affect the way political strategies are designed to address them. Comparing other social categories or choosing other dimensions would reveal differences as well. One need only examine the dimension of choice: we can decide to become Catholic or Islamic tomorrow, or learn to speak a new language, but we cannot "decide" to be old or young. Another dimension is visibility and ascription vs identification: we can hide our sexuality or wealth to some extent, but it is much more difficult to hide poverty or first language. Yet another dimension is the probability and possibility of a change in identity and status in connection to inequalities: we have all been young, and will—hopefully—all become old, while all of us can become disabled and some will even change sex or ethnicity. This also illustrates that these social categories can be unstable and contested: what counts as race or ethnicity in specific contexts, what counts as young or old, is intertwined with power in many ways.

Concluding, there seems to be a wide range of dimensions that differentiate between unequal social categories. It seems wise to ground policy strategies not only in the similarity, but also in the distinctiveness of inequalities. Moreover, these inequalities are not independent, since there are many historical, political, social and cultural intersections. The preceding discussion has also provided starting points for further conceptualization of intersectionality at work. Parallel to the analysis in Table 57.1, we can expect structural intersections to be most important where the location of inequality or the mechanisms (re)producing them are seen to be similar. Furthermore, we can expect political alliances or conflicts to run parallel to differences and similarities in degrees of institutionalization, goals, claims and strategies, as outlined in Table 57.2.

[. . .]

Strategies to Address Differentiated Inequalities

. . . A "one size fits all" approach to multiple discrimination is based on an incorrect assumption of sameness or equivalence of the social categories connected to inequalities and of the mechanisms and processes that constitute them. Focusing on similarities ignores the differentiated character and dynamics of inequalities. It also overlooks the political dimension of equality goals. Moreover, it has become clear that attention to structural mechanisms and the role of the state and private sphere in reproducing inequalities is much needed.

. . . I present some starting points for a more promising strategy to address differentiated inequalities. . . . Moreover, it highlights the necessity of an ongoing struggle over the implementation of such a strategy.

This strategy should start from the following propositions:

Inequalities are found in both the public and private spheres. They are reproduced through identities, behaviours, interactions, norms and symbols, organizations and institutions, including states and state-like institutions.

Inequalities are not equivalent; social categories are connected to inequalities in different ways.

Inequalities are dynamic problems that can be located in various distinct structures, that are experienced differently, and that can be (re)produced in different ways.

Inequalities are not independent, but deeply interconnected, maybe even interdependent.

Inequality policies are subject to vastly different political views and parties (e.g., to annihilate differences or value diversity).

Power struggles between various inequalities will always be present, as this is part of (political) intersectionality.

These hegemonic struggles need to be addressed and anticipated by careful balancing of resources and institutionalization, and by organizing public arenas or institutions for them.

This article has demonstrated that strategies addressing differentiated inequalities at the structural level cannot be "the same," and that an individualistic anti-discrimination policy is insufficient. What is needed is the development of complex methods and tools informed by intersectionality theory, an increase of resources, but also further development of intersectionality theory and a rethinking of the representation and participation of citizens in an era of post-identity politics. This necessitates ongoing organized political articulation, struggle, debate and deliberation.

References

Charter of Fundamental Rights of the European Union. 2000. Solemn Proclamation of the European Parliament, the Commission and the Council of 7 December 2000, OJ 2000 C346/1.

Crenshaw, Kimberlé Williams. 1989. "Demarginalizing the Intersection of Race and Sex: A Black Feminist Critique of Antidiscrimination Doctrine, Feminist Theory and Antiracist Politics." *University of Chicago Legal Forum* 139–67.

Crenshaw, Kimberlé Williams. 1994. "Mapping the Margins: Intersectionality, Identity Politics, and Violence Against Women of Color." Pp. 93–118 in *The Public Nature of Private Violence*, edited by M. A. Fineman and R. Mykitiuk. New York: Routledge.

European Commission. 2004. *Equality and Non-Discrimination in an Enlarged European Union*. Green Paper. Luxembourg: Office for Official Publications of the European Communities.

"Don't Deport Our Daddies"

Gendering State Deportation Practices and Immigrant Organizing

Monisha Das Gupta

On the morning of July 7, 2009, I joined a rally in front of 26 Federal Plaza on Broadway in Manhattan for 52-year-old Brooklyn resident Roxroy Salmon, a Jamaican national and a legal permanent resident (see Figure 58.1). He was appearing that day before an immigration judge for a hearing on his deportation case in one of the courtrooms in the building. The Manhattan-based Families for Freedom (FFF) and the First Presbyterian Church, a new member of the New York's New Sanctuary Coalition, had organized the event. As I drew close to the plaza, I saw a crowd of people holding signs that said, "Broken Hearts, Broken Families. Stop Deportation Now," "Help Keep Children Safe," and "A Family United Is a Happy Family."

As we waited outside on the plaza for Roxroy to appear before the judge, we chanted and sang. The chants and the song focused on the attentiveness with which Roxroy parented his children—three of whom lived with him, the youngest being his 13-year-old son Elijah—and took care of his elderly mother, who suffered from Alzheimer's disease. But, as organizers from FFF had warned us, the judge ruled to deport Roxroy, whose two minor drug convictions from over 20 years ago were grounds for removal. Within a month of the hearing, Roxroy received his deportation order.

Families for Freedom came together in 2002 in New York City to directly organize migrants in deportation proceedings and their families in order to contest the rising tide of deportation that stood at the record high of 409,849 in 2012 (Immigration and Customs Enforcement 2012). Unlike the iconography in the anti-deportation movement that focuses on mothers who are forcibly separated from their children, in its public rallies, vigils, and website, FFF prominently features deported daddies. What did FFF's representations say about its deployment of gender and sexuality? In turn, what did its work say about the place of gender and sexuality in deportation policy and practice?

[. . .]

Monisha Das Gupta. 2014. "'Don't Deport Our Daddies': Gendering State Deportation Practices and Immigrant Organizing." *Gender & Society* 28(1):83–109.

Figure 58.1 Roxroy Salmon addressing a rally held in support of him and his family at the Federal Plaza in Manhattan, New York, in November 2008

Source: Photograph by Mizue Aizeki.

The organization's work reveals that post-entry social control (Kanstroom 2007) has increasingly relied on criminalizing immigrants in order to deport them, and that its members become the targets of deportation *precisely because* they do not and cannot structurally live up to the prescribed gender and sexual arrangements. Criminalization devalues its members' kinship ties. The organization's advocacy on behalf of those with criminal convictions sets it apart from anti-deportation groups that use the rhetoric of innocent family-centered deportees (see Pallares 2010). To offer a grounded reading of FFF's activism, I utilize a strand of queer scholarship that looks at the institutions and discourses that pathologize variations in sexualities and gender relations to mark them as deviating from heteronorms that produce a national culture, the ideal worker, and the ideal citizen (Cohen 2004; Ferguson 2004; Halberstam 2005; Luibhéid 2004).

[...]

About FFF and Deportation Policies

Since its founding, FFF has engaged in a sustained, though difficult, grassroots-driven resistance to the pipeline from police stations, jails, criminal courts, and prisons to privately run federal detention centers and immigration courts. Its members are permanent residents, undocumented migrants, and asylum seekers who are predominantly men of color from Caribbean, Latin American, South Asian, and African nations, reflecting the ethnic makeup of New York City's working-class neighborhoods. The group has played a foundational role in the anti-deportation movement with its Deportation 101 trainings, seeding initiatives in different parts of the country, and, over the years, shifting the terms of the debate among organizers on immigration reform to account for criminalization.

The organization takes up the cause of undocumented and legal permanent residents with criminal convictions, and runs a rights education program in Rikers Island Prison, where inmates are profiled for their immigration status. . . . The organizations align themselves with the U.S. prison abolition movement, and offer a unique analysis of crimmigration—the use of local law enforcement and the criminal justice system to enforce federal immigration law. Unlike Chicago's La Familia Latina Unida (LFLU), which also mobilizes families but focuses on the undocumented and on law-abiding parents—breadwinning and hardworking fathers, and care-taking mothers who raise "good" children (Pallares 2010)—FFF's analysis of criminalization leads it to reject the distinction between criminal and law-abiding migrants. FFF strongly argues that the immigrant rights movement's legislative focus on legalization, which pertains only to undocumented migrants, is too narrow, and does not address pre-9/11 legislation that conjoined criminal law with immigration enforcement, making legal permanent residents vulnerable.

Two federal laws—the 1996 Anti-Terrorism and Death Penalty Act and Illegal Immigration Reform and Immigrant Responsibility Act (IIRIRA)— tightened the knot that has tied immi-gration law to criminal law since 1988 (Kanstroom 2007, 227–31) by deepening post-entry social control over those who had certain types of criminal convictions and ensuring that they be removed with little recourse to due process and judicial review (Kanstroom 2007, 10–17). The USA Patriot Act of 2001 widened and intensified the provisions of the two 1996 laws. The effectiveness of these laws has been greatly enhanced by the interface between local law enforcement and the Department of Homeland Security's arm for interior enforcement, Immigration and Customs Enforcement (ICE). Recent programs like 287(g) allow local police to enforce federal immigration law upon receiving (minimal) training. Since 2008, Secure Communities agreements permit police to cross-check a person's fingerprints with the immi-gration database at the time of booking, and detain the person for ICE if the records show immigration violations. Consequently, the share of immigrants deported on the grounds of having criminal convictions has steadily increased from 35 percent in 2007 to 55 percent in 2011 (Foley 2011).

[. . .]

In the case of deportation policies, criminalization provides the medium to coordinate federal functions of national security and immigration control with state government-level criminal justice systems.

[. . .]

In 1996, the IIRIRA eliminated the Immigration and Naturalization Act's 212(c) waiver that allowed immigration judges to consider the hardship that the deportation of long-term LPRs with criminal records would cause to their U.S. citizen or LPR spouse, children, or parents (Hing 2006, 58–64). The logic of using criminal law to permanently remove migrants without regard for the lives they have built in the United States continues to inform ameliorative poli-cies to address the separation of family members and the 2013 attempt to craft comprehensive immigration legislation (Immigrant Justice Network 2013).

Method: *Testimonios* as Evidence

Since 2009, I have been engaged in action research in Los Angeles and New York City in organiza-tions that reject the mainstream legislative compromise that intensifies border and post-entry enforcement in exchange for a limited legalization program. The data presented in this article are part of this larger study. For my analysis, I draw primarily on an internet archive of 29 narratives from members representing 15 nationalities, and secondarily on interviews conducted in 2009 and 2010 with members of FFF and the New York chapter of the New Sanctuary Movement. Seventeen of the website narratives are in the first person, with six accounts from persons directly targeted for deportation, and 11 from impacted family members. . . .

I characterize the web accounts as *testimonios*—forms of life writing that incite social change. As evidence, *testimonios* tell us what matters to those who, in the act of testifying, give voice to experiences that are otherwise negated in order to impel the audience to action (Beverley 2004). . . .

Methodologically, *testimonios* are instructive because they break down the binary formulation of deliberate, politically geared speech and authentic, unscripted speech. The stories, as uncrafted as they might sound, are framed to do the political work of publicizing the treatment of deportees and their families in order to stop deportation. They challenge us to recognize a truth that is being produced in the politico-experiential telling.

[. . .]

Figuring "Family" in Migration Literature

The traditional literature on the impact of U.S. immigration policies on the ability of minoritized migrants to form families has uncritically lamented the barriers the policies posed to conjugal heterosexuality, thereby naturalizing heteronormative kinship as desired and desirable arrangements (Luibhéid 2004; Manalansan 2006; Ting 1995). A critical treatment of the exclusion and deportation policies that were developed in the late nineteenth and early twentieth centuries has shown how they legislated national anxieties about intimacy, domesticity, and reproduction in ways that devalued and severely disrupted the varied kinship ties of Asian and Mexican migrants (Gee 2003; Lee 2003; Ngai 2004; Shah 2011).

[. . .]

Through the testimonies on its website, FFF publicizes the disruption to social reproduction in migrant families when men—disproportionately targeted, first, by the enforcement of criminal law, and then by immigration law—are deported. Testifying in words and through photographs to the centrality of men's care work in their families lends the emotional content and import to the FFF's web narratives, enabling them to operate as *testimonios*.

[. . .]

The *testimonios* on FFF's website are overwhelmingly (28 out of the 29) about or from incarcerated or deported men. Nationally, men constitute the majority of the detainee population, though the number of women detained has risen from 7 percent in 2001 to 10 percent in 2008 (Human Rights Watch 2009, 11). The predominance of men both in the national statistics on deportees and among its constituency mirrors the targeting of men in encounters with law enforcement. One of the organizers, Manisha Vaze, laid out the gendered tactics of immigration enforcement:

> ICE agents have the discretion about who they pick up; what they might do is pick up the father instead of the mother so that the mother can take care of the kids in the house or so that they don't have to call Child Protective Services. . . . I think it [this exercise of discretion] came out of the flack ICE got for the New Bedford raid. . . . It [the practice of detaining men] mimics prisons. Prisons are mostly filled with men. There aren't as many family facilities [for immigration detention]. They'd rather not have the burden of detaining U.S. citizen children [to keep them with the parent].

In conducting home raids, the ICE agents put in practice the ideology that women are the primary caregivers in their families.

The same ideology about motherhood fuels the public disapproval of detaining women with children. Bad publicity about workplace raids that resulted in mothers being separated from their young and breastfeeding children, as well as legal challenges to the mistreatment of incarcerated women and children in facilities like T. Don Hutto Residential Center in Texas (American Civil Liberties Union 2012), have made it more difficult for ICE to target women. The 2007 ICE raid at a factory in New Bedford, Massachusetts, and the removal to out-of-state detention centers of the women workers, many mothers of young children, provoked widespread outrage (Massachusetts Immigrant and Refugee Advocacy Coalition 2008). The public perception that it was cruel to separate mothers from their children led to pressure from Congress on ICE to issue nonbinding guidelines suggesting that pregnant women, nursing mothers, and sole caregivers among detainees arrested in workplace raids be offered alternatives to detention (National Council of La Raza 2008). The 2011 ICE guidelines further instructed its personnel to exercise prosecutorial discretion in cases where the persons arrested are primary caregivers in the family, or who have spouses who are (Morton 2011, 4). Though the language about caregivers in the prosecutorial guidelines is gender-neutral, it simply formalizes the gendered discretion that ICE officers already exercised.

[. . .]

In comparison, men with criminal convictions present organizations like FFF with a difficult public relations task. What representational strategies would allow criminalized men to be seen in a sympathetic light? One of the biggest challenges for those who advocate on behalf of prisoners is producing them as subjects of rights because of the dominant understanding that those who break laws have no entitlements (Schaffer and Smith 2004). In the case of migrants, this perception is deepened by their legal and symbolic status as "aliens," who are constructed in the public imagination as having no claim on nationstate based rights.

Even in faith communities that ally with FFF, deportees' criminal convictions make their appeals for help questionable. An organizer in the New Sanctuary Movement that lent support to Roxroy Salmon reflected on the challenges of getting support from the congregations when the person in question has a criminal conviction. She laid out the moral difficulties that confront congregants:

> The response is to evaluate the person's story. People start judging. . . . [They] get uncomfortable because these are people who did not do everything by the book. The process of evaluation, to identify whether there was an error made—even progressive people can fixate on that idea, particularly progressive white people, and other ethnicities can also fall into that trap. So we have to figure out a way to displace that tendency.

In the case of FFF, left-behind family members use the affective language of domesticity to resignify their detained or deported loved ones.

In a move that I found initially puzzling, all the *testimonios* emphasized the emotional rather than the material toll of detention and deportation. They highlighted deported men's contribution to social reproduction of their families, and the first-person testimonies of deported men speak to their desire to be good fathers—not in their role as financial providers but as caregivers of their biological and nonbiological children. As in Roxroy's case, some narratives emphasize the deported men's critical role in taking care of an elderly, often disabled, parent. Placing the men and their contributions in the private sphere and publicizing the

Figure 58.2 Joshua speaking at a Children's Vigil organized by Families for Freedom in March 2006 at the Federal Plaza in Manhattan, New York

Source: Photograph by Mizue Aizeki, courtesy of Families for Freedom.

quality of their caregiving become organizing tools that also contest the stereotypical casting of men who have criminal convictions as uncaring and irresponsible.

If home raids work in the private sphere to spread what Buff (2008) characterizes as "deportation terror," then FFF members publicize that invasion. This type of intrusiveness illustrates a basic insight of feminists of color—the private sphere cannot operate as a shield for low-income people of color because their kinship systems and sexuality are suspect and open to intense public policing. In a testimony to the UN Special Rapporteur on the Human Rights of Migrants in 2007, Joshua (see Figure 58.2) paints a vivid picture of the violation of his home, and the traumatic process of learning what happened to his father:

> My name is Joshua. I am 9 years old. My Father was here since he was 12 years old. His mother and sisters and most of his family are still here. The INS took my dad away from me when I was in kindergarten. . . . They came to my house early in the morning and took him while I was sleeping. . . . For many nights after they took my dad, I asked my mom when he was coming back. Then I got it. He was deported to Jamaica almost 3 years ago.

> I miss my dad very much, but the people who took him just don't care. . . . They are leaving families heartbroken. I want them to stop the deportation laws. They should bring my daddy back. And I wish other kids could have their daddies back too. . . . That's why people everywhere should care about families like ours.

From his mother's testimony, we find out that eight federal agents banged on the door early one morning in 2004 to arrest his father, Calvin James. Notably, FFF includes children directly in its organizing work.

While the presence and voices of children serve to underline their innocence and their unjustified suffering, the children's politico-sentimental effectiveness also lies in the encouragement they get from FFF to confront the public with their trauma and demand accountability.

In the adult narratives, one finds compelling accounts of how the deported men helped with the everyday tasks of caring for their children and of their desire to be good fathers. Writing in the first person, Georgiana Facey, a U.S. citizen, described the expedited removal of her husband, Howard, to Jamaica for an outstanding deportation order: "Life has turned upside down since our husbands were taken away. . . . They used to help with everything: pick up the kids from school; take them to the library, the park, McDonald's." In a transcribed telephone conversation from Jamaica carried on the webpage with Georgiana's story, Howard expressed his emotional turmoil on being separated from his wife and three small children: "Even though I'm not locked up, it feels like prison. I worry about the time I used to spend with [my] kids. We spent precious time together. I don't want my kids to grow up without a father." Without any hope of reuniting with his children soon, Howard articulates how deportation has interfered with his ability to be a good father.

Addressing a congregation at St. Paul of the Apostle Church in 2007, Joe, an asylum seeker from China who had lived in Brooklyn for ten years, talked about his and his wife's fears of being separated from their U.S.-born young children. Joe and Mei had been pulled over while driving to Vermont, and had spent four months in detention. In this statement made to seek sanctuary for his family, Joe said:

> I am here representing thousands of families with a similar situation. . . . As parents facing deportation, we feel helpless to protect our own children. . . . We love our children's smiles. We want to see them grow. We want to be in their daily life. . . . I have been working in a restaurant for 10 years. . . . Today I am 28. I am a young father. I want to be a good father. . . . My daughter here—she is the oldest child. She is 2 now. I take her to the playground, even if I am tired. She has a lot of energy. She deserves the best.

Joe expresses his desire to be a good father through his involvement in his children's life in the midst of his taxing work at the restaurant. His reference to the ordinary pleasure he takes in his children's smiles opens up a powerful affective space. Similarly, when testifying with her son, Joshua, to the U.N. Special Rapporteur, Kathy McArdle, who continues to sit on FFF's board, shared a humdrum but tender domestic moment while going through the horrors of Calvin's arrest and its aftermath. She recalled, "Their greatest joy was probably the tickle fights they used to have, and just quiet moments together that can never be duplicated by phone calls." In a more elaborate feature in the magazine *Colorlines,* an older Josh is quoted as remembering his father's cooking: "I miss his cooking. I really liked his rice that he used to make. It had coconut milk in it" (Wessler 2009). Touch, smell, taste, and sight bring to life a daily presence that deportation ends. These details serve to remind readers that those who have been deported or live in the fear of deportation cannot take these daily interactions for granted.

The *testimonios* describe the intimate acts of parenting. They dwell on the mundane details. Even when the *testimonios* mention tasks stereotypical of men when they undertake social reproduction, they underline their complementarity and quality. The attentiveness with which the tasks are done and the physical details of the caregiving form the emotional grain of the narratives, and are evoked to give substance to the men's identity as "good fathers." The *testimonios* from the members of FFF challenge us to apply to their families the feminist insights about kinship arrangements in communities of color where men's place in their families cannot be read straightforwardly through the hegemonic scripts about masculinity that are contingent on breadwinning. As the FFF organizers repeatedly point out, the working-class realities of the members make men's caregiving and household tasks essential for their family's survival.

Enforcement not only targets migrants' livelihood, their biological reproduction, and their activism, but also their ability to care for their family members and households. Once the men are deported, women become solely responsible for care work, and the crisis in social reproduction deepens as they juggle paid work with child care. This, at times, leads to what one study calls the "effective deportation" of left-behind family members, including those who are U.S. citizens (Kremer, Moccio, and Hammell 2009, 81–97). While most members of FFF struggle to survive in the United States because the countries to which the adults were deported are economically depressed and politically unstable, a few, like Georgiana, have decided to send a child away to live with their deported husbands to cope with the increased pressures they face at work and home.

In its *testimonios* and vigils, such as the one for Roxroy and countless others, FFF refuses to treat the suffering and pain of deportation as private. By putting these feelings at the center of its political work, it enacts the political mandate of *testimonios* to mobilize the affective to end incarceration and deportation. The members imbue their presence in physical and virtual space with emotions that give texture to and enliven a slogan that I have gustily shouted over and over in immigrant rights marches, *"¡Alto a las redadas!* [Stop the raids]."

Why Families? Criminality and Illegible Kinships

[. . .]

Given the ways in which "the family" has been constructed and mobilized in political movements to promote rather than challenge heteronormativity, I asked the then executive director, Janis Rosheuvel, why the organization coalesces around "families." She observed that the organization's name reflects those who comprise it—family members outside of detention centers, the majority women, fighting for their incarcerated loved ones. Comparing the investment of its members with that of lawyers and advocates, she pointed out, "People directly affected by the issues fight at a whole other level—that's why it's crucial for families to be at the center of organizing." Pressed further about how the organization defined families, she clarified that the term embraces anyone who is impacted or wants to help a loved one.

Yet, FFF's political analysis does not stop at the assumption that the affective dimensions of kinship make families its "natural" constituency. Since each member's experience with ICE agents, detention centers, criminal and immigration courts, and consulates is singular, it can be fragmenting rather than unifying. Thus, the organization has had to build a political platform that pulls together the skeins of individual experiences to thematize criminalization and deportation as aspects of state violence in the lives of migrants. . . .

Historically, fears about migrant criminality have informed immigration authorities' decisions about whether migrants deserve to reside in the United States (Lee 2003; Ngai 2004, 75–90). In the current wave of deportations, FFF sets itself apart from many other immigrant rights organizations that make morality-based arguments and consequently accept the distinction between violent and nonviolent crimes, and criminal and noncriminal deportees. The organization's internal process has required developing a political vocabulary that reflects this analysis. Laying out the difference in FFF's position on deportation within and outside the movement, Vaze explained that many advocates buy into the reasoning that migrants with criminal convictions are:

worthy of being deported or undeserving of being in the United States. *I hear it all over—we want to keep the hardworking undocumented family-oriented immigrants in this country. But those criminals should be deported. And there is no real analysis of what it means to be a criminal for immigration purposes.* . . . When people are so divided in terms of who is deserving and who is undeserving, it becomes really important that people are politicized [emphasis mine].

In this critique of the immigrant rights movement's acceptance of federal and state government dictated terms of who is a criminal, FFF outrightly rejects the appeal to family as an alibi for respectability.

How does this process of politicization work? According to Vaze, FFF engages its members in continual conversations about the tendency of, say, an asylum seeker with no criminal conviction to distance himself from a legal permanent resident with one, and of both to refuse to see any commonality with an undocumented migrant. In turn, FFF also hears undocumented migrants with no criminal convictions privileging their claims over criminally convicted legal permanent residents. "We are pitted against each other, and it's a constant conversation about how to build unity," especially because FFF is one of the few immigrant rights organizations that make a conscious effort to ensure it represents criminally convicted migrants.

The inclusion, and advocacy on behalf of the criminally convicted requires, as Rosheuvel puts it, internal and public education "to transform the immigrant rights movement and how it views the people who are most marginalized from it—people with criminal convictions—and then also the wider society." Reflecting on the common theme that runs through various FFF programs, she said:

> Part of what we do is unpacking the criminal justice system for people. Why is it unjust that 90 percent of stop-and-frisk in NYC are brown and black men? We debunk a lot of myths about why people are locked up in the first place, why they have contact with the criminal justice system, which can lead to deportation proceedings. . . . We spread the word about the dangerous intersection of criminal justice and immigration.

The public discussion of the racialized and gendered processes through which migrants encounter local law enforcement helps deportees find common ground across immigration status and their particular cases.

Testimonios, in addition to holding out the possibility of solidarity with those who are not directly affected (Beverley 2004, 34–48), serve to build a political community among those who have been differentially affected by deportation and often feel condemned to shame, silence, and isolation. The organizers I interviewed talked about the importance of training members to tell their stories to build leadership *within* the organization and in the immigrant rights movement in order to uncover that "dangerous intersection of criminal justice and immigration." Taking Roxroy as an example, an FFF organizer explained that it took two painstaking years of going public with his story to shore up the solidarity I witnessed on that July day in 2009. As organizing tools, *testimonios* construct a political collectivity, purpose, and vocabulary. In narrating their experiences, the members cannot assume that their sense of loss and grief as criminalized people of color will appear universally legible to those who are safely anchored in their own families through various systems of privilege, including that afforded by U.S. citizenship.

Deportees and their families live in New York City neighborhoods that have been associated with the culture of poverty that was posited by the infamous 1965 Moynihan Report and subsequently popularized by academics and nonacademics. The culture of poverty discourse fundamentally depends on deviant constructions of gender and sexuality, and conjoins failed fatherhood, criminality, and inner city poverty as a "way of life" associated with urban African Americans. Those same neighborhoods are also haunted by the specter, promoted by social scientists, policy makers, and public commentators, of the "downward assimilation" of new immigrants into this culture of poverty, driving a wedge between native-born blacks and their immigrant neighbors (see Jung 2009; Pierre 2004). Families for Freedom realizes that these discursive forces construct *both* native-born people of color and immigrants of color (who are sometimes members of the same family) as pathological, prone to criminality, and, therefore, deserving of the state's intrusiveness into areas of life that are normatively "private."

This political insight helps FFF connect the struggles of native-born people of color against prisons with those against the detention and deportation of immigrants. It also leads Rosheuvel to assert, with a chuckle, as I kept pushing her to tell me how FFF defines families, "We don't define it any way. Particularly for folks who are migrants, the whole notion that there is a so-called normal family is an illusion anyway. . . . We try to get people to think about their lives outside of the context of how mainstream corporate media tells them what a successful family should be." Later in the interview, she reminded me that the daily struggles in the "private" sphere recounted in the *testimonios* arise from the lived experiences of FFF members in their racially and class-segregated neighborhoods. "Before the criminal justice system made their lives into a calamity," she pointed out, "they are, oftentimes, on the margins." Their social and economic marginalization, compounded by their overexposure to the threat of arrest as a result of where they live and work, creates a gulf between what society values as families and their daily practices of providing and caring for their kin. Just as FFF members' place of residence associates them with crime and exposes them to encounters with police, so too the urban blight in the same neighborhoods leads to a reorganization of the gendered division of labor. The circulation in the inner city of domesticating and disciplining notions post-welfare reform of good fathering (Curran and Abrams 2000) instructs us not to limit our understanding of poor and working-class masculinity as breadwinning but to extend it to caregiving that is reserved for middle-class men in dominant narratives. Migrant men's caregiving is an existential reality, an affectively potent quality, and a state-mediated expectation reserved for criminalized men who have to be rescued from their irresponsibility and pathological masculinity.

However, the "deportation nation" (Kanstroom 2007) undercuts this welfare state expectation by removing criminalized men from their children, sometimes indefinitely. Post-1996, immigration court judges can no longer exercise their discretion to cancel a removal order of migrants with a U.S. citizen or LPR spouse or children. The expulsion of the fathers, despite their publicly professed role as caregiver, puts into play national belonging and nonbelonging. The state requires formal U.S. citizenship in addition to heteronormativity to validate the spatial integrity of kinship arrangements. It renders those who forge kinship across immigration status illegible.

[. . .]

FFF's steadfast claim that "our *family* is valuable; our family deserves justice; our family should have access to relief and justice like any other family" rests on the recognition that as migrants of color, these families fall outside of racially marked familial arrangements that are deemed deserving of substantive national membership and rights. This assertion cannot be read simplistically as an appeal to heteronormativity. The stories of FFF members break out of the normative framework that values nuclear, law-abiding, self-sufficient, well-to-do U.S. citizen families, noncriminal migrants over criminal, and nonviolent crimes over violent ones.

[. . .]

References

American Civil Liberties Union. 2012. *ACLU Challenges Prison-Like Conditions at Hutto Detention Center*. Retrieved January 6, 2012 (www.aclu.org/immigrants-rights-racial-justice-prisoners-rights/aclu-challenges-prison-conditions-hutto-detention).

Beverley, John. 2004. *Testimonio*. Minneapolis, MN: University of Minnesota Press.

Buff, Rachel Ida. 2008. "The Deportation Terror." *American Quarterly* 60:523–51.

Cohen, Cathy. 2004. "Deviance as Resistance." *Du Bois Review* 1:27–45.

Curran, Laura and Laura Abrams. 2000. "Making Men into Dads." *Gender & Society* 14:662–78.

Ferguson, Roderick. 2004. *Aberrations in Black*. Minneapolis, MN: University of Minnesota Press.

Foley, Elise. 2011. "Obama Administration Sets Deportation Record." *Huffington Post*, October 18. Retrieved June 1, 2012 (www.huffingtonpost.com/2011/10/8/deportations-customs-remove-record-number_n_1018002.html).

Gee, Jennifer. 2003. "Housewives, Men's Villages, and Sexual Respectability." In *Asian/Pacific Islander Women*, edited by S. Hune and G. M. Nomura. New York: New York University Press.

Halberstam, Judith. 2005. *In a Queer Time and Place*. New York: New York University Press.

Hing, Bill Ong. 2006. *Deporting Our Souls*. New York: Cambridge University Press.

Human Rights Watch. 2009. *Detained and Dismissed*. New York: Human Rights Watch. Retrieved January 5, 2012 (www.hrw.org/reports/2009/03/16/detained-and-dismissed).

Immigrant Justice Network. 2013. *Analysis of S.744 Provisions Impacting Immigrants Accused or Convicted of Crimes*. Retrieved May 25, 2013 (www.ilrc.org/policy-advocacy/ immigrant-justice-network).

Immigration and Customs Enforcement. 2012. *Removal Statistics*. Retrieved December 28, 2012 (www. ice.gov/removal-statistics).

Jung, Moon-Kie. 2009. "The Racial Unconscious of Assimilation Theory." *Du Bois Review* 6:375–95.

Kanstroom, Daniel. 2007. *Deportation Nation*. Cambridge, MA: Harvard University Press.

Kremer, James D., Kathleen A. Moccio, and Joseph Hammell. 2009. *Severing a Lifeline*. Minneapolis, MN: Dorsey & Whitney LLP.

Lee, Erika. 2003. "Exclusion Acts." In *Asian/Pacific Islander Women*, edited by S. Hune and G. M. Nomura. New York: New York University Press.

Luibhéid, Eithne. 2004. "Heteronormativity and Immigration Scholarship." *GLQ* 10:227–35.

Manalansan, Martin F. 2006. "Queer Intersections." *International Migration Review* 40:224–49.

Massachusetts Immigrant and Refugee Advocacy Coalition. 2008. "New Bedford Immigration Raids." *MIRA Coalition*. Retrieved January 5, 2012 (http://web.archive.org/web/20090117191643/http://www.miracoalition.org/home/new-bedford-immigration-raids).

Morton, John. 2011. "Exercising Prosecutorial Discretion Consistent with the Civil Immigration Enforcement Priorities of the Agency for the Apprehension, Detention, and Removal of Aliens." Retrieved January 11, 2012 (www.ice.gov/doclib/secure-communities/pdf/ prosecutorial-discretion-memo.pdf).

National Council of La Raza. 2008. *Implications of Immigration Enforcement on America's Children: A Hearing on ICE Workplace Raids, U.S. House Representatives, 110th Congress*. Retrieved October 18, 2013 (www.nclr.org/images/uploads/publi-cations/52035_file_May_20_testimony_FINAL_1.pdf).

Ngai, Mae M. 2004. *Impossible Subjects*. Princeton, NJ: Princeton University Press.

Pallares, Amalia. 2010. "Representing 'la familia.'" In *¡Marcha!*, edited by A. Pallares and N. Flores-Gonzáles. Urbana, IL: University of Illinois Press.

Pierre, Jemima. 2004. "Black Immigrants in the United States and 'Cultural Narratives' of Ethnicity." *Identities* 11:141–70.

Schaffer, Kay and Sidonie Smith. 2004. *Human Rights and Narrated Lives*. New York: Palgrave Macmillan.

Shah, Nayan. 2011. *Stranger Intimacy*. Berkeley, CA: University of California Press.

Ting, Jennifer. 1995. "Bachelor Societies." In *Privileging Positions*, edited by M. Alquizola, D. F. Rony, W. K. Scott, and G. Y. Okihiro. Pullman: Washington State University Press.

Wessler, Seth. 2009. "Double Punishment." *Colorlines*. Retrieved January 12, 2012 (http://colorlines.com/archives/2009/10/double_punishment.html).

Brothers and Others

Organizing Masculinity,
Disorganizing Workers

Poulami Roychowdhury

© iStockphoto.com/400tmax

A midst the din of an especially well-attended organizing meeting for street vendors, voices called for "brotherhood." Members had gathered to plan a protest. The issue was fines. Having already organized several rallies to no avail, leaders within the organization were pushing for something more drastic. John, an energetic African American board member, rallied members around a 24-hour vigil. "This is it brothers! Let's show them what we're made of." Following John, a newly elected Egyptian board member, Hamid, continued to deploy the brotherly metaphor, exhorting members on the need for fraternal sacrifice. Despite such encouragement, a group of Bangladeshi and Senegalese vendors muttered discontentedly in one corner of the room. To them, the protest exemplified Vendors for Justice's (VFJ) failure to support their efforts at being stable breadwinners. In the end, such

Poulami Roychowdhury. 2014. "Brothers and Others: Organizing Masculinity, Disorganizing Workers." *Social Problems* 61(1):22–41.

reservations outweighed John and Hamid's motivational speeches. Instead of ratifying the protest, the Bangladeshis and Senegalese, two of the largest ethnic groups within the vending community, walked out of the meeting. The campaign imploded.

These interactions took place within the offices of VFJ, an organization that brings together street vendors in New York City. By invoking brotherhood, VFJ leaders John and Hamid were not only invoking familial bonds. They were actively constructing and recruiting members around a collective identity, a notion of masculinity linked to militancy and courage. Yet, their efforts failed. A number of men in the room simply walked out.

Why did this particular group of men fail to agree on a hegemonic masculine identity? How did their identity failures shape solidarity and mobilization? Gender scholars have long argued that hegemonic notions of masculinity help consolidate a sense of superiority among men by excluding women and subordinate men. In the context of social movement organizations these gendered exclusions ostensibly build solidarity among male workers. By conducting boundary work between "us" and "them," movement participants bond with each other and feel motivated to undertake collective risks. My research challenges this scholarship. I argue that the exclusionary processes inherent to collective gender identity formation can undermine hegemony and destabilize collective action, even for men.

The analysis presented here is based on data from ten months of participant observation and 30 semistructured interviews with members of a street vendors' organization in New York City that I call "Vendors for Justice" (VFJ). VFJ's members included a predominantly male, ethnically diverse, and occupationally segmented labor force. Attempting to unify its diverse base and overcome resource constraints, VFJ's leaders rallied members around a collective gendered identity of brotherhood. Despite their collective aspirations, organizers constructed brotherhood through a series of abjections, othering not only femininity but also alternative notions of masculinity that were salient for men within the organization. VFJ members espoused three distinct rhetorics around masculinity, each shaped by the intersection of gender, class, and ethnicity within their lives. Brotherhood selectively recognized two of these three rhetorics as legitimate forms of masculine comportment, sanctioning and censuring errant men. These exclusions rebounded on the organization, fracturing the very collectivity brotherhood was meant to create. Far from unifying members, the boundary work involved in creating a hegemonic masculinity alienated potential participants, further weakening an already unstable organizing climate.

This study highlights the limits organizations face in manipulating gender for institutional purposes. Social movements may fail to recruit believers when they construct gender in overly narrow or exclusive ways. These failures are more likely to occur within voluntary, resource-poor organizations like VFJ that have limited disciplinary powers over their membership base. Within this kind of organizational context discursive exclusions can easily have adverse effects, estranging members and rupturing solidarity.... Deploying masculinity does not always lend itself to hegemonic projects. Like femininity, masculinity may also be a frail and tenuous construction.

[...]

Methodology and Research Context

The analysis offered here is based on ten months of participant observation and 30 semistructured interviews with a racially heterogeneous and occupationally segmented labor force in New York City: street vendors. I used an extended case methodology to understand what the particularities of one organizational context revealed about existing theories of masculinity (Burawoy 1998)....

Operating out of a one-room office under the umbrella of a larger nonprofit, VFJ provided legal aid and policy advocacy for New York City's street vendors. VFJ clinics educated vendors about their legal rights, while organizing drives mobilized vendors against the state's regulatory practices. In addition, systemic advocacy raised awareness among both policy makers and the public about the important role of street vendors in the city.

[. . .]

For a period of ten months, I attended monthly board and bimonthly membership meetings at VFJ, and participated in VFJ's conferences with other state and civil society organizations. My ethnography covered VFJ's publicity and fundraising events, street demonstrations and protests, confrontations with the Green Market, and community board meetings. Every week, I volunteered part time at the VFJ office, and observed how members interacted with VFJ leaders, and with each other.

Participant observation was supplemented by 30 semistructured interviews, including all 11 board members, the executive director, 1 outside consultant, and 17 members. These interviews ran anywhere from one to four hours, and were either conducted over coffee, or at vendors' carts during off-peak hours. I questioned interviewees about their personal histories, and asked them to comment on VFJ and its leadership, including their notions of masculinity and how it relates to brotherhood. . . . In addition to participant observation and interviews, I read VFJ publications to learn more about the membership base.

[. . .]

Boundary Work: Constructing a Hegemonic Masculinity

A typical day at VFJ looked something like this: members dropped by to report tickets and police harassment, discussed protest strategies and fundraising ideas, and kept each other abreast of street closures and festivals. References to brotherhood were common in these relatively mundane exchanges. "Hey, what's up brother?" William, a long time African American member, welcomed Juan to a meeting. When Mohammed later interrupted Juan, Samuel cried out, "Hey, listen up. Our brother Juan here is trying to tell us something. Give the man some respect." During mock altercations between members, those who joined the fray tended to warn the opposing side in similar ways, "Hey step back, that's my brother you talking to!" Meanwhile, Yusuf, a young Egyptian vendor, tried to initiate a conversation with Amadou, a new Senegalese member: "Grab a chair, brother, no need to stay on your feet all day and night!" At the beginning of each membership meeting, Tyron, a long-time African American board member, opened by welcoming new brothers to the group.

While women comprised roughly 20 percent of VFJ's membership base, and three women served on its board, men in leadership positions envisioned brotherhood as a common identity that bridged ethnic and occupational differences between men. When I asked Samuel, VFJ's executive director, how members should ideally relate to one another, he argued that brotherhood could unite a heterogeneous membership base: "We have a lot pulling us apart: different languages, religion, race. Also, different kinds of vendors have different issues. So brotherhood can be a powerful thing. It brings everyone together." As one of the few white men in the organization, Samuel worried that linguistic and racial barriers prevented him from fully connecting with members. By referring to "different kinds of vendors" Samuel alluded to the challenges occupational segregation posed for collective unity.

For Samuel, brotherhood involved specific attributes. Addressing a membership meeting, Samuel fleshed out what he meant by the concept: "We are each other's brothers. That means we watch out for one another, and fight when needed. The city isn't going to pay attention to us unless we show a strong front." By alluding to a "strong front" and the necessity of fighting and "watching out for one another," Samuel marked brotherhood as a gendered category that involved distinctly masculine virtues associated with fraternity, equality, and militancy.

Echoing Samuel, a number of board members articulated brotherhood as a militant fraternity of equals. When I asked John, the African American board member whose calls for brotherhood opened this article, what brotherhood meant to him, he explained: "You got my back, I got yours. If someone's helping you out like a brother should, then you keep fighting the good fight." Likewise, Hamid, a newly elected Egyptian board member, talked about brotherhood by referencing equality and militancy. A tall, handsome man in his fifties, Hamid earned a comfortable income from two hot dog carts. Having introduced a large number of Egyptian vendors to VFJ, Hamid found it relatively easy to command attention. As a result, he frequently addressed membership meetings. Before one particular rally, Hamid attempted to motivate members:

> We cannot just think of ourselves. Think of all your brothers in this room. I hear someone say they have a bad leg and can't go, or their wife is sick. If we are to get anywhere, we all have to do things equal. Brothers fight for each other.

While John indirectly alluded to the relationship between equality and militancy, Hamid more directly connected these two concepts. Within Hamid's address, difference and inequality were compressed into one, and both threatened to undermine collective action.

By emphasizing equality and militancy as manly traits, brotherhood promised to counter the threats that men within the organization faced on the street and at home. Papa, a general vendor who illegally worked in midtown without a license, described how police harassment degraded his sense of manliness. "The police, they'll treat you like a criminal. Someday, we feel real low, hardly like a man." Meanwhile, Amjad, who worked seven days a week at his halal food cart in midtown, admitted that his job created tensions within his family: "My wife wants me to be home more. But how can I? I can tell she is disappointed. This isn't the right job for a man like me. The family I come from, I should have become a doctor. Instead I am on the street." Acutely sensing the relationship between work and masculinity, Amjad articulated how his job on the street made him look like the wrong kind of man to his family. Lacking the professional credentials and status that go along with medicine, Amjad strove to inform his work with a sense of professionalism by donning a chef's hat and an immaculately starched apron. These practices were not just marketing tools, but also a means of recuperating a sense of masculine pride.

[. . .]

Brotherhood within VFJ thus ostensibly functioned in the way collective identities work within a range of social movements, redefining personal experiences in terms of collective grievances (Melucci 2003; Taylor and Whittier 1999). As noted by existing scholarship, gendered identifications within social movements often arise within a crisis of masculinity, and VFJ is no different (Maynard 1989). Brotherhood took men who felt belittled by their experiences at work and helped them learn how to be "strong," independent, and "fight the good fight."

While brotherhood thus served as a promise for otherwise marginalized men, it was constructed through the systematic exclusion and silencing of women. Women were excluded from the boundaries of brotherhood at critical organizational events. Hamid entered the April board meeting late and everyone turned to shake his hand, while Samuel filled him in on the proceedings. Triunfa came in shortly after Hamid, but nobody acknowledged her entrance. The difference in reception was notable given that Triunfa had been a board member longer than Hamid, and continuously demonstrated her dedication to the organization by staying late after meetings to do photocopying and cleanup.

Like Triunfa, other women within the organization felt the effects of exclusion. When Jane, a long-term board member, got run over by a taxi and stopped attending meetings, her inactivity largely went unnoticed. Contrast the board's response to Jane's injuries with Darren's a month later. When Darren, a retired soldier, fell and twisted his bad ankle, Samuel immediately brought his injuries to everyone's attention. A number of other board members, including Fallou, a wealthy Senegalese vendor, suggested that VFJ should "help a brother in need." I was surprised that so much effort was put into ensuring Darren's return since he had never struck me as especially hard working. Meanwhile, Jane always took on the responsibility of reminding members about upcoming meetings, and single-handedly organized VFJ's holiday fundraiser. Despite my assessment of their relative merits, Darren was promptly sent a $250 check along with a fruit basket, while Jane languished in the hospital unattended.

These more overt exclusions punctuated a day-to-day environment where women and women's contributions went unacknowledged. Men frequently occupied the center of the office, their conversations volubly impinging on anybody who walked by. Women rarely talked publicly. Their conversations were housed in nooks and crannies, in front of the drinking fountain, next to the copy machine. The spatial centrality of men's voices and interpersonal relations was no coincidence. Their voice was an artifact of an organizational culture that gave precedence to particular bodies and gendered practices. These exchanges attempted to establish brotherhood as the hegemonic model for masculine comportment within the organization, using boundary work between men and women to recruit men's allegiance.

[. . .]

Interpretive Disagreements: Masculinity as an Intersectional Category

Using overt boundary work between men and women, brotherhood promised to unify men under a hegemonic notion of masculinity connected to equality and militancy. In reality, the category was far from universally appealing. Members responded to brotherhood through three disparate notions of masculinity, shaped by the intersections of gender, class, and ethnicity within their lives. By emphasizing equality and militancy, brotherhood did not appeal to those who interpreted manhood through alternative tropes of familial responsibility and mutual care.

Conversations about brotherhood quickly morphed into discussions of masculinity at large. Tyron, the long-standing African American board member who always opened membership meetings by welcoming new brothers to the fold, was a well-educated, financially successful art vendor. During a long interview at his cart in Harlem, I began to understand how Tyron's approach to brotherhood was shaped by his larger anxieties about masculine conduct. Discussing his training in civil rights and the student movement of the sixties, Tyron explained:

For black men in this country, it used be that you were a boy. Well now, you have the option of being a man, of being equal to any other man. But how do you get there? You got to have some support, but the kind that raises you up. Not the kind that makes you dependent.

In this conceptualization, masculinity is situated within the racialized history of the United States, where black men were treated as boys. Dependency emerges as a critical threat to manhood, and equality its counterpoint. When Tyron argued that men needed "support," he conceptualized an organizational vision for VFJ as an institution that could help men be men by treating them equally. In his actions towards other men in the organization, Tyron was soft-spoken, always polite, and never domineering. In turn, he rarely accepted excuses for missed meetings, asking everyone to participate equally in the organization's success.

Tyron's vision of masculinity as equality existed alongside a second conceptualization of masculinity that floated around VFJ. This notion of masculinity highlighted militancy and aggression. Khaled, an Egyptian vendor who ran a successful Halal food cart, expressed disdain for men who refused to join a protest against fine increases. When I wondered if an alternative strategy would have won more votes, Khaled dismissed my reasoning as misguided. For Khaled, the real problem was that some men were "cowardly," while others were not. "Cowards" always found some kind of excuse, backing out at the last minute: "Some people are weak. They get scared by cold weather. If you're strong, this is no problem. You are always ready to join." Given that some men were simply cowardly, Khaled believed that VFJ needed to forge ahead with whatever strategy the leadership felt was best. In a membership meeting, Khaled took the floor to say as much, confirming that brotherhood involved a community of "strong" men. A group of young Egyptian vendors cheered Khaled's speech. Winking at Stacy and me, the youngest women in the room, they enthusiastically added their names to the rally sign-up sheet while circling the room exuding a sense of virile militancy.

Together, Tyron and Khaled articulated notions of masculinity that mapped on to the internal components of brotherhood. But VFJ also housed a third discourse of masculinity, one that emphasized alternative values of familial responsibility and mutual care. This third interpretation was apparent in a series of statements. Ibrahim, a Senegalese vendor who sold purses in midtown, described his commitments as a husband and father. "Everything I got goes to my wife. I have two children." Likewise, Kumar, a South Indian vendor, admitted that he frequently felt exhausted and disheartened by his occupation, but forced himself to keep going because it was his responsibility as a breadwinner.

These men's alternative rhetoric about masculinity shaped their responses to brotherhood. During our conversation at his fruit and vegetable cart, Farid, a Bangladeshi man in his mid-fifties, argued that brotherhood involved financial responsibility.

> In our country, a brother is someone who takes care of you. I had no brother of my own, so these two boys I grew up with, they were my brothers. They even helped me raise money for my sister's wedding. . . . Boys in our village were just that way. You know how it is, we were raised to feel responsible for our families, and we all did projects around the village. There was a real communal spirit.

Farid began answering my question about brotherhood by strictly talking about brothers as financial providers. His vision of brotherhood, however, was based on a more generalized picture of how boys "were" and "were raised," about the normative dimensions of masculinity at large. Like Ibrahim and Kumar, Farid understood manhood as financial responsibility and mutual care, not only towards one's family but also to the larger community. . . .

One board member went so far as to try and incorporate these alternative elements into the brotherhood promoted at VFJ. Anwar, a Bangladeshi board member who sold hot dogs in front of Ground Zero, staunchly believed that VFJ needed to do more to take care of its neediest members. Arguing that organizing by itself would not protect vendors who were facing financial collapse, Anwar initiated an "Emergency Fund." Towards the end of each meeting, members were asked to voluntarily donate as much as they wanted to the fund, which would then be made available to anyone who needed immediate financial assistance.

But Anwar's attempts to transform brotherhood were overwhelmed by other leaders' concerted efforts to limit the identity to equality and militancy. As a result, the discourse of masculinity as familial responsibility and mutual care frequently came into conflict with brotherhood, challenging its commitments. At the end of a discussion about future protest strategies, I trailed a group of Senegalese vendors out of the office on to the subway. Once out of earshot of VFJ leaders, several of them admitted feeling uncomfortable with the protest, arguing that it might threaten their ability to earn a stable income. Moussa, a middle-aged man with three children and a stay-at-home wife, asked the following question: "Tell me, if I have to do something that harms my family, should I do it?" At that particular moment, Moussa felt he had to choose between two contradictory notions of masculinity: the hegemonic model put forward by VFJ under the rubric of brotherhood and his own conceptualization of himself as a good husband and father.

[. . .]

Members ascribed to three distinct notions of masculinity, only two of which were articulated within brotherhood. Ignoring the way masculinity is an intersectional category, VFJ leaders continued to pursue their hegemonic project, failing to see how intersectional identities could shape conflicting responses to brotherhood. Despite such denial, members' cultural backgrounds and material realities shaped how they normatively approached brotherhood, spelling an ongoing battle between men about what it meant to be a man.

Organizational Disruptions: From Exclusion to Alienation and Disunity

By excluding those who connected masculinity to familial responsibility and care and insisting on brotherhood instead, VFJ's leaders undermined their own collective aspirations. Brotherhood disrupted solidarity in three key ways. First, and least surprisingly, it alienated women, depriving the organization of their input. Second, it alienated men, by making VFJ leaders look insensitive and myopic. Last, it fueled contestation and enmity between those who remained, silencing alternative organizing strategies that may have appealed to a broader base.

As much of the existing literature on hegemonic masculinity would predict, brotherhood systematically excluded women. All three of the women who served on the board during my time at VFJ left the organization, complaining of feeling ignored and slighted. When I visited Jane after she was run over by a taxi, she bitterly commented that VFJ had forgotten about her when she needed the organization the most. She explained, "Nobody wants to keep working without getting the recognition they deserve." Shortly after Jane's departure, Stacy withdrew from the board. She told me privately that she felt pushed into doing work for men in the organization who claimed the credit. She specifically sighted Anwar's pet project, the Emergency Fund, as something she had been forced into managing. Triunfa was the last of the women to leave. Before her departure, she mentioned that she no longer felt her presence was needed at VFJ. I interpreted Triunfa's feelings of uselessness to be integrally connected to the organization's singular lack of recognition of her contributions.

These women's departures exacted serious costs on the organization. Triunfa had helped grease the day-to-day activities at VFJ, voluntarily cleaning the office, making photocopies, and notifying members of upcoming meetings. After she left, many of these duties were neglected, and members regularly complained about not being notified about meetings. Stacy's departure signaled a halt to VFJ's mediation with the Times Square Alliance. A network of businesses that had historically been hostile to street vendors, the Alliance had been inching towards more progressive policies through meetings with VFJ board members. This relationship unraveled after Stacy left. While Triunfa's exit took a toll on daily life at VFJ and Stacy's departure jeopardized external relationships, Jane's withdrawal from the organization rang the death knell of that year's holiday fundraising season. Before her accident, Jane had designed a plan to raise money by selling tins full of candied nuts. When she withdrew from the board, nobody took over the project. Stacked in the corner of the office, the empty tins made a hollow clanging sound when anybody accidentally bumped into them.

Brotherhood not only alienated women, but also made the organization appear ineffectual to particular men. Ibrahim, the Senegalese vendor who highlighted his commitments to his family, characterized brotherhood as a fictitious category with little relevance to his life. Explaining why he did not wish to participate in VFJ protests, Ibrahim directly critiqued brotherhood for setting up unrealistic expectations: "They say we brothers. But what it mean? They say do this, do that, but how can I do? I don't got no license." Referencing the third notion of masculinity that was prevalent at VFJ, a notion of manhood connected to familial obligations, Ibrahim argued that his first priority was being a stable breadwinner. To the extent that brotherhood threatened that stability by putting him in risky situations during protests, Ibrahim rejected the identity and the organizational context that demanded such action.

Like Ibrahim, Mohit, a Bangladeshi vendor in his late thirties, critiqued brotherhood for insisting on equality, while ignoring real material differences between men. Not owning his own cart, Mohit eked out a meager living by working part time at other vendors' carts throughout the city. A long-term member of VFJ, Mohit expressed little interest in being brothers with relatively affluent men in the organization:

> He [Samuel] tells me we are brothers and that we are the same. How can we be the same? He's a lawyer! I'm a poor man from Sylhet [a district in Bangladesh]. He doesn't have a family. I have to think of my mother. My brothers are still in school.

Mohit identified himself as a brother, but pointed out that his real brothers were back in Bangladesh. Pretending to be Samuel's brother only occluded the vast class differences that divided them.

Critiquing VFJ's insistence on militancy, Mohit went on to complain that VFJ didn't "really do anything" for its members:

> There are other organizations that help vendors secure spots [on the street]. They even give their members loans to buy carts. These guys [VFJ] don't do any of that. What good does it do to always be protesting and organizing strikes?

Mohit gestured at the ways brotherhood ignored his most immediate material interests: attaining his own cart and securing a spot. Linking VFJ's discursive commitments to its institutional practices, Mohit rationalized his decision to stop attending organizational events. Samuel lamented Mohit's absence because he had once been an active member. Unfortunately, Samuel blamed Mohit's disappearance on his "bad attitude," ignoring the substantial ways brotherhood had failed to address Mohit's daily challenges.

Finally, brotherhood disrupted unity by breeding constant conflict between men. Tensions erupted within the office whenever either component of brotherhood, equality or militancy, were threatened. During the course of my research, a group of Bangladeshi vendors vocally advocated for a service that would help members pay fines. The campaign was unsurprising given Bangladeshi vendors' tendency to emphasize financial responsibility as a key tenet of masculinity. Before his departure from VFJ, Mohit played a central role within the movement. VFJ leaders, however, were clearly uncomfortable with the service. Anxious about preserving "equality" between men, Tyron feared that fine reimbursements would introduce distinctions between members. Meanwhile, John worried that reimbursements would undermine militancy, transforming VFJ into a service organization and making members into clients. While financial responsibility and mutual care were positive markers of manhood for men like Mohit, these practices threatened the masculine boundaries of brotherhood as defined by the organization. In the end, the voices of board members like John and Tyron overruled Mohit's.

Financial "dependence" posed such a threat to brotherhood, it bred hostility between board members. When Anwar first initiated the Emergency Fund, VFJ's other leaders seemed supportive. But as the fund grew through generous contributions from members, the board was unable to agree on when or who to distribute it to. Many board members worried it might "send the wrong signal," indicating that VFJ would bail out irresponsible vendors at any given moment. Anwar was incensed by the blockade, making several attempts to have the funds released. By the end of my eight months at VFJ, Anwar's earlier enthusiasm about the organization had visibly diminished and the fund remained undisbursed.

Brotherhood not only caused conflict by denying members' financial needs, but also by demanding that men engage in perilous practices. Amadou's expulsion from the organization provided a stark example of the way brotherhood alienated men by placing them at risk while casting them as cowardly when they rebelled. Amadou's estrangement began with an attempt to organize a protest in front of city hall. The "24-hour vigil," which involved rotating shifts of two vendors for an indefinite period of time, intended to force the mayor to reassess the city's fine structure. Despite VFJ leaders' attempts to rally members under the banner of brotherhood during the organizing meeting, Bangladeshi and Senegalese vendors defected from the campaign.

Amadou, a new board member, made the mistake of publicly agreeing with the Bangladeshis and Senegalese. Two days later, he became the focus of an emergency board meeting. Samuel opened the meeting by addressing Amadou in a seemingly apologetic, but largely accusatory fashion.

I lost my temper. But you know who I was mad at? I was mad at you [Amadou]. You were supposed to be leading your Senegalese brothers, but you said you didn't want to fight. You were afraid! If a board member is afraid, all our brothers are going to be afraid too.

By framing Amadou as "afraid," Samuel bypassed the real issue: that Amadou simply disagreed with the adopted strategy, not necessarily with the idea of direct action itself.

Responding to Samuel, Amadou reasoned that the campaign would have created a high-risk situation by isolating shifts of two people. In essence, VFJ was asking individual members to protest without the strength of a group behind them: "You out there at night by yourself. Maybe the police come and lock you up. You never know. They take your stuff and lock you up."

Amadou's personal experiences revealed that the police could and did behave in arbitrary ways. The previous year, Amadou had been arrested when he tried to document police harassment by taking a photograph. The police had handcuffed him, citing New York's post-9/11 anti-terrorist laws. After spending a night in jail and losing a portion of his savings on bail, Amadou remained concerned about individual forms of protest.

While Amadou tried to communicate his reservations about the particular strategy involved, his remarks were chided as "unbrotherly" by a number of board members. John remarked, "brothers don't sell each other out like that," intimating that Amadou had betrayed the brotherhood through his dissent. In a more gentle tone, Cisse reasoned that the board had to set an example of the "bonds that united them." When Amadou rose from his chair to leave, other men on the board agreed that the organization would be better off without him. That was the last time anybody saw Amadou at VFJ.

Amadou's expulsion from the board cost the organization more than a board member. Amadou had served as a contact point between VFJ and other West African vendors on his block. When he dropped out of the organization, these men followed suit. More fundamentally, Amadou's expulsion took place within a context where his voice was not the only one to be silenced. The 24-hour vigil fell apart because those who insisted on equality and militancy refused to accommodate other men's concerns. Instead, these concerns were classified as cowardly and summarily rejected for being unbefitting to brotherly conduct.

A similar set of events transpired a few months after Amadou left. Once again, VFJ leaders' insistence on brotherhood fueled tension between men within the organization. This time, conflict erupted after the board attempted to resuscitate the aborted 24-hour vigil. Despite the earlier skirmish with Amadou and opposition from Bangladeshis and Senegalese, the particularities of the campaign strategy remained unchanged. The plan was, once again, to hold an around-the-clock vigil with rotating shifts of two vendors. Only the venue had changed. Instead of city hall, the vigil would now take place in front of the mayor's house.

A number of Bangladeshi members immediately voiced opposition. Given that it was now the dead of winter, they were reluctant to support a strategy that would expose participants to sub-zero nightly temperatures. Ali, a young and energetic vendor who worked near Canal Street, spoke on behalf of other Bangladeshis. Ali's questions were immediately cut short. "Why don't you just admit you're afraid man?" Darren aggressively asked him. The retired soldier who had been sent a $250 check after twisting his knee, Darren frequently played a key role in policing the boundaries of brotherhood. VFJ's other leaders rarely silenced him, profitably using his intimidation tactics to contain dissenting men. When Ali did not answer, John joined in, chastising him. "Listen this strategy takes guts. You've got to step up to the plate, brother, know what I mean?" Ali sat down and did not speak for the rest of the meeting. A patchy schedule was drawn up for the vigil as members were forced to sign their names to eight-hour shifts.

Before he voiced reservations about the campaign, other men in the organization had commended Ali for his dynamism. When I talked to Ali on the way out of the meeting, he expressed dismay about the way he had been treated at VFJ: "I don't agree with them, so I'm afraid? They say we're brothers, but it's like having a bad brother—the kind that hits you when you do something he doesn't like!" Ali questioned the boundaries of brotherhood. In the process of forming a collectivity, men at VFJ exerted punitive sanctions on other men.

Once again, VFJ's leaders ignored dissent, barreling ahead with their own strategy while rationalizing their choices through a discourse of brotherhood. The night before the protest, everything once again fell apart. The first two shifts, manned largely by Bangladeshi vendors, had withdrawn from the protest. By nine the next morning, I was sitting in Samuel's studio apartment with a small number of demoralized board members. Amadou and Jane had already left the organization by this point. Triunfa and Stacy were on their way out. The remaining board members desperately brainstormed next steps. Without the first two shifts, the 24-hour vigil could hardly get under way. In the end, a bedraggled and confused group walked to the mayor's house to deliver a giant sheet cake with "Please remember us" scrawled in pink loopy letters across the top. The cake failed to make it past the doorman and ended up collecting raindrops as it waited inspection for traces of poison.

Amadou's and Ali's interactions with the organization signal the ways brotherhood not only undermined solidarity by breeding conflict between men, but more broadly created an organizational culture where certain strategies were deemed more masculine despite their strategic value. Instead of recruiting members' allegiance, brotherhood necessitated a series of exclusions that undermined collective identity formation and the solidarity it was intended to create.

Conclusion

[...]

This article has worked through a negative case, analyzing what happens to organizations when notions of masculinity remain relatively rigid and exclusionary. Things may have turned out differently at VFJ if its leaders had incorporated notions of masculine responsibility and care into the rhetoric of brotherhood. An expansive discursive strategy may have helped the organization forge alternative protest strategies and stemmed the rounds of recriminations aimed at members who failed to live up to brotherhood's masculine ideals. This revamped form of brotherhood may have continued to exclude the minority group of women within the organization, but could have proven to be more hegemonic among men, partially living up to the collective potentials for which it was envisioned. To achieve this alternative, VFJ would have had to restructure itself: creating greater opportunities for less privileged vendors to rise the ranks to leadership positions, and institutionalizing new forms of decision making where members had greater voice in movement strategies.

VFJ members faced numerous obstacles to collective action. They were impoverished, over-regulated, and ethnically and occupationally segregated. The promise of a collective identity lay in creating some semblance of unity in the face of all these challenges. Unfortunately, VFJ's discursive choices further aggravated divisions within its membership base, pushing women away and denigrating the concerns and travails of less privileged men. Counter to existing thought on manhood and masculinity, VFJ's story provides a possible explanation for some of the internal dynamics that render hegemonic masculinity a frail and unstable achievement.

References

Burawoy, M. 1998. "The Extended Case Method." *Sociological Theory* 16:4–33.

Maynard, Steven. 1989. "Rough Work and Rugged Men." *Labour/Le Travail* 23:159–69.

Melucci, Alberto. 2003. "The Process of Collective Identity." Pp. 41–63 in *Social Movements and Culture*, edited by H. Johnston and B. Klandermans. New York: Routledge.

Taylor, Verta and Nancy E. Whittier. 1999. "Collective Identity in Social Movement Communities." Pp. 169–94 in *Waves of Protest*, edited by J. Freeman and V. Johnson. Boston, MA: Rowman & Littlefield.

Patriarchal Accommodations

Women's Mobility and Policies of Gender Difference From Urban Iran to Migrant Mexico

Abigail Andrews and Nazanin Shahrokni

In the final decades of the twentieth century, women in the developing world increasingly went "on the move." In areas where mobility at various scales had long been marked as masculine, and where femininity had been associated with fixity, passivity, and the private sphere (Uteng and Cresswell 2008), women started working, studying, and consuming outside the home. As they entered the public arena, local definitions of what was considered "appropriately" feminine also changed.

In some places, perhaps unexpectedly, the expansion of women's mobility coincided with the local government's *reinforcement* of patriarchal public policies—policies, that is, which overtly marked men and women as different, often with reference to "traditional" gender roles. Most scholarship on gender and globalization attributes the growth in women's movement to global economic pressure and—in conjunction—to the spread of egalitarian (Western) gender norms. Therefore, one might expect patriarchal local policies to limit women's autonomy and, in turn, their mobility. Nevertheless, the cases we examine here complicate that story: in the city of Tehran, Iran, women became the majority of public bus riders, just as the city government instituted gender segregation in public transportation. Half a world away, women of the small Mexican village of San Pedro came to predominate among emigrants to the United States, even as the community government codified their exclusion from political participation. Based on these two cases, we examine how patriarchal policies may facilitate the expansion of female mobility in unexpected ways.

[. . .]

Abigail Andrews and Nazanin Shahrokni. 2014. "Patriarchal Accommodations: Women's Mobility and Policies of Gender Difference From Urban Iran to Migrant Mexico." *Journal of Contemporary Ethnography* 43(2):148–75.

We approach this question using what we refer to as linked ethnographies. In an effort to understand the complex, interconnected, local instantiations of global processes, this method puts two in-depth ethnographic studies into dialogue with each other. On one hand, each ethnographer examined the geographically and historically situated process by which women's mobility grew, in a distinct arena (transportation or migration) and in a particular place (Tehran, Iran, or San Pedro, Mexico). In each case, the ethnographer conducted interviews, archival research, and participant observation. Then, to illuminate the unique features of each site as well as their analytical parallels, we put them into conversation across regions.

Through the interconnections between these cases, we trace a similar process: starting in the 1980s, economic liberalization pressured women of Tehran and San Pedro—like many across the world—to work, study, and consume. These practices threatened the boundaries of public and private that had once demarcated male and female, respectively. In response, while purportedly recurring to "tradition," both Tehran and San Pedro re-drew the boundaries of masculinity and femininity. Rather than doing away with unequal gender regimes centered on female modesty or on a male–female division of labor, they extended these "traditional" gender divisions to new forms of mobility. Tehran did so by gender-segregating public space; San Pedro by excluding women from local political responsibilities and thus, de facto, turning them into migrant breadwinners. So doing, both these institutions and their constituents adapted local, gender-differentiated frameworks to accommodate new practices of movement.

We call these policies "patriarchal accommodations." They were patriarchal, because they formally enshrined gender differences associated with male dominance. And, they were accommodations, because, pursuant to the demands of a global economy, they provided space for new forms of female mobility *within* existing standards of "appropriate" masculinity and femininity.

We argue that patriarchal accommodations facilitated women's increased presence as riders on Tehran buses and as emigrants from San Pedro to the United States. They did so because they made it possible for men and women to adapt to the shifting global political economy without violating a gender order that differentiated between them. Women favored these policies, because they could work, study, and consume—but also remain "proper" women. It is beyond the scope of this paper to evaluate whether, on balance, such policies harmed or benefited women. Rather, recognizing the ambivalent effects of gender differences, we focus on extending scholarly understanding of *how*—that is, by what mechanisms—the relationships between femininity, masculinity, and mobility get remade.

[. . .]

Methodology

[. . .]

On one hand, Tehran, the capital city of the Islamic Republic of Iran, is a metropolis of more than twelve million people (Bayat 2010). San Pedro, meanwhile, is a corn-farming village of two thousand people in Southern Mexico. Nevertheless, both were hard-hit in the 1980s and 1990s by neoliberal globalization: Tehran because of the Iran–Iraq War in the 1980s and subsequent market-oriented reforms, and San Pedro because of structural adjustment and North American economic integration.

Furthermore, the institutions we examine—that is, Tehran's bus system and San Pedro's local government—both instituted prime examples of patriarchal policies. Gender segregation is common in the Islamic Republic of Iran, where it covers a wide range of spaces, such as universities, parks, and beaches; we focus on busing in particular, because it was one of the first areas in which Tehran implemented gender segregation and because it affects women across different social classes. Meanwhile, in San Pedro the community government is unusually patriarchal compared to other parts of Mexico—along with those of other, similar villages. As an indigenous community, San Pedro has the right to autonomous self-government. This gives the village the legal right to consider men the political representatives of their female relatives and exclude women from politics. We look at each of these institutions as unique illustrations of the convergence of patriarchal policy and economic globalization, rather than as representative of Iran or Mexico as a whole.

[. . .]

In Tehran, Shahrokni conducted sixteen months of ethnographic research between 2009 and 2011. She rode three bus lines as a participant observer, one connecting the city North–South, one East–West, and one women-only route downtown. . . .

Second, Shahrokni conducted fifty-three informal and seventeen formal interviews with female passengers ranging from age eighteen to seventy-one, whom she recruited using convenience samples during her bus rides. . . .

Finally, Shahrokni reviewed 453 newspaper clippings and government documents on gender segregation from 1979 to 2010 and interviewed twelve city and government officials (two in the bus organization, three city councilors, two deputy mayors, four members of parliament, and one former governor of Tehran). These data allowed her to trace the shift from predominantly male to female bus ridership and the development of the state's gender-segregated busing policy. The archival study and interviews with bureaucrats showed the reorganization of public transportation in Tehran, illustrating how city officials had tried to regulate women's movements but also to accommodate their access to work, education, and consumption.

[. . .]

Meanwhile, in San Pedro, Andrews conducted ten months of participant observation, fifty-two interviews with key informants, a household survey, and archival research. Between 2009 and 2011, Andrews lived as a participant observer for five months in the sending community and five among migrants in Los Angeles. While living with villagers (and then migrants), she observed and took detailed field notes on the ways men and women talked about masculine and feminine roles in relation to political participation and migration, seeking to understand how the village's exclusion of women from local governance restructured gender roles.

Then, Andrews conducted fifty-two in-depth interviews. First, she interviewed ten male community leaders about the gender dimensions of political participation and how decisions were made to exclude or include women. Second, she interviewed forty-two male and female migrants and nonmigrants about how they understood women's and men's roles in politics and migration. . . . Approximately sixty percent of respondents were women and forty percent were men. Half of the respondents had migrated to the United States, and half remained in the sending village. . . .

In conjunction, Andrews conducted a random-sample household survey in San Pedro to illustrate how the gender composition of migration shifted over time. The survey sampled every third household in the village ($n = 121$) and randomly selected a member age fifteen to sixty-five. It gathered data on the histories of 562 migrant family members, examining who migrated and when by gender. It also asked about each family's history of political participation. Finally, this survey provided contact information for family members in the United States, allowing Andrews to conduct a snowball survey of migrants from San Pedro in Los Angeles ($n = 51$).

[. . .]

Tehran and Women's Growing Presence on Public Transportation

Since it began, the Islamic Republic of Iran has emphasized gender difference. Upon its establishment in 1979, the Islamic Republic sought to reconfigure, or in its words, "Islamize" what it considered the "Westoxicated" social order of the previous regime. Women were central to this project. The newly established state revoked laws in favor of women's (liberal) rights, such as the Family Protection Laws of 1967 and 1975 and instead emphasized the complementarity of the sexes and urged women's domesticity and family attachments, instead of work. Consequently, public space was framed as the domain of male breadwinners (Moghadam 1988), and women's presence in public was conditioned upon their donning the veil (Moallem 2005).

In the early 1980s, because of the crowding of public transportation, women's bus ridership was among the practices that the newly established state claimed undermined the "Islamic" public order. . . . While women have been driving in Iran since the 1940s, car ownership was mostly limited to upper-class men. Thus, women, especially of the popular classes, had to rely on public transportation for their commutes. Once established, the Islamic Republic of Iran promised to improve and expand public services, including public transportation. Yet, because of the lack of infrastructure, population growth, and the influx of refugees from the Iran–Iraq war of 1980–1988—all worsened by U.S.-imposed economic sanctions on Iran—public buses were gravely overcrowded. People had to wait in long lines before they could get on a bus, and once on, they were, in the words of several interviewees, "sandwiched by other passengers." The buses looked like "sardine cans," recalled Jaleh, a sixty-eight-year-old retired nurse, and women felt like "sheep being herded into a small space" *(Zan-e Rooz,* November 17, 1984). The crowding allegedly made bus ridership an un-Islamic practice, since in Islam physical contact between unrelated men and women is *haram* (religiously forbidden).

To reinforce the "Islamic" public order, the Islamic Republic of Iran instituted gender segregation policies across the country. In Tehran, busing was one of the first targets, with segregation implemented by the United Bus Company of Tehran (UBCT). The UBCT announced that they had "resolved to implement the gender segregation plan inside the buses to respect the holy boundaries [between the two genders] and to promote appropriate Islamic ethics" *(Zan-e Rooz,* December 23, 1991). To regulate women's movements in public, observe Islamic gender norms, and reduce women's contact with male bus-riders, the UBCT divided bus space into a smaller "women's section" at the back (one-third of the bus) and a more spacious "men's section" in front. The women's section started where the men's section ended. The border was made visible by a metal divider bar.

Meanwhile, in the 1980s and 1990s, downward economic pressure on Iranian families drove increasing numbers of women into the spaces of work, education, and consumption. First, Iran's war with Iraq from 1980 to 1988 compelled women to work. As tens of thousands of men were killed or disabled at war, the number of female-headed households rose. Women household heads were forced to do public tasks or earn income on their own, outside the home. Then, when the Iran–Iraq war ended in 1988, the government of then-President Rafsanjani (1989–1997) began to embrace free-market economic principles. Inspired by World Bank structural adjustment policies, Rafsanjani sought to integrate Iran into the global economy. His government drafted the First Development Plan (1989–1993), which, among other things, aimed at activating the industrial sector and partially privatizing some of the state organizations (Shaditalab 2005). The marriage between "Islamic fundamentalism and market fundamentalism" drove down male wages, leading to an increased demand for women's employment (Bahramitash 2003).

These policy shifts brought more women out into jobs and schools. As Kurzman (2008) indicates, from the 1980s to 1990s, women's labor force participation in Iran rose by a third, and, similar to patterns throughout the Middle East, women's share of public and service sector employment increased rapidly (though women continued to work at a lower rate than men). In 1976—three years prior to the establishment of the Islamic Republic—70 percent of Iranian women were "housewives." By 1996, this number had declined to 59 percent, suggesting that more women were now working (Shaditalab 2005). Also, economic development, state expansion, and oil wealth gave women greater access to education. By 2006, Iranian women outnumbered men both in secondary and tertiary education (*The Report on Women's Situation* 2006).

In this context, bus segregation operated as a patriarchal accommodation. On one hand, it extended gender difference; on the other, it provided the conditions for women, who were hesitant to ride "mixed" public transportation for religious or safety reasons, to adapt to these broader political and economic shifts. Most Iranian women—including both those who were religiously observant and those who were secular—welcomed the gender separation on buses. Often, religiously observant women worried about their purity, and gender-segregated buses enabled them to observe religious norms that forbid male–female contact. Meanwhile, many secular women were concerned about a comfortable, harassment-free ride. For instance, in a 1981 letter to the editor of *Zan-e Rooz,* an Iranian women's magazine, a secular woman named Parivash wrote, "As a woman I cannot bear the idea of standing in close physical contact with these men, brothers, or comrades." She explained that men, whether "brothers" (Islamists) or "comrades" (secular leftists), continued to harass women on the buses, emphasizing that for her, discomfort had nothing to do with religious ethics *(Zan-e Rooz,* June 20, 1981).

Ironically, by providing a religiously appropriate and safe space for women in the public sphere, segregation facilitated their mobility across the city (see also Amir-Ebrahimi 2006). The separate bus space also removed the hassle of competition with men over space. While waiting for buses, riders had previously jostled for position rather than waiting in line. In a 2009 interview with Shahrokni, Zahra Nouri, one of the (female) deputy mayors of Tehran, reflected:

> Under these circumstances, the gender segregation plan came as a blessing. Women have to make sure that their chador [full-body cloak] or headscarf is not falling off. Sometimes they carry a bag, a bunch of books, or their grocery shopping, or a child or even two. It is difficult to compete with men. So, even though the initial planners of gender segregation did not have this in mind, what I find significant is that with segregation women had to compete [only] with women, and *that* was a blessing!

The women's section provided women with an area that they saw as not only religiously respectable but also safer and more comfortable. For instance, Masoomeh, a forty-three-year-old housewife, recounted, "Of course! It [gender segregation] not only made our commute possible but actually made it much easier. Who likes to be rubbed by men on a twenty-minute bus ride? Look what happens in [collective] taxis! When you sit in between two men in the back seat you constantly have to remind them not to lean over you, not to touch you!" Without men in their section, women could avoid being touched, both for personal safety and for religious purity.

Segregation not only made women feel more comfortable but also, as political economic pressures grew, enabled them to adapt to new demands. For example, Neda, a forty-year-old respondent who worked as a bank clerk, explained that her capacity to work relied on her mother's ability to use public transit. Before bus segregation, Neda told Shahrokni, her mother, who rarely talked to men except, in Neda's words, "the bakers and the grocers, who are not strangers," was confined within the house and only went out with her husband or in a relative's car. Neda added, "My father is very strict. He had made it clear that he did not want to see my mother going out of the house alone. He used to tell us that the streets of Tehran are full of wolves. Men like himself, I suppose!" Nevertheless, Neda needed a job, and in order to work she needed her mother's help in caring for her two small children. She said, "I'm married and have two children. I can't afford childcare, so if my mother did not assist me in raising my kids, I probably would have had to quit my job and stay home." The patriarchal accommodation of gender-segregation made it possible for women like Neda and her mother to feel comfortable and proper riding buses and for men like Neda's father to permit this movement. Because Neda's mother and father trust the gender-segregated buses, today, Neda rides one bus to her job at a downtown bank while her mother takes another bus to Neda's home to help with childcare.

[. . .]

The consequences of the UBCT's patriarchal accommodation were that by the mid-1990s far more women rode buses; furthermore, they developed a sense of entitlement to the women's section, demanding even more segregated bus space. Bus segregation and women's increasing presence in public space fueled each other. Thanks to segregation, more women began riding buses. As they did, they demanded additional segregated bus space, and the UBCT expanded its gender segregation plan, extending women's sections to half of the bus, launching women-only buses, and hiring women bus drivers for the first time. In the 1990s, *Zan-e Rooz* magazines—where women had once complained about the unwarranted and illegitimate physical contact with men—were now filled with complaints about the quantity and quality of gender-segregated spaces allocated to them. For instance, in 1996, a female government employee wrote to the magazine: "When we [women] manage to get on the bus, we see men sitting in *our* sections. So, women, in a section that's *theirs,* have to stand on their feet" (*Zan-e Rooz,* May 11, 1996). In this framing, men's presence now represented a threat not to women's purity or safety but rather to their sense of entitlement to the space. By the late 1990s, women were formulating men's intrusion into the women's section as a violation of "women's rights."

Discursively, segregation also enabled mobility to become viewed as "appropriately" feminine. Even official language shifted. Whereas in the early 1980s, the UBCT had framed gender-segregated busing as part of the state's Islamization project, it later came to highlight the importance of women's "rights" to separate, comfortable, safe, religiously pure space. For instance, in 2006, Ahmadi Bafandeh, then director of the UBCT, stated, "Unfortunately, a number of men do not respect women's rights and, indifferent about the existing rules, create problems for women and other passengers by taking seats from the women's section" (*Etemad,* December 17, 2006). Yet, these "rights" were not associated with reducing gender differences, as in the West, but instead with maintaining the separation between genders. By the 2000s, women's presence in public spaces was no longer considered an interruption of the Islamic public order.

Perhaps inadvertently, gender segregation had contributed to the transformation of the gendered terms on which the initial plans were carried out. In a 2010 interview, one of the senior experts at the UBCT commented to Shahrokni that he felt the expansion of women's urban mobility in recent decades was "remarkable." While in previous decades women used buses mainly to move within their own neighborhoods, nowadays, he said, there was a "female flow" across the city. Nevertheless, though larger than before, this "female flow" still occurred within the contours of patriarchal policy.

San Pedro and the Feminization of Migration

Meanwhile, in San Pedro, a patriarchal accommodation also facilitated the feminization of mobility, in this case, women's emigration to Los Angeles. Until the 1980s, women of San Pedro lacked mobility within and outside the village. While women did farmwork with their husbands at home, in order to leave the house alone, a woman was expected to seek her husband's or father's permission. In contrast to many other areas of Mexico where women played central roles in markets (Stephen 2005), in this case, men were the salesman who traveled from town to town to sell produce. . . . If women did leave home without permission, they often faced abuse. For instance, Adelita remembered, "[My husband] went to bring the belt, and he said, 'Who gave you permission to step outside?' Because I had taken the onions and the chilies outside to wash them in the sun. . . . He just wanted me behind the door, in the corner, as if I were a crook, shut in." As a result, women rarely left the village at all, let alone on their own. Thus, early migration out of San Pedro was almost all male. . . .

Meanwhile, women's relative confinement in the home was historically tied to political exclusion. As an indigenous community, San Pedro has the right to self-government under a law practiced since the colonial era and formally recognized in 1995 called *Usos y Costumbres* ("Ways and Customs"). The community is run by male citizens, who serve in public posts on a rotating basis, attend democratic decision-making assemblies, and provide labor for local public works. Despite universal suffrage in Mexico, this autonomy enables San Pedro, like 75 percent of indigenous communities in its home state of Oaxaca, to exclude women from voting, attending village assemblies, and/or serving in public offices (Danielson and Eisenstadt 2009; Velásquez 2004). Rather, such villages consider families as units, and male heads of household represent their wives and daughters in public affairs. In turn, indigenous communities face markedly high sex disparities in education and health, and the state of Oaxaca—primarily rural and indigenous—has Mexico's highest rate of domestic violence (Barrera Bassols 2006).

San Pedro codified this patriarchal exclusion during the 1980s and 1990s. At that time, indigenous communities' rights to legal autonomy and the associated exclusion of women were contested in Mexico's Federal Congress, among different levels of state government, and by other indigenous communities such as the Zapatistas in the state of Chiapas (Speed 2007). Yet, leaders of San Pedro insisted on keeping the political sphere exclusively male. Drawing on a logic some have characterized as "masculinist protection" (Young 2003), men explained that they represented their wives and daughters in the village government in order to protect their female relatives from the burden of political participation. For instance, Ricardo, a past president of San Pedro, said, "We cannot name women [to public posts] because they are our mothers. I would go to the village assembly on behalf of my daughters, but because it is a burden—not to deprive them of their rights." . . . Although the state government repeatedly sent mandates insisting that San Pedro include women, the village leaders demurred.

Meanwhile, many female respondents *also* endorsed this all-male political structure, preferring to remain outside of politics (cf. Worthen 2012). In Andrews's 2011 surveys, more than 55 percent of female respondents in San Pedro said they preferred not to participate in village government. When Genaro, an NGO employee working in the village, proposed that the community include women in political meetings, women themselves rejected the idea. Genaro described, "The *women* said, 'We don't want to come to the assembly—obligation or right. Come here all day? No, better to let it be optional. . . . We'd rather not, because it's too much time and too much work to come to the assemblies.'" Thus, several women *also* affirmed the complementary structure in which women cared for the home and men for civic affairs.

Nevertheless, political economic changes undermined men's and women's traditional positions. In 1982, Mexico defaulted on its debt, cutting real wages in half. In response, the International Monetary Fund began structural adjustment, pushing the Mexican government to roll back agricultural subsidies and privatize land. Then, in 1994, the North American Free Trade Agreement (NAFTA) terminated corn subsidies and flooded the market with cheap U.S. corn. This debilitated San Pedro and other subsistence corn-farming communities, fostering a rapid decline in farm incomes (Barkin 2003). Families needed new wages in order to subsist, so both men and women began leaving to seek work in the United States.

Around this time, the U.S. service and garment sectors also provided growing opportunities for women. In Los Angeles, the primary destination for U.S. migrants from San Pedro, factory and service jobs increasingly sought out female migrants. Respondents in Los Angeles—sixty percent of whom worked in housekeeping and thirty-five percent in garment factories—recalled seeing ads that specifically recruited women ("*se busca muchachas*"). These factors helped draw women out of the village. Raquel, a San Pedro woman who came to the United States in 1982 at the age of fifteen, remembered, "My mother told me, 'You know what? If these girls [other migrants from San Pedro] went to the United States and they're telling you they work sewing jeans and there are people sewing on buttons.' . . . Well, having no idea of the reality, she [my mother] said, 'Sewing buttons is nothing you can't do.'" Changes in the political economy of low-wage labor in the United States were necessary to shift the gender dimensions of migration, but they were not sufficient. Given San Pedro's tradition of male migration and its history of confining women to the home, we must explain how women came to dominate its migration stream.

The case of San Pedro is particularly confounding given the gender patterns of migration in other parts of Mexico. In the majority of Mexican migrant communities, which faced comparable economic "push" and "pull" factors in this period, migration remained predominantly male (Massey et al. 1987; Goldring 2001). Women who did migrate typically came after—or as dependents of—husbands or fathers (Cerrutti and Massey 2001). Furthermore, while prevailing theories suggest that women tend to migrate from the *least* patriarchal hometowns (Massey, Fischer, and Capoferro 2006), San Pedro's highly feminized stream came from one of the *most* gender-unequal areas of Mexico.

We argue that what distinguished San Pedro and pushed the feminization of its migration stream was its patriarchal accommodation. In the 1980s and 1990s, as growing numbers of people from San Pedro left for the United States, ever fewer men remained to staff the village government. Other communities adapted by integrating women into civic affairs, where the women substituted for absent male migrants (Kearney and Besserer 2004). In those cases, men maintained their breadwinner roles, but they forsook their dominion in village governance. There, while masculinity remained associated with mobility, it became delinked from political status. In contrast, San Pedro insisted that the political sphere remain men's domain. Rather than integrating women into civic affairs as substitutes for men, village leaders demanded men's participation. If male migrants did not return home when they were called to staff the village government—or pay a male substitute—the community fined them or cut off the water and electricity in the houses they left behind. In extreme cases, migrant men faced expulsion from the community and lost their rights to land or belonging there. Yet, because women had neither rights nor obligations in village politics, female migrants were exempt from such sanctions.

This local patriarchal policy made the cost of migrating higher for men than for women and set the stage for women to leave. Though men had previously been sent to the U.S. as breadwinners, many male respondents told Andrews that the new community sanctions affected them especially heavily. For instance, twenty-eight-year-old José explained that although he had gone to the United States short-term, he quickly returned. He had been named village policeman and, given the low wages he earned in Los Angeles, he had no way to pay the US$4,000 required to hire a substitute. Like most male respondents, he insisted, "It [migrating] is a big burden, a big burden."

Women, however, had no political responsibilities; therefore, they faced no sanctions and could migrate without violating their duties to the community. Graciela, a fifty-eight-year-old respondent living in Los Angeles who had been one of San Pedro's first female migrants to establish herself in the United States, later finding jobs for other women and encouraging them to follow, explained, "Men have more obligations [in the village government] than us women . . . in *Usos y Costumbres,* it's the man who has to do community service and all the hard labor . . . so we [migrants] were more women than men." When she was thirteen, Graciela recalled, her parents stayed in the village and sent her to work in the United States, hoping that she would make fast money in housekeeping. Because men had to do community service, women like Graciela were more "free" to migrate than their fathers and brothers, enabling them to pursue jobs in Los Angeles and help support their families back home.

Maintaining politics as a male domain allowed men to adapt to the feminization of work and migration, by framing migrant labor as a complement to male participation in the village government—a gendered division of tasks. For example, Ronaldo explained that when the village named him as community land secretary, the responsibility of breadwinning fell to his wife, "When I started to have to serve in public posts, I said to my wife, learn to sew blouses. That's how she started to sell, sell, sell—to support us. Because who is going to pay when we [men] do civil service, and I had to serve in a lot of full-time public posts." . . . By the early 1990s, women represented more than fifty percent of San Pedro's migrants to the United States.

[. . .]

Women of San Pedro who did migrate to Los Angeles began to find jobs in garment factories and housekeeping, where they worked long hours, were paid minimum wage or less, and often faced wage theft and other labor abuses. On the other hand, as ever more relatives arrived in the U.S., women built up a community in Los Angeles, and fewer than ten percent of female migrants returned to live in San Pedro after migrating to the United States. Many, like thirty-two-year-old Estrella, reflected, "In the United States, I feel like a bird with wings; I spread my wings and I'm free—to go out!" Meanwhile, back home, women in the village remained excluded from politics, rates of domestic abuse were higher than elsewhere in Mexico, and as of 2011 the majority of women continued to have to ask permission to leave the house. Nevertheless, parents and relatives recognized the need for remittances from their female relatives, shifting the links between femininity, income, and movement to the United States.

Conclusion

. . . In the face of global economic pressure, seemingly "reactive" patriarchal policies played an important role in facilitating women's access to employment, education, and consumption. We call these policies patriarchal accommodations. They were "accommodations," first, because they responded to men's and women's ongoing investment in gender differences. Tehran helped decouple femininity and domesticity by actively creating and providing new gender-segregated transportation that allowed for more mobile femininity. This enabled women to ride buses without threatening either their feminine status or the masculinity of men. San Pedro, meanwhile, enabled female mobility in a somewhat different way: by default.

Community members on the Mexican side refused to incorporate women into village assemblies and political participation. Yet, the village continued to be squeezed economically. Thus, with men absorbed in politics, women had to migrate for work. As a result, migrants became predominantly female, and the social status of migrants got degraded—disparagingly labeled feminine. To understand the surprising effects of such policies, we must consider that both men and women may be committed to sustaining gender differences, albeit in new and different forms.

[. . .]

The effects of patriarchal accommodations are not straightforwardly "positive" or "negative" for women. Just as the processes that lead to a feminization of mobility reflected the local context of Iranian and Mexican patriarchal policies, the implications of these shifts should also be understood in context. In some ways, these policies offered a means for local states to extend and deepen their control, regulating women's movements in Tehran and perpetuating their exclusion from political voice in San Pedro. Given that mobility emerged through this *extension* of male–female differences, it seems unlikely to increase gender equality. However, in other ways women's mobility gave them new capabilities, ranges of movement, and access to public spaces. Over time, women's new income and remittances may have also offered them greater leverage within families. . . . Still, we would caution that even if women do gain autonomy from their husbands and other male counterparts through this process, global political and economic changes can also shift the locus and scale of male domination.

[. . .]

References

Amir-Ebrahimi, Masserat. 2006. "Conquering Enclosed Public Spaces." *Cities* 23:455–61.

Bahramitash, Roksana. 2003. "Islamic Fundamentalism and Women's Economic Role: The Case of Iran." *International Journal of Politics, Culture, and Society* 16:551–68.

Barkin, David. 2003. "The Reconstruction of a Modern Mexican Peasantry." *Journal of Peasant Studies* 30:73–90.

Barrera Bassols, Dalia. 2006. "Indigenous Women in the Representation System for Elective Posts: The Case of Oaxaca." *Agricultura, Sociedad y Desarrollo*, January:19–37.

Bayat, Asef. 2010. "Tehran: Paradox City." *New Left Review* 66:99–122.

Cerrutti, Marcela and Douglas Massey. 2001. "Migration and Its Consequences: On the Auspices of Female Migration from Mexico to the United States." *Demography* 38:187–200.

Danielson, Michael S. and Todd A. Eisenstadt. 2009. "Walking Together, but in Which Direction? Gender Discrimination and Multicultural Practices in Oaxaca, Mexico." *Politics and Gender* 5:153–84.

Goldring, Luin. 2001. "The Gender and Geography of Citizenship in Mexico-U.S. Transnational Spaces." *Identities: Global Studies in Culture and Power* 7(4):501–37.

Kearney, Michael and Federico Besserer. 2004. "Oaxacan Municipal Governance in Transnational Context." Pp. 483–94 in *Indigenous Mexican Migrants in the United States*, edited by J. Fox and G. Rivera-Salgado. La Jolla: Center for U.S.-Mexican Studies, University of California, San Diego.

Kurzman, Charles. 2008. "A Feminist Generation in Iran?" *Iranian Studies* 41:297–321.

Massey, Douglas, Rafael Alarcon, Jorge Durand, and Roberto González. 1987. *Return to Aztlan: The Social Process of International Migration from Western Mexico*. Berkeley, CA: University of California Press.

Massey, Douglas, Mary Fischer, and Chiara Capoferro. 2006. "International Migration and Gender in Latin America: A Comparative Analysis." *International Migration Review* 44(5):63–91.

Moallem, Minoo. 2005. *Between Warrior Brother and Veiled Sister: Islamic Fundamentalism and the Politics of Patriarchy in Iran*. Berkeley, CA: University of California Press.

Moghadam, Valentine. 1988. "Women, Work, and Ideology in the Islamic Republic." *International Journal of Middle East Studies* 20(2):221–43.

The Report on Women's Situation Between 1976 and 1996. 2006. Tehran, Iran: Presidential Center for Women's and Family Affairs.

Shaditalab, Jaleh. 2005. "Iranian Women: Rising Expectations." *Critique* 14(1):35–55.

Speed, Shannon. 2007. *Rights in Rebellion: Indigenous Struggle and Human Rights in Chiapas.* Stanford, CA: Stanford University Press.

Stephen, Lynn. 2005. *Zapotec Women: Gender, Class and Ethnicity in Globalized Oaxaca.* Durham, NC: Duke University Press.

Uteng, Tanu Priya and Tim Cresswell. 2008. *Gendered Mobilities.* Burlington, VT: Ashgate.

Velásquez, Maria Cristina. 2004. "Migrant Communities, Gender, and Political Power in Oaxaca." Pp. 483–94 in *Indigenous Mexican Migrants in the United States*, edited by J. Fox and G. Rivera-Salgado. La Jolla, CA: Center for U.S.-Mexican Studies, UC San Diego.

Worthen, Holly. 2012. "Mexico's 'New' Rural Women: Gendered Labor and Formulations of Rural Citizenship." PhD dissertation, Geography, University of North Carolina, Chapel Hill, NC.

Young, Iris M. 2003. "The Logic of Masculinist Protection: Reflections on Current Security State." *Signs* 29(1):1–25.